Paris

"All you've got to do is decide to go
and the hardest part is over.

So go!"

TONY WHEELER, COFOUNDER – LONELY PLANET

THIS EDITION WRITTEN AND RESEARCHED BY
Catherine Le Nevez,
Christopher Pitts, Nicola Williams

Contents

(left) **Jardin du Luxembourg p228** Paris' most popular park.

....

(above) **Basilique du Sacré-Cœur p134** The landmark basilica.

....

(right) **Restaurants in Montmartre p140** Exciting dining venues.

....

Welcome to Paris

Paris has a timeless familiarity for visitors, with architectural icons, exquisite cuisine, chic boutiques and priceless artistic treasures.

Iconic Architecture

The wrought-iron spire of the Eiffel Tower, the broad Arc de Triomphe, the Champs-Élysées, the gargoyled Notre Dame cathedral, lamplit bridges spanning the Seine and art nouveau cafes spilling on to wicker-chair-lined terraces are indelibly etched in the minds of anyone who's visited the city – and the imaginations of anyone who hasn't (yet). But despite initial appearances, Paris' cityscape isn't static: there are some stunning modern and contemporary icons too, from the inside-out, industrial-style Centre Pompidou to the *mur végétal* (vertical garden) gracing the striking Musée du Quai Branly.

Glorious Food

Paris' dining is iconic and whether you seek a cosy neighbourhood bistro or a triple-Michelin-starred temple to gastronomy, you'll find every establishment prides itself on exquisite preparation and presentation of quality produce, invariably served with wine. Enticing patisseries, *boulangeries* (bakeries), *fromageries* (cheese shops) and crowded, colourful street markets are perfect for packing a picnic to take to the city's parks and gardens. A host of culinary courses – from home kitchens through to the world's most prestigious cookery schools – offers instruction for all schedules, abilities and budgets.

Stylish Shopping

Paris remains at the forefront of international trends, and browsing emerging and established designer boutiques and flagship *haute couture* houses is a quintessential part of any visit. You'll also find uberhip concept stores, quirky homeware shops, and resplendent art nouveau department stores, along with a trove of vintage shops and flea markets, atmospheric bookshops (including the dark-green *bouquiniste* stalls – second-hand bookshop – lining the riverbanks), adorable children's wear and toy shops, art and antique dealers, venerable shops selling state-of-the-art professional cookware, and, of course, gourmet food and wine shops galore.

Artistic Treasures

Paris is one of the great art repositories of the world, harbouring treasures from antiquity onward. In addition to big hitters like the incomparable Louvre, the Musée d'Orsay's exceptional impressionist collection, and the Centre Pompidou's cache of modern and contemporary art, there are scores of smaller museums housing collections in every imaginable genre, and a diverse range of venues mounting major exhibitions through to off-beat installations.

Why I Love Paris

By Catherine Le Nevez, Writer

Paris' grandeur is inspiring but what I love most about the city is its intimacy. Its *quartiers* (quarters) are like a patchwork of villages, and while it's one of the world's major metropolises – with all of the culture and facilities that go with it – there's a real sense of community at the local shops, markets and cafes that hasn't changed since my childhood. Yet because every little 'village' has its own evolving character, I'm constantly discovering and rediscovering hidden corners of the city.

For more about our writers, see p416

Top: Palais Garnier (p96)

Paris'
Top 16

1

Eiffel Tower *(p82)*

1 No one could imagine Paris today without its signature spire. But Gustave Eiffel only constructed this graceful tower – then the world's tallest, at 320m – as a temporary exhibit for the 1889 Exposition Universelle. Luckily, its popularity assured its survival beyond the World Fair and its elegant art nouveau webbed-metal design has become the defining fixture of the city's skyline. Head here at dusk for the best day and night views of the glittering city, and toast making it to the top at the sparkling Champagne bar.

⊙ *Eiffel Tower & Western Paris*

Arc de Triomphe *(p94)*

2 If anything rivals the Eiffel Tower as the symbol of Paris, it's this magnificent 1836-built monument to Napoléon's 1805 victory at Austerlitz, which he commissioned the following year. The intricately sculpted triumphal arch stands sentinel in the centre of the Étoile (star) roundabout – just be sure to use the pedestrian tunnels below ground to reach it! Some of the best vistas in Paris radiate from the top, including swooping views along the luxury-shop-lined Champs-Élysées, Paris' most glamorous avenue, now car-free on the first Sunday of every month.

⊙ *Champs-Élysées & Grands Boulevards*

Notre Dame (p195)

3 A vision of stained-glass rose windows, flying buttresses and frightening gargoyles, Paris' glorious cathedral, Cathédrale Notre Dame de Paris, on the larger of the two inner-city islands, is the city's geographic, historic and spiritual heart. This Gothic wonder took nearly 200 years to build, but would have been demolished following damage during the French Revolution had it not been for the popularity of Victor Hugo's timely novel, *The Hunchback of Notre Dame* which sparked a petition to save it. Climb its 400-odd spiralling steps for magical rooftop views.

⦿ *The Islands*

Louvre (p108)

4 The *Mona Lisa* and the *Venus de Milo* are just two of the priceless treasures resplendently housed inside the fortress turned royal palace turned France's first national museum, the Musée du Louvre. Stretching along the Seine, this immense museum can seem overwhelming, but there are plenty of ways to experience it even if you don't have nine months to glance at every artwork and artefact here. One of the best is via its thematic trails, from the 'Art of Eating' to 'Love in the Louvre'. JARDIN DES TUILERIES (P118) AND THE LOUVRE

⦿ *Louvre & Les Halles*

Parisian Dining
(p44)

5 Whether you're at an unchanged-in-decades neighbourhood haunt, a beautiful art nouveau brasserie, a switched-on, experimental neobistro or a feted *haute cuisine* establishment helmed by a legendary chef – such as Restaurant Guy Savoy (p238), now ensconced in the neoclassical former mint the Monnaie de Paris – the food and the dining experience are considered inseparable. France pioneered what is still the most influential style of cooking in the Western world and Paris is its showcase par excellence. Do as Parisians do and savour every moment. RESTAURANTS ALONG RUE MOUFFETARD (P210)

✕ *Eating*

Musée Rodin (p230)

6 The lovely Musée Rodin is the most romantic of Paris' museums. Auguste Rodin's former workshop and showroom, the 1730-built, beautifully restored Hôtel Biron, is filled with Rodin's own sculptural masterpieces like *The Kiss,* the marble monument to love, as well as creations by his protégé, sculptor Camille Claudel, and by other artists whose works Rodin collected, Van Gogh and Renoir among them. But the real treat is the mansion's rambling, rose-scented sculpture garden, which provides an entrancing setting for contemplating works like *The Thinker* (pictured below).

⊙ *St-Germain & Les Invalides*

Specialised Shopping (p65)

7 Paris, like any major city, offers international chains (including icons that originated here). But what really sets Parisian shopping apart is its incredible array of specialist shops. Candles from the world's oldest candle maker, pigments from the art-supply shop that developed 'Klein blue' with the artist, soft leather handbags made in the hip Haut Marais, *bouquiniste* (secondhand bookshop; pictured bottom right) stalls lining the banks of the Seine, and fashions displayed beneath the stained-glass dome of grande dame department store Galeries Lafayette are just some of the goodies in store.

🔒 *Shopping*

6

Musée d'Orsay (p224)

8 Against a backdrop of richly coloured walls, the Musée d'Orsay's celebrated canvases by impressionist and postimpressionist masters, including Renoir, Gauguin, Cézanne, Sisley, Manet, Monet, Degas and Toulouse-Lautrec, appear as if they're hung in an intimate home. The Gare d'Orsay – the grand former railway station in which the museum is located that was completed at the turn of the 20th century – is an exemplar of art nouveau architecture, but France's treasured national collection of masterpieces from 1848 to 1914 is the star of the show.

◉ *St-Germain & Les Invalides*

Jardin du Luxembourg (p228)

9 Arguably considered the most attractive park in Paris, the Jardin du Luxembourg, offers a snapshot of Parisian life. Couples stroll through the chestnut groves. Children chase wooden sailing boats around the octagonal pond and laugh at the antics of engaging marionettes. Old men play rapid-fire chess with cherished pieces at weathered tables. Students pore over books between lectures. Office workers snatch some sunshine, lounging in iconic sage-green metal chairs. Musicians strike up in the bandstand. Joggers loop past stately statues. And friends meet and make plans to meet again.

⊙ *St-Germain & Les Invalides*

Sacré-Cœur (p134)

10 Paris' landmark basilica, Basilique du Sacré-Cœur, is a place of pilgrimage in more ways than one. Staircased, ivy-clad streets slink up the hill of the fabled artists' neighbourhood of Montmartre to a funicular gliding up to the church's dove-white domes. The chapel-lined basilica – featuring the shimmering apse mosaic *Christ in Majesty* – crowns the 130m-high Butte de Montmartre (Montmartre Hill). Its lofty position provides dizzying vistas across Paris from the basilica's front steps and, above all, from up inside its main dome.

⊙ *Montmartre & Northern Paris*

The Seine (p74)

11 The city's most beautiful 'boulevard' of all, the Seine, flows through the city's heart, flanked by Parisian-as-it-gets landmarks like the Eiffel Tower, Louvre and Notre Dame. Taking to the water on a cruise or Batobus ferry is an idyllic way to acquaint or reacquaint yourself with the city. Its Unesco World Heritage–listed riverbanks, islands and 37 bridges are perfect for promenading, particularly along the reclaimed car-free stretches on both the left and right banks. Entertainment options abound, including summertime beaches.

⊙ *The Seine*

Centre Pompidou

(p116)

12 The primary-coloured, inside-out Centre Pompidou building, designed by architects Renzo Piano and Richard Rogers, houses France's national modern and contemporary-art museum (Europe's largest), the Musée National d'Art Moderne (MNAM), containing creations from 1905 through to the present day. On display are works from Europeans such as Picasso, Matisse, Chagall, Kandinsky and more, as well as from cross-Atlantic artists such as Kahlo, Warhol and Pollock, plus edgy installation pieces, sculpture and videos. The centre's cutting-edge cultural offerings include temporary exhibition spaces, a public library, cinemas and entertainment venues. Topping it off is the spectacular panorama radiating from the roof.

⊙ *Louvre & Les Halles*

Street Markets *(p66)*

13 Stall after stall of cheeses, punnets of raspberries, stacked baguettes, sun-ripened tomatoes, freshly lopped pigs' trotters, horse-meat sausages, spit-roasted chickens, glass bottles of olives and olive oils, quail eggs, duck eggs, boxes of chanterelle mushrooms and knobbly truffles, long-clawed langoustines and prickly sea urchins on beds of crushed ice – along with belts, boots, wallets, cheap socks, chic hats, colourful scarves, striped T-shirts, wicker baskets, wind-up toys, buckets of flowers... Paris' street markets, such as the wonderful Marché Bastille (p184), are a feast for the senses.

🔒 *Bastille & Eastern Paris*

Père Lachaise *(p157)*

14 Paris is a collection of villages and this sprawl of cobbled lanes and elaborate tombs, with a population (as it were) of over one million, qualifies as one in its own right. The world's most visited cemetery was founded in 1804, and initially attracted few funerals because of its distance from the city centre. The authorities responded by exhuming famous remains and resettling them here. Their marketing ploy worked and Cimetière du Père Lachaise has been Paris' most fashionable final address ever since.

⊙ *Le Marais, Ménilmontant & Belleville*

Versailles (p263)

15 No wonder revolutionaries massacred the Château de Versailles palace guard and ultimately dragged King Louis XVI and his queen, Marie-Antoinette, back to Paris to be guillotined: this monumental, 700-room palace and sprawling estate – with its fountained gardens, ponds and canals – could not have been in starker contrast to taxpayers' average living conditions at the time. A Unesco World Heritage–listed wonder, Versailles is easily reached from central Paris; try to time your visit to catch musical fountain displays and equestrian shows. RIGHT: GALERIE DES GLACES (P266)

⊙ *Day Trips from Paris*

Canal St-Martin (p148)

16 Bordered by shaded towpaths and traversed by iron footbridges, the charming, 4.5km-long Canal St-Martin was slated to be concreted over when barge transportation declined, until local residents rallied to save it. The quaint setting lured artists, designers and students, who set up artists collectives, vintage and offbeat boutiques, and a bevy of neoretro cafes and bars. Enduring maritime legacies include old swing bridges that still pivot 90 degrees when boats pass through the canal's double locks, and a canal cruise is the best way to experience Paris' lesser-known waterway.

⊙ *Montmartre & Northern Paris*

What's New

Lifestyle Hotels

A host of new sleep-drink-dine-dance hotels are making accommodation in Paris a lifestyle choice. Among the newcomers are Le Pigalle (p284), with a destination bar, DJs and in-room turntables; rockstar-hot ex-thermal baths Les Bains (p287), with a sizzling in-house club; cocktail-driven Grand Hôtel Pigalle (p285); and Off Paris Seine (p292), the city's first floating hotel, with a panoramic 400 sq-metre sun terrace, 15m-long swimming pool, bar and lounge.

Ancient Origins

Across from the Eiffel Tower, Paris' newly reopened anthropological museum, the Musee de l'Homme (p85), traces the evolution of humankind through revamped exhibits and an updated layout.

Louvre Renewal

The labyrinthine Louvre (p108) recently embarked on a 30-year renovation plan to make the museum more accessible. A modernised entrance hall and improved navigation are the first priorities.

Car-Free Streets

Green initiatives include closing 3.3km of Right Bank expressway between the Tuileries and Bastille, pedestrianising the Champs-Élysées on the first Sunday of each month and an annual car-free day. (p295)

Flat-Rate Fares

Taxi travel between the city centre and Paris' two main airports has become mercifully simpler with the introduction of fixed-price cab charges. (p330)

Craft Breweries

Paris has embraced the *bière artisanale* (craft beer) trend and the city now has a handful of boundary-pushing breweries, such as Brasserie La Parisienne (p252), offering behind-the-scenes tours and tastings.

Cocktail Dinners

The city's cocktail renaissance has seen a flurry of new restaurants upping the bar with amazing food pairings, such as at Dersou (p188), where each course comes with a custom-created cocktail.

Detox!

Changes in Paris' drinking scene include serious juice bars, such as Le Marais' Wild & the Moon (p171), finally arriving.

Gluten-Free Goodness

Paris' health kick continues with gluten-free options such as *boulangerie* (bakery) Chambelland (p169), baking cakes and breads that are as good as those of any traditional French bakery.

Minted Michelin-Starred Dining

Triple-Michelin-starred culinary icon Guy Savoy's flagship Restaurant Guy Savoy (p238) is now ensconced within the refurbished neoclassical mint, the Monnaie de Paris.

Samaritaine Shopping

Left empty for a decade, landmark art nouveau department store La Samaritaine (p314) is getting ready to reopen its doors by 2018, with a luxury hotel on site too.

For more recommendations and reviews, see **lonelyplanet. com/Paris**

Need to Know

For more information, see Survival Guide (p329)

Currency
Euro (€)

Language
French

Visas
Generally no restrictions for EU citizens. Usually not required for most other nationalities for stays of up to 90 days.

Money
ATMs widely available. Visa and MasterCard accepted in most hotels, shops and restaurants; fewer accept American Express.

Mobile Phones
Check with your provider about roaming costs before you leave home, or ensure your phone's unlocked to use a French SIM card (available cheaply in Paris).

Time
Central European Time (GMT/UTC plus one hour).

Tourist Information
Paris Convention & Visitors Bureau (Office du Tourisme et des Congrès de Paris; Map p372; www.parisinfo.com; 27 rue des Pyramides, 1er; ⊙7am-7pm May-Oct, 10am-7pm Nov-Apr; MPyramides) The main branch is 500m northwest of the Louvre. It sells tickets for tours and several attractions, plus museum and transport passes. Also books accommodation.

Daily Costs

Budget: Less than €100
➡ Dorm bed: €25–50
➡ Coffee/glass of wine/*demi* (half-pint of beer)/cocktail from: €3/3.50/3.50/9
➡ Excellent self-catering options, especially markets
➡ Frequent free concerts and events
➡ Public transport, standby theatre tickets

Midrange: €100–250
➡ Double room: €130–250
➡ Two-course meal: €20–40
➡ Museums: free to around €12
➡ Admission to clubs: free to around €20

Top End: More than €250
➡ Historic luxury hotel double from €250
➡ Gastronomic restaurant *menu* from €40
➡ Designer boutiques
➡ The sky is the limit!

Advance Planning
Two months before Book accommodation, organise opera, ballet or cabaret tickets, check events calendars to find out what festivals will be on, and make reservations for high-end/popular restaurants.

Two weeks before Sign up for a local-led tour and start narrowing down your choice of museums, prepurchasing tickets online where possible.

Two days before Pack your comfiest shoes!

Useful Websites
Lonely Planet (www.lonelyplanet.com/paris) Destination information, hotel bookings, traveller forum and more.

Paris Info (www.parisinfo.com) Comprehensive tourist-authority website.

Secrets of Paris (www.secretsofparis.com) Loads of resources and reviews.

Paris by Mouth (http://parisbymouth.com) Foodie heaven.

Sortiraparis (www.sortiraparis.com) Up-to-date calendar listing what's on around town.

HiP Paris (http://hipparis.com) Not only vacation rentals ('Haven in Paris') but switched-on articles and reviews by expat locals too.

WHEN TO GO

Spring and autumn are ideal. Summer is the main tourist season but many places close during August. Sights are quieter and prices lower during winter.

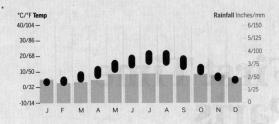

Arriving in Paris

Charles de Gaulle Airport
Trains (RER), buses and night buses to the city centre €6 to €17; taxi €50 to €55, 15% higher evenings and Sundays.

Orly Airport Trains (Orlyval then RER), buses and night buses to the city centre €8 to €12.05; T7 tram to Villejuif-Louis Aragon then metro to centre (€3.60); taxi €30 to €35, 15% higher evenings and Sundays.

Beauvais Airport Buses (€17) to Porte Maillot then metro (€1.90); taxi at least €150 (probably more than the cost of your flight!).

Gare du Nord train station
Within central Paris; served by metro (€1.90).

For much more on **arrival** see p330

Getting Around

Walking is a pleasure in Paris, and the city also has one of the most efficient and inexpensive public-transport systems in the world, making getting around a breeze.

➔ **Metro & RER** The fastest way to get around. Runs from about 5.30am and finishes around 12.35am or 1.15am (to around 2.15am on Friday and Saturday nights), depending on the line.

➔ **Bicycle** Virtually free pick-up, drop-off Vélib' (p333) bikes operate across 1800 stations citywide.

➔ **Bus** Good for parents with prams/strollers and people with limited mobility.

➔ **Boat** The Batobus (p336) is a handy hop-on, hop-off service stopping at nine key destinations along the Seine.

For much more on **getting around** see p332

Sleeping

Paris has a wealth of accommodation, but it's often full well in advance. Reservations are recommended year-round and essential during the warmer months (April to October) and all holidays. Although cheaper, accommodation outside central Paris is invariably a false economy given travel time and costs. Choose somewhere within Paris' 20 *arrondissements* to experience Parisian life the moment you step out the door.

Useful Websites

➔ **Lonely Planet** (www.lonelyplanet.com/france/paris/hotels) Reviews of Lonely Planet's top choices.

➔ **Paris Hotel Service** (www.parishotelservice.com) Boutique-hotel gems.

➔ **Paris Hotel** (www.hotels-paris.fr) Well-organised hotel-booking site with user reviews.

➔ **Room Sélection** (www.room-selection.com) Select apartment rentals centred on Le Marais.

➔ **Paris Attitude** (www.parisattitude.com) Thousands of apartment rentals, professional service, reasonable fees.

For much more on **sleeping** see p278

ARRONDISSEMENTS

Within the *périphérique* (ring road), Paris is divided into 20 *arrondissements* (city districts), which spiral clockwise like a snail shell from the centre. *Arrondissement* numbers (1er, 2e etc) form an integral part of all Parisian addresses. Each *arrondissement* has its own personality, but it's the *quartiers* (quarters, ie neighbourhoods), which often overlap *arrondissement* boundaries, that give Paris its village atmosphere.

First Time Paris

For more information, see Survival Guide (p329)

Checklist

➡ Check passport validity and visa requirements.

➡ Arrange travel insurance.

➡ Confirm airline baggage restrictions.

➡ Book accommodation as well as popular and/or high-end restaurants well ahead.

➡ Buy tickets online for the Louvre, Eiffel Tower etc.

➡ Organise international roaming on your phone if needed (and be sure to check roaming charges).

What to Pack

➡ Comfortable shoes – Paris is best explored on foot.

➡ Phrasebook – the more French you attempt, the more rewarding your visit will be.

➡ Travel plug (adapter).

➡ Corkscrew (corked wine bottles are the norm; screw caps are rare); remember to pack it in your checked baggage for flights.

Top Tips for Your Trip

➡ An unforgettable introduction to the city is a river cruise (or hop-on, hop-off Batobus trip) along the Seine, floating past quintessentially Parisian landmarks like the Eiffel Tower, Louvre and Notre Dame.

➡ The metro is efficient and easy to use. Local buses are a scenic alternative.

➡ Prebook attractions online wherever possible to avoid standing in long ticket queues.

➡ Above all, don't try to cram too much into your schedule. Allow time to soak up the atmosphere of Paris' neighbourhoods – lingering over a coffee on a cafe terrace and exploring the backstreets are as much a part of the Parisian experience as visiting major sights.

What to Wear

As the cradle of *haute couture*, Paris is chic: don your smarter threads (and accessories such as scarves). You'll also stand out as a tourist less and therefore be less of a target for pickpockets. Dress up rather than down for the 'nicer' restaurants, clubs and bars – no jeans, shorts or trainers/sneakers.

Bring sturdy shoes whatever the season – cobbled streets aren't kind on high heels or thin soles.

When visiting religious sites such as Notre Dame, be sure to dress respectfully.

Be Forewarned

In general, Paris is a safe city and random street assaults are rare. The city is generally well lit and there's no reason not to use the metro until it stops running, at some time between 12.30am and just past 1am (2.15am on weekends). Many women do travel on the metro alone, late at night, in most areas.

Pickpocketing is typically the biggest concern. *Always* be alert and take precautions: don't carry more money than you need, and keep your credit cards, passport and other documents in a concealed pouch, a hotel safe or a safe-deposit box.

Money

Visa and MasterCard are the most widely used credit cards; American Express is only accepted by upmarket establishments such as international chain hotels, luxury boutiques and department stores.

Chip-and-pin is the norm for card transactions – few places accept swipe-and-signature. Some foreign chip-and-pin-enabled cards require a signature – ask your bank before you leave. ATMs (*points d'argent* or *distributeurs automatiques de billets*) are everywhere; withdrawals incur international transaction fees.

You can change cash (and travellers cheques) at some banks, post offices and money-exchange offices. Many shops don't accept €200 and €500 bills.

For more information, see p339.

Taxes & Refunds

Prices displayed in shops etc invariably include France's TVA (*taxe sur la valeur ajoutée;* value-added tax).

Non-EU residents can often claim a refund of TVA paid on goods.

Tipping

➡ **Taxis** Drivers expect tips of between 5% and 10% of the fare, though the usual procedure is to round up to the nearest €1.

➡ **Restaurants** Bills include a service charge (usually 15%) and many people leave a few extra euros.

➡ **Bars & Cafes** Not necessary at the bar. If drinks are brought to your table, tip as you would in a restaurant.

➡ **Hotels** Bellhops usually expect €1 to €2 per bag.

Language

Although English is increasingly widespread in Paris, you'll have an infinitely more rewarding experience if you address locals in French, even simply '*bonjour, parlez-vous anglais?*' ('hello, do you speak English?').

1 What are the opening hours?
Quelles sont les heures d'ouverture?
kel son lay zer doo·vair·tewr

French business hours are governed by a maze of regulations, so it's a good idea to check before you make plans.

2 I'd like the set menu, please.
Je voudrais le menu, s'il vous plait.
zher voo·dray ler mer·new seel voo play

The best-value dining in France is the two- or three-course meal at a fixed price. Most restaurants have one on the chalkboard.

3 Which wine would you recommend?
Quel vin vous conseillez?
kel vun voo kon·say·yay

Who better to ask for advice on wine than the French?

4 Can I address you with 'tu'?
Est-ce que je peux vous tutoyer?
es ker zher per voo tew·twa·yay

Before you start addressing someone with the informal 'you' form, it's polite to ask permission first.

5 Do you have plans for tonight/tomorrow?
Vous avez prévu quelque chose ce soir/demain?
voo za·vay pray·vew kel·ker shoz ser swar/der·mun

To arrange to meet up without sounding pushy, ask friends if they're available rather than inviting them directly.

Etiquette

➡ Communication tends to be formal and reserved, but this shouldn't be mistaken for unfriendliness.

➡ Always greet/farewell anyone you interact with, such as shopkeepers, with '*Bonjour* (*bonsoir* at night)/*Au revoir*'.

➡ Particularly in smaller shops, staff may not appreciate you touching the merchandise until invited to do so, nor taking photographs.

➡ Parisians don't speak loudly – modulate your voice to a similarly low pitch.

➡ *Tu* and *vous* both mean 'you' but *tu* is only used with people you know very well, children or animals. Use *vous* until you're invited to use *tu*.

➡ Talking about money (eg salaries or spending outlays) is generally taboo in public.

➡ Never use 'garçon' (literally 'boy') to summon a waiter, rather 'Monsieur' or 'Madame'.

Top Itineraries

Day One

Louvre & Les Halles (p106)

 Start with a stroll through the elegant **Jardin des Tuileries**, stopping to view Monet's enormous *Water Lilies* at the **Musée de l'Orangerie** and/or photography exhibits at the **Jeu de Paume**. IM Pei's glass pyramid is your compass point to enter the labyrinthine **Louvre**.

> **Lunch** Nip out for contemporary cooking at Racines 2 (p126).

Louvre & Les Halles (p106)

 Visiting this monumental museum could easily consume a full day but once you've had your fill, browse the colonnaded arcades of the exquisite **Jardin du Palais Royal**, and visit the beautiful church **Église St-Eustache**. Tap into the soul of the former Les Halles wholesale markets along backstreet legacies like the former oyster market, **rue Montorgueil**. Linger for a drink on **rue Montmartre**, then head to the late-opening **Centre Pompidou** for modern and contemporary art and amazing rooftop views.

> **Dinner** Frenchie (p127) offers walk-in wine-bar dining.

Le Marais, Ménilmontant & Belleville (p154)

There's a wealth to see in Le Marais by day (**Musée Picasso**, **Musée Carnavalet**, **Musée des Arts et Métiers**...) but the neighbourhood really comes into its own at night, with a cornucopia of hip bars and clubs.

Day Two

Champs-Élysées & Grands Boulevards (p92)

 Climb the mighty **Arc de Triomphe** for a pinch-yourself Parisian panorama. Promenade down Paris' most glamorous avenue, the **Champs-Élysées**, and give your credit card a workout in the **Triangle d'Or**, **Galeries Lafayette** or **place de la Madeleine** before catching edgy art exhibitions at **La Pinacothèque**.

> **Lunch** Café Branly (p85): casual yet classy, with ringside tower views.

Eiffel Tower & Western Paris (p80)

 Check out indigenous art and awesome architecture at the **Musée du Quai Branly**. This cultural neighbourhood is also home to the world's largest Monet collection at the **Musée Marmottan-Monet**, contemporary installations at the **Palais de Tokyo**, and Asian treasures at the **Musée Guimet**. Sunset is the best time to ascend the **Eiffel Tower**, to experience both dizzying views during daylight hours, and the glittering *ville lumière* (City of Light) by night.

> **Dinner** Cracking Modern French fare at Le Casse Noix (p254).

Montparnasse & Southern Paris (p246)

Detour for a drink at a historic Montparnasse brasserie like **Le Select** or continue straight down the Seine to party aboard floating nightclubs like **Le Batofar**.

Day Three

The Islands (p193)

 Starting your day at the city's most visited sight, **Notre Dame**, gives you the best chance of beating the crowds. In addition to admiring its stained-glass interior, allow around an hour to visit the top and another to explore the archaeological **crypt**. For even more beautiful stained glass, don't miss nearby **Sainte-Chapelle**. Cross the **Pont St-Louis** to buy a **Berthillon** ice cream before browsing Île St-Louis' enchanting boutiques.

 Lunch Deliciously Parisian hang-out Café Saint Régis (p202).

St-Germain & Les Invalides (p222)

Swoon over impressionist masterpieces in the magnificent **Musée d'Orsay**, scout out the backstreet boutiques and storied shops of St-Germain, sip coffee on the terrace of literary cafes like **Les Deux Magots** and laze in the lovely **Jardin du Luxembourg**, the city's most popular park.

Dinner French classics in the art nouveau jewel Bouillon Racine (p236).

Latin Quarter (p205)

Scour the shelves of late-night bookshops like the legendary **Shakespeare & Company**, then join Parisian students and academics in the Latin Quarter's bars, cafes and pubs on **rue Mouffetard** or hit a jazz club like **Café Universel**.

Day Four

Montmartre & Northern Paris (p132)

 Montmartre's slinking streets and steep staircases lined with crooked ivy-clad buildings are enchanting places to meander, especially in the early morning when tourists are few. Head to the hilltop **Sacré-Cœur** basilica, then brush up on the area's fabled history at the **Musée de Montmartre**.

 Lunch Local favourite Le Miroir (p147) offers fantastic lunchtime *menu* specials.

Montmartre & Northern Paris (p132)

Stroll the shaded towpaths of cafe-lined **Canal St-Martin**, and visit the futuristic **Parc de la Villette**, the kid-friendly **Cité des Sciences** museum and the instrument-filled Musée de la Musique, within the **Cité de la Musique**. Sailing schedules permitting, hop on a **canal cruise** to Bastille.

Dinner Sublime 'small plates' at Le 6 Paul Bert (p186).

Bastille & Eastern Paris (p180)

The Bastille neighbourhood calls for a cafe crawl: classics include the cherry-red **Le Pure Café** and absinthe specialist **La Fée Verte**. Salsa your socks off at the 1936 dance hall **Le Balajo** on nightlife strip **rue de Lappe** or catch electro, funk and hip-hop at **Badaboum**.

If You Like...

Markets

Marché Bastille Arguably the best open-air market in the city. (p184)

Marché d'Aligre Wonderfully chaotic market with all the staples of French cuisine. (p189)

Marché St-Quentin Covered market dating back to 1866. (p144)

Rue Montorgueil Street stalls front the food shops of this pedestrianised strip. (p126)

Marché des Enfants Rouges Glorious maze of food stalls with ready-to-eat dishes from around the globe. (p168)

Marché aux Fleurs Reine Elizabeth II Fragrant flower market. (p203)

Marché Raspail Especially popular for its fabulous Sunday organic market. (p239)

Marché aux Puces de St-Ouen Europe's largest flea market, with over 2500 stalls. (p153)

Rue Mouffetard Atmospheric commercial street with food shops and stalls galore. (p216)

Marché de Belleville Open-air market in business since 1860, in one of Paris' most multicultural, up-and-coming 'hoods. (p170)

Churches

Église St-Eustache Architecturally magnificent and musically outstanding, this church has sent souls soaring for centuries. (p119)

Fountain on Place de la Concorde (p97)

ROMAN_SLAVIK/GETTY IMAGES ©

Cathédrale Notre Dame de Paris Paris' mighty cathedral is without equal. (p195)

Basilique du Sacré-Cœur The city's landmark basilica lords over Montmartre. (p134)

Église de la Madeleine Neoclassical landmark with wondrous concerts. (p99)

Église St-Pierre Where the Jesuit order was founded. (p142)

Sainte-Chapelle Classical concerts provide the perfect opportunity to truly appreciate Sainte-Chapelle's beauty. (p200)

Basilique de St-Denis France's first major Gothic structure and still one of its finest. (p140)

Église St-Germain des Prés Built in the 11th century, this is Paris' oldest church. (p232)

Église St-Sulpice Frescoes by Delacroix and a starring role in *The Da Vinci Code*. (p233)

Cathédrale Notre Dame – Chartres Renowned for its brilliant-blue stained glass. (p273)

Romance

Jardin du Palais Royal Elegant urban garden with arcaded galleries and gravel walkways embraced by the neoclassical Palais Royal. (p120)

Le Grand Véfour Savour the romance of 18th-century Paris in one of the world's most beautiful restaurants. (p124)

Square du Vert-Galant Tiny, triangular park at the tip of the Île de la Cité. (p201)

Île aux Cygnes The city's little-known third island has wonderful Eiffel Tower views. (p250)

Eiffel Tower There's a reason the top platform sees up to

three marriage proposals an hour. (p82)

Canal St-Martin Stroll the shaded towpaths or sit on the banks and watch the boats float by. (p148)

Place St-Sulpice The *place* (square) in front of Église St-Sulpice is an enchanting spot to linger. (p233)

Musée Rodin Swoon over Rodin's marble monument to love, *The Kiss*, and stroll the museum's rose- and sculpture-filled garden. (p230)

Le Pradey With its deep-red walls, frilly bedspread and heart-shaped door frame, the themed Moulin Rouge room at this design hotel is pure romance. (p282)

Literature

Maison de Victor Hugo Visit the elegant home of celebrated novelist and poet Victor Hugo overlooking one of Paris' most sublime city squares. (p160)

Maison de Balzac Balzac's residence and writing studio from 1840–47 is a charmer. (p86)

St-Germain literary addresses Take a literary-loop walking tour through this fabled part of the Left Bank. (p237)

Latin Quarter literary addresses The Latin Quarter is scattered with seminal literary addresses. (p213)

Montparnasse literary addresses Writers, artists and political exiles flocked to Montparnasse's brasseries in its early-20th-century heyday. (p251)

Shakespeare & Company Attend a reading by an established or an emerging author, curl up in the reading library or browse the shelves of this magical bookshop and writers' hub. (p219)

For more top Paris spots, see the following:

➡ Eating (p44)
➡ Drinking & Nightlife (p54)
➡ Entertainment (p60)
➡ Shopping (p65)
➡ Parks & Activities (p72)

Bibliothèque Nationale de France France's national library frequently mounts literary exhibitions. (p250)

Panoramas

Eiffel Tower Each of Paris' landmark tower's three viewing platforms offers a different perspective of the city. (p82)

Tour Montparnasse The views over Paris are the redeeming feature of this smoked-glass skyscraper. (p249)

Galeries Lafayette Some of the best free views of the city are from the top of this grand department store. (p104)

Cathédrale Notre Dame de Paris Get a gargoyle's-eye view by climbing Notre Dame's bell towers. (p195)

Parc de Belleville Climb to the top of the hill in this little-known Belleville park to savour some of the best views of the city. (p162)

Arc de Triomphe Swooping views along the Champs-Élysées. (p94)

Centre Pompidou Although only six storeys high, the Centre Pompidou rooftop's views across low-rise Paris are phenomenal. (p116)

Le Ballon Air de Paris Airborne views from a balloon. (p249)

Palais de Chaillot Front-row Eiffel Tower views. (p86)

Basilique du Sacré-Cœur Superb views from Sacré-Cœur's

steps; even better views from inside its central dome. (p134)

Art Nouveau

Eiffel Tower The graceful latticed metalwork of Paris' 'iron lady' is art nouveau architecture at its best. (p82)

Abbesses metro entrance Hector Guimard's finest remaining glass-canopied metro entrance, illuminated by twin lamps. (p142)

Musée d'Orsay The 1900-built former railway station housing this monumental museum justifies a visit alone. (p224)

Le Train Bleu Resplendent restaurant inside the Gare de Lyon. (p189)

Galeries Lafayette Glorious department store topped by a stunning stained-glass dome. (p104)

Le Carreau du Temple This old covered market in the Marais recently reopened as a cutting-edge cultural and community centre. (p174)

Bofinger Dine amid art nouveau brass, glass and mirrors in Paris' oldest brasserie. (p168)

Musée Maxim's Art nouveau artworks, objets d'art and furniture above belle époque bistro Maxim's. (p97)

Grand Palais A 1900-built beauty with an 8.5-ton glass roof. (p96)

Modern & Contemporary Architecture

Centre Pompidou Designed inside out by Renzo Piano and Richard Rogers in the 1970s, Paris' premier cultural centre is still cutting-edge today. (p116)

La Défense The only place in the city to see a forest of skyscrapers. (p87)

Musée du Quai Branly Striking Seine-side museum designed by Jean Nouvel. (p84)

Institut du Monde Arabe The building that established Nouvel's reputation blends modern and traditional Arab elements with Western influences. (p210)

Fondation Cartier pour l'Art Contemporain Stunning contemporary art space courtesy of Nouvel. (p249)

Philharmonie de Paris Futuristic Nouvel-designed symphonic concert hall in the equally futuristic Parc de la Villette. (p139)

Fondation Louis Vuitton Frank Gehry–designed fine-arts centre, topped by a giant glass 'cloud'. (p90)

Louvre glass pyramid Egypt's original pyramid builders couldn't have imagined this. (p108)

Bibliothèque Nationale de France The national library's four towers are shaped like half-open books. (p250)

Cité de l'Architecture et du Patrimoine Inside the 1937-built Palais du Chaillot, the exhibits cover not only Paris' architectural past and present but also its future. (p85)

Parks & Gardens

Jardin du Luxembourg Paris' most popular inner-city oasis. (p228)

Jardin des Tuileries Meet Monet and revel in Paris at its symmetrical best. (p118)

Promenade Plantée The world's first elevated park, atop a disused 19th-century railway viaduct. (p182)

Maison et Jardins de Claude Monet The flower-filled gardens surrounding Monet's former home take on a palette of hues come spring. (p276)

Parc de la Villette Canal-side 35-hectare pavilion-filled 'park of the future' with state-of-the-art facilities for kids and adults. (p136)

Parc des Buttes-Chaumont Hilly, forested haven in Northern Paris. (p139)

Versailles Designed by André Le Nôtre, the château's gardens are fit for a king. (p263)

Jardin des Plantes The city's beautiful botanic gardens shelter rare plants and 18th-century glass-and-metal greenhouses. (p209)

Bois de Vincennes Paris' eastern woods were once royal hunting grounds. (p183)

Bois de Boulogne Explore Paris' western woods by rowing boat or bicycle. (p90)

French Revolution– Era History

Place de la Bastille Site of the former prison stormed on 14 July 1789, mobilising the Revolution. (p182)

Versailles The October 1789 march on Versailles forced the royal family to leave the château. (p263)

Conciergerie Louis XVI's queen, Marie-Antoinette, was one of the aristocratic prisoners tried and imprisoned here. (p201)

Place de la Concorde Louis XVI and Marie-Antoinette were among thousands guillotined where the obelisk now stands. (p97)

Basilique de St-Denis Louis XVI and Marie-Antoinette's final resting place. (p140)

(Top) Grande Arche de la Défense (p87)
(Below) Gardens at Château de Versailles (p263)

Parc du Champ de Mars This former military training ground was the site of Revolutionary festivals. (p87)

Caveau de la Huchette Long a swinging jazz club, this cellar was used as a courtroom and torture chamber during the Revolution. (p219)

Medieval History

Le Marais The Marais' medieval streets largely escaped Baron Haussmann's reformation. (p79)

Cathédrale Notre Dame de Paris Constructed between 1163 and the early 14th century. (p195)

Louvre Immense fort-turned-palace-turned-museum, constructed 1190–1202. (p108)

Sainte-Chapelle Consecrated in 1248. (p200)

Sorbonne University founded in 1253. (p208)

Musée National du Moyen Âge Partly housed in the 15th-century Hôtel de Cluny, Paris' finest civil medieval building. (p207)

Basilique de St-Denis Work on this Gothic wonder started around 1136. (p140)

Cathédrale Notre Dame – Chartres France's best-preserved medieval cathedral, built in the 13th century. (p273)

Château de Vincennes The only medieval castle in Paris. (p183)

Month By Month

January

The frosty first month of the year isn't the most festive in Paris, but cocktails – as well as the winter *soldes* (sales) – certainly brighten the mood.

🍷 Paris Cocktail Week

Each of the 50-plus cocktail bars all over the city that take part in late January's Paris Cocktail Week (www.pariscocktailweek.fr) creates two signature cocktails for the event. There are also workshops, guest bartenders, masterclasses and food pairings. Sign up for a free pass for cut-price cocktails.

🎆 Chinese New Year

Paris' largest lantern-lit festivities and dragon parades take place in the city's main Chinatown in the 13e in late January or early February. Parades are also held in Belleville and Le Marais.

February

Festivities still aren't in full swing in February, but couples descend on France's romantic capital for Valentine's Day, when virtually all restaurants offer special menus.

🍴 Salon International de l'Agriculture

Appetising nine-day international agricultural fair (www.salon-agriculture.com), with produce (and animals) from all over France turned into delectable fare at the Parc des Expositions at Porte de Versailles, 15e, from late February to early March.

March

Blooms appear in Paris' parks and gardens, leaves start greening the city's avenues and festivities begin to flourish. And days get longer – the last Sunday morning of the month ushers in daylight-saving time.

☆ Printemps du Cinéma

Selected cinemas across Paris offer filmgoers a unique entry fee of €4 per session over three days sometime around the middle of March (www.printempsducinema.com).

☆ Banlieues Bleues

Big-name acts perform during the Suburban Blues (www.banlieuesbleues.org) jazz, blues and R&B festival from mid-March to mid-April at venues in Paris' northern suburbs.

April

Sinatra sang about April in Paris, and the month sees the city's 'charm of spring' in full swing, with chestnuts blossoming and cafe terraces coming into their own.

🎡 Foire du Trône

Dating back some 1000 years (!), this huge funfair (www.foiredutrone.com) is held on the Pelouse de Reuilly of the Bois de Vincennes from around Easter to early June.

🏃 Marathon International de Paris

On your marks...the Paris International Marathon (www.schneiderelectric parismarathon.com), usually held on the second Sunday of April, starts on the av des Champs-Élysées, 8e, and finishes on av Foch, 16e, attracting more than 40,000 runners from over 100 countries.

May

The temperate month of May has more public holidays than any other in France. Watch out for widespread closures, particularly on May Day (1 May).

🍺 Paris Beer Week

Craft beer's popularity in Paris peaks during Paris Beer Week (www.laparis beerweek.com), held during the first week of May, when over 150 events take place across the city's bars, pubs, breweries, specialist beer shops and other venues.

◉ La Nuit Européenne des Musées

Key museums across Paris stay open late for the European Museums Night (http://nuitdesmusees.cul turecommunication.gouv. fr), on one Saturday in mid-May. Most offer free entry.

◉ Portes Ouvertes des Ateliers d'Artistes de Belleville

More than 250 painters, sculptors and other artists in Belleville open their studio doors (www.ateliers-artistes-belleville.fr) to visitors over four days (Friday to Monday) in late May.

🏃 French Open

The glitzy Internationaux de France de Tennis Grand Slam (www.rolandgarros. com) hits up from late May to early June at Stade Roland Garros at the Bois de Boulogne.

June

Paris is positively jumping in June, thanks to warm temperatures and long daylight hours. Come evening, twilight lingering until nearly 11pm is the stuff of dreams.

☆ Festival de St-Denis

Book ahead for this prestigious cycle of classical-music concerts at the Basilique de St-Denis (www.festival-saint-denis.com) and nearby venues held throughout the month.

☆ Fête de la Musique

National music festival (http://fetedelamusique.cul turecommunication.gouv.fr) on the summer solstice (21 June) with staged and impromptu live performances of jazz, reggae, classical and more all over the city.

🎆 Gay Pride March

Late June's colourful Saturday-afternoon Marche des Fiertés (www.gaypride.fr) through Le Marais to Bastille celebrates Gay Pride Day with over-the-top floats and outrageous costumes.

☆ Paris Jazz Festival

Free jazz concerts swing every Saturday and Sunday afternoon in June and July in the Parc Floral de Paris during the Paris Jazz Festival (www.parisjazzfestival.

fr). Park entry for adults/under 25s of €6/3 applies.

☆ La Goutte d'Or en Fête

Raï, reggae and rap feature at this three-day world-music festival (http://goutte dorenfete.wordpress.com) on square Léon in the 18e's Goutte d'Or neighbourhood in late June.

July

During the Parisian summer, 'beaches' – complete with sunbeds, umbrellas, atomisers, lounge chairs and palm trees – line the banks of the Seine, while shoppers hit the summer *soldes* (sales).

🎆 Bastille Day

The capital celebrates France's national day on 14 July with a morning military parade along av des Champs-Élysées accompanied by a fly-past of fighter aircraft and helicopters. *Feux d'artifice* (fireworks) light up the sky above the Champ de Mars by night.

🏃 Paris Plages

From mid-July to early September, 'Paris Beaches' (www.paris.fr) take over the Right Bank between the Louvre, 1er, and Pont de Sully, 4e; and the Rotonde de la Villette and rue de Crimée, 19e. All beaches are open from 8am to midnight.

🏃 Tour de France

The last of the 21 stages of this legendary, 3500km-long cycling event (www.letour.com) finishes with a dash up av des Champs-Élysées on the third or fourth Sunday of July.

August

Parisians desert the city in droves during the summer swelter when, despite an influx of tourists, many restaurants and shops shut. It's a prime time to cycle, with far less traffic on the roads.

☆ Cinéma au Clair de Lune

Film screenings take place under the stars around town in late July/early August during Paris' free 'moonlight cinema', organised by the Forum des Images (www.forumdesimages.fr).

☆ Rock en Seine

Headlining acts rock the Domaine National de St-Cloud, on the city's southwestern edge, at this popular three-day, late-August music festival (www.rockenseine.com).

September

Tourists leave and Parisians come home: *la rentrée* marks residents' return to work and study after the summer break. Cultural life shifts into top gear and the weather is often at its blue-skied best.

☆ Jazz à La Villette

This super two-week jazz festival (www.jazzala villette.com) in the first half of September has sessions in Parc de la Villette, at the Cité de la Musique and at surrounding venues.

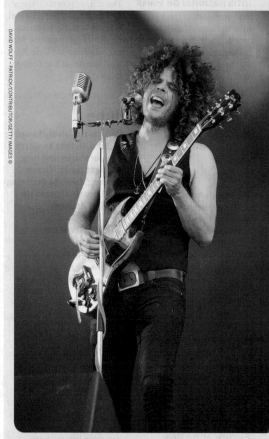

(Below) Andrew Stockdale from Wolfmother performs at Rock en Seine
(Bottom) Champs-Élysées Christmas Market

DAVID WOLFF – PATRICK/CONTRIBUTOR/GETTY IMAGES ©

KIEV.VICTOR/SHUTTERSTOCK ©

☆ Festival d'Automne

The long-running Autumn Festival of arts (www.festival-automne.com), from mid-September to late December, incorporates painting, music, dance and theatre at venues throughout the city.

☆ Techno Parade

On one Saturday in mid-September, floats carrying musicians and DJs pump up the volume as they travel between place de la République and place d'Italie during the Techno Parade (www.technoparade.fr).

☉ Journées Européennes du Patrimoine

The third weekend in September sees Paris open the doors of otherwise off-limits buildings – embassies, government ministries and so forth – during European Heritage Days (journeesdupatrimoine.culturecommunication.gouv.fr).

October

October heralds an autumnal kaleidoscope in the city's parks and gardens, along with bright, crisp days, cool, clear nights and excellent cultural offerings. Daylight saving ends on the last Sunday morning of the month.

☆☆ Nuit Blanche

From sundown until sunrise on the first Saturday and Sunday of October, museums and recreational facilities like swimming pools stay open, along with bars and clubs, for one 'White Night' (ie 'All-Nighter'; www.paris.fr).

☆☆ Fête des Vendanges de Montmartre

The grape harvest from the Clos Montmartre in early October is followed by five days of festivities including a parade (www.fetedesvendangesdemontmartre.com).

☉ Foire Internationale d'Art Contemporain

Scores of galleries are represented at the contemporary-art fair known as FIAC (www.fiac.com), held over four days in late October at venues including the Grand Palais.

November

Dark, chilly days and long, cold nights see Parisians take refuge indoors: the opera and ballet seasons are going strong and there are plenty of cosy bistros and bars.

☆ Africolor

From mid-November to late December, this six-week-long African-music festival (www.africolor.com) is primarily held in outer suburbs, such as St-Denis, St-Ouen and Montreuil.

☐ Beaujolais Nouveau

At midnight on the third Thursday (ie Wednesday night) in November – as soon as French law permits – the opening of the first bottles of cherry-bright, six-week-old Beaujolais Nouveau is celebrated in Paris wine bars, with more celebrations on the Thursday itself.

December

Twinkling fairy lights, brightly decorated Christmas trees and shop windows, and outdoor ice-skating rinks make December a magical month to be in the City of Light.

☐ Champs-Élysées Christmas Market

Paris stages several Christmas markets from mid-November to early January; this one on the Champs-Élysées, with over 100 food, gift and mulled-wine 'chalets' set up along the famous avenue, is the largest.

☆☆ Christmas Eve Mass

Mass is celebrated at midnight on Christmas Eve at many Paris churches, including Notre Dame – arrive early to find a place.

☆☆ Le Festival du Merveilleux

Normally closed to the public, the magical private museum Musée des Arts Forains (www.arts-forains.com), filled with fairground attractions of yesteryear, opens for 11 days from late December to early January, with enchanting rides, attractions and shows.

☆☆ New Year's Eve

Bd St-Michel, 5e; place de la Bastille, 11e; the Eiffel Tower, 7e; and especially av des Champs-Élysées, 8e, are the Parisian hot spots to welcome in the new year, although no New Year's fireworks have taken place in recent years.

With Kids

Paris is extraordinarily child friendly, with an overwhelming choice of creative, educational, culinary and 'pure old-fashioned fun' things to see, do, experience. Plan ahead to get the best out of kid-friendly Paris.

Jardin des Tuileries (p118)

Science Museums

Cité des Sciences

If you have time for just one museum, make it this one (p138). Book interactive Cité des Enfants sessions (for children aged two to 12) in advance to avoid disappointment.

Palais de la Découverte

Collections at this science museum (p97) are a perfect mix of interactive and academic; outstanding science-experiment workshops for over-10s.

Musée des Arts et Métiers

Crammed with instruments and machines, Europe's oldest science and technology museum (p161) is mesmerising. Activity- and experiment-driven workshops are top-notch.

Art Attack

Centre Pompidou

Urban ode to modern art (p116) with great exhibitions, art workshops (for kids aged three to 12) and teen events in Studio 13/16.

Musée en Herbe

Thoughtful art museum (p121) for children with an excellent bookshop and art workshops for kids aged two to 12.

Palais de Tokyo

Palais de Tokyo (p87) offers interactive installations, art workshops (for kids six to 12) and storytelling sessions (for three- to five-year-olds).

Treasure Hunts with THATLou

Give the kids a burst of art adrenalin with a THATLou (p336) treasure hunt at the Louvre or an equivalent THATd'Or hunt at the Musée d'Orsay. Play alone or in teams. Fabulous fun for all ages.

Hands-On Activities

Crafty Happenings at Musée du Quai Branly

Mask-making, boomerang-hurling and experimenting with traditional instruments: the ateliers (for kids aged three to 12) at this Seine-side museum (p84) devoted to

African, Asian and Oceanic art and culture are diverse and creative.

Music at Philharmonie de Paris

Concerts, shows and instrument workshops are part of the world-music repertoire at the city's cutting-edge philharmonic hall (p139) in Parc de la Villette.

Bag Painting with Kasia Dietz

Design and paint a reversible, hand-printed canvas tote with Paris-based New Yorker **Kasia Dietz** (www.kasiadietz-workshops.com; workshop €90-120); ideal for fashion-conscious teens (and parents).

Model Building at Cité de l'Architecture et du Patrimoine

Workshops at Paris' architecture museum (p85) see kids (aged five to 16 years) build art deco houses, châteaux and towers in miniature form.

Animal Mad

Equestrian Shows at Versailles

World-class equestrian shows (p268) at Château de Versailles are mesmerising and magical; combine with a stable visit.

Sharks at Aquarium de Paris Cinéaqua

It's not the best aquarium, but Cinéaqua (p87) has a shark tank and 500-odd fish species.

Ménagerie du Jardin des Plantes

The collection of animals (p208) in Jardin des Plantes includes snow panthers and pandas; combine with the neighbouring Natural History Museum (p209).

Parc Zoologique de Paris

Observe lions, cougars, white rhinos and a whole gaggle of other beasties at this state-of-the-art zoo (p183) in Bois de Vincennes.

Parks & Outdoor Capers

Sailing Boats in Jardin du Luxembourg

Playgrounds, puppet shows, pony rides, chess and an old-fashioned carousel: this

legendary park (p228) has pandered to children for forever. But it is the vintage toy boats to sail that are the real heart-stealer.

Jardin des Tuileries

Light relief after the neighbouring Louvre, this Seine-side park (p118) stages kids' activities (including puppet shows) and a summertime amusement park.

Parc Floral de Paris

Easily the best playground (p183) for kids eight years and older: outdoor concerts, puppet shows, giant climbing webs, 30m-high slides and a zip line, among other high-energy-burning attractions.

Jardin d'Acclimatation

This enormous green area (p90) with cycling paths, forest, lakes and ponds in the Bois de Boulogne is a family must. Renting a pedalo or rowing boat – bring a picnic – is a warm-weather treat, and every child loves the faster-paced amusement park and puppet shows.

Locks on Canal St-Martin

Watching canal boats navigate the many locks (p148) is fun, fascinating and free. Lunch waterside on fish and chips from the Sunken Chip (p143).

Riverside Play on Les Berges de Seine

Giant board games, a climbing wall, a 20m-long blackboard to chalk on, tepees and events 'n' shows galore line this expressway-turned-promenade (p233).

PAWEL LIBERA/GETTY IMAGES ©

Cruising down the Seine

Boat Trips on the Seine

Every kid, big and small, loves a voyage down the Seine with Bateaux-Mouches (p336) or Bateaux Parisiens (p336). But there is something extra special about the one-hour 'Paris Mystery' tours designed especially for children by Vedettes de Paris (p336).

Screen Entertainment

Digital Exhibitions at Gaîté Lyrique

Digital-driven exhibitions (p174), video games for older children and teens, laptops to use in the digitally connected cafe and a library with desks shaped like ducks for kids under five to sit at and draw while older siblings geek.

Comic Art at Art Ludique–Le Musée

Teens will appreciate this refreshingly different art museum (p251) dedicated to comics, video games, animation and live-action cinema.

Special-Effect Movies at Cité des Sciences

Two special-effect cinemas: Géode with 3D movies, and Cinéma Louis-Lumière

screening animation and short films. Top it off with a cinematic trip through the solar system in the Planetarium of the science museum (p138).

Behind-the-Scenes Tour at Le Grand Rex

Whiz-bang special effects stun during behind-the-scenes tours at this iconic 1930s cinema (p131). Stand behind the big screen and muck around in a recording studio.

Theme Parks

The obvious park, best suited for children aged four to 10, is Disneyland Resort Paris (p269). The other hot shot is **Parc Astérix** (☎08 26 46 66 26; www.parcasterix.fr; A1 motorway btwn exit 7 & 8, Plailly; adult/child €47/39; ⊗10am-6pm daily Apr & Jun, 10am-6pm Wed, Sat & Sun May, 10am-7pm daily Jul & Aug, 10am-6pm Sat & Sun Sep & Oct), which is 30km north of Paris. Despite its Gaulish comic-book-inspired name, this park covers the whole gamut from prehistory to the 19th century with its six 'worlds', adrenaline-pumping attractions and shows for all ages.

Easy Eating

Pink Flamingo Pizza Picnic

Where else are you sent away with a pink balloon when you order? Kids adore take-away pizzeria Pink Flamingo (p143) with outlets on Canal St-Martin and in Bastille and Le Marais.

Hand-Pulled Noodles at Les Pâtes Vivantes

Watching nimble-fingered chefs pull traditional **Chinese noodles** (Map p370, E3; ☎01 45 23 10 21; www.lespatesvivantes.net; 46 du Faubourg Montmartre, 9e; noodles €9.80-12; ⊗noon-3pm & 7-11pm; MLe Peletier) by hand is spellbinding.

Le Jardin des Pâtes

This Left Bank address (p212), steps from Jardin des Plantes, cooks up some of Paris' most creative and tasty pasta.

Dip in at Chalet Savoyard

Everyone loves a bubbling pot of cheese, a basket of bread and a fondue fork (p187).

Best Crêpes in Town

The best bit about Breizh Café (p163) is the Breton cider parents can sip while kids tuck into some of Paris' best crêpes.

Three-Course Dining

Le Clown Bar

Enchant children with fantastical paintings, ceramics and murals over gourmet modern French cuisine at this legendary address (p167) next to the city's winter circus in Le Marais.

Historic at La Coupole

The historic 1927 setting (p257) might not overly impress kids, but the lavish children's *menu* and game-filled notebooks to entertain will.

Gourmet at Glou

How refreshing to find a hip wine bar (p168) in Le Marais that serves excellent food and fine wine, *and* caters to children with their own gourmet *menu* (two- or three-course set menu), colouring pencils and paper.

Playful Le Nid

Older children and teens can kick back with board games over a drink, lunch or tasty weekend brunch at this pioneering games cafe (p173) in Le Marais – as much for adults as big kids.

Sweet Dessance

Three-course dining (Map p386, D4; ☎01 42 77 23 62; www.dessance.fr; 74 rue des Archives, 3e; 2-/3-course lunch menu €22/26, tasting menus €36-50; ⊙noon-11pm Wed, Thu & Sun, to midnight Fri & Sat; ; MArts et Métiers) built very much from sweet bites and desserts. How could any child refuse?

Le Jardin des Plumes

Michelin-starred children's *menus* wow at this county estate (p277) in Giverny.

Rainy Day Ideas

Cirque d'Hiver Bouglione

Clowns, trapeze artists and acrobats have entertained children of all ages at the city's winter circus (p175) since 1852. The season runs October to March; performances last around 2½ hours.

Musée des Égouts de Paris

Romping through sewerage tunnels, learning what happens when you flush a loo in Paris and spotting rats is all part of the experience at this quirky museum (p234).

Les Catacombes

Teens generally get a kick out of Paris' most macabre sight (p248), but be warned: guided tours of this underground cemetery packed with more skulls than you can imagine is not for the faint-hearted.

Muséum National d'Histoire Naturelle

No space is better designed for children (aged six to 12) than the inventive Galerie des Enfants inside Paris' first-class Natural History Museum (p209).

An Afternoon at the Theatre

Paris' diverse theatre scene stages bags of *spectacles* (shows), *théâtre classique* (classical theatre) and other performances for kids, some in English; weekly entertainment mag *Pariscope* (€0.70, www.facebook.com/pariscope.fr, or download the free app) lists what's on.

Musée de la Magie

Pure magic (p160)!

Musée de la Poupée

Paris' doll museum (p162) is a one-stop shop for ogling vintage dolls, all shapes and sizes. Doll hospital and hands-on workshops for children and families too.

Like a Local

Paris isn't an urban resort. The city has the highest population density of any European capital, and its parks, cafes and restaurants are its communal backyards and dining rooms, while neighbourhood shops and street markets are cornerstones of local life.

Paris locals in a bar

Dining Like a Local

Parisians are obsessed with talking about, shopping for, preparing and above all eating food. Quality trumps quantity, which is reflected in the small, specialist gourmet food shops thriving all over the city.

Sunday lunch is traditionally France's main meal of the week, but Sunday (and often Saturday) brunch has become a fixture on the weekend's social calendar from around noon to about 4pm. Be sure to prebook popular venues.

Another part of the recent shift towards informal dining is the profusion of casual wine bars where, rather than ordering full *menus* (two- or three-course set menus), locals gather to share small tapas-style plates over *un verre* (a glass).

Drinking Like a Local

For Parisians, alcohol is invariably something to be savoured rather than a means of intoxication. Parisians tend to go to bars with groups of friends, so there's often less mingling than in British-style pubs.

Given Paris' high concentration of city dwellers, most bars and cafes close around 2am due to noise restrictions, and nightclubs in the inner city are few.

Cocktail bars are shaking up Paris' drinking scene, though, with a slew of specialist bars opening across the city in recent years. Craft beer is also staking its claim in this wine-drinking city, with several Parisian breweries in fully fledged operation. **Paris Cocktail Week** (www.paris cocktailweek.fr; ☉Jan) and **Paris Beer Week** (www.laparisbeerweek.com; ☉May) are now fixtures on the city's calendar.

And, although the image of Parisians sipping *un café* on a wicker-chair-lined cafe terrace isn't new, what is new in recent years is the dramatic improvement in the quality of the coffee. A new wave of Parisian roasteries, like pioneers Belleville Brûlerie (p179) and Coutume (p241), sees hip young Parisians attending cupping sessions and buying beans to brew up back home.

Conversing Like a Local

Food and drink aside, conversations between locals often revolve around philosophy, art and sports such as rugby, football (soccer), cycling and tennis. Talking about money (salaries or spending outlays, for example) in public is generally taboo.

Hanging Out Like a Local

Parisians generally work to live rather than the other way round. Thanks to the standard working week of 35 hours (currently being hotly debated), long annual leave (which might be anything up to nine weeks) and a *lot* of public holidays, Parisians aren't driven to make and spend money 24/7/365. Instead, leisure activities factor highly in Parisians' *joie de vivre* (spirited enjoyment of life), along with the company of friends and family (children are treated like little adults and welcomed with open arms just about everywhere).

Cinemas, theatres and concert venues as well as art exhibitions, festivals and special events draw huge local crowds.

Sunday is the main day of rest, when most workplaces (including the majority of shops) close and locals head to museums, parks, and *jardins partagés* (community gardens); visit www.paris.fr for a list (and map) of gardens that are open to the public.

Year-round, you'll find locals kicking back all along the banks of the Seine but never more so than on warm summer evenings with a picnic and bottle of wine.

Meeting the Locals

The best way to get a feel for local life is to head to areas where Parisians work, live and play away from the busy tourist sights. Great neighbourhoods to start exploring:

➡ Bastille

➡ Belleville

➡ Canal St-Martin

➡ Les Halles (especially rues Montorgueil and Montmartre)

➡ Latin Quarter (especially rue Mouffetard)

NEED TO KNOW

Metro Parisians from all walks of life – from students to celebrity chefs – use the metro. If you're in Paris for a week or more, get a Navigo pass to save money and zip through the turnstiles without queuing for tickets.

Vélib' bikes Virtually free Vélib' bikes are hugely popular – Parisians flit all over the city on these pearly-taupe machines.

➡ Ménilmontant

➡ South Pigalle (aka SoPi, centred on rue des Martyrs)

➡ The 13e (especially the villagey Butte aux Cailles and floating clubs on the Seine)

Local-led tours and activities are also a fantastic way to get an insider's perspective of the city.

➡ **Parisien d'un Jour – Paris Greeters** (p337) Run by volunteers.

➡ **Ça Se Visite** (p337) Discover the city's northeastern neighbourhoods on foot or by scooter.

➡ **Localers** (p337) Walks and activities such as *pétanque* (similar to lawn bowls).

➡ **Meeting the French** (p336) Workshops and courses, from backstage cabaret tours to fashion-designer showroom visits and more.

Navigation

A few pointers to help you navigate the city like a local: street numbers notated *bis* (twice), *ter* (thrice) or *quater* (four times) are similar to the English a, b etc. If you're entering an apartment building, you'll generally need the alphanumeric *digicode* (entry code) to open the door. Once inside, apartments are usually unmarked, without any apartment numbers or even occupants' names. To know which door to knock on, you're likely to be given cryptic directions like *cinquième étage, premier à gauche* (5th floor, first on the left) or *troisième étage, droite droite* (3rd floor, turn right twice). In all buildings, the 1st floor is the floor above the *rez-de-chaussée* (ground floor).

For Free

Paris might be home to haute couture, haute cuisine and historic luxury hotels, but if you're still waiting for your lottery numbers to come up, don't despair. There's a wealth of ways to soak up the French capital without spending a centime (or scarcely any, at least).

The Panthéon (p209) dominates the skyline

Free Museums

If you can, time your trip to be here on the first Sunday of the month when you can visit the *musées nationaux* (www.rmn.fr), as well as a handful of monuments, for free (some during certain months only).

European citizens under 26 get free entry to national museums and monuments.

At any time, you can visit the permanent collections of selected *musées municipaux* (www.paris.fr) for free.

Temporary exhibitions at both national and city museums always incur a separate admission fee. Some museums have reduced entry at various times of the day or week.

National Museum & Monument Free Days

The museums and monuments offering free admission on the first Sunday of the month:

➡ Arc de Triomphe (p94); November to March

➡ Basilique de St-Denis (p140); November to March

➡ Château de Versailles (p263); November to March

➡ Cité de l'Architecture et du Patrimoine (p85)

➡ Conciergerie (p201); November to March

➡ Musée de la Chasse et de la Nature (p162)

➡ Musée de l'Histoire de l'Immigration (p183)

➡ Musée de l'Orangerie (p118)

➡ Musée des Arts et Métiers (p161); also free every Thursday from 6pm

➡ Musée des Impressionnismes Giverny (p277)

➡ Musée d'Orsay (p224)

➡ Musée du Louvre (p108); October to March

➡ Musée du Quai Branly (p84)

➡ Musée Guimet des Arts Asiatiques (p86)

➡ Musée National d'Art Moderne (p116); within the Centre Pompidou

➡ Musée National du Moyen Âge (p207)

➡ Musée National Eugène Delacroix (p233)

➡ Musée National Gustave Moreau (p99)

➡ Musée Picasso (p161)

➡ Musée Rodin (p230)

➡ Panthéon (p209); November to March

➡ Sainte-Chapelle (p200); November to March

➡ Tours de Notre Dame (p195); November to March

39

PLAN YOUR TRIP FOR FREE

Other Free Museums

Other freebies include Paris' fascinating town-planning and architectural centre, the Pavillon de l'Arsenal (www.pavillon-arsenal.com) in Le Marais, and the Musée du Parfum (p97), which are free all year.

Admission to the Maison Européenne de la Photographie (p161) is free from 5pm every Wednesday evening.

Free Churches

Some of the city's most magnificent buildings are its churches and other places of worship. Not only exceptional architecturally and historically, they contain exquisite art, artefacts and other priceless treasures. Best of all, entry to general areas within them is, in most cases, free.

Do respect the fact that although many of Paris' places of worship are also major tourist attractions, Parisians come here to pray and celebrate significant events on religious calendars as part of their daily lives. Keep noise to a minimum, obey photography rules (check signs), dress appropriately and try to avoid key times (eg Mass) if you're sightseeing only.

Free Cemeteries

Paris' celebrity-filled cemeteries, including the three largest – Père Lachaise (p157), Cimetière de Montmartre (p137) and Cimetière du Montparnasse (p250) – are free to wander.

Free Entertainment

Free Music

Concerts, DJ sets and recitals regularly take place for free (or for the cost of a drink) at venues throughout the city. Busking musicians and performers entertain crowds on streets and even aboard the metro.

Free Literary Events

This literary-minded city is an inspired place to catch a reading, author signing or writing workshop. English-language bookshops such as Shakespeare & Company (p219) and Abbey Bookshop (p220) host literary events throughout the year and can point you towards others.

Free Fashion Shows

Reserve ahead to attend free weekly fashion shows (p105) at Galeries Lafayette's flagship department store (p104). While you're here, don't miss one of the best free views over the Parisian skyline from Galeries Lafayette's rooftop. Nearby department store Le Printemps (p105) also has amazing – and free – views from the roof.

Free Festivals

Loads of Paris' festivals and events are free, such as the Paris Plages (p29) beaches.

Getting Around

Walking

Paris is an eminently walkable city, with beautiful parks and gardens, awe-inspiring architecture, and markets and shops to check out along the way.

For a free walking tour, contact Paris Greeters (p337) in advance for a personalised excursion led by a resident volunteer.

Cycling (Almost Free)

If you'd rather free-wheel around Paris, the Vélib' (p333) system costs next to nothing for a day's subscription, and the first 30 minutes of each bike rental is free.

Buses (Cheap As Chips)

Instead of taking a bus tour, simply hop on a local bus. Scenic routes include lines 21 and 27 (Opéra–Panthéon), line 29 (Opéra–Gare de Lyon), line 47 (Centre Pompidou–Gobelins), line 63 (Musée d'Orsay–Trocadéro), line 73 (Concorde–Arc de Triomphe) and line 82 (Montparnasse–Eiffel Tower). Time it to avoid peak commuting hours.

NEED TO KNOW

➡ Paris has hundreds of free wi-fi points at popular locations including parks, libraries, local town halls and tourist hot spots. Locations are mapped at www.paris.fr.

➡ Consider investing in a transport or museum pass.

➡ Theatre tickets are sold for half price on the day of performance.

➡ Paris' parks are perfect for picnics made from market fare.

Cité des Sciences (p138), designed by architect Adrien Fainsilber

👁 Museums & Galleries

If there's one thing that rivals a Parisian's obsession with food, it's art. More than 200 museums pepper the city, and whether you prefer the classicism of the Musée du Louvre, the impressionists of the Musée d'Orsay or detailed exhibits of French military history, you can always be sure to find something new just around the corner.

Paris Museum Pass

If you think you'll be visiting more than two or three museums or monuments while in Paris, the single most important investment you can make is the Paris Museum Pass (p338). The pass is valid for entry to some 34 venues in the city, including the Louvre, Centre Pompidou, Musée d'Orsay and the Musée Rodin (but not the Eiffel Tower). It will get you into another 20 places outside the city, including the châteaux at Versailles and Fontainebleau and the Basilique de St-Denis.

One of the best features of the pass is that you can bypass the long ticket queues at major attractions (though not the security queues). But be warned, the pass is valid for a certain number of days, not hours, so if you activate a two-day pass late Friday afternoon, for instance, you will only be able to use it for a full day on Saturday. Also keep in mind that most museums are closed on either Monday or Tuesday, so think twice before you activate a pass on a Sunday.

The Paris Museum Pass is available online as well as at participating museums, tourist desks at the airports, branches of the Paris

Convention & Visitors Bureau, Fnac outlets (www.fnactickets.com) and major metro stations. European citizens under 26 and children under 18 years get free entry to national museums and monuments, so *don't* buy this pass if you belong to one of those categories.

For Free

Municipal museums in Paris (eg Musée Carnavalet) are all free; many other museums have one free day per month (generally the first Sunday of the month, in some cases winter months only). Note that temporary exhibits almost always have a separate admission fee, even at free museums.

Performances

Many museums host excellent musical concerts and performances, with schedules that generally run from September to early June. Some of the top venues:

➡ **Musée du Louvre** (p108) Hosts a series of lunchtime and evening classical concerts throughout the week.

➡ **Musée d'Orsay** (p224) Chamber music every Tuesday at 12.30pm, plus various evening classical performances.

➡ **Musée du Quai Branly** (p84) Folk performances of theatre, dance and music from around the world.

➡ **Musée National du Moyen Âge** (p207) Daytime medieval music performances twice a week plus some additional evening concerts.

➡ **Centre Pompidou** (p116) Film screenings and avant-garde dance and music performances.

➡ **Le 104** (p139) A veritable potpourri of everything from circus and magic to afternoon breakdancing.

Workshops

If you have kids in tow, make sure you check out the day's workshops (atéliers). Although these are often in French, most activities involve hands-on creation, so children should enjoy themselves despite any language barrier. At major museums (eg Centre Pompidou), it's best to sign up in advance.

Dining

Although there are plenty of tourist cafeterias to be found in Paris, the dining options in museums are generally pretty good – some are destinations in themselves. Even if you're not out sightseeing, consider a meal at one of the following:

➡ **Les Ombres** (p91) and **Café Branly** (p83) These two dining options at the Musée du Quai Branly have ringside seats for the Eiffel Tower.

➡ **Tokyo Eat** (p89) and **Monsieur Bleu** (p91) Two hip venues at the Palais du Tokyo.

➡ **Restaurant Musée d'Orsay** (p225) and **Café Campana** (p225) Within the Musée d'Orsay; the former was the art nouveau railway station's showpiece restaurant.

➡ **Mini Palais** (p100) Gorgeous terrace and modern French cuisine in the Grand Palais.

➡ **Musée Jacquemart-André** (p138) Lunch or tea in the sumptuous dining room of a 19th-century mansion.

➡ **Le Bal Café** (p138) Modern British cuisine and superb coffee in a hidden, arty hang-out.

➡ **Le Cristal Room** (p88) Baccarat crystal meets Philippe Starck design in this Galerie-Musée Baccarat stunner.

Public Art

Museums and galleries are not the sole repositories of art in Paris. Indeed, art is all around you, including *murs végétaux* (vertical gardens adorning apartment buildings), and street art ranging from small murals to artworks covering entire high-rises and 'invader' tags (tiled Space Invaders–inspired creations) marking street corners. Enjoying art in Paris is simply a matter of keeping your eyes open.

While the smaller, anonymous works are among the most interesting and unique, there are plenty of big-name installations as well that have become destinations in their own right. Niki de Saint Phalle and Jean Tinguely's playful *Stravinsky Fountain* – a collection of 16 colourful, animated sculptures based on the composer's oeuvre – is located next to the Centre Pompidou. Daniel Buren's zebra-striped columns of varying heights at the Palais Royal is another

NEED TO KNOW

➡ City museums (eg Petit Palais, Musée Cognacq-Jay) are free.

➡ Temporary exhibits almost always have a separate admission fee, even at free museums.

➡ Ask if you qualify for a reduced-price ticket (*tarif réduit*): students, seniors and children generally get discounts or free admission.

TIPS FOR AVOIDING MUSEUM FATIGUE

➡ Wear comfortable shoes and make use of the toilets.

➡ Sit down as often as you can; standing still and walking slowly promote tiredness.

➡ Reflecting on the material and forming associations with it causes information to move from your short- to long-term memory; your experiences will thus amount to more than a series of visual 'bites'. Using an audioguide is a good way to provide context.

➡ Studies suggest that museum-goers spend no more than 10 seconds viewing an exhibit and another 10 seconds reading the label as they try to take in as much as they can. To avoid this, choose a particular period or section to focus on, or join a guided tour of the highlights.

beloved Paris fixture; the installation was originally greeted with derision but has since become an integral part of the historic site. Both the Jardin des Tuileries and the Jardin du Luxembourg are dotted with dozens of sculptures that date from the 19th and early 20th centuries; the Jardin des Tuileries also contains an area with more contemporary works from the likes of Lichtenstein and Magdalena Abakanowicz.

Interestingly, one of the best areas to go hunting for contemporary public art – and architecture – is out in the business district of La Défense, where you'll find some 60 works by well-known artists such as Miró, Calder and Belmondo. Metro stations, too, often contain some iconic or unusual additions, from Hector Guimard's signature art nouveau entrances to the crown-shaped cupolas at the Palais Royal.

Tickets

Consider booking online to avoid queues where possible (eg Musée d'Orsay, Centre Pompidou); preprint tickets if necessary. In some cases you can download the tickets on to a smartphone, but check before you make a purchase. Also ensure you can download more than one ticket on to your phone if need be.

If you can't book online, keep an eye out for automated machines at museum entrances, which generally have shorter queues. Note that credit cards without an embedded smart chip (and some non-European chip-enabled cards) won't work in these machines.

Opening Hours

Most museums are closed on either Monday or Tuesday – it is vital that you verify

opening days before drawing up your day's schedule.

General opening hours are from 10am to 6pm, though all museums shut their gates between 30 minutes and an hour before their actual closing times. Thus, if a museum is listed as closing at 6pm, make sure you get there before 5pm.

Major museums are often open one or two nights a week, which is an excellent time to visit as there are fewer visitors.

Museums & Galleries by Neighbourhood

➡ **Eiffel Tower & Western Paris** (p85) The largest concentration of museums in Paris, from the Quai Branly to Musée Marmottan Monet.

➡ **Champs-Élysées & Grands Boulevards** (p96) Grand Palais, La Pinacothèque, Petit Palais and more.

➡ **Louvre & Les Halles** (p120) The Louvre, Centre Pompidou, Musée de l'Orangerie and others.

➡ **Montmartre & Northern Paris** (p137) Musée Jacquemart-André, Cité des Sciences, Le 104 and others.

➡ **Le Marais, Ménilmontant & Belleville** (p160) Musée National Picasso and Musée Carnavalet, among others.

➡ **Bastille & Eastern Paris** (p182) Cinémathèque Française and others.

➡ **Latin Quarter** (p208) Musée National du Moyen Âge, Muséum National d'Histoire Naturelle, and Institut du Monde Arabe.

➡ **St-Germain & Les Invalides** (p232) Musée d'Orsay, Musée Rodin and more.

➡ **Montparnasse & Southern Paris** (p246) Fondation Cartier and others.

Lonely Planet's Top Choices

Musée du Louvre (p108) The one museum you just can't miss.

Musée d'Orsay (p224) Monet, Van Gogh and company.

Centre Pompidou (p116) One of the top modern-art museums in Europe.

Musée Rodin (p230) Superb collection of Rodin's masterpieces in an intimate setting.

Musée National Picasso (p161) An incomparable overview of Picasso's work and life.

Best Modern Art Museums & Installations

Centre Pompidou (p116) Huge selection of modern art and big-name temporary exhibits.

Grand Palais (p96) Varied exhibitions inside a beautiful, 1900-built art nouveau building.

Palais de Tokyo (p87) Interactive contemporary-art exhibitions and installations against a stark concrete-and-steel backdrop.

Jeu de Paume (p118) Contemporary-photography exhibitions in the Jardin des Tuileries.

Best Unsung Museums

La Pinacothèque (p97) Shaking up the Paris art world with juxtaposed works and a diverse program of exhibitions.

Cité de l'Architecture et du Patrimoine (p85) Standout museum devoted to French architecture and heritage.

Musée Jacquemart-André (p138) Gorgeous 19th-century mansion hung with canvases by Rembrandt, Botticelli and Titian.

Musée des Lettres et Manuscrits (p232) Handwritten letters and works providing a powerful connection to their famous authors.

Best History Museums

Musée National du Moyen Âge (p207) Where medieval history and crafts come to life.

Musée de l'Armée (p231) Within the monumental Hôtel des Invalides complex, commemorating French military history.

Musée de Montmartre (p137) Relive the days of Toulouse-Lautrec and Maurice Utrillo.

Best Museums for Non-European Art

Musée du Quai Branly (p84) Overview of indigenous art from around the world, presented in the most striking of manners.

Musée Guimet (p86) France's foremost Asian art museum.

Musée du Louvre (p108) Mesopotamian, Egyptian and Islamic artefacts.

Institut du Monde Arabe (p210) Art and artisanship from the Middle East and North Africa.

Best Small Museums

Musée de l'Orangerie (p118) For Monet's sublime *Water Lilies* series.

Cinémathèque Française (p182) Props, early equipment

and short clips bring cinematic history to life.

Musée Marmottan Monet (p88) The world's largest Monet collection.

Musée de la Vie Romantique (p138) Dedicated to the work of two Romantic artists.

Best Science Museums

Cité des Sciences (p138) Excellent science-related exhibits and attractions for all ages.

Muséum National d'Histoire Naturelle (p209) Dinosaur skeletons, taxidermic elephants and excellent temporary exhibits.

Palais de la Découverte (p97) Engaging, interactive children's science museum attached to the Grand Palais.

Musée des Arts et Métiers (p161) Europe's oldest science and technology museum.

Best Residence Museums

Musée National Eugène Delacroix (p233) The Romantic artist's home and studio contains many of his more intimate works.

Musée Cognacq-Jay (p161) Treasure trove of artwork and objets d'art.

Musée Nissim de Camondo (p140) Sumptuous mansion housing a private 19th-century collection of art and furnishings.

Musée Bourdelle (p249) Monumental bronzes displayed in the house and workshop of sculptor Antoine Bourdelle.

Maison de Victor Hugo (p160) Victor Hugo's former quarters, overlooking Paris' most elegant square.

 # Eating

The inhabitants of some cities rally around local sports teams, but in Paris, they rally around la table – and everything on it. Pistachio macarons, shots of tomato consommé, decadent bœuf bourguignon, a gooey wedge of Camembert running onto the cheese plate...food is not fuel here, it's the reason you get up in the morning.

Macarons

Paris: A Culinary Renaissance

Home to one of the world's great culinary traditions, France has shaped Western cooking techniques and conceptions of what good food is for centuries – whether it's a multicourse gourmet meal or a crusty baguette. Blessed with a rich and varied landscape, farmers with a strong sense of regional identity and a culture that celebrates life's daily pleasures, it's no surprise that French chefs have long been synonymous with gastronomic genius.

Over the past several decades, though, restaurant culture has started to slip. Frozen and industrially prepared ingredients, stultifying business regulations and an over-reliance on formulaic dishes led to a general decline in both quality and innovation. Alarmed by these foreboding trends, a new generation of chefs has emerged in the past several years, reemphasising market-driven cuisine and displaying a willingness to push the boundaries of traditional tastes, while at the same time downplaying the importance of Michelin stars and the formal, chandelier-studded dining rooms of yesteryear.

Even more significantly, the real change that is taking place in Paris today is that more and more of these chefs – and, just as importantly, more and more diners – are open to culinary traditions originating outside of France. Some have trained abroad (in what is surely one of the greatest examples of Gallic pride-swallowing, French chef Gregory Marchand went to the UK to work for Jamie Oliver), while others aren't even French, originally hailing from Japan,

NEED TO KNOW

Price Ranges

The following price ranges refer to the cost of a two-course meal.

€ less than €20

€€ €20–40

€€€ more than €40

Opening Hours

Restaurants generally open from noon to 2pm for lunch and from 7.30pm to 10.30pm for dinner. Peak Parisian dining times are 1pm and 9pm.

Most restaurants shut for at least one full day (usually Sunday). August is the peak holiday month and many places are consequently closed during this time.

Reservations

➡ Midrange restaurants will usually have a free table for lunch (arrive by 12.30); book a day or two in advance for dinner.

➡ Reservations are absolutely mandatory for lunch and dinner at popular/high-end restaurants – up to one or two months in advance, and you may need to reconfirm on the day.

Tipping

A *pourboire* (tip) on top of the bill is not necessary as service is always included. But it is not uncommon to round up the bill if you were pleased with your waiter.

Paying the Bill

Trying to get *l'addition* (the bill) can be maddeningly slow in many cases. Do not take this personally. The French consider it rude to bring the bill immediately – you have to be persistent when it comes to getting your server's attention.

Prix-Fixe Menus

➡ Daily *formules* or *menus* (prix-fixe menus) typically include two- to four-course meals. In some cases, particularly at market-driven neobistros, there is no *carte* (menu).

➡ Lunch *menus* are often a fantastic deal and allow you to enjoy *haute cuisine* at very affordable prices.

Above: Classic French croissants
Left: Bistro on Île de la Cité (p202)

Eating by Neighbourhood

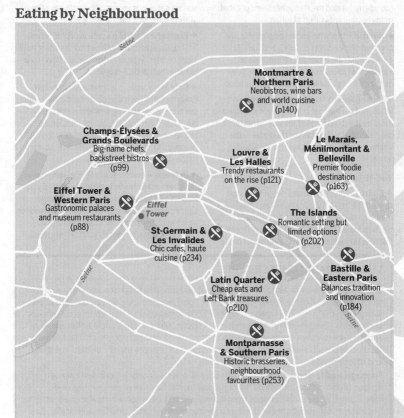

Montmartre & Northern Paris
Neobistros, wine bars and world cuisine (p140)

Champs-Élysées & Grands Boulevards
Big-name chefs, backstreet bistros (p99)

Louvre & Les Halles
Trendy restaurants on the rise (p121)

Le Marais, Ménilmontant & Belleville
Premier foodie destination (p163)

Eiffel Tower & Western Paris
Gastronomic palaces and museum restaurants (p88)

Eiffel Tower

St-Germain & Les Invalides
Chic cafes, haute cuisine (p234)

The Islands
Romantic setting but limited options (p202)

Latin Quarter
Cheap eats and Left Bank treasures (p210)

Bastille & Eastern Paris
Balances tradition and innovation (p184)

Montparnasse & Southern Paris
Historic brasseries, neighbourhood favourites (p253)

the US or elsewhere. The latter group has come to Paris specifically because they love French cooking, but none are so beholden to its traditions that they are afraid to introduce new concepts or techniques from back home. French cuisine has finally come to the realisation that a global future doesn't necessarily mean a loss of identity – decadent work-of-art pastries and the divine selection of pungent cheeses aren't going anywhere. Instead, there is an opportunity to once again create something new.

How to Eat & Drink Like a Parisian

Eating well is of prime importance to most French people, who spend an inordinate amount of time thinking about, discussing and enjoying food and wine. Yet dining out doesn't have to be a ceremonious occasion or one riddled with pitfalls for the uninitiated. Approach food with even half the enthusiasm *les français* do, and you will

be welcomed, encouraged and exceedingly well fed.

WHEN TO EAT

➡ **Petit déjeuner (breakfast)** The French kick-start the day with a *tartine* (slice of baguette smeared with unsalted butter and jam) and *un café* (espresso) or – for kids – hot chocolate. Parisians might grab a coffee and croissant on the way to work, but otherwise croissants (eaten straight, never with butter or jam) are more of a weekend or 4pm treat along with *pains au chocolat* (chocolate-filled croissants) and other *viennoiseries* (sweet pastries).

➡ **Déjeuner (lunch)** The traditional main meal of the day, lunch translates to a starter and main course with wine, followed by a short sharp *café*. During the work week this is less likely to be the case – many busy Parisians now grab a sandwich to go and pop off to run errands – but the standard hour-long lunch break, special prix-fixe *menus* and *tickets restaurant* (company-funded meal vouchers) ensure that many restaurants fill up at lunch.

➡ **Apéritif** Otherwise known as an *apéro*, the premeal drink is sacred. Cafes and bars get packed out from around 5pm onwards as Parisians wrap up work for the day and relax over a chit-chat-fuelled glass of wine or beer.

➡ **Diner (dinner)** Traditionally lighter than lunch, but a meal that is being treated more and more as the main meal of the day. In restaurants the head chef will almost certainly be in the kitchen, which is not always the case during lunch.

WHERE TO EAT

➡ **Bistro** (or *bistrot*) A small neighbourhood restaurant that serves French standards (duck confit, *steak-frites*). The setting is usually casual; if you're looking for a traditional French meal, a bistro is the place to start. Don't expect *haute*

cuisine service; most simply do not have the staff to cater to a diner's every whim.

➡ **Brasserie** Much like a cafe except it serves full meals, drinks and coffee from morning until 11pm or later. Typical fare includes *choucroute* (sauerkraut) and sausages.

➡ **Cafe** Many visitors will naturally gravitate towards cafes (which become bars around 5pm) because of the alluring ambience and buzzy sun-kissed terraces. Meals are inexpensive, but remember they often consist of industrially prepared food that's simply reheated, so stick to the drinks.

➡ **Crêperie** A quintessentially Parisian snack is the street crêpe made to order, slathered with Nutella and folded up in a triangular wedge. Crêpes can be so much more than this, however, as a trip to any authentic crêperie will reveal. Savoury crêpes, known as *galettes*, are made

THE FIVE BASIC CHEESE TYPES

Charles de Gaulle once famously asked how it was possible to govern a country with 246 types of cheese. A more relevant question for non-Frenchies: how do you come to grips with a shop that sells 246 types of cheese? The choices on offer at a *fromagerie* (cheese shop) can be overwhelming, but vendors will always allow you to sample before you buy, and they are usually very generous with their guidance and pairing advice. The following list divides French cheeses into five main groups – as they are usually divided in a shop – and recommends several types in each family to try.

Fromage à pâte demi-dure 'Semi-hard cheese' means uncooked, pressed cheese. Among the finest are Tomme de Savoie, made from either raw or pasteurised cow's milk; Cantal, a cow's-milk cheese from Auvergne that tastes something like cheddar; St-Nectaire, a pressed cheese that has a strong, complex taste; and Ossau-Iraty, a ewe's-milk cheese made in the Basque Country.

Fromage à pâte dure 'Hard cheese' is always cooked and then pressed. Among the most popular are Beaufort, a grainy cow's-milk cheese with a slightly fruity taste from Rhône-Alpes; Comté, a cheese made with raw cow's milk in Franche-Comté; Emmental, a cow's-milk cheese made all over France; and Mimolette, an Edam-like dark-orange cheese from Lille that can be aged for up to 36 months.

Fromage à pâte molle 'Soft cheese' is moulded or rind-washed. Camembert, a classic moulded cheese from Normandy that for many is synonymous with 'French cheese', and Brie de Meaux are both made from raw cow's milk. Munster from Alsace, mild Chaource and strong-smelling Langres from Champagne, and the odorous Époisses de Bourgogne are rind-washed, fine-textured cheeses.

Fromage à pâte persillée 'Marbled' or 'blue cheese' is so called because the veins often resemble *persille* (parsley). Roquefort is a ewe's-milk veined cheese that is to many the king of French cheeses. Fourme d'Ambert is a mild cow's-milk cheese from Rhône-Alpes. Bleu du Haut Jura (also called Bleu de Gex) is a mild, blue-veined mountain cheese.

Fromage de chèvre 'Goat's-milk cheese' is usually creamy and both sweet and slightly salty when fresh, but hardens and gets much saltier as it matures. Among the best varieties are Ste-Maure de Touraine, a creamy, mild cheese from the Loire region; Crottin de Chavignol, a classic though saltier variety from Burgundy; Cabécou de Rocamadour from Midi-Pyrénées, often served warm with salad or marinated in oil and rosemary; and Chabichou, a soft, slightly aged cheese from Poitou.

Above: Al fresco dining in Montmartre (p140)
Right: A selection of cheese being enjoyed

LECHATNOIR/GETTY IMAGES ©

with buckwheat flour; dessert crêpes are made with white flour – usually you order one of each accompanied by a bowl of cider.

→ **Gastronomic** Pierre Gagnaire, Guy Savoy, Pascal Barbot...Paris has one of the highest concentrations of culinary magicians in the world. Designed to amaze your every sense, many of these restaurants are once-in-a-lifetime destinations – even for Parisians – so do your homework and make sure you reserve well in advance.

→ **Market** Fantastic places to wander: here you'll find all the French culinary specialities in the same place, in addition to meals and snacks cooked on site. At last count there were 82 food markets in the city. Most are open twice weekly from 8.30am to 1pm, though covered markets keep longer hours, reopening around 4pm.

→ **Neobistro** Generally small and relatively informal, these are run by young, talented chefs who aren't afraid to experiment and push the envelope. The focus is on market-driven cuisine, hence choices are often limited to one or two dishes per course.

→ **Wine bar/cave à manger** The focus is on sampling wine; the style of cuisine, while often excellent, can be wildly different. Some places serve nothing more than plates of cheese and charcuterie *(saucisson, pâté)*; others are full-on gastronomic destinations with a talented chef running the kitchen.

MENU ADVICE

→ **Carte** Menu, as in the written list of what's cooking, listed in the order you'd eat it: starter, main course, cheese then dessert. Note that an entrée is a starter, not the main course (as in the US).

→ **Menu** Not at all what it means in English, *le menu* in French is a prix-fixe *menu*: a multicourse meal at a fixed price. It's by far the best-value dining there is and most restaurants chalk one on the board. In some cases, particularly at neobistros, there is no *carte* – only a stripped-down *menu* with one or two choices.

→ **À la carte** Order whatever you fancy from the menu (as opposed to opting for a prix-fixe *menu*).

→ **Formule** Similar to a *menu, une formule* is a cheaper lunchtime option comprising a main plus starter or dessert. Wine or coffee is sometimes included.

→ **Plat du jour** Dish of the day, invariably good value.

→ **Menu enfant** Two- or three-course kids' meal (generally up to the age of 12) at a fixed price; usually includes a drink.

Top: Marché Mouffetard (p216)
Above: French bread for sale
Bottom: An assortment of éclairs

DAILY BREAD

Few things in France are as tantalising as the smell of just-baked buttery croissants wafting out of an open bakery door. With roughly 1200 *boulangeries* (bakeries) in Paris – or 11.5 per sq km – you'll likely find yourself inside one at some point during your stay. And, as you'll notice in the extravagant display windows, bakeries bake much more than baguettes: they also sell croissants, chocolate éclairs, quiches, pizzas and an astounding array of pastries and cakes. If you're eating lunch on the cheap or you're after a baguette sandwich to go, a trip to the closest bakery will do you right.

If it's the bread you're after, try to familiarise yourself with the varieties on sale while you're standing in the queue – not all baguettes are created equal. Most Parisians today will ask for a *baguette tradition* (traditional-style baguette), distinguished by its pointy tips and coarse, handcrafted surface. Other breads you'll see include *boules* (round loaves), *pavés* (flattened rectangular loaves) and *ficelles* (skinny loaves that are half the weight of a baguette).

The shape of a baguette (literally 'stick' or 'wand') evolved when Napoleon Bonaparte ordered army bakers to create loaves for soldiers to stuff down their trouser legs on the march.

Every spring *boulangers* (bakers) battle it out in the official Grand Prix de la Meilleure Baguette de Paris (Best Baguette in Paris). The winner is not only awarded a cash prize but also provides the French president with baguettes for a year.

➡ **Menu dégustation** Fixed-price tasting menu served in many top-end restaurants, consisting of five to seven modestly sized courses.

DINING TIPS

➡ **Bread** Order a meal and within seconds a basket of fresh bread will be brought to the table. Butter is rarely an accompaniment. Except in the most upmarket of places, don't expect a side plate – simply put it on the table.

➡ **Water** Asking for *une carafe d'eau* (jug of tap water) is perfectly acceptable, although some waiters will presume you don't know this and only offer mineral water, which you have to pay for. Should bubbles be more your cup of tea, ask for *de l'eau gazeuze* (fizzy mineral water). Ice (*glaçons*) can be hard to come by.

➡ **Service** To state the obvious, France is not a service-oriented country. No one is working for tips here, so to get around this, think like a Parisian – acknowledge the expertise of your *serveur* by asking for advice (even if you don't really want it) and don't be afraid to flirt. In France flirtation is not the same as picking someone up, it is both a game that makes the mundane more enjoyable and a vital life skill to help you get what you want (such as the bill). Being witty and speaking French with an accent will often help your cause.

➡ **Dress** Smart casual is best. How you look is very important, and Parisians favour personal style above all else. But if you're going some place dressy, don't assume this means suit and tie – that's more business-meal attire. At the

other end of the spectrum, running shoes may be too casual, unless, of course, they are more hip than functional, in which case you may fit right in.

Vegetarians, Vegans & Gluten-Free

Vegetarians and vegans make up a small minority in a country where *viande* (meat) once also meant 'food', and they are not particularly well catered for. Specialist vegetarian restaurants are still few in number in Paris, and it's safe to say that vegetarians will still be met with looks of genuine bewilderment at some traditional French bistros. On the up side, more and more modern places are offering vegetarian choices on their set *menus;* another good bet is non-French cuisine. See www.happy-cow.net for a decent guide to veggie options in Paris.

Likewise, gluten-free dining isn't easy: try Noglu (p122) or Helmut Newcake (p100) for starters, and boulangerie Chambelland (p169) for bread and cakes, but do your research ahead of time.

Cooking Classes

What better place to discover the secrets of *la cuisine française* than in Paris, the capital of gastronomy? Courses are available at different levels and durations.

Cook'n With Class (☑01 42 57 22 84 ; www.cooknwithclass.com; 6 rue Baudelique, 18e) A bevy of international chefs, small classes and an

Mes Bocaux food truck

enchanting Montmartre location are ingredients for success at this informal cooking school which organises dessert classes for kids, cheese and wine courses, market visits, gourmet food tours and six-course dinners with the chef and sommelier as well as regular cookery classes. Three-hour cooking classes start from €130.

Le Cordon Bleu (✆01 85 65 15 00; www.cordonbleu.edu/paris; 13-15 quai André Citroën, 15e) One of the world's foremost culinary-arts schools. Prices start from €75 for two-hour classes and €360 for two-day courses.

La Cuisine Paris (✆01 40 51 78 18; www.lacuisineparis.com; 80 quai de l'Hôtel de Ville, 4e) A variety of classes in English, ranging from how to make bread, croissants and macarons, to market classes and gourmet 'foodie walks'. Four-hour cooking classes from €69.

Le Foodist (✆06 71 70 95 22; www.lefoodist.com; 59 rue du Cardinal Lemoine, 5e) Classes at this culinary school include classic French cookery and patisserie courses such as éclairs and choux pastry, macarons or croissants. Market tours and

wine and cheese tastings and pairings are also available. Instruction is in English. Three-hour classes start from €95.

Food Trucks
Street food continues to take the city by storm as food trucks roll out across Paris. Find the day's location online or follow them on Twitter or Facebook.

Le Camion Qui Fume (p124) The 'smoking truck' that started it all, with gourmet burgers grilled by SoCal chef (and now local food celeb) Kristin Frederick, who trained at Paris' prestigious Ferrandi culinary school. Follow @lecamionquifume

Cantine California (www.cantinecalifornia.com) Organic burgers, tacos and homemade desserts from San Fran transplant Jordan Feilders. Follow @CantineCali

Mes Bocaux (www.mesbocaux.fr, 2-/3-course menu €13.80/16.50) Former Michelin-starred Savoyard chef Marc Veyrat upped the takeaway stakes when he put his small fleet of smart black food trucks on the road.

Lonely Planet's Top Choices

Restaurant AT (p215) Abstract-art-like masterpieces made from rare ingredients.

Le 6 Paul Bert (p186) Dazzling bistro dishes that change daily.

Restaurant Guy Savoy (p238) Resplendent triple-Michelin-starred flagship rehoused in the neoclassical mint.

Le Pantruche (p146) Superb modern French cuisine at fantastic value.

Hugo Desnoyer (p89) Feast for meat lovers courtesy of Paris' most famous butcher.

Best by Budget

€

Fric-Frac (p141) Wildly creative croques monsieurs by Canal St-Martin.

Hero (p141) Korean cuisine and cocktails.

La Pâtisserie (p184) Sandwiches and cakes to go by celebrity chef Cyril Lignac.

Au Pied de Fouet (p234) Bistro classics are astonishingly good value at this 150-year-old charmer.

Candelaria (p165) Hipster-favourite *taqueria* (taco restaurant).

Kunitoraya (p121) Paris' best udon noodles.

€€

Ellsworth (p122) Small plates with creative flair.

Uma (p122) For a culinary journey by the Louvre.

Le Casse Noix (p254) Cosy retro interior, affordable prices and exceptional cuisine.

La Bulle (p145) Stunning, under-the-radar address for modern French cuisine.

Matière à. (p145) Seasonal, modern French fare around a shared table.

Le Clos Y (p254) Utterly original daily changing *menus*.

€€€

Restaurant David Toutain (p240) Mystery degustation courses showcasing creative high-end cooking.

Septime (p188) A beacon of modern cuisine.

Dersou (p188) Creative fusion cuisine and bespoke cocktails.

Chez Françoise (p239) Old-school oyster specialist in the Air France building.

Frenchie (p127) The bijou bistro that redefined Parisian dining.

L'Astrance (p89) Dazzling gastronomy for a meal to remember.

Best by Cuisine

Traditional French

À la Biche au Bois (p187) Game, especially *la biche* (doe), is the speciality of the countrified 'doe in the woods'.

Le Miroir (p147) Excellent French standards at this Montmartre favourite.

Bouillon Racine (p236) Art nouveau jewel with traditional fare inspired by age-old recipes.

Le Bon Georges (p101) For those who thrive on nostalgia.

Le Temps au Temps (p187) Traditional and excellent-value bistro fare on foodie street rue Paul Bert.

Brasserie Bofinger (p168) The city's oldest brasserie.

Seafood

L'Écailler du Bistrot (p186) Extraordinary seafood in a traditional setting.

L'Avant Comptoir de la Mer (p234) Chic St-Germain seafood tapas bar.

Le Dôme (p257) Magnificent shellfish platters in a timeless art deco brasserie.

Clamato (p186) Seafood tapas courtesy of Septime's Michelin-starred chef.

Huîtrerie Regis (p236) Oyster heaven.

Veggie

Mûre (p124) Pillow-strewn cafe with fresh juices and yum breakfasts.

Le Bio d'Adam et Eve (p125) Vegan-friendly pit stop.

Tricycle Store (p141) Veggie hot dogs in the 10e.

Bob's Juice Bar (p143) Pioneering Parisian veggie address.

Krishna Bhavan (p211) All-vegetarian Indian fare.

Gentle Gourmet Café (p187) All of the dishes are vegan and most are organic at this light-filled cafe.

Crêpes

Breizh Café (p163) Among the most authentic Breton crêpes in town.

Crêpe Dentelle (p124) Superb crêpes by Les Halles.

Crêperie Pen-Ty (p143) Northern Paris' best crêperie, with traditional Breton aperitifs.

Little Breizh (p234) Innovative twists such as Breton sardines.

Le Pot O'Lait (p212) Great galettes and sweet crêpes in the Latin Quarter.

Pink champagne

🍷 Drinking & Nightlife

For the French, drinking and eating go together like wine and cheese, and the line between a cafe, salon de thé (tearoom), bistro, brasserie, bar, and even bar à vins (wine bar) is blurred. The line between drinking and clubbing is often nonexistent – a cafe that's quiet midafternoon might have DJ sets in the evening and dancing later on.

Cafe on rue Montorgueil (p126)

Drinking

For most Parisians living in tiny flats, cafes and bars have traditionally served as the *salon* they don't have – a place where they can meet with friends over *un verre* (glass of wine), read for hours over a café au lait, debate politics while downing an espresso at a zinc counter, swill cocktails during *apéro* (aperitif; predinner drink) or get the party started aboard a floating club on the Seine.

COFFEE & TEA

Coffee has always been Parisians' drink of choice to kick-start the day. So it's surprising, particularly given France's fixation on quality, that Parisian coffee has lagged behind world standards, with burnt, poor-quality beans and unrefined preparation methods. But the city is in the throes of a coffee revolution, with local roasteries like Belleville Brûlerie and Coutume priming cafes citywide for outstanding brews made by professional baristas, often using cutting-edge extraction techniques. Caffeine fiends are now spoilt for choice and while there's still plenty of substandard coffee in Paris, you don't have to go far to avoid it.

Surprisingly too, tea – more strongly associated with France's northwestern neighbours, the UK and Ireland – is extremely popular in Paris. Tearooms offer copious varieties; learn about its history at the tea museum within the original Marais branch of Mariage Frères (p179).

WINE

Wine is easily the most popular beverage in Paris and house wine can cost less than bottled water. Of France's dozens of wine-

NEED TO KNOW

Tiered Pricing

Drinking in Paris essentially means paying rent for the space you take up. So it costs more to sit at a table than to stand at the counter, more for coveted terrace seats, more on a fancy square than a backstreet, more in the 8e than the 18e.

Average Costs

A coffee starts at around €3, a glass of wine from €3.50, a cocktail €9 to €15 and a *demi* (half-pint) of beer €3.50 to €7. In clubs and chic bars, prices can be double this. Admission to clubs is free to around €20 and is often cheaper before 1am.

Happy Hour

Most mainstream bars and international-styled pubs have a 'happy hour' – called just that (no French translation) – which ushers in reduced-price drinks for a good two or three hours, usually between around 5pm and 8pm.

Closing Times

Closing time for cafes and bars tends to be 2am, though some have licences until dawn. Club hours vary depending on the venue, day and event.

Top Tips

➡ Arrive early: from 10pm many cafes apply a pricier night rate.

➡ Although most places serve at least small plates (often full menus), it's normally fine to order a coffee or alcohol if you're not dining.

➡ The French rarely go drunk-wild and tend to frown upon it.

Coffee Decoded

Un café Single shot of espresso.

Un café allongé Espresso lengthened with hot water (sometimes served separately).

Un café au lait Coffee with milk.

Un café crème Shot of espresso lengthened with steamed milk.

Un double Double shot of espresso.

Une noisette Shot of espresso with a spot of milk.

Above: Tea cannisters at Mariage Frères (p179)
Left: Le Progrès (p150)

Drinking by Neighbourhood

Montmartre & Northern Paris
Local gems include canal-side cafes (p147)

Champs-Élysées & Grands Boulevards
Swanky hotel bars, glam nightclubs (p102)

Louvre & Les Halles
Eclectic mix of bars and clubs (p127)

Le Marais Ménilmontant & Belleville
Hip, edgy bars and nightlife venues (p171)

Eiffel Tower & Western Paris
Classy bars and sunny cafes (p91)

St-Germain & Les Invalides
Historic literary cafes, stylish bars (p240)

The Islands
Quaint tearooms and wine bars (p203)

Bastille & Eastern Paris
Lively clubs and bars galore (p189)

Latin Quarter
Spirited student pubs and bars (p215)

Montparnasse & Southern Paris
Boulevard-facing brasseries and backstreet cafes (p258)

producing regions, the principal ones are Burgundy, Bordeaux, the Rhône and the Loire valleys, Champagne, Languedoc, Provence and Alsace. Wines are generally named after the location of the vineyard rather than the grape varietal. The best wines are Appellation d'Origine Contrôlée (AOC; soon to be relabelled Appellation d'Origine Protégée, AOP), meaning they meet stringent regulations governing where, how and under what conditions they're grown, fermented and bottled.

BEER

Beer hasn't traditionally had a high profile in France and the main French beer you're still likely to encounter is the mass-produced Kronenbourg 1664 (5.5%), brewed in Strasbourg.

There is, however, a growing *bière artisanale* (craft beer) scene, with cafes beginning to offer limited-production brews on

tap and by the bottle – **La Fût Gueuze** (Map p410; 24 rue Dumeril, 13e; ⊗4pm-2am; MCampo-Formio) is a good place to start sampling. The city's artisan beer festival, Paris Beer Week (http://laparisbeerweek.com), takes place in brasseries, bars and specialist beer shops, usually in early May. An excellent resource for hopheads is www.hoppyparis.com, listing local breweries and bars that carry microbrews and Belgian beers.

COCKTAILS

Recent years have seen a resurgence of the cocktail scene across the city, from glitzy hotel bars and neobistros to super-cool backstreet speakeasies – even former hostess bars by Pigalle are getting in on the scene. Sample forgotten French liqueurs, fresh fruit, and homemade infusions and syrups at the best of the bunch. Aficionados won't want to miss Paris Cocktail Week (http://pariscocktailweek.fr), held the last week of January.

NATURAL WINE

The latest trend in wine, *les vins naturels* (natural wines) have a fuzzy definition – no one really agrees on the details, but the general idea is that they are produced using little or no pesticides or additives. This means natural wines do not contain sulphites, which are added as a preservative in most wines. The good news is that this gives natural wines a much more distinct personality (or *terroir*, as the French say), the bad news is that these wines can also be more unpredictable. For more specifics, see the website www.morethanorganic.com.

Nightlife

Paris' residential make-up means nightclubs aren't ubiquitous. Lacking a mainstream scene, clubbing here tends to be underground and extremely mobile. The best DJs and their followings have short stints in a certain venue before moving on, and the scene's hippest *soirées clubbing* (clubbing events) float between venues – including the many dance-driven bars. Dedicated clubbers may also want to check out the growing suburban scene, much more alternative and spontaneous in nature, but harder to reach.

Wherever you wind up, the beat is strong. Electronic music is of particularly high quality in Paris' clubs, with some excellent local house and techno. Funk and groove have given the predominance of dark minimal sounds a good pounding, and the Latin scene is huge; salsa dancing and Latino music nights pack out plenty of clubs. World music also has a following in Paris, where everything – from Algerian raï to Senegalese *mbalax* and West Indian *zouk* – goes at clubs.

BEFORE, L'AFTER & AFTER D'AFTERS

Seasoned Parisian clubbers, who tend to have a finely tuned sense of the absurd, split their night into three parts. First, *la before* – drinks in a bar that has a DJ playing. Second, they head to a club for *la soirée,* which rarely kicks off before 1am or 2am. When the party continues (or begins) at around 5am and goes until midday, it's *l'after.* Invariably, though, given the lack of any clear-cut distinction between Parisian bars and clubs, the before and after can easily blend into one without any real 'during'. *After d'afters,* meanwhile, kicks off in bars and clubs on Sunday afternoons and evenings, with a mix of strung-out hardcore clubbers pressing on amid those looking for a party that doesn't take place in the middle of the night.

CLUBBING WEBSITES

Track tomorrow's hot 'n' happening soirée with these Parisian nightlife links.

➡ **Paris DJs** (www.parisdjs.com) Free downloads to get you in the groove.

➡ **Paris Bouge** (www.parisbouge.com) Comprehensive listings site.

➡ **Parissi** (www.parissi.com) Search by date, then *la before, la soirée* and *l'after.*

➡ **Tribu de Nuit** (www.tribudenuit.com) Parties, club events and concerts galore.

SUBURBAN SCENE

Plug into the indie clubbing scene with the following informal venues and collectives, which organise parties in the northern suburbs.

➡ **Otto 10** (www.otto10.fr)

➡ **75021** (www.facebook.com/75021Paris)

➡ **Le 6B** (www.le6b.fr)

➡ **Alter Paname** (www.facebook.com/AlterPaname80)

Lonely Planet's Top Choices

Le Mary Céleste (p171) There are few hipper places to drink than this fashionable Marais cocktail bar.

Le Baron Rouge (p189) Wonderfully convivial barrel-filled wine bar.

Lockwood (p128) Irrepressibly good all day long, from coffee to cocktails.

Holybelly (p140) The flagbearer for Canal St-Martin's new crop of coffee houses.

Le Batofar (p259) Red-metal tugboat with a rooftop bar and portholed club beneath.

Best Cocktails

Experimental Cocktail Club (p128) Superb cocktails in a setting that exudes spirit and soul.

Tiger Bar (p241) Chic St-German spot with innovative mixed drinks and 45 different gins.

Baranaan (p150) New wave cocktail bar serving Indian cocktails and veggie cuisine in the upcoming 10e.

Lulu White (p147) Absinthe-based drinks in Prohibition-era New Orleans surrounds.

Little Bastards (p217) Phenomenal house creations in a Latin Quarter backstreet.

Les Jardins du Pont-Neuf (p203) Fab floating bar.

Best Coffee

Belleville Brûlerie (p179) Ground-breaking roastery with Saturday-morning tastings and cuppings.

Boot Café (p171) A fashionable must, if only to snap the enchanting facade.

Caffé Juno (p216) Aromatic little Latin Quarter roaster.

Telescope (p128) It may be small, but it packs a punch.

Fondation Café (p173) Belleville beans on a buzzing terrace with Le Marais trendies.

Café Lomi (p150) Coffee roastery and cafe in the multiethnic La Goutte d'Or neighbourhood.

Best Tearooms

Le Loir dans La Théière (p173) Tasty tea in an enchanting, picture-book setting.

Mosquée de Paris (p208) Sip sweet mint tea and nibble delicious pastries in this peaceful haven.

Zen Zoo (p129) Taiwanese bubble tea in the City of Light.

Mariage Frères (p179) Paris' oldest and finest tearoom, founded in 1854.

L'Amaryllis de Gérard Mulot (p235) Wonderful tearoom by patisserie maestro Gérard Mulot.

Best Nightclubs

Le Rex Club (p129) Legendary house and techno club with a phenomenal sound system.

Concrete (p189) Top spot for electro dance music all hours, on a barge by Gare de Lyon.

Social Club (p128) Subterranean fave and a good spot to kick off the night.

Zig Zag Club (p102) Best of the Champs-Élysées venues.

La Dame de Canton (p259) Aboard a three-masted Chinese junk.

Best Wine Bars

Le Garde Robe (p128) Affordable natural wines and unpretentious vibe.

Septime La Cave (p190) Wine and gourmet nibbles just off rue de Charonne.

La Quincave (p242) Bar stools fashioned from wine barrels and over 200 natural wines.

La Cave Paul Bert (p189) Pocket-sized bistro wine bar.

Au Sauvignon (p241) Original zinc bar and hand-painted ceiling.

Best Pavement Terraces

Chez Prune (p148) The boho cafe that put Canal St-Martin on the map.

Café des Anges (p189) Wrap up in a ginger blanket and live the Paris dream.

L'Ebouillanté (p171) On sunny days there is no prettier cafe terrace.

Les Jardins du Pont-Neuf (p203) Glam floating bar with Seine-side terrace seating.

Best Neighbourhood Cafes

Le Petit Fer à Cheval (p171) Pocket-size cafe-bar with 1903 zinc bar and fervent crowd of regulars.

Aux Deux Amis (p174) Famed for its hand-cut horse meat, served Fridays.

Le Progrès (p150) Old-school Montmartre cafe loaded with ambience.

Chez Jeannette (p150) For vintage vibes you don't get better than this 1950s hang-out.

Le Petit Gorille (p258) Fab neoretro bar in the 15e.

Grand Staircase of the Palais Garnier (p96)

 # Entertainment

Catching a performance in Paris is a treat. French and international opera, ballet and theatre companies and cabaret dancers take to the stage in fabled venues, and a flurry of young, passionate, highly creative musicians, thespians and artists make the city's fascinating fringe art scene what it is.

Marion Cotillard performs at the Philharmonie de Paris (p139)

Cabarets

Whirling lines of feather-boa-clad, high-kicking dancers at grand-scale cabarets like cancan creator Moulin Rouge are a quintessential fixture on Paris' entertainment scene – for everyone but Parisians. Still, the dazzling sets, costumes and dancing guarantee an entertaining evening (or matinee).

Tickets to these spectacles start from around €90 (from €200 with dinner) and may include a half-bottle of Champagne for an extra €10. Reserve ahead.

Live Music

Festivals for just about every musical genre ensure that everyone gets to listen in. Street music is a constant in this busker-filled city, with summer adding stirring open-air concerts along the Seine and in city parks to the year-round serenade of accordions.

JAZZ & BLUES

Paris became Europe's most important jazz centre after WWII and the city's best clubs and cellars still lure international stars.

Admission generally ranges from free to around €30 depending on the artist, time and venue.

Download podcasts, tunes, concert information and all that jazz from Paris' jazz radio station, TSF (www.tsfjazz.com).

FRENCH CHANSONS

While *chanson* literally means 'song' in French, it also specifically refers to a style of heartfelt, lyric-driven music typified by Édith Piaf, Maurice Chevalier, Charles Aznavour et al. You'll come across some rousing live covers of their most famous songs

NEED TO KNOW

Listings

Paris' two top listings guides *Pariscope* (€0.70) and *L'Officiel des Spectacles* (www.offi.fr; €0.70), both in French but easy to navigate, are available from news stands on Wednesday, and are crammed with everything that's on in the capital.

Useful Websites

➡ **LYLO** (www.lylo.fr) Short for Les Yeux, Les Oreilles (meaning 'eyes and ears'), offering the low-down on the live-music, concert and clubbing scenes.

➡ **Le Figaro Scope** (http://evene. lefigaro.fr) Music, cinema and theatre listings.

➡ **Paris Nightlife** (www.parisnightlife. fr) All-encompassing listings site.

Tickets

The most convenient place to purchase concert, theatre and other cultural and sporting-event tickets is from electronics and entertainment megashop Fnac (p200), whether in person at the *billeteries* (ticket offices) or by phone or online. There are branches throughout Paris, including in the Forum des Halles.

Tickets generally can't be refunded.

Discount Tickets

On the day of performance, theatre, opera and ballet tickets are sold for half price (plus €3 commission) at the central **Kiosque Théâtre Madeleine** (Map p370; opposite 15 place de la Madeleine, 8e; ⊗12.30-8pm Tue-Sat, to 4pm Sun; Ⓜ Madeleine).

at traditional venues. Contemporary twists on the genre include the fusion of dance beats with traditional *chanson* melodies. The term also covers intimate cabarets such as Montmartre's Au Lapin Agile (p152).

Admission generally ranges from free to around €30 depending on the artist, time and venue.

ROCK, POP & INDIE

AccorHotels Arena (☎01 58 70 16 00; www. accorhotelsarena.com; 8 bd de Bercy, 12e; Ⓜ Bercy), **Stade de France** (☎08 92 70 09 00; www. stadefrance.com; St-Denis La Plaine; stadium tours adult/child €15/10; ⊗9.30am-6pm Tue-Sun; Ⓜ St-Denis-Porte de Paris) and Le Zénith (p136) in

Parc de la Villette are the largest venues but also the most impersonal; it's the smaller concert halls with real history and charm that most fans favour.

CLASSICAL MUSIC

The city hosts dozens of orchestral, organ and chamber-music concerts each week. In addition to theatres and concert halls, Paris' beautiful, centuries-old stone churches have magnificent acoustics and provide a meditative backdrop for classical-music concerts. Posters outside churches advertise upcoming events with ticket information, or visit www.ampconcerts.com, where you can make online reservations. Tickets cost around €23 to €30.

The new Jean Nouvel–designed 2400-seat Philharmonie de Paris (p139) concert hall opened in the Parc de la Villette in 2015.

WORLD & LATINO

Musiques du monde (world music) has a huge following in Paris, where everything – from Algerian raï and other North African music to Senegalese *mbalax* and West Indian *zouk* – goes at clubs. Many venues have salsa classes.

Cinema

The film-lover's ultimate city, Paris has some wonderful movie houses to catch new flicks, avant-garde cinema and priceless classics.

Foreign films (including English-language films) screened in their original language with French subtitles are labelled 'VO' *(version originale)*. Films labelled 'VF' *(version française)* are dubbed in French.

Pariscope and *L'Officiel des Spectacles* list the full crop of Paris' cinematic pickings and screening times; online check out http://cinema.leparisien.fr.

First-run tickets cost around €11.50 for adults (€13.50 for 3D). Students and over 60s get discounted tickets (usually around €8.50) from 7pm Sunday to 7pm Friday. Discounted tickets for children and teens have no restrictions. Most cinemas have across-the-board discounts before noon.

Opera & Ballet

France's Opéra National de Paris and Ballet de l'Opéra National de Paris perform at Paris' two opera houses, the Palais Garnier (p103) and Opéra Bastille (p191). The season runs between September and July.

AccorHotels Arena (p61)

Theatre

The majority of theatre productions in Paris, including those originally written in other languages, are – naturally enough – performed in French. Only occasionally do English-speaking troupes play at smaller venues in and around town. Consult *Pariscope* or *L'Officiel des Spectacles* for details.

Buskers in Paris

Paris' gaggle of clowns, mime artists, living statues, acrobats, in-line skaters, buskers and other street entertainers can be loads of fun and cost substantially less than a theatre ticket (a few coins in the hat is appreciated). Some excellent musicians perform in the long echo-filled corridors of the metro, a highly prized privilege that artists audition for. Outside, you can be sure of a good show at the following:

➡ **Place Georges Pompidou, 4e** The huge square in front of the Centre Pompidou.

➡ **Pont St-Louis, 4e** The bridge linking Paris' two islands (best enjoyed with a Berthillon ice cream in hand).

➡ **Pont au Double, 4e** The pedestrian bridge linking Notre Dame with the Left Bank.

➡ **Place Joachim du Bellay, 1er** Musicians and fire-eaters near the Fontaine des Innocents.

➡ **Parc de la Villette, 19e** African drummers at the weekend.

➡ **Place du Tertre, Montmartre, 18e** Montmartre's original main square is Paris' busiest busker stage.

Entertainment by Neighbourhood

➡ **Eiffel Tower & Western Paris** (p91) Entertainment options are limited in this refined residential area.

➡ **Champs-Élysées & Grands Boulevards** (p103) Famous revues and Paris' palatial 1875-built opera house take top billing here.

➡ **Louvre & Les Halles** (p130) Swinging jazz clubs, centuries-old theatres and cinemas mix it up with pumping nightclubs.

➡ **Montmartre & Northern Paris** (p151) Showstopping cabarets, mythologised concert halls and cutting-edge cultural centres scatter throughout Paris' northern quarters.

➡ **Le Marais, Ménilmontant & Belleville** (p174) Rockin' live-music venues, gay and lesbian clubs, DJs hitting the decks and old-style *chansons*.

➡ **Bastille & Eastern Paris** (p190) Salsa dancing, old-time tea dancing and France's national cinema institute are big drawcards.

➡ **Latin Quarter** (p218) Swing bands, cinema retrospectives and jam sessions are among the Latin Quarter's offerings.

➡ **St-Germain & Les Invalides** (p242) Atmospheric cinemas, cultural centres and theatres inhabit this chic, sophisticated neighbourhood.

➡ **Montparnasse & Southern Paris** (p259) Some of this area's most happening venues are aboard boats moored on the Seine.

Lonely Planet's Top Choices

Palais Garnier (p103) Paris' premier opera house is an artistic inspiration.

Point Éphémère (p152) Uber-cool cultural centre on the banks of Canal St-Martin.

Moulin Rouge (p151) The can-can creator razzle-dazzles with spectacular sets, costumes and choreography.

Le 104 (p139) Cultural tour de force in a former funeral parlour.

La Flèche d'Or (p191) Former railway station club renowned for unearthing new talent.

Café Universel (p218) Brilliant jazz club showcasing a diverse range of styles.

Best Cinemas

Le Cinémathèque Française (p191) The national cinema institute has a host of cinematic offerings.

Le Champo (p219) Beloved art deco icon screening independent films.

Forum des Images (p130) The Paris film archive.

Le Grand Rex (p131) Art deco landmark from the '30s.

Studio Galande (p218) *The Rocky Horror Picture Show* screenings plus other cult flicks.

Cinéma Les Fauvettes (p260) Specialises in long-standing and recent classics.

Best Live Music

Jazz Clubs

Café Universel (p218) Intimate club with unpretentious vibe and no cover.

New Morning (p152) Solid and varied line-up of everything from postbop and Latin to reggae.

Le Baiser Salé (p129) Reputable venue that focuses on Caribbean and Latin sounds.

Sunset & Sunside (p129) Blues, fusion and world sounds, as well as straight-up jazz.

Le Caveau des Oubliettes (p219) Jam sessions in a 12th-century dungeon.

La Java (p175) Live salsa, rock and world music where Édith Piaf got her first break.

Rock, Pop & Indie

Le Trianon (p152) Old Montmartre theatre with great acts and an intimate setting.

Le Divan du Monde (p151) Great indie shows in Pigalle.

Cabaret Sauvage (p152) Giant yurt that hosts hip-hop, funk and world concerts.

Bus Palladium (p152) Eclectic rock venue.

La Maroquinerie (p175) Tiny but trendy venue in Ménilmontant with real cutting-edge gigs.

Nouveau Casino (p175) Underground and up-to-the-minute acts.

French Chansons

Au Limonaire (p103) Perfect Parisian wine bar with *chansons* and French singer-songwriters.

Au Lapin Agile (p152) Legendary Montmartre cabaret.

Le Vieux Belleville (p175) Old-fashioned bistro and *musette* atop Parc de Belleville.

Classical

Philharmonie de Paris (p139) The new home of the Orchestre de Paris.

Sainte-Chapelle (p200) Unforgettable classical concerts amid jewel-like stained glass.

Maison de la Radio (p91) Top performers recorded live for national radio.

Église St-Eustache (p119) Sunday-afternoon organ concerts.

Église de la Madeleine (p99) Memorable organ recitals.

World & Latino

Favela Chic (p172) Latin, funk and Brazilian pop.

Cabaret Sauvage (p152) From reggae and raï to dance-till-dawn DJ nights.

La Java (p175) Live salsa nights followed by Latin and electro DJs.

La Chapelle des Lombards (p191) Afro jazz, reggae and Latin grooves.

Best Cultural Centres

Centre Pompidou (p116) Irresistible cocktail of cutting-edge performances.

Gaîté Lyrique (p174) Unique and fascinating exhibitions create buzz at this vibrant cultural centre in Le Marais.

Le Carreau du Temple (p174) Covered market–turned–cultural centre, well worth a gander for its drop-dead-gorgeous art nouveau ironwork alone.

Petit Bain (p260) Barge that bills itself as a 'floating cultural centre' with diverse events.

Best Theatre, Opera & Dance

Palais Garnier (p103) Fabled home of the phantom of the opera offering an unforgettable experience.

Opéra Bastille (p191) Paris' main, modern opera house, seating an audience of 3400.

Théâtre du Châtelet (p130) Operas, ballets, classical recitals and musicals.

Department store Galeries Lafayette (p104)

Shopping

Paris has it all: broad boulevards lined with international chains, luxury avenues studded with designer fashion houses, famous grands magasins (department stores) and fabulous markets. But the real charm lies in strolling the city's backstreets, where tiny speciality shops and quirky boutiques selling everything from strawberry-scented Wellington boots to heaven-scented candles are wedged between cafes, galleries and churches.

NEED TO KNOW

Opening Hours

Shops generally open between 10am and 7pm Monday to Saturday. Smaller shops often shut on Monday or may close from around noon to 2pm for lunch. Larger stores hold *nocturnes* (late-night shopping), usually on Thursday, until around 10pm. Sunday shopping is limited; the Champs-Élysées, Montmartre and Le Marais are liveliest.

Sales

Paris' twice-yearly *soldes* (sales) generally last five to six weeks, starting around mid-January and again around mid-June.

Tax Refunds

Non-EU residents may be eligible for a TVA (taxe sur la valeur ajoutée; value-added tax) refund (p21).

Top Shopping Tips

➜ Ring the bell to access ultraexclusive designer boutiques.

➜ Head to a *cabine d'essayage* (fitting room), or check sizes at www.online conversion.com/clothing.

➜ Most shops offer free (and very beautiful) gift wrapping – ask for *un paquet cadeau*.

➜ A *ticket de caisse* (receipt) is essential for returning/exchanging an item (within one month of purchase).

➜ Particularly in smaller shops, shopkeepers may not appreciate your touching the merchandise until invited to do so.

➜ If you're happy browsing, tell sales staff *'Je regarde'* – 'I'm just looking'.

➜ Bargaining is only acceptable at flea markets.

Parisian Souvenirs

For authentic quirky and/or nostalgic souvenirs, browse the City of Paris' Paris Rendez-Vous boutique (p176) or online store (http://boutique.paris.fr), which ships worldwide.

At major museums, the Boutiques de Musées (www.boutiquesdemusees.fr) have high-quality replicas and a digital painting-and-frame service: choose one and have it mailed to your home.

Maison Kitsuné (p153)

Fashion

Fashion shopping is Paris' forté. Although its well-groomed residents make the city at times look and feel like a giant catwalk, fashion here is about style and quality first and foremost, rather than status or brand names.

A good place to get an overview of Paris fashion is at the city's famous *grands magasins* such as Le Bon Marché (p244), Galeries Lafayette (p104) and Le Printemps (p105).

FASHION SHOWS

Although tickets for Paris' high-profile *haute couture* and prêt-à-porter fashion shows are like hens' teeth, you can still see some runway action: reserve ahead to attend free weekly fashion shows (p105) at Galeries Lafayette.

DRESSING FOR LESS

Parisian fashion doesn't have to break the bank: there are fantastic bargains at secondhand and vintage boutiques (generally, the more upmarket the area, the better quality the cast-offs), along with outlet shops selling previous seasons' collections, surpluses and seconds by name-brand designers.

Arcades

Dating from the 19th century, Paris' glass-roofed *passages couverts* (covered passages) were the precursors to shopping malls and are treasure chests of small, exquisite boutiques. Be sure to stroll (p123) through some of the Right Bank's best-preserved arcades.

Markets

Nowhere encapsulates Paris' village atmosphere more than its markets. Not simply

Above: Shops along rue Mouffetard
(p216)
Right: Bag from French fashion house
Dior (p104)

CHRISTIAN VIERIG/CONTRIBUTOR/GETTY IMAGES ©

Shopping by Neighbourhood

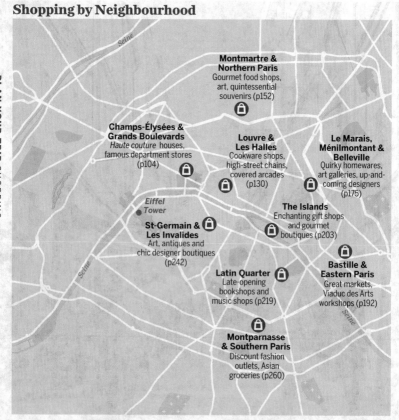

Montmartre & Northern Paris
Gourmet food shops, art, quintessential souvenirs (p152)

Champs-Élysées & Grands Boulevards
Haute couture houses, famous department stores (p104)

Louvre & Les Halles
Cookware shops, high-street chains, covered arcades (p130)

Le Marais, Ménilmontant & Belleville
Quirky homewares, art galleries, up-and-coming designers (p175)

Eiffel Tower

St-Germain & Les Invalides
Art, antiques and chic designer boutiques (p242)

The Islands
Enchanting gift shops and gourmet boutiques (p203)

Latin Quarter
Late-opening bookshops and music shops (p219)

Bastille & Eastern Paris
Great markets, Viaduc des Arts workshops (p192)

Montparnasse & Southern Paris
Discount fashion outlets, Asian groceries (p260)

places to shop, the city's street markets are social gatherings for the entire neighbourhood, and visiting one will give you a true appreciation for Parisian life.

Nearly every little quarter has its own street market at least once a week (never Monday) where tarpaulin-topped trestle tables bow beneath fresh, cooked and preserved delicacies. *Marchés biologiques* (organic markets) are increasingly sprouting up across the city. Many street markets also sell clothes, accessories, homewares and more. Markets in Paris' more multicultural neighbourhoods are filled with the flavours and aromas of continents beyond Europe.

Bric-a-brac, antiques, retro clothing, jewellery, cheap brand-name clothing, footwear, African carvings, DVDs and electronic items and much more are laid out at the city's flea markets. Watch out for pickpockets!

The website www.paris.fr (in French) lists every market by *arrondissement*.

Gourmet Goods

Food, wine and tea shops make for mouthwatering shopping. Pastries might not keep, but items you can take home (customs regulations permitting) include light-as-air macarons, chocolates, jams, preserves, foie gras and, of course, fabulous French cheeses. Many of the best *fromageries* (cheese shops) can provide vacuum packing.

Art, Antiques & Homewares

From venerable antique dealers to edgy art galleries, there are a wealth of places in this artistic city to browse and buy one-off conversation pieces and collectibles.

Paris also has a trove of unique homewares shops selling colourful, quirky innovations to brighten your living and/or working environment.

Lonely Planet's Top Choices

Le Bonbon au Palais (p220) Artisan sweets from throughout France in a geography-classroom-themed boutique.

Didier Ludot (p130) Couture creations of yesteryear.

E Dehillerin (p131) Paris' professional chefs stock up at this 1820-opened cookware shop.

La Grande Épicerie de Paris (p244) Glorious food emporium.

Magasin Sennelier (p245) Historic art-supply shop with paints, canvases and paraphernalia galore.

Shakespeare & Company (p219) A 'wonderland of books', as Henry Miller described it.

Best Concept Stores

Gab & Jo (p242) The country's first concept store stocking only French-made items.

Merci (p176) Fabulously fashionable and unique: all profits go to a children's charity in Madagascar.

Colette (p131) Uber-hip designer fashion and basement 'water bar'.

L'Éclaireur (p176) Part art space, part lounge and part deconstructionist fashion statement; for men and women in separate spaces.

Hermès (p243) Housed in an art deco swimming pool.

Best Fashion

Boutiques

Maison Kitsuné (p175) The secret to looking effortlessly French.

Andrea Crews (p177) Bold art and fashion collective.

La Boutique Extraordinaire (p178) Exquisite hand-knitted garments.

Antoine et Lili (p153) All the colours of the rainbow in this iconic boutique.

Triangle d'Or (p104) Famous fashion houses fill the Golden Triangle.

Pigalle (p153) Leading Parisian menswear brand.

Accessories & Bags

JB Guanti (p243) Gorgeous gloves.

Marie Mercié (p244) Hand-made hats.

Gérard Durand (p245) Bright, bold *collants* and *bas* (tights and stockings).

Alexandra Sojfer (p245) Hand-crafted umbrellas.

Jamin Puech (p177) One-of-a-kind handbags.

Cie Bracelet Montre (p244) Watchbands.

Secondhand, Vintage & Discount Boutiques

L'Habilleur (p179) Discount designer wear.

Frivoli (p148) Brand-name cast-offs by the Canal St-Martin.

Kiliwatch (p131) New and used streetwear; vintage hats and boots.

Chercheminippes (p245) Seven specialist boutiques on one street.

Spree (p153) Superstylish boutique-gallery showcasing 1950s to 1980s vintage fashion.

Catherine B (p244) Stocking only Chanel and Hermès vintage pieces.

Best Gourmet Shops

Place de la Madeleine (p103) Single-item specialist shops and famous emporiums.

La Manufacture de Chocolat (p192) Alain Ducasse's bean-to-bar chocolate factory.

Fromagerie Goncourt (p179) Contemporary *fromagerie* unusually styled like a boutique.

L'Éclair de Génie (p176) Sweet éclairs displayed like art.

Comptoir de la Gastronomie (p131) Foie gras and other gourmet goodies.

La Dernière Goutte (p243) Wines from small, independent French producers.

Best for Kids

Chez Hélène (p176) Old-fashioned *bonbon* (sweet) shop.

Bonton (p177) Vintage-inspired fashion, furnishings and knick-knacks for babies, toddlers and children.

Smallable Concept Store (p245) One-stop shop for babies, children and teens.

Boîtes à Musique Anna Joliet (p131) Swiss music boxes to enchant in the Palais Royale.

Album (p221) Superb collection of *bandes desinées* (graphic novels) and related collectibles.

Finger in the Nose (p244) Streetwise Parisian label for kids.

Best Art & Antiques

Marché aux Puces de St-Ouen (p153) One of Europe's largest flea markets, with over 2500 stalls.

Hôtel Drouot (p105) Famous auction house.

La Maison de Poupée (p244) Adorable antique dolls.

Deyrolle (p243) Historic taxidermist that starred in *Midnight in Paris*.

👁 LGBT Travellers

The city known as 'gay Paree' lives up to its name. Paris is so open that there's less of a defined 'scene' here than in other cities where it's more underground. While Le Marais is the mainstay of gay and lesbian nightlife, you'll find venues right throughout the city attracting a mixed crowd.

Background

Paris was the first European capital to vote in an openly gay mayor when Bertrand Delanoë was elected in 2001, and the city itself is very open – same-sex couples commonly display affection in public and checking into a hotel room is unlikely to raise eyebrows. In fact, the only challenge you may have is working out where straight Paris ends and gay Paris starts, as the city is so stylish and sexy.

In 2013 France became the 13th country in the world to allow same-sex marriage (and adoption by same-sex couples), and polls show the majority of French citizens support marriage equality. Typically at least one partner needs to be a resident to get married here. And, of course, there's no end of romantic places to propose.

Drinking & Nightlife

Le Marais, especially the areas around the intersection of rue Ste-Croix de la Bretonnerie and rue des Archives, and eastwards to rue Vieille du Temple, has been Paris' main centre of gay nightlife for some three decades and is still the epicentre of gay and lesbian life in Paris. There's also a handful of bars and clubs within walking distance of bd de Sébastopol. The lesbian scene is less prominent than its gay counterpart, and centres on a few cafes and bars in Le Marais, particularly along rue des Écouffes. Bars and clubs are generally all gay- and lesbian-friendly.

Events

By far the biggest event on the gay and lesbian calendar is Gay Pride Day, in late June, when the annual **Marche des Fiertés** (Gay Pride March; www.gaypride.fr; ⊙Jun or Jul) through Le Marais to Bastille provides a colourful spectacle, and plenty of parties take place.

Year-round, check gay and lesbian websites or ask at gay bars and other venues to find out about events.

Organisations & Resources

Centre Gai et Lesbien de Paris Île de France (CGL; Map p386; ☎01 43 57 21 47; www.centrelgbt paris.org; 63 rue Beaubourg, 3e; ⊙centre & bar 3.30-8pm Mon-Fri, 1-7pm Sat, library 6-8pm Mon-Wed, 5-7pm Fri & Sat; MRambuteau, Arts et Métiers) is the single best source of information for gay and lesbian travellers in Paris, with a large library of books and periodicals and a sociable bar. Also has details of hotlines, helplines, gay and gay-friendly medical services and politically oriented activist associations, plus they can provide details of transgender resources and workshops

Gay Guided Tours

For an insider's perspective of gay life in Paris and recommendations on where to eat, drink, sightsee and party, take a tour with the **Gay Locals** (www.thegaylocals.com; 3hr tour from €180) – two long-time resident expats who lead tours of Le Marais in English, as well as private tours of other popular neighbourhoods and customised tours based on your interests.

Lonely Planet's Top Choices

Open Café (p172) The wide terrace is prime for talent-watching.

Gibus Club (p172) One of Paris' biggest gay parties.

La Champmeslé (p128) Cabaret nights, fortune-telling and art exhibitions attract an older lesbian crowd.

Queen (p102) Don't miss disco night!

Best Weekend in Le Marais

Loustic (p173) Among the best coffee (and espresso-bar interior design) in town.

Place des Vosges (p160) Charming city square.

Broken Arm (p166) Hipster address with fresh juice- and salad-driven cafe adjoining an achingly cool concept store.

Cimetière du Père Lachaise (p157) Oscar Wilde's winged-angel-topped tomb is a highlight.

La Belle Hortense (p173) Creative wine bar with modish mixed crowd and shelves of books.

Derrière (p168) Play ping-pong between courses at this stellar restaurant.

Best Shopping Sprees

Samuel Coraux (p178) Fabulous and occasionally outrageously kitsch jewellery for guys 'n' gals by one of Paris' funkiest jewel designers.

État Libre d'Orange (p177) Perfumery that screams Marais hipster, with scents bearing

names like Fat Electrician, Jasmin et Cigarette, and Delicious Closet Queen.

L'Éclaireur (p176) Part art space, part lounge and part deconstructionist fashion statement; fashion for men and women.

Best Apéros

L'Étoile Manquante (p172) Trendy, gay-friendly bar with retro interior and fabulous pavement terrace for obligatory after-work drinks.

Open Café (p172) With a four-hour happy hour kicking in daily at 6pm, how can you possibly go wrong?

Le Raidd (p172) Has a laid-back lounge-style ground-floor bar.

Best Gay Hang-Outs

Café Cox (p172) The meeting place for an interesting (and interested) cruisy crowd throughout the evening, from dusk onward.

Le Raidd (p172) Upstairs is a pulsating den of DJs, dancing, themed parties, raunchy shower shows....

Café Voulez-Vous (p172) Sassy New York–styled gay bar and lounge with a mellow vibe.

Best Lesbian Hang-outs

3w Kafé (p172) Flagship cocktail bar-pub on a street with several lesbian bars; weekend dancing downstairs and themed evenings.

Les Jacasses (p172) Mellow music, hard-core evenings and a happy 'hour' that happily lasts for four.

PLAN YOUR TRIP LGBT TRAVELLERS

La Champmeslé (p128) A fixture on Paris' lesbian scene since the '70s.

Best Clubs

Open Café (p172) The only place to be late on a Saturday night.

Le Tango (p172) Mingle with a mixed and cosmopolitan gay and lesbian set in a historic 1930s dancehall.

Gibus Club (p172) Get ready to party.

Best Party Spots Beyond Le Marais

Ménilmontant Edgy urban cool.

Pigalle Montmartre's sexy southern neighbour.

Champs-Élysées Glam bars and clubs.

Bastille Lively local vibe.

Canal St-Martin Arty, indie venues.

Belleville Increasingly hip, multicultural 'hood.

Parks & Activities

Ready to unwind with the Parisians? Take a break from the concrete and check out the city's islands of green, where you'll be able to thwack a tennis ball, stroll in style, admire art, or bust out some wine and cheese. And in true French form, you won't even need to break a sweat.

Parks

➡ **Jardin du Luxembourg** (p228) Paris' most iconic swathe of green, where you can stroll among the statues, play tennis, jog in style and entertain the kids.

➡ **Jardin des Tuileries** (p118) Leafy Seine-side oasis, perfect for picnics, summer carnival rides, jogging and impossibly magnificent vistas.

➡ **Bois de Vincennes** (p183) The erstwhile royal hunting grounds east of Paris. Today it's home to a zoo, the kid-packed Parc Floral and pick-up football matches.

➡ **Bois de Boulogne** (p90) Baron Haussmann's western oasis. Cycle, row, stroll the gardens, hit the amusement park or catch a steeplechase.

➡ **Jardin des Plantes** (p209) Natural-history museum, botanic gardens and sprinkler-dodging picnics.

➡ **Parc des Buttes-Chaumont** (p139) Another Haussmann creation, this quirky local spot has a faux Greek temple, abandoned railway line, dance hall and t'ai chi vibes.

Spectator Sports

Paris hosts a great variety of sporting events throughout the year, from the French Open (www.rolandgarros.com) and BNP Paribas Masters (www.atpworldtour.com) to local football matches. There are a handful of stadiums in and around the city; for upcoming events, click on Sports & Games (under the Going Out menu) at http://en.parisinfo. com. Better yet, if you can read French, sports

daily *L'Équipe* (www.lequipe.fr) will provide more depth. Local teams include Paris Saint-Germain (football; www.psg.fr) and the pink-clad Stade Français Paris (rugby; www.stade. fr). Catch France's national football team, Les Bleus, at the Stade de France.

The city's three horse-racing tracks can make for a thrilling afternoon. The Hippodrome d'Auteuil and the Hippodrome de Longchamp (www.france-galop.com) are in the Bois de Boulogne; the Hippodrome de Paris-Vincennes (www.letrot.com) is in the Bois de Vincennes. Every October the Prix de l'Arc de Triomphe (www.prixarcdetriomphe. com), Europe's most prestigious horse race, is held at the Hippodrome de Longchamp or outside Paris in Chantilly.

Cycling

Everyone knows that the Tour de France races up the Champs-Élysées at the end of July every year, but you don't need Chris Froome's leg muscles to enjoy Paris on two wheels. Between Vélib' (the Paris bike-share scheme; p333) and the hundreds of kilometres of urban bike paths, cycling around the city has never been easier. Sign up for one of the great city bike tours (p335) or hire a bike (p334) yourself. Some streets are closed to vehicle traffic on Sundays – great news for cyclists! Bring your own helmet.

Skating

The next most popular activity after cycling has to be skating, whether on the street or on ice. Rent a pair of in-line skates at Nomadeshop (p179) and join the Friday-evening skate – **Pari Roller** (Map p412; http://pari-roller.com; place Raoul Dautry, 14e; ⊙10pm-1am Fri, arrive 9.30pm; ⓂMontparnasse Bienvenüe) – that streaks through the Paris streets, or join the more laid-back Sunday-afternoon skate – Rollers & Coquillages (p179).

During the winter holidays several temporary outdoor rinks are installed around Paris – the most famous are located in front of the Hôtel de Ville and on the 1st floor of the Eiffel Tower. See www.paris.fr for other locations.

Hammams & Spas

Whether you want to hobnob with the stars at a *spa de luxe* or get a *savon noir* (black soap) exfoliation at the neighbourhood hammam (Turkish steambath), Paris has spaces to suit every whim.

A hammam generally charges an entrance fee, which grants you admission to a steam bath and sauna. Extras – exfoliation scrubs, orange-blossom massages, and mint tea and North African pastries – are tacked on to the initial price (but worth it!). Most hammams are primarily for women; if men are admitted it's usually only once or twice a week, and only rarely at the same time as women.

Swimming

If you want to go swimming at either your hotel or in a public pool, you'll need to don a *bonnet de bain* (bathing cap) – even if you don't have any hair. You shouldn't need to buy one ahead of time as they are generally sold at most pools. Men are required to wear skin-tight trunks (Speedos); loose-fitting Bermuda shorts are not allowed.

Boules

Don't be surprised to see groups of earnest Parisians playing *boules* (France's most popular traditional game, similar to lawn bowls) in the Jardin du Luxembourg and other parks and squares with suitably flat, shady patches of gravel. The Arènes de Lutèce (p217) *boulodrome* in a 2nd-century Roman amphitheatre in the Latin Quarter is a fabulous spot to absorb the scene. There are usually places to play at Paris Plages.

NEED TO KNOW

Resources

The best source of information on sports in Paris can be found on the city hall's website (www.paris.fr/sport), with info on everything from skating and badminton to stadiums and equipment rental. Another website is http://quefaire.paris.fr/sports, which lists venues for underground football, climbing, swimming pools open at night and other activities.

Tickets

Tickets for big events can generally be purchased through the venue's website. Reserve well in advance, before you leave for Paris. If you want to try your luck, head to the box office at the nearest Fnac store (www.fnac.com, follow the Magasins link to locate a branch near you).

Parks & Activities by Neighbourhood

➡ **Eiffel Tower & Western Paris** (p90) Escape to the Bois de Boulogne.

➡ **Louvre & Les Halles** (p118) A funfair and superb vistas in the Jardin des Tuileries.

➡ **Montmartre & Northern Paris** (p136) Two of Paris' largest parks: Parc des Buttes-Chaumont and Parc de la Villette.

➡ **Le Marais, Ménilmontant & Belleville** (p179) Departure point for in-line skating.

➡ **Bastille & Eastern Paris** (p183) The expansive Bois de Vincennes, Parc Floral and a host of other great parks.

➡ **Latin Quarter** (p209) Stroll the Jardin des Plantes.

➡ **St-Germain & Les Invalides** (p228) The city's most iconic swathe of green, the Jardin du Luxembourg.

➡ **Montparnasse & Southern Paris** (p252) The rails-to-trails Petite Ceinture and sprawling Parc Montsouris.

GARDEL BERTRAND/HEMIS.FR/GETTY IMAGES ©

Left Bank of the Seine

◉ The Seine

The lifeline of Paris, the Seine sluices through the city, spanned by 37 bridges. Its Unesco World Heritage–listed riverbanks offer picturesque promenades, parks, activities and events, including sandy summertime beaches. After dark, watch the river dance with the watery reflections of city lights and tourist-boat flood lamps.

Riverbank Rejuvenation

Paris' riverbanks have been reborn in recent years. On the Right Bank, east of the Hôtel de Ville, the former expressway is now home to walkways and cycleways. On the Left Bank from the Pont de l'Alma to the Musée d'Orsay (linked to the water's edge by a grand staircase that doubles as amphitheatre seating), the car-free stretch Les Berges de Seine is now a Parisian hotspot for outdoor activities.

A resounding success since it opened in 2013, this innovative promenade is dotted with restaurants and bars (some aboard boats), chessboard tables, hopscotch and ball-game courts, a skate ramp, kids' climbing wall, a 100m running track and floating gardens on 1800 sq metres of artificial islands (complete with knotted-rope hammocks where you can lie back and soak up the river's reclaimed serenity).

At any time of year, Les Berges de Seine also offers temporary events and activities as diverse as film screenings and knitting workshops, and even wintertime curling on ice.

Promenading & Pausing

The Seine's riverbanks are where Parisians come to cycle, jog, in-line skate and stroll; staircases along the banks lead down to the water's edge.

Particularly picturesque spots for a riverside promenade include the areas around Paris' two elegant inner-city islands, the Île de la Cité and Île Saint-Louis. Up at street level, the banks are lined with the distinctive green-metal *bouquiniste* stalls selling antiquarian books, sheet music and old advertising posters. A lesser-known island stroll is the artificial Île aux Cygnes via its tree-shaded walkway, the Allée des Cygnes (walking from west to east gives you a stunning view of the Eiffel Tower).

The river also acts as a giant backyard for apartment-dwelling Parisians. All along its banks you'll find locals reading, picnicking, canoodling or just basking in the sunshine. Among the best-loved spots is the tiny, triangular park Square du Vert-Galant beneath the Pont Neuf.

Summertime Beaches

Presaging the latest anti-auto revolution that ushered in Les Berges de Seine were the Paris Plages (Paris Beaches), with traffic supplanted by *pétanque* (a variant on the game of bowls) courts, pop-up bars and cafes, sun lounges, parasols, water fountains and sprays, and sand brought in by barges lining the river from mid-July to mid-August.

The Paris Plages were established in 2002 for Parisians who couldn't escape to the coast to cool off in the summer months. They now cover the square in front of the Hôtel de Ville, 1km along the Right Bank (from the Pont des Arts to the Pont de Sully) and the quays by the Bassin de la Villette in the 19e.

Seine-Side Entertainment

In addition to Les Berges de Seine, entertainment options include floating

NEED TO KNOW

➜ There are no fences or barriers along the water's edge. Keep a close eye on children to ensure they don't take an unexpected plunge.

➜ Swimming is strictly forbidden, even during Paris Plages, due to boat traffic and the health hazards posed by the water quality.

➜ Stairs leading to the water can be especially slippery after rain.

nightclubs aboard boats moored in southern Paris, such as the red-metal tugboat Le Batofar (p259), and even a floating swimming pool, Piscine Joséphine Baker (p261).

On the banks, riverside venues include the Docks en Seine (p251), which incorporates the French fashion institute, vast outdoor terraces, uber-hip bars, clubs and restaurants, an entertainment-themed contemporary-art museum and more.

River Cruises & Tours

The best way, of course, to become acquainted with the Seine is to take a cruise along its waters. A plethora of companies run day- and night-time boat tours (p336), usually lasting around an hour, with commentary in multiple languages. Many cruise companies also offer brunch, lunch and dinner cruises, and the standard of cuisine is generally high (this is Paris, after all).

An alternative to traditional boat tours is the Batobus (p334), a handy hop-on, hop-off service that stops at quintessentially Parisian attractions: the Eiffel Tower, Champs-Élysées, Musée d'Orsay, Musée du Louvre, St-Germain des Prés, Hôtel de Ville, Notre Dame and Jardin des Plantes. Single- and multiday tickets allow you to spend as long as you like sightseeing between stops.

Explore Paris

PARIS'
TOP SIGHTS

Neighbourhoods at a Glance

1 Eiffel Tower & Western Paris p80

Home to *very* well-heeled Parisians, this grande dame of a neighbourhood is where you can get up close and personal with the city's symbolic tower as well as more contemporary architecture in the high-rise business district of La Défense just outside the *périphérique* (ring road) encircling central Paris.

2 Champs-Élysées & Grands Boulevards p92

Baron Haussmann famously reshaped the Parisian cityscape around the Arc de Triomphe, from which 12 avenues radiate like the spokes of a wheel. To its east are gourmet shops garlanding the Église de la Madeleine, the palatial Palais Garnier opera house and the Grands Boulevards' art nouveau department stores.

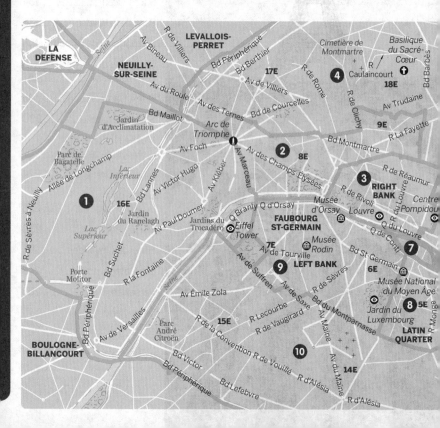

③ Louvre & Les Halles p106

Paris' splendid line of monuments, the *axe historique* (historic axis; also called the grand axis), passes through the Tuileries gardens before reaching IM Pei's glass pyramid at the entrance to the world's most visited museum, the Louvre. Nearby, the Forum des Halles shopping mall has recently emerged from a much-needed makeover.

④ Montmartre & Northern Paris p132

Montmartre's lofty views, wine-producing vines and hidden village squares have lured painters from the 19th century onwards. Crowned by the Sacré-Cœur basilica, Montmartre is the city's steepest *quartier* (quarter), and its slinking streets lined with crooked ivy-clad buildings retain a fairytale charm. The edgy neighbourhoods of Pigalle and Canal St-Martin areas are hotbeds of creativity and have true grit.

⑤ Le Marais, Ménilmontant & Belleville p154

Fashionable bars and restaurants, emerging designers' boutiques and the city's thriving gay and Jewish communities all squeeze into Le Marais' medieval lanes. Neighbouring Ménilmontant has some of the city's most happening nightlife, while hilly Belleville is a vibrant multicultural neighbourhood.

⑥ Bastille & Eastern Paris p180

Fabulous markets, intimate gourmet bistros, and a disused 19th-century railway viaduct with artist studios below and an elevated park (Promenade Plantée) on top make this neighbourhood one of the best places to discover the Parisians' Paris.

⑦ The Islands p193

Paris' geographic and spiritual heart is here in the Seine. The larger of the two inner-city islands, the Île de la Cité, is dominated by Notre Dame. Serene little Île St-Louis is graced with elegant apartments and hotels, and charming eateries and boutiques.

⑧ Latin Quarter p205

The hub of academic life in Paris, the Latin Quarter centres on the Sorbonne's main university campus. It's home to some outstanding museums and churches, and Paris' beautiful art deco mosque and botanic gardens.

⑨ St-Germain & Les Invalides p222

Literary buffs, antique collectors and fashionistas flock to this legendary part of Paris, where the presence of writers such as Sartre, de Beauvoir and Hemingway still lingers, and chic boutiques abound.

⑩ Montparnasse & Southern Paris p246

Montparnasse has surviving brasseries from its mid-20th-century heyday and re-energised backstreets buzzing with local life, while Paris' largest Chinatown, filled with Asian grocers and eateries.

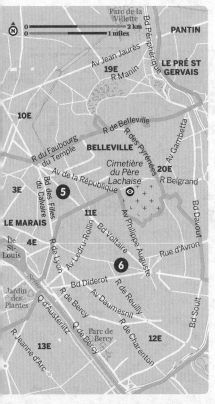

Eiffel Tower & Western Paris

Neighbourhood Top Five

❶ Eiffel Tower (p82) Ascending the icon at dusk to watch its sparkling lights blink across Paris.

❷ Musée du Quai Branly (p84) Finding inspiration in traditional art and craftmanship from around the world.

❸ Cité de l'Architecture et du Patrimoine (p85) Wandering past cathedral portals, gargoyles and intricate scale models in this standout museum dedicated to French architecture.

❹ Bois de Boulogne (p90) Exploring western Paris' oasis of greenery: from bike rides, rowing boats and horse races to an amusement park kids will adore!

❺ Musée Marmottan Monet (p88) Taking a trip to see the world's largest collection of Monet canvases, alongside other impressionist and postimpressionist painters.

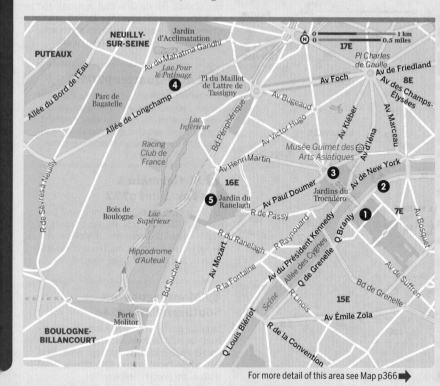

For more detail of this area see Map p366 ➡

Explore: Eiffel Tower & Western Paris

With its hourly sparkles that illuminate the evening skyline, the Eiffel Tower needs no introduction. Ascending to its viewing platforms will offer you a panorama over the whole of Paris, with the prestigious neighbourhood of Passy (the 16e *arrondissement*) stretching along the far banks of the Seine to the west. In the 18th and 19th centuries, Passy was home to luminaries such as Benjamin Franklin and Balzac. Defined by its sober, elegant buildings from the Haussmann era, it was annexed to the city only in 1860.

While most of the area today won't send the same frisson of excitement down your spine as taking the lift to the top of the tower, Passy is nonetheless home to some fabulous museums, and culture fans will certainly be busy. There's the Musée Marmottan Monet, with the world's largest collection of Monet paintings; the hip Palais de Tokyo, with modern art installations; the Musée Guimet des Arts Asiatiques, France's standout Asian art museum; the underrated Cité de l'Architecture et du Patrimoine, with captivating sculptures and murals; and a host of smaller collections devoted to fashion, anthropology, wine and even sub-Saharan art. On the Left Bank is the prominent Musée du Quai Branly, introducing indigenous art and culture from outside Europe, while at the city's western edge is the leafy refuge of the Bois de Boulogne. Beyond this lies the business district of La Défense.

Local Life

➡ **Museum hopping** Parisians flock to this part of town for its fine museums.

➡ **Green space** Leafy Bois de Boulogne is where city-dwellers escape the concrete on bikes, skates or by *footing* (jogging).

➡ **Daily commute** More than 150,000 people squeeze onto morning trains to La Défense, the city's business district, where skyscrapers rub shoulders with art.

Getting There & Away

➡ **Metro** Line 6 runs south from Charles de Gaulle–Étoile past the Eiffel Tower (views are superb from the elevated section); line 9 runs southwest from the Champs-Élysées. Line 1 terminates at La Défense.

➡ **RER** RER A runs west to La Défense; RER C runs along the Left Bank, with a stop at the Eiffel Tower.

➡ **Bus** Scenic bus 69 runs from the Champ de Mars (Eiffel Tower) along the Left Bank, crosses the Seine at the Louvre, and continues east to Père Lachaise.

➡ **Bicycle** Handy Vélib' stations include 2 av Octave Creard and 3 av Bosquet.

➡ **Boat** Eiffel Tower.

Lonely Planet's Top Tip

There are excellent top-end restaurants in the 16e, but it is substantially more affordable – and fun in nice weather – to follow the local flock and picnic. Build your own feast with sweet and savoury goodies from *boulangeries* (bakeries), markets, speciality food shops or takeaway delis.

✗ Best Places to Eat

➡ Hugo Desnoyer (p89)
➡ L'Astrance (p89)
➡ Atelier Vivanda (p89)
➡ Firmin Le Barbier (p89)
➡ Le Jules Verne (p89)

For reviews, see p88. ➡

☉ Best Picnic Spots

➡ Musée du Quai Branly garden (p84)
➡ Parc du Champ de Mars (p87)
➡ Jardins du Trocadéro (p86)
➡ place des États-Unis, opposite Galerie-Musée Baccarat (p88)
➡ Bois de Boulogne (p90)

For reviews, see p85. ➡

☕ Best Places to Drink

➡ St James Paris (p91)
➡ Bô Zinc Café (p91)
➡ Frog XVI (p91)

For reviews, see p91. ➡

TOP SIGHT
EIFFEL TOWER

There are different ways to experience the Eiffel Tower, from an evening ascent amid twinkling lights to a meal in one of its two restaurants. And even though some 6.9 million people come annually, few would dispute that each visit is unique – and something that simply has to be done when in Paris.

Metal Asparagus
Named after its designer, Gustave Eiffel, the Tour Eiffel was built for the 1889 Exposition Universelle (World Fair). It took 300 workers, 2.5 million rivets and two years of nonstop labour to assemble. Upon completion the tower became the tallest human-made structure in the world (324m or 1063ft) – a record held until the completion of the Chrysler Building in New York (1930). A symbol of the modern age, it faced massive opposition from Paris' artistic and literary elite, and the 'metal asparagus', as some Parisians snidely called it, was originally slated to be torn down in 1909. It was spared only because it proved an ideal platform for the transmitting antennas needed for the newfangled science of radiotelegraphy.

1st Floor
Of the tower's three floors, the 1st (57m) has the most space but the least impressive views. The glass-enclosed Pavillon Ferrié – open since summer 2014 – houses an immersion film along with a small cafe and souvenir shop, while the outer walkway features a discovery circuit to help visitors learn more about the tower's ingenious design. Check out

DON'T MISS
➡ 2nd-floor panorama
➡ Top-floor Champagne bar

PRACTICALITIES
➡ Map p366, F5
➡ ☎08 92 70 12 39
➡ www.tour-eiffel.fr
➡ Champ de Mars, 5 av Anatole France, 7e
➡ adult/youth/child lift to top €17/14.50/8, lift to 2nd fl €11/8.50/4, stairs to 2nd fl €7/5/3, lift 2nd fl to top €6
➡ ⏱lifts & stairs 9am-12.45am mid-Jun–Aug, lifts 9.30am-11.45pm, stairs 9.30am-6.30pm Sep–mid-Jun
➡ Ⓜ Bir Hakeim or RER Champ de Mars–Tour Eiffel

the sections of glass flooring that proffer a dizzying view of the antlike people walking on the ground far below.

This level also hosts the **58 Tour Eiffel** (☑01 45 55 20 04; www.restaurants-toureiffel.com; 2-/3-course lunch menu €22.50/27, dinner menu €70/80; ☺11.30am-4.30pm & 6.30-11pm) restaurant.

Not all lifts stop at the 1st floor (check before ascending), but it's an easy walk down from the 2nd floor should you accidentally end up one floor too high.

2nd Floor

Views from the 2nd floor (115m) are the best – impressively high but still close enough to see the details of the city below. Telescopes and panoramic maps placed around the tower pinpoint locations in Paris and beyond. Story windows give an overview of the lifts' mechanics, and the vision well allows you to gaze through glass panels to the ground. Also up here are toilets, a souvenir shop and the Michelin-starred restaurant Jules Verne (p89).

Top Floor

Views from the wind-buffeted top floor (276m) stretch up to 60km on a clear day, though at this height the panoramas are more sweeping than detailed. Celebrate your ascent with a glass of bubbly (€12 to €21) from the champagne bar (open noon to 10pm). Afterwards peep into Gustave Eiffel's restored top-level office where lifelike wax models of Eiffel and his daughter Claire greet Thomas Edison.

To access the top floor, take a separate lift on the 2nd floor (closed during heavy winds).

Ticket Purchases & Queueing Strategies

Ascend as far as the 2nd floor (either on foot or by lift), from where it is lift-only to the top floor. Pushchairs must be folded in lifts and you are not allowed to take bags or backpacks larger than aeroplane-cabin size.

Buying tickets in advance online usually means you avoid the monumental queues at the ticket offices. Print your ticket or show it on a smartphone screen. If you can't reserve your tickets ahead of time, expect waits of well over an hour in high season.

Stair tickets can't be reserved online. They are sold at the south pillar, where the staircase can also be accessed. The climb consists of 360 steps to the 1st floor and another 360 steps to the 2nd floor.

If you have reservations for either restaurant, you are granted direct access to the lifts.

NIGHTLY SPARKLES

Every hour on the hour, the entire tower sparkles for five minutes with 20,000 6-watt lights. They were first installed for Paris' millennium celebration in 2000 – it took 25 mountain climbers five months to install the current bulbs and 40km of electrical cords. For the best view of the light show, head across the Seine to the Jardins du Trocadéro.

Slapping a fresh coat of paint on the tower is no easy feat. It takes a 25-person team 18 months to complete the 60-tonnes-of-paint task, redone every seven years. Painted red and bronze since 1968, it's had six different colours throughout its lifetime, including yellow.

MAN ON A WIRE

In 1989 tightrope artist Philippe Petit walked up an inclined 700m cable across the Seine, from Palais Chaillot to the Eiffel Tower's 2nd floor. The act, performed before an audience of 250,000 people, was held to commemorate the French Republic's bicentennial.

DAVID SAILORS/GETTY IMAGES ©

TOP SIGHT
MUSÉE DU QUAI BRANLY

No other museum in Paris provides such inspiration for travellers, armchair anthropologists and those who simply appreciate the beauty of traditional craftwork. A tribute to the incredible diversity of human culture, the Musée du Quai Branly (designed by architect Jean Nouvel) presents an overview of indigenous and folk art from around the world.

Divided into four main sections (Oceania, Asia, Africa and the Americas) the museum showcases an impressive array of masks, carvings, weapons, jewellery and more, all displayed in a refreshingly unique interior without rooms or high walls. Although its sheer vastness can be intimidating, there are numerous aids on hand to help you navigate the collection and delve deeper into particular sections. Strategically placed multimedia touch screens provide more context for certain pieces, while tailored walks (available online and at the entrance) focus on specific themes, from masks and funerary objects to jewellery and musical instruments.

Highlights to look out for include remarkable carvings from Papua New Guinea (Oceania); clothing, jewellery and textiles from ethnic groups from India to Vietnam (Asia); a life-size 11th-century sculpture of a hermaphrodite (Africa); and artefacts from the great American civilisations – the Mayas, Aztecs and Incas.

Must-sees include temporary exhibits and performances, which are generally excellent.

The museum also contain **Café Branly** (Map p366; 27 quai Branly, 7e; ⏱10am-7pm Tue, Wed & Sun, to 8pm Thu-Sat; Ⓜ Pont de l'Alma, léna), as casual spot with ringside views of the Eiffel Tower and cafe fare to tuck into with a drink or three.

DON'T MISS

➡ The Papua New Guinea collection, Oceania

➡ The Evenk shaman cloak, Asia

➡ The Soninke hermaphrodite, Africa

➡ The grizzly totem pole, Americas

PRACTICALITIES

➡ Map p366, G4

➡ 📞01 56 61 70 00

➡ www.quaibranly.fr

➡ 37 quai Branly, 7e

➡ adult/child €9/free

➡ ⏱11am-7pm Tue, Wed & Sun, 11am-9pm Thu-Sat

➡ Ⓜ Alma Marceau or RER Pont de l'Alma

SIGHTS

EIFFEL TOWER LANDMARK
See p82.

MUSÉE DU QUAI BRANLY MUSEUM
See p84.

**FONDATION PIERRE
BERGÉ-YVES SAINT LAURENT** MUSEUM
Map p366 (www.fondation-pb-ysl.net; 3 rue
Léonce Reynaud, 16e; adult/teen €7/5; ⏰11am-
6pm Tue-Sun; Ⓜ Alma Marceau) This foundation dedicated to preserving the work of the
haute couture legend organises temporary
fashion and art exhibitions.

**GALERIES DU PANTHÉON
BOUDDHIQUE** GALLERY
Map p366 (19 av d'Iéna, 16e; ⏰10am-5.45pm
Wed-Mon, garden to 5pm; Ⓜ Iéna) FREE This excellent and often overlooked Asian art collection is comprised primarily of Japanese
Buddhist paintings and sculptures brought
to Paris in 1876 by collector Émile Guimet.
Housed in the sumptuous Hôtel Heidel-
bach, it's a short distance north of its parent
museum, the Musée Guimet (p86). Don't
miss the wonderful Japanese garden here,
which was completely renovated in 2016; it
sometimes hosts tea ceremonies.

MUSÉE DE LA MARINE MUSEUM
Map p366 (Maritime Museum; ☎01 53 65 69 69;
www.musee-marine.fr; 17 place du Trocadéro
et du 11 Novembre, 16e; adult/child €8.50/free;
⏰11am-6pm Wed-Mon; Ⓜ Trocadéro) Located
in the western wing of Palais de Chaillot,
the Maritime Museum examines France's
naval adventures from the 17th century
until today and boasts one of the world's
finest collections of model ships, as well as
ancient figureheads, compasses, sextants,
telescopes and paintings.

MUSÉE DE L'HOMME MUSEUM
Map p366 (Museum of Humankind; ☎01 44 05
72 72; www.museedelhomme.fr; 17 place Trocadéro et du 11 Novembre, 16e; adult/child €10/free;
⏰Thu-Mon 10am-6pm, Wed to 9pm; Ⓜ Passy,
Iéna) Originally opened in 1882 and recently renovated, this museum traces the
evolution of humankind through artefacts
gathered from around the world. There are
few English labels, and the transitions between exhibits sometimes lack coherency,
but there are nevertheless some fascinating
pieces on display, including a Cro Magnon

EIFFEL TOWER & WESTERN PARIS SIGHTS

 TOP SIGHT **CITÉ DE L'ARCHITECTURE ET DU PATRIMOINE**

In the eastern wing of the Palais de Chaillot, directly
across from the Eiffel Tower, is this standout museum
devoted to French architecture and heritage. The burgundy walls and skylit rooms showcase 350 plaster
casts taken from the country's greatest monuments, a
collection whose seeds were sown following the dese-
cration of many buildings during the French Revolution.

Some of the original details from which the casts
were made, such as sculptures from the Reims Cathedral, were later destroyed in the wars that followed.
Although they're not in situ, wandering through such a
magnificent collection of church portals, gargoyles, and
saints and sinners from around France is an incomparable experience for anyone interested in the elemental
stories that craftspeople chose to preserve in stone.

On display on the upper floors are reproduced murals and stained-glass windows from some of France's
most important monuments, which are arranged in an
intriguing labyrinthine layout. One of the most beautiful
reproductions in this section is the Cathédrale of St-
Etienne cupola.

DON'T MISS
➜ Casts Gallery
➜ Murals and
stained-glass
galleries
➜ Cathédrale of St-
Étienne cupola

PRACTICALITIES
➜ Map p366, E4
➜ www.citechaillot.fr
➜ 1 place du Trocadéro
et du 11 Novembre, 16e
➜ adult/child €8/free
➜ ⏰11am-7pm Wed &
Fri-Mon, to 9pm Thu
➜ Ⓜ Trocadéro

shell necklace, delicately carved mammoth tusks and reindeer jawbones, a variety of Paleolithic stone tools and a Peruvian mummy. Great views of the Eiffel Tower from the ground-floor restaurant and 2nd-floor cafe.

PALAIS DE CHAILLOT
HISTORIC BUILDING

Map p366 (place du Trocadéro et du 11 Novembre, 16e; MTrocadéro) The two curved, colonnaded wings of this building (built for the 1937 International Expo) and the terrace in between them afford an exceptional panorama of the Jardins du Trocadéro, the Seine and the Eiffel Tower. The eastern wing houses the standout Cité de l'Architecture et du Patrimoine (p85), devoted to French architecture and heritage, as well as the Théâtre National de Chaillot (p91), staging dance and theatre. The western wing houses the Musée de la Marine (p85) and the Musée de l'Homme (p85).

MAISON DE BALZAC
MUSEUM

Map p366 (47 rue Raynouard, 16e; ☺10am-6pm Tue-Sun; MPassy or RER Avenue Président Kennedy) **FREE** This pretty, three-storey spa house is where novelist Honoré de Balzac (1799–1850) lived and worked from 1840 to 1847, editing the entire *Comédie Humaine*. There's lots of memorabilia, letters, prints and portraits – perfect for die-hard Balzac fans.

MUSÉE DAPPER
ART MUSEUM

Map p366 (☎01 45 00 91 75; www.dapper.com.fr; 35 rue Paul Valéry, 16e; adult/child €6/free; ☺11am-7pm Wed, Sun & Mon, to 10pm Fri & Sat; MVictor Hugo) Focused on African and Caribbean art, this jewel of a museum is an invitation to leave Paris behind for an hour or two. Exhibits rotate throughout the year, but the permanent collection is superb: ritual and festival masks and costumes accompanied by several video presentations. The auditorium hosts film screenings, concerts, storytelling and other cultural events.

MUSÉE DE LA MODE DE LA VILLE DE PARIS
MUSEUM

Map p366 (☎01 56 52 86 00; www.galliera.paris.fr; 10 av Pierre 1er de Serbie, 16e; adult/child €8/free; ☺10am-6pm Tue-Sun, to 9pm Thu; Mléna) Housed in 19th-century Palais Galliera, Paris' Fashion Museum warehouses some 100,000 outfits and accessories – from canes and umbrellas to fans and gloves – from the 18th century to the present day. The sumptuous Italianate palace and gardens dating

---

TOP SIGHT
MUSÉE GUIMET DES ARTS ASIATIQUES

France's foremost Asian arts museum, the Musée Guimet has a superb collection of sculptures, paintings and religious articles that originated in the vast stretch of land between Afghanistan and Japan. In fact, it's possible to observe the gradual transmission of both Buddhism and artistic styles along the Silk Road in some of the museum's pieces, from the 1st-century Gandhara Buddhas from Afghanistan and Pakistan to the later Central Asian, Chinese and Japanese Buddhist sculptures and art.

Other strong points of the museum include the Southeast Asian statuary on the ground floor (which has the world's largest collection of Khmer artefacts outside Cambodia), the Nepalese and Tibetan bronzes and mandalas, and the vast China collection, which encompasses everything from ink paintings and calligraphy to funerary statuary and early bronzes.

Part of the collection, comprised of Buddhist paintings and sculptures, is housed in the nearby Galeries du Panthéon Bouddhique (p85). Don't miss the wonderful Japanese garden here.

DON'T MISS
➡ Afghan collection
➡ Southeast Asian statuary
➡ China collection
➡ Galeries du Panthéon Bouddhique

PRACTICALITIES
➡ Map p366, F4
➡ ☎01 56 52 54 33
➡ www.guimet.fr
➡ 6 place d'Iéna, 16e
➡ adult/child €7.50/free
➡ ☺10am-6pm Wed-Mon
➡ Mléna

WORTH A DETOUR

LA DÉFENSE

More than just office space, La Défense is an engaging, open-air art gallery. Calder, Miró, Agam, César and Torricini are among the international artists behind the colourful and often-surprising sculptures and murals that pepper the central 1km-long promenade. Pick up a map and excellent booklets in English outlining walks to discover its art and surprising green spaces at **Info Défense** (☏01 46 93 19 00; www.ladefense.fr; place de la Défense; ☉9am-6pm Mon-Fri, 10am-5pm Sat & Sun; ⓜLa Défense), located near the Globe Trotter Cafe at the heart of the promenade.

Grande Arche de la Défense (www.grandearche.com; 1 Parvis de la Défense; ⓜLa Défense) La Défense's landmark edifice is the marble Grande Arche, a cube-like arch built in the 1980s to house government and business offices. The arch marks the western end of the *axe historique* (historic axis), though Danish architect Johan-Otto von Sprekelsen deliberately placed the Grande Arche fractionally out of alignment. After several years of renovations, access to the roof is expected to reopen in 2017.

Musée de la Défense (15 place de la Défense; ⓜLa Défense) This modest museum, located in the basement of the tourist office (p87), evokes the area's development and architecture through drawings, architectural plans and scale models. It is currently closed to the public.

from the mid-19th century are worth a visit in themselves, as are the excellent temporary exhibitions the museum hosts.

PARC DU CHAMP DE MARS PARK
Map p366 (Champ de Mars, 7e; ⓜÉcole Militaire or RER Champ de Mars–Tour Eiffel) Running southeast from the Eiffel Tower, the grassy Champ de Mars – an ideal summer picnic spot – was originally used as a parade ground for the cadets of the 18th-century École Militaire, the vast French-classical building at the southeastern end of the park, which counts Napoleon Bonaparte among its graduates. The steel-and-etched glass 2000 **Wall for Peace memorial** (Map p366; www.wallforpeace.com; ⓜÉcole Militaire or RER Champ de Mars–Tour Eiffel) is by Clara Halter.

PALAIS DE TOKYO ART MUSEUM
Map p366 (www.palaisdetokyo.com; 13 av du Président Wilson, 16e; adult/child €10/free; ☉noon-midnight Wed-Mon; ⓜIéna) The Tokyo Palace, created for the 1937 Exposition Universelle, has no permanent collection. Rather its shell-like interior of concrete and steel is a stark backdrop to interactive contemporary-art exhibitions and installations. Its bookshop is fabulous for art and design magazines, and its eating and drinking options are magic.

MUSÉE D'ART MODERNE DE LA VILLE DE PARIS ART MUSEUM
Map p366 (www.mam.paris.fr; 11 av du Président Wilson, 16e; ☉10am-6pm Tue, Wed, Fri-Sun,

10am-10pm Thu; ⓜIéna) **FREE** The permanent collection at Paris' modern-art museum displays works representative of just about every major artistic movement of the 20th and (nascent) 21st centuries, with works by Modigliani, Matisse, Braque and Soutine. The real jewel, though, is the room hung with canvases by Dufy and Bonnard. Look out for cutting-edge temporary exhibitions (not free).

AQUARIUM DE PARIS CINÉAQUA AQUARIUM
Map p366 (www.cineaqua.com; av des Nations Unies, 16e; adult/child €20.50/13; ☉10am-7pm; ⓜTrocadéro) Paris' aquarium, on the eastern side of the Jardins du Trocadéro, has a shark tank and 500-odd fish species to entertain families on rainy days. Three cinemas screen ocean-related and other films (dubbed in French, with subtitles). Budget tip: show your ticket from the nearby Musée de la Marine or the Musée Guimet to get reduced aquarium admission (adult/child €16.40/10.40).

FLAME OF LIBERTY MEMORIAL MONUMENT
Map p366 (place de l'Alma, 8e; ⓜAlma Marceau) This bronze sculpture, a replica of the one topping the Statue of Liberty, was placed here in 1987 as a symbol of friendship between France and the USA. More famous is its location, above the place d'Alma tunnel where, on 31 August 1997, Diana, Princess of Wales, was killed in a car accident. Graffiti remembering the princess covers the entire wall next to the sculpture.

TOP SIGHT
MUSÉE MARMOTTAN MONET

Housed in the duc de Valmy's former hunting lodge (well, let's call it a mansion), this intimate museum houses the world's largest collection of Monet paintings and sketches. It provides an interesting if patchy cross-section of his work, beginning with paintings such as the seminal *Impression, Soleil levant* (1873) and *Promenade près d'Argenteuil* (1875), passing through numerous water-lily studies, before moving on to the rest of the collection, which is considerably more abstract and dates to the early 1900s. Some of the masterpieces to look out for include *La Barque* (1887), *Cathédrale de Rouen* (1892), *Londres, le Parlement* (1901) and the various *Nymphéas* – many of these were smaller studies for the works now on display in the **Musée de l'Orangerie** (p118).

Temporary exhibitions, included in the admission price and always excellent, are generally shown either in the basement or on the 1st floor. Also on display are a handful of canvases by Renoir, Pissaro, Gauguin and Morisot, and a collection of 13th- through 16th-century illuminations, which are quite lovely if somewhat out of place.

DON'T MISS

➡ *Impression, Soleil levant*

➡ *Promenade près d'Argenteuil*

➡ *Londres, le Parlement*

➡ The illuminations collection

PRACTICALITIES

➡ Map p366, C5

➡ ☎01 44 96 50 33

➡ www.marmottan.fr

➡ 2 rue Louis Boilly, 16e

➡ adult/child €11/6.50

➡ ⊙10am-6pm Tue-Sun, to 9pm Thu

➡ Ⓜ La Muette

GALERIE-MUSÉE BACCARAT   MUSEUM

Map p366 (11 place des États-Unis, 16e; adult/child €10/free; ⊙10am-6pm Mon & Wed-Sat; Ⓜ Boissière, Kléber) Showcasing 1000 stunning pieces of crystal, many of them custom-made for princes and dictators of former colonies, this flashy museum is at home in its striking new rococo-style premises designed by Philippe Starck. It is also home to an upmarket restaurant called – what else? – Le Cristal Room.

✗ EATING

MALITOURNE   PATISSERIE €

Map p366 (☎01 47 20 52 26; www.patisserie-malitourne.com; 30 rue de Chaillot, 16e; ⊙7.30am-7.30pm Mon-Fri, 8am-1pm Sat; Ⓜ Alma-Marceau) Indulge in something sweet at this great little *pâtissier,* chocolate-maker and *traiteur* (caterer). Going strong since 1976, it has the added bonus of street entertainment: watch chocolate-makers at work in their street-side kitchen with a huge window designed to show it all off.

TRAITEUR JEGADO   FAST FOOD €

Map p366 (☎01 47 20 23 83; www.traiteur-jegado.fr; 45 rue de Chaillot, 16e; mains per kg €11-31; ⊙noon-2pm Mon-Fri; Ⓜ Alma Marceau, George V) The sign outside this busy canteen-style *traiteur* (caterer) simply reads *'plats cuisinés'* (cooked dishes), but there's no missing this top-choice takeaway address – just look for the lunchtime line snaking halfway down the street. Delicious salads, starters and hot dishes are prepared in the no-frills kitchen, then bagged to go.

MARCHÉ PRÉSIDENT WILSON   MARKET €

Map p366 (av du Président Wilson, 16e; ⊙7am-2.30pm Wed & Sat; Ⓜ Iéna, Alma-Marceau) This open-air market across from Palais de Tokyo is the most convenient in the neighbourhood. Organic wines, heirloom vegetables and artisanal charcuterie are some of the many temptations.

FIRMIN LE BARBIER   FRENCH €€

Map p366 (☎01 45 51 21 55; www.firminlebarbier.fr; 20 rue de Monttessuy, 7e; mains €26-35; ⊙noon-2pm Wed-Fri & Sun, 7-10.30pm Wed-Sat; Ⓜ Pont de l'Alma) This brick-walled bistro was opened by a retired surgeon turned gourmet, and his passion is apparent in everything from the personable service to the wine list. The menu is traditional French (sirloin steak with polenta, decadent bœuf bourguignon), while the modern interior is bright and cheery with an open kitchen. Find it a five-minute walk from the Eiffel Tower. Reserve.

WAKNINE
FRENCH €€

Map p366 (☑01 47 23 48 18; www.waknine.fr; 9 av Pierre 1er de Serbie, 16e; mains €22.50-31.50; ☺noon-10.30pm; ⓂIéna) It may look unremarkable from the outside, but this cosy hideaway is a local secret. The cuisine and service are both excellent without being overbearing; think steak with a parmesan and truffle emulsion or roast chicken in a delicate wholegrain mustard sauce, followed by Roquefort with confit prunes. Meals bookend tea and pastries in the early afternoon and tapas for *apéro* (premeal drinks).

ATELIER VIVANDA
FRENCH €€

Map p366 (☑01 40 67 10 00; www.ateliervivanda. com; 18 Rue Lauriston, 16e; meal €35; ☺noon-2.30pm & 7.30-10.30 Mon-Fri; ⓂCharles de Gaulle–Étoile) A micro outpost of carnivore heaven, tucked away down an inconspicuous side street 10 minutes from the Arc de Triomphe. The Atelier focuses uniquely on high-quality meat and poultry; the three-course meal (the only option) is a deal in this neighbourhood. Reserve.

TOKYO EAT
FUSION €€

Map p366 (☑01 47 20 00 29; www.palaisdetokyo. com; Palais de Tokyo, 13 av du Président Wilson, 16e; mains €18-31; ☺noon-2am Wed-Tue; ⓂIéna) This artsy canteen attached to contemporary-art museum Palais de Tokyo is industrially chic, with colourful flying saucers hovering above the tables and changing art exhibits on the walls. Cuisine is unpredictable and fun – anything from chicken curry served on a banana leaf to caramelised chicory. DJs hit the decks some evenings. The weekday lunch *plat du jour* (dish of the day; €13) is an excellent deal.

LE PETIT RÉTRO
BISTRO €€

Map p366 (☑01 44 05 06 05; www.petitretro.fr; 5 rue Mesnil, 16e; 2-/3-course menus lunch €26/31, dinner €30/36; ☺noon-2.30pm & 7-10.30pm Mon-Wed, to 11pm Thu-Sat; ⓂVictor Hugo) From the gorgeous 'Petit Rétro' emblazoned on the zinc bar to the ceramic, art nouveau

folk tiles on the wall, this is a handsome old-style bistro. Its fare is French classic: for example, blood sausage, *blanquette de veau* (veal in a butter and cream sauce) and *oreilles de cochon* (pig's ears). Delicious.

★HUGO DESNOYER
MODERN FRENCH €€€

Map p366 (☑01 46 47 83 00; www.hugodesnoyer. fr; 28 rue du Docteur Blanche, 16e; mains from €28; ☺restaurant 11.30am-3.30pm Tue-Sat, 8-11pm Wed; ⓂJasmin) Hugo Desnoyer is Paris' most famous butcher and the trip to his shop in the 16e is well worth it. Arrive by noon or reserve to snag a table and settle down to a *table d'hôte* (set menu at a fixed price) feast of homemade terrines, quiches, foie gras and cold cuts followed by the finest meat in Paris – cooked to perfection *naturellement*.

A more convenient branch, Steak Point (p101), is located in the basement of Galeries Lafayette Gourmet.

★L'ASTRANCE
GASTRONOMY €€€

Map p366 (☑01 40 50 84 40; 4 rue Beethoven, 16e; lunch menus €70-150, dinner €230; ☺12.15-1.15pm & 8.15-9.15pm Tue-Fri; ⓂPassy) It's been over 15 years since Pascal Barbot's dazzling cuisine at the three-star L'Astrance made its debut, but it has shown no signs of losing its cutting edge. Look beyond the complicated descriptions on the menu – what you should expect are teasers of taste that you never even knew existed. Reserve one to two months in advance.

LE JULES VERNE
GASTRONOMY €€€

Map p366 (☑01 45 55 61 44; www.lejulesverne-paris.com; 2nd fl, Eiffel Tower, Champ de Mars, 7e; menus lunch €105, dinner €190-230; ☺noon-1.30pm & 7-9.30pm; ⓂBir Hakeim or RER Champ de Mars–Tour Eiffel) Book way ahead (online only) to feast on Michelin-starred cuisine and the most beautiful view of Paris at this magical address, on the Eiffel Tower's 2nd floor. Cuisine is contemporary, with a five- or six-course 'experience' menu allowing you to taste the best of chef Pascal Féraud's stunning gastronomic repertoire.

MONSIEUR BLEU
MODERN FRENCH €€€

Map p366 (☑01 47 20 90 47; www.monsieurbleu. com; Palais de Tokyo, 20 av de New York, 16e; mains €22-45; ☺noon-2am; ⓂIéna) An 'in' address with the uber-cool fashion set since opening in 2013, this darling of a restaurant has bags going for it: superb interior design by Joseph Dirand, excellent seasonal cuisine and a summer terrace with a monumental

WORTH A DETOUR

BOIS DE BOULOGNE

The 845-hectare **Bois de Boulogne** (Map p366; bd Maillot; Ⓜ Porte Maillot) owes its informal layout to Baron Haussmann, who, inspired by London's Hyde Park, planted 400,000 trees here in the 19th century. Along with various gardens and other sights, the park has 15km of cycle paths and 28km of bridle paths through 125 hectares of forested land.

Be warned that the area becomes a distinctly adult playground after dark, especially along the Allée de Longchamp running northeast from the Étang des Réservoirs (Reservoirs Pond), where all kinds of sex workers cruise for clients.

The Bois de Boulogne is served by metro lines 1 (Porte Maillot, Les Sablons), 2 (Porte Dauphine), 9 (Michel-Ange–Auteuil) and 10 (Michel-Ange–Auteuil, Porte d'Auteuil), and the RER C (Avenue Foch, Avenue Henri Martin). Vélib' stations are found near most of the park entrances, but not within the park itself.

Jardin d'Acclimatation (Map p366; www.jardindacclimatation.fr; av du Mahatma Gandhi; €3, per attraction €2.90; ⊗10am-7pm Apr-Sep, to 6pm Oct-Mar; Ⓜ Les Sablons) Families adore this green and flowery amusement park on the northern fringe of wooded Bois de Boulogne. There are swings, roundabouts and playgrounds for all ages (included in the admission fee), as well as dozens of attractions such as puppet shows, boat rides, funfair rides, a small water park, pony rides, a little train and so on, which you pay extra for.

Le Chalet des Îles (Map p366; 📞01 42 88 04 69; Carrefour du Bout des Lacs; 30/60/90/120min €6/10/15.50/19, plus €50 deposit; ⊗noon-5pm Mon-Fri, 10am-6pm Sat & Sun mid-Feb–Oct; Ⓜ Avenue Henri Martin) Rent an old-fashioned rowing boat to paddle around Lac Inférieur, the largest of Bois de Boulogne's lakes – romance and serenity guaranteed.

Parc et Château de Bagatelle (Map p366; rte de Sèvres à Neuilly, 16e; during events adult/child €6/3 Jun-Oct, free Nov-Apr; ⊗9.30am-8pm, shorter hours winter; Ⓜ Porte Maillot) These enclosed gardens, originally designed as the result of a wager between Marie-Antoinette and the Count of Artois, frame 18th-century **Château de Bagatelle** (rue de Sèvres à Neuilly; tour adult/child €6/free; ⊗tour 3pm Sun Apr-Oct; Ⓜ Porte Maillot), built for the younger brother of Louis XVI. Magnificent irises bloom in May, roses from June to October, and – perhaps most majestically of all – water lilies in August.

Pré Catelan (Catelan Meadow; Map p366; rte de Suresnes, 16e; ⊗9.30am-8pm, Jardin Shakespeare 2-4pm, shorter hours winter; Ⓜ Ranelagh) **FREE** This garden area within Parc de Bagatelle squirrels away the wonderful Jardin Shakespeare, where plants, flowers and trees mentioned in Shakespeare's plays are cultivated. Watch for summertime performances in the garden's small open-air theatre.

Jardin des Serres d'Auteuil (Map p366; av de la Porte d'Auteuil, 16é; ⊗8am-8.30pm summer, shorter hours otherwise; Ⓜ Porte d'Auteuil) **FREE** Located at the southeastern end of the Bois de Boulogne are these impressive conservatories, which opened in 1898 and are home to a large collection of tropical plants. The new **Stade Roland Garros** (Map p366; www.billetterie.fft.fr; 2 av Gordon Bennett, 16e, Bois de Boulogne; Ⓜ Porte d'Auteuil) has begun expansion into the gardens; they will remain open, but visitors should expect construction through at least 2020.

Stade Roland Garros-Musée de la Fédération Française de Tennis (Map p366; www.fft.fr; 2 av Gordon Bennett, 16e; Ⓜ Porte d'Auteuil) The world's most extravagant tennis museum will be closed until stadium renovations are complete (2020).

Fondation Louis Vuitton (Map p366; www.fondationlouisvuitton.fr; 8 av du Mahatma Gandhi, 16e; adult/child €14/5; ⊗10am-8pm Sat-Thu, to 11pm Fri; Ⓜ Les Sablons) Designed by Frank Gehry, this striking contemporary-art centre opened its doors in late 2014. Emerging behind the Jardin d'Acclimatation, the glass-panelled building thus far has proven more interesting than the temporary exhibits it has hosted. Check online for the latest exhibit.

Eiffel Tower view. It's attached to the Palais de Tokyo (enter from av de New York); reserve in advance.

LES OMBRES
MODERN FRENCH €€€

Map p366 (☑01 47 53 68 00; www.lesombres-restaurant.com; 27 quai Branly, 7e; 2-/3-course weekday lunch menu €35/42, dinner menu €71; ⊗noon-2.15pm & 7-10.20pm; Ⓜléna or RER Pont de l'Alma) This glass-enclosed rooftop restaurant on the 5th floor of the Musée du Quai Branly is named the 'Shadows' after the patterns cast by the Eiffel Tower's webbed ironwork. Dramatic Eiffel views are complemented by kitchen creations such as scampi with spicy mango coulis, or beef tenderloin in watercress sauce. Reserve.

🍷 DRINKING & NIGHTLIFE

★ST JAMES PARIS
BAR

Map p366 (☑01 44 05 81 81; www.saint-james-paris.com; 43 av Bugeaud, 16e; drinks €15-25; ⊗7pm-1am Mon-Sat; 🛜; ⓂPorte Dauphine) It might be a hotel bar, but a drink at St James may well be one of your most memorable in Paris. Tucked behind a stone wall, this historic mansion opens its bar each evening to nonguests – and the setting redefines extraordinary. Winter drinks are in the library, in summer they're in the impossibly romantic garden.

FROG XVI
PUB

Map p366 (☑01 47 27 88 88; www.frogpubs.com; 110 av Kléber, 16e; ⊗noon-2am; ⓂTrocadéro) This popular Parisian pub and brewery has seven locations, but for beer drinkers this one is the saving grace, as there simply isn't much else in the way of craft brews in the posh 16e. IPA on tap, a family-friendly menu and live sports on the big screen. Pints are €5 during happy hour (5pm to 8pm).

BÔ ZINC CAFÉ
BAR

Map p366 (☑01 42 24 69 05; 59 av Mozart, 16e; ⊗7am-2am; ⓂRanelagh) With its soft sage-green facade and buzzing pavement terrace, Bô Zinc is one of those great hybrid addresses – perfect for hanging with locals over coffee, tea or after-work cocktails. Seating is a mix of wooden bistro chairs and 'flop-in' armchairs, while potted palm trees – inside and out – add a touch of chic. Top-notch nosh too, served until 11pm.

☆ ENTERTAINMENT

THÉÂTRE NATIONAL DE CHAILLOT
THEATRE

Map p366 (☑01 53 65 30 00; www.theatre-chaillot.fr; 1 place du Trocadéro, 16e; ⓂTrocadéro) French national theatre located beneath the Trocadéro esplanade, primarily staging modern-dance productions.

MAISON DE LA RADIO
LIVE MUSIC

Map p366 (http://maisondelaradio.fr; 116 av du président Kennedy, 16e; concerts €15; ⓂPassy or RER Avenue du Président Kennedy) Catch a classical concert at Radio France's new concert space, opened in December 2014. With some 200 annual performances, expect a wide variety of music, from organ and chamber music to appearances by the national orchestra. To browse performance times on the website, click on 'Agenda'.

If you're fluent in French, check out one of the *émissions en publique* – your chance to sit in on a live radio show.

YOYO
LIVE MUSIC, CINEMA

Map p366 (www.yoyo-paris.com; Palais de Tokyo, 13 av du Président Wilson, 16e; ⊗variable hours; Ⓜléna, Alma Marceau) Be it street-art exhibitions, live-music gigs, fashion shows, club nights or film screenings, this contemporary raw-concrete space inside Palais de Tokyo promises a great night out.

LES MARIONNETTES DU CHAMP DE MARS
PUPPET SHOWS

Map p366 (☑01 48 56 01 44; http://guignoldu champdemars.centerblog.net; allée du Général Margueritte, 7e; €4; ⓂÉcole Militaire or RER Champ de Mars–Tour Eiffel) For time-honoured French entertainment, take the kids to a show in this Napoleon III–style puppet theatre. Shows are in French, but performances still amuse. Check the website for performance times, usually Wednesday, weekends and school holidays.

🔒 SHOPPING

PATRICK ROGER
CHOCOLATE

Map p366 (☑01 45 01 66 71; www.patrickroger.com; 45 av Victor Hugo, 16e; ⊗10.30am-7.30pm Mon-Sat; ⓂVictor Hugo) The creations of chocolate artist and sculptor Patrick Roger are extraordinary (and often very large – 80kg or so), rendering a visit to his boutiques an eye-opening experience. More modest, take-home boxes are as beautiful.

Champs-Élysées & Grands Boulevards

CHAMPS-ÉLYSÉES | GRANDS BOULEVARDS

Neighbourhood Top Five

1 **Arc de Triomphe** (p94) Climbing Napoleon's arch to survey the *axe historique*, extending from the Louvre to La Défense, and paying tribute to the Tomb of the Unknown Soldier.

2 **Palais Garnier** (p96) Taking in a performance or touring the mythic 19th-century opera house, where Chagall's ceiling mural is on display.

3 **Galeries Lafayette** (p104) Catching a free fashion show showcasing seasonal trends at the magnificent art nouveau department store and admiring the rooftop panorama.

4 **Grand Palais** (p96) Viewing exceptional art exhibitions beneath the 8.5-tonne art nouveau glass roof.

5 **Champs-Élysées** (p96) Strolling the over-the-top avenue – you can't leave Paris without doing it once.

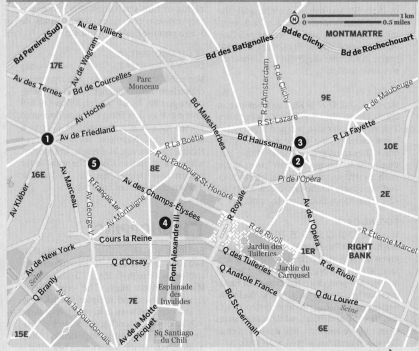

For more detail of this area see Map p368 and p370 ➡

Explore: Champs-Élysées & Grands Boulevards

The Champs-Élysées and Grands Boulevards area is grandiose in layout – it's possible to play an epically proportioned game of connect the dots here. The main landmarks – the Arc de Triomphe, place de la Concorde, place de la Madeleine and the Opéra – are joined by majestic boulevards, each lined with harmonious rows of Haussmann-era buildings.

Monumental vistas will keep your eyes occupied, but high-end shops and elegant department stores are this district's *raison d'être* and many will soon find their gaze slipping to the luxury display windows. Dior, Chanel, Louis Vuitton...fans of *haute couture* will find themselves pulled into the famed Triangle d'Or (Golden Triangle), south from the Champs-Élysées. Further east are the historic *grands magasins* (department stores) such as Le Printemps and Galeries Lafayette, which will appeal to shoppers interested in a broader overview of French fashion.

But there's much more to this area than fashion overload. The vestiges of the 1900 World's Fair – the Grand Palais and Petit Palais (along with the bridge Pont Alexandre III) – play host to a variety of excellent exhibits, which range from contemporary art to a family-friendly science museum.

Entertainment, too, has a strong tradition in this area, the most notable venue being the famed 19th-century opera house, the Palais Garnier. While non-French speakers will skip the theatres along the Grands Boulevards, there are plenty of music venues – from classical to rock – that require no language skills to appreciate.

Local Life

→**Epicurean life** Shop for luxury gourmet goods around Place de la Madeleine (p103).

→**Art life** Parisians' thirst for art is unquenchable – join locals viewing exhibitions in museums like La Pinacothèque (p97).

→**Park life** Seek serenity in the tiny, secreted Jardin de la Nouvelle France (p97).

Getting There & Away

→**Metro & RER** Metro line 1 follows the Champs-Élysées below ground, while lines 8 and 9 serve the Grands Boulevards. RER A stops at Auber (Opéra) and Charles de Gaulle–Étoile.

→**Bicycle** You'll find Vélib' stations on side streets off the Champs-Élysées.

→**Boat** The hop-on, hop-off Batobus' Champs-Élysées stop is just east of Pont Alexandre III.

Lonely Planet's Top Tip

Haute cuisine – and *haute* prices – are the rule in the 8e, but if you eat at one of the finer restaurants for lunch on a weekday, you'll save a bundle and still get to treat your tastebuds to an extraordinary meal. Make sure to reserve.

Best Places to Eat

→ Richer (p101)
→ Le Hide (p99)
→ Floquifil (p102)
→ Mamou (p101)
→ Lasserre (p100)

For reviews, see p99.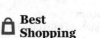

Best Places to Drink

→ PanPan (p103)
→ Blaine (p102)
→ Zig Zag Club (p102)
→ Showcase (p102)

For reviews, see p102.

Best Shopping

→ Galeries Lafayette (p104)
→ Le Printemps (p105)
→ Triangle d'Or (p104)
→ À la Mère de Famille (p105)
→ Place de la Madeleine (p103)

For reviews, see p104.

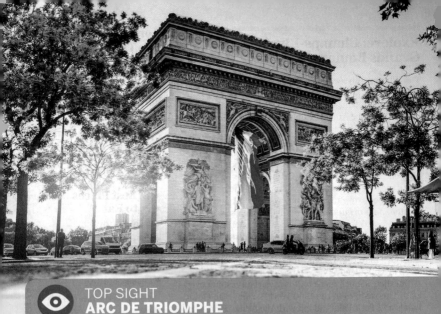

◉ TOP SIGHT
ARC DE TRIOMPHE

Napoléon's armies never did march through the Arc de Triomphe showered in honour, but the monument has nonetheless come to stand as the very symbol of French patriotism. It's not for nationalistic sentiments, however, that so many visitors huff up the narrow, spiralling staircase. Rather it's the sublime panoramas from the top that make the arch such a notable attraction.

DON'T MISS

➡ Tomb of the Unknown Soldier

➡ Multimedia exhibit

➡ Viewing platform

PRACTICALITIES

➡ Map p368, A2

➡ www.monuments-nationaux.fr

➡ place Charles de Gaulle, 8e

➡ adult/child €12/free

➡ ⊙10am-11pm Apr-Sep, to 10.30pm Oct-Mar

➡ Ⓜ Charles de Gaulle–Étoile

History

The arch was first commissioned in 1806 in the style of a Roman triumphal arch, following Napoléon's victory at Austerlitz the year before. At the time, the victory seemed like a watershed moment that confirmed the tactical supremacy of the French army, but a mere decade later, Napoléon had already fallen from power and his empire had crumbled. The Arc de Triomphe was never fully abandoned – simply laying the foundations, after all, had taken an entire two years – and in 1836, after a series of starts and stops under the restored monarchy, the project was finally completed. In 1840 Napoléon's remains were returned to France and passed under the arch before being interred at Invalides.

Beneath the Arch

Beneath the arch at ground level lies the Tomb of the Unknown Soldier. Honouring the 1.3 million French soldiers who lost their lives in WWI, the Unknown Soldier was laid to rest in 1921, beneath an eternal flame that is rekindled daily at 6.30pm.

Also here are a number of bronze plaques laid into the ground. Take the time to try and decipher some: these mark significant moments in modern French history, such as the proclamation of the Third French Republic (4 September 1870) and the return of Alsace and Lorraine to French rule (11 November 1918). The most notable plaque is the text from Charles de Gaulle's famous London broadcast on 18 June 1940, which sparked the French Resistance to life: 'Believe me, I who am speaking to you with full knowledge of the facts, and who tell you that nothing is lost for France. The same means that overcame us can bring us victory one day. For France is not alone! She is not alone!'

Sculptures

The arch is adorned with four main sculptures, six panels in relief, and a frieze running beneath the top. Each was designed by a different artist; the most famous sculpture is the one to the right as you approach from the Champs-Élysées: *La Marseillaise* (Departure of the Volunteers of 1792). Sculpted by François Rude, it depicts soldiers of all ages gathering beneath the wings of victory, en route to drive back the invading armies of Prussia and Austria. The higher panels depict a series of important victories for the Revolutionary and imperial French armies, from Egypt to Austerlitz, while the detailed frieze is divided into two sections: the *Departure of the Armies* and the *Return of the Armies*. Don't miss the multimedia section beneath the viewing platform, which provides more detail and historical background for each of the sculptures.

Viewing Platform

Climb the 284 steps to the viewing platform at the top of the 50m-high arch and you'll be suitably rewarded with magnificent panoramas over western Paris. From here, a dozen broad avenues – many of them named after Napoléonic victories and illustrious generals – radiate towards every compass point. The Arc de Triomphe is the highest point in the line of monuments known as the *axe historique* (historic axis, also called the grand axis); it offers views that swoop east down the Champs-Élysées to the gold-tipped obelisk at place de la Concorde (and beyond to the Louvre's glass pyramid), and west to the skyscraper district of La Défense, where the colossal Grande Arche marks the *axe*'s western terminus.

ARCH ACROBATICS

On 7 August 1919, three weeks after the WWI victory parade, Charles Godefroy flew a biplane through the arch (14.5m wide) to honour the French pilots who had fought in the war. It was no easy feat: Jean Navarre, the pilot originally chosen to perform the flight, crashed his plane while practising and died.

Don't cross the traffic-choked roundabout above ground if you value your life! Stairs lead from the northern side of the Champs-Élysées to pedestrian tunnels (not linked to metro tunnels) that bring you out safely beneath the arch. Tickets to the viewing platform are sold in the tunnel.

BASTILLE DAY CELEBRATION

The military parade commemorating Bastille Day (14 July) kicks off from the arch, which is adorned by a billowing tricolour.

◉ SIGHTS

◉ Champs-Élysées

ARC DE TRIOMPHE   LANDMARK

See p94.

AVENUE DES CHAMPS-ÉLYSÉES   STREET

Map p368 (8e; Ⓜ Charles de Gaulle–Étoile, George V, Franklin D Roosevelt or Champs-Élysées–Clemenceau) No trip to Paris is complete without strolling this broad, tree-shaded avenue lined with luxury shops. Named for the Elysian Fields ('heaven' in Greek mythology), the Champs-Élysées was laid out in the 17th century and is part of the *axe historique*, linking place de la Concorde with the Arc de Triomphe. It's where presidents and soldiers strut their stuff on Bastille Day, where the Tour de France holds its final sprint, and where Paris turns out for organised and impromptu celebrations.

GRAND PALAIS   ART MUSEUM

Map p368 (✆ 01 44 13 17 17; www.grandpalais.fr; 3 av du Général Eisenhower, 8e; adult/child €15/1; ⊙ 10am-8pm Sun, Mon & Thu, to 10pm Wed, Fri & Sat; Ⓜ Champs-Élysées–Clemenceau) Erected for the 1900 Exposition Universelle (World's Fair), the Grand Palais today houses several exhibition spaces beneath its huge 8.5-tonne art nouveau glass roof. Some of Paris' biggest shows (Renoir, Chagall, Turner) are held in the Galeries Nationales, lasting three to four months. Hours, prices and exhibition dates vary significantly for all galleries. Those listed here generally apply to the Galeries Nationales, but always check the website for exact details. Reserving a ticket online for any show is strongly advised.

Other exhibit spaces include the imaginative Nef – which plays host to concerts, art installations, a seasonal amusement park and horse shows – and several other minor galleries, entered from av Winston-Churchill. There's also an MK2 cinema and fabulous restaurant, Mini Palais (p100).

PETIT PALAIS   ART MUSEUM

Map p368 (✆ 01 53 43 40 00; www.petitpalais. paris.fr; av Winston-Churchill, 8e; permanent collections free; ⊙ 10am-6pm Tue-Sun; Ⓜ Champs-Élysées–Clemenceau) **FREE** This architectural stunner was built for the 1900 Exposition Universelle, and is home to the Paris mu-

◉ TOP SIGHT
PALAIS GARNIER

Few other Paris monuments have provided artistic inspiration in the way that the Palais Garnier has. From Degas' ballerinas to Gaston Leroux' Phantom and Chagall's ceiling, the layers of myth painted on gradually over the decades have bestowed a particular air of mystery and drama to its ornate interior. Designed in 1860 by Charles Garnier (then an unknown 35-year-old architect), the opera house was part of Baron Haussmann's massive urban renovation project.

The opera house is open to visitors during the day, and the building is a fascinating place to explore even if you're not taking in a show. Highlights include the opulent Grand Staircase, the library-museum (1st floor) and the horseshoe-shaped auditorium (2nd floor), with its extravagant gilded interior and red velvet seats. Above the massive chandelier is Chagall's gorgeous ceiling mural (1964), which depicts scenes from 14 operas.

Visits are either unguided (audioguides available; €5), or you can reserve a spot on an English-language guided tour. Staff advise showing up at least 30 minutes ahead of time. Check the website for updated schedules.

DON'T MISS

➡ Grand Staircase
➡ Library-Museum
➡ Chagall's ceiling

PRACTICALITIES

➡ Map p370, C4
➡ ✆ 08 25 05 44 05
➡ www.operadeparis.fr
➡ cnr rues Scribe & Auber, 9e
➡ adult/child unguided tour €11/7, guided tour €15.50/11
➡ ⊙ unguided tour 10am-5pm, to 1pm on matinee performance days, guided tour by reservation
➡ Ⓜ Opéra

nicipality's Museum of Fine Arts, the Musée des Beaux-Arts de la Ville de Paris. It specialises in medieval and Renaissance objets d'art, such as porcelain and clocks, tapestries, drawings, and 19th-century French painting and sculpture; and also has paintings by such artists as Rembrandt, Colbert, Cézanne, Monet, Gaugin and Delacroix.

The cafe here has lovely garden seating.

PALAIS DE LA DÉCOUVERTE   SCIENCE MUSEUM
Map p368 (www.palais-decouverte.fr; av Franklin D Roosevelt, 8e; adult/child €9/7; ⊙9.30am-6pm Tue-Sat, 10am-7pm Sun; MChamps-Élysées–Clemenceau) Attached to the Grand Palais, this children's science museum has excellent temporary exhibits (eg moving lifelike dinosaurs) as well as a hands-on, interactive permanent collection focusing on astronomy, biology, physics and the like. Some of the older exhibits have French-only explanations, but overall this is a dependable family outing.

MUSÉE MAXIM'S   MUSEUM
Map p368 (☑01 42 65 30 47; www.maxims-musee-artnouveau.com; 3 rue Royale, 8e; adult/child €20/free; ⊙English tours 2pm Wed-Sun, closed Jul & Aug; MConcorde) During the belle époque, Maxim's bistro was the most glamorous place to be in the capital. The restaurant has lost much of its cachet (though the food is actually excellent), but for art nouveau buffs, the real treasure is the upstairs museum. Opened by Maxim's owner, fashion designer Pierre Cardin, it's filled with some 550 pieces of art nouveau artworks, objets d'art and furniture detailed during one-hour guided tours.

PLACE DE LA CONCORDE   SQUARE
Map p368 (8e; MConcorde) Paris spreads around you, with views of the Eiffel Tower, the Seine and along the Champs-Élysées, when you stand in the city's largest square. Its 3300-year-old pink granite obelisk was a gift from Egypt in 1831. The square was first laid out in 1755 and originally named after King Louis XV, but its royal associations meant that it took centre stage during the Revolution – Louis XVI was the first to be guillotined here in 1793.

During the next two years, 1343 more people, including Marie-Antoinette, Danton and Robespierre, also lost their heads here. The square was given its present name after the Reign of Terror in the hope that it would become a place of peace and

HIDDEN OASIS

Descending rustic, uneven staircases (by the white-marble Alfred de Musset sculpture on av Franklin D Roosevelt, or the upper garden off cours la Reine) brings you to the tiny 0.7-hectare **Jardin de la Nouvelle France** (Map p368; cnr av Franklin D Roosevelt & cours la Reine, 8e; ⊙24hr; MFranklin D Roosevelt), an unexpected wonderland of lilacs, lemon, orange, maple and weeping beech trees, with a wildlife-filled pond, waterfall, wooden footbridge and benches to soak up the serenity.

harmony. The corners of the square are marked by eight statues representing what were once the largest cities in France.

◉ Grands Boulevards

LA PINACOTHÈQUE   ART MUSEUM
Map p370 (www.pinacotheque.com; 28 place de la Madeleine, 8e; adult/child from €13/free; ⊙10.30am-6.30pm Sat-Tue & Thu, to 8.30pm Wed & Fri; MMadeleine) The top private museum in Paris, La Pinacothèque organises three to four major exhibits per year. Its nonlinear approach to art history, with exhibits that range from Mayan masks to retrospectives covering the work of artists such as Edvard Munch, has shaken up the otherwise rigid Paris art world and won over residents used to more formal presentations.

Although the focus is primarily on temporary exhibits, make sure to visit the permanent collection as well. Displayed thematically, it presents artwork rarely seen side by side in most other museums.

NOUVEAU MUSÉE DU PARFUM   MUSEUM
Map p370 (☑01 40 06 10 09; www.nouveau museefragonard.com; 3-5 square de l'Opéra Louis Jouvet, 9e; ⊙9am-5pm Mon-Sat; MOpéra or RER Auber) FREE If the art of perfume-making entices, stop by Fragonard's Perfume Museum. The most recent addition to a trio of Paris locations, it has 30-minute guided tours (in multiple languages) that walk visitors through the history of perfume making, the different layers of perfume composition and the ingenious processes of distilling a flower's fragrance. Tours finish

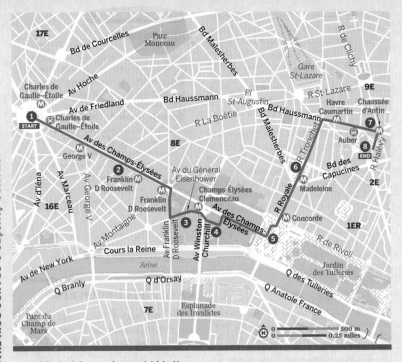

Neighbourhood Walk
Arc de Triomphe to Palais Garnier

START ARC DE TRIOMPHE
END PALAIS GARNIER
LENGTH 3.5KM; TWO HOURS

Paris is at its most glamorous along this walk, which takes you from the Arc de Triomphe along the famed av des Champs-Élysées to the opulent Palais Garnier opera house.

The city's sense of grandeur peaks beneath the mighty **1 Arc de Triomphe** (p94). Just don't try to cross the traffic-choked Étoile (star) roundabout above ground – use the pedestrian tunnels.

A dozen avenues radiate from the Étoile, including the incomparable **2 av des Champs-Élysées** (p96). Take your time strolling this broad, tree-shaded avenue past car showrooms and luxury shops.

Parkland unfolds at the Champs-Élysées Marcel Dassault roundabout; turn right on av Franklin D Roosevelt then left on av du Général Eisenhower: on your right is the gorgeous, glass-roofed **3 Grand Palais** (p96), built for the 1900 Exposition Universelle (World Fair).

Heading across av Winston Churchill, you'll arrive at the smaller but equally striking art nouveau **4 Petit Palais** (p96), also built for the 1900 World's Fair. Today it houses the city's fine-arts museum.

Continue east to **5 place de la Concorde** (p97), the vast square between the Champs-Élysées and the Jardin des Tuileries, with 360-degree views taking in the Eiffel Tower and Seine. In the centre, the pink granite obelisk stands on the site of a French Revolution guillotine.

The Greek-temple-style **6 Église de la Madeleine** (p99) dominates place de la Madeleine. The place is home to some of the city's finest gourmet shops, as well as the colourful Marché aux Fleurs Madeleine flower market, trading since 1832.

On the left of bd Haussmann you'll see the *grands magasins* (department stores) Le Printemps then **7 Galeries Lafayette** (p104) – be sure to head up to the rooftop for a fabulous, free panorama over Paris.

Turn right on rue Halévy to reach the entrance to Paris' resplendent **8 Palais Garnier** (p96) opera house.

in the shop, where you can test your nose on a few different scents.

Two other wings can be found at **rue Scribe** (Map p370; 9 rue Scribe, 9e; ☺9am-6pm Mon-Sat, to 5pm Sun; MOpéra or RER Auber) **FREE**, an old townhouse with a collection of copper distillery vats and antique flacons, and the **Théâtre-Musée des Capucines** (Map p370; 39 blvd des Capucines, 2e; ☺9am-6pm Mon-Sat; MOpéra or RER Auber) **FREE**, which concentrates on the bottling and packaging side of perfume production.

ÉGLISE DE LA MADELEINE CHURCH

Map p370 (Church of St Mary Magdalene; www.eglise-lamadeleine.com; place de la Madeleine, 8e; ☺9.30am-7pm; MMadeleine) Place de la Madeleine is named after the 19th-century neoclassical church at its centre, the Église de la Madeleine. Constructed in the style of a massive Greek temple, 'La Madeleine' was consecrated in 1842 after almost a century of design changes and construction delays.

The church is a popular venue for classical-music concerts (some free); check the posters outside or the website for dates.

On the south side, the monumental staircase affords one of the city's most quintessential Parisian panoramas. From here, you can see down rue Royale to place de la Concorde and its obelisk and across the Seine to the Assemblée Nationale. The Invalides' gold dome appears in the background.

MUSÉE NATIONAL
GUSTAVE MOREAU ART MUSEUM

Map p370 (www.musee-moreau.fr; 14 rue de la Rochefoucauld, 9e; adult/child €6/free; ☺10am-12.45pm & 2-5.15pm Mon, Wed & Thu, 10am-5.15pm Fri-Sun; MTrinité) Symbolist painter Gustave Moreau's former studio is crammed with 4800 of his paintings, drawings and sketches – although symbolism received more attention as a literary movement in France (Baudelaire, Verlaine, Rimbaud). A particular highlight is *La Licorne* (The Unicorn), inspired by *La Dame à la Licorne* (The Lady with the Unicorn) cycle of tapestries in the Musée National du Moyen Âge.

Present a Palais Garnier or Musée d'Orsay ticket for reduced admission.

MUSÉE GRÉVIN MUSEUM

Map p370 (www.grevin.com; 10 bd Montmartre, 9e; adult/child €24.50/17.50; ☺9.30am-7pm, shorter hours winter; MGrands Boulevards) This large (and expensive) waxworks inside the passage Jouffroy has some 300 wax figures.

They largely look more like caricatures than characters but, still, where else do you get to see Marilyn Monroe, Charles de Gaulle and Spiderman face to face, or the original death masks of some of the French Revolution leaders?

✗ EATING

The Champs-Élysées area is known for its big-name chefs (Alain Ducasse, Pierre Gagnaire) and culinary icons (Taillevent), but there are a few under-the-radar restaurants too, where Parisians who live and work in the area dine on a regular basis. Rue de Ponthieu, running parallel to the Champs-Élysées, is a good spot to hunt for casual eateries, bakeries and cafes. Head to the Grands Boulevards for a more diverse dining selection – everything from hole-in-the-wall wine bars to organic cafes.

✗ Champs-Élysées

★LADURÉE PATISSERIE €

Map p368 (www.laduree.com; 75 av des Champs-Élysées, 8e; pastries from €1.50; ☺7.30am-11.30pm Mon-Fri, 8.30am-12.30am Sat, 8.30am-11.30pm Sun; MGeorge V) One of the oldest patisseries in Paris, Ladurée has been around since 1862 and was the original creator of the lighter-than-air macaron. Its tearoom is the classiest spot to indulge on the Champs. Alternatively, pick up some pastries to go – from croissants to its trademark macarons, it's all quite heavenly.

FRAMBOISE CRÊPERIE €

Map p368 (☎01 74 64 02 79; www.creperiefram boise.fr; 7 Rue de Ponthieu, 8e; 2-course lunch €13.50, crêpes from €8.50; ☺11.45am-2.30pm daily, 7-10pm Mon-Fri; MFranklin D Roosevelt) Tucked in among a string of Asian takeaways is this delightful, contemporary crêperie. With an emphasis on quality (eg organic buckwheat flour), this is a top pick for an inexpensive meal off the Champs-Élysées.

LE HIDE FRENCH €€

Map p368 (☎01 45 74 15 81; www.lehide.fr; 10 rue du Général Lanrezac, 17e; 2-/3-course menus €27/35; ☺6-10.30pm Mon-Sat; MCharles de Gaulle–Étoile) A perpetual favourite, Le Hide is a tiny neighbourhood bistro serving scrumptious traditional French fare: snails, baked shoulder of lamb with pumpkin purée or monkfish in lemon butter. Unsurprisingly, this place fills up faster than you can scamper down the steps of the nearby Arc de Triomphe. Reserve well in advance.

MINI PALAIS   MODERN FRENCH €€

Map p368 (☎01 42 56 42 42; www.minipalais. com; av Winston Churchill, 8e; lunch menu €29, mains €17-39; ⊙10am-2am, kitchen to midnight; MChamps-Élysées–Clemenceau, Invalides) Set inside the fabulous Grand Palais, the Mini Palais resembles an artist's studio on a colossal scale, with unvarnished hardwood floors, industrial lights suspended from ceiling beams and a handful of plaster casts on display. Its sizzling success means that the crowd is anything but bohemian; dress to impress for a taste of the lauded modern cuisine.

LE BOUDOIR   FRENCH €€

Map p368 (☎01 43 59 25 29; www.boudoirparis. fr; 25 rue du Colisée, 8e; 2-/3-course lunch menus €32/35, mains €26-33; ⊙12.30-3.30pm Mon-Fri, 7.30-11.30pm Mon-Sat; MSt-Philippe du Roule, Franklin D Roosevelt) Spread across two floors, the quirky salons – Marie-Antoinette, Palme d'Or, le Fumoir – are individual works of art with a style befitting their names. Expect classy bistro fare (quail stuffed with dried fruit and foie gras, chateaubriand steak with chestnut purée) prepared by chef Arnaud Nicolas, a recipient of France's top culinary honour, Meilleur Ouvrier de France.

LASSERRE   GASTRONOMY €€€

Map p368 (☎01 43 59 53 43; www.restaurant-lasserre.com; 17 av Franklin Roosevelt, 8e; lunch menu €90, tasting menu €195, mains €85-120; ⊙noon-2pm Thu & Fri, 7-10pm Tue-Sat; MFranklin D Roosevelt) Since 1942, this exceedingly elegant restaurant in the Triangle d'Or has hosted style icons like Audrey Hepburn and is still a superlative choice for a Michelin-starred meal to remember. A bellhop-attended lift (elevator), white-and-gold chandeliered decor, extraordinary retractable roof and flawless service set the stage for inspired creations from head chef Adrien Trouilloud and pastry chef Guillaume Bousquet. Dress code required.

PHILIPPE &
JEAN-PIERRE   TRADITIONAL FRENCH €€€

Map p368 (☎01 47 23 57 80; www.philippeetjean pierre.fr; 7 rue du Boccador, 8e; 4-/5-course menu €44/54, mains €26-43; ⊙noon-2.15pm Mon-Fri, 7.15-10.45pm Mon-Sat; MAlma Marceau) Philippe graciously oversees the elegant, white-tableclothed dining room, while co-owner Jean-Pierre helms the kitchen. Seasonal menus incorporate dishes like cauliflower cream soup with mushrooms and truffles, sautéed scallops with leek and Granny Smith sauce, and melt-in-the-middle *moelleux au chocolat* cake. Given the service, quality and gilt-edged Triangle d'Or location, prices are almost a bargain.

MAKOTO AOKI   TRADITIONAL FRENCH €€€

Map p368 (☎01 43 59 29 24; 19 rue Jean Mermoz, 8e; 2-/3-course lunch menu €24/38, mains €34-38; ⊙noon-2pm Mon-Fri, 7.30-9.30pm Tue-Sat; MFranklin D Roosevelt) In an *arrondissement* known for grandiose interiors and superstar chefs who are often elsewhere, this intimate neighbourhood restaurant is a real find. The Japanese chef is a French-trained *haute cuisine* perfectionist; lunch might include an extravagant bacon-morel brioche; dinner a divine risotto with John Dory or truffles.

✗ Grands Boulevards

HELMUT NEWCAKE   BOULANGERIE €

Map p370 (☎09 81 31 28 31; www.helmutnew cake.com; 28 rue Vignon, 9e; lunch menus €9.30-13.50; ⊙11.30am-7pm Mon-Sat; MMadeleine) Combining the French genius for pastries with a 100% gluten-free kitchen, Helmut Newcake is one of those Parisian addresses that some will simply have to hang on to. Eclairs, fondants, cheesecake and tarts are some of the dessert options, while you can count on lunch (salads, quiches, soups, pizzas) to be scrumptious and market driven. Takeaway only.

LE VALENTIN   CAFE €

Map p370 (☎01 47 70 88 50; http://restaurant paris9.fr; 30-32 passage Jouffroy, 9e; dishes €8-14; ⊙8.30am-7.30pm Mon-Sat, 10am-7pm Sun; MGrands Boulevards) Inside beautiful covered arcade passage Jouffroy, this enchanting, two-storeyed *salon de thé* (tea house) slash patisserie slash c*hocolaterie* is an equally lovely spot for breakfast, light lunches like quiches, salads, *feuilletés* (savoury-filled puff pastries) and brochettes (skewers), and dozens of varieties of tea, accompanied by exquisite *tartelettes* and delectable cakes.

CHEZ PLUME   ROTISSERIE €

Map p370 (www.chezplume.fr; 6 rue des Martyrs, 9e; dishes €3.50-8.90; ⏲10.15am-2.45pm & 5-9pm Sun-Fri, 9.30am-9pm Sat; MNotre Dame de Lorette) This rotisserie specialises in free-range chicken from southwest France, prepared in a variety of fashions: simply roasted, as a crumble, or even in a quiche or sandwich. It's wonderfully casual: add a side or two (potatoes, polenta, seasonal veggies) and pull up a counter seat.

SUPERNATURE CANTINE   ORGANIC €

Map p370 (📞01 47 70 21 03; www.super-nature. fr; 12 rue de Trévise, 9e; mains €15.50; ⏲noon-2.30pm Mon-Fri, 11.30am-3.30pm Sun; MCadet, Grands Boulevards) 🌿 Clever veggie creations at this funky organic cafe and **restaurant** (Map p370; 📞01 42 46 58 04; 15 rue de Trévise, 9e; mains €17; ⏲noon-2.30pm & 7.30-10pm Mon-Sat) include curried split-pea soup, and cantaloupe, pumpkin seed and feta salad but, being France, it's not all legumes – you can still order a healthy cheeseburger with sprouts.

A takeaway **branch** (Map p370; 8 rue de Trévise, 9e) two doors down serves salads and thick slices of sweet potato and gorgonzola quiche.

LE ZINC DES CAVISTES   CAFE €

Map p370 (📞01 47 70 88 64; 5 rue du Faubourg Montmartre, 9e; lunch menu €16.50, mains €14-17; ⏲kitchen noon-11pm; MGrands Boulevards) Local secret Le Zinc des Cavistes is as good for a full-blown meal (duck confit with mash, chicken fricassee with crushed potatoes) as it is for sampling new vintages.

★**RICHER**   NEOBISTRO €€

Map p370 (www.lericher.com; 2 rue Richer, 9e; mains €19-20; ⏲8am-midnight; MPoissonnière, Bonne Nouvelle) Run by the same team as across-the-street neighbour L'Office (p102), Richer's pared-back, exposed-brick decor is a smart setting for genius creations like trout tartare with cauliflower and tomato and citrus mousse, and quince and lime cheesecake for dessert. It doesn't take reservations, but it serves up snacks, Chinese tea and has a full bar outside meal times. Fantastic value.

MAMOU   NEOBISTRO €€

Map p370 (📞01 44 63 09 25; www.restaurant-mamou.fr; 42 rue Taitbout, 9e; 2-course lunch €19, mains €20-26; ⏲noon-2.30pm Mon-Fri, 7.30-10.30pm Wed-Sat; MChaussée d'Antin)

Fans of *haute cuisine* sans *haute* attitude should seek out this casual bistro by the Palais Garnier. Romain Lalu, who previously worked at the Parisian icon Lasserre (p100), runs the kitchen, and diners can expect all the playful flavour combos of a chef free to follow his whims. Excellent natural wine selection. Reserve ahead.

LE BON GEORGES   BISTRO €€

Map p370 (📞01 48 78 40 30; http://lebongeorges. com; 45 rue Saint-Georges, 9e; 2-course lunch menu €19, mains €24-29; ⏲noon-2.30pm Mon-Fri, 7.30-10.30pm Tue-Fri; MSt-Georges) For a classic French meal, look no further. Le Bon Georges thrives on nostalgia, focusing on personable service (the proprietor works the room himself) and a hearty bistro menu consisting of standards like cheesy onion soup, shoulder of lamb and a delicious steak tartare. Beef from the Polmard butchers (who raise their own cattle) and seasonal produce are guaranteed.

STEAK POINT   STEAK €€

Map p370 (Lafayette Gourmet, bd Haussmann, 9e; mains €14-26; ⏲noon-7.30pm Mon-Sat; MHavre Caumartin or RER Auber) Sizzling steaks and burgers from a branch of Hugo Desnoyer's butcher shop (p89) in the basement of Lafayette Gourmet. Unlimited chips, limited seating.

CAILLEBOTTE   MODERN FRENCH €€

Map p370 (📞01 53 20 88 70; 8 rue Hippolyte Lebas, 9e; 2-/3-course lunch menu €14/19, 3-/5-course dinner menus €36/49; ⏲noon-2.30pm & 7.30-10.30pm Mon-Fri; MNotre Dame de Lorette) Although named for impressionist painter Gustave Caillebotte, the clattering interior – slate tiles, blond wood and tightly packed marble-topped tables – means this isn't the place for a romantic meal. But it is the place for amazing flavour combinations like scallops with creamy fennel and coffee purée and sea urchin foam, by the same team as Le Pantruche (p146).

FLOQUIFIL   TRADITIONAL FRENCH €€

Map p370 (📞01 42 46 11 19; www.floquifil.fr; 17 rue de Montyon, 9e; mains €14-20; ⏲11am-midnight Mon-Fri, from 6pm Sat; MGrands Boulevards) If you were to envision the ultimate backstreet Parisian wine bar, it would probably look a lot like Floquifil: table-strewn terrace, dark timber furniture, aquamarine-painted walls and bottles galore. But while the by-the-glass wines are superb, you're missing out if you don't dine here (on rosemary-roasted lamb with ratatouille or at the very least a charcuterie platter).

AUTOUR D'UN VERRE
BISTRO €€

Map p370 (01 48 24 43 74; 21 rue de Trévise, 9e; lunch/dinner menus €16/25; ⊗noon-2.30pm Tue-Fri, 7.30-10.30pm Tue-Sun; Ⓜ Cadet, Grands Boulevards) You'd be forgiven for thinking that Autour d'un Verre is one of those pop-up places: the interior doesn't appear to have been renovated since the 1950s. But that's all part of its undercover appeal – and after a few glasses of Clos du Tue-Boeuf, who cares about decoration anyway? The selection of natural wines is superb (as is the food).

L'OFFICE
MODERN FRENCH €€

Map p370 (01 47 70 67 31; 3 rue Richer, 9e; 2-/3-course lunch menus €22/28, dinner menus €27/34; ⊗noon-2.30pm & 7.30-10.30pm Mon-Fri; Ⓜ Poissonière, Bonne Nouvelle) Don't judge this one by the simple chalkboard descriptions ('beef/polenta'), which belie the rich and complex flavours emerging from the kitchen. The market-inspired menu is mercifully short – as in there are only two choices for lunch – but outstanding. Alternatively, cross the street to its new, sleek sibling, Richer (p101).

DRINKING & NIGHTLIFE

The Champs-Élysées is home to a mix of exclusive nightspots, tourist haunts and a handful of large dance clubs that party all night. As a rule, you'll want to look as chic as possible to get in the door.

🍷 Champs-Élysées

ZIG ZAG CLUB
CLUB

Map p368 (www.zigzagclub.fr; 32 rue Marbeuf, 8e; ⊗11.30pm-7am Fri & Sat; Ⓜ Franklin D Roosevelt) Some of the hippest electro beats in western Paris, with star DJs, a great sound and light system, and a spacious dance floor. It can be pricey, but it still fills up quickly, so don't start the party too late.

BLAINE
COCKTAIL BAR

Map p368 (65 rue Pierre Charron, 8e; ⊗8pm-5am Tue-Sat; Ⓜ Franklin D Roosevelt) Hidden

in plain sight is this underground speakeasy: enter through an unmarked black door, relay the password (hint: research on social media) and enter into a recreated Prohibition-era bar. Good cocktails (from €13) and occasional live jazz and DJ sets.

WINE BY ONE
WINE BAR

Map p368 (01 45 63 18 98; www.winebyone.com; 27 rue de Marignan, 8e; ⊗noon-11pm Mon-Sat; Ⓜ Franklin D Roosevelt) Serve-yourself-wine off the Champs-Élysées? While it may not be quite the experience you had in mind when planning your tour of French vineyards, there's no doubt this is a fun, casual way to sample a variety of vintages without spending too much or feeling overly intimidated. Substantial cheese-and-charcuterie plates could easily turn a visit into a full meal.

Load up a card (€2 deposit) with the amount you'd like to spend, then browse the bottles lining the walls and serve yourself by choosing one of three tasting sizes. Prices run from roughly €1 to €10.

SHOWCASE
CLUB

Map p368 (www.showcase.fr; Port des Champs-Élysées, 8e; ⊗11.30pm-6am Thu-Sat; Ⓜ Invalides, Champs-Élysées–Clemenceau) This gigantic electro club has solved the neighbour-versus-noise problem that haunts so many Parisian nightlife spots: it's secreted beneath the Pont Alexandre III bridge alongside the Seine. Unlike other exclusive Champs backstreet clubs, the Showcase can pack 'em in (up to 1500 clubbers) and is less stringent about its door policy, though you'll still want to look like a star.

LA BAROCHE
CAFE

Map p368 (01 43 59 69 57; http://brasserie-baroche.com; 101 rue de la Boëtie, 8e; ⊗7.15am-2am; Ⓜ Franklin D Roosevelt) This dependable brick-walled cafe is a pleasant spot to rest your legs along the Champs. It serves breakfast, salads, full meals and drinks, and stays open late.

QUEEN
CLUB

Map p368 (01 53 89 08 90; www.queen.fr; 79 av des Champs-Élysées, 8e; ⊗11.30pm-6.30am; Ⓜ George V) These days this doyen of a club is as popular with a straight crowd as it is with its namesake clientele, but Monday's disco nights are still prime dancing-queen territory. While right on the Champs-Élysées, it's not quite as inaccessible as the other nearby clubs.

GOURMET FOOD SHOPS

Ultragourmet food shops garland **Place de la Madeleine** (Map p370; M Madeleine); many have in-house dining options too. Notable names include truffle dealers **La Maison de la Truffe** (Map p370; 📞 01 42 65 53 22; www.maison-de-la-truffe.com; 19 place de la Madeleine, 8e; ⊙10am-10pm Mon-Sat; M Madeleine); luxury food shop **Hédiard** (Map p370; www.hediard.fr; 21 place de la Madeleine, 8e; ⊙9am-8pm Mon-Sat; M Madeleine); mustard specialist **Boutique Maille** (Map p370; 📞 01 40 15 06 00; www.maille.com; 6 place de la Madeleine, 8e; ⊙10am-7pm Mon-Sat; M Madeleine); and Paris' most famous caterer, **Fauchon** (Map p370; 📞 01 70 39 38 00; www.fauchon.fr; 26 & 30 place de la Madeleine, 8e; ⊙10am-8.30pm Mon-Sat; M Madeleine), selling incredibly mouthwatering delicacies, from foie gras to jams, chocolates and pastries. Check out the extravagant chocolate sculptures at **Patrick Roger** (Map p370; www.patrickroger.com; 3 place de la Madeleine; ⊙10.30am-7.30pm; M Madeleine).

🍴 Grands Boulevards

PANPAN
BAR

Map p370 (📞 01 42 46 36 06; 32 rue Drouot, 9e; ⊙11am-2am Mon-Fri, 6pm-2am Sat; M Le Peletier) This unassuming locals' hang-out doesn't even bother with a sign, but it keeps things interesting with a variety of activities throughout the week. Favourites include the cocktail workshop on Mondays (where you learn to mix your own, in French, *bien sûr*) and the Thursday-night *aperitivo* (from 7pm), where you can nibble on quiche, charcuterie and the like for €1.

AU GÉNÉRAL LA FAYETTE
BRASSERIE

Map p370 (52 rue la Fayette, 9e; ⊙10am-3am Mon-Sat, to 2am Sun; M Le Peletier) With its archetypal belle époque decor (brass fittings, polished wood, large murals) and excellent wines by the glass, this old-style brasserie is an atmospheric spot for an afternoon coffee or evening drink.

☆ ENTERTAINMENT

Entertainment in the Champs-Élysées and Grands Boulevards neighbourhoods revolves around the landmark Palais Garnier, which stages opera and ballet performances. A handful of smaller music venues are located further east, where you can catch lesser-known acts passing through Paris.

PALAIS GARNIER
OPERA, BALLET

Map p370 (📞 08 92 89 90 90; www.operadeparis. fr; place de l'Opéra, 9e; M Opéra) The city's original opera house is smaller than its Bastille counterpart, but has perfect acoustics. Due to its odd shape, some seats have limited or no visibility – book carefully. Ticket prices and conditions (including last-minute discounts) are available from the **box office** (Map p370; cnr rues Scribe & Auber; ⊙11am-6.30pm Mon-Sat; M Opéra).

L'OLYMPIA
LIVE MUSIC

Map p370 (📞 08 92 68 33 68; www.olympiahall. com; 28 bd des Capucines, 9e; M Opéra) Opened by the founder of the Moulin Rouge in 1888, the Olympia has hosted all the big names over the years, from Édith Piaf to Jimi Hendrix and Jeff Buckley, though it's small enough to put on a fairly intimate show.

AU LIMONAIRE
LIVE MUSIC

Map p370 (📞 01 45 23 33 33; http://limonaire. free.fr; 18 cité Bergère, 9e; ⊙6pm-2am Tue-Sat, from 7pm Sun & Mon; M Grands Boulevards) This perfect little wine bar is one of the best places to listen to traditional *chansons* (French songs) and local singer-songwriters. Performances begin at 10pm Tuesday to Saturday and 7pm on Sunday. Entry is free; reservations are recommended if you plan on dining.

FOLIES-BERGÈRE
LIVE MUSIC

Map p370 (📞 08 92 68 16 50; www.foliesbergere. com; 32 rue Richer, 9e; M Cadet) This is the legendary club where Charlie Chaplin, WC Fields and Stan Laurel appeared on stage together one night in 1911, and where Josephine Baker – accompanied by her diamond-collared pet cheetah and wearing only stilettos and a skirt made from bananas – bewitched audience members, including Hemingway. Today shows span solo acts such as Ben Harper to musicals.

 SHOPPING

Global chains line the Champs-Élysées, but it's the luxury fashion houses in the Triangle d'Or and on rue du Faubourg St-Honoré that have made Paris famous. The area around Opéra and the Grands Boulevards is where you'll find flagship *grands magasins* (department stores).

GALERIES LAFAYETTE   DEPARTMENT STORE
Map p370 (http://haussmann.galerieslafayette. com; 40 bd Haussmann, 9e; ⊙9.30am-8pm Mon-Sat, to 9pm Thu; 🐾; MChaussée d'Antin or RER Auber) Grande dame department store Galeries Lafayette is spread across the main store (whose magnificent stained-glass dome is over a century old), **men's store** (Map p370; MChaussée d'Antin or RER Auber) and **homewares store** (Map p370; MHavre Caumartin or RER Auber), and includes a **gourmet emporium** (Map p370).

Catch modern art in the **gallery** (Map p370; www.galeriedesgaleries.com; 1st fl; ⊙11am-7pm Tue-Sat; MChaussée d'Antin or RER Auber) FREE, take in a **fashion show** (📞0142 82 30 25; ⊙3pm Fri Mar-Jun & Sep-Dec by reservation), ascend to a free, windswept rooftop panorama, or take a break at one of its 24 restaurants and cafes.

À LA MÈRE DE FAMILLE   FOOD & DRINKS
Map p370 (www.lameredefamille.com; 35 rue du Faubourg Montmartre, 9e; ⊙9.30am-8pm Mon-Sat, 10am-1pm Sun; MLe Peletier) Founded in 1761, this is the original location of Paris' oldest chocolatier. Its beautiful belle époque facade is as enchanting as the rainbow of sweets, caramels and chocolates inside.

PUBLICIS DRUGSTORE   CONCEPT STORE
Map p368 (www.publicisdrugstore.com; 133 av des Champs-Élysées, 8e; ⊙8am-2am; MCharles de Gaulle-Étoile) An institution since 1958, Publicis incorporates cinemas and late-

---

HISTORIC HAUTE COUTURE

A stroll around the legendary Triangle d'Or (bordered by avs George V, Champs-Élysées and Montaigne, 8e) or on rue du Faubourg St-Honoré constitutes the walk of fame of top French fashion. Rubbing shoulders with the world's top international designers are Paris' most influential French fashion houses:

Chanel (Map p368; www.chanel.com; 42 av Montaigne, 8e; ⊙10am-7pm Mon-Sat; MGeorge V) Box jackets and little black dresses, chic ever since their first appearance in the 1920s.

Chloé (Map p368; www.chloe.com; 44 av Montaigne, 8e; ⊙10.30am-7pm Mon-Sat; MFranklin D Roosevelt) Bold prints, bohemian layers and uneven hemlines have given street cred to this Parisian label.

Dior (Map p368; www.dior.com; 30 av Montaigne, 8e; ⊙10am-7pm Mon-Sat; MGeorge V) Post-WWII, Christian Dior's creations dictated style, re-establishing Paris as the world fashion capital.

Givenchy (Map p368; www.givenchy.com; 36 av Montaigne, 8e; ⊙10am-7pm Mon-Sat; MGeorge V) The first to present a luxurious collection of women's prêt-à-porter.

Hermès (Map p368; www.hermes.com; 24 rue du Faubourg St-Honoré, 8e; ⊙10.30am-6.30pm Mon-Sat; MConcorde) Founded in 1837 by a saddle-maker, Hermès' famous scarves are *the* fashion accessory.

Lanvin (Map p368; www.lanvin.com; 22 rue du Faubourg St-Honoré, 8e; ⊙10.30am-7pm Mon-Sat; MConcorde) One of Paris' oldest fashion houses, established in 1909.

Louis Vuitton (Map p368; www.louisvuitton.com; 101 av des Champs-Élysées, 8e; ⊙10am-8pm Mon-Sat, 11am-7pm Sun; MGeorge V) Take home a real McCoy canvas bag with the 'LV' monogram.

Saint Laurent (Map p368; www.ysl.com; 38 rue du Faubourg St-Honoré, 8e; ⊙11am-7pm Mon, 10.30am-7pm Tue-Sat; MConcorde) One of the top Parisian designers from the 1960s on, Yves Saint Laurent was the first to incorporate non-European styles into his work.

opening shops, including an *épicerie* (specialist grocer), pharmacy, beauty counter, international newsagent, a wine *cave* (cellar) and cigar bar. At street level there's a glassed-in brasserie and steakhouse; downstairs is the overrated black-and-red Étoile branch of L'Atelier de Joël Robuchon.

LANCEL   FASHION & ACCESSORIES

Map p368 (www.lancel.com; 127 av des Champs-Élysées, 8e; ⊙10am-8pm Mon-Sat, to 7pm Sun; ⓂCharles de Gaulle–Étoile) Open racks of luscious totes fill this handbag designer's gleaming premises.

PASSAGE VERDEAU   SHOPPING ARCADE

Map p370 (6 rue de la Grange Batelière, 9e; ⓂGrands Boulevards) There's lots to explore in this *passage:* vintage comicbooks, antiques, old postcards and more.

PASSAGE JOUFFROY   SHOPPING ARCADE

Map p370 (10-12 bd Montmartre, 9e; ⓂGrands Boulevards) This was the last major *passage* (1847) built in Paris. There's a wax museum, the Musée Grévin (p99) and wonderful boutiques, including bookshops, silversmiths and M&G Segas, where Toulouse-Lautrec bought his walking sticks.

LA MAISON DU MIEL   FOOD & DRINKS

Map p370 (☏01 47 42 26 70; www.maisondumiel. com; 24 rue Vignon, 9e; ⊙9.30am-7pm Mon-Sat; ⓂMadeleine) In this sticky, very sweet business since 1898, 'the Honey House' stocks more than 50 kinds of honey, with such flavours as Corsican chestnut flower, Turkish pine and Tasmanian leatherwood.

HÔTEL DROUOT   ART, ANTIQUES

Map p370 (www.drouot.com; 7-9 rue Drouot, 9e; ⊙11am-6pm Mon-Fri, to 9pm Thu; ⓂRichelieu Drouot) Selling everything from antiques and jewellery to rare books and art, Paris' most established auction house has been in business for more than a century. Viewings are from 11am to 6pm the day before and from 11am to noon the morning of the auction. Pick up the catalogue *Gazette de l'Hôtel Drouot*, published Fridays, in-house or at newsstands.

LES CAVES AUGÉ   WINE

Map p368 (www.cavesauge.com; 116 bd Haussmann, 8e; ⊙10am-7.30pm Mon-Sat; ⓂSt-Augustin) Founded in 1850, this fantastic wine shop with bottles stacked in every conceivable nook and cranny should be your first choice if you trust the taste of Marcel Proust, who was a regular customer. The shop organises tastings every other Saturday (see website), where you can meet local winemakers from different regions.

ERES   FASHION & ACCESSORIES

Map p370 (www.eresparis.com; 2 rue Tronchet, 8e; ⊙10am-7pm Mon-Sat; ⓂMadeleine) Anyone who has despaired of buying a swimsuit in the past will understand why those designed by ERES have become a must-have item. The stunning suits are cut to flatter all shapes and sizes, with bikini tops and bottoms sold separately. It also stocks magnificent lingerie.

GUERLAIN   PERFUME

Map p368 (☏spa 01 45 62 11 21; www.guerlain. com; 68 av des Champs-Élysées, 8e; ⊙10.30am-8pm Mon-Sat, noon-7pm Sun; ⓂFranklin D Roosevelt) Guerlain is Paris' most famous parfumerie, and its shop (dating from 1912) is one of the most beautiful in the city. With its shimmering mirror and marble art deco interior, it's a reminder of the former glory of the Champs-Élysées. For total indulgence, make an appointment at its decadent spa.

LE PRINTEMPS   DEPARTMENT STORE

Map p370 (www.printemps.com; 64 bd Haussmann, 9e; ⊙9.35am-8pm Mon-Wed & Fri-Sat, to 8.45pm Thu; 🛈; ⓂHavre Caumartin) Famous department store Le Printemps encompasses Le Printemps de la Mode (women's fashion), menswear at **Le Printemps de l'Homme** (Map p370; rue de Provence, 9e; ⓂHavre Caumartin) (men's fashion), both with established and up-and-coming designer wear, and Le Printemps de la Beauté et Maison (beauty and homewares), offering a staggering display of perfume, cosmetics and accessories. There's a free panoramic rooftop terrace and luxury eateries, including Ladurée.

MARCHÉ AUX FLEURS MADELEINE   MARKET

Map p370 (place de la Madeleine, 8e; ⊙8am-7.30pm Mon-Sat; ⓂMadeleine) This colourful flower market has been trading since 1832.

Louvre & Les Halles

LOUVRE | LES HALLES

Neighbourhood Top Five

1 **Musée du Louvre**
(p108) Getting lost in the
mother of all museums,
with timeless masterpieces
every which way you turn.

2 **Centre Pompidou**
(p116) Contemplating Eu-
rope's largest collection of
modern art and admiring
the view from the top of one

of the city's most whimsical
buildings.

3 **Jardin des Tuileries**
(p118) Meeting Monet's
waterlilies, picnicing in the
park and revelling in Paris
at its symmetrical best.

4 **Église St-Eustache**
(p119) Feasting on exquisite
sacred art and soulful music
in this Gothic landmark.

5 **Jardin du Palais Royal**
(p120) Browsing designer
boutiques beneath the
arcaded galleries and let-
ting the kids run free amid
Daniel Buren's zebra-striped
columns.

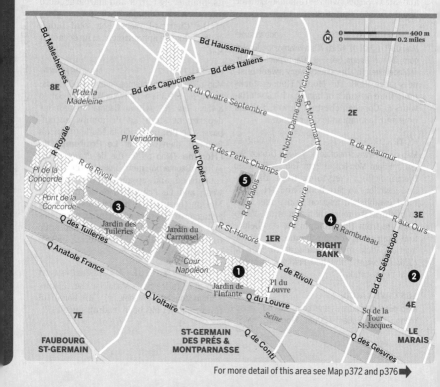

For more detail of this area see Map p372 and p376

Explore: Louvre & Les Halles

The banks of the Seine make an enchanting starting point. A wonderful exploratory loop snakes westwards along quai des Tuileries, past the sculptures and green lawns, pools and fountains of Jardin des Tuileries, to the Musée de l'Orangerie and Jeu du Paume. Continue on foot north to ritzy place Vendôme, then loop back east along shop-chic rue St-Honoré to the Palais Royal.

Set aside at least half a day for the Musée du Louvre. Avoid museum fatigue by combining the often-intimidating art gallery with a long lunch or a picnic and invigorating mooch around the designer galleries and manicured gardens of Jardin du Palais Royal. Serious art lovers will likewise want to set aside another half-day minimum for the Centre Pompidou.

Once you cross into Les Halles, the timeless sophistication of the Louvre area disappears. Instead, unwary passers-by are solicited with bright lights, jostling crowds, painted ladies and the swinging jazz clubs of rue des Lombards. Day and night the mainly pedestrian zone between the Centre Pompidou and Forum des Halles is packed with people, just as it was for the 850-odd years when Paris' main *halles* (marketplace) for foodstuffs was here.

Local Life

➞**After-work drinks** Rue Montorgueil has a good selection of cafe-bars, but it is rue St-Saveur's cocktail clubs (p128) and the hip bars on rue Montmartre that steal the late-night show.

➞**Museums** Forget Tuesday when the Louvre (p108) and Centre Pompidou (p116) are closed; go local and visit during late-night openings (less crowded) or one-off cultural events and happenings.

➞**Japantown** Busy rue St-Anne, just west of Jardin du Palais Royal, is loaded with Asian eateries, though the best choices are found in the side streets.

Getting There & Away

➞**Metro & RER** The Louvre has two metro stations: Palais Royal–Musée du Louvre (lines 1 and 7) and Louvre Rivoli (line 1). Numerous metro and RER lines converge at Paris' main hub, Châtelet–Les Halles.

➞**Bus** Major bus lines include the 27 from rue de Rivoli (for bd St-Michel and place d'Italie) and the 69 near the Louvre Rivoli metro (for Invalides and Eiffel Tower).

➞**Bicycle** Stations at 1 place Ste-Marguerite de Navarre and 2 rue de Turbigo are best placed for the Châtelet–Les Halles metro/RER hub; for the Louvre pedal to/from 165 rue St-Honoré.

➞**Boat** The hop-on, hop-off Batobus (p334) stops outside the Louvre.

Lonely Planet's Top Tip

Some of Paris' top tables are here, but you need to book in advance: plan at least a month ahead for a table at Frenchie (p127), Yam'Tcha (p127), **Spring** (p127) or Verjus (p122). Frenchie has a neighbouring wine bar where you simply rock up and wait for a stool to feast on lighter creations from the same talented chefs.

  Best Places to Eat

➞ Frenchie (p127)
➞ Yam'Tcha (p127)
➞ Verjus (p122)
➞ Spring (p127)
➞ Uma (p122)

For reviews, see p121.➞

🍷 **Best Places to Drink**

➞ Experimental Cocktail Club (p128)
➞ Lockwood (p128)
➞ Telescope (p128)
➞ Le Garde Robe (p128)
➞ L'Ivress (p129)

For reviews, see p127.➞

☆ **Best Entertainment**

➞ Le Grand Rex (p131)
➞ Comédie Française (p130)
➞ Louvre Auditorium (p130)
➞ Le Baiser Salé (p129)
➞ Théâtre du Châtelet (p130)

For reviews, see p130.➞

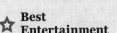

LOUVRE & LES HALLES

⊙ TOP SIGHT
THE LOUVRE

Few art galleries are as prized or daunting as the Musée du Louvre, Paris' pièce de résistance that no first-time visitor to the city can resist. This is, after all, one of the world's largest and most diverse museums. Showcasing 35,000 works of art, it would take nine months to glance at every piece, rendering advance planning essential.

Palais du Louvre

The Louvre today rambles over four floors and through three wings: the **Sully Wing** creates the four sides of the Cour Carrée (literally 'Square Courtyard') at the eastern end of the complex; the **Denon Wing** stretches 800m along the Seine to the south; and the northern **Richelieu Wing** skirts rue de Rivoli. The building started life as a fortress built by Philippe-Auguste in the 12th century – medieval remnants are still visible on the lower ground floor (Sully). In the 16th century it became a royal residence and after the Revolution, in 1793, it was turned it into a national museum. Its booty was no more than 2500 paintings and objets d'art.

Over the centuries French governments amassed the paintings, sculptures and artefacts displayed today. The 'Grand Louvre' project inaugurated by the late President Mitterrand in 1989 doubled the museum's exhibition space, and both new and renovated galleries have since opened, including the state-of-the-art **Islamic art galleries** (lower ground floor, Denon) in the stunningly restored Cour Visconti.

Mona Lisa

Easily the Louvre's most admired work (and world's most famous painting) is Leonardo da Vinci's *La Joconde* (in French; *La Gioconda* in Italian), the lady with that enigmatic smile

DON'T MISS

➡ Mesopotamian and Egyptian collections
➡ 1st floor, Denon Wing
➡ *Mona Lisa*

PRACTICALITIES

➡ Map p372, F7
➡ ☎ 01 40 20 53 17
➡ www.louvre.fr
➡ rue de Rivoli & quai des Tuileries, 1er
➡ adult/child €15/free
➡ ⊙ 9am-6pm Mon, Thu, Sat & Sun, to 9.45pm Wed & Fri
➡ Ⓜ Palais Royal–Musée du Louvre

known as *Mona Lisa* (Room 6, 1st floor, Denon). For centuries admirers speculated on everything from the possibility that the subject was mourning the death of a loved one to the possibility that she might have been in love or in bed with her portraitist.

Mona (*monna* in Italian) is a contraction of *madonna*, and Gioconda is the feminine form of the surname Giocondo. Canadian scientists used infrared technology to peer through paint layers and confirm Mona Lisa's identity as Lisa Gherardini (1479–1542?), wife of Florentine merchant Francesco de Giocondo. Scientists also discovered that her dress was covered in a transparent gauze veil typically worn in early-16th-century Italy by pregnant women or new mothers; it's surmised that the work was painted to commemorate the birth of her second son around 1503, when she was aged about 24.

Priceless Antiquities

Whatever your plans are, don't rush by the Louvre's astonishing cache of treasures from antiquity: both **Mesopotamia** (ground floor, Richelieu) and **Egypt** (ground and 1st floors, Sully) are well represented, as seen in the *Code of Hammurabi* (Room 3, ground floor, Richelieu) and the *Seated Scribe* (Room 22, 1st floor, Sully). Room 12 (ground floor, Sackler Wing) holds impressive friezes and an enormous **two-headed-bull column** from the Darius Palace in ancient Iran, while an enormous seated statue of Pharaoh Ramesses II highlights the temple room (Room 12, Sully).

Also worth a look are the mosaics and figurines from the Byzantine empire (lower ground floor, Denon), and the Greek statuary collection, culminating with the world's most famous armless duo, the **Venus de Milo** (Room 16, ground floor, Sully) and the **Winged Victory of Samothrace** (top of Daru staircase, 1st floor, Denon).

French & Italian Masterpieces

The **1st floor of the Denon Wing**, where the *Mona Lisa* is found, is easily the most popular part of the Louvre – and with good reason. Rooms 75 through 77 are hung with monumental French paintings, many iconic: look for the *Consecration of the Emperor Napoleon I* (David), *The Raft of the Medusa* (Géricault) and *Grande Odalisque* (Ingres).

Rooms 1, 3, 5 and 8 are also must-visits. Filled with classic works by **Renaissance** masters (Raphael, Titian, Uccello, Botticini), this area culminates with the crowds around the *Mona Lisa*. But you'll find plenty else to contemplate, from Botticelli's graceful frescoes (Room 1) to the superbly detailed *Wedding Feast at Cana* (Room 6). On the ground

RENOVATING THE LOUVRE

In late 2014 the Louvre embarked on a 30-year renovation plan, with the aim of modernising the museum to make it more accessible. Phase 1 increased the number of main entrances to reduce security wait times (even still, buy tickets online or use the Paris Museum Pass; lines at the underground Carrousel du Louvre entrance are often shorter). It also revamped the central Hall Napoléon to vastly improve what was previously bewildering chaos. Important changes to come include increasing the number of English-language signs and artwork texts to aid navigation.

The Louvre

A HALF-DAY TOUR

Successfully visiting the Louvre is a fine art. Its complex labyrinth of galleries and staircases spiralling three wings and four floors renders discovery a snakes-and-ladders experience. Initiate yourself with this three-hour itinerary – a playful mix of Mona Lisa obvious and up-to-the-minute unexpected.

Arriving in the newly renovated **Hall Napoléon ❶** beneath IM Pei's glass pyramid, pick up colour-coded floor plans at an information stand, then ride the escalator up to the Sully Wing and swap passport or credit card for multimedia guide (there are limited descriptions in the galleries) at the wing entrance.

The Louvre is as much about spectacular architecture as masterly art. To appreciate this zip up and down Sully's Escalier Henri II to admire **Venus de Milo ❷**, then up parallel Escalier Henri IV to the palatial displays in **Cour Khorsabad ❸**. Cross room 1 to find the escalator up to the 1st floor and the opulent **Napoleon III apartments ❹**. Next traverse 25 consecutive galleries (thank you, floor plan!) to flip conventional contemplation on its head with Cy Twombly's **The Ceiling ❺**, and the hypnotic **Winged Victory of Samothrace sculpture ❻**, which brazenly insists on being admired from all angles. End with the impossibly famous **The Raft of the Medusa ❼**, **Mona Lisa ❽** and **Virgin & Child ❾**.

TOP TIPS

» **Floor Plans** Don't even consider entering the Louvre's maze of galleries without a Plan/Information Louvre brochure, free from the information desk in the Hall Napoléon

» **Crowd dodgers** The Denon Wing is always packed; visit on late nights Wednesday or Friday or trade Denon in for the notably quieter Richelieu Wing

» **2nd floor** Not for first-timers: save its more specialist works for subsequent visits

MISSION MONA LISA

If you just want to venerate the Louvre's most famous lady, use the Porte des Lions entrance (closed Wednesday and Friday), from where it's a five-minute walk. Go up one flight of stairs and through rooms 26, 14 and 13 to the Grande Galerie and adjoining room 6.

Napoleon III Apartments
1st Floor, Richelieu
Napoleon III's gorgeous gilt apartments were built from 1854 to 1861, featuring an over-the-top decor of gold leaf, stucco and crystal chandeliers that reaches a dizzying climax in the Grand Salon and State Dining Room.

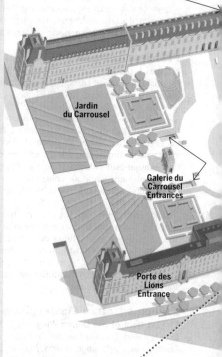

Rue de Rivoli Entrance

Jardin du Carrousel

Galerie du Carrousel Entrances

Porte des Lions Entrance

The Raft of the Medusa
Room 77, 1st Floor, Denon
Decipher the politics behind French romanticism in Théodore Géricault's *Raft of the Medusa*.

DEA/G DAGLI ORTI/GETTY IMAGES ©

Mona Lisa
Room 6, 1st Floor, Denon
No smile is as enigmatic or bewitching as hers. Da Vinci's diminutive *La Joconde* hangs opposite the largest painting in the Louvre – sumptuous, fellow Italian Renaissance artwork *The Wedding at Cana*.

Cour Khorsabad
Ground Floor, Richelieu
Time travel with a pair of winged human-headed bulls to view some of the world's oldest Mesopotamian art. **DETOUR»** Night-lit statues in Cour Puget.

The Ceiling
Room 32, 1st Floor, Sully
Admire the blue shock of Cy Twombly's 400-sq-metre contemporary ceiling fresco – the Louvre's latest, daring commission. **DETOUR»** *The Braque Ceiling*, room 33.

③ Cour Khorsabad

Cour Puget

Cour Marly

④

Cour Carrée

RICHELIEU WING

SULLY WING

Cour Napoléon ①

Pyramid Main Entrance

⑤

Inverted Pyramid

②

⑥

⑦ ⑧

Cour Visconti

⑨

Pont des Arts

DENON WING

Pont du Carrousel

Virgin & Child
Grande Galerie, 1st Floor, Denon
In the spirit of artistic devotion save the Louvre's most famous gallery for last: a feast of Virgin-and-child paintings by Raphael, Domenico Ghirlandaio, Giovanni Bellini and Francesco Botticini.

Winged Victory of Samothrace
Escalier Daru, 1st Floor, Sully
Draw breath at the aggressive dynamism of this headless, handless Hellenistic goddess. **DETOUR»** The razzle-dazzle of the Apollo Gallery's crown jewels.

Venus de Milo
Room 16, Ground Floor, Sully
No one knows who sculpted this seductively realistic goddess from Greek antiquity. Naked to the hips, she is a Hellenistic masterpiece.

112

PETER WILL/GETTY IMAGES ©

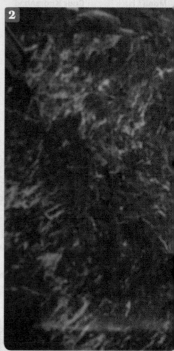

1. The Lacemaker
Jan Vermeer's painting can be found in Room 38.

2. Venus de Milo
The seductively realistic Hellenic masterpiece.

3. The Winged Victory of Samothrace
Part of the Greek statuary collection and half of the world's most famous

armless pair (the other is Venus de Milo).

4. Room 77
Filled with masterpieces from French romanticism, including Théodore Géricault's *Raft of the Medusa*.

3

LOUVRE

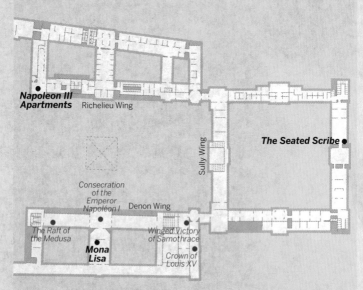

Napoleon III Apartments   Richelieu Wing

Sully Wing

The Seated Scribe ●

Consecration of the Emperor Napoléon I   Denon Wing

The Raft of the Medusa

Mona Lisa

Winged Victory of Samothrace

Crown of Louis XV

First Floor

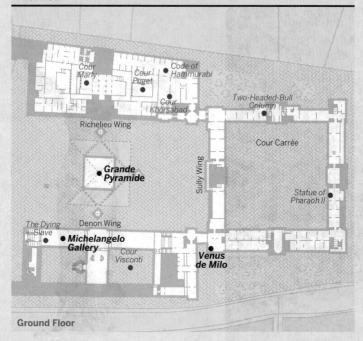

Cour Marly

Cour Puget

Code of Hammurabi

Cour Khorsabad

Two-Headed-Bull Column

Richelieu Wing

Cour Carrée

Sully Wing

Grande Pyramide

The Dying Slave

Denon Wing

Michelangelo Gallery

Cour Visconti

Statue of Pharaoh II

Venus de Milo

Ground Floor

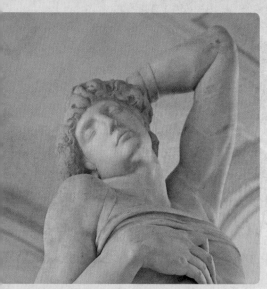

Michelangelo's *The Dying Slave*

floor of the Denon Wing, take time for the Italian sculptures, including Michelangelo's *The Dying Slave* and Canova's *Psyche and Cupid* (Room 4).

Northern European Painting

The 2nd floor of the Richelieu Wing, directly above the gilt and crystal of the **Napoleon III Apartments** (1st floor), allows for a quieter meander through the Louvre's inspirational collection of Flemish and Dutch paintings spearheaded by works by Peter Paul Rubens and Pieter Bruegel the Elder. Vermeer's *The Lacemaker* can be found in Room 38, while Room 31 is devoted chiefly to works by Rembrandt.

Trails & Tours

Self-guided thematic trails range from Louvre masterpieces and the art of eating to family-friendly topics. Download trail brochures in advance from the website. Another good option is to rent a Nintendo 3DS multimedia guide (adult/child €5/3; ID required). More formal, English-language **guided tours** (☑01 40 20 51 77; adult/child €12/5; ☺11.30am & 2pm except 1st Sun of month) depart from the Hall Napoléon. Reserve a spot up to 14 days in advance or sign up on arrival at the museum.

THE PYRAMID INSIDE & OUT

Almost as stunning as the masterpieces inside is the 21m-high glass pyramid designed by Chinese-born American architect IM Pei that bedecks the main entrance to the Louvre in a dazzling crown. Beneath Pei's Grande Pyramide is the **Hall Napoléon**, the museum's main entrance area. To revel in another Pei pyramid of equally dramatic dimensions, head towards the **Carrousel du Louvre** (Map p372; www.carrouseldulouvre.com; ☺8.30am-11pm, shops 10am-8pm; ☎), a busy shopping mall that loops underground from the Grande Pyramide to the **Arc de Triomphe du Carrousel** (Map p372) – its centrepiece is Pei's **Pyramide Inversée** (inverted glass pyramid).

French kings wore their crowns only once – at their coronation. Lined with embroidered satin and topped with openwork arches and a fleur-de-lis, Louis XV's 1722-crafted crown (Room 66, 1st floor, Denon) was originally adorned with pearls, sapphires, rubies, topazes, emeralds and diamonds.

TOP SIGHT
CENTRE POMPIDOU

The Centre Pompidou has amazed and delighted visitors ever since it opened in 1977, not just for its outstanding collection of modern art but also for its radical architectural statement. The dynamic and vibrant arts centre delights and enthrals with its irresistible cocktail of galleries and exhibitions, hands-on workshops, dance performances, bookshop, design boutique, cinemas and other entertainment venues.

Musée National d'Art Moderne

Europe's largest collection of modern art fills the bright and airy, well-lit galleries of the National Museum of Modern Art, covering two complete floors of the Pompidou. For art lovers, this is one of the jewels of Paris. On a par with the permanent collection are the two temporary exhibition halls (on the ground floor/basement and the top floor), which showcase some memorable blockbuster exhibits. Also of note is the fabulous children's gallery on the 1st floor.

The permanent collection changes every two years, but the basic layout generally stays the same. The 5th floor showcases artists active between 1905 and 1970 (give or take a decade); the 4th floor focuses on more contemporary creations, roughly from the 1990s onward.

The dynamic presentation of the 5th floor mixes up works by Picasso, Matisse, Chagall and Kandinsky with lesser-known contemporaries from as far afield as Argentina and Japan, as well as more famous cross-Atlantic names such as Arbus, Warhol, Pollock and Rothko.

DON'T MISS

- The Musée National d'Art Moderne
- Cutting-edge temporary exhibitions
- The 6th floor and its sweeping panorama of Paris

PRACTICALITIES

- Map p376, G6
- ☎01 44 78 12 33
- www.centrepompidou.fr
- place Georges Pompidou, 4e
- museum, exhibitions & panorama adult/child €14/free
- 11am-10pm Wed-Mon
- (wi-fi)
- Ⓜ Rambuteau

One floor down on the 4th, you'll find monumental paintings, installation pieces, sculpture and video take centre stage. The focus here is on contemporary art, architecture and design. The 4th floor also has an Espace des Collections Nouveaux Médias et Film, where visitors can discover 40 years of image and sound experimentation.

Architecture & Views

Former French President Georges Pompidou wanted an ultracontemporary artistic hub and he got it: competition-winning architects Renzo Piano and Richard Rogers (Studio Piano & Rogers) designed the building inside out, with utilitarian features like plumbing, pipes, air vents and electrical cables forming part of the external facade. The building was completed in 1977.

Viewed from a distance (such as from Sacré-Cœur), the Centre Pompidou's primary-coloured, boxlike form amid a sea of muted grey Parisian rooftops makes it look like a child's Meccano set abandoned on someone's elegant living-room rug. Although the Centre Pompidou is just six storeys high, the city's low-rise cityscape means stupendous views extend from its roof (reached by external escalators enclosed in tubes). Rooftop admission is included in museum and exhibition admission – or buy a panorama ticket (€3; 11am to 10pm Wednesday to Monday) just for the roof.

Atelier Brancusi

West of the Centre Pompidou main building, this reconstruction of the **studio** (Map p376; 55 rue Rambuteau, 4e; ⊙2-6pm Wed-Mon; Ⓜ Rambuteau) FREE of Romanian-born sculptor Constantin Brancusi (1876–1957) – known for works such as *The Kiss* and *Bird in Space* – contains over 100 sculptures in stone and wood. You'll also find drawings, pedestals and photographic plates from his original Paris studio.

Tours & Guides

Guided tours are only in French (the information desk in the central hall on the ground floor has details), but the gap is easily filled by the excellent multimedia guide (adult/child under 13 years €5/3), which explains selected works in the Musée National d'Art Moderne in detail on a 1½-hour trail. There is also a guide for each temporary exhibit; another covering the unique architecture of the Centre Pompidou; and one created with kids (ages eight to 12) in mind.

REFRESHMENTS

Georges' outdoor terrace on the 6th floor is a fabulous spot for a drink with a view, though it's not so great for dining. For a meal or a casual drink, head to nearby Café La Fusée (p129) or Dame Tartine (p125).

The full-monty Pompidou experience is as much about hanging out in the busy streets and squares around it, packed with souvenir shops and people, as absorbing the centre's contents. West of the Centre Pompidou, fun-packed place Georges Pompidou and its nearby pedestrian streets attract bags of buskers, musicians, jugglers and mime artists. Don't miss place Igor Stravinsky with its fanciful mechanical fountains of skeletons, hearts, treble clefs, and a big pair of ruby-red lips by Jean Tinguely and Niki de St-Phalle.

LOUVRE & LES HALLES CENTRE POMPIDOU

TOP SIGHT
JARDIN DES TUILERIES

Filled with fountains, classical sculptures and magnificent panoramas every way you turn, this quintessentially Parisian park was laid out in 1664 by André Le Nôtre, architect of the gardens at Versailles.

The 16th-century Palais des Tuileries (home to Napoléon, among others) stood at the garden's western end until 1871, when it was razed during the upheaval of the Paris Commune. All that remains of the palace today are two buildings, now both museums.

The **Musée de l'Orangerie** (Map p372; ☎01 44 77 80 07; www.musee-orangerie.fr; adult/child €9/free; ◷9am-6pm Wed-Mon), set in a 19th-century edifice built to shelter the garden's orange trees in winter, is a treat. The two oval rooms of the purpose-built top floor are the show-stealer; here you'll find eight of Monet's enormous, ethereal *Water Lilies* canvases bathed in natural light.

Downstairs is the private collection of art dealer Paul Guillaume (1891–1934), with works by all the big names of early modern art: Cézanne, Matisse, Picasso, Renoir, Modigliani, Soutine and Utrillo.

There's always a queue, so arrive early. A combination ticket covering admission to the Musée d'Orsay costs €16.

The other museum is the wonderfully airy **Jeu de Paume** (Map p372; ☎01 47 03 12 50; www.jeudepaume.org; adult/child €10/free; ◷11am-9pm Tue, to 7pm Wed-Sun), set in the palace's erstwhile royal tennis court. It stages innovative photography exhibitions.

DON'T MISS

➡ Monet's *Water Lilies*
➡ Paul Guillaume collection
➡ Picnic or stroll in the park

PRACTICALITIES

➡ Map p372, C5
➡ ◷7am-11pm Jun-Aug, shorter hours Sep-May
➡ 🚹
➡ Ⓜ Tuileries, Concorde

TOP SIGHT
ÉGLISE ST-EUSTACHE

Just north of the gardens snuggling up to the city's old marketplace, now the Forum des Halles, is one of the most beautiful churches in Paris. Majestic, architecturally magnificent and musically outstanding, St-Eustache has made spirits soar for centuries.

Tales of spiritual pomp and circumstance are plentiful. Richelieu and Molière were baptised here, Louis XIV celebrated his first Holy Communion here and Colbert was buried here. Mozart chose St-Eustache for the funeral Mass of his mother and in 1855 Berlioz's *Te Deum* premiered here – the church's acoustics are extraordinary.

Built between 1532 and 1637, the church is primarily Gothic. Artistic highlights include a work by Rubens, Raymond Mason's colourful bas-relief of market vendors (1969) and Keith Haring's bronze triptych (1990) in the side chapels. Outside is a gigantic sculpture of a head and hand entitled *L'Écoute* (Listen; 1986) by Henri de Miller. Audioguides are available for €3.

One of France's largest organs is above the church's western entrance; it has 101 stops and 8000 pipes dating from 1854. Free organ recitals at 5.30pm on Sunday are a must for music lovers, as is June's Festival des 36 Heures de St-Eustache – 36 hours of nonstop music embracing a symphony of genres.

DON'T MISS

➡ *L'Écoute*
➡ Free Sunday-afternoon organ recitals
➡ Artwork in the side chapels

PRACTICALITIES

➡ Map p376, C4
➡ www.st-eustache.org
➡ 2 impasse St-Eustache, 1er
➡ ⊙9.30am-7pm Mon-Fri, 9am-7pm Sat & Sun
➡ Ⓜ Les Halles

◉ SIGHTS

History and culture meet head on along the banks of the Seine in the 1er *arrondissement*, home to some of the most important sights for visitors to Paris, including the world-renowned Louvre and Centre Pompidou. It was in this same neighbourhood that Louis VI created *halles* (markets) in 1137 for the merchants who converged on the city centre to sell their wares, and for over 800 years they were, in the words of Émile Zola, the 'belly of Paris'. The wholesalers were moved lox, stock and cabbage out to the suburbs in 1971.

◉ Louvre

MUSÉE DU LOUVRE　　　　MUSEUM
See p108.

JARDIN DES TUILERIES　　　　PARK
See p118.

JARDIN DU PALAIS ROYAL　　GARDENS
Map p372 (2 place Colette, 1er; ⊘7am-10.15pm Apr-May, to 11pm Jun-Aug, shorter hours Sep-Mar; ♿; Ⓜ Palais Royal–Musée du Louvre) FREE The Jardin du Palais Royal is a perfect spot to sit, contemplate and picnic between boxed hedges, or shop in the trio of arcades that frame the garden so beautifully: the Galerie de Valois (east), Galerie de Montpensier (west) and Galerie Beaujolais. However, it's the southern end of the complex, polka-dotted with sculptor Daniel Buren's 260 black-and-white striped columns, that has become the garden's signature feature.

This elegant urban space is fronted by the neoclassical Palais Royal (closed to the public), constructed in 1633 by Cardinal Richelieu but mostly dating to the late 18th century. Louis XIV hung out here in the 1640s; today it is home to the Conseil d'État (State Council; Map p372).

The *Galerie de Valois* is the most up-market arcade with designer boutiques like Stella McCartney and Pierre Hardy. Across the garden, in the Galerie de Montpensier, the Revolution broke out on a warm mid-July day, just three years after the galleries opened, in the Café du Foy. The third arcade, tiny Galerie Beaujolais, is crossed by Passage du Perron, a passageway above which the writer Colette (1873–1954) lived out the last dozen years of her life.

LES ARTS DÉCORATIFS　　ART MUSEUM
Map p372 (www.lesartsdecoratifs.fr; 107 rue de Rivoli, 1er; adult/child €11/free; ⊘11am-6pm Tue-Sun, to 9pm Thu; Ⓜ Palais Royal–Musée du Louvre) A trio of privately administered collections – Applied Arts, Advertising and Fashion & Textiles – sit in the Rohan Wing of the vast Palais du Louvre. They are collectively known as the Decorative Arts; admission includes entry to all three. For an extra €2, you can scoop up a combo ticket that also includes the Musée Nissim de Camondo (p140) in the 8e.

The Arts Décoratifs (Applied Arts) section takes up the majority of the space and displays furniture, jewellery and such objets d'art as ceramics and glassware from the Middle Ages and the Renaissance through the art nouveau and art deco periods to modern times. Its collections span from Europe to East Asia.

On the other side of the building is the smaller Musée de la Publicité (Advertising Museum), which has some 100,000 posters in its collection dating as far back as the 13th century and innumerable promotional materials. Most of the space is given over to special exhibitions.

Haute couture (high fashion) creations by the likes of Chanel and Jean-Paul Gaultier can be ogled in the Musée de la Mode et du Textile (Museum of Fashion & Textiles), home to some 16,000 costumes from the 16th century to the present day. Items are only on display during regularly scheduled themed exhibitions.

◉ Les Halles

ÉGLISE ST-EUSTACHE　　　　CHURCH
See p119.

CENTRE POMPIDOU　　　　MUSEUM
See p116.

TOUR JEAN SANS PEUR　　　　TOWER
Map p376 (Tower of John the Fearless; www.tourjeansanspeur.com; 20 rue Étienne Marcel, 2e; adult/7-18yr €5/3; ⊘1.30-6pm Wed-Sun; Ⓜ Étienne Marcel) This 29m-high Gothic tower was built during the Hundred Years' War by the Duke of Bourgogne so that he could take refuge from his enemies – such as the supporters of the Duke of Orléans, whom he had assassinated. Part of a splendid mansion in the early 15th century, it is one of the few examples of feudal military architec-

ture extant in Paris. Climb 140 steps up the spiral staircase to the top turret (no views).

MUSÉE EN HERBE   ART MUSEUM

Map p376 (☑01 40 67 97 66; www.musee-en-herbe.com; 23 rue de l'Arbre-Sec, 1er; €6; ☺10am-7pm Fri-Wed, to 9pm Thu; 🚼; MLouvre Rivoli, Châtelet) One of the city's great back-street secrets, this children's museum – which moved to a new, larger locale in 2016 – is a surprise gem for art lovers of every age, not just kids. Its permanent exhibition changes throughout the year and focuses on the work of one artist or theme through a series of interactive displays.

Captions are in English as well as French, children get a *jeu de piste* (activity sheet) to guide and entertain, and additional work-shops and guided visits for kids and adults – think hands-on art workshops, afternoon tea, early-evening aperitifs and so on (€6 to €10, reserve in advance) – add to the experience.

FORUM DES HALLES   SHOPPING MALL

Map p376 (www.forumdeshalles.com; 1 rue Pierre Lescot, 1er; ☺shops 10am-8pm Mon-Sat; MChâtelet–Les Halles) Paris' main wholesale food market stood here for nearly 800 years before being replaced by this underground shopping mall in 1971. Long considered an eyesore by many Parisians, the mall's exterior was finally demolished in 2011 to make way for the new golden-hued translucent canopy, unveiled in 2016. Below, four floors of stores, cafes and a cinema extend down to the city's busiest metro hub.

Spilling out from the curvilinear, leaflike rooftop are new gardens, with *pétanque* (a variant on the game of bowls) and chess tables, a central patio and pedestrian walk-ways. The project has also opened up the shopping centre, allowing for more natural light.

TOUR ST-JACQUES   TOWER

Map p376 (☑01 83 96 15 05; 39 rue de Rivoli, 4e; adult/child €10/8; ☺10am-5pm Fri-Sun Jun-Sep; MChâtelet) Just north of place du Châtelet, the Flamboyant Gothic, 54m-high St James Tower is all that remains of the Église St-Jacques la Boucherie, built by the powerful butchers guild in 1523 as a starting point for pilgrims setting out for the shrine of St James at Santiago de Compostela in Spain. The tower has recently been restored, and guided 50-minute tours (in French) take visitors up 300 stairs to an expansive pano-rama. Children must be 10 years or older.

ART IN THE MAKING: 59 RUE DE RIVOLI

In such a classical part of Paris crammed with elegant historic architecture, **59 Rivoli** (Map p376; http://59rivoli-eng.org; 59 rue de Rivoli, 1er; ☺1pm-8pm; MLouvre-Rivoli) is quite the bohemian breath of fresh air. Take time out to watch artists at work in the 30 ateliers (studios) strung on six floors of the long-abandoned bank building, now a legalised squat where some of Paris' most creative talent works (but doesn't live).

The ground-floor gallery hosts a new exhibition every fortnight and free gigs, concerts and shows pack the place out most weekends. Look for the sculpted facade festooned with catchy drapes, banners and unconventional recycled piping above the shop fronts.

✖ EATING

The dining scene in central Paris is excellent, and there is no shortage of choices, from eat-on-the-go bakeries to casual foodie favourites to Michelin-starred cuisine. By all means reserve a table at a big-name restaurant, but also try wandering market streets like rue Montorgueil or, for something different, sample ramen or udon at one of the innumerable Japanese noodle shops along rue St-Anne.

✖ Louvre

KUNITORAYA   JAPANESE €

Map p372 (www.kunitoraya.com; 1 rue Villedo, 1er; noodles €10-20; ☺noon-5.30pm & 7-11.15pm Thu-Tue; MPyramides) Some of Paris' best udon (thick Japanese noodles) is what this buzzing brick-walled address is all about. Grab a seat at one of the communal tables and watch the young chefs strut their stuff over steaming bowls laced with battered prawns, sweet duck and curry. Arrive well before 1pm (or 8pm) or risk leaving disap-pointed. Cash only and no reservations.

ACE GOURMET BENTO   KOREAN €

Map p372 (18 rue Thérèse, 1er; lunch €9-13; ☺noon-10pm Mon-Sat; MPyramides) It's as cheap as chips, a mug of sweet lemon tea gets you change from €2, and punters can eat in or take away. In the heart of Paris' Japantown, Ace Gourmet Bento is a bijou Korean canteen-bistro with bright white walls, flowery pop-art deco and an unbeatable-value lunch deal.

UMA — FUSION €€

Map p372 (☎01 40 15 08 15; http://uma-restaurant.fr; 7 rue du 29 Juillet, 1er; 2-/3-course lunch €25/29, mains €23-25; ⏰12.30-2.30pm & 7.30-10.30pm Tue-Sat; ⓂTuileries) Embark on a culinary voyage at Uma, where chef Lucas Felzine infuses contemporary French sensibilities with Nikkei: Peruvian-Japanese fusion food. The lunch menu comes with two exquisitely prepared starters (think ceviche with daikon radish or smoked duck with lychees and *huacatay*); grab a table upstairs to spy on the open kitchen. Mezcal, pisco and vodka cocktails served until 1.30am. Reserve.

ELLSWORTH — MODERN AMERICAN €€

Map p372 (☎01 42 60 59 66; www.ellsworthparis.com; 34 rue de Richelieu, 1er; 2-/3-course lunch menu €20/26, mains €11-15; ⏰12.30-2.30pm Tue-Sat, 7-10.30pm Mon-Sat, 11.30am-3pm Sun; ⓂPyramides) Casual cousin of the sleek Verjus (p122), Ellsworth has carved out its own niche in the Parisian ecosystem with a delectable take on American faves: fried buttermilk chicken, braised pork with corn bread, kale salad and possibly the best Brussels sprouts you'll ever taste – roasted with beer, harissa and *buerre noisette* (brown butter). Full lunch menu; small plates for dinner. Reserve.

JUVENILES — BISTRO €€

Map p372 (☎01 42 97 46 49; http://juvenileswinebar.com; 47 rue de Richelieu, 1er; lunch menu €16.50, mains €18-21; ⏰noon-11pm Tue-Sat; ⓂPyramides) Likely the only place in Paris where you'll find haggis 2.0, this low-key wine bar is a hallowed retreat by the Palais Royal. Don't be deterred if sheep innards aren't your thing, as hostess Margaux and chef Romain offer a variety of other, more accessible dishes, such as butternut-squash gnocchi or *magret de canard* (duck breast) and sweet potatoes. Unusual wine list.

RACINES — FRENCH €€

Map p372 (☎01 40 13 06 41; www.racinesparis.com; 8 Passage des Panoramas, 2e; mains €24-32; ⏰noon-2.30pm & 7.30-10.30pm Mon-Fri; ⓂGrands Boulevards, Richelieu-Drouot) Snug inside a former 19th-century *marchand de vin* (wine merchant's; look up to admire the lovely old gold lettering above the door), Racines (meaning 'Roots') is an address that shouts Paris at every turn. Shelves of wine bottles curtain the windows, the old patterned floor smacks of feasting and merriment, and the menu chalked on the blackboard is straightforward.

It's first and foremost a wine bar, though, notable for its excellent choice of organic and natural *vins*.

NOGLU — MODERN FRENCH €€

Map p372 (☎01 40 26 41 24; www.noglu.fr; 16 Passage des Panoramas, 2e; mains €16-25; ⏰noon-3pm Mon-Sat, 7.30-10.30pm Tue-Sat; 🖉; ⓂRichelieu-Drouot, Grands Boulevards) Gluten-free kitchens are hard to find in France, but that's only one of the reasons that Noglu is such a jewel – this chic address builds on French tradition (bœuf bourguignon) while simultaneously drawing on newer culinary trends from across the Atlantic to create some devilishly good pastries, vegetarian plates, and superb pizzas and salads. Don't skip the chocolate-passion tart. Reserve.

The Noglu bakery is located just across the passage.

L'ARDOISE — BISTRO €€

Map p372 (☎01 42 96 28 18; www.lardoise-paris.com; 28 rue du Mont Thabor, 1er; menu €38; ⏰noon-2.30pm Mon-Sat, 6.30-10.30pm daily; ⓂConcorde, Tuileries) This is a lovely little bistro with no menu as such (*ardoise* means 'blackboard', which is all there is), but who cares? The food – fricassee of corn-fed chicken with morels, pork cheeks in ginger, hare in black pepper, prepared dexterously by chef Pierre Jay (ex-Tour d'Argent) – is superb.

★VERJUS — MODERN AMERICAN €€€

Map p372 (☎01 42 97 54 40; www.verjusparis.com; 52 rue de Richelieu, 1er; prix-fixe menu €68; ⏰7-11pm Mon-Fri; ⓂBourse, Palais Royal–Musée du Louvre) Opened by American duo Braden Perkins and Laura Adrian, Verjus was born out of a wildly successful clandestine supper club known as the Hidden Kitchen. The restaurant builds on that tradition, offering a chance to sample some excellent, creative cuisine in a casual space. The tasting menu is a series of small plates, using ingredients sourced straight from producers.

If you're just after an apéritif or a prelude to dinner, the downstairs **Verjus Bar à**

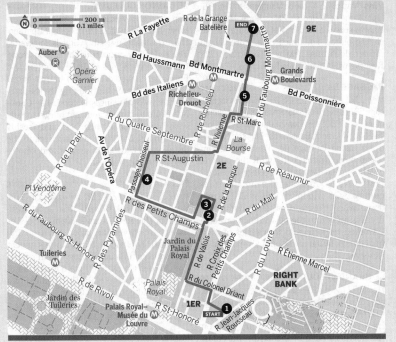

🏃 Neighbourhood Walk
Right Bank Covered Passages

START GALERIE VÉRO DODAT
END PASSAGE VERDEAU
LENGTH 3KM; TWO HOURS

The Right Bank's sumptuously decorated *passages couverts* (covered arcades) offer a walk through early-19th-century Paris. Avoid Sundays, when some are shut.

At 19 rue Jean-Jacques Rousseau, the 1823 **❶ Galerie Véro Dodat** retains its 19th-century skylights, ceiling murals, Corinthian columns, tiled floor, gas globe fittings (now electric) and bijou shopfronts. Continue to the Jardin du Palais Royal, and follow the arcades to Passage des Deux Pavillons and up the stairs to rue des Petits Champs. Duck into **❷ Galerie Vivienne** (1826), decorated with floor mosaics and bas-reliefs on the walls. Don't miss wine shop Legrand Filles & Fils, Wolff et Descourtis, selling silk scarves, and the Emilio Robba flower shop.

Exit on rue Vivienne and peek in at **❸ Galerie Colbert**, featuring a huge glass dome and rotunda. West along rue des Petits Champs is **❹ Passage Choi-** seul (1824), a 45m-long covered arcade, now filled with cheap eateries. Comedies are performed at the Théâtre des Bouffes Parisiens, near the passage's northern end. Paul Verlaine (1844–96) drank absinthe here and Céline (1894–1961) grew up in his mother's lace shop at No 62.

Passing La Bourse will take you to **❺ Passage des Panoramas** (1800), Paris' oldest covered arcade and the first to be lit by gas (1817). It was expanded in 1834 with four interconnecting passages – Feydeau, Montmartre, St-Marc and Variétés – and is full of excellent eateries and unusual shops.

Enter **❻ Passage Jouffroy** (p105), Paris' last major passage (1847). There's a wax museum, the Musée Grévin, and wonderful boutiques, including bookshops, silversmiths and M&G Segas, where Toulouse-Lautrec bought his walking sticks.

Cross the road to **❼ Passage Verdeau** (p105), the last of this stretch of covered arcades. There's lots to explore: vintage comic books, antiques, old postcards and more. The northern exit is at 31bis rue du Faubourg Montmartre.

Vins (Map p372; 47 rue de Montpensier, 1er; ⏰6-11pm Mon-Fri; ⓂBourse, Palais Royal–Musée du Louvre) serves a handful of charcuterie and cheese plates. For lunch or a more casual dinner, don't miss nearby Ellsworth (p122). Reserve well in advance for Verjus.

PASSAGE 53   MODERN FRENCH €€€

Map p372 (✆01 42 33 04 35; www.passage53. com; 53 Passage des Panoramas, 2e; lunch/dinner menu €70/150; ⏰noon-2.30pm & 8-10.30pm Tue-Sat; ⓂGrands Boulevards, Bourse) No address inside Passage des Panoramas contrasts more dramatically with the outside hustle and bustle than this elegant restaurant at No 53. An oasis of calm and tranquillity (with window blinds pulled firmly down when closed), this gastronomic address is an ode to the best French produce – worked to perfection in a series of tasting courses by Japanese chef Shinichi Sato. Reserve.

LE GRAND VÉFOUR   TRADITIONAL FRENCH €€€

Map p372 (✆01 42 96 56 27; www.grand-vefour. com; 17 rue de Beaujolais, 1er; lunch/dinner menu €115/315; ⏰noon-2.30pm & 7.30-10.30pm Mon-Fri; ⓂPyramides) This 18th-century jewel on the northern edge of the Jardin du Palais Royal has been a dining favourite of the Parisian elite since 1784; just look at who gets their names ascribed to each table – from Napoleon and Victor Hugo to Colette (who lived next door). The food is tip-top; expect a voyage of discovery in one of the most beautiful restaurants in the world.

✖ Les Halles

ENZA & FAMIGLIA   ITALIAN €

Map p376 (✆01 40 41 06 25; 89 rue St-Honoré, 1er; pasta €15-20; ⏰noon-2.30pm & 7.30-10.30pm Mon-Sat; ⓂChâtelet–Les Halles) If you're lucky, you'll be able to snag a table at this pocket-sized trattoria, but if not, that's OK too. The superb fresh pasta dishes are also available to go (for under €10), and choice picnic spots – eg the tip of the Île de la Cité – are a mere two blocks and a bridge away.

Two doors down is the sister restaurant, with more elaborate dishes (€13 to €30), while around the corner is a **pizzeria** (Map p376; ✆01 40 26 71 25; 19 rue du Roule, 1er; pizzas €13-18; ⏰noon-3pm & 6-11pm Mon-Sat; ⓂChâtelet–Les Halles), serving a scrumptious choice of wood-fired pizzas.

LE CAMION QUI FUME   FAST FOOD €

Map p372 (http://lecamionquifume.com; 168 rue Montmartre, 2e; burgers €9-11; ⏰11am-11pm Sun-Thu, to midnight Fri & Sat; ⓂGrands Boulevards) The sedentary outpost of the famous **food truck** (burger & fries €11), Le Camion Qui Fume has staked a claim on burger-happy rue Montmartre, and judging by the late-night crowds, business is good. The Camion's claim to fame is gourmet burgers made with high-grade French beef and freshly baked buns, but you'll also appreciate the draught beer, friendly service and smothered chilli cheese fries.

FILAKIA   FAST FOOD €

Map p376 (✆01 42 21 42 88; www.filakia.fr; 9 rue Mandar, 2e; souvlaki €7; ⏰11.30am-3pm & 6.30-10.30pm Mon-Fri, 11.30am-10.30pm Sat; ⓂLes Halles, Sentier) On the prowl for a quality €10 meal? Look no further than this upbeat souvlaki spot off rue Montorgueil. It's more French then Greek, but that's a minor detail – what really counts is the the excellent pita bread, hand-cut fries (€3) and selection of finger-licking locavore fillings (including a vegetarian zucchini and feta option).

MÛRE   ORGANIC €

Map p372 (www.mure-restaurant.com; 6 rue St-Marc, 2e; mains €7.10; ⏰8.30am-5pm Mon-Fri, 11am-5pm Sat; 🛜🖊; ⓂGrands Boulevards, Bourse) Get your kefir fix at Mûre, a cosy, pillow-strewn cafe offering a healthy counterpoint to the onslaught of burger stands on nearby rue Montmartre. Fresh juices, homemade vegetarian dishes for lunch and yum breakfasts are all on offer.

CRÊPE DENTELLE   CRÊPERIE €

Map p376 (✆01 40 41 04 23; 10 rue Léopold Bellan, 2e; crêpes €5-15, lunch menu €11.50; ⏰noon-3pm & 7.30-11pm Mon-Fri; 🖊; ⓂSentier) Named after a style of crêpe that's as delicate as fine lace (dentelle), this is probably not the place to go if you're starving. However, it is an excellent choice for a light and inexpensive lunch, and is certainly the best bet for crêpes near the Louvre. Arrive by 12.15pm or you may not get a seat.

FRENCHIE TO GO   FAST FOOD €

Map p376 (www.frenchietogo.com; 9 rue du Nil, 2e; sandwiches €11-14; ⏰8.30am-4.30pm Mon-Fri, 9.30am-5.30pm Sat & Sun; 🛜; ⓂSentier) Despite the drawbacks – limited seating, eye-poppingly expensive doughnuts – the

RUE D'ARGOUT & RUE MONTMARTRE
....

Rue d'Argout is a slip of a street from the 13th century, but it's one of those short, stumble-upon strips where Paris' young bright things like to be.

Favourite hang-outs here include **Blend** (Map p376; www.blendhamburger.com; 44 rue d'Argout, 2e; burger €9-11, fries €4-5; ⊙noon-11pm; Ⓜ Sentier), a gourmet burger bar the size of a pocket handkerchief that is still going strong following its 2012 opening. Easy to spot by the hungry crowd lingering outside waiting for a table, the sharp, smart, black and wood space cooks up bijou-sized burgers with homemade buns and meat from celebrity butcher Yves-Marie Le Bourdonnec.

Up the street is the colourful and always busy **Fée Nature** (Map p376; Ⓙ01 42 21 44 36; www.feenature.com; 67 rue d'Argout, 2e; plat du jour €8.50; ⊙noon-4pm Mon-Fri; ☎; Ⓜ Sentier), with its inventive, wholly 'bio et sain' (organic and healthy) menu – there are even a few gluten-free options.

Just beyond is rue Montmartre, clad with numerous places to sip coffee and cocktails. Two of the longest running are the Crazy Heart, aka **Le Cœur Fou** (Map p376; Ⓙ01 42 33 04 98; 55 rue Montmartre, 2e; ⊙5pm-2am; Ⓜ Étienne Marcel), a tiny gallery-bar with candles nestled in whitewashed walls. A few doors down, **Le Tambour** (Map p376; Ⓙ01 42 33 06 90; 41 rue Montmartre, 2e; ⊙8.30am-6am; Ⓜ Étienne Marcel, Sentier) is a vintage mecca for Parisian night owls with its long hours (food until 3.30 or 4am) and hip mix of recycled street furniture and old metro maps.

fast-food outpost of the burgeoning Frenchie (p127) empire is a wildly popular destination. Bilingual staff transform choice ingredients (eg cuts of meat from the Ginger Pig in Yorkshire) into American classics like pulled-pork and pastrami sandwiches, accompanied by cornets of fries, coleslaw and pickled veggies.

LE BIO D'ADAM ET EVE   VEGETARIAN €
Map p376 (Ⓙ09 82 36 94 57; 41 rue St Honoré, 1er; meals from €8; ⊙11.30am-8pm Mon-Sat; Ⓙ; Ⓜ Châtelet) 🥦 If you're having trouble finding dining options that go beyond the rigidly circumscribed boundaries of traditional French cuisine (gluten-free, dairy-free), this vegan-friendly pit stop will do you right, with a creative selection of organic, feel-good smoothies, soups, salads and sandwiches. A buffet of just-cooked dishes is also available for lunch and early dinner.

DAME TARTINE   CAFE €
Map p376 (Ⓙ01 42 77 32 22; 2 rue Brisemiche, 4e; tartines €9.90-13.50; ⊙9am-11.30pm; ☎; Ⓜ Hôtel de Ville) One of the few reasonable dining options near the Centre Pompidou, Dame Tartine makes the most of its lively location across from the whimsical Stravinsky Fountain. Don't expect miracles on the culinary front, but its speciality – the tartine (open-face sandwich) – will hit the spot after a morning in the museum.

A NOSTE   REGIONAL FRENCH €€
Map p372 (Ⓙ01 47 03 91 91; www.a-noste.com; 6bis rue du Quatre Septembre, 2e; tapas €9-18, taloa sandwich €6.50; ⊙noon-11pm; Ⓜ Bourse) Pull up a stool at one of A Noste's communal tables and feast on original Gascon- and Basque-style tapas: from the airy cornmeal fougasse with smoked duck and goat cheese to the deep-fried panisse (chickpea flour) and chorizo nuggets.

Not content with one way of doing things, owner Julien Duboué has also installed a 1960s red-and-white Renault along one wall – yes, an indoor food truck – where you can pick up taloa (stuffed corn tortillas flavoured with espelette peppers and rosemary) to go. The more refined restaurant upstairs ensures that a return trip is in order.

**LA TOUR DE MONTLHÉRY –
CHEZ DENISE**   TRADITIONAL FRENCH €€
Map p376 (Ⓙ01 42 36 21 82; 5 rue des Prouvaires, 1er; mains €23-28; ⊙noon-2.30pm & 7.30pm-5am Mon-Fri; Ⓜ Châtelet) The most traditional eatery near the former Les Halles marketplace, this boisterous old bistro with red-chequered tablecloths has been run by the same team for 30-some years. If you've just arrived and are ready to feast on all the French classics – snails in garlic sauce, veal liver, steak tartare, braised beef cheeks and housemade pâtés – reservations are in order. Open till dawn.

RACINES 2   MODERN FRENCH €€
Map p376 (📞01 42 60 77 34; www.racinesparis.
com; 39 rue de l'Arbre Sec, 1er; 2-/3-course lunch
menu €28/32, mains €24-31; ⏱noon-2.30pm
Mon-Fri, 7.30-10.30pm Mon-Sat; Ⓜ Louvre Rivoli)
R2 is a cousin of Racines (p122) in Passage
des Panoramas, but that is about the extent
of the family resemblance. No 2 is a thoroughly modern, urban bistro with a contemporary, Philippe Starck interior and an
open stainless-steel kitchen where you can
watch the hip, young, black-dressed chefs,
tattoos and all, at work.

What's cooking – just two or three choices for each course – is chalked on the board,
and the Louvre, handily so, is just around
the corner.

**LA MAUVAISE
RÉPUTATION**   MODERN FRENCH €€
Map p376 (📞01 42 36 92 44; www.lamauvaise
reputation.fr; 28 rue Léopold-Bellan, 2e;
2-/3-course lunch menu €18/22, mains €16-24;
⏱noon-2.30pm Mon-Fri, 7.30-10.30pm Tue-Sat;
📶; Ⓜ Sentier) The name alone – Bad Reputation (yep, also a Georges Brassens album)
– makes you want to poke your nose in and

RUE MONTORGUEIL

A splinter of the historic Les Halles, rue Montorgueil was once the oyster market and
the final stop for seafood merchants hailing from the coast. Immortalised by Balzac in
La Comédie humaine, this compelling strip still draws Parisians to eat and shop – it's
lined with *fromageries* (cheese shops), cafes, and street stalls selling fruit, veg and
other foodstuffs.

Aux Tonneaux des Halles (Map p376; 📞01 42 33 36 19; 28 Rue Montorgueil, 1er; mains
€17-25; ⏱noon-11pm Mon-Sat; Ⓜ Les Halles) Originally a hotel, Aux Tonneaux only became a cafe in the 1920s – a relatively recent addition compared to some of the other
addresses here. It features a fine outdoor terrace, as well as classic bistro fare such
as *steak-frites.*

Charles Chocolatier (Map p376; 15 Rue Montorgueil, 1er; ⏱10am-7.45pm Tue-Sat; Ⓜ Les
Halles) Delectable artisan chocolates made with 100% cocoa butter (no milk, butter
or cream).

Caldo Freddo (Map p376; 34 Rue Montorgueil, 1er; pizza slices €4-5.50; ⏱11am-midnight;
🧒; Ⓜ Les Halles) Pizzas by the pie and the slice (with a truffle topping!) along with
arancini (fried rice balls), antipasti and panini.

Stohrer (Map p376; www.stohrer.fr; 51 rue Montorgueil, 2e; ⏱7.30am-8.30pm; Ⓜ Étienne
Marcel, Sentier) This bakery was opened in 1730 by the Polish pastry chef of queen
consort Marie Leczinska (wife of Louis XV). Specialities include its very own *baba au
rhum* (sponge cake soaked in rum-flavoured syrup) and *puits d'amour* (puff pasty with
vanilla cream and caramel).

Au Rocher de Cancale (Map p376; 📞01 42 33 50 29; 78 rue Montorgueil, 2e; dozen oysters €19, seafood platter €30; ⏱8am-2am; Ⓜ Sentier, Les Halles) This 19th-century timber-
lined restaurant (first opened in 1804 at No 59) is the last remaining legacy of the old
oyster market. You can feast on oysters and seafood from Cancale (in Brittany) as
well as other *plats du jour.*

À La Mère de Famille (Map p376; www.lameredefamille.com; 82 rue Montorgueil, 2e;
⏱10am-8pm Mon-Sat, to 1pm Sun; Ⓜ Sentier, Les Halles) The oldest confectionery house
in Paris, with over 250 years of experience creating chocolates, bonbons and other
sweet temptations.

La Fermette (Map p376; 86 rue Montorgueil, 2e; ⏱4-8pm Mon, 8.30am-8pm Tue-Sat,
8.30am-2pm Sun; Ⓜ Sentier, Les Halles) Not the most stylish *fromagerie* in town, but it
always has great deals out the front, where you can pick up a preselected assortment
of cheese for under €10.

Nysa (Map p376; www.nysa.fr; 94 rue de Montorgueil, 2e; ⏱10.30am-2pm & 4-9pm; Ⓜ Sentier) This unpretentious wine store supports independent vineyards and has an interesting selection of bottles for under €15.

see what's happening behind that bright-orange canopy and oyster-grey facade just footsteps from rue Montorgueil. The answer is great bistro cooking and warm, engaging service in a catchy designer space with coloured spots on the wall and fresh flowers on each table.

CLAUS   BREAKFAST €€
Map p376 (📞01 42 33 55 10; www.clausparis.com; 14 rue Jean-Jacques Rousseau, 1er; breakfasts €16.50-31.50; ⏱7.30am-5pm Mon-Fri, 9.30am-5pm Sat & Sun; MÉtienne Marcel) Dubbed the '*haute-couture* breakfast specialist' in Parisian foodie circles, this inspired *épicerie du petit-dej* (breakfast grocery shop) has everything you could possibly desire for the ultimate gourmet breakfast and brunch – organic mueslis and cereals, fresh juices, jams, honey and so on.

Breakfast or brunch on-site, shop at Claus to create your own or ask for a luxury breakfast hamper to be delivered to your door. Its lunchtime salads, soups and tarts are equally tasty. There's a takeaway shop across the street.

★FRENCHIE   BISTRO €€€
Map p376 (📞01 40 39 96 19; www.frenchie-restaurant.com; 5-6 rue du Nil, 2e; prix-fixe menu €68; ⏱7-11pm Mon-Fri; MSentier) Tucked down an alley you wouldn't venture down otherwise, this bijou bistro with wooden tables and old stone walls is iconic. Frenchie is always packed and for good reason: excellent-value dishes are modern, market-driven and prepared with just the right dose of unpretentious creative flair by French chef Gregory Marchand.

The only hiccup is snagging a table: reserve well in advance; arrive at 6.30pm and pray for a cancellation (it does happen); or – failing that – share tapas-style small plates with friends across the street at **Frenchie Bar à Vins** (Map p376; dishes €9-23; ⏱7-11pm Mon-Fri). No reservations at the latter – write your name on the sheet of paper strung outside, loiter in the alley and wait for your name to be called.

YAM'TCHA   FUSION €€€
Map p376 (📞01 40 26 08 07; www.yamtcha.com; 121 rue St Honoré, 1er; prix-fixe menu lunch/dinner €65/135; ⏱noon-2.30pm Wed-Fri, 7.30-10.30pm Tue-Sat; MLouvre Rivoli) Adeline Grattard's ingeniously fused French and Cantonese flavours (fried squid with sweet-potato noodles) has earned the female chef no

shortage of critical praise. Pair dishes on the frequently changing menu with wine or tea, or indulge in the famous steamed buns (*bāozi*) over a pot of oolong at the **Boutique Yam'Tcha** (Map p376; 📞01 40 26 06 06; 4 rue Sauval, 1er; steamed buns from €3; ⏱11.30am-10pm Wed-Sat; MLouvre Rivoli). Reserve up to two months in advance.

SPRING   MODERN FRENCH €€€
Map p376 (📞01 45 96 05 72; www.springparis.fr; 6 rue Bailleul, 1er; prix-fixe menu €84; ⏱6.30-10.30pm Tue-Sat; MPalais Royal–Musée du Louvre) One of the Right Bank's talk-of-the-town addresses, with Chicago-born Daniel Rose in the open kitchen and stunning food. It has no printed menu, meaning hungry gourmets put their appetites in the hands of the chefs and allow multilingual waiting staff to reveal what's cooking as each course is served. Reserve well in advance.

PIROUETTE   NEOBISTRO €€€
Map p376 (📞01 40 26 47 81; 5 rue Mondétour, 1er; lunch menu €20, 3-/6-course dinner menu €42/62; ⏱noon-2.30pm & 7.30-10.30pm Mon-Sat; MLes Halles) In one of the best restaurants in the vicinity of the old 'belly of Paris', chef Tomy Gousset's kitchen crew works wonders at this cool loftlike space, serving tantalising creations that range from seared duck, asparagus and Buddha's hand fruit to *baba au rhum* (sponge cake soaked in rum-flavoured syrup) with chantilly and lime. Some unique ingredients and a new spin for French cuisine.

🍷🍸 DRINKING & NIGHTLIFE

The area north of Les Halles is a prime destination for night owls. Cocktails predominate, but you'll also find wine and champagne bars, studenty hangouts, open-till-dawn local dives and a smattering of fun nightclubs. Rue Montmartre, rue Montorgueil and rue St-Sauveur are the best streets to explore.

🍷 Louvre

BAR DU MOULIN   CAFE
Map p376 (10 place des Petits Pères, 2e; ⏱7am-midnight; MBourse) Looking out onto a perfect

THE CITY'S MOST FAMOUS HOT CHOCOLATE

Clink china with lunching ladies, their posturing poodles and half the students from Tokyo University at **Angelina** (Map p372; 226 rue de Rivoli, 1er; ⊗8am-7pm Mon-Fri, 9am-7pm Sat & Sun; MTuileries), a grand dame of a tearoom dating to 1903. Decadent pastries are served here, but it's the superthick, decadently sickening 'African' hot chocolate (€8.20), which comes with a pot of whipped cream and a carafe of water, that prompts the constant queue for a table.

Parisian square, this cafe is a pleasant stop for alfresco drinks or a casual meal (salads, tartines, croques). Don't miss the lovely art nouveau bakery next door.

TELESCOPE   CAFE
Map p372 (☑01 42 61 33 14; 5 rue Villedo, 1er; ⊗8.30am-5pm Mon-Fri, 9.30am-6pm Sat; MPyramides) The barista delivers at this minimalist coffee shop, which brews frothy cappuccinos and serves pastries and light lunch to boot.

LA CHAMPMESLÉ   BAR
Map p372 (4 rue Chabanais, 2e; ⊗4pm-dawn Mon-Sat; MPyramides) The grande dame of Parisian dyke bars, around since 1979, is a cosy, relaxed spot that attracts an older crowd (about 75% are lesbians, the rest mostly gay men). Cabaret nights, tarot-card reading and fortune-telling sessions, and art exhibitions.

SOCIAL CLUB   CLUB
(www.parissocialclub.com; 142 rue Montmartre, 2e; ⊗11pm-6am Thu-Sat; MBourse) These subterranean cube-themed rooms showcasing electro, hip-hop, funk and live acts are a magnet for young clubbers who take their music seriously. Thursdays showcase local DJs; Fridays are gay nights.

HARRY'S NEW YORK BAR   COCKTAIL BAR
Map p372 (☑01 42 61 71 14; 5 rue Daunou, 2e; ⊗noon-2am; MOpéra) One of the most popular American-style bars in the prewar years, Harry's once welcomed writers like F Scott Fitzgerald and Ernest Hemingway, who no doubt sampled the bar's unique cocktail and creation: the Bloody Mary. The Cuban mahogany interior dates from the mid-19th

century and was brought over from a Manhattan bar in 1911.

There's a basement piano bar called Ivories where Gershwin supposedly composed *An American in Paris* and, for the peckish, old-school hot dogs and generous club sandwiches to snack on. The occasional advertisement for Harry's that appears in print still reads 'Tell the Taxi Driver Sank Roo Doe Noo'.

Les Halles

★LOCKWOOD   CAFE
Map p376 (☑01 77 32 97 21; 73 rue d'Aboukir, 2e; ⊗8am-2am Mon-Sat, 10am-4pm Sun; MSentier) A happening address for hip coffee lovers. Savour beans from the Belleville Brûlerie during the day, brunch on weekends and well-mixed cocktails in the subterranean candle-lit *cave* (wine cellar) at night.

★EXPERIMENTAL COCKTAIL CLUB   COCKTAIL BAR
Map p376 (37 rue St-Saveur, 2e; ⊗7pm-2am; MRéaumur-Sébastopol) Called ECC by trendies, this fabulous speakeasy with a black curtain for a facade and old-beamed ceiling is effortlessly hip. Oozing spirit and soul, the cocktail bar – with retro-chic decor by American interior designer Cuoco Black and sister bars in London and New York – is a sophisticated flashback to those *années folles* (crazy years) of Prohibition New York.

Cocktails (€13 to €15) are individual and fabulous, and DJs set the space partying until dawn at weekends. It's not a large space, however, and fills to capacity quickly.

LE GARDE ROBE   WINE BAR
Map p376 (☑01 49 26 90 60; 41 rue de l'Arbre Sec, 1er; ⊗12.30-2.30pm Mon-Fri, 6.30-midnight Mon-Sat; MLouvre Rivoli) The Garde Robe is possibly the only bar in the world to serve alcohol alongside a detox menu. While you probably shouldn't come here for the full-on cleansing experience, you can definitely expect excellent, affordable natural wines, a casual atmosphere and a good selection of eats, ranging from the standard cheese and charcuterie plates to more adventurous veg-friendly options.

MA CAVE FLEURY   WINE BAR
Map p376 (☑01 40 28 03 39; https://macave fleury.wordpress.com; 177 rue St-Denis, 2e; ⊗5-9pm Mon, 11am-1pm & 5-10pm Tue-Fri, noon-

9pm Sat; **M**Réaumur Sébastopol) Morgane Fleury opened this welcoming little place in 2009 to promote organic and biodynamic wines. The emphasis is on Champagne – her family has been producing biodynamic Champagne for 20 years now – but you can also sample a decent selection of organic wines from around France, with a strong emphasis on the Loire region.

LA CORDONNERIE
BAR

Map p376 (📞01 40 28 95 35; 28 rue Greneta, 2e; ⏰8am-2am; **M**Réaumur Sébastopol) If you're counting the centimes in your pocket, La Cordonnerie is your spot for cheap drinks and a good time. The €3 pints during happy hour (5pm to 8.30pm) and free couscous on Thursdays mean crowds spilling out onto the pavement late into the night.

L'IVRESS
WINE BAR

(📞06 61 40 27 97; http://livress.fr; 5 rue Poissonnière, 2e; ⏰6pm-1am Mon-Sat; **M**Sentier) Make sure to reserve an armchair or oak barrel (for those who prefer to stand) at this cosy bar and wine shop, otherwise your chances of getting a table may be slim. Expect a choice selection of wines from independent vineyards and enough quality nibbles to keep the after-work crowd lingering long past happy hour. Book by text message.

AVEK
COCKTAIL BAR

Map p376 (21 rue St-Sauveur, 2e; ⏰6pm-2am Tue-Sat; **M**Sentier) Original cocktails for €8 and a kick-back vibe ensures a hip crowd every night of the week. Service can be slow, but the barkeeps win points for friendliness.

LE FORUM
COCKTAIL BAR

Map p376 (📞01 42 65 37 86; www.bar-le-forum. com; 29 rue du Louvre, 2e; ⏰6pm-1am Mon-Thu, to 2am Fri & Sat; **M**Sentier) More than 80 cocktails are detailed on the menu of this classy cocktail bar. They don't come cheap, but all are painstakingly made to order and worth the wait and the price.

Ô CHATEAU
WINE BAR

Map p376 (www.o-chateau.com; 68 rue Jean-Jacques Rousseau, 1er; ⏰4pm-midnight Mon-Sat; 📱; **M**Les Halles, Étienne Marcel) Wine aficionados can thank this young, fun, cosmopolitan wine bar for bringing affordable tasting to Paris. Sit at the long, trendy bar and savour your pick of 40-odd *grands vins* served by the glass (or 500-odd by the bottle!). Or sign up in advance for an intro to

French wine (€30) or a guided cellar tasting in English over lunch (€75) or dinner (€100).

CAFÉ LA FUSÉE
BAR

Map p376 (📞01 42 76 93 99; 168 rue St-Martin, 3e; ⏰8am-2am; **M**Rambuteau, Étienne Marcel) A short walk from the Pompidou, the Rocket is a lively, laid-back indie hang-out with a red-and-white striped awning strung with fairy lights outside, and paint-peeling, tobacco-coloured walls indoors. You can grab simple meals here (€8 to €13), and it's got a decent wine selection by the glass.

LE REX CLUB
CLUB

(www.rexclub.com; 5 bd Poissonnière, 2e; ⏰midnight-7am Thu-Sat; **M**Bonne Nouvelle) Attached to the art deco Grand Rex cinema, this is Paris' premier house and techno venue where some of the world's hottest DJs strut their stuff on a 70-speaker, multidiffusion sound system.

LE COCHON À L'OREILLE
CAFE €€

Map p376 (📞01 42 36 07 56; 15 rue Montmartre, 1er; 2-course lunch €17, 3-course dinner €32; ⏰10am-2am Tue-Sat; **M**Les Halles) A Parisian jewel, the heritage-listed hole-in-the-wall Le Cochon à l'Oreille retains 1890-laid tiles depicting vibrant market scenes of the old *halles*. Hours can vary.

ZEN ZOO
TEAHOUSE

Map p372 (📞01 42 96 27 28; www.zen-zoo.com; 13 rue Chabanais, 2e; ⏰11am-10pm Mon-Sat; 📱;

JAZZ DUO

Rue des Lombards is the street to swing by for live jazz.

Le Baiser Salé (Map p376; 📞01 42 33 37 71; www.lebaisersale.com; 58 rue des Lombards, 1er; ⏰daily; **M**Châtelet) Known for its Afro and Latin jazz, and jazz fusion concerts, the Salty Kiss combines big names and unknown artists. The place has a relaxed vibe, with sets usually starting at 7.30pm or 9.30pm.

Sunset & Sunside (Map p376; 📞01 40 26 46 60; www.sunset-sunside.com; 60 rue des Lombards, 1er; ⏰daily; **M**Châtelet) Two venues in one at this trendy, well-respected club: electric jazz, fusion and the odd salsa session downstairs; acoustics and concerts upstairs.

Quatre Septembre) Taiwan's fabulously addictive bubble tea *(zhēnzhū nǎichá)* has finally made it to Paris. If you're not familiar with the drink, consisting of sweet milk tea and chewy tapioca balls sucked up through an unusually large straw, by all means pencil Zen Zoo into your Right Bank itinerary, either at tea time (dim sum served) or for a scrumptious Chinese lunch (from €11.50).

⭐ ENTERTAINMENT

LOUVRE AUDITORIUM — LIVE MUSIC

Map p372 (📞01 40 20 55 00; www.louvre.fr/musiques; Hall Napoléon, Louvre, 1er; Ⓜ Palais Royal–Musée du Louvre) Excellent classical-music concerts are staged several times a week at the Louvre Auditorium (off the main entrance hall). Don't miss the Thursday lunchtime concerts, which cost a mere €6 to €15. The season runs from September to April or May, depending on the concert series.

THÉÂTRE DE LA VILLE — DANCE

Map p376 (📞01 42 74 22 77; www.theatredelaville-paris.com; 2 place du Châtelet, 4e; Ⓜ Châtelet) It hosts theatre and music too, but this theatre is best known for its contemporary dance productions.

THÉÂTRE DU CHÂTELET — CLASSICAL MUSIC

Map p376 (📞01 40 28 28 40; www.chatelet-theatre.com; 1 place du Châtelet, 1er; Ⓜ Châtelet) This venue hosts concerts as well as operas, musicals, theatre, ballet and popular Sunday-morning concerts.

PARIS' FILM ARCHIVE

Cinemas showing films set in Paris are the centrepiece of the city's film archive at **Forum des Images** (Map p376; www.forumdesimages.fr; 1 Grande Galerie, Porte St-Eustache, Forum des Halles, 1er; ⏱1-9pm Tue-Fri, from 2pm Sat & Sun; Ⓜ Les Halles). Created in 1988 to establish 'an audiovisual memory bank of Paris', and renovated in dramatic shades of pink, grey and black, the five-screen centre has a library and research centre with newsreels, documentaries and advertising.

Check its program online for thematic series and frequent festivals and events.

COMÉDIE FRANÇAISE — THEATRE

Map p372 (www.comedie-francaise.fr; place Colette, 1er; Ⓜ Palais Royal–Musée du Louvre) Founded in 1680 under Louis XIV, this state-run theatre bases its repertoire around the works of classic French playwrights. The theatre has its roots in an earlier company directed by Molière at the Palais Royal.

The French playwright and actor was seized by a convulsion on stage during the fourth performance of the *Imaginary Invalid* in 1673 and died later at his home on nearby rue de Richelieu.

OPÉRA COMIQUE — OPERA

Map p372 (www.opera-comique.com; 1 place Boïeldieu, 2e; Ⓜ Richelieu Drouot) This century-old hall (renovated in 2016) has premiered many important French operas and continues to host classic and less-known works.

🛍 SHOPPING

The 1er and 2e *arrondissements* are mostly about fashion. Indeed the Sentier district is something of a garment heaven, while rue Étienne Marcel, place des Victoires and rue du Jour flaunt prominent labels and shoe shops. Nearby rue Montmartre and rue Tiquetonne are the streets to shop for streetwear and avant-garde designs; the easternmost part of the 1er around Palais Royal, for fancy period and conservative label fashion.

⭐ DIDIER LUDOT — FASHION & ACCESSORIES

Map p372 (📞01 42 96 06 56; www.didierludot.fr; 19-20 & 23-24 Galerie de Montpensier, 1er; ⏱10.30am-7pm Mon-Sat; Ⓜ Palais Royal–Musée du Louvre) In the rag trade since 1975, collector Didier Ludot sells the city's finest couture creations of yesteryear in his exclusive twinset of boutiques, hosts exhibitions and has published a book portraying the evolution of the little black dress.

NOSE — PERFUME

Map p376 (📞01 40 26 46 03; http://nose.fr; 20 rue Bachaumont, 2e; ⏱10.30am-7.30pm Mon-Sat; Ⓜ Sentier) Come to this concept shop for a personal perfume diagnosis, after which the knowledgeable staff (English spoken) will be able to narrow down a selection of fragrances that suit you best. You could easily spend over an hour here, so come with time to spare. Perfumes and cosmetics available for both men and women.

MORA
HOMEWARES

Map p376 (13 Rue Montmartre, 1er; ⊘9am-6.15pm Mon-Fri, 10am-1pm & 1.45-6.30pm Sat; MLes Halles) Both amateur and professional pastry chefs will want to stop by MORA to pick up all manner of specialist culinary items, from unique cake and pastry moulds to macaron mats, pasta makers, piping bags and cream chargers (in case you're considering some fresh-baked éclairs back home).

COMPTOIR DE LA GASTRONOMIE
FOOD & DRINKS

Map p376 (☑01 42 33 31 32; www.comptoir delagastronomie.com; 34 rue Montmartre, 1er; ⊘6am-8pm Mon-Sat; MLes Halles) This elegant *épicerie fine* (specialist grocer) stocks a scrumptious array of gourmet goods to take away; it adjoins a striking art nouveau dining room dating to 1894.

GALIGNANI
BOOKS

Map p372 (☑01 42 60 76 07; http://galignani. com; 224 rue de Rivoli, 1er; ⊘10am-7pm Mon-Sat; MConcorde) Proudly claiming to be the 'first English bookshop established on the continent', this ode to literature stocks French and English books and is a good spot to pick up just-published titles.

BOÎTES À MUSIQUE ANNA JOLIET
GIFTS & SOUVENIRS

Map p372 (Passage du Perron, 1er; ⊘noon-7pm Tue-Sat; MPyramides) This wonderful shop at the northern end of the Jardin du Palais Royal specialises in music boxes, new and old, from Switzerland.

LEGRAND FILLES & FILS
FOOD & DRINKS

Map p372 (www.caves-legrand.com; 1 rue de la Banque, 2e; ⊘10am-7.30pm Tue-Sat, 11am-7pm Sun; MPyramides) Tucked within Galerie Vivienne since 1880, Legrand sells fine wine and all the accoutrements: corkscrews, tasting glasses, decanters etc. It also has a fancy wine bar, *école du vin* (wine school) and *espace dégustation* with several tastings a month; check its website for details.

KILIWATCH
FASHION & ACCESSORIES

Map p376 (☑01 42 21 17 37; http://espacekili-watch.fr; 64 rue Tiquetonne, 2e; ⊘10.30am-7pm Mon, to 7.30pm Tue-Sat; MÉtienne Marcel) A Parisian institution, Kiliwatch gets jam-

---

---

packed with hip guys and gals rummaging through racks of new and used streetwear. Startling vintage range of hats and boots plus art/photography books, eyewear and the latest sneakers.

ANTOINE
FASHION & ACCESSORIES

Map p372 (10 av de l'Opéra, 1er; ⊘10.30am-1pm & 2-6.30pm Mon-Sat; MPyramides, Palais Royal–Musée du Louvre) Antoine has been the Parisian master of bespoke canes, umbrellas, fans and gloves since 1745.

E DEHILLERIN
HOMEWARES

Map p376 (www.e-dehillerin.fr; 18-20 rue Coquillière, 1er; ⊘9am-12.30pm & 2-6pm Mon, 9am-6pm Tue-Sat; MLes Halles) Founded in 1820, this extraordinary two-level store – think old-fashioned warehouse rather than shiny, chic boutique – carries an incredible selection of professional-quality *matériel de cuisine* (kitchenware). Poultry scissors, turbot poacher, professional copper cookware or Eiffel Tower–shaped cake tin – it's all here.

COLETTE
CONCEPT STORE

Map p372 (www.colette.fr; 213 rue St-Honoré, 1er; ⊘11am-7pm Mon-Sat; MTuileries) Uber-hip is an understatement. Ogle designer fashion on the 1st floor, and streetwear, limited-edition sneakers, art books, music, gadgets and other high-tech, inventive and/or plain unusual items on the ground floor. End with a drink in the basement 'water bar' and pick up free design magazines and flyers for some of the city's hippest happenings by the door upon leaving.

Montmartre & Northern Paris

Neighbourhood Top Five

❶ Basilique du Sacré-Cœur (p134) Hiking up the steps for panoramic city views and some of the city's finest street entertainers outside, and a glittering mosaic within.

❷ Parc de la Villette (p136) Treating the kids to a day in the capital's world-class science museum and

enjoying a performance or exhibit at the city's largest cultural playground.

❸ Musée Jacquemart-André (p138) Stepping into opulent surrounds at this elegant art museum, a rare snapshot of 19th-century Parisian high society, climaxing with afternoon tea in the lavish tearoom.

❹ Basilique de St-Denis (p140) Discovering the tombs of French royalty in St-Denis.

❺ Le Mur des je t'aime (p142) Declaring 'I love you' to someone you love or learning how to say it in every language under the sun in a pretty city park in Montmartre.

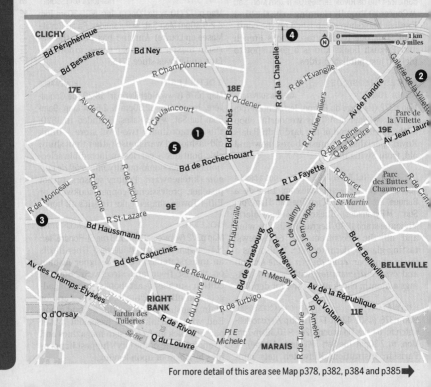

For more detail of this area see Map p378, p382, p384 and p385 ➡

Explore: Montmartre & Northern Paris

One of the wellsprings of Parisian myth, Montmartre has always stood apart. Bohemians, revolutionaries, artists, cancan girls and headless martyrs have all played a role in its story, and while it belongs to Paris today, vestiges of the original village – ivy-clad buildings, steep narrow streets – remain. Crowned by the white-domed Sacré-Cœur, dragged back to earth by red-light Pigalle, it has forever encompassed contrast and conflict.

An ideal place to base yourself, Montmartre is rich in sights, cuisine, shopping and entertainment. Most visitors spend half a day or more exploring the side streets, searching valiantly for that one perfect vista to snap a selfie looking out over the city.

After dark, night owls will enjoy drinking and dining in style in south Pigalle, or 'SoPi' as Parisian hipsters know it. This edgy but increasingly fashionable area bustles with local life in the shape of its sensational cocktail bars. For a taste of fully fledged, grown-up *bobo* (bourgeois bohemian) lifestyle, head east again to Canal St-Martin, a vibrant 'hood that today has everything from all-day brunches to late-night drinks to casual shopping and romantic waterside strolls.

Local Life

➡ **SoPi cocktails** Old girlie bars in trendy south Pigalle (SoPi) have morphed into some of the city's most exciting cocktail bars: fashionistas start their crawl with Lulu White (p147) and Glass (p143) on rue Frochot, ending at the bar at the Grand Hôtel Pigalle (p285).

➡ **Neobistros** Canal St-Martin and south Pigalle are two of the most exciting places to dine and now a pocket of the 10e around rue du Faubourg St-Martin and rue du Faubourg St-Denis has joined in the party.

➡ **Canal lounging** On spring and summer weekends, it feels like the entire neighbourhood can be found around Canal St-Martin (p148).

➡ **Little Africa** Locals love the colourful, predominantly north African *quartier* of La Goutte d'Or for its craft-beer brewery Brasserie la Goutte d'Or (p139) and artisan coffee-bean roastery Café Lomi (p150).

Getting There & Away

➡ **Metro** Lines 2 and 12 serve Montmartre; lines 5 and 7 serve northeastern Paris (Canal St-Martin and La Villette). Further west, Clichy can be accessed via line 2.

➡ **RER** RER B links Gare du Nord with central Paris.

➡ **Bicycle** There are quite a few stations along the Canal St-Martin, including place République and 8 place Jacques Bonsergent.

Lonely Planet's Top Tip

Although gritty, the neighbourhoods in the north and northeast of Paris are still fairly safe as far as big cities go, providing you behave sensibly. If there are places you really need to stay on your guard, it's at the foot of the hill that leads up to Sacré-Cœur and also on Montmartre's place du Tertre. It's not unusual for pickpockets and con artists to work the crowds here.

Best Places to Eat

➡ 52 Faubourg St-Denis (p140)
➡ La Bulle (p145)
➡ Matière à. (p145)
➡ Grand Amour Hôtel (p144)
➡ Le Verre Volé (p144)

For reviews, see p140.➡

Best Places to Drink

➡ Le Très Particulier (p149)
➡ CopperBay (p149)
➡ Gravity Bar (p147)
➡ Lulu White (p147)
➡ Hardware Société (p149)

For reviews, see p147.➡

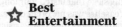

Best Entertainment

➡ Philharmonie de Paris (p151)
➡ Le Divan du Monde (p151)
➡ Point Éphémère (p152)
➡ La Cigale (p151)
➡ Moulin Rouge (p151)

For reviews, see p151.➡

TOP SIGHT
BASILIQUE DU SACRÉ-CŒUR

Although some may poke fun at Sacré-Cœur's unsubtle design, the city panorama from its parvis (in front of the church) is a perfect Paris postcard. More than just a basilica, Sacré-Cœur is a veritable experience, from the buskers and street artists performing on the steps to the groups of friends picnicking on the hillside park. Touristy, yes, but gold.

History

It may appear to be a place of peacefulness and worship today, but in truth Sacré-Cœur's foundations were laid amid bloodshed and controversy. Its construction began in 1875, in the wake of France's humiliating defeat by Prussia and the subsequent chaos of the Paris Commune. Following Napoléon III's surrender to von Bismarck in September 1870, angry Parisians, with the help of the National Guard, continued to hold out against Prussian forces – a harrowing siege that lasted four long winter months. By the time a ceasefire was negotiated in early 1871, the split between the radical working-class Parisians (supported by the National Guard) and the conservative national government (supported by the French army) had become insurmountable.

Over the next several months, the rebels, known as Communards, managed to overthrow the reactionary government and take over the city. It was a particularly chaotic and bloody moment in Parisian history, with mass executions on both sides and a wave of rampant destruction that spread throughout Paris. Montmartre was a key Communard stronghold. It was on the future site of Sacré-Cœur that the rebels won their first victory and it was consequently the first neighbourhood to be targeted when the French army

DON'T MISS

➡ The views from the parvis
➡ The apse mosaic *Christ in Majesty*
➡ The dome

PRACTICALITIES

➡ Map p378, F3
➡ ☎ 01 53 41 89 00
➡ www.sacre-coeur-montmartre.com
➡ place du Parvis du Sacré-Cœur
➡ dome adult/child €6/4, cash only
➡ ⏰ 6am-10.30pm, dome 8.30am-8pm May-Sep, to 5pm Oct-Apr
➡ Ⓜ Anvers

returned in full force in May 1871. Ultimately, many Communards were buried alive in the gypsum mines beneath the Butte.

Basilica

Within the historical context, the construction of an enormous basilica to expiate the city's sins seemed like a gesture of peace and forgiveness – indeed, the seven million French francs needed to construct the church's foundations came solely from the contributions of local Catholics. However, the Montmartre location was certainly no coincidence: the conservative old guard desperately wanted to assert its power in what was then a hotbed of revolution. The battle between the two camps – Catholic versus secular, royalist versus republican – raged on and in 1882 the construction of the basilica was even voted down by the city council on the grounds that it would continue to fan the flames of civil war. It was overturned in the end by a technicality.

Six successive architects oversaw construction of the Romano-Byzantine–style basilica, and it wasn't until 1919 that Sacré-Cœur was finally consecrated, even then standing in utter contrast to the bohemian lifestyle that surrounded it. While criticism of its design and white travertine stone has continued throughout the decades (one poet called it a giant baby's bottle for angels), the interior is enlivened by the glittering apse mosaic *Christ in Majesty*, designed by Luc-Olivier Merson in 1922 and one of the largest in the world.

Dome & Crypt

Outside, some 234 spiralling steps lead you to the basilica's dome, which affords one of Paris' most spectacular panoramas; it's said you can see for 30km on a clear day. Weighing in at 19 tonnes, the bell called La Savoyarde in the tower above is the largest in France. The chapel-lined crypt, visited in conjunction with the dome (for an additional €2), is huge but not very interesting.

A PLACE OF PILGRIMAGE

In a sense, atonement here has never stopped: a prayer 'cycle' that began in 1885 before the basilica's completion still continues around the clock, with perpetual adoration of the Blessed Sacrament continually on display above the high altar. The basilica's travertine stone exudes calcite, ensuring it remains white despite weathering and pollution.

In 1944, 13 Allied bombs were dropped on Montmartre, falling just next to Sacré-Cœur. Although the stained-glass windows all shattered from the force of the explosions, miraculously no one died and the basilica sustained no other damage.

MONTMARTRE & NORTHERN PARIS BASILIQUE DU SACRÉ-CŒUR

TOP SIGHT
PARC DE LA VILLETTE

The vast green Parc de la Villette (designed by architect Bernard Tschumi) is a cultural centre, kids playground and landscaped urban space rolled into one. The French love of geometric forms defines the layout – the colossal mirror-like sphere of the Géode cinema, an undulating strip of corrugated steel stretching for hundreds of metres, the bright-red cubical pavilions known as *folies* – but the intersection of two canals, the Ourcq and the St-Denis, brings the most natural and popular element: water. Although it's a fair hike from central Paris, consider the trip here if you have children, or to attend one of the many events (world, rock and classical music concerts; art exhibits; outdoor cinema; circuses; modern dance).

Events throughout the year are staged in the wonderful old Grande Halle (pictured above), **Le Zénith** (Map p384; ☎01 55 80 09 38, 08 90 71 02 07; www.le-zenith.com; ⊘variable), the Cabaret Sauvage (p152) and Paris' stunning, cutting-edge Philharmonie de Paris (p139).

When the weather's pleasant, children (and adults) will enjoy exploring the numerous themed gardens, the best of which double as playgrounds. However, for the young ones, the star attraction is Cité des Sciences (p138) and its attached cinemas. The brilliant Cité des Enfants is probably the most popular section, with a construction site, TV studio, robots and water-based physics experiments all designed for children.

DON'T MISS

→ Evening performances

→ The themed gardens

→ Cité des Sciences

PRACTICALITIES

→ Map p384, C1

→ www.villette.com

→ 211 av Jean Jaurès, 19e

→ ⊘6am-1am

→ 🚼

→ Ⓜ Porte de la Villette, Porte de Pantin

⊙ SIGHTS

The hilltop neighbourhood of Montmartre safeguards some of Paris' most iconic sights, including the white domed Sacré-Cœur basilica and one of the city's few vineyards. The *quartier's* museums evoke its fabled artistic heritage and it is easy to get around between them on foot. West, past place de Clichy and beyond to the Parisian joggers' paradise of Parc Monceau, there are a couple of excellent lesser-known art museums at home in historic mansions. Canal St-Martin, a sight in itself with its vintage bridges and canal boats, is in the opposite direction to the east.

BASILIQUE DU SACRÉ-CŒUR   BASILICA
See p134.

PARC DE LA VILLETTE   PARK
See p136.

MUSÉE DE MONTMARTRE   MUSEUM
Map p378 (☏01 49 25 89 39; www.museede montmartre.fr; 12 rue Cortot, 18e; adult/child €9.50/5.50; ☉10am-6pm; ⓜLamarck-Caulaincourt) One of Paris' most romantic spots, this enchanting 'village' museum showcases paintings, lithographs and documents illustrating Montmartre's bohemian, artistic and hedonistic past – one room is dedicated entirely to the French cancan! The museum is in a 17th-century manor where several artists, including Renoir and Raoul Dufy, had their studios in the 19th century. You can also visit the studio of pioneering female painter Suzanne Valadon, who lived and worked here with her son Maurice Utrillo and partner André Utter between 1912 and 1926.

Allow ample time to stroll the museum gardens, named after Renoir, who painted his masterpieces *Bal du Moulin de la Galette* and *Jardin de la rue Cortot* while working in his studio here from 1875 to 1877. Find the tree strung with a swing to evoke the impressionist painter's famous work, *La Balançoire,* also painted here. Follow the path to the end of the garden for a stunning 'secret' view of the Clos Montmartre vineyards. Museum admission includes an audioguide.

CIMETIÈRE DE MONTMARTRE   CEMETERY
Map p378 (2 av Rachel, 18e; ☉8am-6pm Mon-Fri, 8.30am-6pm Sat, 9am-6pm Sun; ⓜPlace de Clichy) This 11-hectare cemetery opened in 1798. It contains the graves of writers Émile Zola (whose ashes are now in the Panthéon), Alexandre Dumas (fils) and Stendhal; composers Jacques Offenbach and Hector Berlioz, artist Edgar Degas, film director François Truffaut and dancer Vaslav Nijinsky, among others. Steps from the rue Caulaincourt road bridge lead down to the entrance on av Rachel, just off bd de Clichy.

PLACE DU TERTRE   SQUARE
Map p378 (place du Tertre, 18e; ⓜAbbesses) It would be hard to miss this busy square, one of the most touristy spots in all of Paris. Although today it's filled with visitors, buskers and portrait artists, place du Tertre was originally the main square of the village of Montmartre before it was incorporated into the city proper.

One of the more popular claims of Montmartre mythology is staked to La Mère Catherine at No 6: in 1814, so it's said, Cossack soldiers first introduced the term *bistro* (Russian for 'quickly') into the French lexicon. Another big moment came on Christmas Eve 1898, when Louis Renault's first car was driven up the Butte to the place du Tertre, igniting the start of the French auto industry.

ESPACE DALÍ   ART MUSEUM
Map p378 (☏01 42 64 40 10; www.daliparis.com; 11 rue Poulbot, 18e; adult/child €11.50/6.50; ☉10am-6pm, to 8pm Jul & Aug; ⓜAbbesses) More than 300 works by Salvador Dalí (1904–89), the flamboyant Catalan surrealist printmaker, painter, sculptor and self-promoter, are on display at this surrealist-style basement museum located just west of place du Tertre. The collection includes Dalí's strange sculptures, lithograph, and many of his illustrations and furniture, including the famous Mae West Lips Sofa.

HALLE ST-PIERRE   ART MUSEUM
Map p378 (www.hallesaintpierre.org; 2 rue Ronsard, 18e; adult/child €8/6.50; ☉11am-6pm Mon-Fri, 11am-7pm Sat, noon-6pm Sun; ⓜAnvers) Founded in 1986, this museum and gallery is in the lovely old covered St Peter's Market. It focuses on the primitive and Art Brut schools; there is no permanent collection, but the museum stages three temporary exhibitions a year. It also has an auditorium, cafe and bookshop.

MUSÉE DE L'ÉROTISME   MUSEUM
Map p378 (www.musee-erotisme.com; 72 bd de Clichy, 18e; adult/reduced €10/6; ☉10am-2am;

Ⓜ Blanche) The Museum of Erotic Art attempts to raise around 2000 titillating statuary, stimulating sexual aids and fetishist items to a loftier plane, with antique and modern erotic art from four continents spread out across five floors. Some of the exhibits are, well, breathtaking.

MUSÉE DE LA VIE ROMANTIQUE   MUSEUM
Map p378 (☑ 01 55 31 95 67; www.vie-romantique. paris.fr; 16 rue Chaptal, 9e; ⊙10am-6pm Tue-Sun; Ⓜ Blanche, St-Georges) **FREE** This romantic mansion with green shutters and tangled garden sits in a cobbled courtyard at the end of a tree-shaded alley. Writer George Sand and painter Ary Scheffer lived here, and the objects exhibited create a wonderful flashback to romantic-era Paris when Chopin (Sand's lover), Delacroix et al attended salons in the house. End your literary visit with tea and cake in the museum's enchanting garden cafe, open spring to autumn.

LE BAL   GALLERY
Map p385 (www.le-bal.fr; 6 impasse de la Défense, 18e; adult/child €6/free; ⊙noon-9pm Wed, noon-10pm Thu, noon-8pm Fri, 11am-8pm Sat,

11am-7pm Sun; Ⓜ Place de Clichy) A two-floor gallery specialising in contemporary photography exhibits, with an excellent bookstore and neighbouring cafe serving lunch and weekend brunch (great chocolate Guinness cake!). Watch for film screenings, performances and artistic soirées organised by Le Bal Lab.

CITÉ DES SCIENCES   SCIENCE MUSEUM
Map p384 (☑ 01 56 43 20 20; www.cite-sciences. fr; 30 av Corentin Cariou, 19e, Parc de la Villette; adult/child €9/7, La Géode €12/9; ⊙10am-6pm Tue-Sat, to 7pm Sun, La Géode 10.30am-8.30pm Tue-Sun; ♿; Ⓜ Porte de la Villette) This is the city's top museum for kids, with three floors of hands-on exhibits for children aged two and up, special-effect cinema **La Géode**, a planetarium and retired submarine. Each exhibit has a separate admission fee (combined tickets exist), so research online beforehand to work out what's most appropriate. Be sure to reserve tickets in advance for both weekend and school-holiday visits, plus for the fabulous **Cité des Enfants** educative play sessions (1½ hours, ages two to seven years or five to 12 years) year-round.

TOP SIGHT
MUSÉE JACQUEMART-ANDRÉ

If you belonged to the cream of Parisian society in the late 19th century, chances are you would have been invited to one of the dazzling soirées held at this mansion. The home of art collectors Nélie Jacquemart and Édouard André, this opulent residence was designed in the then-fashionable eclectic style, which combined elements from different eras – seen here in the presence of Greek and Roman antiquities, Egyptian artefacts, period furnishings and portraits by Dutch masters.

A wander through the 16 rooms offers a glimpse of the lifestyle and tastes of Parisian high society: from the library, hung with canvases by Rembrandt and Van Dyck, to the marvellous Jardin d'Hiver – a glass-paned garden room backed by a magnificent double-helix staircase. Upstairs is an impressive collection of Italian Renaissance works by Botticelli, Donatello and Titian, among others.

The mansion's architect, Henri Parent, was nearly hired to work on the Paris opera house, the Palais Garnier – he was beat out only by the then-unknown Charles Garnier.

After the tour, stop in at the **salon de thé** (open 11.45am to 5.30pm Monday to Friday, from 11am Saturday and Sunday), which serves lunch, brunch and pastries as extravagant as the decor.

DON'T MISS

➡ The library
➡ The Jardin d'Hiver
➡ The 2nd floor Italian art collection
➡ The tearoom

PRACTICALITIES

➡ Map p385, C4
➡ ☑ 01 45 62 11 59
➡ www.musee-jacque mart-andre.com
➡ 158 bd Haussmann, 8e
➡ adult/child €12/10
➡ ⊙10am-6pm, to 8.30pm Mon during temporary exhibitions
➡ Ⓜ Miromesnil

Packing a picnic is also a good idea. Otherwise, several chain restaurants grace shopping-centre complex Vill'up (complete with cinema and freefall simulator – parents you've been warned).

MUSÉE DE LA MUSIQUE   MUSIC MUSEUM
Map p384 (www.cite-musique.fr; 221 av Jean Jaurès, 19e; adult/child €7/free; ⊙noon-6pm Tue-Sat, 10am-6pm Sun; MPorte de Pantin) This music museum squats inside the Philharmonie 2 (previously called Cité de la Musique) building on the complex of the **Philharmonie de Paris** (Map p384; www.phil harmoniedeparis.com; ⊙2-6pm Tue-Fri, 10am-6pm Sat & Sun, plus concerts) on the southern edge of Parc de la Villette. It displays some 900 rare musical instruments; you can hear many of them being played on the audioguide. Temporary exhibitions command an additional entrance fee.

PARC DES BUTTES-CHAUMONT   PARK
Map p384 (rue Manin & rue Botzaris, 19e; ⊙7am-10pm May-Sep, to 8pm Oct-Apr; MButtes-Chaumont, Botzaris) This quirky park is one of the city's largest green spaces; its landscaped slopes hide grottoes, waterfalls, a lake and even an island topped with a temple to Sybil. Once a gypsum quarry and rubbish dump, it was given its present form by Baron Haussmann in time for the opening of the 1867 Exposition Universelle. The tracks of an abandoned 19th-century railway line (La Petite Ceinture, which once circled Paris) run through the park.

It's a favourite with Parisians, who come here to practise t'ai chi, take the kids to a puppet show or simply to relax with a bottle of wine and a sundown picnic.

BRASSERIE LA GOUTTE D'OR   BREWERY
Map p382 (☑09 80 64 23 51; www.brasserie lagouttedor.com; 28 rue la Goutte d'Or, 18e; ⊙5-7pm Thu & Fri, 2-7pm Sat; MChâteau Rouge) FREE No address is such an earthy reflection of the gutsy, multiethnic *quartier* of La Goutte d'Or than this craft brewery, with brewmaster Thierry Roche at the helm. In business since 2012, it turns to the local 'hood for inspiration: spicy red beer Château Rouge is named after the local metro station; fruity India pale ale L'Ernestine evokes the street where La Goutte d'Or's early beers were brewed in the early 1900s; aromatic and bitter La Môme is a nod to a local restaurant.

Guided tours are free and include tastings around a simple chipboard bar.

INSTITUT DES CULTURES
D'ISLAM-LÉON   CULTURAL CENTRE
Map p382 (ICIC; www.institut-cultures-islam.org; 19-23 rue Léon, 18e; walking tours adult/child €12/8; ⊙1-8pm Tue-Thu, 4-8pm Fri, 10am-8pm Sat & Sun; MChâteau Rouge) The Islam Cultural Institute, in the heart of the Goutte d'Or neighbourhood, hosts concerts, poetry readings, film screenings, temporary exhibitions, art workshops and cooking classes, all generally related to north Africa or the Middle East. There's a pleasant cafe on site and the institute runs fascinating two-hour walking tours of the Goutte d'Or neighbourhood. The ICIC has a **second building** (Map p382; ☑01 53 09 99 84; 56 rue Stéphenson, 18e; ⊙1-8pm Tue-Thu, 4-8pm Fri, 10am-8pm Sat & Sun; MMarx Dormoy, Château Rouge) FREE nearby with more exhibition space, a hammam and a trio of beehives on its roof.

LE 104   GALLERY
(☑01 53 35 50 00; www.104.fr; 104 rue d'Aubervilliers or 5 rue Curial, 19e; ⊙noon-7pm Tue-Fri, 11am-7pm Sat & Sun; 🛜; MStalingrad, Crimée) FREE A former funeral parlour turned city-funded alternative art space, Le 104 is a hive of activity. It essentially supports and encourages young artists, and a random wander through its public areas uncovers breakdancers, wacky art installations and rehearsing actors. Check the schedule for events to make the most of it: there's theatre, circus, music, monthly balls and even magic shows. Some things are free; others require admission. Also on site are a pizza truck, a retro 1950s-styled cafe and an industrial loft-like restaurant-bar.

MUSÉE CERNUSCHI   ART MUSEUM
Map p385 (www.cernuschi.paris.fr; 7 av Vélasquez, 8e; ⊙10am-6pm Tue-Sun; MVilliers) FREE The Cernuschi Museum comprises an excellent and rare collection of ancient Chinese art (funerary statues, bronzes, ceramics), much of which pre-dates the Tang dynasty (618–907), in addition to diverse pieces from Japan. Milan banker and philanthropist Henri Cernuschi (1821–96), who settled in Paris before the unification of Italy, assembled the collection during an 1871–73 world tour.

WORTH A DETOUR

BASILIQUE DE ST-DENIS

Once one of France's most sacred sites, **Basilique de St-Denis** (www.saint-denis-basilique.fr; 1 rue de la Légion d'Honneur; basilica free, tombs adult/child €8.50/free; ⊙10am-6.15pm Mon-Sat, noon-6.15pm Sun Apr-Sep, 10am-5.15pm Mon-Sat, noon-5.15pm Sun Oct-Mar; Ⓜ Basilique de St-Denis) was built atop the tomb of St Denis, the 3rd-century martyr and alleged first bishop of Paris who was beheaded by Roman priests. By the 6th century it had become the royal necropolis. Almost all of France's kings and queens from Dagobert I (r 629–39) to Louis XVIII (r 1814–24) are buried here, including Louis XVI and Marie-Antoinette (42 kings and 32 queens in total).

The single-towered basilica, begun around 1136, was the first major structure in France to be built in the Gothic style, serving as a model for other 12th-century French cathedrals. Features illustrating the transition from Romanesque to Gothic can be seen in the choir and double ambulatory, which are adorned with a number of 12th-century stained-glass windows.

The tombs in the crypt are Europe's largest collection of funerary art and the real reason to make the trip out here. Adorned with *gisants* (recumbent figures), those made after 1285 were carved from death masks and are thus fairly lifelike; earlier sculptures are depictions of how earlier rulers might have looked.

An audioguide costs €4.50.

MUSÉE NISSIM DE CAMONDO   ART MUSEUM

Map p385 (☑ 01 44 55 57 50; www.lesartsdecoratifs.fr; 63 rue de Monceau, 8e; adult/child €9/free; ⊙11am-5.30pm Wed-Sun; Ⓜ Monceau, Villiers) This museum, housed in a sumptuous mansion modelled on the Petit Trianon at Versailles, displays 18th-century furniture, wood panelling, tapestries, porcelain and other objets d'art collected by Count Moïse de Camondo, a Sephardic Jewish banker who moved from Constantinople to Paris in the late 19th century. He bequeathed the mansion and his collection to the state on the proviso that it would be turned into a museum named in memory of his son Nissim (1892–1917), a pilot killed in action during WWI.

🍴 EATING

Not much changes in the staid western Paris culinary scene, but once you cross over that invisible border somewhere in the middle of the 9th *arrondissement*, it's a different world. It seems there is a constant flurry of new openings in edgy south Pigalle, along Canal St-Martin and in the overtly working-class and cosmopolitan 10e west of place de la République: young chefs at work here boast some of the most exciting dining venues in contemporary Paris.

⭐52 FAUBOURG ST-DENIS   MODERN FRENCH €

Map p382 (www.faubourgstdenis.com; 52 rue du Faubourg St-Denis, 10e; mains €16-20; ⊙8am-midnight, kitchen noon-2.30pm & 7-11pm; 🐾; Ⓜ Château d'Eau) This thoroughly contemporary, neighbourhood cafe-restaurant is simply a brilliant space to hang out in at any time of day. Be it for breakfast, coffee, a zingy fresh-sage infusion, dinner or drinks, 52 Faubourg, as locals call it, gets it just right. Cuisine is modern and creative, and the chef is not shy in mixing veg with fruit in every course – including dessert. No reservations.

⭐HOLYBELLY   INTERNATIONAL €

Map p382 (www.holybel.ly; 19 rue Lucien Sampaix, 10e; breakfast €5-11.50, lunch mains €13.50-16.50; ⊙9am-6pm Thu, Fri, Mon, from 10am Sat & Sun; Ⓜ Jacques Bonsergent) This outstanding barista-run coffee shop and kitchen is always rammed with a buoyant crowd, who never tire of Holybelly's exceptional service, Belleville-roasted coffee and cuisine. Sarah's breakfast pancakes served with egg, bacon, homemade bourbon butter and maple syrup are legendary, while her lunch menu features everything from traditional braised veal shank to squid *à la plancha*.

Breakfast is served until noon weekdays and all day at weekends; lunchtime is noon to 3pm. No reservations.

★ **SOUL KITCHEN**   VEGETARIAN €

Map p378 (www.soulkitchenparis.fr; 33 rue Lamarck, 18e; lunch menu €13.50; ⏰8.30am-6pm Tue-Fri, 10am-6.30pm Sat & Sun; 🛜📷♿; Ⓜ Lamarck-Caulaincourt) This vegetarian eatery with shabby-chic vintage interior and tiny open kitchen is as soulful as its name suggests. Market-driven dishes include feisty bowls of creative salads, homemade soups, savoury tarts, burritos and wraps – all gargantuan in size and packed with seasonal veggies. Round off lunch or snack between meals on muffins, cakes and the finest mint-laced *citronnade maison* (homemade lemonade) in town.

Families, note: feel free to rifle through the playful content of the sage-green 'games' cupboard.

★ **TRICYCLE STORE**   FAST FOOD €

Map p382 (www.letricycle.fr; 51 rue Paradis, 10e; hot dogs €5; ⏰noon-6pm Mon-Fri, to 4pm Sun; 🛜📷; Ⓜ Poissonnière) What began life as a hot-dog stand on wheels – three wheels to be precise – pedalled around town by flame-haired Coralie and partner Daqui has now morphed into a fully fledged shop with upstairs seating. Dogs are 100% vegetarian with names inspired by hip-hop artists. House special Dogtor Dre is a corn and smoked-soya sausage smothered in creamy avocado, coriander, onions and tomato.

LE VERRE VOLÉ SUR MER   SEAFOOD €

Map p382 (📞01 48 03 21 38; 53 rue de Lancry, 10e; bentos €14, small plates €8-15; ⏰noon-2pm & 7.30-11pm; Ⓜ Jacques Bonsergent) This minuscule seafood-inspired wine bar with barstool seating is a rare catch in urban Paris, but with celebrated traditional wine bar Le Verre Volé (p144) as its big sister, its pedigree is golden. Join locals for a lunchtime bento of salmon tartare laced with lemon and coriander, or after-work plates of freshly shucked oysters and raw and cooked fish.

FLAT IRON   BISTRO €

Map p382 (📞01 40 18 02 57; http://flatiron.fr; 38 rue de Sambre et Meuse, 10e; mains €14; ⏰9.30am-1.30am Tue-Sat, noon-3.30pm Sun; Ⓜ Belleville, Colonel Fabien) For a taste of Manhattan in Belleville, people-watch at this New York–style hang-out in the retro interior with red-brick wall and wooden bistro chairs, or al fresco in summer when the action spills onto the pavement outside. Contrary to the Big Apple vibe, the kitchen is deeply rooted in France – think *entrecôte* (steak), braised endives and *poisson du jour* (fish of the day).

Sunday brunch is a fun affair, as are wintertime oyster-themed aperitif soirées.

FRIC-FRAC   SANDWICHES €

Map p382 (http://fricfrac.fr; 79 quai de Valmy, 10e; sandwiches €11.50-14.50; ⏰noon-3pm & 8-11pm Tue-Fri, noon-11pm Sat, noon-7pm Sun; Ⓜ Jacques Bonsergent) Traditional snack croque monsieur (a toasted cheese and ham sandwich) gets a contemporary makeover at this quayside space. Grab a toasted sandwich to munch on along the canal banks or eat in: gourmet Winnie (Crottin de Chavignol cheese, dried fruit, chestnut honey, chives and rosemary) and exotic Shaolin (king prawns and Thai chutney) are among the creative combos served with salad and fries.

HERO   KOREAN €

(www.heroparis.com; 289 rue St-Denis, 2e; cocktails €8-12, chicken €12.50-18; ⏰noon-

---

CANAL CRUISES

Everyone takes the river boats down the Seine, but if you're up for something slightly different, why not try a canal cruise? Two companies run seasonal 2½-hour trips along the Canal St-Martin, chugging back and forth between central Paris and Parc de la Villette. Boats go at a leisurely pace, passing through four double locks, two swing bridges and an underground section (livened up somewhat by an art installation).

Canauxrama (Map p382; www.canauxrama.com; 13 quai de la Loire, 19e; adult/child €18/9; Ⓜ Jaurès) Cruises depart from the Bassin de la Villette near Parc de la Villette and from the **Port de l'Arsenal** (Map p394; www.canauxrama.com; opposite 50 bd de la Bastille, 12e, Port de l'Arsenal; adult/child €18/9; Ⓜ Bastille); summertime evening weekend cruises are particularly enchanting. Gourmand and thematic cruises too.

Paris Canal Croisières (Map p384; 📞01 42 40 96 97; www.pariscanal.com; Parc de la Villette, 19e; adult/child €20/13; ⏰mid-Mar–mid-Nov; Ⓜ Porte de Pantin) Cruises depart from Parc de la Villette and from quai Anatole France near the Musée d'Orsay.

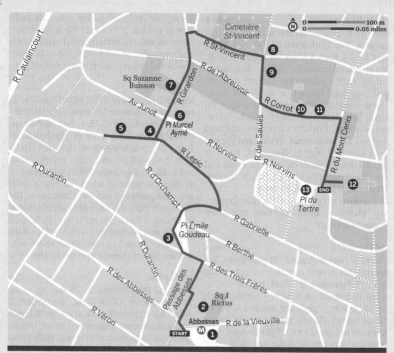

Neighbourhood Walk
Mythic Montmartre

START ABBESSES METRO STATION
END PLACE DU TERTRE
LENGTH 1KM; ONE HOUR

Begin on **1 place des Abbesses**, where Hector Guimard's iconic art-nouveau metro entrance (1900) still stands. Deep underground, beneath a maze of gypsum mines, it is one of Paris' deepest metro stations. Learn how to say 'I love you!' in another language or 10 with **2 Le Mur des je t'aime**, hidden in Sq Jehan Rictus, on place des Abbesses.

On place Émile Goudeau you'll find **3 Le Bateau Lavoir** at At No 11bis, where Max Jacob, Amedeo Modigliani and Pablo Picasso – who painted his seminal Les Demoiselles d'Avignon (1907) here – once had art studios.

Continue the climb up rue Lepic to Montmartre's two surviving windmills: **4 Moulin Radet** (now a restaurant) and, 100m west, **5 Moulin Blute Fin**. In the 19th century, the latter became the open-air dance hall Le Moulin de la Galette, immortalised by Renoir in his 1876 tableau Bal du Moulin de la Galette (in the Musée d'Orsay).

Just north of the windmills watch a man pop out of a stone wall. This **6 Passe-Muraille statue** portrays Dutilleul, the hero of Marcel Aymé's short story Le Passe-Muraille (The Walker through Walls). Aymé lived in the adjacent building from 1902 until 1967. Continue along rue Girardon to Sq Suzanne Buisson, home to a **7 statue of St-Denis**, the 3rd-century martyr and patron saint of France beheaded by Roman priests.

After passing by Cimetière St-Vincent you'll come upon the celebrated cabaret **8 Au Lapin Agile** (p152), with a mural of a rabbit jumping out of a cooking pot by caricaturist André Gill. Opposite is **9 Clos Montmartre**, a vineyard dating from 1933.

Uphill is Montmartre's oldest building, a 17th-century manor house. Once home to Renoir, Utrillo and Raoul Dufy, it's now the **10 Musée de Montmartre** (p137). Continue on past composer **11 Eric Satie's former residence** (No 6) and turn right onto rue du Mont Cenis; you'll soon come to historic **12 Église St-Pierre de Montmartre**. End on busy **13 place du Tertre** (p137), the former main square of the village.

2.30pm & 7-11pm Tue-Sun; MStrasbourg-St-Denis) The creative team behind Le Mary Céleste (p171) and **Glass** (Map p378; www.glass paris.com; 7 rue Frochot, 9e; ⊙7pm-2am; MPigalle) are behind this unique drinking and dining space. Hero cooks up *yangnyeom* (crispy fried Korean chicken) in sweet and sour, garlicky or fiery *gochu yang* sauces. Tasty salads and snacks pad out the menu, all to be washed down with a truly fabulous cocktail or shot of traditional Korean soju (distilled rice liquor).

Internet reservations for dinner only.

ROCOCO
KEBAB €

Map p382 (www.rococokebab.fr; 10 rue du Faubourg St-Martin, 10e; kebabs €9, lunch menu €12; ⊙noon-midnight; 🔊🖋; MStrasbourg-St-Denis, Jacques Bonsergent) With its black minimalist interior and creative kebabs to eat in or to go, Rococo casts a great new spin on fast food. Everything from the tasty bread buns and pickles to the tangy herb salsa and aubergine caviar doused on the meats is homemade. Meats are spit-roasted and marinated in orange and mustard, and lemon and spices among others.

There's a felafel option for vegetarians.

MARCHÉ BIOLOGIQUE DES BATIGNOLLES
MARKET €

Map p385 (34 bd des Batignolles, 17e; ⊙9am-3pm Sat; MPlace de Clichy) Abuzz with market stalls, this busy boulevard in northern Paris had its own covered market from 1846 until 1867 (when it shut and moved to its current location on nearby rue Lemercier). These days it's the organic produce that pulls in the punters fast and thick. Dozens of the 50 or so stalls offer tastings and everything is super fresh.

SUNKEN CHIP
FAST FOOD €

Map p382 (🖉01 53 26 74 46; www.thesunken chip.com; 39 rue des Vinaigriers, 10e; fish & chips €12-14; ⊙noon-2.30pm & 7-10pm Tue-Fri, noon-3.30pm & 7-10pm Sat & Sun; MJacques Bonsergent) It's hard to argue with the battered, fried goodness at this ideally located fish 'n' chip shop near Canal St-Martin. Nothing is frozen here: it's all line-caught fish fresh from Brittany (three varieties per day), accompanied with thick-cut chips (peeled and chopped *sur place*), brown malt vinegar and minty mushy peas. Pickled eggs and onions are optional. Takeaway is available.

L'ÉTÉ EN PENTE DOUCE
CAFE €

Map p378 (🖉01 42 64 02 67; 23 rue Muller, 18e; mains €10.30-18.30; ⊙noon-midnight; MAnvers) Parisian terraces don't get much better than Summer on a Gentle Slope, named after the 1987 French film: a secret square wedged in between two flights of steep staircases on the backside of Montmartre, in a neighbourhood that's very much the real thing. Quiches, giant salads and classic dishes like Niçois-style stuffed veggies make up the menu.

BOB'S JUICE BAR
VEGETARIAN €

Map p382 (🖉09 50 06 36 18; www.bobsjuicebar. com; 15 rue Lucien Sampaix, 10e; juices €4-7.50, bagels €4.50; ⊙7.30am-3pm Mon-Fri, 8.30am-4pm Sat; 🖋; MJacques Bonsergent) Craving a protein shake or green smoothie? This pocket-sized space with bags of rice flour and flaxseed lining the walls is the original hot spot in Paris for smoothies, cold-pressed organic juices, vegan breakfasts, hummus sandwiches, gluten-free muffins and generously filled bagels.

PINK FLAMINGO
PIZZA €

Map p382 (🖉01 42 02 31 70; www.pinkflamingo pizza.com; 67 rue Bichat, 10e; pizzas €11.50-17; ⊙7-11.30pm Mon-Thu, noon-3pm & 7-11.30pm Fri-Sun; MJacques Bonsergent) Once the weather warms up, the Flamingo unveils its secret weapon – pink helium balloons that the delivery guy uses to locate you and your perfect canal-side picnic spot (GPS not needed). Order a Poulidor (duck, apple and chèvre) or a Basquiat (gorgonzola, figs and cured ham), pop into Le Verre Volé (p144) across the canal for the perfect bottle of vino and you're set.

LE GRENIER À PAIN
BOULANGERIE €

Map p378 (38 rue des Abbesses, 18e; sandwiches €3-4.10; ⊙7.30am-8pm Thu-Mon; MAbbesses) Past winner of Paris' annual 'best baguette' prize, this enchanting bakery with semi-open kitchen is the finest picnic stop in Montmartre. Join the queue for takeaway crusty baguette sandwiches, succulent *fougasses* and alluring mini breads topped with fig and goat's cheese or bacon and olives. End on a sweet high with a fruit-bejewelled loaf cake.

CRÊPERIE PEN-TY
CRÊPERIE €

Map p378 (🖉01 48 74 18 49; 65 rue de Douai, 9e; galettes €3-10.90, crêpes €3.90-8.90; ⊙noon-2.30pm & 7.30-11pm Mon-Fri, 12.30-4pm & 6.30-11.30pm Sat, 12.30-4pm & 6.30-10.30pm Sun;

M Place de Clichy) Hailed as the best crêperie in northern Paris, the Pen-Ty is worth the detour. Book ahead, and don't miss the selection of authentic Breton aperitifs like *chouchen* (a type of mead) and *pastis marin* (an aniseed and seaweed liquor). Savoury *galettes* (made with buckwheat flour) and sweet crêpes are pricier in the evening and at weekends. There is a takeaway window too.

BRASSERIE BARBÈS
CAFE €

Map p382 (📞01 42 64 52 23; www.brasserie barbes.com; 2 bd Barbès, 18e; ⏰8.30am-2am; 📶; M Barbès-Rochechouart) This bright brasserie-style cafe with vintage ceiling fans, potted plants and a wonderful glass rotunda provides a welcome retreat from the hustle and bustle of the raucous Marché Barbès that brings chaos to the 'hood Wednesday and Saturday mornings. Indulge in an egg-and-bacon breakfast, reuben-sandwich brunch or a green detox juice.

When the sun shines tables on the rooftop terrace are prime real estate.

MARCHÉ ST-MARTIN
MARKET €

Map p382 (31-33 rue du Château d'Eau, 10e; ⏰9am-8pm Tue-Sat, 9am-2pm Sun; M Château d'Eau) This lovely covered market, built in 1859 and revamped in 1880, is a delightful spot to mooch around stalls selling high-quality food produce. Join locals afterwards for breakfast, brunch or a burger lunch at **Allen's Market**, a New York–style cafe in the market with a delightful pavement terrace.

MARCHÉ ST-QUENTIN
FOOD MARKET €

Map p382 (85bis bd de Magenta, 10e; ⏰8am-8pm Tue-Sat, to 1.30pm Sun; M Gare de l'Est) This iron-and-glass covered market, built in 1866, has the usual range of French specialities and produce, as well as affordable lunches at a variety of stalls (including African and Lebanese).

LA MÔME
NORTH AFRICAN €

Map p382 (📞01 42 23 35 64; 16 rue Stéphenson, 18e; tajines €13-18; ⏰noon-3pm & 7-10.30pm Mon-Sat; M La Chapelle, Barbès Rochechouart) For authentic Moroccan *pastillas* (sweet and savoury meat pies) and *tajines* running from chicken and pears to duck with cherries and pistachios, head to this unassuming neighbourhood cafe with cracked tile floors and cosy interior in the vibrant, predominantly north African neighbourhood of La Goutte d'Or.

Begin on the pavement terrace with a locally brewed La Môme artisan beer, crafted specially for this local institution.

LE RELAIS GASCON
TRADITIONAL FRENCH €

Map p378 (📞01 42 58 58 22; www.lerelaisgascon. fr; 6 rue des Abbesses, 18e; lunch/dinner menu €17.50/27.50; ⏰10am-2am; M Abbesses) Situated a short stroll from place des Abbesses, Le Relais Gascon has a relaxed atmosphere and authentic regional cuisine at reasonable prices. The giant salads and *confit de canard* will satisfy big eaters, while the traditional *cassoulet* (potatoes, cheese and bacon baked in a casserole) and *tartiflette* (rich bean, pork and duck stew) are equally delicious. It does not accept credit cards, but its branch on nearby rue Joseph de Maistre does.

KRISHNA BHAVAN
INDIAN €

Map p382 (📞01 42 05 78 43; www.krishna-bhavan.com; 24 rue Cail, 10e; lunch/dinner menu €14.50/19, dishes €6-7.50; ⏰11am-11pm; 📶; M La Chapelle) This is about as authentic an Indian vegetarian canteen as you'll find in Paris. If in doubt as to what to order, ask for a *thaali*, a circular steel tray with samosas, dosas and other wrapped goodies. Wash it all down with a yoghurt-based lassi, which comes in five flavours, including mango and rose.

★LE VERRE VOLÉ
BISTRO €€

Map p382 (📞01 48 03 17 34; http://leverrevole. fr; 67 rue de Lancry, 10e; mains €15-25; ⏰bistro 12.30-2pm & 7.30-10.30pm, wine cellar 9am-1am; M Jacques Bonsergent) The tiny 'Stolen Glass' – a wine shop with a few tables – is just about the most perfect wine-bar-restaurant in Paris, with top wines and expert advice. Unpretentious and hearty *plats du jour* (dishes of the day) are excellent. Reserve well in advance for meals, or stop by to pick up a bottle.

★GRAND AMOUR HÔTEL
NEOBISTRO €€

Map p382 (📞01 44 16 03 30; www.hotelamour paris.fr; 18 rue de la Fidélité, 10e; 2-course lunch €18, mains €14-22; ⏰8am-12.30am; 📶; M Gare de l'Est) Track down in-the-know Parisians in this hipster neobistro beneath Hôtel Grand Amour, an address that is rapidly turning the 10e into *the* place to be in Paris. Breakfast – French, English or vegetarian – opens the day, followed by an enticing mix of food served all day: think vegetarian risotto, pastrami sandwiches, hake roasted with parsnip and avocado, or steak and fries.

Reservations for weekend brunch, served from noon to 6pm, are vital.

★ LA BULLE   MODERN FRENCH €€

Map p382 (☑01 40 37 34 51; www.restolabulle.fr; 48 rue Louis Blanc, 10e; 2-/3-course lunch menu €18.50/24, dinner menus €43 & €55; ⊘noon-2.30pm & 7.30-10.30pm Mon-Sat; MLouis Blanc) It's worth the short detour to this contemporary corner bistro with oyster-grey facade, lime-green seating on a sunny pavement terrrace, and talented young chef Romain Perrollaz in the kitchen. His cuisine is creative and strictly *fait maison* (homemade), with lots of tempting combos like beef with dill-spiked spelt risotto or pork *pot au feu* with old-time veg, watercress and peanut vinaigrette.

The most expensive *menu* is a six-course tasting feast.

★ MATIÈRE À.   MODERN FRENCH €€

Map p382 (☑09 83 07 37 85; 15 rue Marie et Louise, 10e; 2-/3-course lunch menu €19/23, dinner menu €44; ⊘noon-2.30pm & 7.30pm-1am Mon-Fri, 7pm-1am Sat; MRépublique) The short but stunning seasonal menu changes daily at this unique space. *Table d'hôte*–style memorable dining for no more than 14 is around a shared oak table lit by dozens of naked light bulbs. In the kitchen is young chef Anthony Courteille, who prides himself on doing everything *fait maison* (homemade), including bread and butter to die for. Reservations essential.

LA GRILLE   FRENCH €€

Map p382 (☑01 45 81 08 49; www.lagrille faubourg.fr; 80 rue du Faubourg Poissonnière, 10e; mains €16-42; ⊘noon-2.30pm & 6pm-2am Tue-Fri, 5pm-2am Sat; ⌘☎; MPoissonnière) Around for 50-odd years, this up-to-the-minute brasserie with huge people-watching windows markets itself as a top-end gastropub today. *Turbot au beurre blanc* (turbot in a white wine and butter sauce) is the kitchen's signature dish and the bar menu cooks up frog legs, snails, bone marrow or simple sides of fries and mayo to nibble on. Don't miss the cocktail list.

ABRI   NEOBISTRO €€

Map p382 (☑01 83 97 00 00; 92 rue du Faubourg Poissonnière, 9e; lunch/dinner menus €26/46; ⊘12.30-2pm Mon, 12.30-2pm & 8-10pm Tue-Sat; MPoissonnière) It's no bigger than a shoebox

and the decor is borderline nonexistent, but that's all part of the charm. Katsuaki Okiyama is a seriously talented chef with an artistic flair, and his surprise tasting menus (three courses at lunch, six at dinner) are exceptional. On Monday and Saturday, a giant gourmet sandwich is all that's served for lunch. Reserve well in advance.

VIVANT   MODERN FRENCH €€

Map p382 (☑01 42 46 43 55; http://vivantparis. com; 43 rue des Petites Écuries, 10e; mains €23-29; ⊘noon-2pm & 7-10.30pm Mon-Sat; MPoissonnière, Bonne Nouvelle) Simple but elegant dishes – creamy burrata, crispy duck leg with mashed potatoes, foie gras and roasted onion – showcase the carefully sourced ingredients used at this small but chic restaurant, inside a century-old exotic-bird shop with a stunning ceramic wall and ceiling. Swiss-born Pierre Jancou is a natural-wine activist and at least one glass of *vin* is an essential part of the meal here. Reserve ahead.

SOL SEMILLA   VEGETARIAN €€

Map p382 (www.sol-semilla.fr; 23 rue des Vinaigriers, 10e; menus €19.50-23.50, soups & mains €11-15.50; ⊘noon-4pm Tue, Wed & Sun, noon-4pm & 7-10pm Thu-Sat; ☑; MJacques Bonsergent, Gare de l'Est) 🍃 Superfood specialist Sol Semilla is both a boutique and canteen. Here you'll find organic supersoups (vitality, detox), vegan-friendly seasonal salads and stir-fries, açaí berry smoothies and raw-cocoa desserts.

LES VINAIGRIERS   MODERN FRENCH €€

Map p382 (☑01 46 07 97 12; www.lesvinaigriers. fr; 42 rue des Vinaigriers, 10e; 2-/3-course lunch menu €19/23, dinner mains €20-25; ⊘noon-2.30pm & 7.30-10.30pm Tue-Sat, noon-4pm Sun; MJacques Bonsergent, Gare de l'Est) This darling dining room, anchored by the vintage corkscrew staircase in the back and an open kitchen facing the street, offers one of the canal's best-value lunch deals. The modern French cuisine is excellent – think delicate pumpkin soup with mint and chèvre emulsion, or orecchiette pasta with a rich white-wine-based cream of chicken. Book ahead.

JEANNE B   DELI €€

Map p378 (☑01 42 51 17 53; www.jeanne-b-comestibles.com; 61 rue Lepic, 18e; 2-/3-course lunch €19/24, dinner €25/29; ⊘9.30am-10.30pm; ☎⌘; MAbbesses, Lamarck-Caulaincourt) Choose among the homemade terrines, stuffed veggies, salads, meat pies or roasted lamb and chicken at this gourmet sit-down deli. There's no overwrought buzz about the place, and even if the menu feels pricey, the dishes don't disappoint. House speciality, *croq 'homard de Jeanne,* is a chunky lobster sandwich. Between meals drop in for morning coffee and cakes or afternoon *goûter.*

Jeanne B caters for children with a €15 roast-chicken-and-fries *menu.*

PHILOU BISTRO €€

Map p382 (☑01 42 38 00 13; 12 av Richerand, 10e; 2-/3-course menu €27/34; ☺noon-2.30pm & 8-10.30pm Mon-Fri; ⓜJacques Bonsergent) The walls at this swanky bistro are nearly 100% chalkboard, with the day's temptations writ large. The brainchild of seasoned chef Philippe Damas – the man who founded Le Square Trousseau (p188) – Philou steers away from the latest trends, instead preferring succulent French comfort food prepared with top-of-the-line ingredients.

LE COQ RICO POULTRY €€

Map p378 (☑01 42 59 82 89; www.lecoqrico. com; 98 rue Lepic, 18e; mains €24-41, whole roast chicken €98; ☺noon-2pm & 7-11pm; ⓜAbbesses) Le Coq Rico cooks up poultry, but not any old poultry. Be prepared to sink your teeth into *belles volailles* – red-ribbon birds raised in luxurious five-star chicken coops – at this rare *haute cuisine* address in Montmartre. France's finest chickens from Bourg-en-Bresse are served here, as are *pintades* (guinea fowl) and much sought-after pigeons from Mesquer in western France.

A selection of eggs, gizzards, bouillons, foie gras ravioli and other delicacies whet the appetite before the arrival of the pièce de résistance: an entire just-roasted chicken or guinea fowl, which can be split up to four ways.

LA MASCOTTE SEAFOOD €€

Map p378 (☑01 46 06 28 15; www.la-mascotte-montmartre.com; 52 rue des Abbesses, 18e; lunch/dinner menus €29/49; ☺8am-11.30pm; 🛗; ⓜAbbesses) Founded in 1889, this unassuming bar with candy-striped awning is as authentic as it gets in Montmartre. It specialises in quality seafood – oysters, lobster, scallops – and French regional dishes like Auvergne sausage. Or pull up a seat at the bar for a simple glass of wine and a plate of charcuterie. The children's *menu* is €20.

LE GARDE TEMPS MODERN FRENCH €€

Map p378 (☑09 77 40 34 13; www.restaurant-legardetemps.fr; 19bis rue Pierre Fontaine, 9e; 2-/3-course menu €29/35; ☺noon-2pm & 7-10.30pm Mon-Fri, 7-10.30pm Sat; ⓜPigalle) The chalkboard menus at this contemporary bistro are framed and hung on the walls, and thankfully the promise of gastronomic art doesn't disappoint. Old bistro standards are swept away in favour of more imaginative creations (fondant of red cabbage with quail confit) and – here's where Le Garde Temps scores big points – dinner prices aren't much more than that ho-hum cafe down the street.

LE PANTRUCHE BISTRO €€

Map p378 (☑01 48 78 55 60; www.facebook. com/LePantruche; 3 rue Victor Massé, 9e; lunch/dinner menus €19/36; ☺12.30-2.30pm & 7.30-10.30pm Mon-Fri; ⓜPigalle) Named after a nearby 19th-century theatre, classy Pantruche woos foodies in the dining hotspot of south Pigalle with seasonal bistro fare, reasonable prices and an intimate setting. The menu runs from classics (steak with Béarnaise sauce) to more daring creations (scallops served in a parmesan broth with cauliflower mousseline). Reserve well in advance.

JAMBO AFRICAN €€

Map p382 (☑01 42 45 46 55; 23 rue Ste-Marthe, 10e; 3-course menu €28; ☺7.30-10.30pm Tue-Sun; ⓜBelleville) This charming restaurant, decorated with shields and masks from different parts of Africa, was opened by former aid worker Pierre-Olivier (known as Pop to regulars) and his Rwandan wife Dada. The food is inspired by Central African cuisine; many of the ingredients are imported direct from Kigali, the Rwandan capital.

CHEZ MICHEL BRETON, SEAFOOD €€

Map p382 (☑01 44 53 06 20; 10 rue de Belzunce, 10e; lunch/dinner €29/35; ☺7pm-midnight Mon, noon-2.30pm & 7pm-midnight Tue-Fri; ⓜGare du Nord) If all you know about Breton cuisine is crêpes and cider, a visit to Chez Michel is in order. The only option is to order the four-course *menu,* which features excellent seafood (scallop tartare, hake with Breton white beans) as well as numerous specialities like *kig ha farz* (Breton pot au feu), *keuz breizh* (Breton cheeses) and *kouign* (butter cake).

BISTRO DES DAMES — BISTRO €€

Map p385 (01 45 22 13 42; 18 rue des Dames, 17e; mains €16-21; noon-2am summer, noon-3pm & 7pm-2am winter; Place de Clichy) This charming little party bistro will appeal to lovers of simple, authentic cuisine, with hearty salads, tortillas and glorious charcuterie platters of *pâté de campagne* and paper-thin Serrano ham. The dining room, which looks out onto the street, is lovely, but in summer it's the cool and tranquillity of the small back garden that pulls in the punters.

CHEZ TOINETTE — TRADITIONAL FRENCH €€

Map p378 (01 42 54 44 36; 20 rue Germain Pilon, 18e; mains €19-24; 7-11.30pm Mon-Sat; Abbesses) The atmosphere of this convivial restaurant is rivalled only by its fine cuisine (seared duck with honey, venison with foie gras). In the heart of one of the capital's most touristy neighbourhoods, Chez Toinette has kept alive the tradition of old Montmartre with its simplicity and culinary expertise. An excellent if touristy choice for a traditional French meal.

LA ROTONDE — BRASSERIE €€

Map p382 (01 80 48 33 40; www.larotonde.com; 6-8 place de la Bataille de Stalingrad, 19e; 2-/3-course lunch menu €15/18, mains €14-22; 9am-midnight Tue-Sat, noon-8pm Sun; Stalingrad) Standing proud by the Bassin de la Villette, this striking 18th-century pavilion has gone from customs station to police barracks to salt warehouse to elegant brasserie. The light-filled circular atrium is the show stealer, but it's the Sunday brunch (€23) and the huge summer terrace of the casual cafe-bar La Rotonde that really draw the crowds.

La Rotonde is open from 6pm to midnight Wednesday and Thursday, and 6pm to 2am Friday and Saturday.

LE MIROIR — BISTRO €€

Map p378 (01 46 06 50 73; www.restaurant-miroir.com; 94 rue des Martyrs, 18e; lunch menu €19.50, dinner menus €35-46; noon-2pm & 7.30-10pm; Abbesses) This modern bistro is a local favourite, smack in the middle of the Montmartre tourist trail. There are lots of delightful pâtés and *rillettes* to start with – guinea hen with dates, duck with mushrooms, haddock and lemon – followed by well-prepared standards like stuffed veal shoulder. Excellent wine list, sourced from the Mirror's wine shop across the street.

LE CHANSONNIER — FRENCH €€

Map p382 (01 42 09 40 58; http://lechansonnier.wix.com/lechansonnier; 14 rue Eugène Varlin, 10e; lunch/dinner menus €12.20/26, mains €17.50; noon-2.30pm & 6.30-11pm; Château Landon, Louis Blanc) The 'Singer' (named after the 19th-century Lyonnais socialist singer-songwriter Pierre Dupont) could be a film set, with its curved zinc bar and art-nouveau mouldings. Refreshingly unhip, the food is old-school French and very substantial with mains that range from *noix St-Jacques provençal* (scallops in herbed tomato sauce) and bouillabaisse to *daube de sanglier* (boar stew). The bistro dates to 1920.

DRINKING & NIGHTLIFE

Crowded around place Pigalle (at the foot of Montmartre) you'll find an eclectic selection of nightlife options, from local cafes and hipster dives to dance clubs and hostess bars. In contrast, the trend around the Canal St-Martin is more barista-run cafes, though wonderful summer nights (and days) see everyone decamp to the canal-side quays with blankets, baguettes and bottles of wine. In the 10e, parallel rue du Faubourg St-Martin and rue du Faubourg St-Denis and surrounding streets are speckled with ubercool cocktail bars, hybrid bistro-bars and coffee shops.

★ LULU WHITE — COCKTAIL BAR

Map p378 (www.luluwhite.bar; 12 rue Frochot, 9e; 7pm-3am Mon-Sat; Pigalle) Sip absinthe-based cocktails in Prohibition-era New Orleans surrounds at this elegant, serious and supremely busy cocktail bar on rue Frochot; several more line the same street, making for a fabulous evening out. Should you be wondering, Lulu White was an infamous African-American brothel owner in early 20th-century New Orleans.

★ GRAVITY BAR — COCKTAIL BAR

Map p382 (44 rue des Vinaigriers, 10e; 7pm-2am Tue-Sat; Jacques Bonsergent, Gare de l'Est) Catching the wave is the theme behind this trendsetting, surfing- and water-sports-themed bar near Canal St-Martin. Indeed, the stunning wave-like interior crafted from soft wood threatens to distract from

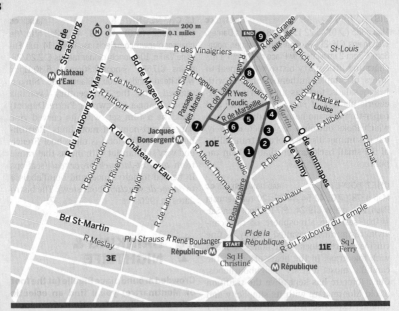

🏃 Local Life
Exploring the Canal St-Martin

Bordered by shaded towpaths and criss-crossed with iron footbridges, Canal St-Martin wends through the city's northern neighbourhoods. You can float by on a canal cruise, but strolling among this rejuvenated *quartier's* cool cafes, offbeat boutiques and hip bars lets you see why it's beloved by young Parisians.

❶ Rock 'n' Roll Fashion

Kick off on the boutique-lined rue Beaurepaire. One of the first designers to open up a store here was **Liza Korn** (www.liza-korn.com; 19 rue Beaurepaire, 10e; ⊘11am-2pm & 3-7.30pm Mon-Sat; Ⓜ Jacques Bonsergent), whose tiny store is a portal into a rich and playful imagination.

❷ Go Retro

Flip through colour-coded racks of brand-name cast-offs at vintage boutique **Frivoli** (26 rue Beaurepaire, 10e; ⊘11am-7pm Wed-Fri, 2-7pm Sat; Ⓜ Jacques Bonsergent) – among the best deals you'll find in the neighbourhood.

❸ Culture Vulture

Local artwork is often on display at **Espace Beaurepaire** (☑ 01 42 45 59 64; www.espacebeaurepaire.com; 28 rue Beaurepaire, 10e; ⊘variable; Ⓜ Jacques Bonsergent) **FREE**, a gallery and cultural centre that also hosts events such as book signings, pop-up concept stores and dance performances.

❹ Canal-side Cafes

Watch the passing boats from **Chez Prune** (71 quai de Valmy, 10e; ⊘8am-2am Mon-Sat, 10am-2am Sun; Ⓜ République), the rough-around-the-edges cafe that put Canal St-Martin on the map over a decade ago.

❺ Alternative Medecine

Rue de Marseille is another great shopping street. You'll find a trio of famous Parisian brands here – Maje, Agnès B and APC – but don't overlook **Medecine Douce** (www.bijouxmedecinedouce.com; 14 rue de Marseille, 10e; ⊘11am-7pm Tue-Sat; Ⓜ République, Jacques Bonsergent), a studio-showroom displaying gorgeous jewellery handmade on site.

❻ L'Heure du Gôuter

Kids pour into the belle époque bakery **Du Pain et Des Ideés** (www.dupainetdesidees.com; 34 rue Yves Toudic, 10e; ⊘6.45am-8pm Mon-Fri; Ⓜ Jacques Bonsergent), seeking out the lemon and blackberry *escargots* ('snails'), croissants and naturally leavened bread.

the business at hand – serious cocktails, best partaken in the company of some excellent tapas-style small plates (€5 to €12).

★ HARDWARE SOCIÉTÉ · COFFEE

Map p378 (☎01 42 51 69 03; 10 rue Lamarck, 18e; ⏰9am-4.30pm Thu-Mon, kitchen 9am-3.30pm Thu-Mon; 🛜; ⓜChâteau Rouge, Lamarck-Caulaincourt) With its black-and-white floor, Christian Lacroix butterflies fluttering across one wall and perfect love-heart-embossed cappuccinos, there's no finer spot around the Sacré-Cœur to linger over superb barista-crafted coffee (yes, that is a Slayer espresso machine). This is the Paris outpost of Melbourne's Hardware Société, with feisty breakfasts and brunches cooked up by Di and Will complementing the coffee.

★ LE TRÈS PARTICULIER · COCKTAIL BAR

Map p378 (☎01 53 41 81 40; www.hotel-particulier-montmartre.com; 23 av Junot, 18e, Pavillon D; ⏰6pm-2am Tue-Sun; ⓜLamarck-Caulaincourt) There is possibly no more enchanting spot for a summertime al fresco cocktail than Le Très Particulier, the utterly unique and clandestine cocktail bar of Hôtel Particulier Montmartre (p285). Ring the buzzer at the unmarked black gated entrance to get in and make a beeline for the 1871 mansion's flowery walled garden bar with conservatory-style interior. DJs spin tunes from 10pm every Friday and Saturday.

★ COPPERBAY · COCKTAIL BAR

Map p382 (www.copperbay.fr; 5 rue Bouchardon, 10e; ⏰6pm-2am Tue-Sat; ⓜStrasbourg-St-Denis, République) This sleek, faintly playful cocktail bar's floor-to-ceiling windows, polished pale-wood decor and glistening copper fixtures and fittings inject a generous dose of design flair into proceedings. The cocktail menu mixes classics with house specials like the fig-and-blackberry Black Julep.

BLACKBURN COFFEE · COFFEE

Map p382 (☎01 42 41 73 31; www.blackburn-paris.com; 52 rue du Faubourg St-Martin, 10e; ⏰9am-6pm Mon-Fri, 10am-7pm Sat & Sun; 🛜; ⓜStrasbourg-St-Denis) Be it an Aeropress, Dirty Chai or macchiato you're craving, this specialist coffee shop in the increasingly foodie 10e doesn't disappoint. Its stylish interior is a mellow space to hang out in over detox juices, gourmet *tartines* (open sandwiches) and healthy meal-sized salads. Weekend brunch (€24) – an egg, taco, veggie side and

Barge in a lock, Canal St-Martin

7 Say Cheese

If you're in need of supplies for a picnic pop into local deli **La Crèmerie** (41 rue de Lancry, 10e; ⏰9.30am-1.30pm & 4-8pm Tue-Fri, 10am-8pm Sat; ⓜJacques Bonsergeant) for heavenly cheeses, *saucisson* (dried cured sausage) and housemade jams.

8 Designer Books & Looks

Artzazt (www.artazart.com; 83 quai de Valmy, 10e; ⏰10.30am-7.30pm Mon-Fri, 11am-7.30pm Sat, 1-7.30pm Sun; ⓜRépublique, Jacques Bonsergent) is the leading design bookshop in Paris and, along with a fabulous collection of design and photography books in French and English, it stocks quirky collector's items such as pinhole cameras, sleek kitchen utensils and sunflowers from a bag.

9 Historic Hotel & Cafe

Hôtel du Nord (Map p382; www.hotel-dunord.org; 102 quai de Jemmapes, 10e; ⏰9am-1.30am; 🛜; ⓜJacques Bonsergent) is the setting for Marcel Carné's 1938 film of the same name, which depicted the intersecting lives of those living in the hotel. Author Eugène Dabit, whose stories formed the film's basis, once lived here. It's now a book-lined cafe.

MONTMARTRE & NORTHERN PARIS DRINKING & NIGHTLIFE

BRUNO DE HOGUES/GETTY IMAGES ©

savoury tart affair – is a big draw for the local hipster crowd.

LE PROGRÈS   BAR
Map p378 (7 rue des Trois Frères, 18e; ⏰9am-2am; Ⓜ Abbesses) A real live *café du quartier* perched in the heart of Abbesses, the Progress occupies a corner site with huge windows and simple seating and attracts a relaxed mix of local artists, shop staff, writers and hangers-on. It's great for convivial evenings, but it's also a good place to come for meals (mains €17.90 to €20.50), coffee and well-priced cocktails (€9).

CAFÉ LOMI   COFFEE
(☎09 80 39 56 24; www.cafelomi.com; 3ter rue Marcadet, 18e; ⏰10am-7pm; Ⓜ Marcadet Poissonniers) Curious coffee aficionados in Paris have to visit Café Lomi at least once. The coffee roastery and adjoining industrial-styled cafe is far away from the madding crowd, in the multiethnic La Goutte d'Or neighbourhood, but its coffee beans are personally sourced halfway around the world and roasted back home in Paris.

Alongside the regular espresso, noisette, latte and so forth, it serves filter coffee (mug, Aeropress or Chemex) and a whole host of wacky coffee creations like Bleu d'Auvergne cheese dipped in espresso or espresso tonic (tonic water with espresso). Breakfast, lunch and weekend brunch too.

BARANAAN   CAFE, COCKTAIL BAR
Map p382 (☎01 40 38 97 57; www.elaichicafe.com; 7 rue du Faubourg St-Martin, 10e; ⏰cafe 3pm-12.30am Tue-Thu & Sun, 3pm-1.30am Fri & Sat, bar 6.30pm-2am Mon-Sat; 🛜; Ⓜ Strasbourg-St-Denis, Jacques Bonsergent) One address, two ubercool identities: by day Baranaan is the hip **Elaichi Café**, serving tasty vegetarian food and lassi, chai and fresh juices in a smart contemporary setting. Come dusk, the space morphs into one of Paris' most exciting new-wave cocktail bars, serving Indian cocktails and well-filled naan breads to a keen hipster crowd. Check Baranaan's Facebook page for events and happenings.

LE COQ   COCKTAIL BAR
Map p382 (12 rue du Château d'Eau, 10e; ⏰6pm-2am Tue-Sat; Ⓜ République, Jacques Bonsergent) 🏷 Pop art and concrete walls set the stage for the 10e's trendy cocktail bar with austere black facade. Signature tipples incorporate French spirits – consider a Les Fleurs du Mal (absinthe and rose-infused vodka) or Initials BB (Bénédictine and bourbon). Aspiring mixologists can learn how to shake their own during Saturday-afternoon cocktail workshops; reserve in advance.

CHEZ JEANNETTE   BAR
Map p382 (47 rue du Faubourg St-Denis, 10e; ⏰8am-2am; Ⓜ Château d'Eau) For vintage vibe you don't get better than Jeannette's. Cracked tile floors and original 1950s decor have turned this local neighbourhood cafe-bar into one of the 10e's most popular hotspots. Local hang-out by day, pints by night and reasonably priced meals around the clock.

LUCIEN LA CHANCE   WINE BAR
Map p385 (☎09 73 52 07 14; www.facebook.com/lucienlachance.restaurant; 8 rue des Dames, 17e; ⏰6pm-1am Mon-Sat; Ⓜ Place de Clichy) For a taste of old-world Paris, linger over a glass of *vin naturel* (natural wine) at this delightfully retro wine bar with spotted shabby-chic mirrors and wooden bistro tables between bottle-filled shelves. French-styled tapas (small plates €6 to €9), to be shared among the table, completes the gourmet experience: think raw fattened liver with pistachio-laced porto, mushrooms with hazelnuts and lemon confit, octopus with black pasta...

25* EST   CAFE, BAR
Map p382 (www.25est.com; 10 place de la Bataille de Stalingrad, 19e; ⏰10am-2am; Ⓜ Stalingrad) This charismatic all-rounder is at its best in summer when Parisians crowd its quayside terrace by the murky water of Canal St-Martin to snack on crêpes, drink cocktails or simply hang out. Be it breakfast, lunch (2-/3-course lunch menu €11.80/14.80), dinner or drinks galore, this waterside cafe-bar ticks the box.

ARTISAN   COCKTAIL BAR
Map p378 (☎01 48 74 65 38; www.artisan-bar.fr; 14 rue Bochart de Saron, 9e; ⏰7pm-2am Tue-Sat; Ⓜ Anvers) For a sophisticated drink in trendy SoPi (south Pigalle), white-walled Artisan fits the bill with delicious small plates, wines by the glass, well-mixed shaken or stirred cocktails (€13), and formidable Hot Gin and Philadelphia Fish House punches to share.

LA MACHINE DU MOULIN ROUGE   CLUB
Map p378 (www.lamachinedumoulinrouge.com; 90 bd de Clichy, 18e; admission €9 to €15; ⏰11pm-

6am Fri & Sat, variable Sun-Thu; MBlanche) Part of the original Moulin Rouge (well, the boiler room, anyway), this club packs 'em in on weekends with a dance floor, concert hall, Champagne bar and outdoor terrace. Check the agenda online for weekday soirées and happenings.

CAFÉ CHÉRIE
BAR

Map p382 (www.facebook.com/cafe.cherie; 44 bd de la Villette, 19e; ⊙6pm-2am; MBelleville) An imaginative, colourful bar with its signature red lighting, infamous mojitos and caipirinhas and commitment to quality tunes, Chérie is everyone's *chérie* (darling) in this part of town. A gritty art-chic crowd and electro DJs Thursday to Saturday.

CAFÉ DES DEUX MOULINS
CAFE

Map p378 (15 rue Lepic, 18e; ⊙8am-1am; MBlanche) Midway along food-shop-lined rue Lepic is neon-lit Café des Deux Moulins; this is the much-loved cafe where Amélie worked in the eponymous film. Join tourists posing for photographs on the candyfloss-pink chairs outside or push your way into the cinematic interior and join locals for drinks, lunch (2-/3-course *menu* €14.90/17.90) or weekend brunch (€21).

LA FOURMI
BAR

Map p378 (74 rue des Martyrs, 18e; ⊙8am-1am Mon-Thu, to 3am Fri & Sat, 10am-1am Sun; MPigalle) A Pigalle institution, La Fourmi hits the mark with its high ceilings, long zinc bar and unpretentious vibe. Get up to speed on live music and club nights or sit down for a reasonably priced meal and drinks.

☆ ENTERTAINMENT

★PHILHARMONIE DE PARIS
CONCERT VENUE

Map p384 (☎01 44 84 44 84; www.philharmoniedeparis.fr; 221 av Jean Jaurès, 19e; ⊙box office noon-6pm Tue-Fri, 10am-6pm Sat & Sun; MPorte de Pantin) This major complex, comprising the new Philharmonie 1 building by architect Jean Nouvel and the neighbouring Philharmonie 2 building (previously called Cité de la Musique), hosts an eclectic range of concerts in its main 1200-seat Grande Salle and smaller concert halls. There's every imaginable type of music and dance, from classical to North African and Japanese.

Equally entertaining are its atmospheric *ciné* concerts, when a symphonic orchestra, jazz ensemble or organist accompanies a classic film or new box-office film screening.

LE DIVAN DU MONDE
LIVE MUSIC

Map p378 (☎01 40 05 06 99; www.divandumonde.com; 75 rue des Martyrs, 18e; ⊙variable; MPigalle) Take some cinematographic events and *nouvelles chansons françaises* (new French songs). Add in soul/funk fiestas, air-guitar face-offs and rock parties of the Arctic Monkeys/Killers/Libertines persuasion and stir with an Amy Winehouse swizzle stick. You may now be getting some idea of the inventive, open-minded approach at this excellent cross-cultural venue in Pigalle.

MOULIN ROUGE
CABARET

Map p378 (☎01 53 09 82 82; www.moulinrouge.fr; 82 bd de Clichy, 18e; show €105-130, dinner show from €190; ⊙shows 9pm & 11pm summer, 9pm Sun-Thu, 9pm & 11pm Fri & Sat winter; MBlanche) Immortalised in the posters of Toulouse-Lautrec and later on screen by Baz Luhrmann, Paris' mythical cabaret club twinkles beneath a 1925 replica of its original red windmill. Yes, it's rife with bus-tour crowds. But from the opening bars of music to the last high cancan-girl kick, it's a whirl of fantastical costumes, sets, choreography and Champagne.

Book in advance online and dress smart (jacket and tie is advised for men, but not obligatory). No entry for children under six.

LA CIGALE
LIVE MUSIC

Map p378 (☎01 49 25 89 99; www.lacigale.fr; 120 bd de Rochechouart, 18e; tickets €25-75; MAnvers, Pigalle) Now classed as a historical monument, this music hall dates from 1887 but was redecorated 100 years later by Philippe Starck. Artists who have performed here include Rufus Wainwright, Ryan Adams and Ibrahim Maalouf.

LA SCÈNE DU CANAL
CONCERT VENUE

Map p382 (☎01 48 03 33 22; www.lascenedu canal.com; 116 quai de Jemmapes, 10e; MGare de l'Est) French hip-hop, slam and *chanson* blasts on stage inside edgy concert venue **Espace Jemmapes** within La Scène on Canal St-Martin.

ROSA BONHEUR
DANCE HALL

Map p384 (www.rosabonheur.fr; Parc des Buttes Chaumont, 19e; ⊙noon-midnight Thu & Fri, 10am-midnight Sat & Sun; MBotzaris) This

MONTMARTRE & NORTHERN PARIS ENTERTAINMENT

self-styled *guinguette* (old-fashioned dance hall) morphs from outdoor cafe by day into a jam-packed dance floor by night. Its setting inside the Parc des Buttes Chaumont is surely the most bucolic getaway in the city and, even if the tapas aren't to die for, good vibes are virtually guaranteed. If the park is closed, enter at 7 rue Botzaris.

BUS PALLADIUM — LIVE MUSIC

Map p378 (www.lebuspalladium.com; 6 rue Pierre Fontaine, 9e; ⊙variable; MBlanche) The place to be in the 1960s, the Bus is now back in business 50 years later, with funky DJs and a mixed bag of performances by indie and pop groups.

ALHAMBRA — LIVE MUSIC

Map p382 (www.alhambra-paris.com; 21 rue Yves Toudic, 10e; ⊙variable; MRépublique, Jacques Bonsergent) The Subways and Tom Odell are among the artists who have played at this 1930s cinema-theatre, which now serves as a music hall for pop, rock and soul concerts.

POINT ÉPHÉMÈRE — LIVE MUSIC

Map p382 (☎01 40 34 02 48; www.pointephemere. org; 200 quai de Valmy, 10e; ⊙12.30pm-2am Mon-Sat, 12.30-11pm Sun; ☎; MLouis Blanc) This arts and music venue by the Canal St-Martin attracts an underground crowd for drinks, meals, concerts, dance nights and even art exhibitions.

NEW MORNING — JAZZ, BLUES

Map p382 (www.newmorning.com; 7 & 9 rue des Petites Écuries, 10e; ⊙variable; MChâteau d'Eau) This highly regarded auditorium with excellent acoustics that hosts big-name jazz concerts (Ravi Coltrane, Lake Street Dive) as well as a variety of blues, rock, funk, salsa, Afro-Cuban and Brazilian music.

CABARET SAUVAGE — WORLD MUSIC

Map p384 (www.cabaretsauvage.com; 221 av Jean Jaurès, 19e; ⊙variable; MPorte de la Villette) This very cool space in the Parc de la Villette (it looks like a gigantic yurt) is host to African, reggae and raï concerts as well as DJ nights that last till dawn. Occasional hip-hop and indie acts also pass through.

AU LAPIN AGILE — CABARET

Map p378 (☎01 46 06 85 87 www.au-lapin-agile. com; 22 rue des Saules, 18e; adult €28, student except Sat €20; ⊙9pm-1am Tue-Sun; MLamarck-Caulaincour) This rustic cabaret venue was favoured by artists and intellectuals in the early 20th century and traditional chansons are still performed here. The evening-long show includes singing and poetry. Some love it, others feel it's a bit of a trap.

It's named after Le Lapin à Gill, a mural of a rabbit jumping out of a cooking pot by caricaturist André Gill, which can still be seen on the western exterior wall.

LE TRIANON — LIVE MUSIC

Map p378 (☎01 44 92 78 00; www.letrianon.fr; 80 bd de Rochechouart, 18e; ⊙variable; MAnvers) This century-old music hall features two levels of balconies as well as a main floor area. An intimate spot to catch a quality show: think Dr John, John Butler and – flashback – Tower of Power.

🛍 SHOPPING

There are a growing number of boutiques in the Pigalle area – the ultimate cool souvenir is a 'Pigalle' hoodie – but by far the finest strips for fashion lovers are rue Beaurepaire and rue de Marseille by Canal St-Martin. Montmartre has its fair share of souvenir shops aimed squarely at tourists in search of Eiffel Tower keyrings, but for discerning shoppers there are some exquisite specialist boutiques selling everything from handcrafted jewellery to antique perfume bottles and vintage fashion.

★ BELLE DU JOUR — FASHION & ACCESSORIES

Map p378 (www.belle-de-jour.fr; 7 rue Tardieu, 18e; ⊙10.30am-1pm & 2-7pm Tue-Fri, 10.30am-1pm & 2-6pm Sat; MAnvers) Be whisked back in time to the elegance of belle époque Paris with this sweet-smelling Montmartre shop specialising in perfume bottles. Gorgeous 19th-century atomisers, smelling salts and powder boxes in engraved or enamelled Bohemian, Baccarat and Saint-Louis crystal jostle for the limelight with more contemporary designs. Whether you're after art deco or art nouveau, pink-frosted or painted glass, it's here.

★ PIGALLE — FASHION & ACCESSORIES

Map p378 (www.pigalle-paris.com; 7 rue Henry Monnier, 9e; ⊙noon-8pm Mon-Sat, 2-8pm Sun; MPigalle) Blend in with local hipsters with a hoodie emblazoned with the B&W Pigalle logo from this leading Parisian menswear brand, created by wild-child designer and amateur basketball player Stéphane Ashpool, who grew up in the 'hood.

⭐ **MAISON KITSUNÉ** FASHION & ACCESSORIES

Map p378 (www.shop.kitsune.fr; 68 rue Condorcet, 9e; ⏰1.30-7pm Mon-Sat, noon-6.30pm Sun; Ⓜ Pigalle) Paris fashion label Kitsuné is the secret to looking effortlessly French. Shop here for ready-to-wear fashion, accessories and must-have everyday items for men and women.

⭐ **FROMAGERIE ALLÉOSSE** CHEESE

Map p385 (www.alleosse.com; 13 rue Poncelet, 17e; ⏰9am-1.15pm & 3-7.15pm Tue-Fri, 9am-7pm Sat, 9am-1pm Sun; Ⓜ Ternes) Although there are cheese shops throughout the city, this one is actually worth a trip across town. Cheeses are sold as they should be, grouped into five main categories: *fromage de chèvre* (goat's-milk cheese), *fromage à pâte persillée* (veined or blue cheese), *fromage à pâte molle* (soft cheese), *fromage à pâte demi-dure* (semihard cheese) and *fromage à pâte dure* (hard cheese).

SPREE FASHION & ACCESSORIES

Map p378 (☎01 42 23 41 40; www.spree.fr; 16 rue de la Vieuville, 18e; ⏰11am-7.30pm Tue-Sat, 3-7pm Mon & Sun; Ⓜ Abbesses) Sift through Montmartre's tourist shops to find its superstylish boutique-gallery, with a carefully curated collection of vintage fashion (1950s to 1980s) put together by Paris stylist Roberta Oprandi. What makes shopping here fun is that all the furniture – several lovely 1950s and 1960s pieces by Eames et al – is also for sale, as is the contemporary artwork on the walls.

Allow plenty of time to mooch.

JEREMIE BARTHOD JEWELLERY

Map p378 (www.jeremiebarthod.com; 7 rue des Trois Frères, 18e; ⏰11.15am-7.15pm; Ⓜ Abbesses) Fantasy necklaces, bracelets and other jewellery pieces are crafted from metal springs dipped in antique silver, bronze or copper at this hybrid boutique-atelier (workshop) in Montmartre.

TOMBÉES DU CAMION GIFTS & SOUVENIRS

Map p378 (www.tombeesducamion.com; 17 rue Joseph de Maistre, 18e; ⏰1-8pm; Ⓜ Place de Clichy) For something different, rummage through the trays of secondhand and vintage knick-knacks – miniature toys, bottles, dolls, ornaments, pillboxes, everything you can imagine – arranged with military

WORTH A DETOUR

MARCHÉ AUX PUCES DE ST-OUEN

Vast flea market **Marché aux Puces de St-Ouen** (www.marcheauxpuces-saintouen.com; rue des Rosiers; ⏰variable; Ⓜ Porte de Clignancourt), founded in the late 19th century and said to be Europe's largest, has more than 2500 stalls grouped into 15 *marchés* (markets), each with its own speciality (eg Marché Paul Bert Serpette for 17th-century furniture, Marché Malik for casual clothing, Marché Biron for Asian art). Each market has different opening hours – check the website for details.

precision in this tiny specialist shop. Its tongue-in-cheek name translates as 'Fallen off the Truck'.

CENTRE COMMERCIAL FASHION & ACCESSORIES

Map p382 (www.centrecommercial.cc; 2 rue de Marseille, 10e; ⏰1-7.30pm Mon, 11am-8pm Tue-Sat, 2-7pm Sun; Ⓜ Jacques Bonsergent) This cucumber-cool concept store near Canal St-Martin is first choice for sustainable French-made fashion for men and women, and lifestyle objects for the home. Its peppermint- and pine-perfumed mug candles, handmade in Paris, make beautiful gifts to take home.

ANTOINE ET LILI FASHION & ACCESSORIES, HOMEWARES

Map p382 (www.antoineetlili.com; 95 quai de Valmy, 10e; ⏰11am-8pm Tue-Fri, to 7pm Sun & Mon; Ⓜ Jacques Bonsergent, Gare de l'Est) All the colours of the rainbow and all the patterns in the world congregate in this wonderful Parisian institution with designer clothing for women (pink store) and children (green store), and hip home decorations (yellow store).

MAJE STOCK FASHION & ACCESSORIES

Map p382 (6 rue de Marseille, 10e; ⏰11am-8pm Mon-Sat, 1.30-7.30pm Sun; Ⓜ Jacques Bonsergent) A Parisian prêt-à-porter brand featured regularly on the pages of *Elle, Glamour* and *Marie Claire,* Maje doesn't come cheaply – that is, unless you know about this outlet store, which sells most items at a 30% discount.

Le Marais, Ménilmontant & Belleville

LE MARAIS | MÉNILMONTANT & BELLEVILLE

Neighbourhood Top Five

1 Cimetière du Père Lachaise (p157) Admiring incredible sculptures and tomb art while paying your respects to the rich, famous and infamous buried in the world's most visited cemetery.

2 Place des Vosges (p160) Appreciating the exquisite architecture surrounding Paris' oldest square.

3 Musée National Picasso (p161) Immersing yourself in the life and art of one of the world's most eccentric modern artists, Pablo Picasso, and admiring the museum's exquisitely grand, 17th-century home.

4 Hôtel de Ville (p160) Living the high life for free with a world-class art exhibition at Paris' neo-Renaissance city hall followed by twirling on ice or flopping on a Seine-side beach.

5 Mémorial de la Shoah (p156) Learning about German-occupied Paris and Holocaust horrors.

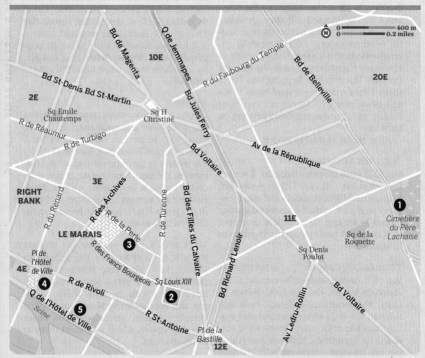

For more detail of this area see Map p386 and p390 ➡

Explore: Le Marais, Ménilmontant & Belleville

Sublime place des Vosges is a perfect starting point – the city square is a triumph of architectural symmetry and of that understated *bon goût* Paris does so well. Meander west along rue de Rivoli or rue du Roi de Sicile, a parallel twinset with shops, cafes and bars. Essential for history buffs is the Mémorial de la Shoah, a two-minute walk from some of the city's best coffee at La Caféothèque.

Bearing north towards the Haut Marais, hipster strips laden with drinking and dining options include rue Vieille du Temple near the Musée National Picasso, rue du Bourg Tibourg, and rue des Rosiers in the heart of the historic Jewish quarter Pletzl.

Bar-busy rue Oberkampf and rue Jean-Pierre Timbaud duck east into the working-class district of Ménilmontant and, further on, increasingly appealing Belleville.

In summer, make a point of heading to the river for a flop on the sand on the Seine-side quays immediately west of Pont de Sully – host to Paris Plages in July and August.

Local Life

→**Cafe life** No single address promises complete immersion into local life quite like the open-all-hours Fluctuat Nec Mergitur (p171), an unpretentious cafe with the perfect people-watching terrace.

→**A market lunch** Lunch with locals around communal tables in Paris' oldest covered market, Marché des Enfants Rouges (p168).

→**Belleville** Leave the crowds behind in this vibrant, multicultural and staunchly working-class 'village', old haunt of Édith Piaf and new haunt of trendsetters.

→**Detox!** Juice bars, organic cafes and gluten-free bakeries have arrived in Le Marais, much to the joy of local hipsters who can't get enough of Wild & the Moon (p171), Café Pinson (p163) and Chambelland (p169).

Getting There & Away

→**Metro** Stops for the lower Marais include Hôtel de Ville and St-Paul (line 1), Rambuteau (line 11), or Filles du Calvaire and St-Sébastien-Froissart (line 8). For the Haut Marais, get off at Temple (line 3); for Ménilmontant, hop off at Belleville (lines 2 and 11), Couronnes or Ménilmontant (line 2), or Oberkampf (line 5).

→**Bus** Le Marais is well served by buses, including bus 29 from rue des Francs Bourgeois to Bastille and Gare de Lyon, and bus 76 from rue de Rivoli to the 20e and Porte de Bagnolet.

→**Bicycle** Handy Vélib' stations: 7 place de l'Hôtel de Ville, 49 rue Rambuteau and place Pasdeloup (next to Filles du Calvaire). In Ménilmontant try 81bis rue Jean-Pierre Timbaud or 137 bd de Ménilmontant.

Lonely Planet's Top Tip

When the hip crowd gets too much, take a break with a peaceful Parisian picnic. Grab a sandwich or fast-food bite and picnic in the Musée des Archives Nationales gardens; by the Seine on a wooden lounger or sun deck between Pont d'Arcole and Pont Louis-Philippe; with sweeping city views in Parc de Belleville; or between flowers on Square de la Roquette, 11e.

 Best Places to Eat

→ Breizh Café (p163)

→ Le Clown Bar (p167)

→ Pierre Sang Boyer (p170)

→ Au Passage (p167)

For reviews, see p163. ➡

 Best Places to Drink

→ Le Mary Céleste (p171)

→ Wild & the Moon (p171)

→ Fluctuat Nec Mergitur (p171)

→ L'Ebouillanté (p171)

→ Le Petit Fer à Cheval (p171)

For reviews, see p171. ➡

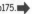 **Best Shopping**

→ Merci (p176)

→ Les Exprimeurs (p176)

→ Maison Kitsuné (p175)

→ Made by Moi (p179)

→ Paris Rendez-Vous (p176)

For reviews, see p175. ➡

TOP SIGHT
MÉMORIAL DE LA SHOAH

No single sight in Paris is as exhaustive or emotionally exhausting as this. Founded in 1956 as a memorial to the unknown Jewish martyr, the Mémorial de la Shoah is now one of Europe's most important Holocaust museums and documentation centres. A vast permanent collection and well-thought-out temporary exhibits all pertain to the Holocaust and the German occupation of parts of France and Paris during WWII.

The entrance to the Mémorial de la Shoah remembers the victims of the Shoah – a Hebrew word meaning 'catastrophe' that's synonymous in France with the Holocaust – with the Mur des Noms (Wall of Names; 2006), a wall inscribed with the names of 76,000 Jews, including 11,000 children, deported from France to Nazi extermination camps during WWII. Most died in Auschwitz and other camps between 1942 and 1944; only 2500 survived deportation.

Deep in the appropriately sombre, bunker-like building lies the crypt and tomb to the unknown Jewish martyr – all six million Jews with no grave of their own. Ashes from some Jews who died in death camps and also the Warsaw ghetto are entombed in the star of David, sculpted from black marble and pierced in its centre with an eternal flame.

DON'T MISS

➤ Mur des Noms
➤ Crypt
➤ Guided tours in English, 3pm second Sunday of month

PRACTICALITIES

➤ Map p386, B7
➤ www.memorialdelashoah.org
➤ 17 rue Geoffroy l'Asnier, 4e
➤ admission free
➤ ⏰10am-6pm Sun-Wed & Fri, to 10pm Thu
➤ Ⓜ St-Paul

TOP SIGHT
CIMETIÈRE DU PÈRE LACHAISE

The world's most visited cemetery opened in 1804. Its 44 hectares hold more than 70,000 ornate tombs – a stroll here is akin to exploring a verdant sculpture garden. Père Lachaise was intended for Parisians as a response to local neighbourhood graveyards being full. It was ground-breaking for Parisians to be buried outside the *quartier* in which they'd lived.

Paris residency was the only criterion needed to be buried in Père Lachaise, hence the cemetery's cosmopolitan population. Among the 800,000-odd buried here are the composer Chopin; the playwright Molière; the poet Apollinaire; writers Balzac, Proust, Gertrude Stein and Colette; the actors Simone Signoret, Sarah Bernhardt and Yves Montand; the painters Pissarro, Seurat, Modigliani and Delacroix; the *chanteuse* Édith Piaf alongside her two-year-old daughter; and the dancer Isadora Duncan.

The grave of Irish playwright and humorist Oscar Wilde (1854–1900), division 89, is among the most visited (as the unfortunate glass barrier erected around his sculpted tomb, designed to prevent fans impregnating the stone with red lipstick imprints, attests). The other big hitter, likewise barricaded from over-zealous fans, is 1960s rock star Jim Morrison (1943–71) who died in his Le Marais home (Map p386; 17 rue Beautreillis, 4e; Ⓜ St-Paul), in division 6.

Up in division 92, protests saw the removal of a fence around the grave of Monsieur Noir, aka journalist Yvan Salman (1848–70), shot aged 22 by Pierre Bonaparte, great-nephew of Napoléon. Legend says women who stroke the amply filled crotch of Monsieur Noir's prostrate bronze effigy will enjoy a better sex life and fertility.

Commemorative memorials to victims of almost every war in modern history form a poignant alley alongside the Mur des Fédérés, an unmemorable plain brick wall against which Communard insurgents were lined up, shot and buried in a mass grave in 1871.

DON'T MISS

➡ Jim Morrison
➡ Édith Piaf
➡ Oscar Wilde
➡ Monsieur Noir
➡ Mur des Fédérés and commemorative war memorials

PRACTICALITIES

➡ ☑ 01 55 25 82 10
➡ www.pere-lachaise.com
➡ 16 rue du Repos & 8 bd de Ménilmontant, 20e
➡ ⊘ 8am-6pm Mon-Fri, 8.30am-6pm Sat, 9am-6pm Sun, shorter hours winter
➡ Ⓜ Père Lachaise, Gambetta

Cimetière du Père Lachaise

A HALF-DAY TOUR

There is a certain romance to getting lost in Cimetière du Père Lachaise, a grave jungle spun from centuries of tales. But to search for one grave among one million in this 44-hectare land of the dead is no joke – narrow the search with this itinerary.

From the main bd de Ménilmontant entrance (metro Père Lachaise or Philippe Auguste), head up av Principale, turn right onto av du Puits and collect a map from the **Bureaux de la Conservation ❶**.

Backtrack along av du Puits, turn right onto av Latérale du Sud, scale the stairs and bear right along chemin Denon to New Realist artist **Arman ❷**, film director **Claude Chabrol ❸** and **Chopin ❹**.

Follow chemin Méhul downhill, cross av Casimir Périer and bear right onto chemin Serré. Take the second left (chemin Lebrun – unsigned), head uphill and near the top leave the footpath to weave through graves on your right to rock star **Jim Morrison ❺**. Back on chemin Lauriston, continue uphill to roundabout **Rond-Point Casimir Périer ❻**.

Admire the funerary art of contemporary photographer **André Chabot ❼**, av de la Chapelle. Continue uphill for energising city views from the **chapel ❽** steps, then zig-zag to **Molière & La Fontaine ❾**, on chemin Molière.

Cut between graves onto av Tranversale No 1 – spot potatoes atop **Parmentier's ❿** headstone. Continue straight onto av Greffülhe and left onto av Tranversale No 2 to rub **Monsieur Noir's ⓫** shiny crotch.

Navigation to **Édith Piaf ⓬** and the **Mur des Fédérés ⓭** is straightforward. End with lipstick-kissed **Oscar Wilde ⓮** near the Porte Gambetta entrance.

TOP TIPS

➡ **Say 'Cheese!'** Père Lachaise is photography paradise any time of day/year, but best are sunny autumn mornings after the rain.

➡ **Guided Tours** Cemetery lovers will appreciate themed guided tours (two hours) led by entertaining cemetery historian Thierry Le Roi (www.necro-romantiques.com).

BRUNO DE HOGUES / GETTY IMAGES ©

Chopin, Division 11
Add a devotional note to the handwritten letters and flowers brightening the marble tomb of Polish composer/pianist Frédéric Chopin (1810–49), who spent his short adult life in Paris. His heart is buried in Warsaw.

Jim Morrison, Division 6
The original bust adorning the disgracefully dishevelled grave of Jim Morrison (1943–71), lead singer of The Doors, was stolen. Pay your respects to rock's greatest legend – no chewing gum or padlocks please.

DAN HERRICK / GETTY IMAGES ©

André Chabot, Division 20
Contemporary photographer André Chabot (b 1941) shoots funerary art, hence the bijou 19th-century chapel he's equipped with monumental granite camera in preparation for the day he departs – and a QR code.

Molière & La Fontaine, Division 25
Parisians refused to leave their local *quartier* for Père Lachaise so in 1817 the authorities moved in popular playwright Molière (1622–73) and poet Jean de la Fontaine (1621–95). The marketing strategy worked.

Oscar Wilde, Division 89
Homosexual Irish writer Oscar Wilde (1854–1900) was forever scandalous: check the enormous packet of the sphinx on his tomb, sculpted by British-American sculptor Jacob Epstein 11 years after he died.

Monsieur Noir, Division 92
Cemetery sex stud Mr Black, alias 21-year-old journalist Victor Noir (1848–70), was shot by Napolèon III's nephew in a botched duel. Urban myth means women rub his crotch to boost fertility.

Édith Piaf, Division 97
The archbishop of Paris might have refused Parisian diva Édith Piaf (1915–63) the Catholic rite of burial, but that didn't stop more than 100,000 mourners attending her internment at Père Lachaise.

Mur des Fédérés, Division 76
This plain brick wall was where 147 Communard insurgents were lined up and shot in 1871. Equally emotive is the sculpted walkway of commemorative war memorials surrounding the mass grave.

Chapel

av des Combattants Étrangers morts pour la France

Porte Gambetta Entrance

Crematorium

av Circulaire

av Tranversale No 3

chemin Bertholle

av de Saint Morys

av Tranversale No 1

av Tranversale No 2

chemin Molière

av Greffülhe

Rond-Point Casimir Périer

av Pacthod

chemin Lauriston

Commemorative war memorials

chemin Lebrun

Porte de la Réunion

av Circulaire

BRUNO DE HOGUES / GETTY IMAGES ©
ALAIN COPSON / GETTY IMAGES ©

⊙ SIGHTS

The Marais (meaning 'marsh' or 'swamp' in French) was exactly what its name implies right up until the 13th century, when it was converted to farmland. In the early 17th century Henri IV built place Royale (today's place des Vosges), turning the area into Paris' most fashionable residential address. When the aristocracy moved out of Paris to Versailles and Faubourg St-Germain, the Marais and its townhouses passed into the hands of ordinary Parisians. The 110-hectare area was given a major facelift in the late 1960s and early '70s, and today it is one of the city's most coveted addresses.

⊙ Le Marais

MÉMORIAL DE LA SHOAH   MUSEUM

See p156.

HÔTEL DE VILLE   ARCHITECTURE

Map p386 (www.paris.fr; place de l'Hôtel de Ville, 4e; Ⓜ Hôtel de Ville) FREE Paris' beautiful town hall was gutted during the Paris Commune of 1871 and rebuilt in luxurious neo-Renaissance style between 1874 and 1882. The ornate facade is decorated with 108 statues of illustrious Parisians, and the outstanding temporary exhibitions (admission free) held inside in its Salle St-Jean almost always have a Parisian theme.

During most winters from December to early March, an ice-skating rink is set up outside this beautiful building, creating a real picture-book experience.

★PLACE DES VOSGES   SQUARE

Map p386 (place des Vosges, 4e; Ⓜ St-Paul, Bastille) Inaugurated in 1612 as place Royale and thus Paris' oldest square, place des Vosges is a strikingly elegant ensemble of 36 symmetrical houses with ground-floor arcades, steep slate roofs and large dormer windows arranged around a leafy square with four symmetrical fountains and an 1829 copy of a mounted statue of Louis XIII. The square received its present name in 1800 to honour the Vosges *département* (administrative division) for being the first in France to pay its taxes.

In Paris, only the earliest houses were built of brick; to save time, the rest were given timber frames and faced with plaster, later painted to resemble brick.

MAISON DE VICTOR HUGO   MUSEUM

Map p386 (www.musee-hugo.paris.fr; 6 place des Vosges, 4e; ◷10am-6pm Tue-Sun; Ⓜ St-Paul, Bastille) FREE Between 1832 and 1848 the writer Victor Hugo lived in an apartment in Hôtel de Rohan-Guéménée, a townhouse overlooking one of Paris' most elegant squares. He moved here a year after the publication of *Notre Dame de Paris* (The Hunchback of Notre Dame), completing *Ruy Blas* during his stay. His house is now a museum devoted to the life of this celebrated novelist and poet, with an impressive collection of his personal drawings and portraits. Temporary exhibitions command an admission fee.

HÔTEL DE SULLY   HISTORIC MANSION

Map p386 (62 rue St-Antoine, 4e; Ⓜ St-Paul, Bastille) In the southwestern corner of place des Vosges is the back entrance to this aristocratic mansion, built in 1625 and home to the headquarters of the Centre des Monuments Nationaux, responsible for many of France's historical monuments. From the square, duck beneath the arch and be instantly wooed by two beautifully decorated, late-Renaissance courtyards, both festooned with allegorical reliefs of the seasons and the elements.

In the northern courtyard look to the southern side for spring (flowers and a bird in hand) and summer (wheat sheaves); in the southern courtyard turn to the northern side for autumn (grapes) and winter, with a symbol representing both the end of the year and the end of life. In the second courtyard are symbols for the elements: on the western side 'air' on the left and 'fire' on the right, and on the eastern side 'earth' on the left and 'water' on the right.

MUSÉE DE LA MAGIE   MUSEUM

Map p386 (☎01 42 72 13 26; www.museedelamagie.com; 11 rue St-Paul, 4e; adult/child €9/7; ◷2-7pm Wed, Sat & Sun; Ⓜ St-Paul) The ancient arts of magic, optical illusion and sleight of hand are explored in this museum, in the 16th-century *caves* (cellars) of the Marquis de Sade's former home. Admission includes a magic show, and a combination ticket covering entry to the adjoining Musée des Automates – a collection of antique wind-up toys – is also available (adult/child €12/9).

★MUSÉE NATIONAL PICASSO ART MUSEUM
Map p386 (☎01 85 56 00 36; www.museepi-cassoparis.fr; 5 rue de Thorigny, 3e; adult/child €12.50/free; ⊙11.30am-6pm Tue-Fri, 9.30am-6pm Sat & Sun; MSt-Paul, Chemin Vert) One of Paris' most beloved art collections is showcased inside the mid-17th-century Hôtel Salé, an exquisite private mansion owned by the city since 1964. Inside is the Musée National Picasso, a staggering art museum devoted to the eccentric Spanish artist, Pablo Picasso (1881–1973), who spent much of his life living and working in Paris. The collection includes more than 5000 drawings, engravings, paintings, ceramic works and sculptures by the *grand maître* (great master), although they're not all displayed at the same time.

The extraordinary collection was donated to the French government by the artist's heirs in lieu of paying inheritance tax. Until the end of 2016 there is no permanent collection in the museum – instead it is hosting one or two exhibitions each year focusing on a different aspect of Picasso's work (from 2017 it is hoped that this will change and a permanent collection will be established). End your visit with a coffee in the rooftop cafe, eye to eye with an ancient stone sphinx.

MUSÉE COGNACQ-JAY MUSEUM
Map p386 (www.cognacq-jay.paris.fr; 8 rue Elzévir, 3e; ⊙10am-6pm Tue-Sun; MSt-Paul, Chemin Vert) FREE This museum inside Hôtel de Donon displays oil paintings, pastels, sculpture, objets d'art, jewellery, porcelain and furniture from the 18th century assembled by Ernest Cognacq (1839–1928), founder of La Samaritaine department store, and his wife Louise Jay.

Although Cognacq appreciated little of his collection, boasting that he had never visited the Louvre and was only acquiring collections for the status, the artwork and objets d'art give a good idea of upper-class tastes during the Age of Enlightenment.

MAISON EUROPÉENNE DE LA
PHOTOGRAPHIE MUSEUM
Map p386 (www.mep-fr.org; 5-7 rue de Fourcy, 4e; adult/child €8/4.50; ⊙11am-7.45pm Wed-Sun; MSt-Paul, Pont Marie) The European House of Photography, housed in the overly renovated Hôtel Hénault de Cantobre (dating – believe it or not – from the early 18th century), has cutting-edge temporary exhibits (usually retrospectives on single photographers), as well as an enormous permanent collection on the history of photography and its connections with France.

There are frequent showings of short films and documentaries on weekend afternoons. The Japanese garden at the entrance is a delight.

★MUSÉE DES ARTS ET MÉTIERS MUSEUM
Map p386 (www.arts-et-metiers.net; 60 rue de Réaumur, 3e; adult/child €8/free; ⊙10am-6pm Tue, Wed & Fri-Sun, to 9.30pm Thu; ♿; MArts et

---

JEWISH PLETZL

Expensive boutiques elbow Jewish bookshops and shops selling religious goods, *cacher* (kosher) grocery shops, butchers, restaurants and takeaway felafel joints in Pletzl (from the Yiddish for 'little square'), the colourful Jewish quarter where the Marais' long-established Jewish community is right at home. It starts in rue des Rosiers and continues along rue Ste-Croix de la Bretonnerie to rue du Temple. Don't miss the **art nouveau synagogue** (Map p386; 10 rue Pavée, 4e; MSt-Paul) designed in 1913 by Hector Guimard, who was also responsible for the city's famous metro entrances.

To delve into the historic heart of this long-established Jewish community, visit the **Musée d'Art et d'Histoire du Judaïsme** (Map p386; ☎01 53 01 86 62; www.mahj.org; 71 rue du Temple, 4e; adult/child €8/free; ⊙11am-6pm Mon-Fri, 10am-6pm Sun; MRambuteau), housed in Pletzl's sumptuous Hôtel de St-Aignan, dating from 1650. The Museum of the Art and History of Judaism traces the evolution of Jewish communities from the Middle Ages to the present, with particular emphasis on French Jewish history and the history of Jewish communities in other parts of Europe and North Africa. Highlights include documents relating to the Dreyfus Affair and works by Chagall, Modigliani and Soutine. A creative array of music, writing and history workshops for children, adults and families complement the excellent exhibitions; see its website for details.

Métiers) The Arts and Crafts Museum, dating to 1794 and Europe's oldest science and technology museum, is a must for anyone with kids – or an interest in how things tick or work. Housed inside the sublime 18th-century priory of St-Martin des Champs, some 3000 instruments, machines and working models from the 18th to 20th centuries are displayed across three floors. In the attached church of St-Martin des Champs is Foucault's original pendulum, introduced to the world at the Universal Exhibition in Paris 1855.

Louis Blériot's monoplane from 1909 is also here. Guided tours are in French only but the excellent English audioguides (€5) – one for adults and another aimed squarely at children aged seven to 12 years – more than compensates.

MUSÉE DES ARCHIVES
NATIONALES   MUSEUM
Map p386 (☎01 40 27 60 96; www.archives-nationales.culture.gouv.fr; 60 rue des Francs Bourgeois, 3e; adult/child €3/free; ⊙10am-5.30pm Mon & Wed-Fri, 2-5.30pm Sat & Sun; MRambuteau, St-Paul) The greatest appeal of the National Archives and its small museum is the stunning twinset of *hôtels particuliers* (mansions) they are squirreled away in along with their stunning gardens. Dating from the early 18th century, Hôtel de Rohan and Hôtel de Soubise are extravagantly painted and gilded in the rococo style inside, with antique furniture and 18th-century paintings alongside a rather dry collection of documents on display (the most interesting and precious are hidden away in the archives).

Admission is more expensive during temporary exhibitions.

MUSÉE DE LA CHASSE
ET DE LA NATURE   MUSEUM
Map p386 (www.chassenature.org; 62 rue des Archives, 3e; adult/child €8/free; ⊙11am-6pm Tue, Thu-Sun, to 9.30pm Wed; MRambuteau, Hôtel de Ville) The Hunting and Nature Museum, inside the delightful Hôtel de Guénégaud (1651), is positively crammed with weapons, paintings, sculptures and objets d'art related to hunting and, of course, lots and lots of trophies (horns, antlers, heads). Particularly appealing are its nature-themed workshops for children.

MUSÉE DE LA POUPÉE   MUSEUM
Map p386 (☎01 42 72 73 11; www.museedela poupeeparis.com; Impasse Berthaud, 3e; adult/child €8/4; ⊙1-6pm Tue-Sat; ⊕; MRambuteau) Frightening to some – all those beady little eyes and silent screams – the Doll Museum is as much for adults as it is for kids. Ogle at 500-odd dolls dating back to 1800, arranged in scenes representing the Parises of yesteryear. Well worth looking into are the creative, one-hour workshops it runs for children (€10 to €15).

◉ Ménilmontant & Belleville

CIMETIÈRE DU PÈRE LACHAISE   CEMETERY
See p157.

BRASSERIE BAPBAP   BREWERY
Map p390 (☎01 77 17 52 97; www.bapbap.paris; 79 rue St-Maur, 11e; guided tour €10; ⊙5-7pm Mon-Fri, 2-7pm Sat; MSt-Maur) This young microbrewery, whose name means 'Brassée à Paris, Bue à Paris' (Brewed in Paris, Beloved in Paris), brews craft beer in an early-20th-century warehouse-turned-garage with an Eiffel-style metal structure. Saturday brewery visits (one hour; book online) include a peek at the filtering, boiling, whirlpool and fermentation tanks in the Brew House where the beer comes to life, plus tastings. If the brewery is shut when you pass by, nip into neighbouring **Hop Malt Market** (Map p390; ☎01 55 28 77 24; www.facebook.com/hmmarket75; 79 rue Saint-Maur, 11e; ⊙9.30am-

> **LOCAL KNOWLEDGE**
>
> ## BELLEVILLE STREET ART
>
> From Belleville metro station, walk east uphill along rue de Belleville and look for the red neon lights of **Aux Folies** (Map p390; ☏06 28 55 89 40; www.aux-folies-belleville.fr; 8 rue de Belleville, 19e; ⊙7am-2am; ⓂBelleville), the Belleville neighbourhood cafe where Édith Piaf used to sing. Turn right onto pedestrian rue Dénoyez, 20e, to be mesmerised by some of Paris' most dazzling street art. Everything on the small pedestrian street, from litter bins and flower pots to lamp posts and window shutters, is covered in colourful graffiti. Artists' workshops pepper the street where local kids kick footballs around and street art 'happenings' break out on sultry summer nights. Break for a drink or lunch at **Le Barbouquin** (Map p390; ☏09 84 32 13 21; www.lebarbouquin.fr; 1 rue Dénoyez, 20e; ⊙9am-7pm Mon-Fri, 10am-8pm Sat & Sun; ⓂBelleville) or **Felicity Lemon** (Map p390; ☏01 71 32 71 11; www.facebook.com/felictylemon.restaurant; 4 rue Lemon, 20e; 2/3 courses €13.50/18; ⊙noon-2.30pm Wed-Sat, plus 7-10.30pm Tue-Sat; ⓂBelleville).

2pm & 3.30pm-1.30am; ⓂSt-Maur) to buy some bottles.

Blue-labelled BapBap Originale is a fruity pale ale mixing wheat and barley malts with hops; yellow-labelled Blanc Bec is like an American wheat beer; while red Vertigo is a dry India pale ale with lots of fabulous hoppy body.

MUSÉE ÉDITH PIAF
MUSEUM

Map p390 (☏01 43 55 52 72; 5 rue Crespin du Gast, 11e; adult/child €4/free; ⊙by apt 1-6pm Mon-Wed; ⓂMénilmontant) **FREE** This private museum in Ménilmontant, some 1.5km from the birthplace of the iconic singer Édith Piaf and closer to her final resting place in Cimetière du Père Lachaise, follows the life and career of the 'urchin sparrow' through memorabilia, recordings, personal objects, letters and other documentation. Admission by reservation, at least eight days in advance.

✖ EATING

Packed with restaurants and bistros of every imaginable type, Le Marais is one of Paris' premier dining neighbourhoods with many addresses requiring an advance reservation. Despite the huge concentration of eating addresses, new openings pop up seemingly every week. Multiethnic Belleville is tops for tasty Asian fare. Looking east, some of Paris' hippest addresses in the Bastille and Eastern Paris neighbourhood are easy walking distance from Cimetière du Père Lachaise – perfect for lunch or dinner post-grave walking.

✖ Le Marais

★JACQUES GENIN
PATISSERIE €

Map p386 (☏01 45 77 29 01; 133 rue de Turenne, 3e; pastry €9; ⊙11am-7pm Tue-Sun; ⓂOberkampf) Wildly creative *chocolatier* Jacques Genin is famed for his flavoured caramels, *pâtes de fruits* (fruit jellies) and exquisitely embossed *bonbons de chocolat* (chocolate sweets). But what completely steals the show at his elegant chocolate showroom is the *salon de dégustation* (aka tearoom), where you can order a pot of outrageously thick hot chocolate and legendary Genin millefeuille, assembled to order.

★BREIZH CAFÉ
CRÊPERIE €

Map p386 (www.breizhcafe.com; 109 rue Vieille du Temple, 3e; crêpes & galettes €6.50-18; ⊙11.30am-11pm Wed-Sat, to 10pm Sun; ⓂSt-Sébastien-Froissart) It is a well-known fact among Parisians: everything at the Breton Café (*breizh* is 'Breton' in Breton) is 100% authentic, rendering it the top spot in the city for authentic crêpes. Be it the Cancale oysters, 20 types of cider or the buttery organic-flour crêpes, everything here is cooked to perfection. If you fail to snag a table, try **L'Épicerie** (Map p386; http://breizh-cafe.com; 111 rue Vieille du Temple, 3e; crêpes & galettes €6.50-17.80; ⊙11.30am-9pm; ⓂSt-Sébastien-Froissart) next door.

★CAFÉ PINSON
CAFE €

Map p386 (☏09 83 82 53 53; www.cafepinson.fr; 6 rue du Forez, 3e; mains €14; ⊙9am-10pm Mon-Fri, 10am-10pm Sat, noon-6pm Sun; 🛜🕹; ⓂFilles du Calvaire) 🍃 This small lifestyle cafe, with an interior by celebrity designer Dorothée Meilichzon, is tucked down an alley in the

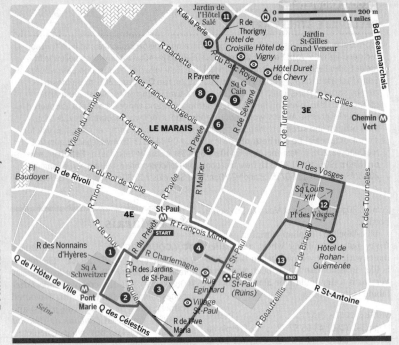

Neighbourhood Walk
Medieval Marais Meanderings

START METRO ST-PAUL
END HÔTEL DE SULLY
LENGTH 2KM; 1½ HOURS

While Henri IV was busy having place Royale (today's place des Vosges) built, aristocrats were commissioning gold-brick *hôtels particuliers* – the city's most beautiful Renaissance structures that lend the Marais a particular architectural harmony.

At 7 rue de Jouy stands majestic **❶ Hôtel d'Aumont**, built around 1650 for a financier. Continue south along rue des Nonnains d'Hyères and turn left onto rue de l'Hôtel de Ville. At 1 rue du Figuier is **❷ Hôtel de Sens**, the oldest Marais mansion, with geometric gardens and a neo-Gothic turret. Begun around 1475, it was built as digs for the archbishops of Sens. It was restored in mock Gothic style in 1911.

Continue southeast along rue de l'Ave Maria, then northeast along rue des Jardins de St-Paul. To the left, two truncated towers are all that remain of Philippe-Auguste's **❸ enceinte**, a fortified wall built in 1190 and

once guarded by 39 towers. Cross rue Charlemagne, duck into rue Eginhard and follow it to rue St-Paul and **❹ Église St-Paul St-Louis** (1641). At the end of rue St-Paul, turn left, then walk north up rue Malher and rue Pavée, the first cobbled road in Paris. At No 24 is the late Renaissance **❺ Hôtel Lamoignon**, built for Diane de France (1538–1619), the legitimised daughter of Henri II.

North along rue Payenne is the back of the **❻ Musée Carnavalet** (closed until 2019 for renovations); the Revolutionary-era 'Temple of Reason' **❼ Chapelle de l'Humanité** at No 5; and the rear of the **❽ Musée Cognacq-Jay** (p161). From grassy **❾ Sq George Cain** opposite 11 rue Payenne, walk northwest to more spectacular 17th-century *hôtels particuliers*: **❿ Hôtel de Libéral Bruant** at 1 rue de la Perle, and **⓫ Hôtel Salé**, crammed with Picassos, at 5 rue de Thorigny.

Retrace your steps to rue du Parc Royal, walk south down rue de Sévigné and follow rue des Francs Bourgeois eastwards to end with sublime **⓬ place des Vosges** (p160) and **⓭ Hôtel de Sully** (p160).

fashionable Haut Marais. A trendy lunchtime crowd flocks here for sweet potato felafel, pumpkin-spiked couscous, creative salads and an organic, market-driven menu that changes daily. Its freshly squeezed juices are predictably excellent, and vegetarians and vegans are well catered for. Superb weekend brunch.

★CANDELARIA   MEXICAN €
Map p386 (☏01 42 74 41 28; www.candelaria paris.com; 52 rue de Saintonge, 3e; tacos €3-5; ☺12.30pm-11pm Sun-Wed, 12.30pm-midnight Thu-Sat, bar 6pm-2am; MFilles du Calvaire) You need to know about this terribly cool *taqueria* to find it. Made of pure, unadulterated hipness in that brazenly nonchalant manner Paris does so well, clandestine Candelaria serves delicious homemade tacos, quesadillas and tostadas in a laid-back setting – squat at the bar in the front or lounge out back around a shared table with bar stools or at low coffee tables.

Come dark, the party kicks off with occasional DJ sets, tastings, post-gallery drinks and some of the best cocktails (€12 to €13) in town. Regulars swear by the Bloody Mary and cocktail-fuelled brunch, served until 4pm on weekends.

PROFITEROLE CHÉRIE   PATISSERIE €
Map p386 (https://profiterolecherie.fr; 17 rue Debelleyme, 3e; profiterole €6; ☺12.30-8pm Tue-Fri, 10am-8pm Sat & Sun; MFilles du Calvaire) Celebrity chef Philippe Urraca's shiny boutique is a one-stop shop for the profiterole of your dreams. Fantastical caramel-glazed puffs of choux pastry filled with praline, whipped vanilla cream, strawberry sorbet, caramel and other devilish creams are assembled to order (meaning you can watch the pastry chef in action), and then packed in silver-lined boxes to eat or take away.

A glass of tart, homemade lemonade is the perfect chaser.

SACHA FINKELSZTAJN   DELI €
Map p386 (☏01 42 72 78 91; www.laboutiquejaune.com; rue des Rosiers, 4e; pasties & sandwiches from €4; ☺10am-7pm Wed-Mon; MSt-Paul) Tempting smells waft from the canary-yellow facade of this third-generation delicatessen and bakery, opened by a Polish couple in 1946. Viennese apple strudel, *borek* (pasties) oozing warm goat's cheese, Yiddish sandwiches, plain or meaty *latkes* (fried potato cakes traditionally eaten at Hanukkah), and *pirojki* with cabbage, aubergine or spinach are some of the eastern and central European specialities baked by their grandson today.

Eat in on a couple of bar stools or take away.

MIZNON   ISRAELI €
Map p386 (☏01 42 74 83 58; 22 rue des Écoffes, 4e; pita sandwiches €9-12; ☺noon-1.30pm Sun-Fri; MHôtel de Ville) Parisians cannot get enough of this hip, shabby-chic hangout whose big sister is none other than the Tel Aviv restaurant of celebrity Israeli chef Eyal Shani. Push your way past the grocery crates and cauliflowers to the bar, order a pita or lamb kebab, or a side of the finest hummus in town.

Do not leave without ending on a sweet *banane au chocolat* pita.

MG ROAD   INDIAN €
(☏01 42 76 04 32; http://mgroadrestaurant.com; 205 rue St-Martin, 4e; mains €18-22; ☺noon-midnight Tue-Sat, 11am-3.30pm Sun; MArts et Métiers) With a light and airy vintage decor inspired by the art deco 'Irani' cafes of Bombay in the late 19th century and a creative Indi-Brit menu by London chef Manoj Sharma, this contemporary Indian restaurant has found the winning formula. Between meals the space doubles as a laid-back cafe. Sunday brunch packs the place out; consider reserving in advance.

GIRAUDET   FRENCH €
Map p386 (☏01 42 78 71 62; www.giraudet.fr; 6 rue du Pas de la Mule, 3e; lunch menus €11.50-14.40; ☺10am-7.30pm Tue-Sat, 11am-7pm Sun; ☑; MChemin Vert) Grab a bar stool at a brightly coloured table, sit back, and savour one of France's most unique specialities in this stylish dumpling bar. Pick your quenelles (dumplings) – plain or fish-, poultry- or cheese-flavoured – then select your sauce to go with it, together with a creative homemade soup (chicory and aniseed, chestnut, lobster and vegetable...) and freshly squeezed juice.

Vegetarians are well-catered for with unusual chestnut or vegetable quenelles. If it is sunny, consider a takeaway to enjoy on the green lawns of nearby place des Vosges.

OKOMUSU   JAPANESE €
Map p386 (☏01 57 40 97 27; www.okomusu.com; 11 rue Charlot, 3e; mains €11-17; ☺7-10.30pm Tue, noon-2.30pm & 7-10.30pm Wed-Sun; ☑; MSt-Sébastien-Froissart) Once full – which hap-

pens within seconds of young Japanese chef Hiroko Tabuchi opening her *table d'hôte* – the door is amusingly wedged shut with a spoon. All eyes are then on the chef as she deftly whips up her speciality *okonomiyaki* (a wheat-flour patty with cabbage, chives, ginger, dried fish shavings and pork, prawn or squid), while diners sit hungrily at the bar. Vegetarians can order the non-meat version.

KRAFT HOTDOG   FAST FOOD €

Map p386 (http://krafthotdog.com; 15 rue des Archives, 4e; hot dogs €3.50-5.50; ⊙noon-11pm Mon-Thu & Sun, noon-midnight Fri & Sat; MHôtel de Ville) Based on the line that frequently stretches halfway down the street, Parisians clearly cannot get enough of the gourmet hot dogs rolled out of this New York–style deli in Le Marais. Dogs come in four types plus a choice of sides including nachos. Our current fave: a hot dog smothered in coleslaw, guacamole and honey mustard. Watch for the daily special.

CLASICO ARGENTINO   ARGENTINE €

Map p386 (⏰01 44 61 00 56; www.clasico-argentino.com; 56 rue de Saintonge, 3e; lunch menu €12.50, empanadas €4; ⊙noon-11pm Mon-Sat; ⏺; MFilles du Calvaire) In the finest Argentinian street-food tradition, *empanadas* (pasties stuffed with different savoury fillings) and *helados* (ice cream) form the backbone of this stylish eatery in the Haut Marais, an ode to Argentina with its blue-and-white decor reflecting the country flag, *cinta-pampa*-embossed ceiling and traditional wooden *tablitas* (benches).

Eat in or take away, and watch out for the Clasico Argentino food truck roaming the town.

HURÉ   BOULANGERIE €

Map p386 (⏰01 42 72 32 18; www.hure-createur.fr; 18 rue Rambuteau, 3e; sandwiches €5-10; ⊙6.30am-8.30pm Tue-Sat; MRambuteau) This is a brilliantly contemporary bakery with graffitied red-brick wall, super-stuffed bread rolls, lavish quiches, buxom fruit tarts and éclairs every colour of the rainbow. With your booty stashed, leg it to the bench-clad courtyard garden of the nearby Musée des Archives Nationales (p162) for lunch in the sun.

BROKEN ARM   CAFE €

Map p386 (⏰01 44 61 53 60; 2 rue Perrée, 3e; mains €7.50-18.50; ⊙9am-6pm Tue-Sat, lunch noon-3.30pm; ⏺; MTemple, Arts et Métiers) Kick off with a fresh apple, kiwi and mint juice and congratulate yourself on scoring a table – inside or out – at this overpoweringly hipster address where chic Marais folk lunch after making an appearance in the adjoining concept store. The menu is limited but packed with goodness: imaginative salads, cold platters and cakes. Between meals, snack on designer *tartines* (open sandwiches).

CAFÉ MARAIS   MODERN FRENCH €

Map p386 (⏰01 42 71 61 46; 10 rue des Haudriettes, 3e; lunch/dinner menu €16.50/18.50; ⊙noon-3.30pm Mon & Tue, noon-3.30pm & 7-11pm Wed-Fri, 7-11pm Sat; MArts et Métiers) Exposed stone, a beamed ceiling and silent B&W Charlie Chaplin movies screened on one wall create an appealing vintage feel in this small and excellent bistro – one of the best-value spots for dining in Le Marais. The round of Camembert roasted with honey, homemade courgette gratin and parmesan crème brûlée are all excellent.

NANASHI   FUSION €

Map p386 (⏰09 60 00 25 59; www.nanashi.fr; 57 rue Charlot, 3e; bentos €14-19; ⊙noon-3pm & 7.30-11pm Mon-Fri, noon-4pm & 7.30-11pm Sat & Sun; MFilles du Calvaire) An address that packs a punch in the Haut Marais, this hip industrial space with large street-facing windows and concrete floor is ubercool, ultrahealthy and brilliant value. Pick from the creative salads, soups and bento boxes – always one meat, one fish and one veggie option – chalked on the board. Don't miss the freshly squeezed, frothy-topped apple, carrot and ginger juice.

ROBERT ET LOUISE   TRADITIONAL FRENCH €

Map p386 (⏰01 42 78 55 89; http://robertetlouise.com; 64 rue Vieille du Temple, 4e; mains €13-21; ⊙7-11pm Tue & Wed, noon-3pm & 7-11pm Thu-Sat, noon-11pm Sun; MSt-Sébastien-Froissart) This 'country inn' with red gingham curtains offers simple and inexpensive French food, including *côte de bœuf* (side of beef for two or three people, €46) cooked on an open fire. Arrive early to snag the farmhouse table next to the fireplace – the makings of a real jolly Rabelaisian evening.

L'AS DU FALLAFEL   JEWISH €

Map p386 (34 rue des Rosiers, 4e; takeaway €6-8.50; ⊙noon-midnight Sun-Thu, to 5pm Fri; MSt-Paul) The lunchtime queue stretching halfway down the street from this place says it all. This Parisian favourite, 100% worth the inevitable wait, is *the* address for kosher, perfectly deep-fried felafel (chickpea balls; €6) and turkey or lamb shawarma sandwiches (€8.50). Do as every Parisian does and get takeaway.

HANK   BURGERS €
Map p386 (☑09 72 44 03 99; http://hankburger. com; 55 rue des Archives, 3e; menus €11.80 & €13.80; ☻noon-10pm; ☑; MHôtel de Ville, Rambuteau) There is no meat involved in the burgers rolled out to an appreciative veggie-loving crowd at Hank's. The stylish space is a pleasure to linger in and the kitchen works strictly with fresh, organic and, where possible, local produce.

LA BRICIOLA   PIZZA €
Map p386 (☑01 42 77 34 10; 64 rue Charlot, 3e; pizzas €9.50-15; ☻noon-2.30pm & 7.30pm-midnight Mon-Sat; MOberkampf) Tuck into excellent pizzas, salads and wine at this friendly Italian eatery in the Haut Marais. Don't miss the blackboard, chalked up each day with a different pizza, pasta and salad special.

BOBOLI   ITALIAN €
Map p386 (☑01 42 77 89 27; www.caffeboboli. com; 13 rue du Roi de Sicile, 4e; mains €15; ☻noon-3pm & 7-11pm; MSt-Paul) Affordable, creative Italian fare is good reason to dine at this small, elegant restaurant run by two young Florentines (hence the name, evocative of the beautiful Boboli Gardens in Florence). Lighting is subtle, tables are dark wood, and the menu is short but delicious: the Parma ham and gooey mozzarella wrapped in grilled courgette strips are delicious.

POZZETTO   ICE CREAM €
Map p386 (www.pozzetto.biz; 16 rue Vieille du Temple, 4e; cone or pot €4-7; ☻noon-11.30pm Mon-Thu, to 12.45am Fri & Sat, to midnight Sun; MSt-Paul) Urban myth says this gelato maker opened when friends from northern Italy couldn't find their favourite ice cream in Paris so they imported the ingredients to make it themselves. The 12 flavours – spatula'd, not scooped – include *gianduia* (hazelnut chocolate from Turin) and *zabaione*, made from egg yolks, sugar and sweet Marsala wine. Great Italian *caffè* too.

★AU PASSAGE   BISTRO €€
Map p386 (☑01 73 20 23 23; www.restaurant-au-passage.fr; 1bis passage St-Sébastien, 11e; small plates €7-14, meats to share €18-70; ☻7-11.30pm Mon-Sat; MSt-Sébastien-Froissart) Spawned by talented Australian chef James Henry, who went on to open Bones then Parisian bistro Belon in Hong Kong, this *petit bar de quartier* (neighbourhood bar) is still raved about. Pick from a good-value, uncomplicated choice selection *of petites assiettes* (small plates designed to be shared) featuring various market produce – cold meats, raw or cooked fish, vegetables and so on. Advance reservations essential.

★LE CLOWN BAR   MODERN FRENCH €€
Map p386 (☑01 43 55 87 35; www.clown-bar-paris.fr; 114 rue Amelot, 11e; mains €25-30; ☻noon-2.30pm & 7-10.30pm Wed-Sun; MFilles du Calvaire) Le Clown is a historic monument next to the city's winter circus, the Cirque d'Hiver (1852), and is practically a museum with its ceramics, mosaics, original zinc bar and purist art deco style. This legendary address, which has been a restaurant for decades, now serves up fabulous modern French cuisine and excellent natural wines for a jovial crowd. Its pavement terrace gets packed out on sunny days.

If you fail to snag a table for lunch or dinner, return between meals to admire the decor while you enjoy an early morning *café* with regulars (the bar opens at 8am) or a glass of *vin naturel*.

SOON   KOREAN €€
Map p386 (☑01 42 77 13 56; http://soon-grill. com; 78 rue des Tournelles, 3e; 2-/3-course lunch menu €19/25, mains €19-25; ☻noon-2.30pm & 7-11.30pm; MChemin Vert) When you cannot eat another too-blue steak, head to this contemporary and oh-so-elegant Korean restaurant where diners barbecue their meat on a hot plate in the centre of each table. Just ensure the dazzling feng shui decor – a mirage of beautiful ceramics by Jeongmee Lee, mother of pearl tableware and luxuriant leather seating – does not distract.

ASIAN EAT STREET
If it's a steaming bowl of noodles you fancy, make a beeline for **rue au Maire, 3e** (MArts et Métiers), a small restaurant- and shop-lined street known for cooking authentic Chinese food and saving the trek to the larger Chinatown in the 13e.

LOCAL KNOWLEDGE

MARCHÉ DES ENFANTS ROUGES

Built in 1615, Paris' oldest covered market **Marché des Enfants Rouges** (Map p386; 39 rue de Bretagne & 33bis rue Charlot, 3e; 🕑8.30am-1pm & 4-7.30pm Tue-Fri, 4-8pm Sat, 8.30am-2pm Sun; MFilles du Calvaire) is secreted behind an inconspicuous green metal gate – and for good reason. A glorious maze of 20-odd food stalls selling ready-to-eat dishes from around the globe, it is a great place to come for a meander and munch with locals. Grab a Moroccan couscous or Caribbean platter and consume at communal tables.

Weave your way through the makeshift kitchens inside Marché des Enfants Rouges to find Alain, a retired baker with grey surfer locks and T-shirt with attitude, at **Chez Alain Miam Miam** (Map p386; www.facebook.com/ChezAlainMiamMiam; 39 rue de Bretagne & 33bis rue Charlot, 3e, Marché des Enfants Rouges; sandwiches €8; 🕑9am-3.30pm Wed-Fri, to 5.30pm Sat, to 3pm Sun; MFilles du Calvaire). Watch him prepare you a monster sandwich or *galette* (savoury pancake) on a sizzling crêpe griddle from a bespoke combo of fresh, organic ingredients – grated fennel, smoked air-dried beef, avocado, sesame salt and carefully curated honeys.

His passion, humour and crêpes are legendary in equal measure. Five-star vegetarian choices too.

LES CHOUETTES
MODERN FRENCH €€

Map p386 (📞01 44 61 73 21; www.restaurant-les-chouettes-paris.fr; 32 rue de Picardie, 3e; 2-course lunch €24, mains €23; 🕑8am-1am, kitchen noon-2.30pm & 7-11pm; 🖥; MOberkampf, République) Dine on inventive French cuisine beneath a fabulous Eiffel-style glass atrium at Les Chouettes, a former jewellery *atelier* (workshop) turned stunning art deco lounge in Le Marais. Between meals a fashionable crowd lingers for coffee, cakes or cocktails on the people-watching pavement terrace or inside around the fireplace, in the library or at the vintage bar. *'Chouette'* means both 'owl' and 'cool, great!'.

GLOU
MODERN FRENCH €€

Map p386 (📞01 42 74 44 32; www.glou-resto.com; 101 rue Vieille du Temple, 3e; lunch menus €18 & €22, mains €17-27; 🕑noon-2.30pm & 7.30-11pm Mon-Fri, noon-5pm & 7.30-11.30pm Sat & Sun; 🖥; MSt-Sébastien-Froissart) Handy for the Musée National Picasso and fashion boutiques of rue Vieille du Temple, Glou cooks modern French cuisine with a welcome twist. Begin with lentil soup sprinkled with smoked haddock flakes perhaps, followed by succulent roast veal. Despite its fashion-chic velour, Glou is super family-friendly – think colouring pens for the kids and an excellent-value €15 children's menu.

DERRIÈRE
MODERN FRENCH €€

Map p386 (📞01 44 61 91 95; www.derriere-resto.com; 69 rue des Gravilliers, 3e; 2-/3-course lunch menu €25/30, mains €19-30; 🕑noon-2.30pm & 8-11.30pm Mon-Sat, noon-4.30pm & 8-11pm Sun; MArts et Métiers) Play table tennis, sit on the side of the bed, glass of champers in hand, or lounge between book cases – such is the nature of this restaurant. Chilled vibe in a trendy 'shoes-off' style aside, Derrière (literally 'behind') is deadly serious in the kitchen. Classic French bistro dishes and more inventive creations are excellent, as is Sunday brunch.

Find Derrière tucked off rue des Gravilliers in a beautiful courtyard – wonderful for lunch when the sun shines.

CHEZ NÉNESSE
BISTRO €€

Map p386 (📞01 42 78 46 49; 17 rue de Saintonge, 3e; mains €22; 🕑noon-2.30pm & 8-10.30pm Mon-Fri; MFilles du Calvaire) 'Old-world bistro' is the atmosphere at this tiny spot with lace curtains and a quality kitchen cooking classic French dishes that have been around for centuries. Its *salade de canard au vinaigre d'hydromel* (duck salad in honey vinegar) and sweet *médaillons de veau au miel* (veal medallions pan fried in honey) are not to be scoffed at.

BRASSERIE BOFINGER
BRASSERIE €€

Map p386 (📞01 42 72 87 82; www.bofingerparis.com; 5-7 rue de la Bastille, 4e; menus €31 & €56; 🕑noon-2pm & 6.30pm-midnight Mon-Sat, noon-11pm Sun; 🖥; MBastille) Founded in 1864, Bofinger is reputedly Paris' oldest brasserie, though its polished art nouveau brass, glass and mirrors indicates redecoration a few decades later. Specialities include Alsatian-inspired dishes like *choucroute* (sauerkraut), oysters (from €27.90 for a dozen) and magnificent seafood platters (€29.90 to €122). Ask for a seat downstairs beneath the *coupole* (stained-glass dome). Kids are catered for with a €14.50 children's *menu*.

CHEZ JANOU   PROVENCAL €€

Map p386 (☑01 42 72 28 41; www.chezjanou.com; 2 rue Roger Verlomme, 3e; mains €18-24; ⏰noon-3pm & 7pm-midnight; Ⓜ Chemin Vert) Push your way in, order a kir from the jam-packed bar while you wait for a table, and revel in the buzz of this busy spot. The cuisine is as close as you'll get to Provençal in Paris, with all the southern classics like *brandade de morue* (salt-cod purée with potatoes), ratatouille and lavender-scented crème brûlée.

It also offers 80 different pastis types. And it is not recommended for the claustrophobic (unless it's summer and you succeed in nabbing a seat on the terrace).

CHEZ JENNY   BRASSERIE €€

Map p386 (☑01 44 54 39 00; www.chezjenny.com; 39 bd du Temple, 3e; lunch menu €20.80, mains €20-30; ⏰noon-midnight Sun-Thu, to 1am Fri & Sat; 🚸; Ⓜ République) Feast on huge Alsatian *choucroute garnie* (sauerkraut with smoked or salted pork, frankfurters and potatoes), *baeckeoffe* (Alsatian meat and veg stew) and stunning marquetry of Alsatian scenes by Charles Spindler on the 1st floor at this cavernous brasserie from 1932. Families will appreciate the €11 children's *menu*.

LE DÔME DU MARAIS   TRADITIONAL FRENCH €€

Map p386 (☑01 42 74 54 17; www.ledomedu-marais.fr; 53bis rue des Francs Bourgeois, 4e; mains €16-33; ⏰noon-11pm; Ⓜ Rambuteau) This place serves classic French dishes in a sublime, pre-Revolution building and former auction room with a glassed-in courtyard and knock-out, octagonal-shaped dining room. At weekend brunch, help yourself to as much as you can eat for €30.

CHEZ MARIANNE   JEWISH €€

Map p386 (2 rue des Hospitalières St-Gervais, 4e; mains €18-25; ⏰noon-midnight; Ⓜ St-Paul) Heaving at lunchtime, Chez Marianne translates as elbow-to-elbow dining beneath age-old beams on copious portions of felafel, hummus, aubergine purée and 25-odd other *zakouski* (hors d'oeuvre). Fare is Sephardic rather than Ashkenazi (the norm at most Pletzl eateries), not Beth Din kosher. A hole-in-the-wall window sells felafel in pita (€7) to munch on the move.

✖ Ménilmontant & Belleville

★ CHAMBELLAND   BOULANGERIE €

Map p390 (☑01 43 55 07 30; www.chambelland.com; 14 rue Ternaux, 11e; lunch menu €12; ⏰9am-8pm Tue-Sun; Ⓜ Parmentier) In a city known for its bakeries, it's only right there's Chambelland – a 100% gluten-free bakery with serious breads to die for. Using rice and buckwheat flour milled at the bakery's very own mill in southern France, this pioneering bakery creates exquisite cakes and pastries as well as sourdough loaves and brioches (sweet breads) peppered with nuts, seeds, chocolate and fruit.

LA CANTINE BELLEVILLE   FRENCH €

Map p390 (☑01 43 15 99 29; http://lacantine belleville.fr; 108 bd de Belleville, 20e; 2-/3-course lunch €12/14, dinner €14/18; ⏰8am-2am; 🛜; Ⓜ Belleville) For a taste of how trendy the edgy Belleville neighbourhood is becoming, hit its local 'canteen', a vibrant one-stop shop for dining, drinking and dancing after dark. Old-school chairs, vintage lighting and a mix of red brick and graffitied concrete give the place an appealing garage vibe. Cuisine is classic French, with particularly excellent steaks – two meat lovers can share the *côte de boeuf*.

Check its website or Facebook page for concerts.

LA CAVE DE L'INSOLITÉ   BISTRO €

Map p390 (☑01 53 36 08 33; www.lacavede linsolite.fr; 30 Rue de la Folie Méricourt, 11e; 2-/3-course lunch €18/20, mains €18-20; ⏰noon-2.30pm & 7-10.30pm Tue-Sat, noon-4pm & 7-10pm Sun; 🛜; Ⓜ St-Ambroise, Parmentier) Fresh artisan products form the backbone of the imaginative dishes – shiitake risotto, cod in ginger broth, banana and cumin *nems* – at this attractive wine bar, run by brothers Axel and Arnaud. The contemporary interior is rustic chic, with wooden tables, a wood-burning stove and the odd decorative grocery crate overflowing with shiny fresh fruit or veg. Natural wine lovers will be in heaven.

CHATOMAT
MODERN FRENCH €€

Map p390 (📞01 47 97 25 77; 6 rue Victor Letalle, 20e; mains €15-20; ⊘7.30-10.30pm Tue-Sat & 1st Sun of mth; Ⓜ Ménilmontant, Couronnes, Père Lachaise) No dinner address is worth the trek to Belleville more than this contemporary bistro with plain white walls, post-industrial flavour and bags of foodie buzz. In the kitchen of the old shop-turned-restaurant, Alice and Victor cook up just three starters, three mains and three desserts each night – and none disappoint. Book in advance.

MARCHÉ DE BELLEVILLE
MARKET €

Map p390 (bd de Belleville, 11e & 20e; ⊘7am-2.30pm Tue & Fri; Ⓜ Belleville) Belleville Market has filled busy thoroughfare bd de Belleville with open-air fruit, veg and other fresh-produce stalls since 1860. Shopping for food aside, it provides a fascinating entry into the large, vibrant community of this eastern neighbourhood, home to artists, students and immigrants from Africa, Asia and the Middle East.

ZOÉ BOUILLON
VEGETARIAN €

(📞01 42 02 02 83; www.zoebouillon.fr; 66 rue Rébeval, 19e; menus €11-14; ⊘11.30am-3.30pm & 6.30-10pm Mon-Fri, 11.30am-3.30pm Sat; Ⓜ Pyrénées, Belleville) Delicious homemade soups, quiches, savoury cakes and tarts are what this enchanting space with a baby-blue facade on a Belleville backstreet does best. Pile in with locals, order at the bar, grab some cutlery and enjoy the mellow vibe while your lunch cooks.

★ PIERRE SANG BOYER
MODERN FRENCH €€

Map p390 (📞09 67 31 96 80; http://pierresangboyer.com; 55 rue Oberkampf, 11e; 2-/3-/5-course lunch €20/25/35, 4-/6-course dinner €35/50;

⊘noon-3pm & 7-11pm Tue-Sat; Ⓜ Oberkampf) *Top Chef* finalist Pierre Sang Boyer stars at his kitchen restaurant where foodies sit on bar stools and watch the French–South Korean chef perform. Cuisine is modern French with a strong fusion lilt, and the vibe is fun and casual. If the place is full, nip around the corner to Sang's 'atelier' annex on rue Gambey.

The celebrity chef also runs Korean and French cooking classes for adults, children and families. He also does market visits and fun aperitif *ateliers* (workshops), which naturally include wine or Champagne.

SOYA
VEGETARIAN, VEGAN €€

Map p390 (📞01 48 06 33 02; www.facebook.com/soyacantinebio; 20 rue de la Pierre Levée, 11e; weekday lunch menu €15-22, brunch €27; ⊘7-11pm Tue, noon-3.30pm & 7-11pm Wed-Fri, 11.30am-11pm Sat, 11.30am-4pm Sun; 🎏; Ⓜ Goncourt, République) A favourite for its ubercool location in an industrial *atelier* (with bare cement, metal columns and big windows), Soya is a full-on *cantine bio* (organic eatery) in what was once a staunchly working-class district. Dishes, many tofu-based, are vegetarian and the weekend brunch buffet is deliciously lazy and languid. A glass floor floods the basement area with light.

LE BARATIN
BISTRO €€

Map p390 (📞01 43 49 39 70; 3 rue Jouye-Rouve, 20e; lunch menu €19, mains €20-30; ⊘noon-2.30pm Tue-Fri, plus 7.30-11.15pm Tue-Sat; Ⓜ Pyrénées, Belleville) *Baratin* (chatter) rhymes with *bar à vin*s (wine bar) in French and this animated venue located just steps from the lively Belleville quarter does both awfully well. In addition it offers some of the best (and very affordable) French food in the 20e with its ever-changing blackboard options. The selection of wine (some organic) by the glass or carafe is excellent.

LE CHATEAUBRIAND
NEOBISTRO €€€

Map p390 (📞01 43 57 45 95; www.lechateaubriand.net; 129 av Parmentier, 11e; menu €70; ⊘7.30-11pm Tue-Sat; Ⓜ Goncourt) Le Chateaubriand is an elegantly tiled, art deco dining room with strikingly imaginative cuisine. Basque chef Iñaki Aizpitarte is well travelled and his dishes display global exposure again and again in their unexpected combinations (watermelon and mackerel, milk-fed veal with langoustines and truffles). Reservations 21 days in advance are essential; if you don't have one, try your luck but only after 9.30pm.

AT DUSK

As the bewitching hour for that all-essential early evening *apéro* (predinner drink) beckons, there is no lovelier city square in which to sit beneath fairy lights and lap up local life than pedestrian **place du Marché Ste-Catherine**, 4e (Ⓜ St-Paul). Clad with benches and trees, it is framed on three sides by atmospheric cafe pavement terraces – perfect for a simple *pression* (glass of draught beer) or kir (white wine and cassis) at dusk.

DRINKING & NIGHTLIFE

Le Marais is a spot par excellence when it comes to a good night out, the lively scene embracing everything from gay-friendly and gay-only to bourgeois arty cafes, eclectic bars and raucous pubs. Rue Oberkampf and parallel rue Jean-Pierre Timbaud are hubs of the Ménilmontant bar crawl, a scene that is edging out steadily through cosmopolitan Belleville.

♥ Le Marais

★LE MARY CÉLESTE   COCKTAIL BAR

Map p386 (www.lemaryceleste.com; 1 rue Commines, 3e; ⊙6pm-1.30am; MFilles du Calvaire) Predictably there's a distinct nautical feel to this fashionable, ubercool cocktail bar in the Marais. Snag a stool at the central circular bar or play savvy and reserve one of a handful of tables (in advance online). Cocktails (€12 to €13) are creative and the perfect partner to a dozen oysters or your pick of tapas-style 'small plates' designed to be shared (€8 to €15).

★FLUCTUAT NEC MERGITUR   CAFE

Map p386 (✆01 42 06 44 07; http://fluctuat-cafe.paris; place de la République, 10e; ⊙7.30am-2am; 🛜; MRépublique) No address guarantees a fuller immersion into local life than Fluctuat (formerly Café Monde et Média) all shiny, new and rebranded with an edgy name after a kitchen fire in February 2015 wrecked the popular cafe and after-work hot spot. Its enviable location on pedestrian esplanade place de la République means it's always buzzing with Parisians chatting over drinks.

★WILD & THE MOON   JUICE BAR

Map p386 (www.wildandthemoon.com; 55 rue Charlot, 3e; ⊙8am-7pm Mon-Fri, 10am-7pm Sat, 11am-5pm Sun; MFilles du Calvaire) A beautiful crowd hobnobs over nut milks, vitality shots, smoothies, cold-pressed juices and raw food in this sleek new juice bar in the fashionable Haut Marais. Ingredients are fresh, seasonal and organic, and it is one of the few places in town where you can have moon porridge or avocado slices on almond and rosemary crackers for breakfast.

★L'EBOUILLANTÉ   CAFE

Map p386 (http://ebouillante.pagesperso-orange.fr; 6 rue des Barres, 4e; ⊙noon-10pm summer, to 7pm winter; MHôtel de Ville) On sunny days there is no prettier cafe terrace. Enjoying a privileged position on a pedestrian, stone-flagged street just footsteps from the Seine, L'Ebouillanté buzzes with savvy Parisians sipping refreshing glasses of homemade *citronnade* (ginger lemonade), hibiscus-flower cordial and herbal teas. Delicious cakes, jumbo salads, savoury crêpes and Sunday brunch (€21) complement the long drinks menu.

★LE PETIT FER À CHEVAL   BAR

Map p386 (www.cafeine.com/petit-fer-a-cheval; 30 rue Vieille du Temple, 4e; ⊙9am-2am; MHôtel de Ville, St-Paul) A Marais institution, the Little Horseshoe is a minute cafe-bar with an original horseshoe-shaped zinc bar from 1903. The place overflows with regulars from dawn to dark. Great *apéro* (predinner drink) spot and great WC – stainless-steel toilet stalls straight out of a Flash Gordon film (actually inspired by the interior of the *Nautilus* submarine in Jules Verne's *20,000 Leagues under the Sea*).

BOOT CAFÉ   COFFEE

Map p386 (19 rue du Pont aux Choux, 3e; ⊙10am-6pm; MSt-Sébastien-Froissart) The charm of this three-table ode to good coffee is its facade, which must win a prize for 'most photographed'. An old cobbler's shop, its original washed-blue exterior, 'Cordonnerie' lettering and fantastic red boot sign above are beautifully preserved. Excellent coffee, roasted in Paris, to boot.

PASDELOUP   COCKTAIL BAR

Map p386 (✆09 54 74 16 36; www.facebook.com/pasdelouparis; 108 rue Amelot, 11e; ⊙6pm-2am Tue-Sun; MFilles du Calvaire) This trendy cocktail bar next to the Cirque d'Hiver in Le Marais is a small place with a simple wood bar and copper-tube shelving evoking Scandinavia in its design. But what makes it stand out for the city's increasingly discerning cocktail crowd is its interesting and superbly gourmet food pairings (from €10).

OH-LA-DI   COFFEE

Map p386 (54 rue de Saintonge, 3e; ⊙8am-5pm Tue-Fri, 9am-6pm Sat & Sun; MTemple) Serious coffee roasted by Paris' very own Café Lomi in the 18e is the big draw of this pocket-sized coffee shop, clad with vintage

GAY & LESBIAN MARAIS

L'Étoile Manquante (Map p386; www.cafeine.com/etoile-manquante; 34 rue Vieille du Temple, 4e; ⊙9am-2am; MHôtel de Ville, St-Paul) With its fabulous pavement terrace, spilling onto rue Ste-Croix de la Bretonnerie, the Missing Star is a trendy, gay-friendly bar with a retro interior topped by starlit vaults.

Café Voulez-Vous (Map p386; ☑01 83 62 22 20; www.facebook.com/cafevoulezvous; 18 rue du Temple, 4e; ⊙11am-2am Mon-Thu & Sun, to 3am Fri, to 4am Sat; MHôtel de Ville) There are few more mellow gay addresses in which to hang out and enjoy the fashionable vibe of Le Marais cafe life over a coffee, Champagne cocktail or bubblegum-flavoured vodka shot than at this New York–styled gay bar and lounge. Attracting a mixed crowd, this sassy all-rounder lends phone cables to customers, has glossy lifestyle magazines to read and offers an awesome Sunday brunch.

Le Raidd (Map p386; www.raiddbar.com; 23 rue du Temple, 4e; ⊙6pm-4am, to 5am Fri & Sat; MHôtel de Ville) Don't be deceived by the laid-back lounge atmosphere of the ground-floor bar, it's one of the busiest gay hang-outs in Le Marais. Upstairs, it is a pulsating den of DJs and electro dance music, themed parties, disco nights, Brazilian soirées, raunchy shower shows and all sorts.

Gibus Club (Map p386; ☑01 47 00 59 14; www.scream-paris.com; 18 rue du Faubourg du Temple, 11e; ⊙11pm-7am Thu-Sat; MRépublique) What started out as a summer party thrown by Scream Club has now morphed into a permanent fixture on the city's gay scene, re-branded as Gibus Club and still working hard to stay top dog as one of Paris' biggest gay parties (admission €15 to €20). Follow the gay crowd to the basement of **Favela Chic** (Map p386; ☑01 40 21 38 14; www.favelachic.com; ⊙7.30pm-2am Tue-Thu, to 5am Fri & Sat).

Open Café (Map p386; www.opencafe.fr; 17 rue des Archives, 4e; ⊙11am-2am; MHôtel de Ville) A gay venue for all types at all hours, this spacious bar-cafe, with twinkling disco balls strung from the starry ceiling, has bags of appeal – including a big buzzing pavement terrace, a kitchen serving breakfast, all-day *tartines* and a four-hour happy 'hour' kicking in daily at 6pm.

Café Cox (Map p386; www.coxbar.fr; 15 rue des Archives, 4e; ⊙5pm-2am; MHôtel de Ville) This small gay bar with decor that changes every quarter is *the* meeting place for an interesting (and interested) cruisy crowd throughout the evening from dusk onwards. OK, we don't like the in-your-face name either, but what's a boy to do? Happy hour runs from 6pm to 10pm (until 2am Sunday).

Le Tango (Map p386; www.boiteafrissons.fr; 13 rue au Maire, 3e; ⊙10.30pm-5am Fri & Sat, 6-11pm Sun; MArts et Métiers) Billing itself as a *boîte à frissons* (club of thrills), Le Tango (admission €6) hosts a mixed and cosmopolitan, gay and lesbian crowd in a historic 1930s dancehall. Its atmosphere and style is retro and festive, with waltzing, salsa and tango getting going from the moment it opens. From about 12.30am onwards DJs play. Sunday's gay tea dance is legendary.

Quetzal (Map p386; 10 rue de la Verrerie, 4e; ⊙5pm-2am; MHôtel de Ville) This perennial favourite gay bar is opposite rue des Mauvais Garçons (Bad Boys' Street), a road named after the brigands who congregated here in 1540. It's always busy, with house and dance music playing at night, and cruisy at all hours; plate-glass windows allow you to check out the talent before it arrives.

3w Kafé (Map p386; 8 rue des Écouffes, 4e; ⊙7pm-3am Wed & Sun, to 4am Thu, to 6.30am Fri & Sat; MSt-Paul) The name of this flagship cocktail-bar-pub on a street with several lesbian bars means 'women with women'. It's relaxed and there's no ban on men (but they must be accompanied by a woman). On weekends there's dancing downstairs with a DJ and themed evenings take place regularly. Check its Facebook page for events.

Les Jacasses (Map p386; 5 rue des Écouffes, 4e; ⊙5pm-2am Wed-Sun; MSt-Paul) Girls will love this sister bar to 3w Kafé – it looks like it's been transplanted directly from Normandy. It has softer music, hard-core evenings and a happy 'hour' that happily lasts for four (from 5pm). Tasty tapas too.

mirrors, geometric blue-and-white floor tiles and glass vases of fresh flowers. The stylish space is not designed for hanging out with your laptop, but the crowd is hip, and the *café*, cookies, cakes and fruity granola superb.

LE NID
BAR

(📞07 82 75 23 00; http://lenid-coconludique. com; 227 rue St-Martin, 3e; ⏰5.30pm-1am Mon-Fri, noon-1am Sat, noon-8.30pm Sun; MArts et Métiers, Rambuteau) This ingenious *'cocon ludique'* (playful cocoon) is, in fact, a fun games bar and cafe where you can play board games over a drink or tasty weekend brunch. Pay €3, snag a table, order your free drink and indulge the inner kid in you with a choice of 500-odd games. There is a shop too where you can buy the latest releases.

LOUSTIC
COFFEE

Map p386 (40 rue Chapon, 3e; ⏰8am-6pm Mon-Fri, 9am-6pm Sat, 10am-6pm Sun; 📶; MArts et Métiers, Rambuteau) This pocket-sized espresso bar with Londoner Channa at its helm has been cleverly designed (by Parisian hot-shot Dorothée Meilichzon) for lounging over excellent coffee (roasted in Belgium, ground to coffee-lover perfection on a Florentine Marzocco machine in situ), or a revitalising cup of chai tea latte with a Swedish cinnamon roll or wedge of carrot cake. 'Loustic' is old Breton for 'smart Alec'.

FONDATION CAFÉ
COFFEE

Map p386 (www.facebook.com/fondationcafe; 16 rue Dupetit Thouars, 3e; ⏰8am-6pm Mon-Fri, 9am-6pm Sat & Sun; MTemple) It is easily one of the city's smallest cafes – just three teeny tables inside and four on the pavement outside – plus it has no toilet. Yet that doesn't stop Paris' international set flocking here for excellent coffee brewed from Belleville-roasted beans and served in a peppermint-green cup. Pair with a sublime slice of warm, buttered banana bread for a match made in heaven.

LA BELLE HORTENSE
BAR

Map p386 (www.cafeine.com/belle-hortense; 31 rue Vieille du Temple, 4e; ⏰5pm-2am; MHôtel de Ville, St-Paul) This creative wine bar named after a Jacques Roubaud novel fuses shelf after shelf of good books to read with an excellent wine list and an enriching weekly agenda of book readings, signings and art events. A zinc bar and original 19th-century ceiling set the mood perfectly.

LA CAFÉOTHÈQUE
COFFEE

Map p386 (📞01 53 01 83 84; www.lacafeotheque. com; 52 rue de l'Hôtel de Ville, 4e; ⏰8.30am-7.30pm Mon-Fri, 10am-7.30pm Sat & Sun; 📶; MSt-Paul, Hôtel de Ville) From the industrial grinder to elaborate tasting notes, this coffee house is serious. Grab a seat, pick your bean, and get it served just the way you like it (espresso, ristretto, latte etc). The coffee of the day keeps well-travelled tastebuds on their toes and there are tastings of different *crus*. Two-hour Saturday-morning tasting initiations cost €60.

FRAGMENTS
COFFEE

Map p386 (76 rue des Tournelles, 3e; ⏰8am-6pm Mon-Fri, 10am-6pm Sat & Sun; 📶; MChemin Vert) Arrive early to snag one of half a dozen vintage wooden tables inside this pocket-sized cafe, a hot address with hipsters for excellent coffee and healthy weekend brunches. If you want to talk coffee, it is laid-back owner and barista Youssef you need to look out for.

LE BARAV
WINE BAR

Map p386 (📞01 48 04 57 59; www.lebarav.fr; 6 rue Charles-François Dupuis, 3e; ⏰noon-3pm & 6pm-12.30am Mon-Fri, 6pm-12.30am Sat; MTemple) This hipster *bar à vins*, smart in the trendy Haut Marais, oozes atmosphere – and has one of the city's loveliest pavement terraces. Its extensive wine list is complemented by tasty food ranging from *croques* (toasted sandwiches) and salads to classic French meaty mains.

CAFÉ LA PERLE
BAR

Map p386 (http://cafelaperle.com; 78 rue Vieille du Temple, 3e; ⏰9am-2am; MSt-Paul, Chemin Vert) This party bar – buzzing neighbourhood cafe by day – is where *bobos* (bohemian bourgeois) come to slum it over *un rouge* (a glass of red wine) at the original zinc bar until the DJ arrives to liven things up. Unique trademarks: the (for real) distressed look of the place, the model locomotive over the bar and the bright orange bar stools.

LE LOIR DANS LA THÉIÈRE
CAFE

Map p386 (http://leloirdanslatheiere.com; 3 rue des Rosiers, 4e; ⏰9am-7.30pm; MSt-Paul) Its cutesy name (Dormouse in the Teapot) notwithstanding, this is a wonderful old space filled with retro toys, comfy couches and scenes of *Through the Looking Glass* on the walls. Its dozen different types of tea poured in the company of excellent savoury tarts and crumble-type desserts ensure a constant queue on the street outside. Breakfast and brunch too.

LA TARTINE   WINE BAR
Map p386 (24 rue de Rivoli & 17 rue du Roi de Sicile, 4e; ⊘7.30am-2am; MSt-Paul) A wine bar where little has changed since the days of gas lighting, this busy place offers 15 selected reds, whites and rosés by the *pot* (46cL). Its fabulous choice of *tartines* (open-faced sandwiches) served on Poilâne bread make it a hot choice for lunch.

LE PICK-CLOPS   BAR
Map p386 (16 rue Vieille du Temple, 4e; ⊘7am-2am Mon-Sat, 8am-2am Sun; ☎; MHôtel de Ville, St-Paul) This buzzy 1950s-styled bar-cafe – all shades of yellow and lit by neon – has formica tables, ancient bar stools and plenty of mirrors. Attracting a friendly flow of locals and passers-by, it's a great place for morning or afternoon coffee, or that last drink alone or with friends.

🍴 Ménilmontant & Belleville

AUX DEUX AMIS   CAFE, BAR
Map p390 (☑01 58 30 38 13; 45 rue Oberkampf, 11e; ⊘8am-2am Tue-Sat; MOberkampf) From the well-worn, tiled floor to the day's menu scrawled in marker on the vintage mirror behind the bar, Aux Deux Amis is the quintessential Parisian neighbourhood bar. It's perfect for a coffee any time and come dusk it serves tapas-style dishes. Friday brings the house speciality – *tartare de cheval* (hand-chopped horse-meat seasoned with a secret mix of herbs).

LA CARAVANE   BAR
Map p390 (www.lacaravane.eu; 35 rue de la Fontaine au Roi, 11e; ⊘11am-2am Mon-Sat, 5pm-2am Sun; ☎; MGoncourt) This kitsch bar and restaurant is a colourful little jewel tucked between République and Oberkampf; look for the tiny campervan above the door and the vintage powder-blue vehicle parked up in front. Lunch with a relaxed local crowd on curried chicken, Thai beef and an eclectic choice of other world-food dishes, or join the party after work for drinks, DJs and concerts.

CAFÉ CHARBON   BAR
Map p390 (www.facebook.com/cafe.charbon. oberkampf; 109 rue Oberkampf, 11e; ⊘9am-

2am Mon-Wed & Sun, 9am-4am Thu-Sat; ☎; MParmentier) With its post-industrial belle époque ambience, the Charbon was the first of the hip cafes and bars to catch on in Ménilmontant. It's always crowded and worth heading to for the distressed decor with high ceilings, chandeliers and perched DJ booth.

☆ ENTERTAINMENT

LA BELLEVILLOISE   CULTURAL CENTRE
(☑01 46 36 07 07; www.labellevilloise.com; 19-21 rue Boyer, 20e; ⊘7pm-1am Wed & Thu, 7pm-2am Fri, 6pm-2am Sat, 11.30am-midnight Sun; MMénilmontant) Gigs, concerts, theatrical performances, exhibitions, readings, dance classes and workshops: this arts centre is where it all happens after dark in Ménilmontant. The trendy cafe-restaurant, with its sunlit tables beneath 100-year-old olive trees, is packed during Sunday brunch, which is accompanied by live jazz. Advance reservations recommended.

LE CARREAU DU TEMPLE   CULTURAL CENTRE
Map p386 (☑01 83 81 93 30; www.carreaudutemple.eu; 4 rue Eugène Spuller, 3e; ⊘box office 2-6pm Mon-Sat; MTemple) The quarter's old covered market with gorgeous art nouveau ironwork is now the city's most architecturally appealing cultural centre and entertainment venue. The place where silks, lace, leather and other materials were sold in the 19th century is now a vast stage for exhibitions, concerts, sports classes and theatre. Check the program online.

L'ALIMENTATION GÉNÉRALE   LIVE MUSIC
Map p390 (☑01 43 55 42 50; http://alimentation-generale.net; 64 rue Jean-Pierre Timbaud, 11e; Fri & Sat €10; ⊘7pm-2am Wed, Thu & Sun, 7pm-5am Fri & Sat; MParmentier) This true hybrid, known as the Grocery Store to Anglophones, is a massive space, fronted on street level by its achingly cool, in-house Italianate canteen-bar with big glass windows and retro 1960s Belgian furniture. But music is the big deal here, with an impressive line-up of live gigs and DJs spinning pop, rock, electro, soul and funk to a packed dance floor.

GAÎTÉ LYRIQUE   CULTURAL CENTRE
Map p386 (☑01 53 01 51 51; www.gaite-lyrique.net; 3bis rue Papin, 3e; exhibitions €7.50, concerts

vary; ⊘2-8pm Tue-Sat, noon-6pm Sun; MArts et Métiers, Réaumur-Sébastopol) Unique and fascinating exhibitions – usually art or installation-art orientated – are the mainstay of this vibrant cultural centre in the Marais. Families with teens will find it particularly appealing; post-exhibition, don't miss the video-game room and library.

LA MAROQUINERIE   LIVE MUSIC
(🖉01 40 33 64 85; http://lamaroquinerie.fr; 23 rue Boyer, 20e; ⊘7-11.30pm; MMénilmontant) This tiny but trendy venue in Ménilmontant entices a staunchly local, in-the-know set with real cutting-edge gigs – many bands kick off their European tours here. The alfresco courtyard and restaurant renders La Maroquinerie an address impossible to resist; to see for yourself, head east along rue de Ménilmontant and take the second right after place de Ménilmontant.

NOUVEAU CASINO   LIVE MUSIC
Map p390 (🖉01 43 57 57 40; www.nouveau casino.net; 109 rue Oberkampf, 11e; ⊘Tue-Sun; MParmentier) This club-concert annexe of Café Charbon (p174) has made a name for itself amid the bars of Oberkampf with its live-music concerts (usually Tuesday, Thursday and Friday) and lively club nights on weekends. Electro, pop, deep house, rock – the program is eclectic, underground and always up to the minute. Check the website for listings.

LA JAVA   WORLD MUSIC
Map p390 (www.la-java.fr; 105 rue du Faubourg du Temple, 11e; MGoncourt) Built in 1922, this is the dance hall where Édith Piaf got her first break, and it now reverberates to the sound of live salsa, rock and world music. Live concerts usually take place at 8pm or 9pm during the week. Afterwards a festive crowd gets dancing to electro, house, disco and Latino DJs.

CIRQUE D'HIVER BOUGLIONE   CIRCUS
Map p386 (🖉01 47 00 28 81; www.cirquedhiver. com; 110 rue Amelot, 11e; MFilles du Calvaire) Clowns, trapeze artists and acrobats have entertained children of all ages at the city's circus in Le Marais since 1852. The season runs from October to March, and performances last around 2½ hours.

LE VIEUX BELLEVILLE   LIVE MUSIC
Map p390 (www.le-vieux-belleville.com; 12 rue des Envierges, 20e; ⊘11am-3pm Mon-Fri, 8pm-

2am Thu-Sat; MPyrénées) This old-fashioned bistro and *musette* at the top of Parc de Belleville is an atmospheric venue for performances of *chansons* featuring accordions and an organ grinder three times a week. It's a lively favourite with locals, so booking ahead is advised.

🔒 SHOPPING

The Marais boasts excellent speciality stores and an ever-expanding fashion presence. Hip young designers have colonised the upper reaches of the 3e towards rue Charlot as well as rue de Turenne. Meanwhile, rue des Francs Bourgeois and, towards the other side of rue de Rivoli, rue François Mirron in the 4e, have well-established boutique shopping for clothing, hats, home furnishings and stationery. Place des Vosges is lined with very high-end art and antique galleries with some amazing sculptures for sale.

🔒 Le Marais

★MAISON KITSUNÉ   FASHION & ACCESSORIES
Map p386 (🖉01 58 30 12 37; https://shop.kitsune. fr; 18 bd des Filles du Calvaire, 11e; ⊘10.30am-7.30pm Mon-Sat, 11am-6pm Sun; MFilles du Calvaire) One of the city's most fashionable labels for men and women, Maison Kitsuné pulls out all the stops with its flagship store in Le Marais. The glorious white space evokes a Californian villa with its seamless maze of rooms, culminating in a magnificent white marble staircase leading downstairs to the Parisian brand's very own **Café Kitsuné** on rue Amelot.

★AUX MERVEILLEUX   FOOD
Map p386 (www.auxmerveilleux.com; 24 rue du Pont Louis-Philippe, 4e; ⊘9am-8pm Tue-Sat, 9am-7pm Sun; MHôtel de Ville) It's hard to say

> ### ❶ LE MARAIS SHOPPING HOURS
> Contrary to elsewhere in the city, many shops in Le Marais only open at 11am and close at 7pm or a little later. Many are also open Sunday afternoon, typically from 2pm to 7pm.

what will send you running for the smelling salts more: the stunning period decor lit by a giant crystal chandelier, or the trays of sinfully gooey cakes, as decadent and rebellious as the 18th-century Merveilleuse (brazen new-society folk with a complete disregard for modesty) and Incroyables (effeminate folk who lived for pleasure) that inspired them.

The cakes were created in the north of France by chef Frédéric Vaucamps. Watch them being assembled – two small meringues are pasted together with whipped cream, then rolled in more cream and chocolate chips, caramelised hazelnuts or almonds. There are several flavours and a box of six/10/15 costs €11/17/25.

★ **MERCI** CONCEPT STORE

Map p386 (☎01 42 77 00 33; www.merci-merci. com; 111 bd Beaumarchais, 3e; ◷10am-7pm Mon-Sat; ⓂSt-Sébastien-Froissart) A Fiat Cinquecento marks the entrance to this unique concept store, which donates all its profits to a children's charity in Madagascar. Shop for fashion, accessories, linens, lamps and nifty designs for the home; and complete the experience with a coffee in its hybrid used-book-shop-cafe or lunch in its stylish basement **La Cantine de Mercia** (Map p386; ☎01 42 77 79 28; www.merci-merci.com; 111 bd Beaumarchais, 3e; soups €8-10, salads & tarts €10-17; ◷noon-6pm Mon-Sat; ⓂSt-Sébastien-Froissart).

★ **L'ÉCLAIR DE GÉNIE** FOOD

Map p386 (http://leclairdegenie.com; 14 rue Pavée, 4e; ◷11am-7pm Mon-Fri, 10am-7.30pm Sat & Sun; ⓂSt-Paul) You will never look at a simple éclair again after visiting the swish boutique of highly creative pastry chef Christophe Adam. Exquisitely filled and decorated éclairs are displayed with military precision in rows beneath glass. Like fashion, flavours change with the seasons. Count on between €5 and €7 a shot.

★ **LES EXPRIMEURS** ARTS, SOUVENIRS

Map p386 (www.lesexprimeurs.fr; 4 rue du Pont Louis-Philippe, 4e; ◷9am-1pm & 2-6pm Tue, Thu & Fri, 9am-noon Wed, 11am-1pm & 2-7pm Sat; ⓂHôtel de Ville) For an exquisite paper cutout of the Eiffel Tower, a bookmark shaped like the Panthéon rooftop or a quality sketchbook or ink pen, look no further than this wonderful stationery shop. It sells both fabulously classy souvenirs as well as daily essentials.

★ **PARIS RENDEZ-VOUS** CONCEPT STORE

Map p386 (www.rendezvous.paris.fr; 29 rue de Rivoli, 4e; ◷10am-7pm Mon-Sat; ⓂHôtel de Ville) Only the city of Paris could be so chic as to have its own designer line of souvenirs, sold in its own ubercool concept store inside Hôtel de Ville (city hall). Shop here for everything from clothing and homewares to Paris-themed books, toy sailing boats and signature Jardin du Luxembourg's Fermob chairs. *Quel style!*

★ **CHEZ HÉLÈNE** CONFECTIONERY

Map p386 (www.chezhelene-paris.com; 28 rue Saint-Gilles, 3e; ◷11am-2pm & 3-7.30pm Mon-Sat; ⓂChemin Vert) Pure indulgence is what this irresistible *bonbon* boutique – a child's dream come true – is about. Old-fashioned toffees and caramels, fudge, liquorice, Eiffel Tower sugar cubes, designer lollipops, artisanal marshmallows, Provençal *calissons...* the choice of quality, well-made *bonbons* (sweets) and *gourmandises* (sweet treats) is outstanding.

★ **FLEUX** HOMEWARES

Map p386 (www.fleux.com; 39 & 52 rue Ste-Croix de la Bretonnerie, 4e; ◷10.45am-7.30pm Mon-Fri, 10.30am-8pm Sat, 1.30-7.30pm Sun; ⓂHôtel de Ville) Innovative designs for the home by European designers fill this twinset of big white mazes. Products range from super chic to kitsch, clever and plain crazy. Its e-boutique stocks about 10% of what you see on the shop floor, but Fleux can post most Paris purchases home for you (at a price, *bien sûr*).

★ **L'ÉCLAIREUR** CONCEPT STORE

Map p386 (☎01 48 87 10 22; www.leclaireur.com; 40 rue de Sévigné, 3e; ◷11am-7pm Mon-Sat; ⓂSt-Paul) Part art space, part lounge and part deconstructionist fashion statement, this shop is known for having the next big thing first. Two tons of wooden planks, 147 TV screens and walls that move to reveal the men's and women's collection all form part of the stunning interior design by Belgian artist Arne Quinze.

VIOLETTE ET LÉONIE FASHION & ACCESSORIES

Map p386 (☎01 44 59 87 35; www.violetteleonie. com; 114 rue de Turenne, 3e; ◷1-7.30pm Mon, 11am-7.30pm Tue-Sat, 2-7pm Sun; ⓂFilles du Calvaire) So chic and of such high quality that it really does not seem like second-hand, Violette et Léonie is a first-class *depôt-vente*

LOCAL KNOWLEDGE

SECRET SHOPPING

Some of the Marais' sweetest boutique shopping is secreted down peaceful alleyways and courtyards, free of cars, as they were centuries ago. Take **Rue du Trésor**, a pedestrian dead-end passage off rue du Vieille du Temple, encrusted with an exclusive handful of hip boutiques like **Trésor** (Map p386; 5 rue du Trésor, 4e; ⊘11am-7.30pm Tue-Sat; MHôtel de Ville, St-Paul) by Brigitte Masson, a bohemian boutique with a catchy salmon-orange facade strung with old-fashioned fairy lights and fresh, individual women's fashion inside. End with a drink or lunch on the buzzing pavement terrace of **La Chaise au Plafond** (Map p386; 10 rue du Trésor, 4e; ⊘9am-2am; MHôtel de Ville, St-Paul) or neighbouring **Les Philosophes** (Map p386; www.cafeine.com/philosophes; 28 rue Vieille du Temple, 4e; ⊘9am-2am, kitchen noon-1.15am; ☎; MHôtel de Ville).

From Monday to Friday its cobbled alleys are mostly mouse quiet, but come the weekend savvy trendsetters mingle at **Village St-Paul** (Map p386; rue St-Paul, des rue Jardins St-Paul & rue Charlemagne, 4e; MSt-Paul), a designer set of five vintage courtyards, refashioned in the 1970s from the 14th-century walled gardens of King Charles V. Meander away Saturday afternoon with a courtyard-to-courtyard stroll, with old stone paving, ancient fountains and tiny artisan boutiques, galleries and antique shops.

concept store specialising in vintage. Shop in its wonderfully spacious boutique in Le Marais or online.

ODETTA VINTAGE
FASHION & ACCESSORIES

Map p386 (www.odettavintage.com; 76 rue des Tournelles, 3e; ⊘2-7.30pm Tue-Sat, 3-7pm Sun; MChemin Vert) One of the top fashionista addresses in the Marais, this boutique specialises in luxury vintage from the 1960s to 1980s. If you're going to find a runway sample, it's here. Think women's shoes, accessories and clothing fashion, as well as the odd piece of remarkable vintage furniture.

ÉTAT LIBRE D'ORANGE
PERFUME

Map p386 (www.etatlibredorange.com; 69 rue des Archives, 3e; ⊘noon-7.30pm Tue-Sat; MArts et Métiers) This perfumery screams Marais hipster. And with scents bearing names such as Fat Electrician, Jasmin et Cigarette, Malaise of the 1970s and Delicious Closet Queen, there really is something for everyone.

MAISON GEORGES LARNICOL
CHOCOLATE

Map p386 (www.chocolaterielarnicol.fr; 14 rue de Rivoli, 4e; ⊘10am-10pm; MSt-Paul) Coco-ginger bites, caramels and chocolate sculptures are among the sweet treats created by this master chocolate maker from Brittany. But it's his syrupy, chewy *kouignettes* (Breton butter cakes unusually made in mini dimensions and different flavours) that steal the show. Oh, and the glass jars of *caramel au beurre salé* (butter caramel) sold with a small spoon...

ANDREA CREWS
FASHION & ACCESSORIES

Map p386 (www.andreacrews.com; 83 rue de Turenne, 3e; ⊘11am-7pm Mon-Fri, 12.30-7.30pm Sat; MSt-Sébastien-Froissart) Using everything from discarded clothing to electrical fittings and household bric-a-brac, this bold art and fashion collective sews, recycles and reinvents to create the most extraordinary pieces. Watch out for 'happenings' in this Marais boutique.

BONTON
CHILDREN, FASHION

Map p386 (www.bonton.fr; 5 bd des Filles du Calvaire, 3e; ⊘10am-7pm Tue-Sat; MSt-Sébastien-Froissart) Chic and stylish, this concept store stocks vintage-inspired fashion, furnishings and knick-knacks for babies, toddlers and children. Don't leave without donning an old-fashioned, floppy sunhat or pair of oversized sunglasses and getting your photo snapped in its retro photo booth. Parents note: loo with changing mat in the basement.

JAMIN PUECH
FASHION & ACCESSORIES

Map p386 (www.jamin-puech.com; 68 rue Vieille du Temple, 4e; ⊘10am-7.30pm Mon-Sat, 1-7pm Sun; MSt-Sébastian-Froissart) A girl's best friend in *bobo* circles, this Parisian design house creates beautiful handbags in all manner of bold colours, textures and textiles. Isabelle Puech and Benoît Jamin are the duo behind the catchy, ethno-urban look. For vintage pieces from the 1990s, head to the couple's first boutique at 61 rue d'Hauteville, 10e.

LOCAL KNOWLEDGE

SOLE DESIGN

The real joy of mooching around Le Marais and neighbouring Ménilmontant is stumbling across tiny *ateliers* (workshops) and boutiques to watch just-established or rising designers at work.

Koché (Map p390; www.koche.fr; 8 Cité du Labyrinthe, 20e; ⊙by appointment; MMénilmontant) The name that rocked Paris Fashion Week in 2016, with an *atelier* far from the madding fashion crowd in edgy Ménilmontant and rapidly rising designer Christelle Kocher at the helm. Contemporary art and traditional French craftsmanship heavily influence her funky, ready-to-wear street gear that mixes denim, jersey and other easy fabrics with elaborately crocheted feathers, chiffon, beads and sequins.

Moon Young Hee (Map p386; 62 rue Charlot, 3e; ⊙11am-7pm Mon-Sat; MFilles du Calvaire) Watch fanciful 'origami' creations being cut by hand in the studio of Korean designer Moon Young Hee. Ancient beams, exposed stone walls and huge street-facing windows form the perfect stage. To view her work in its full glory, head to her flagship store in the 6e, on the banks of the Seine, opposite the Louvre.

Valentine Gauthier (Map p386; www.valentinegauthier.com; 58 rue Charlot, 3e; ⊙9.30am-7.30pm Mon-Sat; MFilles du Calvaire) Go green with jackets, mules, cowboy boots and other romantic, natural and urban designs by one of Paris' most talented ecoconscious designers.

Kate Mack (Map p386; www.kate-mack.com; 15 rue Oberkampf, 11e; ⊙noon-2pm & 3-8pm Tue-Sat; MOberkampf) A hard-core address for getting to the core of Parisian trends, this studio-boutique of Kate Mack is a real delight. Ogle silver-skinned mannequins modelling overtly feminine but funky, femme-fatale designs.

Samuel Coraux (Map p386; www.corauxparis.book.fr; 18 rue Ste-Anastase, 3e; ⊙10am-6pm Mon-Fri; MSt-Sébastien-Froissart) The stark black facade at this hybrid boutique-workshop provides a dramatic contrast to the brilliantly coloured, contemporary creations crafted inside by jewellery designer Samuel Coraux. Every material stars here and shiny plastic appears to be a hot favourite.

LA BOUTIQUE EXTRAORDINAIRE
FASHION & ACCESSORIES

Map p386 (www.laboutiqueextraordinaire.com; 67 rue Charlot, 3e; ⊙11am-8pm Tue-Sat, 3-7pm Sun; MFilles du Calvaire) Mohair, silk and other natural, organic and ethical materials are hand-knitted into exquisite garments, almost too precious to wear, at this unusual and captivating Haut Marais boutique.

LOSCO
FASHION & ACCESSORIES

Map p386 (www.losco.fr; 20 rue de Sévigné, 4e; ⊙2-7pm Mon & Tue, 11am-1pm & 2-7pm Wed-Fri, 11am-7pm Sat, 2-7pm Sun; MSt-Paul) This artisan *ceinturier* epitomises the main draw of shopping in Paris – stumbling upon tiny boutique-workshops selling 101 quality variations of one single item, in this case *ceintures* (belts). Pick a leather type (lizard, python, croc etc), length and buckle to suit just you. Expect to pay anything upwards of €160.

LE BHV
DEPARTMENT STORE

Map p386 (www.bhv.fr; 52 rue de Rivoli, 4e; ⊙9.30am-8pm Mon, Tue & Thu-Sat, to 9pm Wed; MHôtel de Ville) BHV (bay-ash-vay) is a straightforward and vast department store in Le Marais where you can buy everything from guidebooks on Paris to clothes, accessories and every imaginable type of hammer, power tool, nail, plug and hinge.

VERT D'ABSINTHE
DRINKS

Map p386 (www.vertdabsinthe.com; 11 rue d'Ormesson, 4e; ⊙noon-7pm Tue-Sat; MSt-Paul) Fans of the *fée verte* (green fairy), as absinthe was known during the belle époque, will think they've died and gone to heaven. Here, you can buy not only bottles of the best-quality hooch but all the paraphernalia as well: glasses, water jugs and tiny slotted spoons for the all-important sugar cube.

TUMBLEWEED
TOYS, FASHION

Map p386 (19 rue de Turenne, 4e; ⊙11am-7pm; MSt-Paul, Chemin Vert) This little shop specialises in leather slippers for kids and *l'artisanat d'art ludique* (crafts of the playing art): think handmade wooden toys and exquisitely made brain teasers and puzzles for adults, such as Japanese 'spin' and 'secret' boxes that defy entry.

L'HABILLEUR   FASHION & ACCESSORIES

Map p386 (www.facebook.com/LHabilleurParis; 44 rue de Poitou, 3e; ⊙noon-7.30pm Mon-Sat; MSt-Sébastien-Froissart) Discount designer wear – 50% to 70% off original prices – is the lure of this veteran boutique. It generally stocks last season's collections.

MARIAGE FRÈRES   DRINKS

Map p386 (www.mariagefreres.com; 30, 32 & 35 rue du Bourg Tibourg, 4e; ⊙10am-7.30pm; MHôtel de Ville) Founded in 1854, this is Paris's first and arguably finest teashop. Choose from more than 500 varieties of tea sourced from some 35 countries. Mariage Frères has four other outlets, including branches in the 6e and 8e.

📍 Ménilmontant & Belleville

⭐ FROMAGERIE GONCOURT   CHEESE

Map p390 (🕾01 43 57 91 28; 1 rue Abel Rabaud, 11e; ⊙9am-1pm & 4-8.30pm Tue-Fri, 9am-8pm Sat; MGoncourt) Styled like a boutique, this contemporary *fromagerie* (cheese shop) is a must-discover. Clément Brossault ditched a career in banking to become a *fromager* and his cheese selection – 70-odd types – is superb. Cheeses flagged with a bicycle symbol are varieties he discovered in situ during a two-month French cheese tour he embarked on as part of his training.

⭐ MADE BY MOI   FASHION, HOMEWARES

Map p390 (🕾01 58 30 95 78; www.madebymoi.fr; 86 rue Oberkampf, 11e; ⊙2.30-8pm Mon, 10am-8pm Tue-Sat; MParmentier) 'Made by Me', aka handmade, is the driver of this appealing boutique on trendy rue Oberkampf – a perfect address to buy unusual gifts. Mooch here for women's fashion, homewares and other beautiful objects like coloured glass carafes, feathered head dresses, funky contact-lens boxes and retro dial telephones. The ultimate Paris souvenir: 'Bobo brunch' scented candles by Bougies La Française.

BELLEVILLE BRÛLERIE   COFFEE

(🕾09 83 75 60 80; http://cafesbelleville.com; 10 rue Pradier, 19e; ⊙11.30am-5.30pm Sat; MBelleville) With its understated steel-grey

facade, this ground-breaking roastery in Belleville is easy to miss. Don't! These are the guys who brought good coffee to Paris and its beans go into some of the best espressos and cappucinos in town. Taste the week's selection, compare tasting notes, and buy a bag to take home. Online shop too.

BOUTIQUE OBUT   GAMES

Map p390 (www.labouleobut.com; 60 av de la République, 11e; ⊙10am-noon & 12.30-6.30pm Tue-Sat; MParmentier) This is the Parisian mecca for fans of *pétanque* or the similar (though more formal) game of *boules*, a form of bowls played with heavy steel balls wherever a bit of flat and shady ground can be found. It will kit you out with all the equipment necessary to get a game going and even has team uniforms. Pay anything from €40 to €300 for a three-ball set.

🏃 SPORTS & ACTIVITIES

HÔTEL DE VILLE
ICE-SKATING RINK   SKATING

Map p386 (Patinoire de l'Hôtel de Ville; Parvis de l'Hôtel de Ville, 4e; entry free, skate rental €6; ⊙noon-10pm Mon & Thu, 10am-10pm Tue, Wed & Sun, 10am-midnight Fri & Sat mid-Dec–early Mar; MHôtel de Ville) From December to early March, an ice-skating rink sets up outside the beautiful Hôtel de Ville, creating something of a picture-book experience.

ROLLERS & COQUILLAGES   SKATING

Map p386 (www.rollers-coquillages.org; 37 bd Bourdon, 4e; MBastille) This skate club organises a weekly three-hour 'Randonnée en Rollers' (a 23km skate around town), departing on Sunday at 2.30pm from skate shop Nomadeshop.

NOMADESHOP   SKATING

Map p386 (🕾01 44 54 07 44; www.nomadeshop. com; 37 bd Bourdon, 4e; half-/full day from €5/8; ⊙11am-1.30pm & 2.30-7.30pm Tue-Fri, 10am-7pm Sat, noon-6pm Sun; MBastille) Nomadeshop rents and sells equipment and accessories, including wheels, helmets, elbow and knee guards. The shop is also the departure point for Sunday's 'Randonnée en Rollers' around Paris.

Bastille & Eastern Paris

Neighbourhood Top Five

❶ Opéra Bastille (p191) Taking in a backstage tour and opera, ballet or concert recital at this modern monolith, on the landmark square where revolutionaries stormed the Bastille in 1789.

❷ Promenade Plantée (p182) Joining Parisians for a weekend jog or stroll along the foliage-laced path of this elevated city park, uniquely at home atop a 19th-century railway viaduct.

❸ Château de Vincennes (p183) Exploring Paris' only medieval castle, complete with prerequisite keep and sublime 16th-century royal chapel.

❹ Parc Zoologique de Paris (p183) Thrilling the children with lion, white rhino, giraffe and wolverine spottings through camouflaged spy towers at the city's state-of-the-art zoo.

❺ Cinémathèque Française (p182) Catching timeless cinematic classics at this little-known cinema museum, an ode to Parisians' beloved seventh art.

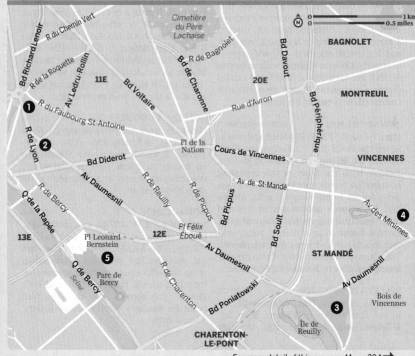

For more detail of this area see Map p394 ➡

Explore: Bastille & Eastern Paris

Bastille isn't known for its sights, but it's nonetheless a fascinating area to explore on foot. As it's still authentically residential in most parts, a wander will give you a taste of everyday life in one of Paris' most dynamic neighbourhoods. For a more voyeuristic glimpse, ascend to elevated park Promenade Plantée, which looks down on the streets around you and offers the occasional peek through an apartment window.

Bastille's main attraction is not aimless *flâneurie* (urban strolling), however: this former working-class district doesn't exactly have the same visual knockout factor as central Paris. It's best for dipping your toes into a vibrant restaurant scene dominated by young, creative chefs; its scores of popular, inexpensive bars and cafes; and the profusion of evening entertainment, from avant-garde opera to indie rock and dancing on a Seine-moored barge.

You may be reluctant to leave the city behind with so much to explore, but an easy trip to the Bois de Vincennes, the city's largest park, never disappoints. From a castle and zoo to outdoor concerts, bike excursions, pick-up football matches and picnics, it's one of the most-loved spots in the capital to unwind al fresco.

Local Life

→**Bistro life** The 11e and 12e have an unusually high number of old-school bistros that have preserved much of their original decor, such as the much-celebrated Chez Paul (p187) and neighbourhood favourites like Au Vieux Chêne (p186).

→**Market life** Fabulous markets include classic Parisian street markets like the Marché Bastille (p184), and Marché d'Aligre (p189), where food shops, wine bars and restaurants fan out into the surrounding streets.

→**Green spaces** Eastern Paris just might have the city's best collection of parks. The Promenade Plantée (p182) and Parc de Bercy (p184) are easy escapes, but on weekends many Parisians decamp to the much larger Bois de Vincennes, with beautifully landscaped Parc Floral de Paris (p183) at its green heart.

Getting There & Away

→**Metro** Lines 1, 8 and 9 are major east–west arteries, while line 5 heads south across the Seine and north to the Gare du Nord. Line 14 serves Bercy.

→**RER** The east–west RER A stops at Nation and Gare de Lyon en route to central and western Paris.

→**Bicycle** There are three Vélib' stations around place de la Bastille: on bd Richard Lenoir, bd Bourdon and rue de Lyon.

Lonely Planet's Top Tip

While the area immediately surrounding the Bastille has spawned a clutch of faceless bars and restaurant chains, walking east along trendy rue de Charonne or along rue du Faubourg St-Antoine to Ledru-Rollin and Faidherbe-Chaligny brings you to a much more interesting neighbourhood, filled with exciting dining addresses, atmospheric cafes and all the quirky, unusual shops that make a city great. Tiny rue St-Nicolas is a particularly tasty street for foodies.

BASTILLE & EASTERN PARIS

✕ Best Places to Eat

→ Dersou (p188)
→ Le 6 Paul Bert (p186)
→ Clamato (p186)
→ Septime (p188)
→ L'Écailler du Bistrot (p186)

For reviews, see p184.➡

♟ Best Places to Drink

→ Le Baron Rouge (p189)
→ La Cave Paul Bert (p189)
→ Café des Anges (p189)
→ Concrete (p189)
→ Septime La Cave (p190)

For reviews, see p189.➡

☆ Best Entertainment

→ Opéra Bastille (p191)
→ La Cinémathèque Française (p191)
→ La Flèche d'Or (p191)
→ Badaboum (p191)

For reviews, see p191.➡

⊙ SIGHTS

Historic place de la Bastille – actually at the intersection of the 4e, 11e and 12e *arrondissements* – is the obvious place to start exploring. A waterside stroll south along the city's only pleasure port, Port de l'Arsenal, brings you to Maison Rouge, host to some fabulous contemporary art exhibitions. Southeast of here is the busy Gare de Lyon station area, with the unusual Promenade Plantée, which can be followed on foot for 4.5km to Bois de Vincennes on the far eastern fringe of this neighbourhood. Several key sights are clustered in the green urban woodland.

PLACE DE LA BASTILLE   SQUARE
Map p394 (place de la Bastille, 12e; MBastille) The Bastille, a 14th-century fortress built to protect the city gates, is the most famous Parisian monument that no longer exists. Nothing remains of the prison it became under Cardinal Richelieu, which was mobbed on 14 July 1789, igniting the French Revolution. Today a skirmishly busy roundabout, traffic flies around the 52m-high **Colonne de Juillet** (Map p394; place de la Bastille, 12e; MBastille) in its centre. The unmissable green-bronze column is topped by a gilded, winged Liberty and revolutionaries from the uprising of 1830 are buried beneath.

If you're interested in finding the Bastille's one-time foundations, look for a triple row of paving stones that traces the building's outline on the ground between bd Henri IV and rue St-Antoine. The foundations are also marked below ground in the Bastille metro station, on the platform of line 5.

OPÉRA BASTILLE   NOTABLE BUILDING
Map p394 (📞01 40 01 19 70; www.operadeparis. fr; 2-6 place de la Bastille, 12e; guided tours adult/child €15/7; MBastille) Delve behind the scenes of this landmark 340-seat venue – that looks absolutely nothing like an opera house in the conventional sense of the word – during a 90-minute backstage guided tour. One of the late President Mitterand's pet projects, the building was intended to strip opera of its elitist airs – hence its notable 13 July 1989 inauguration on the eve of the 200th anniversary of the storming of the Bastille.

Tour schedules are online and the box office inside the opera house sells tickets 10 minutes before tours start.

PROMENADE PLANTÉE   PARK
Map p394 (La Coulée Verte René-Dumont; cnr rue de Lyon & av Daumesnil, 12e; ⊕8am-9.30pm May-Aug, to 5.30pm Sep-Apr; MBastille, Gare de Lyon) The disused 19th-century Vincennes railway viaduct has been reborn as the world's first elevated park, planted with a fragrant profusion of cherry trees, maples, rose trellises, bamboo corridors and lavender. Three storeys above ground, it provides a unique aerial vantage point on the city. Access is via staircase and it starts just south of place de la Bastille on rue de Lyon. Along the first section, above av Daumesnil, chic art-gallery-workshops squat gracefully beneath the arches to form the Viaduc des Arts (p192).

Waking south, look out for the spectacular art deco police station at the start of rue de Rambouillet, topped with a dozen huge, identical marble caryatids. The viaduct later drops back to street level at Jardin de Reuilly (1.5km), but it's possible to follow the line all the way to the Bois de Vincennes (4.5km). This latter section can also be done on a bike or in-line skates.

PETITE CEINTURE DU 12E   PARK
(PC 12; 21 rue Rottembourg, 12e; ⊕8.30am-5pm Mon & Tue, 8.30am-10.45pm Wed-Sun; MMichel Bizot) On sq Charles Péguy, behind the table-tennis tables, you can access a tiny 200m section of the now-abandoned railway line that encircled central Paris from the second half of the 19th century until 1934 when the line was closed. Called the Petite Ceinture, the section here is known as the Petite Ceinture du 12e. Today it is a lovely green park with a nature trail and *jardin partagé* (community garden).

CINÉMATHÈQUE FRANÇAISE   MUSEUM
(www.cinematheque.fr; 51 rue de Bercy, 12e; adult/child €5/2.50, with film €8; ⊕noon-7pm Mon & Wed-Sat, to 8pm Sun; 📶; MBercy) A little-known gem near Parc de Bercy, the Cinémathèque Française was originally created in 1936 by film archivist Henri Langlois. On site are two museums, one presenting temporary exhibitions (usually taking a behind-the-scenes look at a particular film) and the other devoted to the history of cinema, with props (including some from Méliès' classic *A Trip to the Moon,* featured in *Hugo*), early equipment and short clips of a few classics. Enter via place Léonard-Bernstein by the park.

A cinema screens up to 10 films daily.

BOIS DE VINCENNES

Paris is flanked by two large woodlands, Bois de Boulogne in the west and Bois de Vincennes in the east. Originally royal hunting grounds, Bois de Vincennes was annexed by the army following the Revolution and then donated to the city in 1860 by Napoléon III.

A fabulous place to escape the endless stretches of Parisian concrete, Bois de Vincennes also contains a handful of notable sights, and is close to the **Musée de l'Histoire de l'Immigration** (www.histoire-immigration.fr; 293 av Daumesnil, 12e; adult/child €4.50/free, with Aquarium Tropical €8; ⏰10am-5.30pm Tue-Fri, to 7pm Sat & Sun; M Porte Dorée) and **Aquarium Tropical** (www.aquarium-portedoree.fr; 293 av Daumesnil, 12e; adult/child €5/3.50, with Musée de l'Histoire de l'Immigration €8; ⏰10am-5.30pm Tue-Fri, to 7pm Sat & Sun; ⏪; M Porte Dorée). Metro lines 1 (St-Mandé, Château de Vincennes) and 8 (Porte Dorée, Porte de Charenton) will get you to the edges of the park. Pick up picnic supplies on rue de Midi, Vincennes' main shopping street.

Château de Vincennes (☎01 48 08 31 20; http://vincennes.monuments-nationaux.fr; av de Paris, Vincennes; guided tour adult/child €8.50/free; ⏰10am-6pm mid-May–mid-Sep, to 5pm mid-Sep–mid-May; M Château de Vincennes) Originally a meagre 12th-century hunting lodge, this fortified royal residence was expanded several times throughout the centuries until it reached its present size under Louis XIV. Notable features of the medieval chateau complex include its beautiful 52m-high keep (1370) and the royal chapel (1552), which can be explored on a guided visit. Note the chapel is only open between 11am and noon, and 3pm and 4pm.

Parc Zoologique de Paris (Zoo de Vincennes; ☎08 11 22 41 22; http://parczoologique deparis.fr; cnr av Daumesnil & rte de Ceinture du Lac, 12e; adult/child €22/14; ⏰9.30am-7.30pm summer, shorter hours rest of year; M Porte Dorée) Paris' largest, now state-of-the-art zoo focuses on the conservation of species and habitats, with camouflaged vantage points (no peering through fences). Its biozones include Patagonia, with sea lions and cougars; the savannah of Sahel-Sudan, with lions, white rhinos and giraffes; forested Europe, with wolves, lynxes and wolverines; a Guiana rainforest with jaguars, monkeys and anacondas; and Madagascar, home to lemurs. Other highlights include Australian marsupials and manatees (sea cows).

Parc Floral de Paris (☎01 49 57 24 81; www.parcfloraldeparisjeux.com; Esplanade du Chateau de Vincennes or rte de la Pyramide; adult/child €5.50/2.75; ⏰9.30am-8pm summer, shorter hrs rest of year; ⏪; M Château de Vincennes) This magnificent botanical park is a Bois de Vincennes highlight. Natural landscaping and a magnificent collection of plants keep amateur gardeners happy, while Paris' largest play area (giant climbing webs and slides, jungle gyms, sandboxes) thrills families with young children. For bigger kids, there is mini-golf, tree-climbing, table tennis and other activities (not included in the park admission). Free open-air concerts are staged throughout summer, making it a first-rate picnic destination.

Lac Daumesnil (☎01 43 28 19 20; rte de Ceinture du Lac Daumesnil, 20e, Bois de Vincennes; hourly boat hire for 2-/4-person boat €12.20/13.20; ⏰boat hire 10am-8pm summer, to 7pm off season, closed Nov–mid-Feb; M Porte Dorée) Like something out of a Renoir painting, the largest lake in Bois de Vincennes is a popular destination for walks and rowboat excursions in warmer months (hourly boat hire €12.20/13.20 for a two-/four-person boat). A Buddhist temple is nearby.

MAISON ROUGE GALLERY
Map p394 (☎01 40 01 08 81; www.lamaisonrouge. org; 10 bd de la Bastille, 12e; adult/child €10/7; ⏰11am-7pm Wed, Fri-Sun, to 9pm Thu; ⏪; M Quai de la Rapée) Subtitled 'Fondation Antoine de Galbert' after the man who endowed it, this cutting-edge gallery shows contemporary artists and seldom-seen works from private collections. For art and design titles, the gallery's Bookstorming bookshop is an excellent port of call. Note that everything closes between exhibitions.

PARC DE BERCY
PARK

(rue Paul Belmondo; ☉8am-sunset Mon-Fri, from 9am Sat & Sun; 🔊🏍; Ⓜ Cour St-Émilion, Bercy) Built atop the site of a former wine depot, this large, well-landscaped park is a great place to break for a picnic and let the kids run free. Bercy reached its height as the 'world's wine cellar' in the 19th century: it was right on the Seine, close to Paris yet outside the city walls, meaning that shipping was convenient and commerce tax-free.

Vestiges of its former incarnation are spread across the park and the Cour St-Émilion, where the warehouses were located. In some spots you'll see the old railroad tracks; in others you'll find grape vines.

LA MANUFACTURE 111
CULTURAL CENTRE

(📞01 40 33 01 36; www.manufacture111.com; 111 rue des Pyrénées, 20e; ☉6-10pm Fri, noon-10pm Sat, noon-8pm Sun, but variable; Ⓜ Maraîchers) A massive 1500-sq-metre former garage now houses this cutting-edge urban cultural centre. Street art and hip-hop are at the heart of its temporary exhibitions, events and soirées, which can be anything from a music gig to live painting and performances. Here you can also catch a food truck, art workshops, a bookshop and the most creative Sunday brunch in town (11.30am to 3pm, €25). Check its Facebook page or Twitter feed for updates.

🍴 EATING

Bastille dining tends to swing between a highly lauded group of up-and-coming chefs, who run the hip new neobistros that have reinspired Parisian cooking, and the die-hard traditionalists, who rarely venture beyond the much-loved standards of French cuisine. The neighbourrhood caters to all budgets, tastes and time constraints – you'll find several 'fast food' gourmet sandwich and pizza addresses in the mix too.

MARCHÉ BASTILLE
MARKET €

Map p394 (http://equipement.paris.fr/marche-bastille-5477; bd Richard Lenoir, 11e; ☉7am-2.30pm Thu, 7am-3pm Sun; Ⓜ Bastille, Richard Lenoir) If you only get to one open-air street market in Paris, this one – stretching between the Bastille and Richard Lenoir metro stations – is among the city's very best.

LA PÂTISSERIE
SANDWICHES €

Map p394 (www.lapatisseriecyrillignac.com; 24 rue Paul Bert, 11e; lunch menus €9.50-12; ☉7am-8pm; Ⓜ Charonne) This is no ordinary patisserie (cake shop). This is the temple of celebrity chef Cyril Lignac, whose freshly baked breads, well-filled baguette sandwiches and extraordinary cakes in the form of artworks have all the promise of the ultimate gourmet Paris picnic. Indulge.

YARD
MODERN FRENCH €

Map p394 (📞01 40 09 70 30; www.yardparis.com; 6 rue de Mont Louis, 11e; 2-/3-course lunch menus €16/19, mains €15-18; ☉noon-2.30pm & 8-10.30pm Mon-Fri, tapas 6pm-midnight Mon-Fri; Ⓜ Philippe Auguste) This modern bistro near the Père Lachaise cemetery is squirrelled away in a former construction yard, hence its name. The short but inventive menu changes daily, incorporating seasonal dishes such as spring lamb with leeks or a wintery wild boar *mijoté* (stew) with olives and polenta. To watch the chefs cook in the tiny open kitchen, sit at the bar.

Come dusk Yard cooks up tapas dishes over drinks in its neighbouring wine bar; for a lunchtime sandwich to go (unusual fillings are always a reflection of what's cooking that day in the bistro), nip into its next-door sandwich bar.

CHEZALINE
SANDWICHES €

Map p394 (85 rue de la Roquette, 11e; sandwiches €5.50-8; ☉11am-5.30pm Mon-Fri; Ⓜ Voltaire) A former horse-meat butcher's shop (*chevaline*, hence the spin on the name) is now a fabulous deli creating seasonally changing baguettes filled with ingredients like ham and house-made pesto. Other delicacies include salads and homemade terrines. There's a handful of seats (and plenty of parks nearby). Prepare to queue.

ASSAPORARE
ITALIAN €

Map p394 (📞01 44 67 75 77; 7 rue St-Nicolas, 12e; mains €15-20; ☉12.30-2.30pm Mon & Tue, 12.30-2.30pm & 7.30-10.30pm Wed-Fri, 7.30-10.30pm Sat; Ⓜ Ledru-Rollin) For an authentic taste of Italian 'slow food', make a beeline for this well-established Italian bistro, the life and love of Neapolitan architect Giuseppe Lo Casale. From the products cooked in the open kitchen to the white designer chairs sitting comfortably at home between beamed ceiling and vintage flooring, everything is as effortlessly stylish as one would expect of an Italian pure-bred.

PARIS HANOÏ
VIETNAMESE €

Map p394 (☎01 47 00 47 59; www.parishanoi.fr; 74 rue de Charonne, 11e; mains €11-13.50; ☺noon-2.30pm & 7-10.30pm; Ⓜ Charonne) This upbeat restaurant with a cheery canary-yellow facade is one of the city's best addresses for *pho* (soup noodles with beef) and other classic Vietnamese dishes. It doesn't take reservations and the place is a veritable legend, so be prepared to join the queue and dine jaw to jowl with other appreciative foodies. No credit cards.

LOUIE LOUIE
PIZZA €

Map p394 (☎09 73 58 14 36; www.louielouie.paris; 78 rue de Charonne, 11e; pizza €10-15; ☺noon-2.30pm & 7-11.30pm Mon-Fri, noon-12.30am Sat & Sun; Ⓜ Ledru-Rollin, Charonne) In a pared-down interior with light-wood Scandinavian furniture and caramel walls, this pizzeria on trendy rue de Charonne is minimalist, attractive and chic. The menu is simple: cocktails, wine and a dozen-odd different wood-oven-fired pizzas, best accompanied by a bare-bones but ingenious €2 *bol de salade* (a bowl of lettuce leaves dressed in vinaigrette only the French can do).

CHEZ GLADINES
BASQUE €

Map p394 (☎01 58 30 63 52; http://chezgladines-charonne.fr; 64 rue de Charonne, 11e; mains €12-19; ☺noon-11pm Mon-Thu, noon-11.30pm Fri & Sat, 11am-11pm Sun; ☎; Ⓜ Charonne) Colourful formica tables and disco balls strung from the ceiling add a retro ambience to this hipster address near Bastille. The kitchen cooks up a fiery cuisine from the Basque Country in France's hot southwest – the *chipirons à la biscaïna* (squid in a peppery, garlic-laced tomato sauce) is excellent – alongside tamer dishes like salads, snails, charcuterie, steaks and burgers.

Between meals Chez Gladines doubles as a bright and airy neighbourhood cafe.

LES GALOPINS
BISTRO €

Map p394 (☎01 47 00 45 35; http://www.les-galopins.fr/bastille; 24 rue des Taillandiers, 11e; 2-/3-course menus €14.50/19, mains €14.50-17.50; ☺noon-2.30pm Mon-Wed, noon-2.30pm & 7.30-11pm Thu & Sun, noon-2.30pm & 7.30-11.30pm Fri & Sat; Ⓜ Bastille) Push through the black facade to uncover a warm and buzzing, sunflower-gold interior, packed with locals feasting on huge platefuls of traditional French country fare. Vintage posters on the wall inject a retro ambience and staff go out of their way to please. Feisty ap-

petites should order the handsome *côté de bœuf* for two, served with Béarnaise sauce.

BLOOM
INTERNATIONAL €

Map p394 (☎01 43 72 87 88; www.bloom-restaurant.fr; 25 rue de la Forge Royale, 11e; 2-/3-course lunch menu €13/15.50; ☺noon-3pm Tue-Fri, to 4pm Sat & Sun; ☎; Ⓜ Ledru-Rollin) 🖋 Local, organic and strictly *fait maison* (homemade) is the mantra of this delightful little lunchtime spot, happily squirreled away on a quiet street opposite a pretty bench-clad park landscaped like a labyrinth. Vegetarian lasagne, meatballs, tasty quiches and savoury tarts are the order of the day, all made with produce from Île de France. Weekend brunch (€19.50 to €23.50) is a veritable feast.

PIZZERIA DEI CIOPPI
PIZZA €

Map p394 (☎01 84 48 14 58; 44 rue Trousseau, 11e; pizza €8.50-14; ☺noon-2.30pm & 7.30-10pm; Ⓜ Ledru-Rollin) Authentic Italian pizzas are lovingly prepared by Italian chef-owner Fabrizio Ferrara at his tiny pizzeria off rue de Charonne. Ten pizza types tour taste buds around the regions of Italy and are peppered with authentic Italian products. Think Linosa capers, Mazara anchovies and creamy mozzarella from Apulia. Buy *al taglio* (by the slice) to takeaway or eat in at a retro formica table.

CRÊPERIE BRETONNE
CRÊPERIE €

Map p394 (☎01 43 55 02 29; 67 rue de Charonne, 12e; crêpes €2.90-10.90; ☺noon-2pm & 7-11pm Mon-Sat, 7-11pm Sun; Ⓜ Charonne) Authentic down to its well-filled, savoury buckwheat *galettes* and sweet crêpes smothered in whatever filling you fancy, this delightful Breton pancake house with royal blue facade is filled with emotive B&W photos of Brittany. Joy of joys, it even serves dry Val de Rance cider. *Yec'hed mat* (cheers)!

LE BAR À SOUPES
SOUP €

Map p394 (www.lebarasoupes.com; 33 rue de Charonne, 11e; soups €5.50-6, lunch menu €11.30; ☺noon-3pm & 6.30-11pm Mon-Sat; Ⓜ Ledru-Rollin) With 36 varieties of soup served per week (six daily), chances are you'll always find something here to warm you up and please your palate. Stalwarts include pumpkin-chestnut borscht, creamed red lentils and coconut milk, cauliflower and Bleu d'Auvergne cheese, and the Bloody Marys.

MAMA SHELTER
PIZZA €

(☎01 43 48 48 48; www.mamashelter.com; 109 rue de Bagnolet, 20e; pizzas €9-16; ⊘noon-1am; ☏🅿; 🚌76, Ⓜ Alexandre Dumas, Gambetta) If you're headed to a concert at La Flèche d'Or (p191), kick off the evening with pizzas and beer on the summertime rooftop terrace at Mama Shelter, just across the street. The pizzeria itself is on the ground floor and features a wood-fired oven and superb pies. Save room for the Italian coffee ice cream. Great hours.

LE SIFFLEUR DE BALLONS
FRENCH €

Map p394 (☎01 58 51 14 04; www.lesiffleurde ballons.net; 34 rue de Citeaux, 12e; lunch menu €14, platters €8-16; ⊘10.30am-3pm & 5.30-11pm Tue-Fri, 10.30am-11pm Sat; Ⓜ Faidherbe-Chaligny) The *épicerie* (specialist grocer) arm of chef Thomas Dufour and Thierry Bruneau's gourmet bistro across the street, this contemporary *cave à manger* is an ode to fine wine and fine morsels to eat. French wines – all natural – are paired with toasted sandwiches, soups, lentil salads with truffle oil, cheese and charcuterie platters. Look out for tastings with winemakers. Does not take reservations.

À LA RENAISSANCE
CAFE €

Map p394 (☎01 43 79 83 09; 87 rue de la Roquette, 11e; 2-/3-course lunch menu €19/22; ⊘8am-2am, kitchen noon-2.30pm & 7.30-11pm; Ⓜ Voltaire) This vintage neighbourhood cafe with curvaceous zinc bar, ceramic tile floor and buzzing pavement terrace is a great place to dine on quintessential Paris cafe fare with locals. Along with wine and plates of cheese, it serves mackerel rillettes, steak tartare and all-time favourite *œufs à la coq aux tartines* (soft-boiled eggs with toast). Natural wines dominate a surprisingly excellent wine list.

LES DOMAINES QUI MONTENT
FRENCH €

Map p394 (☎01 43 56 89 15; www.lesdomaines quimontent.com; 136 bd Voltaire, 11e; lunch menu €15.90; ⊘shop 10am-8pm Mon-Sat, kitchen noon-2pm Mon-Sat; Ⓜ Voltaire) Les Domaines Qui Montent was around before the *cave à manger* trend began, and although it's not quite as trendy as most newcomers, it is very much the real thing. Above all a wine shop, it offers simple two-course *menus* at lunch that you can pair with any of its available bottles.

AU VIEUX CHÊNE
BISTRO €

Map p394 (☎01 43 71 67 69; www.vieuxchene.fr; 7 rue du Dahomey, 11e; 2-/3-course lunch menu €15/19, dinner €28/33; ⊘noon-2pm & 8-10.30pm Mon-Fri; Ⓜ Faidherbe-Chaligny) Along a quiet side street in a neighbourhood full of traditional woodworking studios, this retro bistro offers an excellent seasonal menu, with specialities like rabbit stuffed with foie gras, and some well-chosen wines. Three of the cast-iron columns holding the place up are registered monuments.

★LE 6 PAUL BERT
BISTRO €€

Map p394 (☎01 43 79 14 32; 6 rue Paul Bert, 12e; 2-/3-course weekday lunch menu €18/19, 4-course dinner menu €44, mains €24-26; ⊘7.30-11pm Tue, noon-2pm & 7.30-11pm Wed-Sat; Ⓜ Faidherbe-Chaligny) Opened by Bertrand Auboyneau of nearby Le Bistrot Paul Bert (p187), this retro bistro with peeling-red-paint facade serves staggering modern cuisine. Exquisite creations prepared by Louis-Philippe Riel from Quebec and Japanese chef Kosuke Tada in an open kitchen change daily, but exciting pairings are a given: think pork and clementine, octopus with kale and raspberry, artichoke and white chocolate. Reservations essential.

★CLAMATO
SEAFOOD €€

Map p394 (www.septime-charonne.fr; 80 rue de Charonne, 11e; tapas €7-20; ⊘7-11pm Wed-Fri, noon-11pm Sat & Sun; Ⓜ Charonne) Arrive early: unlike its raved-about sister restaurant Septime (p188) next door, Clamato doesn't take reservations and you don't want to miss out on Bertrand Grébaut and Théo Pourriat's seafood tapas. Sit at the bar or nab a table in the minimalist retro dining room and feast on creative combos like chickpeas with haddock and artisan feta or mussels with onion confit and saffron.

★L'ÉCAILLER DU BISTROT
SEAFOOD €€

Map p394 (☎01 43 72 76 77; 22 rue Paul Bert, 11e; weekday lunch menu €19, mains €17-34; ⊘noon-2.30pm & 7.30-11pm Tue-Sat; Ⓜ Faidherbe-Chaligny) Oyster lovers should make a beeline for this famous seafood annexe of Le Bistrot Paul Bert (p187), a rustic maritime spot serving a dozen varieties of fresh bivalves, freshly shucked and accompanied by a little lemon juice. Other delights are platters of seafood, a half-dozen *oursins* (sea urchins), minute-cooked tuna steak with sesame oil and the *très* extravagant lobster *menu* (€65).

Freshly shucked oysters to go, too.

LE BISTROT PAUL BERT
BISTRO €€

Map p394 (☎01 43 72 24 01; 18 rue Paul Bert, 11e; 2-/3-course lunch/dinner menu €19/41;

noon-2pm & 7.30-11pm Tue-Sat; MFaidherbe-Chaligny) When food writers list Paris' best bistros, one name that consistently pops up is Paul Bert. The timeless vintage decor and perfectly executed classic dishes like *steak-frites* and hazelnut-cream Paris-Brest pastry merit booking ahead. Look out for its siblings L'Écailler du Bistrot (p186; seafood), La Cave Paul Bert (p189; wine bar with small plates) and Le 6 Paul Bert (p186; modern cuisine) in the same street.

LE TEMPS AU TEMPS BISTRO €€

Map p394 (☑01 43 79 63 40; 13 rue Paul Bert, 11e; 2-/3-course lunch menu €19/21, dinner menu €28/32; ⏱noon-1.30pm & 8-10.30pm Wed-Sun; MFaidherbe-Chaligny) Foodie street rue Paul Bert is the perfect spot for this delightfully traditional and excellent-value bistro with quaint ginger facade and menu chalked on a blackboard outside. Lunch *menus* include a glass of wine – just the job for washing down a deliciously garlicky snail fricasee, roast leg of lamb, or scallops with braised endives and spicy chorizo.

CHEZ PAUL BISTRO €€

Map p394 (☑01 47 00 34 57; www.chezpaul.com; 13 rue de Charonne, 11e; 2-/3-course lunch menu €18/21, mains €17-27; ⏱noon-12.30am; MLedru-Rollin) This is Paris as your grandmother knew it: chequered red-and-white napkins, faded photographs on the walls, old red banquettes and traditional French dishes that could well make your hair curl: pig trotters, *andouillette* (a fiesty tripe sausage), *tête de veau et cervelle* (calf head and brains) and the like. Less offal: a steaming bowl of *pot au feu* (beef stew).

CAPUCINE CAFETTE BISTRO €€

Map p394 (☑01 43 46 10 14; 159 rue du Faubourg St-Antoine, 11e, Passage St-Bernard; mains €15-20; ⏱9am-10pm Tue-Sat, kitchen 12.30-2pm & 7.30-10pm; MLedru-Rollin) For simple homemade cuisine with an Italian edge, served in a delightfully quiet and quaint back alley, try this pocket-sized *'cafette'*. Run with passion and charm by young Sardinian chef Stefania Melis – Steffi to regulars – and her sister, Italianate Capucine is refreshingly different. Between meals, warm up on good coffee and gourmet hot chocolate – the white chocolate and Piedmontese hazelnut is divine.

GENTLE GOURMET CAFÉ VEGAN €€

Map p394 (☑01 43 43 48 49; www.gentlegourmetcafe.com; 24 bd de la Bastille, 12e; 2-course lunch menu €21, mains €18-22; ⏱noon-2.30pm & 6.30-10pm Wed-Sun; 🔒📶♿; MBastille) 🌿 Dishes are 100% vegan, mostly organic and refreshingly gourmet at this restaurant with large windows and lots of natural light across a busy road from the Seine. Indulge in almond-encrusted tofu, estragon-laced beetroot ravioli or a 'meaty' portobello-mushroom burger in sesame brioche bun, all washed down with a lovely choice of fruit juices and teas.

For young appetites there is an €11 menu comprising pan-fried gnocchi and organic fruit juice.

LE COTTE RÔTI NEOBISTRO €€

Map p394 (☑01 43 45 06 37; 1 rue de Cotte, 12e; 2-/3-course lunch menu €22/26, dinner menu €46; ⏱noon-2.30pm & 8-11pm Tue-Fri, 8-11pm Sat; MLedru-Rollin) Contemporary cooking by Nicolas Michel and a chic charcoal-hued dining space ensure this attractive restaurant near Gare de Lyon is always full. Indulge in Michel's signature *épaule d'agneau confite* (shoulder of lamb cooked slowly in its own fat) or another modern French main like roast pigeon with Jerusalem artichokes or scallops *à la plancha* with citrus-spiced braised chicory. Desserts are equally tasty. Reserve.

À LA BICHE AU BOIS TRADITIONAL FRENCH €€

Map p394 (☑01 43 43 34 38; 45 av Ledru-Rollin, 12e; 2-/3-course lunch menu €19/21.50, dinner menu €31.50; ⏱7-10.45pm Mon, noon-2.30pm & 7-10.45pm Tue-Sat; MGare de Lyon) Game, especially *la biche* (venison), is the speciality of convivial 'doe in the woods', but dishes like foie gras and coq au vin also add to the countryside ambience, as do the green awning and potted plants out front. The cheeses and wines are excellent, but game aside, top honours have to go to the sensational *frites* (fries).

CHALET SAVOYARD FONDUE €€

Map p394 (☑01 48 05 13 13; www.chalet-savoyard.fr; 58 rue de Charonne, 11e; 3-course menu €31, mains €17-23; ⏱noon-2.30pm & 7-11pm Sun-Thu, to midnight Fri & Sat; MLedru-Rollin) Fill up on hearty alpine specialities like *tartiflette* (melted Reblochon cheese and bacon baked with potatoes), cheese fondue (served with bread and potatoes) and *raclette* (another type of melted cheese served with potatoes and cold meats) at this Savoyard restaurant. Cheese aficionados will enjoy dipping into a seasonal Mont d'Or, a 'hot box' of raw-milk cheese oven-baked with white wine and garlic.

Great courtyard seating in summer.

L'ÉBAUCHOIR
BISTRO €€

Map p394 (☑01 43 42 49 31; www.lebauchoir.com; 43-45 rue de Cîteaux, 12e; lunch menus €13.50 & €25, mains €19-28; ⊗8-11pm Mon, noon-2.30pm & 8-11pm Tue-Thu, noon-2.30pm & 7.30-11pm Fri & Sat; ⓜFaidherbe-Chaligny) At this convivial gourmet bistro, a little off the beaten track, regulars drop in for inventive creations from chef Thomas Dufour. French classics form the base of his dishes, such as scallops in a sublime saffron cream or *tête de veau* (rolled calf head) in a herb-laced ravigote sauce, and there's usually one main on the evening à la carte menu.

LE SQUARE TROUSSEAU
FRENCH €€

Map p394 (☑01 43 43 06 00; www.squaretrousseau.com; 1 rue Antoine Vollon, 12e; mains €22-34; ⊗8am-2am, kitchen noon-2.30pm & 7-10pm; 🛜; ⓜLedru-Rollin) With etched glass, zinc bar and polished wood panelling, this elegant cafe-restaurant harking back to circa 1900 is a Parisian landmark of sorts. A real all-rounder, this is a place where Parisians flock for a coffee-and-croissant breakfast or drink over the day's newspaper, a classic French meal like frogs' legs or hare stew, or an after-work drink on the delightful terrace overlooking a lovely leafy square.

À LA BANANE IVOIRIENNE
AFRICAN €€

Map p394 (☑01 43 70 49 90; https://www.facebook.com/ALaBananeIvoirienne; 10 rue de la Forge Royale, 11e; menu €29.50, mains €12.50-17; ⊗7-11pm Tue-Thu, to 1am Fri & Sat; 🎵; ⓜLedru-Rollin) An institution in Paris for over two decades, À la Banane Ivoirienne dishes up the best Ivorian food in Paris along with fabulous live music and dancing on Friday nights. West African specialities – including stuffed crab, braised *attiéké* (fermented cassava pulp), *alloco* (fried plaintain) and plenty of fiery meats and fish – are dished up in a colourful interior bristling with gewgaws.

LE VIADUC CAFÉ
INTERNATIONAL €€

Map p394 (☑01 44 74 70 70; www.leviaduc-cafe.com; 43 av Daumesnil, 12e; 2-course lunch menu €15.50, mains €12-22, jazz brunch €20; ⊗9am-4am, kitchen 11am-3pm; 🛜🚼; ⓜGare de Lyon) In one of the glassed-in arches of the Viaduc des Arts (p192), this cavernous cafe is always a great spot to while away the hours

or people-watch from the terrace. It buzzes with local workers at lunchtime and caters to families with an €11 children's *menu*. Sunday's jazz brunch (noon to 4pm) rocks.

⭐DERSOU
NEOBISTRO €€€

Map p394 (☑09 81 01 12 73; www.dersouparis.com; 21 rue St-Nicolas, 12e; 5-/6-/7-course tasting menu incl drinks €95/115/135; ⊗7.30pm-midnight Tue-Fri, noon-3.30pm & 7.30pm-midnight Sat, noon-3.30pm Sun; ⓜLedru-Rollin) Leave any preconceptions you might have at the door, ignore or enjoy the brutishly understated decor, and be wooed by the creative fusion cuisine of Taku Sekine. Much of the seating is at the counter, meaning first-class views of the Japanese chef at work, and options are limited to tasting menus, with each course exquisitely paired with a bespoke cocktail. Reservations essential.

Sunday brunch is an appealing à la carte mixed bag of granola, fruit, pancakes (with bacon, fried egg and maple syrup), toast (with avocado, feta and poached egg), bagels (with raw horse mackerel) etc; €8 to €19 per dish.

⭐SEPTIME
MODERN FRENCH €€€

Map p394 (☑01 43 67 38 29; www.septime-charonne.fr; 80 rue de Charonne, 11e; lunch menus €28 & €55, dinner menu €58; ⊗7.30-10pm Mon, 12.15-2pm & 7.30-10pm Tue-Fri; ⓜCharonne) The alchemists in Bertrand Grébaut's Michelin-starred kitchen produce truly beautiful creations, while blue-smocked waitstaff ensure culinary surprises are all pleasant ones: each dish on the menu is a mere listing of three ingredients, while the mystery *carte blanche* menu puts your taste buds in the hands of the innovative chef. Snagging a table requires planning and perseverance – book three weeks in advance.

For a pre- or post-meal drink, drop by its nearby wine bar Septime La Cave (p190). For stunning seafood tapas, its sister restaurant Clamato (p186) is right next door.

TABLE
MODERN FRENCH €€€

Map p394 (☑01 43 43 12 26; www.tablerestaurant.fr; 3 rue de Prague, 12e; lunch menu €29, mains €32-49; ⊗noon-3pm & 7.45-10.30pm Mon-Fri; ⓜLedru-Rollin) Unusual and rare artisan products sourced from all over France decide the day's menu at this appealing eatery, styled very much like a *table d'hôte*, with diners sitting at the curvaceous zinc bar while talented chef Bruno Verjus performs in his open kitchen. Delicious meats come out of his rotisserie and the chef delights in talking food with diners.

To enter, press the button and wait for the striking glass door to slide open.

LE TRAIN BLEU   FRENCH €€€

Map p394 (☎01 43 43 09 06; www.le-train-bleu. com; 26 place Louis Armand, 12e; Gare de Lyon; menus €65 & €105, mains €25-45; ⏾restaurant 11.30am-2.45pm & 7-10.45pm, bar 7.30am-10.30pm Mon-Sat, 9am-10.30pm Sun; 🛜; ⓂGare de Lyon) This ravishing, belle époque train-station restaurant has been an elegant port of call for hungry travellers and city workers since 1901. Cuisine is traditional French – Charolais beef tartare is prepared at your table – and even if you can't dine here, indulging in a silver pot of tea or cocktail in its comfortable lounge bar is well worth the top-end prices.

🍷⚚ DRINKING & NIGHTLIFE

Place de la Bastille has become increasingly crass over the years, but it invariably draws a crowd, particularly along rue de Lappe just east, which is literally lined with bars. Continue further east and the options become much more stylish and appealing.

★CAFÉ DES ANGES   CAFE

Map p394 (☎01 73 20 21 10; www.cafedesanges paris.com; 66 rue de la Roquette, 11e; ⏾7.30am-2am; ⓂBastille) With its aqua-blue paintwork and locals sipping coffee beneath the terracotta awning on its busy pavement terrace, Angels Cafe lives up to the 'quintessential Paris cafe' dream. In winter wrap up beneath a ginger blanket outside, or push your way through the crowds at the zinc bar to snag a coveted table inside – for breakfast, a burger lunch, steak dinner (mains €10 to €17) and everything in between.

★LA CAVE PAUL BERT   WINE BAR

Map p394 (☎01 58 53 30 92; 16 rue Paul Bert, 11e; ⏾noon-midnight, kitchen noon-2pm & 7.30-11.30pm; ⓂFaidherbe-Chaligny) It is strictly no reservations and standing only at the latest addition to the gourmet Paul Bert empire. This bijou wine bar has eight wines by the glass (predominantly French; €5 to €8), and cheeses, charcuterie, anchovies etc to nibble on. The real gourmet action kicks in

MARCHÉ D'ALIGRE

All the staples of French cuisine can be found in chaotic street market **Marché d'Aligre** (Map p394; http://marched aligre.free.fr; rue d'Aligre, 12e; ⏾8am-1pm Tue-Sun; ⓂLedru-Rollin), a real favourite with Parisians: cheese, coffee, chocolate, wine, charcuterie, even Tunisian pastries. At weekends follow locals into the historic covered market hall – signposted **Marché Beauvau** (Map p394; place d'Aligre, 12e; ⏾9am-1pm & 4-7.30pm Tue-Fri, 9am-1pm & 3.30-7.30pm Sat, 9am-1.30pm Sun; ⓂLedru-Rollin) – for a glass of white wine and platter of freshly shucked oysters.

The morning flea market **Marché aux Puces d'Aligre** (Map p394; place d'Aligre, 12e; ⏾8am-1pm Tue-Sun; ⓂLedru-Rollin) takes place on the square.

at 7.30pm: stylish small plates of bedevilled eggs with truffles, veal sweetbreads with clams and more.

★CONCRETE   CLUB

Map p394 (www.concreteparis.fr; 60 Port de la Rapée, 12e; ⏾10pm-7am; ⓂGare de Lyon) This hugely popular, wild-child club with different dance floors lures a young international set to a boat on the Seine, firmly moored by Gare de Lyon. Notorious for introducing an 'after-hours' element to Paris' somewhat staid clubbing scene, Concrete is the trendy place to party all night until sunrise and beyond. Watch for all-weekend events with electronic dance music around the clock.

Admission is usually free before midnight. Check for world-class electro DJ events on its Facebook page.

★LE BARON ROUGE   WINE BAR

Map p394 (☎01 43 43 14 32; 1 rue Théophile Roussel, 12e; ⏾10am-2pm & 5-10pm Tue-Fri, 10am-10pm Sat, 10am-4pm Sun; ⓂLedru-Rollin) Just about the ultimate Parisian wine-bar experience, this place has barrels stacked against the bottle-lined walls. As unpretentious as you'll find, it's a local meeting place where everyone is welcome and it's especially busy on Sunday after the Marché d'Aligre (p189) wraps up. All the usual suspects – cheese, charcuterie and oysters – will keep your belly full.

LOCAL KNOWLEDGE

RUE DE LAPPE

Although at night it's one of the rowdiest bar-hopping streets in Paris, rue de Lappe is actually quite peaceful during the day and worth a quick wander. Like most streets in the area, it dates back to the 17th century and was originally home to cabinetmakers, who first moved into the area to escape the taxes and restrictions imposed by guilds operating within city limits.

In the centuries that followed, the street was gradually taken over by metalworkers, who equipped the city with its zinc bars, copper piping and the like: one of the busiest bars on the street, **Bar des Ferrailleurs** (Map p394; ☑01 48 07 89 12; 18 rue de Lappe, 11e; ☺5pm-2am Mon-Fri, 3pm-2am Sat & Sun; ⒨Bastille), is a hip homage to these workers. At the same time, immigrants from the central French region of Auvergne also moved in, opening up *cafés-charbons*, places where you could go for a drink and buy coal at the same time. In this way the street eventually became a popular drinking strip, and its accordion-driven dance halls, which hosted *bals-musettes*, were to become famous throughout Paris. The dance hall **Le Balajo** dates back to 1936 and continues to host a weekly *bal-musette*.

You can still find an Auvergne speciality shop here, **Chez Teil** (Map p394; 6 rue de Lappe, 11e; ☺10am-1pm & 4-7.30pm Tue-Sat), at No 6, as well as a beautiful old cafe-bar and bistro, **Les Sans-Culottes** (Map p394; 27 rue de Lappe, 11e; ☺noon-2.30pm & 7.30-11.30pm), at No 27.

For a small deposit, you can fill up 1L bottles straight from the barrel for under €5.

LE 49.3
BAR

Map p394 (☑06 23 16 92 23; http://le49-3.com; 3 Cité de Phalsbourg, 11e; ☺5.30pm-2am Mon-Sat; ⒨Charonne) Worn wooden parquet, vintage zinc bar, a leather Chesterfield sofa and old metal chairs picked up at the flea market strike the perfect shabby-chic chord at this appealing new beer bar. The selection of craft beers – 49 to be precise, plus three different types of gin, rum, whisky and tequila – span the globe, and bar staff are clearly *bière* aficionados.

SEPTIME LA CAVE
WINE BAR

Map p394 (☑01 43 67 14 87; www.septime-charonne.fr; 3 rue Basfroi, 11e; ☺4-11pm Tue-Sat, 5-10pm Sun; ⒨Charonne) This bijou wine bar is an atmospheric spot to linger over an *apéro* while waiting for a table at one of the hip dining addresses around the corner on foodie rue de Charonne. Sit at the bar or around an upcycled vegetable crate and enjoy carefully curated French wines (€5 to €8 by the glass), paired with gourmet nibbles (tapas €6 to €12).

PAUSE CAFÉ
BAR

Map p394 (☑01 48 06 80 33; 41 rue de Charonne, 11e; ☺7.30am-2am Mon-Sat, 9am-8pm Sun; ⒨Ledru-Rollin) Those in search of a quintessential neighbourhood cafe will adore this happening all-rounder. Come here for drinks, meals, coffee and brunch. The exceedingly generous terrace, covered (and unfortunately smoke-filled) in winter, fills up fast with fashionable locals and the almost famous. French film buffs may recognise it from the Gen-X hit *Chacun cherche son chat* (When the Cat's Away; 1996).

TWENTY ONE SOUND BAR
CLUB

Map p394 (☑01 43 70 78 01; http://twentyone-soundbar.com; 20 rue de la Forge Royale, 11e; ☺9pm-2am Tue, Wed, Fri & Sat, 8pm-2am Thu; ⒨Faidherbe-Chaligny) Stark steel and concrete amp up the acoustics at this hip-hop haven, with regular drinks specials and big-name DJs mixing on the decks.

LA FÉE VERTE
BAR

Map p394 (☑01 43 72 31 24; 108 rue de la Roquette, 11e; ☺7am-2am; ☎; ⒨Voltaire) Absinthe, predictably, is the speciality of the Green Fairy, a thronging neighbourhood bar that serves good food (burgers, salads) as well as 20-odd different types of the devilish drink (traditionally, with spoons and sugar cubes). Sunday brunch too.

LE BISTROT DU PEINTRE
BAR

Map p394 (www.bistrotdupeintre.com; 116 av Ledru-Rollin, 11e; ☺7am-2am; ☎; ⒨Ledru-Rollin) This lovely belle époque bistro and wine bar could just as easily count as a restaurant rather than a drinking place; the Auvergne-inspired dishes (mains €12 to €17.50) are delicious. But it's the 1902 art nouveau bar, elegant terrace, spot-on service and creative *grignotage* ('nibbles') menu that have put it on the aperitif A-list of local artists, *bobos* and celebs.

LE PURE CAFÉ
CAFE

Map p394 (www.lepurecafe.fr; 14 rue Jean Macé, 11e; ⊙7am-1am Mon-Fri, 8am-1am Sat, 9am-midnight Sun; MCharonne) With a vintage wood and zinc bar, this cherry-red Parisian corner cafe is an easy spot to drop into for a morning coffee, aperitif, meal (mains €13 to €16) or copious Sunday brunch (€19). Its selection of natural and organic wines by the glass is particularly good. Film buffs: spot its quaint cinematic facade and traditional interior used in the film *Before Sunset*.

BARRIO LATINO
CLUB

Map p394 (⌖01 55 78 84 75; www.barrio-latino. com; 46-48 rue du Faubourg St-Antoine, 11e; ⊙noon-2am Sun-Thu, noon-2.30am Fri, noon-3am Sat; MBastille) This enormous bar-restaurant with serious salsa dancing is spread over three highly impressive floors. It attracts Latinos, Latino wannabes, Latino wannahaves and a gay crowd. Don't arrive too late; the queue to get in can be formidably long. Table reservations recommended.

 # ENTERTAINMENT

OPÉRA BASTILLE
OPERA, CLASSICAL MUSIC

Map p394 (⌖08 92 89 90 90, 01 40 01 19 70; www.operadeparis.fr; 2-6 place de la Bastille, 12e; guided tour €15; ⊙box office 2.30-6.30pm Mon-Sat; MBastille) This 3400-seat venue is the city's main opera hall; it also stages ballet and classical concerts. Tickets go on sale online up to two weeks before they're available by telephone or at the box office. Standing-only tickets (*places débouts;* €5) are available 90 minutes before performances begin. By day, explore the eyesore opera house with a 90-minute guided tour backstage; check hours online.

BADABOUM
LIVE MUSIC

Map p394 (www.badaboum-paris.com; 2bis rue des Taillandiers, 11e; ⊙cocktail bar 7pm-2am Wed-Sat, club & concerts vary; MBastille, Ledru-Rollin) Formerly La Scène Bastille and freshly refitted, the onomatopoeically named Badaboum hosts a mixed bag of concerts on its up-close-and-personal stage, but focuses on electro, funk and hip-hop. Great atmosphere, super cocktails and a secret room upstairs.

LA FLÈCHE D'OR
LIVE MUSIC

(⌖01 44 64 01 02; www.flechedor.fr; 102bis rue de Bagnolet, 20e; ⊙variable; MAlexandre Dumas, Gambetta) Just over 1km northeast of place de la Nation in a former railway station on central Paris' outer edge, this awesome music venue hosts both indie rock concerts and house/electro DJ nights. The Golden Arrow – named for the train to Calais in the 1930s – has a solid reputation for promoting new talent.

LA CINÉMATHÈQUE FRANÇAISE
CINEMA

(www.cinemathequefrancaise.com; 51 rue de Bercy, 12e; ⊙noon-7pm Mon & Wed-Sat, 10am-5pm Sun; MBercy) This national institution is a temple to the 'seventh art' and always screens its foreign offerings in their original versions. Up to 10 movies a day are shown, usually retrospectives (Spielberg, Altman, Eastwood) mixed in with related but more obscure films.

LE MOTEL
LIVE MUSIC

Map p394 (www.lemotel.fr; 8 passage Josset, 11e; ⊙6pm-2am Tue-Sun; MLedru-Rollin) This hole-in-the wall venue in the hot-to-boiling-point 11e has become the go-to indie bar around Bastille. It's particularly well loved for its comfy sofas, inexpensive but quality drinks (Belgian beers on tap and indie cocktails) and excellent music. Live bands and DJs throughout the week.

LA CHAPELLE DES LOMBARDS
LIVE MUSIC

Map p394 (www.la-chapelle-des-lombards.com; 19 rue de Lappe, 11e; admission incl drink €20; ⊙11pm-5am Wed, Thu & Sun, to 6am Fri & Sat; MBastille) World music dominates this perennially popular Bastille dance club, with happening Latino DJs and reggae, funk and Afro jazz concerts. Performances usually take place on Friday and Saturday. Gals get in free before 2am on Friday and Saturday nights.

LE BALAJO
LIVE MUSIC

Map p394 (www.balajo.fr; 9 rue de Lappe, 11e; ⊙variable; MBastille) A mainstay of Parisian nightlife since 1936, this ancient ballroom is devoted to salsa classes and Latino music during the week, with an R&B slant on weekends when the dance floor rocks until *aube* (dawn). But the best time to visit is for its old-fashioned *musette* (accordion music) gigs on Monday afternoon from 2pm to 7pm.

 SHOPPING

VIRGINIE MONROE
FASHION & ACCESSORIES

Map p394 (www.virginiemonroe.com; 30 rue de Charonne, 11e; ☑12.30-7.30pm Mon, 11.30am-7.30pm Tue-Fri, 11am-7.30pm Sat; ⓜLedru-Rollin) Delicate rows of beads, lace-fine bracelets and other colourfully beaded pieces are the mainstay of this chic jewellery designer whose creative life was born in Brazil. She now has boutiques in Paris, Marseille and Lille.

ALT + GO
JEWELLERY

Map p394 (☑01 43 46 55 73; www.alt-go.fr; 21 rue de Cotte, 12e; ☑hours vary; ⓜLedru-Rollin) This French jewellery brand was created in Paris by Russian-born designers Svet Lana, Alexandre and Youlia. Pieces are fantastical and use a plethora of unexpected materials – thermoformed polished acrylic in every colour of the rainbow is a striking favourite. Call ahead to check if they're open (if the designers are showing elsewhere, the shop is closed).

LA COCOTTE
HOMEWARES

Map p394 (www.lacocotte.net; 5 rue Paul Bert, 11e; ☑noon-7pm Tue-Sat; ⓜFaidherbe-Chaligny) If the slew of gourmet restaurants along rue Paul Bert has inspired you to get into the kitchen, stop by this cute boutique for stylish, often Paris- and/or French-themed accoutrements such as tea towels, oven mitts, aprons, cookware, mugs, shopping bags and more.

MY CRAZY POP
FOOD

Map p394 (☑01 48 07 89 08; www.mycrazypop. com; 15 rue Trousseau, 11e; ☑1-7pm Wed-Fri, 11am-8pm Sat; ⓜLedru-Rollin) Roquefort and walnut, parmesan, barbecue and olive tapenade are among the amazing savoury flavours at this popcorn shop (a French first); sweet styles include gingerbread praline, salted-butter caramel, and orange and cinnamon. Wander through to the viewing window at the back to watch the kernels being popped using heat and pressure only (no oil).

LA MANUFACTURE DE CHOCOLAT
FOOD

Map p394 (www.lechocolat-alainducasse.com; 40 rue de la Roquette, 11e; ☑10.30am-7pm Tue-Sat; ⓜBastille) If you dine at superstar chef Alain Ducasse's restaurants, the chocolate will have been made here at Ducasse's own chocolate factory (the first in Paris to produce 'bean-to-bar' chocolate), which he set up with his former executive pastry chef Nicolas Berger. Deliberate over ganaches, pralines and truffles and no fewer than 44 flavours of chocolate bar.

You can also buy Ducasse's chocolates at his Left Bank boutique, **Le Chocolat Alain Ducasse** (Map p402; 26 rue St-Benoît, 6e; ☑1.30-7.30pm Mon, 10.30am-7.30pm Tue-Sat; ⓜSt Germain des Prés).

VIADUC DES ARTS
ARTS & CRAFTS

Map p394 (www.leviaducdesarts.com; 1-129 av Daumesnil, 12e; ☑hours vary; ⓜBastille, Gare de Lyon) Located beneath the red-brick arches of Promenade Plantée (p182) is the Viaduc des Arts, a line-up of craft shops where traditional artisans and contemporary designers carry out antique renovations and create new items using traditional methods. Artisans include furniture and tapestry restorers, interior designers, cabinetmakers, violin- and flute-makers, embroiderers and jewellers.

FERMOB
HOMEWARES

Map p394 (www.paris.fermob.com; 81-83 av Ledru-Rollin, 12e; ☑10am-7pm Mon-Sat; ⓜLedru-Rollin) If you want to create the 'Jardin du Luxembourg look' in your own garden, head for Fermob. It makes French-park-style benches and folding chairs in a range of great colours – from carrot and lemon to fuchsia and aubergine. Lovely cushions, rugs, throws, lamps and accessories for the home, too.

BERCY VILLAGE
MALL

(www.bercyvillage.com; Cour St-Émilion, 12e; ☑shops 11am-9pm Mon-Sat, restaurants & bars 11am-2am; ⓜCour St-Émilion) Set in the former Bercy wine warehouses, this popular outdoor mall has an 18-screen cinema, restaurants, bars and a string of stores catering to the needs of Parisian families: home design, clever kitchen supplies, quality toy stores and more.

The Islands

EATING | DRINKING & NIGHTLIFE | SHOPPING

Neighbourhood Top Five

❶ **Cathédrale Notre Dame de Paris** (p195) Revelling in the crowning glory of medieval Gothic architecture before ascending the cathedral's towers to take in the awe-inspiring panoramas.

❷ **Sainte-Chapelle** (p200) Reading richly coloured biblical tales, exquisitely

told through stained-glass imagery with a grace and beauty impossible to find elsewhere.

❸ **Conciergerie** (p201) Learning how Marie-Antoinette and thousands of others lived out their final days at this 14th-century palace-turned-prison before being beheaded.

❹ **Crypte Archéologique** (p198) Delving underground to discover fascinating Gallo-Roman, medieval and Haussmanian archaeological remains.

❺ **Berthillon** (p202) Savouring the sweetness of this famous Parisian ice cream during a stroll along the riverbanks.

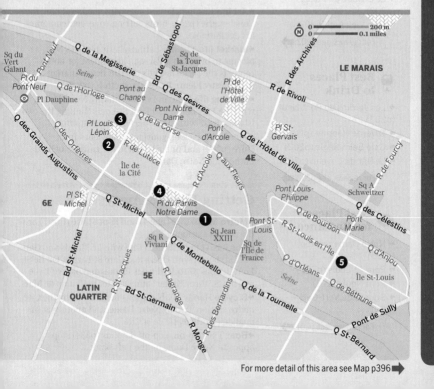

For more detail of this area see Map p396 ➡

Lonely Planet's Top Tip

Queues to see the sunlight stream through spectacular stained glass at Sainte-Chapelle can be staggeringly long. To speed things up, first visit the Conciergerie and buy a combination ticket covering admission to both the old prison and the chapel. With this *billet jumelé* you can skip Sainte-Chapelle's ticket queue and enter via the line for museum-pass holders and combination tickets. You'll still need to go through a security check.

⚔ Best Places to Eat

➡ Berthillon (p202)
➡ Café Saint Régis (p202)
➡ Les Voyelles (p202)
➡ Le Caveau du Palais (p202)
➡ Mon Vieil Ami (p203)

For reviews, see p202.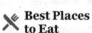

⬤ Best Places to Drink

➡ Les Jardins du Pont-Neuf (p203)
➡ Taverne Henri IV (p203)
➡ Café Saint Régis (p202)
➡ Le Bar du Caveau (p203)

For reviews, see p203.

⊙ Best Places for Romance

➡ Notre Dame rooftop (p195)
➡ Pont St-Louis (p202)
➡ Pont Neuf (p201)
➡ Square du Vert-Galant (p201)

For reviews, see p201.

THE ISLANDS

Explore: the Islands

Paris' landmark cathedral, Notre Dame, dominates the Île de la Cité, so where better to start your explorations? (Heading here first also means you'll beat the crowds.) In addition to viewing its stained-glass interior, allow around an hour to climb the spiralling stairs to the top of the towers, and another to explore the archaeological crypt.

For even more beautiful stained glass, don't miss the nearby exquisite chapel, Sainte-Chapelle, a few footsteps from the intriguing prison the Conciergerie.

Cross the Pont St-Louis to the enchanting little Île St-Louis. After lunch at the deliciously Parisian hang-out Café Saint Régis, browse the island's boutiques and buy an iconic Berthillon ice cream from its flagship premises to take to the water's edge.

After a traditional French meal at 'old friend' Mon Vieil Ami, stroll back over the Pont St-Louis, where you're likely to catch buskers, for a glass of wine at the Île de la Cité's venerable wine bar Taverne Henri IV or a cocktail at its new floating bar Les Jardins du Pont-Neuf. If you're still going strong, cross the Pont Neuf for entertainment options on either side of the Seine.

Local Life

➡ **Art life** Europe's largest surviving medieval hall, the Conciergerie (p201), hosts cutting-edge, contemporary art exhibitions.

➡ **Market life** The most atmospheric place to buy blooms to brighten a Parisian apartment (or hotel room) is the Île de la Cité's ancient flower market, Marché aux Fleurs Reine Elizabeth II (p203).

➡ **Busking life** Pont au Double (linking Notre Dame with the Left Bank) and Pont St-Louis (linking the two islands) buzz with street performers in summer.

➡ **Picnic life** Pick up gourmet sandwiches from Huré (p203) and find a bench in the gardens behind Cathédrale Notre Dame.

Getting There & Away

➡ **Metro** Metro Cité (line 4) and Pont Marie (line 7) are the closest stations.

➡ **Bus** Bus 47 links Île de la Cité with Le Marais and Gare de l'Est; bus 21 with Opéra and Gare St-Lazare. On Île St-Louis it's bus 67 to Jardin des Plantes and place d'Italie, and bus 87 through the Latin Quarter to Champ de Mars.

➡ **Bicycle** Handy Vélib' stations include one by the Cité metro station, two by Notre Dame, and another at 41 quai de l'Horloge, Île de la Cité.

➡ **Boat** The hop-on, hop-off Batobus (p334) stops opposite Notre Dame on the Left Bank.

TOP SIGHT
NOTRE DAME

Paris' most visited unticketed site, with upwards of 14 million crossing its threshold a year, is a masterpiece of French Gothic architecture. Highlights of the mighty cathedral include its three spectacular rose windows, treasury and bell towers. From the North Tower, 400-odd steps spiral to the top of the western facade, with frightening gargoyles and a spectacular view of Paris.

DON'T MISS

➡ Rose windows
➡ Treasury
➡ Bell towers
➡ Flying buttresses

PRACTICALITIES

➡ Map p396, D4
➡ ☎ 01 42 34 56 10
➡ www.cathedralede paris.com
➡ 6 place du Parvis Notre Dame, 4e
➡ cathedral free, adult/child towers €8.50/free, treasury €2/1
➡ ⊘ cathedral 8am-6.45pm Mon-Fri, to 7.15pm Sat & Sun, towers 10am-6.30pm Sun-Thu, to 11pm Fri & Sat Jul & Aug, 10am-6.30pm Apr-Jun & Sep, 10am-5pm Oct-Mar, treasury 9.30am-6pm Apr-Sep, 10am-5.30pm Oct-Mar
➡ Ⓜ Cité

Architecture

Built on a site occupied by earlier churches and, a millennium prior, a Gallo-Roman temple, Notre Dame was begun in 1163 and largely completed by the early 14th century. The cathedral was badly damaged during the Revolution, prompting architect Eugène Emmanuel Viollet-le-Duc to oversee extensive renovations between 1845 and 1864. Enter the magnificent forest of ornate flying buttresses that encircle the cathedral chancel and support its walls and roof.

Notre Dame is known for its sublime balance, though if you look closely you'll see all sorts of minor asymmetrical elements introduced to avoid monotony, in accordance with standard Gothic practice. These include the slightly different shapes of each of the three main portals, whose statues were once brightly coloured to make them more effective as a *Biblia pauperum* – a 'Bible of the poor' to help the illiterate faithful understand Old Testament stories, the Passion of the Christ and the lives of the saints.

Rose Windows

When you enter the cathedral its grand dimensions are immediately evident: the interior alone is 127m long, 48m wide and 35m high, and can accommodate some 6000 worshippers.

The most spectacular interior features are three rose windows, particularly the 10m-wide window over the western facade above the organ – one of the largest in the world, with 7800 pipes (900 of which have historical classification), 111 stops, five 56-key manuals and a 32-key pedalboard – and the window on the northern side of the transept (virtually unchanged since the 13th century).

Towers

A constant queue marks the entrance to the Tours de Notre Dame, the cathedral's bell towers. Climb the 400-odd spiralling steps to the top of the western facade of the North Tower, where you'll find yourself on the rooftop Galerie des Chimères (Gargoyles Gallery), face-to-face with frightening and fantastic gargoyles. These grotesque statues divert rainwater from the roof to prevent masonry damage, with the water exiting through the elongated, open mouth; they also, purportedly, ward off evil spirits. Although they appear medieval, they were installed by Eugène Viollet-le-Duc in the 19th century. From the rooftop there's a spectacular view over Paris.

In the South Tower hangs Emmanuel, the cathedral's original 13-tonne bourdon bell (all of the cathedral's bells are named). During the night of 24 August 1944, when the Île de la Cité was retaken by French, Allied and Resistance troops, the tolling of the Emmanuel announced Paris' approaching liberation. Emmanuel's peal purity comes from the precious

Notre Dame

TIMELINE

1160 Maurice de Sully becomes bishop of Paris. Mission: to grace growing Paris with a lofty new cathedral.

1182–90 The **choir with double ambulatory** 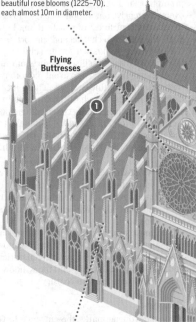 is finished and work starts on the nave and side chapels.

1200–50 The **west facade** ❷, with rose window, three portals and two soaring towers, goes up. Everyone is stunned.

1345 Some 180 years after the foundation stone was laid, the Cathédrale de Notre Dame is complete. It is dedicated to notre dame (our lady), the Virgin Mary.

1789 Revolutionaries smash the original **Gallery of Kings** ❸, pillage the cathedral and melt all its bells except the great bell Emmanuel. The cathedral becomes a Temple of Reason then a warehouse.

1831 Victor Hugo's novel *The Hunchback of Notre Dame* inspires new interest in the half-ruined Gothic cathedral.

1845–50 Architect Viollet-le-Duc undertakes its restoration. Twenty-eight new kings are sculpted for the west facade. The heavily decorated **portals** ❹ and **spire** ❺ are reconstructed. The neo-Gothic **treasury** ❻ is built.

1860 The area in front of Notre Dame is cleared to create the parvis, an al fresco classroom where Parisians can learn a catechism illustrated on sculpted stone portals.

1935 A rooster bearing part of the relics of the Crown of Thorns, St Denis and Ste Geneviève is put on top of the cathedral spire to protect those who pray inside.

1991 The architectural masterpiece of Notre Dame and its Seine-side riverbanks become a Unesco World Heritage Site.

2013 Notre Dame celebrates 850 years since construction began with a bevy of new bells and restoration works.

Virgin & Child
Spot all 37 artworks representing the Virgin Mary. Pilgrims have revered the pearly-cream sculpture of her in the sanctuary since the 14th century. Light a devotional candle and write some words to the *Livre de Vie* (Book of Life).

North Rose Window
See prophets, judges, kings and priests venerate Mary in vivid blue and violet glass, one of three beautiful rose blooms (1225–70), each almost 10m in diameter.

Flying Buttresses

Choir Screen
No part of the cathedral weaves biblical tales more evocatively than these ornate wooden panels, carved in the 14th century after the Black Death killed half the country's population. The faintly gaudy colours were restored in the 1960s.

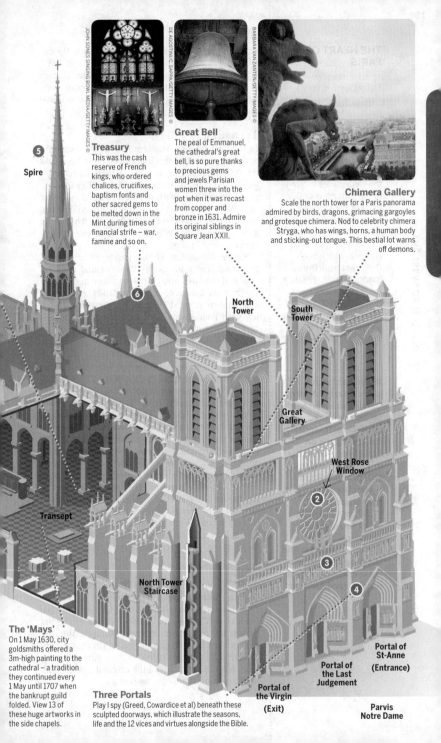

Spire

Treasury
This was the cash reserve of French kings, who ordered chalices, crucifixes, baptism fonts and other sacred gems to be melted down in the Mint during times of financial strife – war, famine and so on.

Great Bell
The peal of Emmanuel, the cathedral's great bell, is so pure thanks to precious gems and jewels Parisian women threw into the pot when it was recast from copper and bronze in 1631. Admire its original siblings in Square Jean XXIII.

Chimera Gallery
Scale the north tower for a Paris panorama admired by birds, dragons, grimacing gargoyles and grotesque chimera. Nod to celebrity chimera Stryga, who has wings, horns, a human body and sticking-out tongue. This bestial lot warns off demons.

North Tower

South Tower

Great Gallery

West Rose Window

Transept

North Tower Staircase

The 'Mays'
On 1 May 1630, city goldsmiths offered a 3m-high painting to the cathedral – a tradition they continued every 1 May until 1707 when the bankrupt guild folded. View 13 of these huge artworks in the side chapels.

Three Portals
Play I spy (Greed, Cowardice et al) beneath these sculpted doorways, which illustrate the seasons, life and the 12 vices and virtues alongside the Bible.

Portal of the Virgin (Exit)

Portal of the Last Judgement

Portal of St-Anne (Entrance)

Parvis Notre Dame

THE HEART OF PARIS

Notre Dame is very much the heart of Paris – so much so that distances from Paris to every part of metropolitan France are measured from place du Parvis Notre Dame, the vast square in front of the Cathedral of Our Lady of Paris, where crowds gather in the afternoon sun to admire the cathedral's facade. A bronze star across the street from the cathedral's main entrance marks the exact location of **Point Zéro des Routes de France** (Map p396; 6 place de Parvis Notre Dame, 4e; M Cité).

Music has been a sacred part of Notre Dame's soul since birth. The best day to appreciate its musical heritage is on Sunday at a Gregorian or polyphonic Mass (10am and 6.30pm respectively) or a free organ recital (4.30pm). From October to June the cathedral stages evening concerts; find the program online at www.musique-sacree-notredameparis.fr.

gems and jewels Parisian women threw into the pot when it was recast from copper and bronze in 1631.

As part of 2013's celebrations for Notre Dame's 850th anniversary since construction began, nine new bells were installed, replicating the original medieval chimes.

Treasury

In the southeastern transept, the *trésor* (treasury) contains artwork, liturgical objects and first-class relics; pay a small fee to enter. Among its religious jewels and gems is the Ste-Couronne (Holy Crown), purportedly the wreath of thorns placed on Jesus' head before he was crucified. It is exhibited between 3pm and 4pm on the first Friday of each month, 3pm to 4pm every Friday during Lent, and 10am to 5pm on Good Friday.

Easier to admire is the treasury's wonderful collection, Les Camées des Papes (Papal cameos). Sculpted with incredible finesse in shell and framed in silver, the 268-piece collection depicts every pope in miniature from St Pierre to the present day, ending with Pope Benoit XVI. Note the different posture, hand gestures and clothes of each pope.

The Mays

Walk past the **choir**, with its carved wooden stalls and statues representing the Passion of the Christ, to admire the cathedral's wonderful collection of paintings in its nave side chapels. From 1449 onwards, city goldsmiths offered to the cathedral each year on 1 May a tree strung with devotional ribbons and banners to honour the Virgin Mary – to whom Notre Dame (Our Lady) is dedicated. Fifty years later the goldsmiths' annual gift, known as a May, had become a tabernacle decorated with scenes from the Old Testament, and, from 1630, a large canvas – 3m tall – commemorating one of the Acts of the Apostles, accompanied by a poem or literary explanation. By the early 18th century, when the brotherhood of goldsmiths was dissolved, the cathedral had received 76 such monumental paintings – just 13 can be admired today.

Crypt

Under the square in front of Notre Dame lies the **Crypte Archéologique** (Archaeological Crypt; Map p396; www.crypte.paris.fr; adult/child €7/5; ☉10am-6pm Tue-Sun), a 117m-long and 28m-wide area displaying *in situ* the remains of structures built on this site during the Gallo-Roman period, a 4th-century enclosure wall, the foundations of the medieval foundlings hospice and a few of the original sewers sunk by Haussmann. Audioguides cost €5.

CATHÉDRALE NOTRE DAME DE PARIS

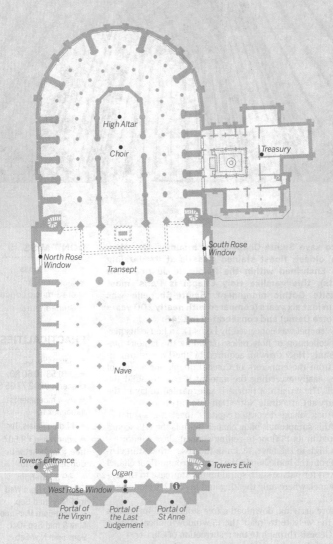

High Altar

Choir

Treasury

North Rose Window

South Rose Window

Transept

Nave

Towers Entrance

Towers Exit

Organ

West Rose Window

Portal of the Virgin

Portal of the Last Judgement

Portal of St Anne

Western Facade

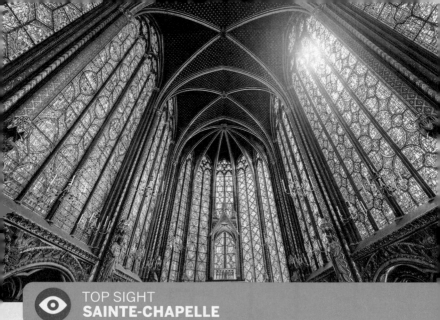

TOP SIGHT
SAINTE-CHAPELLE

Try to save Sainte-Chapelle for a sunny day, when Paris' oldest, finest stained glass is at its dazzling best. Enshrined within the Palais de Justice (Law Courts), this gemlike Holy Chapel is Paris' most exquisite Gothic monument. Sainte-Chapelle was built in just six years (compared with nearly 200 years for Notre Dame) and consecrated in 1248.

The chapel was conceived by Louis IX to house his personal collection of holy relics, including the famous Ste-Couronne (Holy Crown), acquired by the French king in 1239 from the emperors of Constantinople for a sum of money easily exceeding the amount it cost to build the chapel! The wreath of thorns is safeguarded today in the treasury at Cathédrale Notre Dame de Paris.

Statues, foliage-decorated capitals, angels and so on decorate this sumptuous, bijou chapel. But it is the 1113 scenes depicted in its 15 floor-to-ceiling stained-glass windows – 15.5m high in the nave, 13.5m in the apse – that stun visitors. From the bookshop in the former ground-floor chapel reserved for palace staff, spiral up the staircase to the upper chapel, where only the king and his close friends were allowed.

Before arriving, download a free storyboard in English from the website to 'read' the 15-window biblical story – from Genesis through to the resurrection of Christ.

Classical- and sacred-music concerts held here are a soul-stirring experience really not to be missed. Check schedules and buy tickets at **Fnac** (☏08 92 68 36 22; www.fnactickets.com).

DON'T MISS

➡ Stained glass
➡ Classical- and sacred-music concerts
➡ Guided tours

PRACTICALITIES

➡ Map p396, C2
➡ ☏01 53 40 60 80, concerts 01 42 77 65 65
➡ www.monuments-nationaux.fr
➡ 4 bd du Palais, 1er
➡ adult/child €8.50/ free, joint ticket with Conciergerie €15
➡ ⊙9.30am-6pm Thu-Tue, to 9pm Wed mid-May–mid-Sep, 9.30am-6pm Mar–mid-May & mid-Sep–Oct, 9am-5pm Nov-Feb
➡ Ⓜ Cité

⊙ SIGHTS

Île de la Cité was the site of the first settlement in Paris (c 3rd century BC) and later the centre of Roman Lutetia. The island remained the hub of royal and ecclesiastical power, even after the city spread to both banks of the Seine in the Middle Ages. Smaller Île St-Louis was actually two uninhabited islets called Île Notre Dame (Our Lady Isle) and Île aux Vaches (Cows Island) in the early 17th century – until a building contractor and two financiers worked out a deal with Louis XIII to create one island and build two stone bridges to the mainland.

CATHÉDRALE NOTRE DAME DE PARIS   CATHEDRAL
See p195.

SAINTE-CHAPELLE   CHAPEL
See p200.

CONCIERGERIE   MONUMENT
Map p396 (www.monuments-nationaux.fr; 2 bd du Palais, 1er; adult/child €8.50/free, joint ticket with Sainte-Chapelle €15; ⊙9.30am-6pm; Ⓜ Cité) A royal palace in the 14th century, the Conciergerie later became a prison. During the Reign of Terror (1793–94) alleged enemies of the Revolution were incarcerated here before being brought before the Revolutionary Tribunal next door in the Palais de Justice. Top-billing exhibitions take place in the beautiful, Rayonnant Gothic Salle des Gens d'Armes, Europe's largest surviving medieval hall.

Of the almost 2800 prisoners held in the dungeons during the Reign of Terror (in various 'classes' of cells, no less) before being sent in tumbrels to the guillotine, star prisoner was Queen Marie-Antoinette – see a reproduction of her cell. As the Revolution began to turn on its own, radicals Danton and Robespierre made an appearance at the Conciergerie and, finally, the judges of the tribunal themselves.

SQUARE DU VERT-GALANT   PARK
Map p396 (place du Pont Neuf; ⊙24hr; Ⓜ Pont Neuf) Chestnut, yew, black walnut and weeping willow trees grace this picturesque park at the westernmost tip of the Île de la Cité, along with migratory birds including mute swans, pochard and tufted ducks, black-headed gulls and wagtails. Sitting at the islands' original level, 7m below their current height, the waterside park is reached by stairs leading down from the Pont Neuf. It's romantic at any time of day but especially in the evening watching the sun set over the river.

MÉMORIAL DES MARTYRS DE LA DÉPORTATION   MONUMENT
Map p396 (www.cheminsdememoire.gouv.fr; square de l'Île de France, 1er; ⊙10am-7pm Apr-Sep, to 5pm Tue-Sun Oct-Mar; Ⓜ Cité, Ⓡ RER St-Michel–Notre Dame) FREE The Memorial to the Victims of the Deportation, erected in 1962, remembers the 200,000 French residents (including 76,000 Jews, of whom 11,000 were children) who were deported to and murdered in Nazi concentration camps during WWII. A single barred 'window' separates the bleak, rough-concrete courtyard from the waters of the Seine. Inside lies the Tomb of the Unknown Deportee.

ÉGLISE ST-LOUIS EN L'ÎLE   CHURCH
Map p396 (www.saintlouisenlile.catholique.fr; 19 rue St-Louis en l'Île; ⊙9.30am-1pm & 2-7.30pm Mon-Sat, 9am-1pm & 2-7pm Sun; Ⓜ Pont Marie) The French baroque Église St-Louis en l'Île was built between 1664 and 1726. Classical music concerts take place some Sundays (tickets €14 to €30); check the agenda online.

PONT NEUF   BRIDGE
Map p396 (Ⓜ Pont Neuf) Paris' oldest bridge, ironically named 'New Bridge', has linked the western end of Île de la Cité with both riverbanks since 1607, when the king, Henri IV, inaugurated it by crossing the bridge on a white stallion.

View the bridge's arches (seven on the northern stretch and five on the southern span), decorated with 381 *mascarons* (grotesque figures) depicting barbers, dentists, pickpockets, loiterers etc, from a spot along the river or afloat.

The inaugural crossing is commemorated by an equestrian statue of Henri IV, known to his subjects as the Vert Galant ('jolly rogue' or 'dirty old man', perspective depending).

Pont Neuf and nearby place Dauphine were used for public exhibitions in the 18th century. In the last century the bridge became an objet d'art in 1963, when School of Paris artist Nonda built, exhibited and lived in a huge Trojan horse of steel and wood on the bridge; in 1985 when Bulgarian-born 'environmental sculptor' Christo famously wrapped the bridge in beige fabric; and in

1994 when Japanese designer Kenzo covered it with flowers.

PONT ST-LOUIS BRIDGE

Map p396 (MPont Marie) The Île de la Cité and Île St-Louis are connected by the postcard-perfect Pont St-Louis.

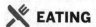 EATING

Île St-Louis is a pleasant if pricey and often touristy place to dine. Otherwise barren of decent eating places, Île de la Cité has a handful of lovely addresses on its western tip. Self-caterers will find a couple of *fromageries* on rue St-Louis en l'Île, 4e, as well as a small supermarket.

★ BERTHILLON ICE CREAM €

Map p396 (www.berthillon.fr; 31 rue St-Louis en l'Île, 4e; 1/2/3 scoops take away €3/4/6.50, eat-in €4.50/7.50/10.50; ⊗10am-8pm Wed-Sun, closed Aug; MPont Marie) Founded here in 1954, this esteemed *glacier* (ice-cream maker) is still run by the same family today. Its 70 all-natural, chemical-free flavours include fruit sorbets such as blackcurrant or pink grapefruit, and richer ice creams made from fresh milk and eggs, such as salted caramel, *marrons glacés* (candied chestnuts) and Agenaise (Armagnac and prunes), along with seasonal flavours like gingerbread.

If you eat on-site in the sweet timber-fronted tearoom, ice creams come with Chantilly (cream whipped with sugar) and coulis.

★ CAFÉ SAINT RÉGIS CAFE €

Map p396 (www.cafesaintregisparis.com; 6 rue Jean du Bellay, 4e; breakfast & snacks €3.50-14.50, mains €18-32; ⊗8am-2am; ☏; MPont Marie) Waiters in long white aprons, a white ceramic-tiled interior and retro vintage decor make hip Le Saint Régis (as regulars call it) a deliciously Parisian hang-out any time of day – from breakfast pastries to mid-morning pancakes, lunchtime salads and burgers and early-evening oyster platters. Come midnight it morphs into a late-night hotspot.

Sunday brunch and happy hour (7pm to 9pm daily) both pack in the crowds.

LE CAVEAU DU PALAIS MODERN FRENCH €€

Map p396 (☏01 43 26 04 28; www.caveaudu palais.fr; 19 place Dauphine, 1er; mains €21-27; ⊗noon-2.30pm & 7-10pm Mon-Sat; MPont Neuf) Even when the western Île de la Cité shows few other signs of life, the Caveau's half-timbered dining areas and (weather permitting) al fresco terrace are packed with diners tucking into bountiful fresh fare: steak tartare with quail's egg, artichoke and mushroom risotto with braised spinach, turbot with sweet potato and sea salt mash, and deconstructed lemon tart.

More informal dishes are served up at its adjacent wine bar, Le Bar du Caveau (p203).

MA SALLE À MANGER BISTRO €

Map p396 (☏01 43 29 52 34; www.masallea manger.fr; 26 place Dauphine, 1er; 2-/3-course lunch menus €20.50/25.50, dinner menus €23.50/28.50; ⊗9am-10.30pm; MPont Neuf) Framed by a pretty-as-a-picture blue-and-white striped awning and pavement tables, on tucked-away Place Dauphine, convivial little bistro-wine bar 'My Dining Room' chalks its changing menu on the blackboard. Simple yet inspired dishes might include French onion soup, Camembert baked with wine, confit of duck with baked apple, filet Mignon with potato dauphinoise (thinly sliced baked potatoes) and a feather-light crème brûlée.

L'ÎLOT VACHE TRADITIONAL FRENCH €€

Map p396 (☏01 73 20 21 64; www.lilotvache.fr; 35 rue St-Louis en l'Île, 4e; 3-course menu €39, mains €24.50-35; ⊗7-11.30pm; ☏; MPont Marie) Named for one of the Île St-Louis' previous two islands and decorated with cow statuettes, this former butcher shop flickers with candles that give its exposed stone and wooden beams a romantic glow. Traditional French classics span Burgundy snails with parsley butter to bœuf bourguignon, duck breast with raspberry jus, and roast seasonal fruits with blackcurrant sorbet.

HURÉ BOULANGERIE €

Map p396 (www.hure-createur.fr; 1 rue d'Arcole, 4e; takeaway lunch menus €8.50-9.50, sandwiches €3-6; ⊗6.30am-8pm Mon-Sat; MSt-Michel Notre Dame, Châtelet) Feisty savoury tarts and quiches, jumbo salads bursting with fresh veggies, mountains of giant meringues piled high on the counter, giant cookies and cakes every colour of the rainbow: if you're after a light al fresco lunch, you'll be hard-pushed to find a better *boulangerie* near Notre Dame.

There are two other branches in Paris.

LES VOYELLES MODERN FRENCH €€

Map p396 (☏01 46 33 69 75; www.les-voyelles. com; 74 quai des Orfèvres, 4e; 2-/3-course menus

THE ISLANDS EATING

€17/22.50; ⊗noon-3pm & 7-10.30pm Tue-Sat; Ⓜ Pont Neuf) Worth the short walk from Notre Dame, the Vowels – spot the letters scattered between books and beautiful objects on the shelves lining the intimate 'library' dining room – is thoroughly contemporary, with fare ranging from finger food (including a daily burger) to full-blown *menus*, which might feature *onglet de bœuf* (hanger steak) with Béarnaise sauce. Its pavement terrace is Paris gold.

Saturdays from noon to 3pm see it host a buffet brunch (€26; with Champagne €35).

LES FOUS DE L'ÎLE   BRASSERIE €€
Map p396 (☏01 43 25 76 67; www.lesfousde lile.com; 33 rue des Deux Ponts, 4e; 2-/3-course menus lunch €20/26, dinner €25/30; ⊗10am-2am; ☏; Ⓜ Pont Marie) This plum-coloured brasserie is a popular family address with an open kitchen and a cockerel theme celebrating the French national symbol, with knickknacks throughout. Hearty fare like *cassoulet* (traditional Languedoc stew with beans and meat) and blackened free-range Challans chicken is served continuously between noon and 11pm. On Sundays, brunch (€25; €29 with a cocktail) buzzes between noon and 4pm.

MON VIEIL AMI   TRADITIONAL FRENCH €€€
Map p396 (☏01 40 46 01 35; www.mon-vieil-ami. com; 69 rue St-Louis en l'Île, 4e; menu €48, mains €14-25; ⊗noon-2.30pm & 7-11pm; ☏; Ⓜ Pont Marie) Alsatian chef Antoine Westermann is the creative talent behind this sleek black neobistro where guests are treated like old friends (hence the name) and vegetables get star billing. From Wednesday to Sunday only, the good-value lunchtime *plat du jour* (dish of the day), such as wintertime kale with smoked bacon and roast chicken, is a perfect reflection of the season.

🍷 DRINKING & NIGHTLIFE

Drinking venues on the islands are in short supply. They do exist, but use them as a starting point as very few places stay open late.

LES JARDINS DU PONT-NEUF   COCKTAIL BAR
Map p396 (www.jdp9.com; quai de l'Horloge, 1er; ⊗7pm-2am Tue-Sat; ☏; Ⓜ Pont Neuf) Island life became more glamorous with the opening of this ultra-chic floating cocktail bar aboard a barge moored by the Pont Neuf. Decked out with art-nouveau-inspired decor including rattan furniture and hanging plants, its two vast terraces overlook the Seine. There's also a dance floor; check the website for upcoming soirées.

TAVERNE HENRI IV   WINE BAR
Map p396 (13 place du Pont Neuf, 1er; ⊗noon-11pm Mon-Sat, closed Aug; Ⓜ Pont Neuf) Dating from 1885, this venerable wine bar lures legal types from the nearby Palais de Justice (not to mention celeb writers and actors, as the autographed snaps testify). A choice of *tartines* (open sandwiches), charcuterie (cold cooked meats) and aromatic cheese platters complement its extensive wine list.

LE BAR DU CAVEAU   WINE BAR
Map p396 (www.caveaudupalais.fr; 17 place Dauphine, 1er; ⊗8am-6.30pm Mon-Wed & Fri, 8am-10pm Thu; Ⓜ Pont Neuf) The wine bar for neighbour Le Caveau du Palais (p202) is not only a good spot for a glass of wine from France's flagship regions but also small, inexpensive dishes like salads, *tartines* (open-faced sandwiches), and croques madam and monsieur (toasted ham and cheese sandwiches, the former with a fried egg on top).

LE FLORE EN L'ÎLE   CAFE
Map p396 (www.lefloreenlile.fr; 42 quai d'Orléans, 4e; ⊗7am-2am; Ⓜ Pont Marie) A tourist crowd piles into this green-and-gold awning-shaded, old-world people-watching spot with prime views of the buskers on Pont St-Louis. There's an extensive menu of brasserie-style fare spanning salads to steaks; if you're looking to linger over a Berthillon ice cream, be aware that it's pricier here than other spots around the island, including Berthillon's own premises.

🔒 SHOPPING

Île St-Louis is a shopper's delight for craft-filled boutiques and tiny, charming specialist stores. Head to Île de la Cité for souvenirs and tourist kitsch.

★MARCHÉ AUX FLEURS REINE ELIZABETH II   MARKET
Map p396 (place Louis Lépin, 4e; ⊗8am-7.30pm Mon-Sat; Ⓜ Cité) Blooms have been sold at this flower market since 1808, making it the

oldest market of any kind in Paris. On Sunday, between 8am and 7pm, it transforms into a cacophonous bird market, the **Marché aux Oiseaux** (Map p396; ⊙8am-7pm Sun).

⭐**38 SAINT LOUIS** FOOD & DRINKS
Map p396 (38 rue St-Louis en l'Île, 4e; ⊙8.30am-10pm Tue-Sat, 9.30am-4pm Sun; ⓂPont Marie) Not only does this contemporary, creamy white-fronted *fromagerie* run by a young, dynamic, food-driven duo have an absolutely superb selection of first-class French *fromage* (cheese), it also offers Saturday wine tastings, artisan fruit juices and prepared dishes to go such as sheep's-cheese salad with truffle oil, and wooden boxes filled with vacuum-packed cheese to take home.

L'ÎLES AUX IMAGES ART
Map p396 (☑01 56 24 15 22; www.lileauximages.com; 51 rue Saint-Louis en l'Île, 4e; ⊙2-7pm Mon-Sat & by appointment; ⓂPont Marie) Original and rare vintage posters, photographs and lithographs dating from 1850 onwards from artists including Man Ray, Salvador Dalí, Paul Gauguin and Picasso are stocked at this gallery-boutique. Many depict Parisian scenes and make evocative home decorations. Framing can be arranged.

CLAIR DE RÊVE TOYS
Map p396 (www.clairdereve.com; 35 rue St-Louis en l'Île, 4e; ⊙11am-1pm & 1.30-7.15pm Mon-Sat; ⓂPont Marie) Stringed marionettes made of papier mâché, leather and porcelain bob

from the ceiling of this endearing little shop. It also sells wind-up toys and music boxes.

IL CAMPIELLO ARTS & CRAFTS
Map p396 (www.ilcampiello.com; 88 rue St-Louis en l'Île, 4e; ⊙noon-7pm; ⓂPont Marie) Venetian carnival masks – intricately crafted from papier mâché, ceramics and leather – are the speciality of this exquisite shop, which also sells jewellery made from Murano glass beads. It was established by a native of Venice, to which the Île St-Louis bears more than a passing resemblance.

PREMIÈRE PRESSION PROVENCE FOOD
Map p396 (www.ppp-olive.com; 51 rue St-Louis en l'Île, 4e; ⊙10.30am-2pm & 3-7.30pm Mon-Fri, 11am-2pm & 3-8pm Sat & Sun; ⓂPont Marie) Its name evokes the first pressing of olives to make olive oil in the south of France, which is what this gourmet boutique stocks – as oil or in any number of spreads and sauces (pesto, tapenade etc).

LIBRAIRIE ULYSSE BOOKS
Map p396 (www.ulysse.fr; 26 rue St-Louis en l'Île, 4e; ⊙2-8pm Tue-Fri; ⓂPont Marie) You can barely move in between this shop's antiquarian and new travel guides, *National Geographic* back editions and maps. Opened in 1971 by the intrepid Catherine Domaine, this was the world's first travel bookshop. Hours vary, but ring the bell and Catherine will open up if she's around.

Latin Quarter

Neighbourhood Top Five

❶ Musée National du Moyen Âge (p207) Time-travelling back to the Middle Ages at France's foremost medieval museum.

❷ Institut du Monde Arabe (p210) Visiting the fascinating exhibits inside the stunning Jean Nouvel-designed building before heading to the top to catch the incredible panorama from the roof.

❸ Jardin des Plantes (p209) Strolling around Paris' sprawling botanic gardens and visiting its historic greenhouses, zoo and the many branches of the Natural History Museum located here.

❹ Shakespeare & Company (p219) Browsing the shelves of Paris' most magical bookshop and refuelling at its wonderful new literary-themed cafe.

❺ Panthéon (p209) Paying homage to France's greatest thinkers buried beneath this domed neoclassical mausoleum.

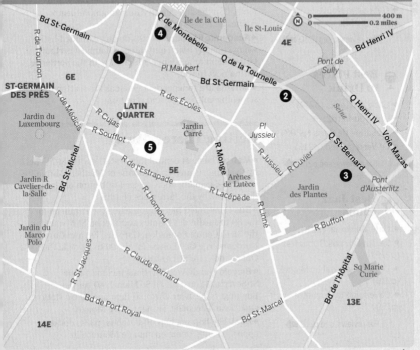

For more detail of this area see Map p398 and p400 ➡

Lonely Planet's Top Tip

While hungry first-time visitors are often drawn into the maze of tiny streets between the Seine, rue St-Jacques and bd St-Germain, you'd be wise to simply avoid this area altogether. Instead, consider grabbing some bread, cheese, charcuterie and wine from local speciality shops and enjoy some multimillion-dollar views with lunch or dinner. Best bets? The quays along the Seine, the place du Panthéon (a fave with students) and the leafy Jardin des Plantes.

✕ Best Places to Eat

➡ Restaurant AT (p215)

➡ Shakespeare & Company Café (p210)

➡ Sola (p215)

➡ Café de la Nouvelle Mairie (p212)

For reviews, see p210.➡

☕ Best Places to Drink

➡ Little Bastards (p217)

➡ Caffé Juno (p216)

➡ Mosquée de Paris (p208)

➡ Le Verre à Pied (p216)

For reviews, see p215.➡

☆ Best Jazz Clubs

➡ Café Universel (p218)

➡ Le Caveau des Oubliettes (p219)

➡ Le Petit Journal St-Michel (p219)

➡ Caveau de la Huchette (p219)

For reviews, see p218.➡

LATIN QUARTER

Explore: Latin Quarter

The centre of Parisian higher education since the Middle Ages, the Latin Quarter takes its name from the classical language spoken here by students and professors until the French Revolution. A serene spot to begin the day is in the botanic gardens, the Jardin des Plantes, before sipping sweet mint tea in the Mosquée de Paris or strolling through the engaging Arab World Institute.

But there's no better strip to see, smell and taste the Latin Quarter than the thriving market street rue Mouffetard, so it's worth combining a flit from food stall to fabulous food shop with lunch at one of the restaurants utilising its produce (skip it on Mondays, when the market stalls are shut).

After admiring the Panthéon's vast interior, the hollow of the afternoon is a contemplative time to meander through the Musée National du Moyen Âge for the ultimate medieval history lesson.

After dinner at a local bistro, head down into a medieval cellar (many used as Revolutionary prisons) for jazz and jam sessions, or join the area's students in the quarter's lively pubs.

Local Life

➡ **Sporting life** Join the locals playing boules and football in the 2nd-century Roman amphitheatre Arènes de Lutèce (p217).

➡ **Academic life** Clink drinks during extended Latin Quarter happy hours and there will almost certainly be a student or academic affiliated with the Sorbonne sitting next to you.

➡ **Cinema life** Independent cinemas are scattered, screening cult, classic and rare films.

Getting There & Away

➡ **Metro** The most central metro stations are St-Michel by the Seine; Cluny–La Sorbonne or Maubert-Mutualité on bd St-Germain; and Censier Daubenton or Gare d'Austerlitz by the Jardin des Plantes.

➡ **Bus** Convenient bus stops include the Panthéon for the 89 to Jardin des Plantes and 13e; bd St-Michel for the 38 to Centre Pompidou, Gare de l'Est and Gare du Nord; and rue Gay Lussac for the 27 to Île de la Cité, Opéra and Gare St-Lazare.

➡ **Bicycle** Handy Vélib' stations include 42 rue St-Severin, 5e, just off bd St-Michel; 40 rue des Boulangers, 5e, near Cardinal Lemoine metro station; and 27 rue Lacépède, 5e, near place Monge.

➡ **Boat** The hop-on, hop-off Batobus (p334) docks opposite Notre Dame on quai de Montebello.

TOP SIGHT
MUSÉE NATIONAL DU MOYEN ÂGE

Sublime treasures at the National Museum of the Middle Ages span medieval statuary, stained glass and objets d'art to its celebrated series of tapestries, *The Lady with the Unicorn*. Evocatively housed in an ornate 15th-century mansion (the Hôtel de Cluny) and the much older *frigidarium* (cold room) of an enormous Roman-era bathhouse, this is one of Paris' top small museums.

Initially the residential quarters of the Cluny Abbots, the Hôtel de Cluny was later occupied by Alexandre du Sommerard, who moved here in 1833 with his collection of medieval and Renaissance objects. Bought by the state after his death, the museum opened a decade later, retaining the Hôtel de Cluny's original layout and features.

The restored 1st-floor late-Gothic chapel, La Chapelle de l'Hôtel de Cluny – with rich carvings of Christ on the cross, 13 angels, floral and foliage ornaments – has direct access to the garden.

The museum's northwestern corner is where you'll find the remains of the Gallo-Roman bathhouse, built around AD 200. Look for the display of the fragment of mosaic *Love Riding a Dolphin*, as well as a gorgeous marble bathtub from Rome. Outside the museum, remnants of the other rooms – a *palestra* (exercise room), *tepidarium* (warm bath) and *calidarium* (hot bath) – are visible.

DON'T MISS

➡ Tapestries
➡ Hôtel de Cluny
➡ Gallo-Roman bathhouse
➡ Gardens

PRACTICALITIES

➡ Map p398, B2
➡ www.musee-moyenage.fr
➡ 6 place Paul Painlevé, 5e
➡ adult/child €8/free, during temporary exhibitions €9/free
➡ ⏲9.15am-5.45pm Wed-Mon
➡ Ⓜ Cluny–La Sorbonne

Upstairs on the 1st floor (room 13) are the unicorn tapestries, representing the five senses and an enigmatic sixth, perhaps the heart. It's believed that they were originally commissioned around 1500 by the Le Viste family in Paris. Discovered in 1814 in the Chateau de Boussac, they were acquired by the museum in 1882 and have since provided inspiration to many, from Prosper Mérimée and George Sand to, most recently, Tracy Chevalier.

Small gardens to the museum's northeast, including the Jardin Céleste (Celestial Garden) and the Jardin d'Amour (Garden of Love), are planted with flowers, herbs and shrubs that appear in works hanging throughout the museum.

◉ SIGHTS

The Latin Quarter's Roman and medieval roots can be seen throughout the neighbourhood but especially at its premier museum, the Musée National du Moyen Âge. Natural history buffs won't want to miss the museums making up the Muséum National d'Histoire Naturelle in the beautiful botanical gardens, the Jardin des Plantes.

MUSÉE NATIONAL DU MOYEN ÂGE   MUSEUM
See p207.

SORBONNE   UNIVERSITY
Map p398 (www.sorbonne.fr; 12 rue de la Sorbonne, 5e; Ⓜ Cluny–La Sorbonne or RER Luxembourg) The crème de la crème of academia flock to this distinguished university, one of the world's most famous. Today 'La Sorbonne' embraces most of the 13 autonomous universities – some 45,215 students in all – created when the University of Paris was reorganised after the student protests of 1968. Visitors are not permitted to enter.

The original Sorbonne was founded in 1253 by Robert de Sorbon, confessor to Louis IX, as a college for 16 impoverished theology students; soon after it grew into a powerful body with its own government and laws.

The Chapelle de la Sorbonne (Map p398), the university's distinctive domed church, was built between 1635 and 1642. The remains of Cardinal Richelieu (1585–1642) lie in a tomb with an effigy of a cardinal's hat suspended above.

SQUARE RENÉ VIVIANI   PARK
Map p398 (quai de Montebello, 5e; ⊙24hr; Ⓜ St-Michel) Opened in 1928 on the site of the former graveyard of adjoining church Église St-Julien-le-Pauvre, this picturesque little park is home to the oldest tree in Paris. The black locust *(Robinia pseudoacacia)* was planted here in 1602 by Henri III, Henri IV and Louis XII's gardener, Jean Robin, and is now supported by concrete pillars disguised as branches and trunks.

A 1995-installed bronze fountain by Georges Jeanclos depicts the legend of Saint Julien. Roses bloom in spring and summer.

MOSQUÉE DE PARIS   MOSQUE
Map p400 (☎01 43 31 14 32; www.la-mosquee.com; 2bis place du Puits de l'Ermite, 5e; adult/child €3/2; ⊙9am-noon & 2-7pm Sat-Thu Apr-Sep, 9am-noon & 2-6pm Sat-Thu Oct-Mar; Ⓜ Place Monge) Paris' central mosque, with a striking 26m-high minaret, was completed in 1926 in an ornate art deco Moorish style. You can visit the interior to admire the intricate tile work and calligraphy. A separate entrance leads to the wonderful North African–style **hammam** (Map p400; 39 rue Geoffroy-St-Hilaire, 5e; admission €18; spa package from €43; ⊙10am-9pm Mon, Wed, Thu & Sat, 2-9pm Fri), **restaurant** (Map p400; mains €15-26; ⊙kitchen noon-2.30pm & 7.30-10.30pm) and **tearoom** (Map p400; ⊙9am-11.30pm), and a small *souk* (actually more of a gift shop). Visitors must be modestly dressed.

MÉNAGERIE DU JARDIN DES PLANTES   ZOO
Map p400 (www.mnhn.fr; 57 rue Cuvier, 5e; adult/child €13/9; ⊙9am-6pm Mon-Fri, to 6.30pm Sat & Sun Easter-Oct, to 5pm Nov-Easter; Ⓜ Gare d'Austerlitz) Like the Jardin des Plantes (p209) in which it's located, this 1000-animal zoo is more than a tourist attraction, also doubling as a research centre for the reproduction of rare and endangered species. During the Prussian siege of 1870, the animals of the day were themselves endangered, when almost all were eaten by starving Parisians.

Do note that the recently renovated zoo (p183) in Vincennes is considerably larger.

ÉGLISE ST ÉTIENNE DU MONT   CHURCH
Map p400 (www.saintetiennedumont.fr; 1 place Ste-Geneviève, 5e; ⊙8.45am-7.45pm Tue-Fri, 8.45am-noon & 2-7.45pm Sat, 8.45am-12.15pm & 2.30-7.45pm Sun; Ⓜ Cardinal Lemoine) FREE The Church of Mount St Stephen, built between 1492 and 1655, contains Paris' only surviving rood screen (1535), separating the chancel from the nave; the others were removed during the late Renaissance because they prevented the faithful in the nave from seeing the priest celebrate Mass.

In the nave's southeastern corner, the tomb of Ste Geneviève lies in a chapel.

The patron of Paris, Ste Geneviève was born at Nanterre in AD 422 and turned away Attila the Hun from Paris in AD 451. A highly decorated reliquary near her tomb contains all that is left of her earthly remains – a finger bone.

Fans of the Woody Allen film *Midnight in Paris* will recognise the stone steps on the northwestern corner as the place where Owen Wilson's character is collected by vintage car and transported back to the 1920s.

JARDIN DES PLANTES GARDENS

Map p400 (www.jardinesplantes.net; place Valhubert & 36 rue Geoffroy-St-Hilaire, 5e; ⊙7.30am-8pm Apr-Oct, 8am-5.30pm Nov-Mar; MGare d'Austerlitz, Censier Daubenton, Jussieu) **FREE** Founded in 1626 as a medicinal herb garden for Louis XIII, Paris' 24-hectare botanic gardens – visually defined by the double alley of plane trees that run the length of the park – are an idyllic spot to stroll around, break for a picnic (watch out for the automatic sprinklers!) and escape the city concrete for a spell. Upping its appeal are three museums from the Muséum National d'Histoire Naturelle and a small zoo.

Other attractions include peony and rose gardens, an alpine garden, and the gardens of the École de Botanique, used by students of the school and green-fingered Parisians. The beautiful glass-and-metal **Grandes Serres** (Map p400; adult/child €6/4; ⊙10am-6pm), a series of four greenhouses, have been in use since 1714, and several of Henri Rousseau's jungle paintings, sometimes on display in the Musée d'Orsay, were inspired by his frequent visits here.

MUSÉUM NATIONAL D'HISTOIRE NATURELLE MUSEUM

Map p400 (www.mnhn.fr; place Valhubert & 36 rue Geoffroy-St-Hilaire, 5e; MGare d'Austerlitz, Censier Daubenton, Jussieu) Despite the name, the Natural History Museum is not a single building, but a collection of sites throughout France. Its historic home is in the Jardin des Plantes, and it's here you'll find the greatest number of branches: taxidermied animals in the excellent **Grande Galerie de l'Évolution** (Map p400; adult/child €9/free; ⊙10am-6pm Wed-Mon), fossils and dinosaur skeletons in the **Galeries d'Anatomie Comparée et de Paléontologie** (Map p400; 2 rue Buffon, 5e; adult/child €7/free; ⊙10am-5pm Mon & Wed-Fri, to 6pm Sat & Sun Apr-Sep, 10am-5pm Wed-Mon Oct-Mar) and meteorites and crystals in the **Galerie de Minéralogie et de Géologie** (Map p400; adult/child €6/free; ⊙10am-5pm Mon & Wed-Fri, to 6pm Sat & Sun Apr-Sep, 10am-5pm Wed-Mon Oct-Mar).

Created in 1793, the National Museum of Natural History became a site of significant scientific research in the 19th century. Of the three museums here, the four-floor Grande Galerie de l'Évolution is a particular

LATIN QUARTER SIGHTS

TOP SIGHT
PANTHÉON

The Panthéon's stately neoclassical dome stands out as one of the most recognisable icons in the Parisian skyline. Louis XV originally commissioned the vast architectural masterpiece around 1750 as an abbey dedicated to Ste Geneviève in thanksgiving for his recovery from an illness. However, due to financial and structural problems, it wasn't completed until 1789 – not a good year for church openings in Paris.

It reverted to religious duties twice after the Revolution but has played a secular role ever since 1885, and the crypt now serves as the resting place of some of France's greatest thinkers, including Voltaire, Rousseau, Braille and Hugo. The first woman to be interred in the Panthéon based on achievement was two-time Nobel Prize– winner Marie Curie (1867–1934), reburied here, along with her husband, Pierre, in 1995.

Its four newest 'residents' are Resistance fighters Germaine Tillion, Genèvieve de Gaulle-Anthonioz, Pierre Brossolette and Jean Zay, who joined Resistance leader Jean Moulin in 2015.

A copy of Foucault's pendulum, first hung from the dome in 1851 to demonstrate the rotation of the earth, takes pride of place.

DON'T MISS

➡ The architecture
➡ Foucault's Pendulum
➡ Crypt

PRACTICALITIES

➡ Map p400, C1
➡ www.monum.fr
➡ place du Panthéon, 5e
➡ adult/child €8.50/free
➡ ⊙10am-6.30pm Apr-Sep, to 6pm Oct-Mar
➡ MMaubert-Mutualité or RER Luxembourg

TOP SIGHT
INSTITUT DU MONDE ARABE

The Arab World Institute was jointly founded by France and 18 Middle Eastern and North African nations in 1980, with the aim of promoting cross-cultural dialogue. In addition to hosting concerts, film screenings and a research centre, the stunning landmark is also home to a new museum and temporary exhibition space.

You certainly can't miss the building: architect Jean Nouvel took his inspiration from traditional latticed wood windows, creating thousands of modern *mashrabiya*, photo-electrically sensitive apertures built into the glass walls that allow you to see out without being seen. The apertures are opened and closed by electric motors in order to regulate the amount of light and heat that reach the institute's interior.

The museum (4th to 7th floors) introduces elements from disparate time periods and cultures, focusing on art, artisanship and science. You'll find everything from pre-Islamic ceramics to ancient astronomical instruments, and from regional music displays to Arabic calligraphy.

From the top (9th) floor **observation terrace**, incredible views stretch across the Seine. There's a panoramic restaurant here, as well as a cafeteria and tearoom (no views) and decent cafe (ground floor).

DON'T MISS

➡ Museum
➡ Observation Terrace

PRACTICALITIES

➡ Arab World Institute
➡ Map p398, F3
➡ www.imarabe.org
➡ 1 place Mohammed V, 5e
➡ adult/child €8/4
➡ ⏱10am-6pm Tue-Thu, to 9.30pm Fri, to 7pm Sat & Sun
➡ Ⓜ Jussieu

---

winner if you're travelling with kids: life-sized elephants, tigers and rhinos play safari, and imaginative exhibits on evolution, extinction and global warming fill 6000 sq metres. The temporary exhibits are generally excellent. Within this building is a separate attraction, the **Galerie des Enfants** (Map p400; adult/child €11/9; ⏱10am-6pm, last entry 5pm) – a hands-on science museum tailored to children from ages six to 12.

COLLÈGE DES BERNARDINS
HISTORIC BUILDING

Map p398 (www.collegedesbernardins.fr; 18-24 rue de Poissy, 5e; ⏱10am-6pm Mon-Sat, 2-6pm Sun; Ⓜ Cardinal Lemoine) FREE Dating back to 1248, this former Cistercian college originally served as living quarters and place of study for novice monks. It's now an art gallery and centre for Christian culture with events ranging from lectures to film screenings and music performances; check schedules online.

MUSÉE DE LA SCULPTURE EN PLEIN AIR
MUSEUM

Map p398 (quai St-Bernard, 5e; Ⓜ Gare d'Austerlitz) FREE Along quai St-Bernard,

this open-air sculpture museum (also known as the Jardin Tino Rossi) has more than 50 late-20th-century unfenced sculptures, and makes a great picnic spot. A salad beneath a César or a baguette beside a Brancusi is a pretty classy way to see the Seine up close.

EATING

From chandelier-lit palaces loaded with history to cheap-eat student haunts, the 5e *arrondissement* (city district) caters to every budget and culinary taste. Rue Mouffetard is famed for its food market and food shops, though you'll have to trek down side streets for the neighbourhood's best meals.

★SHAKESPEARE & COMPANY CAFÉ
CAFE €

Map p398 (www.shakespeareandcompany.com; 2 rue St-Julien le Pauvre, 5e; dishes €4-9.50; ⏱10am-6.30pm Mon-Fri, to 7.30pm Sat & Sun; 🛜📷♿; Ⓜ St-Michel) 🌿 Instant history was made when this light-filled, literary-inspired cafe opened in 2015 adjacent to magical bookshop Shakespeare & Company (p219), designed from long-lost sketches to fulfil a dream of late bookshop founder George Whitman from the 1960s. Its primarily vegetarian menu (with vegan and gluten-free dishes available) includes homemade bagels, rye bread, soups, salads and pastries, plus Parisian-roasted Café Lomi coffee.

Picnic hampers (named 'A Moveable Feast' and including a short story) are in the works.

BAR À VINS AT
MODERN FRENCH €

Map p398 (☑01 56 81 94 08; http://atsushi tanaka.com; 4 rue du Cardinal Lemoine, 5e; dishes €12-16; ⊘7pm-2am Tue-Sun; MCardinal Lemoine) Six to eight wines are available by the glass at this cellar wine bar, but the real reason to come is the chance to try the incomparable cuisine of chef Atsushi Tanaka, whose Restaurant AT (p215) is upstairs, at bargain prices. Cold (only) dishes served here might include raw beef with powdered and puréed smoked artichokes, or ribboned beetroot and fennel.

BOULANGERIE
BRUNO SOLQUES
BOULANGERIE, PATISSERIE €

Map p400 (243 rue St-Jacques, 5e; ⊘6.45am-8pm Mon-Fri; 🖈; MPlace Monge or RER Luxembourg) 🗩 Inventive *pâtissier* Bruno Solques crafts wonderfully rustic breads (sold by weight measured on old-fashioned scales) using only organic flours. The small, bareboards shop is also filled with Solques' creatively shaped flat tarts with mashed fruit, fruit-filled brioches and subtly spiced gingerbread. It's on the pricey side but worth it – kids from the school across the way can't get enough.

ODETTE
PATISSERIE €

Map p398 (www.odette-paris.com; 77 rue Galande, 5e; 1/6/12 pastry puffs €1.90/9.90/19.80; ⊘10.30am-7.30pm; MSt-Michel) Odette's ground-floor space sells *choux* (pastry puffs) with seasonal flavoured cream fillings (nine at any one time), such as coffee, lemon, green tea, salted caramel, pistachio and forest berries. Upstairs, its art deco tearoom plays 1920s music and serves *choux* along with tea, coffee and Champagne. The black-painted timber facade, fronted by tables, and geranium-filled 1st-floor window box are charming.

FROGBURGER
BURGERS €

Map p398 (www.frogburger.com; 18 rue St-Séverin, 5e; burgers €11-13, sides €3.50-5; ⊘11.30am-11pm Sun-Thu, to midnight Fri & Sat; MSt-Michel) FrogPubs (famed for its Parisian microbreweries) is behind this cut-above spot sizzling up burgers including Revolution (beef, smoked pulled pork and coleslaw), da Vinci (beef, Serrano ham, mozzarella and pesto mayo), Crunchy Chicken (with rocket, cheddar and salsa) and Veggie (halloumi, red peppers and grilled mushrooms), with gluten-free bun options and Frog's own-brewed beers.

Sides span onion rings to fries (potato and sweet potato), cheesy nachos and desserts like New York cheesecake.

PHO 67
VIETNAMESE €

Map p398 (☑01 43 25 56 69; 59 rue Galande, 5e; mains €10-17; ⊘6.30-11pm Mon, noon-3pm & 6.30-11pm Tue-Sun; MCluny–La Sorbonne) Tuck into delicious Vietnamese dishes, such as fried boned eel, lacquered duck and prawns grilled in sugarcane leaves, amid the burgundy walls and suspended rattan lamps of this unpretentious little gem where everything is cooked to order. It's hidden away in a small backstreet away from the overtouristy little maze of restaurants that surrounds rue de la Huchette. Cash only.

KRISHNA BHAVAN
INDIAN €

Map p398 (☑01 43 29 87 93; www.krishna-bhavan. com; 25 rue Galande, 5e; mains €6-14; ⊘12.30-2pm & 6.30-11pm; 🖈; MMaubert-Mutualité) In northern Paris' 'little India' neighbourhood, Krishna Bhavan (p144) has spawned a string of neighbouring canteens. Here on the Left Bank it's an upmarket affair with a plush interior, but the menu remains identical, including Punjabi favourites such as *paneer dosa* (fermented rice and lentil crêpes stuffed with cottage cheese), lentil-based *dal makhani* and potato-and-pea *aloo mutter* in creamy sauce.

BONJOUR VIETNAM
VIETNAMESE €

Map p400 (☑01 43 54 78 04; 6 rue Thouin, 5e; mains €10-14; ⊘noon-3pm & 7-11pm Wed-Mon; MCardinal Lemoine) Stop by this lauded Vietnamese spot for a bowl of *pho* (noodle soup with thin slices of rare beef, mint, anise and lime) or *bobun* (cold rice-noodle salad with marinated beef). There's only a handful of tables, so best to reserve.

LE POT O'LAIT   CRÊPERIE €

Map p400 (www.lepotolait.com; 41 rue Censier, 5e; lunch menus €10-12.90, crêpes €3-11.50; ⊙11am-2.30pm & 7-10.30pm Tue-Sat; 🚸; Ⓜ️Censier Daubenton) A bright, contemporary spot, the Milk Can is the business when it comes to *galettes* (savoury buckwheat crêpes) – try smoked salmon or goat's cheese and bacon – and sweet crêpes (pistachio ice cream, zesty orange, hot chocolate and whipped cream). Salads are spectacular; kids will love the ice-cream sundaes.

LA SALLE À MANGER   TRADITIONAL FRENCH €

Map p400 (📞01 55 43 91 99; 138 rue Mouffetard, 5e; mains €10-15, weekend brunch €22; ⊙8.30am-6.30pm; Ⓜ️Censier Daubenton) With a sunny pavement terrace beneath trees enviably placed at the foot of foodie street rue Mouffetard, the 'Dining Room' is prime real estate. Its 360-degree outlook – market stalls, fountain, church and garden with a playground for tots – couldn't be prettier, and its salads, *tartines* (open sandwiches), tarts and pastries ensure packed tables at breakfast, lunch and weekend brunch.

LE COMPTOIR DU PANTHÉON   CAFE €

Map p400 (📞01 43 54 75 36; 5 rue Soufflot, 5e; salads €11-13, mains €12.40-15.40; ⊙kitchen 7am-11pm Mon-Sat, 8am-11pm Sun; 🛜; Ⓜ️Cardinal Lemoine or RER Luxembourg) Enormous, creative meal-size salads are the reason to choose this as a dining spot. Magnificently placed across from the domed Panthéon on the shady side of the street, its pavement terrace is big, busy and quintessentially Parisian – turn your head away from Voltaire's burial place and the Eiffel Tower pops into view. The bar closes at 1.45am every day.

LE JARDIN DES PÂTES   ORGANIC, PASTA €

Map p400 (📞01 43 31 50 71; 4 rue Lacépède, 5e; pasta €12-15; ⊙noon-2.30pm & 7-11pm; 🚸; Ⓜ️Place Monge) 🍽 A crisp white-and-green facade handily adjacent to a Vélib' station flags the Pasta Garden, a simple, smart 100% *bio* (organic) place where pasta comes in every guise imaginable – barley, buckwheat, rye, wheat, rice, chestnut and so on. Try the *pâtes de chataignes* (chestnut pasta) with duck breast, nutmeg, crème fraîche and mushrooms.

LE PUITS DE LÉGUMES   VEGETARIAN, ORGANIC €

Map p398 (📞01 43 25 50 95; www.lepuitsde legumesbio.fr; 18 rue du Cardinal Lemoine, 5e; mains €11-18; ⊙noon-4pm & 7-10pm Mon-Sat; 🚸; Ⓜ️Cardinal Lemoine) 🍽 Homemade tarts, quiches and rice dishes loaded with fresh seasonal vegetables are the draw of the 'Vegetable Well', an all-organic vegetarian (plus fish) student favourite. From the tiny kitchen out the back a comforting waft of homemade cooking pervades the simple dining room, which is filled with a handful of condiment-laden tables. Specials are chalked on the board outside.

★CAFÉ DE LA NOUVELLE MAIRIE   CAFE €€

Map p400 (📞01 44 07 04 41; 19 rue des Fossés St-Jacques, 5e; mains €12-32; ⊙kitchen 8am-midnight Mon-Fri; Ⓜ️Cardinal Lemoine) Shhhh...just around the corner from the Panthéon but hidden away on a small, fountained square, this narrow wine bar is a neighbourhood secret, serving blackboard-chalked natural wines by the glass and delicious seasonal bistro fare from oysters and ribs (*à la française*) to grilled lamb sausage over lentils. It takes reservations for dinner but not lunch – arrive early.

PROSPER ET FORTUNÉE   MODERN FRENCH €€

Map p400 (📞01 43 37 70 39; 50 rue Broca, 5e; lunch/dinner menus €23/45; ⊙noon-3pm & 7-10.30pm Tue-Fri, 7-10.30pm Sat Sep-Jul; Ⓜ️Les Gobelins) 🍽 Chef Eric Lévy's 12-seat premises is effectively a clandestine supper club. Dining at this tucked-away little restaurant is an intimate experience, from watching Lévy prepare daily changing dishes (raw mackerel with yuzu and lemon confit; prime fillet with black radish) using mostly organic premium produce in his open kitchen to then personally delivering each course (and bill). Prior reservations are essential.

LES PAPILLES   BISTRO €€

Map p400 (📞01 43 25 20 79; www.lespapilles paris.com; 30 rue Gay Lussac, 5e; 2-/3-course menus from €20/35, mains €18-35; ⊙noon-2pm & 7-10.30pm Tue-Sat; Ⓜ️Raspail or RER Luxembourg) This hybrid bistro, wine cellar and *épicerie* (specialist grocer) with a sunflower-yellow facade is one of those fabulous Parisian dining experiences. Meals are served at simply dressed tables wedged beneath bottle-lined walls, and fare is market driven: each weekday cooks up a different *marmite du marché* (market casserole). But what really sets it apart is its exceptional wine list.

It only seats around 15 people; reserve a few days in advance to guarantee a table.

After your meal, stock your own *cave* (wine cellar) at Les Papilles' *cave à vin*.

LE PRÉ VERRE
BISTRO €€

Map p398 (☑01 43 54 59 47; www.lepreverre. com; 8 rue Thénard, 5e; lunch menu €14.50, mains €20; ☻noon-2pm & 7.30-10.30pm Tue-Sat; ⛧⟨⟩; ⓂMaubert-Mutualité) Noisy, busy and buzzing, the Delacourcelle brothers' jovial bistro plunges diners into the heart of a Parisian's Paris. At lunchtime join the flock and go for the fabulous-value *formule dejéuner* (lunch menu), which might feature truffle chestnut soup, pollack and purple carrots, and for dessert pineapple minestrone, served with a glass of wine and loads of ultracrusty, ultrachewy baguette (the best).

Asian spices mingle with traditional French ingredients, thanks to chef Philippe's extended sojourns in China, Malaysia, Japan and India. Marc is the man behind the interesting wine list, which focuses on France's small independent *vignerons* (wine producers).

There's a heated terrace; phone and laptop chargers are (rare for Paris) available on request.

LE COUPE-CHOU
FRENCH €€

Map p398 (☑01 46 33 68 69; www.lecoupechou. com; 9 & 11 rue de Lanneau, 5e; 2-/3-course menus €27/33; ☻noon-2pm & 7-10.45pm Sep-Jul, 7-10.45pm Aug; ⓂMaubert-Mutualité) This maze of candlelit rooms inside a vine-clad 17th-century townhouse is overwhelmingly romantic. Ceilings are beamed, furnishings are antique, open fireplaces crackle and background classical music mingles with the intimate chatter of diners. As in the days when Marlene Dietrich dined here, advance reservations are essential. Timeless French dishes include Burgundy snails, steak tartare and bœuf bourguignon.

Finish off with fabulous cheeses sourced from *fromagerie* (cheese shop) Quatrehomme and a silken crème brûlée.

Le Coupe-Chou, incidentally, has nothing to do with cabbage *(chou)*; rather it's named after the barber's razor once wielded in one of its seven rooms.

L'AOC
TRADITIONAL FRENCH €€

Map p398 (☑01 43 54 22 52; www.restoaoc.com; 14 rue des Fossés St-Bernard, 5e; 2-/3-course lunch menus €21/29, mains €19-34; ☻noon-

---

LATIN QUARTER LITERARY ADDRESSES

Like its Left Bank neighbours, the Latin Quarter is steeped in literary history.

James Joyce's flat (Map p400; 71 rue du Cardinal Lemoine, 5e; ⓂCardinal Lemoine) Peer down the passageway at 71 rue du Cardinal Lemoine: Irish writer James Joyce (1882–1941) lived in the courtyard flat at the back marked 'E' when he arrived in Paris in 1921; he finished editing *Ulysses* here.

Ernest Hemingway's apartment (Map p400; 74 rue du Cardinal Lemoine, 5e; ⓂCardinal Lemoine) At 74 rue du Cardinal Lemoine is the apartment where Ernest Hemingway (1899–1961) lived with his first wife, Hadley, from January 1922 until August 1923. Just below was Bal au Printemps, a popular *bal musette* (dancing club) that served as the model for the one where Jake Barnes meets Brett Ashley in Hemingway's *The Sun Also Rises*.

Paul Verlaine's garret (Map p400; 39 rue Descartes, 5e; ⓂCardinal Lemoine) Hemingway wrote in a top-floor garret of a hotel (round the corner from his apartment) at 39 rue Descartes, the very hotel where the poet Paul Verlaine (1844–96) died. Ignore the incorrect plaque.

Place de la Contrescarpe Rue Descartes runs south into place de la Contrescarpe (place Monge), now a well-scrubbed square with four Judas trees and a fountain, but once a 'cesspool' (said Hemingway), especially Café des Amateurs at 2 to 4 place de la Contrescarpe, now **Café Delmas** (Map p400; www.cafedelmasparis.com; ☻7.30am-2am Sun-Thu, to 4am Fri & Sat; ⛧; ⓂPlace Monge).

George Orwell's boarding house (Map p400; 6 rue du Pot de Fer, 5e; ⓂPlace Monge) In 1928 George Orwell (1903–50) stayed in a cheap boarding house above 6 rue du Pot de Fer while working as a dishwasher. Read about it and the street, which he called 'rue du Coq d'Or' (Street of the Golden Rooster), in *Down and Out in Paris and London* (1933).

2pm & 7.30-11pm Tue-Sat; Ⓜ Cardinal Lemoine) *'Bistrot carnivore'* is the strapline of this ingenious restaurant concocted around France's most respected culinary products. The concept is Appellation d'Origine Contrôlée (AOC), the French precursor to Europe-wide AOP, meaning everything has been reared or produced according to strict guidelines. The results are outstanding. Choose between favourites (steak tartare) or the rotisserie menu, ranging from roast chicken to suckling pig.

LA RÔTISSERIE   ROTISSERIE €€

Map p398 (📞 01 43 54 17 47; www.larotisserie-delatour.com; 19 quai de la Tournelle, 5e; mains €22-28; ⊙ noon-2.15pm & 7-10.30pm; Ⓜ Cardinal Lemoine) Spit-roasted suckling pigs, chickens, ducks, shoulder of lamb and more turn on rotating skewers on an open flame within view of your table at this relaxed, chequered-tableclothed, quayside bistro run by its Michelin-starred neighbour La Tour d'Argent (p215). Order off the daily chalkboard and save room for classic desserts like crème brûlée. There's an extensive – and excellent – wine list.

TERROIR PARISIEN   BISTRO €€

Map p398 (📞 01 44 31 54 54; www.yannick-alleno.com; 20 rue St-Victor, 5e; 2-/3-course lunch menus €24/32, mains €16-29; ⊙ noon-2.30pm & 7-10.15pm; Ⓜ Maubert-Mutualité) 🍃 A focus on exclusively Île-de-France-sourced ingredients and an airy, modern interior make for a winning combination. Contemporary creations span pan-seared scallops with Jerusalem artichoke purée, ham and chicory gratin to green cabbage stuffed with roast pigeon. A few quick bites (eg croque monsieur) are also served. Do note that portions are small.

LENGUÉ   JAPANESE €€

Map p398 (📞 01 46 33 75 10; http://lengue.fr; 31 rue de la Parcheminerie, 5e; menus lunch/dinner €18/40; ⊙ noon-3pm & 7-11pm Tue-Sat, 7-11pm Sun; Ⓜ Cluny-La Sorbonne) This modish Japanese *izakaya* bar is incongruously set in medieval French surrounds, with exposed wooden beams, old stone walls and a downstairs cellar. In the evening, expect communal tapas-style dishes (vegetable dumplings, prawn tempura) accompanied by wine and sake; for lunch, it's one hot main and several cold sides, served bento (lunchbox) style. Be sure to reserve.

DANS LES LANDES   BASQUE, TAPAS €€

Map p400 (📞 01 45 87 06 00; http://danslelandes.fr; 119bis rue Monge, 5e; tapas €9-19; ⊙ noon-2.30pm & 7-11pm Mon-Fri, noon-11pm Sat & Sun; Ⓜ Censier Daubenton) Treat yourself to a trip to the Basque Country: Gascogne chef Julien Duboué presents his artful, tapas-size take on southwestern cuisine, with whimsical dishes that range from smoked duck with polenta and chilli-smothered *xistoria* (Basque sausages) to truffle and marrow risotto, duck-neck confit and jars of foie gras. It's one of the best places in Paris for Basque wines.

MOISSONNIER   LYONNAIS €€

Map p398 (📞 01 43 29 87 65; 28 rue des Fossés St-Bernard, 5e; mains €19-38; ⊙ noon-2.30pm & 7.30-10.30pm Tue-Sat; Ⓜ Cardinal Lemoine) It's Lyon, not Paris, that French gourmets venerate as the French food capital. Take one bite of a big, fat *andouillette* (pig-intestine sausage), *tablier de sapeur* (breaded, fried stomach), traditional *quenelles* (dumplings) or *boudin noir aux pommes* (black pudding with apples) and you'll realise why. A perfect reflection of one of France's most unforgettable regional cuisines in monumental portions.

L'AGRUME   NEOBISTRO €€

Map p400 (📞 01 43 31 86 48; 15 rue des Fossés St-Marcel, 5e; 2-/3-course lunch menus €22/25, dinner menu €45; ⊙ 12.15-2.30pm & 7.30-10.30pm Tue-Sat; Ⓜ Censier Daubenton) Snagging a table at L'Agrume can be tough; reserve several days ahead. The reward is watching chefs work with seasonal products in the open kitchen while you dine at a table, bar stool or *comptoir* (counter). Lunch is magnificent value and a real gourmet experience. Evening dining is an exquisite, daily changing no-choice *dégustation* (tasting) melody of five courses.

LES PIPOS   TRADITIONAL FRENCH €€

Map p398 (📞 01 43 54 11 40; www.les-pipos.com; 2 rue de l'École Polytechnique, 5e; mains €11-30; ⊙ 8am-2am Mon-Sat; Ⓜ Maubert-Mutualité) Natural wines are the speciality of this *bar à vins*, which it keeps in its vaulted stone cellar. First-rate food includes a fish of the day and oysters from Brittany, along with standards like confit of duck and a mouthwatering cheese board, which includes all the gourmet names (bleu d'Auvergne, brie de Meaux, Rocamadour and St-Marcellin). No credit cards.

LE BUISSON ARDENT
MODERN FRENCH €€

Map p400 (📞01 43 54 93 02; www.lebuisson ardent.fr; 25 rue Jussieu, 5e; 2-/3-course lunch menus €25/28, 3-course dinner menu €40; ⏰noon-2.30pm & 7.30-10.30pm; 🚇Jussieu) Housed in a former coach house, this time-worn bistro (murals in the front room date to the 1920s) serves classy, exciting French fare, from parmesan-crusted scallops with split-pea crème or pork tenderloin with sage mash and roast pear to desserts like *baba au rhum* (rum-drenched yeast-based cake) with sultana syrup.

It will also provide you with a bag to take your unfinished open bottle of wine away with you.

LE PETIT PONTOISE
BISTRO €€

Map p398 (📞01 43 29 25 20; www.lepetit pontoise.fr; 9 rue de Pontoise, 5e; 2-/3-course midweek lunch menus €23/29, 3-course weekend lunch menu €34, mains €22-30; ⏰noon-2.30pm & 6.30-10.30pm; 🚇Maubert-Mutualité) Take a seat at a wooden table behind the lace curtains screening out the world to indulge in simple but fantastic old-fashioned classics, like *rognons de veau à l'ancienne* (calf kidneys), *joues de cochon miellées aux épices douces* (pig cheeks with honey and spices) and *carré d'agneau en croute et ail des ouis* (garlic-crusted rack of lamb).

⭐RESTAURANT AT
GASTRONOMY €€€

Map p398 (📞01 56 81 94 08; www.atsushitanaka. com; 4 rue du Cardinal Lemoine, 5e; 4-/6-course lunch menus €35/55, 12-course dinner tasting menu €95; ⏰12.15-2pm & 8-9.30pm Tue-Sat; 🚇Cardinal Lemoine) Trained by some of the biggest names in gastronomy (Pierre Gagnaire included), chef Atsushi Tanaka showcases abstract artlike masterpieces incorporating rare ingredients (charred bamboo, kohlrabi turnip cabbage, juniper berry powder, wild purple fennel, Nepalese Timut pepper) in a blank-canvas-style dining space on stunning outsized plates. Just off the entrance, steps lead to his cellar wine bar, Bar à Vins AT (p211).

⭐SOLA
FUSION €€€

Map p398 (📞dinner 01 43 29 59 04, lunch 09 65 01 73 68; www.restaurant-sola.com; 12 rue de l'Hôtel Colbert, 5e; menus lunch €48-78, dinner €98; ⏰noon-1.30pm & 7.30-9pm Tue-Sat; 🚇St-Michel) Pedigreed chef Hiroki Yoshitake combines French technique with Japanese sensibility, resulting in gorgeous signature

creations (such as miso-marinated foie gras on *feuille de brick* served on sliced tree trunk). The artful presentations and attentive service make this a perfect choice for a romantic meal – go for the full experience and reserve a table in the Japanese dining room downstairs.

LA TRUFFIÈRE
GASTRONOMY €€€

Map p400 (📞01 46 33 29 82; www.latruffiere. fr; 4 rue Blainville, 5e; 2-/3-course lunch menus €32/40, 3-/5-/7-course dinner menus €65/125/165; ⏰noon-2pm & 7-10.30pm Tue-Sat; 🚇Place Monge) As its name implies, truffles are the centrepiece of this Michelin-starred restaurant's menu, featuring in most (albeit not all) of its weekly changing dishes, from classic Italian gnocchi to miso and sake-marinated tuna with samphire, roast venison with juniper berries and smoked Jerusalem artichokes, and oxtail stew with mash. To go all-out, order the seven-course black truffle tasting menu (€280).

LA TOUR D'ARGENT
GASTRONOMY €€€

Map p398 (📞01 43 54 23 31; www.latourdargent. com; 15 quai de la Tournelle, 5e; menus lunch €85, dinner €180-200, mains €75-100; ⏰12.30-2pm & 7-10.30pm Tue-Sat Sep-Jul; 🚇Cardinal Lemoine) The venerable Michelin-starred 'Silver Tower' is famous for its *caneton* (duckling), rooftop garden with glimmering Notre Dame views and fabulous history harking back to 1582 – from Henry III's inauguration of the first fork in France to inspiration for the winsome animated film *Ratatouille*. Its wine cellar is one of Paris' best; dining is dressy and exceedingly fine.

Reserve eight to 10 days ahead for lunch, three weeks ahead for dinner – and don't miss its chocolate soufflé with bitter orange ice cream for dessert.

Buy fine food and accessories in La Tour d'Argent's **boutique** (Map p398; 2 rue du Cardinal Lemoine, 5e; ⏰11.15am-7.15pm Tue-Sat; 🚇Cardinal Lemoine) directly across the street, near its casual bistro La Rôtisserie (p214).

🍷 DRINKING & NIGHTLIFE

Rive Gauche romantics, well-heeled cafe-society types and students by the gallon drink in the 5e *arrondissement*, where nostalgic haunts, some swish new bars and a deluge of early-evening

LATIN QUARTER DRINKING & NIGHTLIFE

happy hours ensure a quintessential Parisian soirée.

CAFFÉ JUNO   COFFEE

Map p400 (www.caffe-juno.com; 58 rue Henri Barbusse, 5e; ⊘9am-7pm Mon-Sat; 📶; Ⓜ Raspail or RER Port Royal) 🍴 Hole-in-the-wall Caffé Juno roasts its own Ethiopian, Indonesian, Colombian and Cameroonian beans and specialises in espressos, filters and lattes. Prices are impressively reasonable to drink on-site in the industrial-style space strewn with hessian bags; you can also buy beans to take home.

STRADA CAFÉ   COFFEE

Map p398 (www.stradacafe.fr; 24 rue Monge, 5e; ⊘8am-6.30pm Mon-Fri, 10am-6.30pm Sat & Sun; 📶; Ⓜ Cardinal Lemoine) Beans from Parisian roastery l'Arbre à Café (Brazilian, Ethiopian and Costa Rican espresso blend, and Ethiopian filter blend), Lyon roastery Mokxa (Honduran bio single-origin espresso) and hot new Amsterdam roastery White Label (Rwandan filter) underpin the success of sunlit corner cafe Strada. Electrical sockets are plentiful and the international baristas are passionate about their brews.

LE VERRE À PIED   CAFE

Map p400 (http://leverreapied.fr; 118bis rue Mouffetard, 5e; ⊘9am-9pm Tue-Sat, 9.30am-4pm Sun; Ⓜ Censier Daubenton) This café-tabac is a pearl of a place where little has changed since 1870. Its nicotine-hued mirrored wall, moulded cornices and original bar make it part of a dying breed, but it epitomises the charm, glamour and romance of an old Paris everyone loves, including stallholders from the rue Mouffetard market who yo-yo in and out.

Contemporary photography and art adorns one wall. Lunch is a busy, lively affair, and live music quickens the pulse a couple of evenings a week.

LE VIOLON DINGUE   PUB

Map p398 (46 rue de la Montagne Ste-Geneviève, 5e; ⊘7pm-5am Tue-Sat; Ⓜ Maubert-Mutualité) A loud, lively bar, the 'Crazy Violin' is adopted by revolving generations of students for big-screen sports upstairs and the flirty 'Dingue Lounge' downstairs. The name is a pun on the expression *le violon d'Ingres,* meaning 'hobby' in French because the celebrated painter Jean-Auguste-Dominique Ingres played fiddle in his spare time. Happy hour is 7pm to 10pm Tuesday to Saturday.

🏃 Local Life
A Stroll Along Rue Mouffetard

Originally a Roman road, cobbled rue Mouffetard acquired its name in the 18th century, when the now underground River Bièvre became the communal waste disposal. The odours gave rise to the name Mouffette ('skunk'), which evolved into Mouffetard. The street's now filled with market stalls (bar Mondays), cheap eateries and lively bars.

❶ Market Shopping
Today the aromas on 'La Mouffe', as it's nicknamed by locals, are infinitely more enticing. Grocers, butchers, fishmongers and other food purveyors set their goods out on street stalls during the **Marché Mouffetard** (Map p400; rue Mouffetard, 5e; ⊘8am-7.30pm Tue-Sat, to noon Sun; Ⓜ Censier Daubenton).

❷ Fine Cheeses
You won't even have to worry about the aromas if you're taking home the scrumptious cheeses from *fromagerie* **Androuet** (Map p400; http://androuet.com; 134 rue Mouffetard, 5e; ⊘9.30am-1pm & 4-7.30pm Tue-Fri, 9.30am-7.30pm Sat, to 9.30am-1.30pm Sun; Ⓜ Censier Daubenton) – all of its cheeses can be vacuum-packed for free.

❸ Delicious Deli
Stuffed olives, capsicums and marinated aubergine are among the picnic goodies at **Delizius** (Map p400; 134 rue Mouffetard, 5e; ⊘9.30am-8pm Tue-Fri, 9am-8pm Sat, 9am-2pm Sun; Ⓜ Censier Daubenton).

❹ Movie Time
A small doorway leads to cinema **L'Epée de Bois** (Map p400; http://epee-de-bois. cine-movida.com; 100 rue Mouffetard, 5e; tickets adult/child Mon & Wed €5.50/4, Tue & Thu-Sun €7.50/4; Ⓜ Censier Daubenton), which screens both art-house flicks and big-budget blockbusters.

❺ Sweet Treats
Light, luscious macarons and a mouthwatering range of chocolates are laid out like jewels at **Chocolats Mococha** (Map p400; www.chocolatsmococha.com; 89 rue Mouffetard, 5e; ⊘11am-8pm Tue-Sun; Ⓜ Censier Daubenton).

Marché Mouffetard

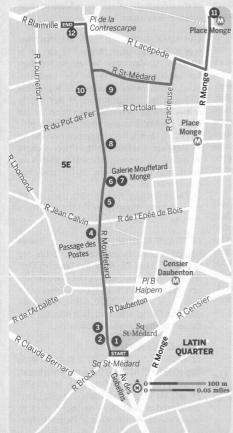

LATIN QUARTER

➏ Caffeine Fix

Get a potent dose of caffeine at hip new corner spot **Dose** (Map p400; www.dosedealerdecafe.fr; 73 rue Mouffetard, 5e; ⏱8am-6pm Mon-Fri, 9am-7pm Sat & Sun; 🛜; Ⓜ Place Monge), which uses award-winning beans and offers a choice of milk.

➐ Bowled Over

Join locals skittling pins in friendly **Bowling Mouffetard** (Map p400; 📞01 43 31 09 35; www.bowling-mouf fetard.fr; 73 rue Mouffetard, 5e; games €4-6.50, shoes €2; ⏱3pm-2am Mon-Fri, 10am-2am Sat & Sun; Ⓜ Place Monge).

➑ Revolutionary Apéro

Host to revolutionary meetings in 1848, these days **Le Vieux Chêne** (Map p400; 69 rue Mouffetard, 5e; ⏱4pm-2am Sun-Thu, to 5am Fri & Sat; Ⓜ Place Monge) is a student favourite, especially during happy hour (4pm to 9pm Tuesday to Sunday, and from 4pm until closing on Monday).

➒ Floral Ice Cream

Stop at **Gelati d'Alberto** (Map p400; www.gelatidalberto.com; 45 rue Mouffetard, 5e; ⏱noon-midnight Apr-Sep, closed Oct-Mar; 👶; Ⓜ Place Monge), where Italian ice-cream wizards shape your cone into a flower.

➓ Crêpe Artistry

If you prefer savoury to sweet or hot to cold, check the signboard outside crêpe artist Nicos' unassuming little shop **Chez Nicos** (Map p400; 44 rue Mouffetard, 5e; crêpes €3-6; ⏱noon-2am; 👶; Ⓜ Place Monge) – it lists dozens of fillings.

⓫ Roman History

For a park with a difference, head to 2nd-century Roman amphitheatre **Arènes de Lutèce** (Map p400; www. arenesdelutece.com; 49 rue Monge, 5e; ⏱8am-9.30pm Apr-Oct, to 5.30pm Nov-Mar; Ⓜ Place Monge). Originally seating 10,000 for gladiatorial combats, it was discovered by accident in 1869.

⓬ Cocktail Hour

Enjoy a unique house-speciality cocktail at uberhip bar **Little Bastards** (Map p400; 5 rue Blainville, 5e; ⏱6pm-2am Mon-Thu, to 4am Fri & Sat; Ⓜ Place Monge).

LE PUB ST-HILAIRE   PUB

Map p398 (2 rue Valette, 5e; ⏱3pm-2am Mon-Thu, 4pm-5am Fri & Sat; Ⓜ Maubert-Mutualité) 'Buzzing' fails to do justice to the pulsating vibe inside this student-loved pub. Generous happy hours last from 5pm to 9pm and the place is kept packed with a trio of pool tables, board games, music on two floors, hearty bar food and various gimmicks to rev up the party crowd (a metre of cocktails, 'be your own barman' etc).

CAVE LA BOURGOGNE   BAR

Map p400 (144 rue Mouffetard, 5e; ⏱7am-2am Mon-Sat, to 11pm Sun; Ⓜ Censier Daubenton) A prime spot for soaking up rue Mouffetard's contagious 'saunter-all-day' spirit, this neighbourhood hang out sits on square St-Médard, one of the Latin Quarter's loveliest, with flower-bedecked fountain, centuries-old church and market stalls spilling across one side. Inside, locals and their pet dogs meet for coffee around dark wood tables alongside a local wine-sipping set. In summer everything spills outside.

LE CROCODILE   BAR

Map p400 (6 rue Royer-Collard, 5e; ⏱6pm-2am Mon-Sat; Ⓜ Odén or RER Luxembourg) This green-shuttered bar has been dispensing affordable cocktails (363 at last count, with gummy-'bear' crocodiles in the glass) since 1966. Arrive late for a truly eclectic crowd, including lots of students, and raucous revelry. Hours can vary (dawn closings are common). Happy hour runs from 6pm to 11pm Monday to Thursday and 6pm to 10pm Friday and Saturday.

LE PIANO VACHE   BAR

Map p398 (http://lepianovache.fr; 8 rue Laplace, 5e; ⏱6pm-2am Mon-Sat; Ⓜ Maubert-Mutualité) Down the hill from the Panthéon, this underground bar is covered in old posters above old couches and drenched in 1970s and '80s rock ambience. A real student fave, it has bands and DJs playing mainly rock, plus some Goth, reggae and pop. Happy hour runs from 6pm to 9pm.

☆ ENTERTAINMENT

Jazz and independent cinema are the twin strengths of the Latin Quarter's entertainment scene, with a host of venues for both.

★ CAFÉ UNIVERSEL   JAZZ, BLUES

Map p400 (☎01 43 25 74 20; www.cafeuniversel. com; 267 rue St-Jacques, 5e; ⏱9pm-2am Mon-Sat; ☏; Ⓜ Censier Daubenton or RER Port Royal) Café Universel hosts a brilliant array of live concerts with everything from bebop and Latin sounds to vocal jazz sessions. Plenty of freedom is given to young producers and artists, and its convivial relaxed atmosphere attracts a mix of students and jazz lovers. Concerts are free, but tip the artists when they pass the hat around.

STUDIO GALANDE   CINEMA

Map p398 (☎01 43 54 72 71; http://studiogalande. wordpress.com; 42 rue Galande, 5e; tickets €8.50-11; Ⓜ Cluny–La Sorbonne) Do the time warp again at this cult cinema, which, since the early 1980s, has screened *The Rocky Horror Picture Show* (in English) without interruption every Friday and Saturday night from 10pm (BYO costumes and props). The rest of the week it shows art-house films in their original languages.

LA LUCHA LIBRE   SPECTATOR SPORT

Map p398 (www.laluchalibre.fr; 10 rue de la Montagne Ste-Geneviève, 5e; ⏱5pm-2am Tue-Sat; Ⓜ Maubert-Mutualité) On the first and third Friday of the month at 10.30pm this high-spirited Mexican-themed bar really comes into its own when its vaulted cellar hosts masked-and-costumed Mexican pro-wrestling shows, which are as entertaining as they are a serious competition. Tickets go on sale from 8pm; afterwards there's an open ring where anyone in the audience can give it a go.

The wrestling ring is also open to all from 8.30pm Tuesday to Friday and from 5pm on Saturday.

LE GRAND ACTION   CINEMA

Map p398 (www.legrandaction.com; 5 rue des Écoles, 5e; tickets €9; Ⓜ Cardinal Lemoine) Cult films both recent (such as the Coen brothers' *Hail, Caesar!*) and not *(Apocalypse Now, East of Eden, 2001: A Space Odyssey* and *The Thing)* screen in their original languages at this cinephiles' favourite.

ÉGLISE ST-JULIEN
LE PAUVRE   CLASSICAL MUSIC

Map p398 (☎01 42 26 00 00; www.concertinparis.com; 1 rue St-Julien le Pauvre, 5e; tickets €18-23; Ⓜ St-Michel) Piano recitals (Chopin, Liszt) are staged at least two evenings a week in one of the oldest churches in Paris. Higher-priced tickets directly face the stage. Payment is by cash only at the door.

LE CAVEAU DES OUBLIETTES   JAZZ, BLUES

Map p398 (☎01 46 34 24 09; https://lecaveaudes oubliettes.wordpress.com; 52 rue Galande, 5e; ⊙5pm-2am Sun-Tue, to 4am Wed-Sat; MSt-Michel) From the 16th-century ground-floor pub (with a happy hour from 5pm to 9pm), descend to the 12th-century dungeon for jazz, blues and funk concerts, and jam sessions (from 10pm).

LE PETIT JOURNAL ST-MICHEL   JAZZ, BLUES

Map p400 (☎01 43 26 28 59; www.petitjournal saintmichel.com; 71 bd St-Michel, 5e; admission incl 1 drink €20, with dinner €49-57; ⊙7.30pm-1am Mon-Sat; MCluny–La Sorbonne or RER Luxembourg) Classic jazz concerts kick off at 9.15pm in the atmospheric downstairs cellar of this sophisticated jazz venue across from the Jardin du Luxembourg. Everything ranging from Dixieland and vocals to big band and swing sets patrons' toes tapping. Dinner is served at 8pm (but it's the music that's the real draw).

CAVEAU DE LA HUCHETTE   JAZZ, BLUES

Map p398 (☎01 43 26 65 05; www.caveaude lahuchette.fr; 5 rue de la Huchette, 5e; Sun-Thu €13, Fri & Sat €15; ⊙9.30pm-2.30am Sun-Wed, to 4am Thu-Sat; MSt-Michel) Housed in a medieval *caveau* (cellar) used as a courtroom and torture chamber during the Revolution, this club is where virtually all the jazz greats (Georges Brassens, Thibault...) have played since the end of WWII. It attracts its fair share of tourists, but the atmosphere

can be more electric than at the more serious jazz clubs. Sessions start at 10pm.

LE CHAMPO   CINEMA

Map p398 (www.lechampo.com; 51 rue des Écoles, 5e; tickets adult/child €9/4; MCluny–La Sorbonne) This is one of the most popular of the many Latin Quarter cinemas, featuring classics and retrospectives looking at the films of such actors and directors as Alfred Hitchcock, Jacques Tati, Alain Resnais, Frank Capra, Tim Burton and Woody Allen. One of the two *salles* (cinemas) has wheelchair access.

A couple of times a month Le Champo screens films for night owls, kicking off at midnight (three films plus breakfast €15).

 # SHOPPING

Bookworms in particular will love this part of the Left Bank, which is home to some wonderful bookshops. Other student-frequented shops include camping stores, comic shops, old-school music shops where collectors browse for hours and cheap, colourful homewares stores, interspersed with the occasional *droguerie-quincaillerie* (hardware store) – easily spotted by the jumble of laundry baskets, buckets etc piled on the pavement out the front.

★SHAKESPEARE & COMPANY   BOOKS

Map p398 (☎01 43 25 40 93; www.shakespeare andcompany.com; 37 rue de la Bûcherie, 5e; ⊙10am-11pm; MSt-Michel) Shakespeare's en-

---

BOUQUINISTES

With some 3km of forest-green boxes lining the Seine – containing over 300,000 secondhand (and often out-of-print) books, rare magazines, postcards and old advertising posters – Paris' **bouquinistes** (⊙11.30am-dusk), or used-book sellers, are as integral to the cityscape as Notre Dame. Many open only from spring to autumn (and many shut in August), but year-round you'll still find some to browse.

The *bouquinistes* have been in business since the 16th century, when they were itinerant peddlers selling their wares on Parisian bridges; back then their sometimes subversive (eg Protestant) materials could get them in trouble with the authorities. By 1859 the city had finally wised up: official licenses were issued, space was rented (10 metres of railing) and eventually the permanent green boxes were installed.

Today, *bouquinistes* (the official count ranges from 200 to 240) are allowed to have four boxes, only one of which can be used to sell souvenirs. Look hard enough and you just might find some real treasures: old comic books, forgotten first editions, maps, stamps, erotica and prewar newspapers – as in centuries past, it's all there, waiting to be rediscovered.

chanting nooks and crannies overflow with new and secondhand English-language books. The original shop (12 rue l'Odéon, 6e; closed by the Nazis in 1941) was run by Sylvia Beach and became the meeting point for Hemingway's 'Lost Generation'. Readings by emerging and illustrious authors take place at 7pm most Mondays. There's a wonderful cafe (p210) and various workshops and festivals.

The bookshop is fabled for nurturing writers, and at night its couches turn into beds where writers stay in exchange for stacking shelves.

American-born George Whitman opened the present incarnation in 1951, attracting a beat-poet clientele, and scores of authors have since passed through its doors. In 2006 Whitman was awarded the Officier des Arts et Lettres by the French Minister of Culture, recognising his 'significant contribution to the enrichment of the French cultural inheritance'. Whitman died in 2011, aged 98; he is buried in division 73 of Cimetière du Père Lachaise. Today his daughter, Sylvia Beach Whitman, maintains Shakespeare & Company's serendipitous magic.

★ LE BONBON AU PALAIS   SWEETS

Map p398 (www.bonbonsaupalais.fr; 19 rue Monge, 5e; ⊙10.30am-7.30pm Tue-Sat; Ⓜ Cardinal Lemoine) Kids and kids-at-heart will adore this sugar-fuelled *tour de France*. The school-geography-themed boutique stocks rainbows of artisan sweets from around the country. Old-fashioned glass jars brim with treats like *calissons* (diamond-shaped, icing-sugar-topped ground fruit and almonds from Aix-en-Provence), *rigolettes* (fruit-filled pillows from Nantes), *berlingots* (striped, triangular boiled sweets from Carpentras and elsewhere) and *papalines* (herbal liqueur-filled pink-chocolate balls from Avignon),

★ BIÈRES CULTES   DRINKS

Map p400 (www.bierescultes.fr; 44 rue des Boulangers, 5e; ⊙3-8pm Mon, 11am-2pm & 3-9pm Tue-Thu, 11am-9pm Fri & Sat; Ⓜ Cardinal Lemoine) At any one time this beer-lovers' fantasyland stocks over 400 different craft and/or international brews, and it also has two on tap to taste on the spot. Just some of its wares when you visit might include US-brewed Alaskan Smoked Porter, German smoked Aecht Schlenkerla Rauchbier from Bamberg and New Zealand Monteith's. Check its website for events and seasonal releases.

FROMAGERIE MAURY   CHEESE

Map p400 (1 rue des Feuillantines, 5e; ⊙2-9pm Tue-Thu, 10.30am-1.30pm & 3-8.30pm Fri & Sat; Ⓜ Censier Daubenton or RER Port Royal) 🖉 This wonderful little *fromagerie* feels more like a farm shop you'd find in the countryside than an inner-city Parisian boutique. Organic eggs sit in straw baskets (cartons are available) and owner Christophe Maury insists that you try his amazing range of carefully selected cheeses from small-scale producers in southwestern France, the Jura mountains, Corsica, Italy and Spain before you buy.

FROMAGERIE LAURENT
DUBOIS   CHEESE

Map p398 (www.fromageslaurentdubois.fr; 47ter bd St-Germain, 5e; ⊙8am-7.45pm Tue-Sat, 8.30am-1pm Sun; Ⓜ Maubert-Mutualité) One of the best *fromageries* in Paris, this cheese-lover's nirvana is filled with to-die-for delicacies, such as St-Félicien with Périgord truffles. Rare, limited-production cheeses include blue Termignon and Tarentaise goat's cheese. All are appropriately cellared in warm, humid or cold environments. There's also a 15e **branch** (Map p414; 2 rue de Lourmel, 15e; ⊙9am-1pm & 4-7.45pm Tue-Fri, 8.30am-7.45pm Sat, 9am-1pm Sun; Ⓜ Dupleix).

ABBEY BOOKSHOP   BOOKS

Map p398 (🖉 01 46 33 16 24; 29 rue de la Parcheminerie, 5e; ⊙10am-7pm Mon-Sat, 2-7pm Sun; Ⓜ Cluny–La Sorbonne) In a heritage-listed townhouse, this welcoming Canadian-run bookshop serves free coffee (sweetened with maple syrup) to sip while you browse tens of thousands of new and used books. It also organises literary events and countryside hikes.

PARFUMS DE NICOLAÏ   PERFUME

Map p400 (www.pnicolai.com; 240 rue St-Jacques, 5e; ⊙10.30am-2pm & 2.30-7pm Mon-Sat; Ⓜ Place Monge) Established in Paris in 1986 by esteemed *parfumeuse* Patricia de Nicolaï, whose great-grandfather Pierre-François Pascal Guerlain founded Guerlain a century-and-a-half earlier, Nicolaï remains a family-run business today. Recent fragrance releases include Cococabana (with notes of ylang-ylang, palm, vanilla and tonka flower), Kiss Me Tender (with orange blossom, almond, jasmine and cloves) and Musc Monoï (lemon, magnolia, coconut and sandalwood).

CROCODISC
MUSIC

Map p398 (www.crocodisc.com; 40 & 42 rue des Écoles, 5e; ⊙11am-7pm Tue-Sat mid-Aug–late Jul; ⓂMaubert-Mutualité) Music might be more accessible than ever before in the digital age, but for many it will never replace rummaging through racks for treasures. New and secondhand CDs and vinyl discs at 40 rue des Écoles span world music, rap, reggae, salsa, soul and disco, while No 42 has pop, rock, punk, new wave, electro and soundtracks.

Its nearby sister shop **Crocojazz** (Map p398; www.crocodisc.com; 64 rue de la Montagne Ste-Geneviève, 5e; ⊙11am-1pm & 2-7pm Tue-Sat mid-Aug–late Jul; ⓂMaubert-Mutualité) specialises in jazz, blues, gospel and timeless crooners, with books and DVDs as well as recordings.

AU VIEUX CAMPEUR
SPORTS & OUTDOORS

Map p398 (www.auvieuxcampeur.fr; 48 rue des Écoles, 5e; ⊙11am-7.30pm Mon-Wed & Fri, 11am-9pm Thu, 10am-7.30pm Sat; ⓂMaubert-Mutualité) This outdoor store has colonised the Latin Quarter, with 30-and-counting different outlets scattered about. Each is devoted to your favourite sport: climbing, skiing, diving, camping, biking and so on. While it's a great resource if you need any gear, the many boutiques make shopping something of a treasure hunt – especially as many outlets change what they sell with the seasons.

Ask for directions to other branches at this flagship store (or any other that you come across), which generally sells mountaineering equipment.

MAYETTE LA BOUTIQUE DE LA MAGIE
GAMES, HOBBIES

Map p398 (☑01 43 54 13 63; www.mayette.com; 8 rue des Carmes, 5e; ⊙2-7.30pm Tue-Sat; ⓂMaubert-Mutualité) One of a kind, this 1808-established magic shop is said to be the world's oldest. Since 1991 it's been in the hands of world-famous magic pro Dominique Duvivier. Professional and hobbyist magicians flock here to discuss king sandwiches, reverse assemblies, false cuts and other card tricks with him and his daughter, Alexandra.

Should you want to learn the tricks of the trade, Duvivier has magic courses up his sleeve.

ALBUM
COMICS

Map p398 (www.album.fr; 67 bd St-Germain, 5e; ⊙10am-8pm Mon-Sat, noon-7pm Sun; ⓂCluny–La Sorbonne) Album specialises in *bandes dessinées* (comics and graphic novels), which have an enormous following in France, with everything from Tintin and Babar to erotic comics and the latest Japanese manga. Serious comic collectors – and anyone excited by Harry Potter wands, Star Wars, Superman and other superhero figurines and T-shirts (you know who you are!) – shouldn't miss it.

LIBRAIRIE EYROLLES
BOOKS

Map p398 (www.eyrolles.com; 61 bd St-Germain, 5e; ⊙9.30am-7.30pm Mon-Fri, to 8pm Sat; ⓂMaubert-Mutualité) Art, design, architecture, dictionaries and kids' books are the mainstay of this large bookshop with titles in English and stacks of browsing space.

For maps, guides and travel lit hop across the street to its **Librairie de Voyage** (Map p398; 63 bd St-Germain, 5e; ⊙9.30am-7.30pm Mon-Fri, to 8pm Sat; ⓂMaubert-Mutualité).

🏃 SPORTS & ACTIVITIES

WINE TASTING IN PARIS
WINE

Map p400 (☑06 76 93 32 88; www.wine-tasting-in-paris.com; 14 rue des Boulangers, 5e; 2hr tastings from €60; ⊙tastings 5-7pm Tue, Thu & Sat; ⓂJussieu) Situated on a winding cobblestone Latin Quarter backstreet, this wine-tasting school offers various options for tastings, including its popular French Wine Tour (two hours, six wines), during which you'll learn about tasting methodology, wine vocabulary and interpreting wine labels as well as French wine-growing regions. All classes are in English.

PISCINE PONTOISE
SWIMMING

Map p398 (☑01 55 42 77 88; http://piscine.equipement.paris.fr; 19 rue de Pontoise, 5e; adult/child €4.80/2.90; ⊙hours vary; ⓂMaubert-Mutualité) A beautiful art-deco-style indoor pool in the heart of the Latin Quarter. An €11.10 evening ticket (from 8pm) covers entry to the pool, gym and sauna. It has shorter hours during term time – check schedules online.

St-Germain & Les Invalides

ST-GERMAIN | LES INVALIDES

Neighbourhood Top Five

1 **Musée d'Orsay** (p224) Revelling in a wealth of world-famous impressionist masterpieces and art nouveau architecture at this glorious national museum.

2 **Jardin du Luxembourg** (p228) Strolling through the chestnut groves and orchards, past ponds and statues, at the city's most popular park.

3 **Musée Rodin** (p230) Indulging in an exquisitely Parisian moment in the sculpture-filled gardens of the renovated private mansion, the 1730 Hôtel Biron.

4 **La Grande Épicerie de Paris** (p246) Feasting your eyes on the fantastical food displays at this food emporium attached to Paris' first department store, Le Bon Marché, designed by Gustave Eiffel.

5 **Hôtel des Invalides** (p231) Visiting Napoléon's elaborate tomb within the monumental complex housing France's largest military museum.

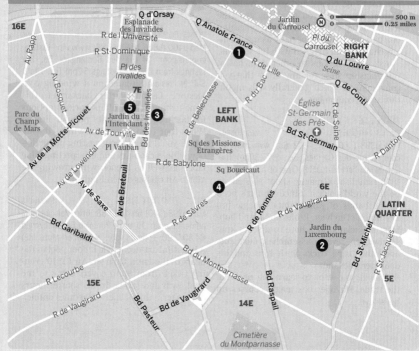

For more detail of this area see Map p402 and p406 ➡

Explore: St-Germain & Les Invalides

Despite gentrification since its early-20th-century bohemian days, there remains a startling cinematic quality to this soulful part of the Left Bank where artists, writers, actors and musicians cross paths and *la vie germano-pratine* (St-Germain life) is *belle*.

This is one of those neighbourhoods whose very fabric is an attraction in itself, so allow plenty of time to stroll its side streets and stop at its fabled literary cafes, prêt-à-porter stores, gourmet shops and grand department store Le Bon Marché with its vast white spaces showcasing interior design. In between, view Delacroix's works at the Église St-Sulpice and his former studio, the Musée National Eugène Delacroix; linger in the masterpiece-filled sculpture garden of the Musée Rodin; and be moved by the handwritten letters and annotations of renowned scientists, musicians, artists, authors and other historical figures at the Musée des Lettres et Manuscrits.

Entry to the Musée d'Orsay is cheaper in the late afternoon, so it's an ideal time to check out its breathtaking collections, before dining at the area's stylish restaurants and swizzling cocktails at its bars.

Local Life

➡**River life** Join locals sprinting, skating, cycling, bar-hopping or just Zenning out along the riverside promenade Les Berges de Seine (p233).

➡**Market life** Street markets where St-Germain denizens stock up on bountiful fresh produce include Marché Raspail (p239) and rue Cler (p238).

➡**Fashion life** Scour the racks for designer cast-offs at St-Germain's secondhand boutiques (p242).

Getting There & Away

➡**Metro** This area is especially well served by metro and RER. Get off at metro stations St-Germain des Prés, Mabillon or Odéon for its busy bd St-Germain heart. RER line C shadows the Seine along the Left Bank and is a fast way to get from St-Michel–Notre Dame to the Musée d'Orsay.

➡**Bicycle** Convenient Vélib' stations include 141 bd St-Germain, 6e; opposite 2 bd Raspail, 6e; and 62 rue de Lille, 7e.

➡**Boat** Batobus boats dock by quai Malaquais for St-Germain des Prés and quai de Solférino for the Musée d'Orsay.

Lonely Planet's Top Tip

The St-Germain and Les Invalides neighbourhood's two biggest-hitting museums – the impressionist-filled Musée d'Orsay and magnificently renovated Musée Rodin – offer a discounted combination ticket costing €18. But you don't need to cram both into one day; the joint ticket is valid for a single visit to each museum within three months.

✖ Best Places to Eat

➡ Restaurant Guy Savoy (p238)
➡ Clover (p236)
➡ Restaurant David Toutain (p240)
➡ Bouillon Racine (p236)
➡ L'Avant Comptoir de la Mer (p234)
➡ Huîtrerie Regis (p236)

For reviews, see p234.

🍷 Best Places to Drink

➡ Les Deux Magots (p240)
➡ Coutume (p241)
➡ Tiger Bar (p241)
➡ Au Sauvignon (p241)
➡ Castor Club (p241)

For reviews, see p240.

🛍 Best Shopping

➡ La Grande Épicerie de Paris (p246)
➡ Magasin Sennelier (p245)
➡ Gab & Jo (p242)
➡ Cire Trudon (p243)
➡ Cantin (p245)

For reviews, see p242.

TOP SIGHT
MUSÉE D'ORSAY

The home of France's national collection from the impressionist, postimpressionist and art nouveau movements spanning the 1840s to 1914 is the glorious former Gare d'Orsay – itself an art nouveau showpiece – where a roll call of masters and their world-famous works are on display.

History

The Gare d'Orsay was designed by competition-winning architect Victor Laloux. Even on its completion, just in time for the 1900 Exposition Universelle, painter Edouard Detaille declared that the new station looked like a Palais des Beaux Arts. But although it had all the mod-cons of the day – including luggage lifts and passenger elevators – by 1939 the increasing electrification of the rail network meant the platforms were too short for mainline trains, and within a few years all rail services ceased.

The station was used as a mailing centre during WWII, and in 1962 Orson Welles filmed Kafka's *The Trial* in the then-abandoned building. Fortunately, it was saved from being demolished and replaced with a hotel complex by a Historical Monument listing in 1973, before the government set about establishing the palatial museum.

Transforming the languishing building into the country's premier showcase for art from 1848 to 1914 was the grand project of President Valéry Giscard d'Estaing, who signed off on it in 1977. The museum opened its doors in 1986.

Far from resting on its laurels, the Musée d'Orsay's recent renovations incorporated a re-energised layout and increased exhibition space. Rather than being lost in a sea of white, prized paintings now gleam from richly coloured walls that create an intimate, stately-

DON'T MISS

➡ The building
➡ Painting collections
➡ Decorative-arts collections
➡ Sculptures
➡ Graphic-arts collections

PRACTICALITIES

➡ Map p406, G2
➡ www.musee-orsay.fr
➡ 62 rue de Lille, 7e
➡ adult/child €12/free
➡ ⊘9.30am-6pm Tue, Wed & Fri-Sun, to 9.45pm Thu
➡ ⓂAssemblée Nationale or RER Musée d'Orsay

home-like atmosphere, with high-tech illumination literally casting the masterpieces in a new light.

Paintings

Top of every visitor's must-see list is the world's largest collection of impressionist and postimpressionist art. Just some of its highlights include Manet's *On the Beach* and *Woman with Fans;* Monet's gardens at Giverny and *Rue Montorgueil, Paris, Celebration of June 30, 1878;* Cézanne's card players, *Green Apples* and *Blue Vase;* Renoir's *Ball at the Moulin de la Galette* and *Young Girls at the Piano;* Degas' ballerinas; Toulouse-Lautrec's cabaret dancers; Pissarro's *The Seine and the Louvre;* Sisley's *View of the Canal St-Martin;* and Van Gogh's self-portraits, *Bedroom in Arles* and *Starry Night over the Rhône.* One of the museum's newer acquisitions is James Tissot's 1868 painting *The Circle of the Rue Royale,* classified a National Treasure.

Decorative & Graphic Arts

Household items such as hat and coat stands, candlesticks, desks, chairs, bookcases, vases, pot-plant holders, freestanding screens, wall mirrors, water pitchers, plates, goblets and bowls become works of art in the hands of their creators from the era, incorporating exquisite design elements.

Drawings, pastels and sketches from major artists are another of the d'Orsay's lesser-known highlights. Look for Georges Seurat's *The Black Bow* (c 1882), which uses crayon on paper to define forms by contrasting between black and white, and Paul Gaugin's poignant self-portrait (c 1902–03), drawn near the end of his life.

Sculptures

The cavernous former station is a magnificent setting for sculptures, including works by Degas, Gaugin, Camille Claudel, Renoir and Rodin.

Guided Tours

For a thorough introduction to the museum, 90-minute 'Masterpieces of the Musée d'Orsay' guided tours (€6) in English run at 11.30am and 2.30pm on Tuesday and 11.30am from Wednesday to Saturday; 90-minute '19th-Century Art' tours (€6) are also available at the same hours. Kids under 13 aren't permitted on tours.

An audioguide costs €5.

Views

Don't miss the Parisian panorama through the former railway station's giant glass clock face, and from the adjacent terrace.

SAVINGS TIPS

Combined tickets with the Musée de l'Orangerie (p118) cost €14, while combined tickets with the Musée Rodin (p230) are €18; both combination tickets are valid for a single visit to the museums within three months. Musée d'Orsay admission drops to €9 after 4.30pm (after 6pm on Thursday). The museum is busiest on Tuesday and Sunday. Save time by buying tickets online and head to entrance C.

Photography of all kinds (including from mobile phones) is forbidden, to avoid crowd bottlenecks. If you want something more than memories to take away, there's an excellent book and gift shop.

DINING OPTIONS

Designed like a fantasy underwater world, on-site **Café Campana** (Map p406; dishes €9-18; ⏲10.30am-5pm Tue, Wed & Fri-Sun, 11am-9pm Thu) serves a short, stylish menu. Time has scarcely changed the museum's sumptuous **Restaurant Musée d'Orsay** (Map p406; ☎01 45 49 47 03; 2-/3-course lunch menus €22/32, mains €16-23; ⏲11.45am-5.30pm Tue, Wed & Fri-Sun, 11.45am-2.45pm & 7-9.30pm Thu).

PRINT COLLECTOR/CONTRIBUTOR/GETTY IMAGES ©

1. The Ballet Class
One of Edgar Degas' many ballerina masterpieces.

2. The Flower Garden at Giverny
Claude Monet created many paintings of his garden in Giverny.

3. Self-Portrait
Several of Vincent Van Gogh's famous paintings are on display in the museum.

4. Bal du Moulin de la Galette
Pierre-Auguste Renoir's.1876 painting portrays Parisian life.

3

TOP SIGHT
JARDIN DU LUXEMBOURG

This inner-city oasis of formal terraces, chestnut groves and lush lawns has a special place in Parisians' hearts. Napoléon dedicated the 23 gracefully laid-out hectares of the Luxembourg Gardens to the children of Paris, and many residents spent their childhood prodding little wooden sailboats with long sticks on the octagonal pond, watching puppet shows and riding the carousel or ponies.

DON'T MISS

➡ Grand Bassin
➡ Puppet shows
➡ Orchards
➡ Palais du Luxembourg
➡ Musée du Luxembourg

PRACTICALITIES

➡ Map p402, D7
➡ www.senat.fr/visite/jardin
➡ numerous entrances
➡ ⊙vary
➡ Ⓜ Mabillon, St-Sulpice, Rennes, Notre Dame des Champs or RER Luxembourg

History

The Jardin du Luxembourg's history stretches further back than Napoléon's dedication. The gardens are a backdrop to the Palais du Luxembourg, built in the 1620s for Marie de Médici, Henri IV's consort, to assuage her longing for the Pitti Palace in Florence. The Palais is now home to the French Senate, which, in addition to parliamentary-assembly activities like voting on legislation, is charged with promoting the palace and its gardens.

Numerous overhauls over the centuries have given the Jardin du Luxembourg a blend of traditional French- and English-style gardens that is unique in Paris.

All of the gardens' nostalgic childhood activities are still here today, as well as modern play equipment, tennis and other sporting and games venues.

Grand Bassin

All ages love the octagonal **Grand Bassin** (Map p402), a serene ornamental pond where adults can lounge and kids can play with 1920s **toy sailboats** (Map p402; 30/60min €2/3.30; ⊙Apr-Oct). Nearby, littlies can take **pony rides** (Map p402; €3.50; ⊙3-6pm Wed, Sat, Sun & school holidays) or romp around the **playgrounds** (Map p402; adult/child €1.20/2.50; ⊙hours vary) – the green half is for kids aged seven to 12 years, the blue half for under-sevens.

Puppet Shows

You don't have to be a kid or be able to speak French to be delighted by marionette shows, which have entertained audiences in France since the Middle Ages. The lively puppets perform in the Jardin du Luxembourg's little **Théâtre du Luxembourg** (Map p402; www.marionnettesduluxembourg.fr; tickets €6; ⊙usually 2pm Wed, Sat & Sun, plus 4pm daily during school holidays). Show times can vary; check the program online and arrive half an hour ahead.

Orchards

Dozens of apple varieties grow in the **orchards** (Map p402) in the gardens' south. Bees have produced honey in the nearby apiary, the **Rucher du Luxembourg** (Map p402), since the 19th century. The annual Fête du Miel (Honey Festival) offers two days of tasting and buying its sweet harvest around late September in the ornate **Pavillon Davioud** (Map p402; 55bis rue d'Assas, 6e).

Palais du Luxembourg

The **Palais du Luxembourg** (Map p402; www.senat.fr; rue de Vaugirard, 6e) was built in the 1620s and has been home to the Sénat (French Senate) since 1958. It's occasionally visitable by guided tour.

East of the palace is the ornate, Italianate **Fontaine des Médici** (Map p402), built in 1630. During Baron Haussmann's 19th-century reshaping of the roads, the fountain was moved 30m and the pond and dramatic statues of the giant bronze Polyphemus discovering the white-marble lovers Acis and Galatea were added.

Musée du Luxembourg

Prestigious temporary art exhibitions, such as 'Cézanne et Paris', take place in the beautiful **Musée du Luxembourg** (Map p402; www.museeduluxembourg.fr; 19 rue de Vaugirard, 6e; most exhibitions adult/child €13.50/9; ⊙10am-7pm Tue-Thu, Sat & Sun, to 9.30pm Fri & Mon).

Around the back of the museum, lemon and orange trees, palms, grenadiers and oleanders shelter from the cold in the palace's **orangery** (Map p402). Nearby, the heavily guarded Hôtel du Petit Luxembourg was where Marie de Médici lived while the Palais du Luxembourg was being built. The president of the Senate has called it home since 1825.

PICNICKING

Kiosks and cafes are dotted throughout the park, including places selling candy floss. If you're planning on picnicking, forget bringing a blanket – the elegantly manicured lawns are off-limits apart from a small wedge on the southern boundary. Instead, do as Parisians do, and corral one of the iconic 1923-designed green metal chairs and find your own favourite part of the park.

If you fancy taking home a classic Jardin du Luxembourg chair, pick one up from Fermob (p244).

SCULPTURES

The gardens are studded with over 100 sculptures. Look out for statues of Stendhal, Chopin, Baudelaire and Delacroix.

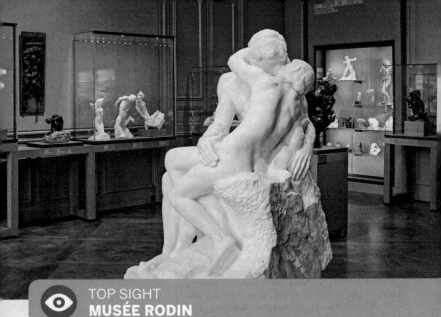

Sculptor, painter, sketcher, engraver and collector Auguste Rodin donated his entire collection to the French state in 1908 on the proviso that they dedicate his former workshop and showroom, the beautiful Hôtel Biron (1730), to displaying his works. They're now installed in the mansion and in its rose-filled garden – one of the most peaceful places in central Paris.

Sculptures

The first large-scale cast of Rodin's famous sculpture The Thinker (*Le Penseur*), made in 1902, resides in the garden – the perfect place to contemplate this heroic naked figure conceived by Rodin to represent intellect and poetry (it was originally titled *The Poet*).

The Gates of Hell (*La Porte de l'Enfer*) was commissioned in 1880 as the entrance for a never-built museum, and Rodin worked on his sculptural masterwork up until his death in 1917. Standing 6m high by 4m wide, its 180 figures comprise an intricate scene from Dante's *Inferno*.

The Kiss (*Le Baiser*; pictured above) was originally part of *The Gates of Hell*. The marble sculpture's entwined lovers caused controversy on its completion due to Rodin's then-radical approach of depicting women as equal partners in ardour.

Collections

In addition to Rodin's own paintings and sketches, don't miss his prized collection of works by artists including Van Gogh and Renoir.

Rodin at the Hôtel Biron

The 'Rodin at the Hôtel Biron' room incorporates original furniture to recreate the space as it was when he lived and worked here.

DON'T MISS

→ *The Thinker*
→ *The Gates of Hell*
→ *The Kiss*
→ Camille Claudel sculptures
→ Collections

PRACTICALITIES

→ Map p406, D4
→ www.musee-rodin.fr
→ 79 rue de Varenne, 7e
→ adult/child museum incl garden €10/7, garden only €4/2
→ ⊙10am-5.45pm Tue & Thu-Sun, to 8.45pm Wed
→ Ⓜ Varenne

TOP SIGHT
HÔTEL DES INVALIDES

Flanked by the 500m-long Esplanade des Invalides lawns, the Hôtel des Invalides was built in the 1670s by Louis XIV to house 4000 *invalides* (disabled war veterans). On 14 July 1789, a mob broke into the building and seized 32,000 rifles before heading on to the prison at Bastille and the start of the French Revolution.

Église du Dôme
South of the main courtyard is the **Église du Dôme** (Map p406), which, with its sparkling golden dome (1677–1735), is one of the finest religious edifices erected under Louis XIV.

Also south of the main courtyard is the Église St-Louis des Invalides, once used by soldiers.

Tombeau de Napoléon 1er
The very extravagant Tombeau de Napoléon 1er (Napoléon's Tomb), in the centre of the Église du Dôme, comprises six coffins fitting into one another like a Russian doll.

Musée de l'Armée
North of the main courtyard is the **Musée de l'Armée** (Army Museum; Map p406), containing the nation's largest collection on French military history. Sobering wartime footage screens at this army museum, which also has weaponry, flag and medal displays as well as a multimedia area dedicated to Charles de Gaulle.

Musée des Plans-Reliefs
Within the Hôtel des Invalides itself, the esoteric Musée des Plans-Reliefs is full of scale models of towns, fortresses and châteaux across France.

DON'T MISS
➡ Musée de l'Armée
➡ Église du Dôme
➡ Tombeau de Napoléon 1er
➡ Musée des Plans-Reliefs

PRACTICALITIES
➡ Map p406, C4
➡ www.musee-armee.fr
➡ 129 rue de Grenelle, 7e
➡ adult/child €11/free
➡ ⏱10am-6pm Apr-Oct, to 5pm Nov-Mar, hours can vary
➡ Ⓜ Varenne

SIGHTS

Chart-topping sights in this stately neighbourhood include the impressionist-art-filled Musée d'Orsay, massive military complex Hôtel des Invalides (home to Napoléon's tomb) and sculpture-strewn Musée Rodin. Look out for smaller, lesser-known gems too, such as the Musée National Eugène Delacroix, Musée des Lettres et Manuscrits and some exquisite churches – and don't miss a stroll in the city's most beautiful park, the delightful Jardin du Luxembourg.

◉ St-Germain

JARDIN DU LUXEMBOURG   PARK
See p228.

LE BATEAU IVRE   MONUMENT
Map p402 (4 rue Ferou, 6e; MSt-Sulpice) Arthur Rimbaud's 1871 poem *Le Bateau Ivre* (*The Drunken Boat*), depicting a fantastical and frightening sea voyage of a sinking boat from the first-person narration of the boat itself using rich imagery and symbolism, occupies a 300m-long wall spanning an entire block in the heart of St-Germain. Rimbaud wrote the poem at age 16 after being inspired by Jules Verne's recently published novel *Twenty Thousand Leagues Under the Sea*. The 100-line poem was hand painted on the wall in 2012.

MUSÉE DES LETTRES ET MANUSCRITS   MUSEUM
Map p402 (MLM; Letters & Manuscripts Museum; 222 bd St-Germain, 7e; adult/child €7/5; ⊘10am-7pm Tue, Wed & Fri-Sun, to 9.30pm Thu May-Sep, shorter hours Oct-Apr; MRue du Bac) Grouped into five themes – history, science, music, art and literature – the handwritten and annotated letters and works on display at this captivating museum provide a powerful emotional connection to their authors. They include Napoléon, Charles de Gaulle, Marie Curie, Albert Einstein, Mozart, Beethoven, Piaf, Monet, Toulouse-Lautrec, Van Gogh, Victor Hugo, Hemingway and F Scott Fitzgerald; there are many, many more. It's thoroughly absorbing – allow at least a couple of hours. Temporary exhibitions also take place regularly.

◉ TOP SIGHT
ÉGLISE ST-GERMAIN DES PRÉS

Paris' oldest standing church, the Romanesque *Église St-Germain des Prés* (*St Germanus of the Fields*) (p232) was built in the 11th century on the site of a 6th-century abbey and was the dominant place of worship in Paris until the arrival of Notre Dame. It's undergone numerous alterations since, but the *Chapelle de St-Symphorien* (to the right as you enter) was part of the original abbey.

The Chapelle de St-Symphorien is believed to be the resting place of St Germanus (496–576), the first bishop of Paris. The Merovingian kings were buried here during the 6th and 7th centuries, but their tombs disappeared during the Revolution.

Over the western entrance, the bell tower has changed little since 990, although the spire dates only from the 19th century.

Until the late 17th century the abbey owned most of the land in the Left Bank west of what's now bd St-Michel, and donated some of its lands along the Seine – the Pré aux Clercs (Fields of the Scholars) – to house the University of Paris (hence the names of the nearby streets, rues du Pré aux Clercs and de l'Université).

DON'T MISS
➡ Chapelle de St-Symphorien
➡ Bell tower

PRACTICALITIES
➡ Map p402, D3
➡ www.eglise-stgermaindespres.fr
➡ 3 place St-Germain des Prés, 6e
➡ ⊘8am-7.45pm
➡ MSt-Germain des Prés

MUSÉE NATIONAL EUGÈNE DELACROIX
MUSEUM

Map p402 (www.musee-delacroix.fr; 6 rue de Furstenberg, 6e; adult/child €7/free; ⊙9.30am-5pm Wed-Mon; MMabillon) In a courtyard off a magnolia-shaded square, this museum is housed in the romantic artist's home and studio at the time of his death in 1863. It contains a collection of his oil paintings, watercolours, pastels and drawings, including many of his more intimate works, such as *An Unmade Bed* (1828) and his paintings of Morocco.

A ticket from the Musée du Louvre (p108) allows entry to the museum on the same day (you can also buy tickets here and skip the Louvre's ticket queues).

As well as the Musée du Louvre, you can see Delacroix's works at the Musée d'Orsay (p224) and frescoes at Église St-Sulpice.

ÉGLISE ST-SULPICE
CHURCH

Map p402 (www.pss75.fr/saint-sulpice-paris; place St-Sulpice, 6e; ⊙7.30am-7.30pm; MSt-Sulpice) In 1646 work started on the twin-towered Church of St Sulpicius, lined inside with 21 side chapels, and it took six architects 150 years to finish. It's famed for its striking Italianate facade with two rows of superimposed columns, its Counter-Reformation-influenced neoclassical decor and its frescoes by Eugène Delacroix – and its setting for a murderous scene in Dan Brown's *The Da Vinci Code*.

You can hear the monumental, 1781-built organ during 10.30am Mass on Sunday or the occasional Sunday-afternoon concert.

The frescoes in the Chapelle des Sts-Anges (Chapel of the Holy Angels), first to the right as you enter the chapel, depict Jacob wrestling with the angel (to the left) and Michael the Archangel doing battle with Satan (to the right), and were painted by Delacroix between 1855 and 1861.

MUSÉE ATELIER ZADKINE
MUSEUM

Map p402 (www.zadkine.paris.fr; 100bis rue d'Assas, 6e; ⊙10am-6pm Tue-Sun; MVavin) FREE Russian cubist sculptor Ossip Zadkine (1890–1967) arrived in Paris in 1908 and lived and worked in this cottage for almost 40 years. Zadkine produced an enormous catalogue of sculptures made from clay, stone, bronze and wood. The museum covers his life and work; one room displays figures he sculpted in contrasting walnut, pear, ebony, acacia, elm and oak.

MONNAIE DE PARIS
MUSEUM

Map p402 (☏01 40 46 56 66; www.monnaiede paris.fr; 11 quai de Conti, 6e; MPont Neuf) The 18th-century royal mint, the Monnaie de Paris – still used by the Ministry of Finance to produce commemorative medals and coins – houses the Musée de la Monnaie (Parisian Mint Museum), showcasing the history of French coinage from antiquity onwards. The overhaul of this sumptuous neoclassical building, with one of the longest facades on the Seine, incorporates interior streets, the restoration of an aristocratic townhouse built by Jules Hardouin Mansart in 1690, and Guy Savoy's flagship restaurant (p238) and courtyard brasserie.

BIBLIOTHÈQUE MAZARINE
LIBRARY

Map p402 (☏01 44 41 44 06; www.bibliotheque-mazarine.fr; 23 quai de Conti, 6e; 5-day pass free; ⊙10am-6pm Mon-Fri; MMabillon) Within the Institut de France, the Mazarine Library is France's oldest public library, founded in 1643. You can visit the bust-lined, late-17th-century reading room or consult the library's collection of 500,000 volumes, using an admission pass valid for five consecutive days obtained by providing ID. Schedules for free 1½-hour guided tours in English are posted on its website.

⊙ Les Invalides

MUSÉE D'ORSAY
MUSEUM

See p224.

MUSÉE RODIN
MUSEUM, GARDEN

See p230.

HÔTEL DES INVALIDES
MONUMENT, MUSEUM

See p231.

FONDATION DUBUFFET
ART MUSEUM

Map p406 (www.dubuffetfondation.com; 137 rue de Sèvres, 6e; adult/child €6/4; ⊙2-6pm Mon-Fri Sep-Jul; MDuroc) Situated in a lovely 19th-century *hôtel particulier* (private mansion) at the end of a courtyard, the foundation houses the collection of Jean Dubuffet (1901–85), chief of the Art Brut school (a term he himself coined to describe all works of artistic expression not officially recognised). Much of his work is incredibly modern and expressive.

LES BERGES DE SEINE
PROMENADE

Map p406 (btwn Musée d'Orsay & Pont de l'Alma, 7e; ⊙information point noon-7pm Sun-Thu,

10am-10pm Fri & Sat May-Sep, shorter hours Oct-Apr; M Solférino, Assemblée Nationale, Invalides) A breath of fresh air, this 2.3km-long expressway-turned-riverside-promenade is now a favourite spot to run, cycle, skate, play board games or take part in a packed program of events. Equally it's simply a great place to hang out – in a Zzz shipping-container hut (reserve at the information point just west of the Musée d'Orsay), on the archipelago of floating gardens, or at the burgeoning restaurants and bars (some floating aboard boats and barges).

MUSÉE DES ÉGOUTS DE PARIS   MUSEUM

Map p406 (http://equipment.paris.fr/musee-des-egouts-5059; place de la Résistance, 7e; adult/child €4.40/3.60; ⊙11am-5pm Tue & Wed May-Sep, 11am-4pm Tue & Wed Oct-Dec & Feb-Apr; M Alma Marceau or RER Pont de l'Alma) Raw sewage flows beneath your feet as you walk through 480m of odoriferous tunnels in this working sewer museum. Exhibitions cover the development of Paris' waste-water-disposal system, including its resident rats (there's an estimated one sewer rat for every Parisian above ground). Enter via a rectangular maintenance hole topped with a kiosk across the street from 93 quai d'Orsay, 7e.

The sewers are closed when rain floods the tunnels. Toy rats are sold at its gift shop.

✕ EATING

The picnicking turf of the Jardin de Luxembourg is complemented by some fabulous places to buy picnic ingredients. Even if it's not picnic weather, the neighbourhood's streets are lined with everything from quintessential Parisian bistros to chic designer restaurants and flagship establishments with Michelin-starred chefs. Some charming places hide inside Cour du Commerce St-André, a glass-covered passageway built in 1735 to link two *jeu de paume* (old-style tennis) courts.

✕ St-Germain

L'AVANT COMPTOIR   FRENCH TAPAS €

Map p402 (www.hotel-paris-relais-saint-germain.com; 3 Carrefour de l'Odéon, 6e; tapas €5-10; ⊙noon-midnight; M Odéon) Squeeze in around the zinc bar (there are no seats and it's tiny) and order off the menu suspended from the ceiling to feast on amazing tapas (crab custard tarts with Pernod foam, Iberian ham or salmon tartare croquettes, duck confit hot dogs, blood-sausage macarons, and prosciutto and artichoke waffles), with wines by the glass, in a chaotically sociable atmosphere.

For seafood tapas, head to neighbouring **L'Avant Comptoir de la Mer** (Map p402; tapas €4-30; ⊙noon-11pm), or for gourmet bistro dining, try for a lunchtime table or evening reservation at **Le Comptoir du Relais** (Map p402; 📞01 44 27 07 97; mains €14-39, dinner menu €60; ⊙noon-6pm & 8.30-11.30pm Mon-Fri, noon-11pm Sat & Sun;).

LITTLE BREIZH   CRÊPERIE €

Map p402 (📞01 43 54 60 74; 11 rue Grégoire de Tours, 6e; crêpes €4.70-12; ⊙noon-2.15pm & 7-10.15pm; 📞; M Odéon) As authentic as you'd find in Brittany, but with some innovative twists (such as Breton sardines, olive oil and sundried tomatoes; goat's cheese, stewed apple, hazelnuts, rosemary and honey; smoked salmon, dill cream, pink peppercorns and lemon), the crêpes at this sweet spot are infinitely more enticing than those sold on nearby street corners. Hours can fluctuate; book ahead.

AU PIED DE FOUET   BISTRO €

Map p402 (📞01 43 54 87 83; www.aupiedde fouet.com; 3 rue St-Benoît, 6e; mains €9-12.50; ⊙noon-2.30pm & 7-11pm Mon-Sat; M St-Germain des Prés) At this tiny, lively, cherry-red-coloured bistro, wholly classic dishes such as *entrecôte* (steak), *confit de canard* (duck cooked slowly in its own fat) with creamy potatoes and *foie de volailles sauté* (pan-fried chicken livers) are astonishingly good value. Round off your meal with a *tarte Tatin* (upside-down apple tart), wine-soaked prunes, or deliciously rich *fondant au chocolat*.

POILÂNE   BOULANGERIE €

Map p402 (www.poilane.com; 8 rue du Cherche Midi, 6e; ⊙7.15am-8.15pm Mon-Sat; M Sèvres-Babylone) Pierre Poilâne opened his *boulangerie* (bakery) upon arriving from Normandy in 1932. Today his granddaughter Apollonia runs the company, which still turns out wood-fired, rounded sourdough loaves made with stone-milled flour and Guérande sea salt. A clutch of other outlets include one in the 15e (p254).

PARIS' OLDEST RESTAURANT & CAFE

St-Germain claims both the city's oldest restaurant and its oldest cafe.

À la Petite Chaise (Map p402; ☎01 42 22 13 35; www.alapetitechaise.fr; 36 rue de Grenelle, 6e; menus lunch/dinner €25/33, mains €21; ⊙noon-2pm & 7-11pm; MSèvres-Babylone) This restaurant hides behind an iron gate that's been here since it opened in 1680, when wine merchant Georges Rameau served food to the public to accompany his wares. Classical decor and cuisine (onion soup, foie gras, duck, lamb and unexpected delights like venison terrine with hazelnuts) make it worth a visit above and beyond its history.

Le Procope (Map p402; ☎01 40 46 79 00; www.procope.com; 13 rue de l'Ancienne Comédie, 6e; 2-/3-course menus from €21/28; ⊙11.30am-midnight Sun-Wed, to 1am Thu-Sat; 📶; MOdéon) The city's oldest cafe welcomed its first patrons in 1686, and was frequented by Voltaire, Molière and Balzac et al. Its chandeliered interior also has an entrance onto the 1735-built glass-roofed passageway Cour du Commerce St-André. House specialities include coq au vin, calf's-head casserole in veal stock, calf kidneys with violet mustard, and homemade ice cream.

L'AMARYLLIS DE GÉRARD MULOT
PATISSERIE €

Map p402 (www.gerard-mulot.com; 12 rue des Quartre Vents, 6e; dishes €6.60-20, lunch menu €25; ⊙11am-6.30pm Tue-Sat; MOdéon) Pastry maestro Gérard Mulot has three boutiques in Paris, including one on nearby **rue de Seine** (Map p402; 76 rue de Seine, 6e; ⊙6.45am-8pm Thu-Tue; MMabillon), but this branch also incorporates a *salon de thé* (tearoom) where you can sit down to savour his famous fruit tarts on the spot. Other dishes include quiches, gourmet salads, omelettes and more filling lunch meals including a meat or fish *suggestion du chef.*

IL GELATO DEL MARCHESE
GELATERIA €

Map p402 (3 rue des Quatre-Vents, 6e; ice cream per 1/2/3 scoops €3.90/4.50/6.50; ⊙11am-11pm May-Sep, shorter hours Oct-Apr; MOdéon) Sardinian ricotta and honeyed almonds, Piedmont hazelnut truffle, coffee and cardamom, and caipirinha (yes, the Brazilian cocktail of cachaça, sugar and lime) are among the amazing flavours of gelato scooped up to take away or eat in the attached tearoom. If it's not ice cream weather, go for a deliciously thick hot chocolate, made from noon onwards.

LA MAISON DU CHOU
PATISSERIE €

Map p402 (7 Rue de Furstenberg, 6e; 1/3/6/12 filled choux €2/5/10/18; ⊙11am-8pm; MMabillon) At this little boutique, crisp, crunchy *choux* (pastry puffs) are piped to order with *fromage-blanc*-based fillings flavoured with everything from chocolate to caramel, praline and coffee. There's a handful of seats on-site; otherwise the *choux* make perfect picnic fare.

JSFP TRAITEUR
DELI €

Map p402 (8 rue de Buci, 6e; dishes €3.70-6.20; ⊙9.30am-8.30pm; 📶; MMabillon) Brimming with big bowls of salad, terrines, pâté and other prepared delicacies, this deli is a brilliant bet for quality Parisian 'fast food' such as quiches in a variety of flavour combinations (courgette and chive, mozzarella and basil, salmon and spinach...) to take to a nearby park, square or stretch of riverfront.

LA BOTTEGA DI PASTAVINO
ITALIAN €

Map p402 (☎01 44 07 09 56; 18 rue de Buci, 6e; deli dishes €5.50-7.50, restaurant mains €19-36; ⊙deli 9.30am-8.15pm Mon-Sat, restaurant 8-11.30pm Mon-Sat; MMabillon) Crammed with imported Italian groceries – marinated capsicums, artichokes and olives, dozens of varieties of dried and fresh pasta, white-truffle cream and bottles of Italian *vino* – this Aladdin's-cave deli also dishes up freshly cooked pasta, salads, and piping-hot panini for lunch on the run. At the back, up a spiral staircase, is its 20-seat restaurant, L'Étage.

CUISINE DE BAR
SANDWICHES €

Map p402 (www.cuisinedebar.fr; 8 rue du Cherche Midi, 6e; dishes €9.20-13.50; ⊙8.30am-7pm Mon-Sat, 9.30am-3.30pm Sun; 📶; MSèvres-Babylone) As next-door neighbour to one of Paris' most famous bakers, this isn't your average sandwich bar. Instead, between shopping in designer boutiques, it's an ultrachic spot to lunch on open sandwiches cut from that celebrated Poilâne bread (p234) and fabulously topped with gourmet goodies such as foie gras, smoked duck, gooey St-Marcellin cheese and Bayonne ham.

★BOUILLON RACINE BRASSERIE €€

Map p402 (📞01 73 20 21 12; www.bouillonracine. com; 3 rue Racine, 6e; weekday lunch menu €16, menus €31-42; ⊙noon-11pm; ♿; MCluny-La Sorbonne) Inconspicuously situated in a quiet street, this heritage-listed 1906 art nouveau 'soup kitchen', with mirrored walls, floral motifs and ceramic tiling, was built in 1906 to feed market workers. Despite the magnificent interior, the food – inspired by age-old recipes – is no afterthought but superbly executed (stuffed, spit-roasted suckling pig, pork shank in Rodenbach red beer, scallops and shrimps with lobster coulis).

Finish off your foray into gastronomic history with an old-fashioned sherbet. Two-course children's menus mean kids don't miss out.

★CLOVER NEOBISTRO €€

Map p402 (📞01 75 50 00 05; www.clover-paris. com; 5 rue Perronet, 7e; 2-/3-course lunch menus €28/42, 3-/5-course dinner menus €58/73; ⊙12.30-2pm & 7.30-10pm Tue-Sat; MSt-Germain des Prés) Dining at hot-shot chef Jean-François Piège's casual bistro is like attending a private party: the galley-style open kitchen adjoining the 20 seats (reserve ahead!) is part of the dining-room decor, putting customers at the front and centre of the culinary action. Light, luscious dishes span quinoa chips with aubergine and black sesame to cabbage leaves with smoked herring *crème* and chestnuts.

★SEMILLA NEOBISTRO €€

Map p402 (📞01 43 54 34 50; 54 rue de Seine, 6e; lunch menu €24, mains €20-50; ⊙12.30-2.30pm & 7-10.45pm; MMabillon) Stark concrete, exposed pipes and an open kitchen (in front of which you can book front-row 'chef seats') set the factory-style scene for edgy, modern, daily changing dishes such as pork spare ribs with sweet potato and cinnamon, mushrooms in hazelnut butter, and trout with passionfruit and ginger (all suppliers are listed). Desserts here are outstanding. Be sure to book.

If you haven't made a reservation, head to its adjoining walk-in wine bar, **Freddy's** (Map p402; 54 rue de Seine, 6e; small plates €5-15; ⊙noon-midnight; MSt-Germain des Prés), serving small tapas-style plates.

★HUÎTRERIE REGIS SEAFOOD €€

Map p402 (http://huitrerieregis.com; 3 rue de Montfaucon, 6e; dozen oysters from €16; ⊙noon-2.30pm & 6.30-10.30pm Mon-Fri, noon-10.45pm Sat, noon-10pm Sun; MMabillon) Hip, trendy, tiny and white, this is *the* spot for slurping oysters on crisp winter days. The oysters come only by the dozen, along with fresh bread and butter, but wash them down with a glass of chilled Muscadet and *voilà*, one perfect lunch. A twinset of tables loiter on the pavement; otherwise it's all inside. No reservations, so arrive early.

LE TIMBRE NEOBISTRO €€

Map p402 (📞01 45 49 10 40; www.restaurant letimbre.com; 3 rue Ste-Beuve, 6e; 3-course lunch menu €26, 3-/4-/5-course dinner menus €36/43/49; ⊙noon-3pm & 7.30-11pm Tue-Sat; MVavin) As tiny as the postage stamp for which it's named, Le Timbre is run by husband-and-wife team Charles Danet (in the kitchen) and Agnès Peyre (front of house) and has a local following for its daily changing menu of original dishes (caramelised endives with parmesan *crème* and brioche; and turbot and clams with marinated cabbage and potato terrine).

Desserts like chocolate and honey ganache and homemade brioche ice cream are dazzling; the wine list, chalked on the blackboard, changes daily too.

LA CUISINE DE PHILIPPE BISTRO €€

Map p402 (📞01 43 29 76 37; 25 rue Servandoni, 6e; 2-/3-course lunch menus €25/28, dinner menus €35/40; ⊙noon-2.15pm & 7-10.15pm Tue-Sat; MSt-Sulpice) Look up to see the beautiful muralled ceiling at this mustard-walled, tiled-floored old-style bistro. Soufflés – goat's cheese and basil; lobster, crab and tarragon; wild mushroom; rhubarb; pistachio – are a speciality. Other dishes include guinea fowl marinated in honey and spices; Madeira-flambéed veal kidneys; and eggs poached in red wine with bacon and croutons. Lunch *menus* include a glass of wine.

LE BON SAINT POURCAIN NEOBISTRO €€

Map p402 (📞01 42 01 78 24; 10bis rue Servandoni, 6e; mains €24-27; ⊙noon-2.30pm & 7-10.30pm Tue-Sat; MSt-Sulpice) Right at home in this chic neighbourhood, behind a French navy-blue facade, Le Bon Saint Pourcain has a daily changing chalkboard menu listing three to four starters, mains and desserts, which you can watch being cooked up in the central open kitchen. Meats such as *porcelet*

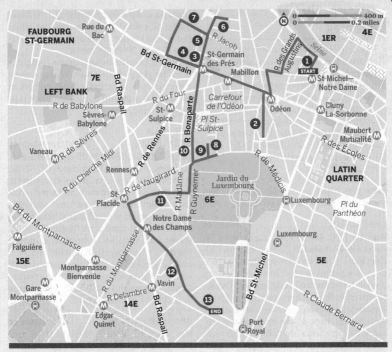

Neighbourhood Walk
Left Bank Literary Loop

START QUAI DES GRANDS AUGUSTINS
END 113 RUE NOTRE DAMES DES CHAMPS
LENGTH 5KM; ONE TO TWO HOURS

To retrace the footsteps of Left Bank literary luminaries, begin by following the Seine west past the *bouquinistes* (secondhand booksellers) that Ernest Hemingway loved.

South is the 'Beat Hotel', now the **❶ Relais Hôtel du Vieux Paris**, where Allen Ginsberg, Jack Kerouac, William S Burroughs and others holed up in the 1950s.

At **❷ 12 rue de l'Odéon** stood the original Shakespeare & Company bookshop where owner Sylvia Beach lent books to Hemingway, and edited, retyped and published *Ulysses* for James Joyce in 1922. It was closed during the occupation when Beach refused to sell her last copy of Joyce's *Finnegan's Wake* to a Nazi officer.

Bd St-Germain's **❸ Les Deux Magots** (p240) and **❹ Café de Flore** (p241) were favourite cafes of postwar intellectuals Jean-Paul Sartre and Simone de Beauvoir.

At **❺ 36 rue Bonaparte** Henry Miller stayed in a 5th-floor mansard room in 1930, which he later wrote about in *Letters to Emil* (1989). **❻ L'Hôtel** (p291), the former Hôtel d'Alsace, is where Oscar Wilde died in 1900. Hemingway spent his first night in Paris in room 14 of the **❼ Hôtel d'Angleterre** (p291) in 1921.

In 1925 William Faulkner stayed several months at what's now the posh **❽ Hôtel Luxembourg Parc**, and Hemingway's last years in Paris were at **❾ 6 rue Férou**. F Scott and Zelda Fitzgerald lived at **❿ 58 rue de Vaugirard** in 1928, near **⓫ 27 rue de Fleurus**, where Gertrude Stein lived and entertained artists and writers including Matisse, Picasso, Braque, Gauguin, Fitzgerald, Hemingway and Ezra Pound.

Pound lived in **⓬ 70bis rue Notre Dame des Champs** in a flat filled with Japanese paintings and packing crates, while Hemingway's first apartment in this area was above a sawmill at **⓭ 113 rue Notre Dames des Champs**.

RUE CLER

Pick up fresh bread, sandwich fillings, pastries and wine for a picnic along the typically Parisian commercial street rue Cler, 7e, which buzzes with local shoppers, especially on weekends.

Interspersed between the *boulangeries*, *fromageries*, grocers, butchers, delis and other food shops (many with pavement stalls), lively cafe terraces overflow with locals too.

(baby pig), pigeon and rabbit as well as fish are married with seasonal produce.

CHEZ MARCEL
LYONNAIS €€

Map p402 (☑01 45 48 29 94; 7 rue Stanislas, 6e; menus €19-42, mains €19-26; ◷noon-2pm & 7.30-10pm Mon-Fri; ⓂNotre Dame des Champs) Since 1919, this picture-perfect bistro, with worn timber furniture and paintings on the sepia-toned walls, has been serving up Lyon's signature *bouchon* (Lyonnais bistro) dishes such as pigs' ears, coarse *andouillette* sausages, pike *quenelles* (dumplings) with *nantua* crayfish sauce, and sugary pink praline tart. Ownership changes over the years have not only preserved but increased its appeal.

WADJA
BISTRO €€

Map p402 (☑01 46 33 02 02; 10 rue de la Grande Chaumière, 6e; 2-/3-course lunch menus €20/22, 3-course dinner menu €40; ◷12.15-2pm & 7.30-10.30pm Mon-Fri, 7.30-10.30pm Sat; ⓂVavin) Behind a honey-coloured timber facade, an evocative Parisian setting is created by a zinc bar backed by soaring mirrors, some 1930s lithographs and patterned floor tiles. This tucked-away little treasure is off even most foodies' radars. Updated French classics include pan-fried scallops with caramelised blood orange; veal brain with lemon and caper confit; and cardamom crêpes with roasted apple.

POLIDOR
TRADITIONAL FRENCH €€

Map p402 (☑01 43 26 95 34; www.polidor.com; 41 rue Monsieur le Prince, 6e; menus €22-35, mains €12-20; ◷noon-2.30pm & 7pm-12.30am Mon-Sat, noon-2.30pm & 7-11pm Sun; 🚻; ⓂOdéon) A meal at this quintessentially Parisian *crèmerie-restaurant* is like a trip to Victor Hugo's Paris: the restaurant and its decor date from 1845. *Menus* of tasty, family-style French cuisine ensure a stream of diners

eager to sample *bœuf bourguignon, blanquette de veau à l'ancienne* (veal in white sauce) and Polidor's famous *tarte Tatin*. Expect to wait. No credit cards.

Midnight in Paris fans might recognise it as the place where Owen Wilson's character meets Hemingway (who dined here in his day). Over 20,000 bottles are stocked in its wine cellar.

ROGER LA GRENOUILLE
TRADITIONAL FRENCH €€

Map p402 (☑01 56 24 24 34; 26-28 rue des Grands Augustins, 6e; menus lunch/dinner €27.50/32, mains €18-29.50; ◷noon-2pm & 7-11pm Mon-Fri, noon-11pm Sat; ⓂSt-Michel) Scattered with frog sculptures, B&W pictures of 1920s Paris and an array of old lamps, time-worn, sepia-coloured institution 'Roger the Frog' serves nine varieties of frogs' legs, including *à la Provençale* (with tomato) and *Normande* (cooked in cider and served with apple). If you're squeamish about devouring Roger, alternatives include dishes such as veal kidneys or lamb shanks.

BRASSERIE LIPP
BRASSERIE €€

Map p402 (☑01 45 48 53 91; 151 bd St-Germain, 6e; mains €22-38; ◷8.30am-1am, kitchen 11.45am-12.45am; ⓂSt-Germain des Prés) Waiters in black waistcoats, bow ties and long white aprons serve brasserie favourites like *choucroute garnie* (dressed sauerkraut) and *jarret de porc aux lentilles* (pork knuckle with lentils) at this illustrious wood-panelled establishment. (Arrive hungry: salads aren't allowed as meals.) Opened by Léonard Lipp in 1880, the brasserie achieved immortality when Hemingway sang its praises in *A Moveable Feast*.

★RESTAURANT GUY SAVOY
GASTRONOMY €€€

Map p402 (☑01 43 80 40 61; www.guysavoy.com; Monnaie de Paris, 11 quai de Conti, 6e; lunch menu via online booking €110, 12-/18-course tasting menus €420/490; ◷noon-2pm & 7-10.30pm Tue-Fri, 7-10.30pm Sat; ⓂPont Neuf) If you're considering visiting a three-Michelin-star temple of gastronomy, this should certainly be on your list. The world-famous chef needs no introduction (he trained Gordon Ramsay, among others) but now his flagship, entered via a red-carpeted staircase, is ensconced in the gorgeously refurbished neoclassical Monnaie de Paris (p233). Monumental cuisine to match includes Savoy icons like artichoke and black-truffle soup with layered brioche.

Look out for Guy Savoy's casual courtyard brasserie/cafe on the same site. Or try his famed brioche for a fraction of the price in his eponymous restaurant by heading around the corner to his brioche boutique, **Goût de Brioche** (Map p402; www.goutde brioche.com; 54 rue Mazarine, 6e; brioche €4-7; ⊙8.30am-7.30pm Tue-Fri, 8am-7.30pm Sat & Sun; MOdéon).

✗ Les Invalides

LE BAC À GLACES ICE CREAM €
Map p406 (www.bacaglaces.com; 109 rue du Bac, 7e; ice cream per 1/2/3 scoops €3.50/4.50/5.50; ⊙11am-7pm Mon-Fri, to 7.30pm Sat; MSèvres-Babylone) Apricot and thyme, lemon and basil, strawberry and rose, and a triple hit of orange, Grand Marnier and chocolate are among the 60 flavours of all-natural ice creams at this luscious *glacière* (ice-cream maker). A cloud of Chantilly sugar-whipped cream costs an extra €0.50.

MAISON DE LA CHANTILLY DESSERTS €
Map p406 (www.maisondelachantilly.com; 47 rue Cler, 7e; dishes €1.50-5.50; ⊙10am-7pm Tue-Sun; MÉcole Militaire) Cloudlike *crème Chantilly* (cream whipped with icing and vanilla sugars), which originated at the namesake château near Paris, is the star of this little sky-blue-and-white cafe, whether served in cornets with fresh strawberries, on meringues and cakes, or as a decadent accompaniment to coffee. You can also buy it by the container to take away.

BESNIER BOULANGERIE €
Map p406 (40 rue de Bourgogne, 7e; ⊙7am-8pm Mon-Fri Sep-Jul; MVarenne) You can watch baguettes being made through the viewing window of this award-winning *boulangerie*. Fig bread made from chestnut flour is a speciality. Expect to queue around lunchtime.

MARCHÉ RASPAIL MARKET €
Map p406 (bd Raspail btwn rue de Rennes & rue du Cherche Midi, 6e; ⊙regular market 7am-2.30pm Tue & Fri, organic market 9am-2pm Sun; MRennes) ✎ A traditional open-air market on Tuesday and Friday, Marché Raspail is especially popular on Sunday, when it's filled with *biologique* (organic) produce.

★CHEZ FRANÇOISE TRADITIONAL FRENCH €€
Map p406 (☏01 47 05 49 03; www.chezfrancoise. com; Aérogare des Invalides, 7e; 2-/3-course menus from €28/33, oysters per half-dozen €15.50-29; ⊙noon-3pm & 7pm-midnight; MInvalides) Buried beneath the enormous Air France building but opening to a retractable-roofed terrace, this old-school 1949-opened restaurant – a favourite with parliamentary workers from the Assemblée Nationale – recalls the early glamour of air travel, the era when it was established at this former off-site terminal for transiting passengers. Specialities include *entrecôte de bœuf* and sublime oysters.

CHEZ DUMONET BISTRO €€
Map p406 (Joséphine; ☏01 45 48 52 40; 117 rue du Cherche Midi, 6e; mains €25-42; ⊙noon-2.30pm & 7.30-9.30pm Mon-Fri; MDuroc) Fondly known by its former name, Joséphine, this lace-curtained, mosaic-tiled place with white-clothed tables inside and out is the Parisian bistro of many people's dreams, serving timeless standards such as confit of duck, *millefeuille* of pigeon, and grilled *châteaubriand* steak with Béarnaise sauce. Be sure to order its enormous signature Grand Marnier soufflé at the start of your meal.

During truffle season (November to March), though, it's hard to go past its aromatic truffle menus (€49 to €105).

LES FABLES DE LA FONTAINE GASTRONOMY €€
Map p406 (☏01 44 18 37 55; www.lesfablesdela-fontaine.net; 131 rue St-Dominique, 7e; 2-course lunch menu €25, mains €21-29; ⊙noon-2.30pm & 7-10.30pm; MÉcole Militaire or RER Pont de l'Alma) Prices at this Michelin-starred restaurant are a serious bargain and the lunchtime *menu* (available midweek only) is an absolute steal. Chefs Julia Sedefdjian and David Bottreau create true works of art: on-the-shell oysters in vivid green cucumber jelly with green apple and lemon caviar; almond-crusted veal with mashed artichokes and king trumpet mushrooms; and banana soufflé with rum ice cream.

LA GRANDE CRÈMERIE FRENCH €€
Map p402 (☏01 43 26 09 09; www.lagrandec-remerie.fr; 8 rue Grégoire de Tours, 6e; mains €14-30; ⊙6.30-11pm; MOdéon) The success of Serge Mathieu's tiny *cave gourmande* (gourmet wine cellar) **La Crèmerie** (Map p402; 9 rue des Quatre-Vents, 6e; ⊙shop 3.30-8.30pm Mon, 11am-10pm Tue-Sat; MOdéon), prompted the opening of this larger rustic space serving the earthy flavours of the French countryside on cold platters (duck,

rabbit, pork, seafood or cheese) designed for sharing, along with splendid wines.

CAFÉ TRAMA
MODERN FRENCH €€

Map p406 (📞01 45 48 33 71; 83 rue du Cherche Midi, 6e; mains €16-24; ⏰11am-10.30pm, kitchen 11.30am-2.15pm & 7-10pm Tue-Sat; Ⓜ Vaneau) Cafe classics come with a contemporary twist at this black-awning-framed local with mellow lighting, chequered tiles, vintage furniture and pavement tables. Try the pan-fried squid with rocket and orange segments, croque monsieur with truffle salt on premium Poujauran bread, or ginger and basil beef tartare with meat from famed Parisian butcher Hugo Desnoyer, along with all-natural wines.

TRUFFES FOLIES
MODERN EUROPEAN €€

Map p406 (📞01 44 18 05 41; www.truffesfolies. fr; 37 rue Malar, 7e; mains €19-32; ⏰restaurant noon-3pm & 6.30-9.30pm Mon-Fri, noon-3pm Sat, deli 11am-10pm Mon-Fri; Ⓜ La Tour-Maubourg) Truffle fans will be in raptures at this restaurant/deli. The prized fungi appears in everything imaginable, from sandwiches to dishes like œufs en cocotte (eggs in ramekins), scallop carpaccio, paramesan and sage ravioli, and wild mushroom risotto, as well as swoon-worthy desserts (crème brûlée; brioche pudding with salted caramel and truffle ice cream). Truffles also appear in every product its deli stocks.

Pick up olive oil, salt, butter, honey, vinegar, polenta, mayo, cheeses, Périgord black truffles or Alba white truffles to create your own truffled delicacies.

★ RESTAURANT DAVID TOUTAIN
GASTRONOMY €€€

Map p406 (📞01 45 51 11 10; www.davidtoutain. com; 29 rue Surcouf, 7e; 9-/15-course tasting menus €80/110; ⏰noon-2pm & 8-10pm Mon-Fri; Ⓜ Invalides) Prepare to be wowed: David Toutain pushes the envelope at his eponymous Michelin-starred restaurant with some of the most creative high-end cooking in Paris. Mystery degustation courses include unlikely combinations such as smoked eel in green-apple-and-black-sesame mousse, cauliflower, white chocolate and coconut truffles, or candied celery and truffled rice pudding with artichoke praline (stunning wine pairings available).

LES CLIMATS
TRADITIONAL FRENCH €€€

Map p406 (📞01 58 62 10 08; www.lesclimats. fr; 41 rue de Lille, 7e; 2-/3-course lunch menus €36/42, 5-course dinner menu €98, mains €44-58, bar snacks €7-22; ⏰restaurant noon-2.30pm & 7-10pm Tue-Sat, bar noon-2.30pm & 7-10.30pm Tue-Sat; Ⓜ Solférino) Like the neighbouring Musée d'Orsay, this is a magnificent art nouveau treasure – a 1905-built former home for female telephone, telegram and postal workers – featuring soaring vaulted ceilings and original stained glass, along with a lunchtime summer garden and glassed-in winter garden. Exquisite Michelin-starred dishes complement its 150-page list of wines, sparkling wines and whiskies purely from the Burgundy region.

DRINKING & NIGHTLIFE

St-Germain's Carrefour de l'Odéon has a cluster of lively bars and cafes. Rues de Buci, St-André des Arts and de l'Odéon enjoy a fair slice of night action with arty cafes and busy pubs, while place St-Germain des Prés buzzes with the pavement terraces of fabled literary cafes. Rue Princesse attracts a student crowd with its bevy of pubs, microbreweries and cocktail bars. Les Invalides is a day- rather than night-time venue, with government ministries and embassies outweighing drinking venues. Particularly in summer, however, look out for bars along Les Berges de Seine (p233).

🍷 St-Germain

★ LES DEUX MAGOTS
CAFE

Map p402 (www.lesdeuxmagots.fr; 170 bd St-Germain, 6e; ⏰7.30am-1am; Ⓜ St-Germain des Prés) If ever there was a cafe that summed up St-Germain des Prés' early-20th-century literary scene, it's this former hang-out of anyone who was anyone. You will spend beaucoup to sip a coffee in a wicker chair on the terrace shaded by dark-green awnings and geraniums spilling from window boxes, but it's an undeniable piece of Parisian history.

★ TIGER BAR
COCKTAIL BAR

Map p402 (www.tiger-paris.com; 13 rue Princesse, 6e; ⏰6pm-2am Tue-Sat; Ⓜ Mabillon) Suspended bare-bulb lights and fretted timber make this split-level space a stylish spot for specialist gins (45 different varieties). Its 24 cocktails include a Breakfast Martini (gin, triple sec, orange marmalade and lemon juice) and Oh My Dog (white-pepper-infused gin, lime juice, raspberry and rose cordial and ginger ale). You can also sip Japanese sake, wine and craft beer.

AU SAUVIGNON
WINE BAR

Map p402 (www.ausauvignon.com; 80 rue des Sts-Pères, 7e; ☺8am-11pm Mon-Sat, 9am-10pm Sun; MSèvres-Babylone) Grab a table in the evening light at this wonderfully authentic *bar à vins* or head to the quintessential bistro interior, with an original zinc bar, tightly packed tables and hand-painted ceiling celebrating French viticultural tradition. A plate of *casse-croûtes au pain Poilâne* – toast with ham, pâté, terrine, smoked salmon and foie gras – is the perfect accompaniment.

CAFÉ DE FLORE
CAFE

Map p402 (172 bd St-Germain, 6e; ☺7am-2am; MSt-Germain des Prés) The red upholstered benches, mirrors and marble walls at this art deco landmark haven't changed much since the days when Jean-Paul Sartre and Simone de Beauvoir essentially set up office here, writing in its warmth during the Nazi occupation. It also hosts a monthly English-language *philocafé* (philosophy discussion) session.

FROG & PRINCESS
MICROBREWERY, PUB

Map p402 (www.frogpubs.com; 9 rue Princesse, 6e; ☺5.30pm-2am Mon-Fri, 11.30am-2am Sat & Sun; MMabillon) Part of the Frog family that includes several Parisian microbreweries, this good-time pub on one of the Left Bank's liveliest drinking streets is popular for its own brewed beers (several of which recently took out medals at the World Beer Awards), burgers, American barbecue and soul food, and sports screenings.

CASTOR CLUB
COCKTAIL BAR

Map p402 (14 rue Hautefeuille, 6e; ☺7pm-4am Tue-Sat; MOdéon) Discreetly signed, this underground cocktail bar has an intimate upstairs bar and 18th-century cellar with hole-in-the-wall booths where you can sip superb-value cocktails (custom made, if you like) and groove to smooth '50s, '60s and '70s tracks. Very cool.

LE 10
PUB

Map p402 (www.lebar10.com; 10 rue de l'Odéon, 6e; ☺2pm-2am; ☎; MOdéon) Plastered with

STARS OF THE FUTURE

Founded in 1920 by Paris' chamber of commerce and industry, **Restaurants d'Application de Ferrandi** (Map p406; www.ferrandi-paris.fr; 28 rue de l'Abbé Grégoire, 6e; menus Le Premier lunch/dinner €25/40, Le 28 lunch €30-32, dinner €30-45; ☺by online reservation; closed school holidays; MSt-Placide) is arguably France's most prestigious culinary school, turning out a who's who of industry professionals. You can taste these future Michelin-starred chefs' creations at bargain prices at the school's two training restaurants, Le Premier (focusing on classical French cookery) and Le 28 (high-level gastronomy), overseen by Ferrandi's esteemed professors.

Hours often vary; bookings are only available via the online calendar.

posters, cellar pub 'Le Dix' is a student favourite, not least for its cheap sangria. An eclectic selection emerges from the jukebox – everything from jazz and the Doors to traditional French *chansons* (à la Édith Piaf). It's the ideal spot for plotting the next revolution or conquering a lonely heart.

🍷 Les Invalides

★COUTUME
COFFEE

Map p406 (www.coutumecafe.com; 47 rue de Babylone, 7e; ☺8am-7pm Mon-Fri, 10am-7pm Sat & Sun; ☎; MSt-François Xavier) ⟋ The dramatic improvement in Parisian coffee in recent years is thanks in no small part to Coutume, artisan roaster of premium beans for scores of establishments around town. Its flagship café – a bright, light-filled, postindustrial space – is ground zero for innovative preparation methods including cold extraction and siphon brews. Fabulous organic fare and pastries too.

LA QUINCAVE
WINE BAR

Map p402 (17 rue Bréa, 6e; ☺11am-1pm & 5-11.30pm Tue-Thu, 11am-11.30pm Fri & Sat; MVavin) Bar stools at this lively wine bar/shop are fashioned from wine barrels, but on summer evenings most of the action spills onto the tiny street out front. Over

200 varieties of natural wines are available by the bottle, ranging from €9 to €35 (corkage costs €7), along with charcuterie and cheese platters to soak them up.

CLUB   COCKTAIL BAR

Map p406 (www.the-club.fr; 24 rue Surcouf, 7e; ⊙noon-1.30am Mon-Fri, 6.30pm-1.30am Sat; ⓂLa Tour-Maubourg) At street level the Club has New York–warehouse brickwork and big timber cabinets, but the lounge-like basement, strewn with red and black sofas, is even cooler. Cocktails include the house-speciality Club (lime, fresh ginger, and Jack Daniels honey liqueur) and seasonally changing creations, or ask for the bar staff to surprise you with their own concoctions.

☆ ENTERTAINMENT

St-Germain and especially Les Invalides aren't major nightlife destinations – eating, drinking and, above all, shopping are the main entertainments here. For live music, check for events in bars along Les Berges de Seine (p233), or head to the Latin Quarter or the floating nightclubs in the 13e. Cinema-goers are well catered for, with multiplexes concentrated around the Odéon metro station on bd St-Germain.

CHEZ PAPA   JAZZ

Map p402 (✆01 42 86 99 63; www.papajazzclub-paris.fr; 3 rue St-Benoît, 6e; concerts €12; ⊙concerts 9pm-1am Mon-Thu, 9.30pm-1.30pm Fri & Sat; ⓂSt-Germain des Prés) The doors of this snug St-Germain jazz club regularly stay open until dawn. Piano duets, blues, sax solos and singers regularly feature on the bill. Its restaurant, serving traditional French dishes (snails, foie gras, tartare, veal stew), opens from noon to 3.30pm and 7.30pm to 10.30pm Monday to Saturday.

LE LUCERNAIRE   CULTURAL CENTRE

Map p402 (✆reservations 01 45 44 57 34; www.lucernaire.fr; 53 rue Notre Dame des Champs, 6e; ⊙bar 11am-9pm Mon, 11am-12.30am Tue-Fri, 4pm-12.30am Sat, 4-10pm Sun; ⓂNotre Dame des Champs) Sunday-evening concerts are a fixture on the impressive repertoire of the dynamic Centre National d'Art et d'Essai (National Arts Centre). Whether it's classical guitar, baroque, French *chansons* or east Asian music, these weekly concerts starting from 4pm (hours vary) are a real treat. Art and photography exhibitions, cinema, theatre, lectures, debates and guided walks round off the packed cultural agenda.

COMÉDIE FRANÇAISE THÉÂTRE DU VIEUX COLOMBIER   THEATRE

Map p402 (✆01 44 58 15 15, tickets 01 44 39 87 00; www.comedie-francaise.fr; 21 rue du Vieux Colombier, 6e; ⊙Sep-Jul; ⓂSt-Sulpice) One of three Comédie Française venues (p130), along with the Right Bank's main Salle Richelieu and Studio Théâtre. Founded in 1680, it presents works by classic French playwrights such as Molière.

🛍 SHOPPING

The northern wedge of the 6e between Église St-Germain des Prés and the Seine is a dream to mooch with its bijou art galleries, antique shops, stylish vintage clothes shops, and designer boutiques (Vanessa Bruno, Isabel Marant et al). St-Germain's style continues along the western half of bd St-Germain and rue du Bac with a striking collection of contemporary furniture, kitchen and design shops. Gourmet food and wine shops galore make it a foodie's paradise.

🛍 St-Germain

★ GAB & JO   CONCEPT STORE

Map p402 (www.gabjo.fr; 28 rue Jacob, 6e; ⊙11am-7pm Mon-Sat; ⓂSt-Germain des Prés) ✿ Forget mass-produced, imported souvenirs: for quality local gifts, browse the shelves of the country's first-ever concept store stocking only made-in-France items. Designers include La Note Parisienne (scented candles for each Parisian *arrondissement*, such as the 6e, with notes of lipstick, cognac, orange blossom, tuberose, jasmine, rose and fig), Marius Fabre (Marseille soaps), Germaine-des-Prés (lingerie), MILF (sunglasses) and Monsieur Marcel (T-shirts).

CIRE TRUDON   CANDLES

Map p402 (https://trudon.com; 78 rue de Seine, 6e; ⊙10am-7pm Mon-Sat; ⓂOdéon) Claude Trudon began selling candles here in 1643, and the company – which officially supplied Versailles and Napoléon with light – is now the world's oldest candle-maker (look for the plaque to the left of the shop's awning).

A rainbow of candles and candlesticks fill the shelves inside.

DEYROLLE   ANTIQUES, HOMEWARES

Map p402 (www.deyrolle.com; 46 rue du Bac, 7e; ⊙10am-1pm & 2-7pm Mon, 10am-7pm Tue-Sat; ⓜRue du Bac) Overrun with creatures including lions, tigers, zebras and storks, taxidermist Deyrolle opened in 1831. In addition to stuffed animals (for rent and sale), it stocks minerals, shells, corals and crustaceans, stand-mounted ostrich eggs and pedagogical storyboards. There are also rare and unusual seeds (including many old types of tomato), gardening tools and accessories.

AU PLAT D'ÉTAIN   GAMES

Map p402 (www.auplatdetain.sitew.com; 16 rue Guisarde, 6e; ⊙10.30am-6.30pm Tue-Sat; ⓜMabillon) Tiny tin *(étain)* and lead soldiers, snipers, cavaliers, military drummers and musicians (great for chessboard pieces) cram this fascinating boutique. In business since 1775, the shop itself is practically a collectable.

JB GUANTI   FASHION & ACCESSORIES

Map p402 (www.jbguanti.com; 59 rue de Rennes, 6e; ⊙10am-7pm Mon-Sat; ⓜSt-Sulpice) For the ultimate finishing touch, the men's and women's gloves at this boutique, which specialises solely in gloves, are the epitome of both style and comfort, whether unlined, silk lined, cashmere lined, lambskin lined or trimmed with rabbit fur.

HERMÈS   CONCEPT STORE

Map p402 (www.hermes.com; 17 rue de Sèvres, 6e; ⊙10.30am-7pm Mon-Sat; ⓜSèvres-Babylone) A stunning art deco swimming pool now houses luxury label Hermès' inaugural concept store. Retaining its original mosaic tiles and iron balustrades, and adding enormous timber pod-like 'huts', the vast, tiered space showcases new directions in home furnishings, including fabrics and wallpaper, along with classic lines such as its signature scarves. There's also an appropriately chic cafe, Le Plongeoir (the Diving Board).

LA DERNIÈRE GOUTTE   WINE

Map p402 (✆01 43 29 11 62; www.ladernieregoutte.net; 6 rue du Bourbon le Château, 6e; ⊙3-8pm Mon, 10.30am-1.30pm & 3-8pm Tue-Fri, 11am-7pm Sat; ⓜMabillon) 'The Last Drop' is the brainchild of Cuban-American sommelier Juan Sánchez, whose tiny wine shop is packed with exciting, mostly organic French *vins de propriétaires* (estate-bottled wines) made by small independent producers. Wine classes lasting two hours (seven tastings) take place in English from Wednesday to Saturday (per person €55); check the website for the program.

PIERRE HERMÉ   FOOD

Map p402 (www.pierreherme.com; 72 rue Bonaparte, 6e; ⊙10am-8pm; ⓜOdéon) It's the size of a chocolate box, but once you're in Pierre Hermé your taste buds will go wild. This boutique, one of Paris' top chocolatiers, is a veritable feast of perfectly presented petits fours, cakes, chocolates, nougats, macarons and jams. There are several other branches around Paris.

FINGER IN THE NOSE   CHILDREN, FASHION

Map p402 (www.fingerinthenose.com; 11 rue de l'Échaudé, 6e; ⊙2.30-7pm Mon, 11am-7.30pm Tue-Sat; ⓜMabillon) This finger-on-the-pulse Parisian children's-wear label thumbs its nose at convention and offers edgy streetwear for kids, such as graphic T-shirts, fleeces

---

ART & ANTIQUE STREETS

St-Germain's narrow streets are filled with art and antique shops. Meander along rue Mazarine, rue Jacques Callot, rue des Beaux Arts and rue de Seine for art galleries.

Edgier galleries include **Galerie Loft** (Map p402; www.galerieloft.com; 3bis rue des Beaux Arts, 6e; ⊙10am-1pm & 2.30-6pm Tue-Fri, 10.30am-1pm & 2.30-6pm Sat; ⓜSt-Germain des Prés), with all forms of art (digital video and performance photography included) by contemporary Chinese artists on show at this courtyard gallery.

Art and antique dealers congregate within the Carré Rive Gauche. Bounded by quai Voltaire and rues de l'Université, des St-Pères and du Bac, this 'Left Bank square' is home to more than 120 specialised merchants. Antiques fairs are usually held in spring, while exhibitions take place during the year.

A collector's delight the size of a pocket handkerchief, **Hapart** (Map p402; www.antiquetoysparis.com; 72 rue Mazarine, 6e; ⊙2-7pm Tue-Sun; ⓜOdéon) recalls lost childhood with its romantic selection of old and antique toys.

EIFFEL-DESIGNED LE BON MARCHÉ

Built by Gustave Eiffel as Paris' first department store in 1852, **Le Bon Marché** (Map p406; www.bonmarche.com; 24 rue de Sèvres, 7e; ⊙10am-8pm Mon-Wed & Sat, to 9pm Thu & Fri; ⓜSèvres-Babylone) is the epitome of style, with a superb concentration of men's and women's fashions, beautiful homewares, stationery, books and toys as well as chic dining options.

The icing on the cake is its glorious food hall, **La Grande Épicerie de Paris** (Map p406; www.lagrandeepicerie.com; 36 rue de Sèvres, 7e; ⊙8.30am-9pm Mon-Sat; ⓜSèvres-Babylone) It sells 30,000 rare and luxury gourmet products, including 60 different types of bread and delicacies such as caviar ravioli. Its fantastical displays of chocolates, pastries, biscuits, cheeses, fresh fruit and vegetables and deli goods are a Parisian sight in themselves. Wine tastings take place in the basement.

and jackets along with sophisticated twists like its line of LBDs ('little black dresses') for teenage girls. There's another location in Le Marais near its HQ.

CATHERINE B
VINTAGE

Map p402 (http://les3marchesdecatherineb. com; 1-3 rue Guisarde, 6e; ⊙11am-7pm Mon-Sat; ⓜMabillon) Luxury vintage goods from just two labels – Chanel and Hermès – are stocked by Catherine B, whose constantly changing, worldwide-sourced collection at any one time contains around 1500 pieces (scarves, jewellery, footwear, clothing, handbags, belts and more). Catherine is a font of knowledge on both fashion houses, and, while items here aren't cheap, all are 100% authentic (no knock-offs).

FERMOB
HOMEWARES

Map p402 (www.paris.fermob.com; 17 bd Raspail, 7e; ⊙10am-7pm Mon-Sat Apr-Oct, 10am-1pm & 2-7pm Tue-Sat Nov-Mar; ⓜRue du Bac) Famed for manufacturing iconic French garden furniture, including the Jardin du Luxembourg's signature chairs, Fermob has now opened this large, white 120-sq-metre Left Bank boutique in addition to its Bastille premises (p192). Choose from a spectacular array of colours (23 at last count) for your own garden or terrace. Seasonal opening hours can vary.

LA MAISON DE POUPÉE
ANTIQUES

Map p402 (☑06 09 65 58 68; 40 rue de Vaugirard, 6e; ⊙2.30-7pm Mon-Sat, by appointment Sun; ⓜSt-Sulpice or RER Luxembourg) Opposite the residence of the French Senate's president, this delightful little shop sells its namesake dolls' houses as well as *poupées anciennes* (antique dolls).

CIE BRACELET MONTRE
FASHION & ACCESSORIES

Map p402 (www.cie-bracelet-montre.com; 25 rue du Dragon, 6e; ⊙11am-7pm Mon-Fri; ⓜSt-Germain des Prés) If you're already in awe of Paris' incredible array of specialist shops stocking just one item, you'll be amazed at this niche boutique, which simply sells watch bands. They come in a rainbow of colours and range of materials (alligator, crocodile, lizard, ostrich, shark), for both men and women. It was established by vintage Rolex dealer Hady Ouaiss.

There are 8000 watch bands in stock, which can be fitted on the spot, or you can have one custom made.

MARIE MERCIÉ
FASHION & ACCESSORIES

Map p402 (www.mariemercie.com; 23 rue St-Sulpice, 6e; ⊙11am-7pm Mon-Sat; ⓜMabillon) Stand out in the crowd in a unique hat handcrafted by Fontainebleau-born milliner Marie Mercié, who has collaborated with designers including Hermès, Kenzo, John Galliano and Agnès B, and combines traditional methods with modern materials and humorous twists. She's also authored two books on her work and the history of millinery.

MES DEMOISELLES
FASHION & ACCESSORIES

Map p402 (www.mesdemoiselles.fr; 21 rue St-Sulpice, 6e; ⊙10am-7pm Mon-Sat; ⓜMabillon) Antique cuts of silks, wools and cottons are transformed into floaty bohemian-influenced women's fashion (dresses, knitwear, coats and other separates) by designer Anita Radovanovic, who founded the Mes Demoiselles label here in Paris in 2006. There are two other boutiques in the city.

SMALLABLE CONCEPT STORE CHILDREN
Map p406 (www.smallable.com; 81 rue du Cherche Midi, 6e; ⊙2-7.30pm Mon, 10.30am-7.30pm Tue-Sat; Ⓜ Vaneau) Set back behind a covered polished-concrete courtyard, this deceptively large Parisian-chic space is a one-stop-shop for babies, children and teens, with over 20,000 items (strollers, shoes, furniture, clothes and toys) from 450 premium brands (Little Eleven, Chloé Kids, Petit Bateau, Pom d'Api, Zadig and many more).

ALEXANDRA SOJFER FASHION & ACCESSORIES
Map p402 (www.alexandrasojfer.com; 218 bd St-Germain, 7e; ⊙10am-7pm Mon-Sat; Ⓜ Rue du Bac) Become Parisian chic with a frivolous, frilly, fantastical or frightfully fashionable *parapluie* (umbrella), parasol or walking cane handcrafted by Alexandra Sojfer from this St-Germain boutique, in the trade since 1834.

GÉRARD DURAND FASHION & ACCESSORIES
Map p406 (www.accessoires-mode.com; 75-77 rue du Bac, 7e; ⊙9am-7pm Mon-Sat; Ⓜ Rue du Bac) Brightly coloured, boldly printed *collants* and *bas* (tights and stockings) are the speciality of this boutique, which also stocks equally vibrant socks, scarves and gloves.

SABBIA ROSA FASHION & ACCESSORIES
Map p402 (☑01 45 48 88 37; 73 rue des Sts-Pères, 6e; ⊙10am-7pm Mon-Sat; Ⓜ St-Germain des Prés) Only French-sourced fabrics (silk from Lyon, lace from Calais) are used by lingerie designer Sabbia Rosa for her ultra-luxe range. Every piece is unique; measurements can be taken and gorgeous items custom made in just 48 hours. The list of celebrity clients reads like a who's who: Madonna, Naomi Campbell, Claudia Schiffer and George Clooney have all shopped here.

🏛 Les Invalides

★**MAGASIN SENNELIER** ARTS & CRAFTS
Map p402 (www.magasinsennelier.com; 3 quai Voltaire, 7e; ⊙2-6.30pm Mon, 10am-12.45pm & 2-6.30pm Tue-Sat; Ⓜ St-Germain des Prés) Cézanne and Picasso were among the artists who helped develop products for this venerable 1887-founded art supplier on the banks of the Seine, and it remains an exceptional place to pick up canvases, brushes, watercolours, oils, pastels, charcoals and more. The shop's forest-green facade with gold lettering, exquisite original timber cabinetry and glass display cases also fuel artistic inspiration.

CANTIN CHEESE
Map p406 (www.cantin.fr; 12 rue du Champs de Mars, 7e; ⊙2-7.30pm Mon, 8.30am-7.30pm Tue-Sat, 8.30am-1pm Sun; Ⓜ École Militaire) 🍴 Opened in 1950 and still run by the same family today, this exceptional *fromagerie* stocks cheeses only made in limited quantities on small rural farms. They're then painstakingly ripened in Cantin's own cellars (from two weeks up to two years) before being displayed for sale.

CHAPON CHOCOLATE
Map p406 (www.chocolat-chapon.com; 69 rue du Bac, 7e; ⊙9am-8pm Mon-Sat, to 7pm Sun; Ⓜ Rue du Bac) Chocolate-making moulds cover the walls at this prize-winning chocolatier, which sells seasonal speciality creations (Easter eggs et al), pralines, chocolate Eiffel Towers and roasted cocoa beans. But it's most renowned for its incredible chocolate mousse (Ecuadorian, Venezuelan, Madagascan, Peruvian, or a blend of Ecuadorian and Ghanaian chocolate). Look out for its chocolate-mousse food truck at parks and events around Paris.

BONPOINT FIN DE SÉRIES CHILDREN'S CLOTHING
Map p402 (www.bonpoint.com; 42 rue de l'Université, 7e; ⊙10am-7pm Mon-Sat; Ⓜ Rue du Bac) Bonpoint clothes for babies and children through to teens aged 16 come with price tags that match their quality and cachet, which makes this *fin de séries* (outlet) shop a fantastic find for much more affordable discounted end-of-season lines.

CHERCHEMINIPPES VINTAGE
Map p406 (www.chercheminippes.com; 102, 106, 109-111, 114 & 124 rue du Cherche Midi, 6e; ⊙11am-7pm Mon-Sat; Ⓜ Vaneau) Scattered along one street, these seven beautifully presented boutiques sell secondhand pieces by current designers. Each specialises in a different genre (*haute couture*, kids, menswear etc); items are perfectly ordered by size and designer. There are changing rooms.

Montparnasse & Southern Paris

MONTPARNASSE & 15E | PLACE D'ITALIE & CHINATOWN | MONTPARNASSE & SOUTHERN PARIS

Neighbourhood Top Five

❶ Tour Montparnasse (p249) Ignoring the 1970s smoked-glass exterior of this un-Parisian skyscraper and zipping to the top for a glass of Champagne on the terrace while taking in one of the finest panoramas over the city.

❷ Les Catacombes (p248) Prowling the spine-prickling, skull-and-bone-packed subterranean tunnels of Paris' creepy ossuary.

❸ Cimetière du Montparnasse (p250) Visiting the resting places of local luminaries, including Jean-Paul Sartre, Simone de Beauvoir and Serge Gainsbourg.

❹ Île aux Cygnes (p250) Traversing the tiny, tree-lined inner-city island from the Statue of Liberty replica towards the Eiffel Tower.

❺ Bibliothèque Nationale de France (p250) Catching superb literary-themed exhibitions at France's book-shaped national library.

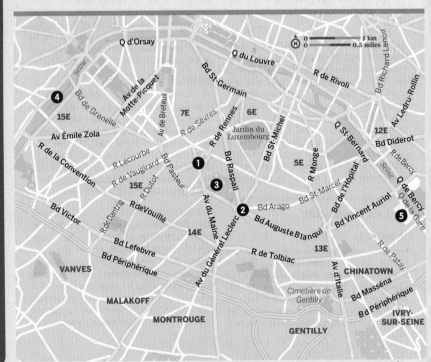

For more detail of this area see Map p410, 412 and p414 ➡

Explore: Montparnasse & Southern Paris

Tour Montparnasse is an unavoidable sight, but its observation deck offers an unrivalled spot for getting to grips with the lay of the land. At its feet are the cafes, brasseries and backstreets, now swathed by urban grit, where some of the early-20th-century's most seminal artists and writers hung out. The area's tree-filled cemetery is a peaceful spot to escape to – and to visit the graves of many of those same visionaries.

West in the tranquil 15e, take in more great views by strolling the Île aux Cygnes or boarding a balloon 'flight' in the Parc André-Citroën, one of the capital's most innovative open spaces. Other wonderful local parks in this greenified area include Parc Georges Brassens, with rose gardens and even a vineyard and apiary, as well as a stretch of the former Petite Ceinture steam railway line.

To Montparnasse's east, the ever-regenerating 13e is home to the country's national library, Paris' largest Chinatown and some striking street art.

The entire area is strewn with exciting neobistros. No matter where you end up for dinner, head back to the river to dance until dawn on the floating bars and nightclubs moored on the Seine's quays.

Local Life

→**Street life** Join locals shopping for flowers, cheese, charcuterie and more along traditional commercial street rue Daguerre (p255).

→**Track life** Explore Paris' former steam railway line on the parkland stretch Petite Ceinture du 15e (p252).

→**Breton life** Take a crêperie crawl through Montparnasse's 'Little Brittany' (p256).

→**Art life** Delve into the 13e's street art scene starting at Galerie Itinerrance (p250).

Getting There & Away

→**Metro** Montparnasse Bienvenüe is the metro hub for Montparnasse and the 15e. Bibliothèque and Place d'Italie are convenient 13e stops.

→**Bus** Buses fill the gap in areas lacking comprehensive metro coverage. From Gare Montparnasse, bus 91 goes to Bastille. Bus 62 travels from Bibliothèque to Javel via the southern *quartiers*. Bus 21 runs from Glacière to Chatelet. Bus 42 links Balard with Gare du Nord via the western 15e and Eiffel Tower.

→**Bicycle** Handy Vélib' stations include 5-7 rue d'Odessa, 14e; 13 bd Edgar Quinet, 14e; 2 av René Coty, 14e; and two facing place d'Italie, 13e.

→**Boat** The hop-on, hop-off Batobus has docks at Port de Javel Haut, 15e and quai d'Austerlitz, 13e.

Lonely Planet's Top Tip

The metro is tailor-made for cross-town trips, but to whizz around Paris' perimeter, hop on the T3 tram. From the Pont du Garigliano, 15e, it currently skims the city's edge as far as Porte de la Chapelle, 18e. An extension to Porte d'Asnières, 17e, is due for completion at the end of 2017, encircling some three-quarters of the city. Passengers use standard t+ tickets. For updates on Paris' trams, visit www.tramway.paris.fr.

Best Places to Eat

→ Le Clos Y (p254)
→ Le Beurre Noisette (p254)
→ Le Casse Noix (p254)
→ Le Grand Pan (p254)
→ Jeu de Quilles (p254)

For reviews, see p253.➡

Best Places to Drink

→ Le Petit Gorille (p258)
→ Félicie (p259)
→ Le Rosebud (p259)
→ Le Select (p259)
→ Le Merle Moqueur (p259)

For reviews, see p258.➡

Best Floating Clubs

→ Le Batofar (p259)
→ La Dame de Canton (p259)
→ La Plage Parisienne (p259)

For reviews, see p259.➡

MONTPARNASSE & SOUTHERN PARIS

 TOP SIGHT
LES CATACOMBES

Paris' most macabre sight is its series of underground tunnels lined with skulls and bones. In 1785 it was decided to rectify the hygiene problems of Paris' overflowing cemeteries by exhuming the bones and storing them in disused quarry tunnels; the Catacombes were created in 1810. Bear in mind that it's not suitable for young children (nor anyone faint-hearted!).

Tunnels

The route through Les Catacombes begins at a small, dark-green belle époque building in the centre of a grassy area of av Colonel Henri Roi-Tanguy, adjacent to place Denfert Rochereau. After descending 20m (via 130 narrow, dizzying spiral steps) below street level, you follow the dark, subterranean passages to reach the ossuary itself, with a mind-boggling amount of bones and skulls of millions of Parisians neatly packed along the walls. You'll traverse 2km of tunnels in all; the temperature is a cool 14°C below ground.

The exit is back up 83 steps onto rue Rémy Dumoncel, 14e (metro Mouton-Duvernet), 700m southwest of av Colonel Henri Roi-Tanguy. Bag searches are carried out to prevent visitors 'souveniring' bones. A **gift shop** (Map p412; www.compoirdescatacombes.com; 31 rue Rémy Dumoncel, 14e; ☺10.30am-8.30pm Tue-Sun; ⓂAlésia) selling quirky skull-and-bone-themed items (Jenga, candles, shot glasses) is across the street from the exit.

DID YOU KNOW?

➡ During WWII these tunnels were used as a headquarters by the Resistance.

➡ Thrill-seeking cataphiles are often caught (and fined) roaming the tunnels at night.

PRACTICALITIES

➡ Map p412, F4

➡ www.catacombes. paris.fr

➡ 1 av Colonel Henri Roi-Tanguy, 14e

➡ adult/child €12/free

➡ ☺10am-8pm Tue-Sun

➡ Ⓜ Denfert Rochereau

⊙ SIGHTS

This vast swathe of southern Paris is a perfect place to explore if you're looking for a local experience away from the tourist crowds, but there are also some big-hitting sights here too, from the creepy skull-and-bone-packed underground tunnels of Les Catacombes to France's national library, Bibliothèque Nationale de France.

⊙ Montparnasse & 15e

LES CATACOMBES   CEMETERY
See p248.

TOUR MONTPARNASSE   VIEWPOINT
Map p412 (www.tourmontparnasse56.com; 33 av du Maine, 15e; adult/child €15/9.50; ⊙9.30am-11.30pm daily Apr-Sep, to 10.30pm Sun-Thu, to 11pm Fri & Sat Oct-Mar; Ⓜ Montparnasse Bienvenüe) Spectacular views unfold from this 209m-high smoked-glass and steel office block, built in 1973. (Bonus: it's about the only spot in the city you can't see this startlingly ugly skyscraper, which dwarfs lowrise Paris.) A speedy lift/elevator whisks visitors up in 38 seconds to the indoor observatory on the 56th floor, with multimedia displays. Finish with a hike up the stairs to the 59th-floor open-air terrace (with a sheltered walkway) and bubbly at the terrace's Champagne bar.

The tower also houses the city's highest restaurant, Le Ciel de Paris (p257).

FONDATION HENRI CARTIER-BRESSON   MUSEUM
Map p412 (www.henricartierbresson.org; 2 impasse Lebouis, 14e; adult/child €7/4; ⊙1-6.30pm Tue, Thu, Fri & Sun, 1-8.30pm Wed, 11am-6.45pm Sat; Ⓜ Gaîté) Founded by renowned French humanist photographer Henri Cartier-Bresson (1908–2004) and his portrait-photographer wife Martine Franck (1938–2012), this intimate gallery has a small permanent collection of their works and also mounts rotating exhibitions by French and international photographers, including the winner of the Henri Cartier-Bresson Award every two years. Cartier-Bresson pioneered artistic photojournalism, set up a photography department for the Resistance and co-founded the collective agency Magnum. Take the laneway leading off rue Lebouis to find it tucked in a courtyard.

MUSÉE BOURDELLE   MUSEUM
Map p412 (www.bourdelle.paris.fr; 18 rue Antoine Bourdelle, 15e; ⊙10am-6pm Tue-Sun; Ⓜ Falguière) FREE Monumental bronzes fill the house and workshop where sculptor Antoine Bourdelle (1861–1929), a pupil of Rodin, lived and worked. The three sculpture gardens are particularly lovely, with a flavour of belle époque and post-WWI Montparnasse. The museum usually has a temporary exhibition (attracting an admission fee) going on alongside its free permanent collection.

FONDATION CARTIER POUR L'ART CONTEMPORAIN   ART MUSEUM
Map p412 (http://fondation.cartier.com; 261 bd Raspail, 14e; adult/child €10.50/7; ⊙11am-10pm Tue, to 8pm Wed-Sun; Ⓜ Raspail) Designed by Jean Nouvel, this stunning glass-and-steel building is a work of art in itself. It hosts temporary exhibits on contemporary art (from the 1980s to today) in a diverse variety of media – from painting and photography to video and fashion, as well as performance art. Artist Lothar Baumgarten created the wonderfully rambling garden.

PARC ANDRÉ-CITROËN   PARK
Map p414 (2 rue Cauchy, 15e; ⊙8am-9.30pm May-Aug, shorter hours rest of year; Ⓜ Balard) In 1915 automotive entrepreneur André Citroën built a vast car manufacturing plant here in the 15e. After it closed in the 1970s, the vacated site was eventually turned into this forward-looking 14-hectare urban park. Its central lawn is flanked by greenhouses, dancing fountains, an elevated reflecting pool, and smaller gardens themed around movement and the (six) senses. The helium-filled sightseeing balloon Le Ballon Air de Paris (p249) is located here. Check seasonal hours signposted at the entrances.

LE BALLON AIR DE PARIS   SCENIC BALLOON
Map p414 (☑01 44 26 20 00; www.ballondeparis.com; Parc André Citroën, 2 rue de la Montagne de la Fage, 15e; adult/child €12/6; ⊙9am-9pm May-Aug, shorter hours Sep-Apr; Ⓜ Balard, Lourmel) ✈ Drift up and up but not away – this helium-filled balloon in Parc André Citroën remains tethered to the ground as it lifts you 150m into the air for spectacular panoramas over Paris. The balloon plays an active environmental role, changing colour depending on the air quality and pollution levels. From September to May, the last 'flight' is 30 minutes before the park closes.

Confirm ahead any time of year as the balloon doesn't ascend in windy conditions.

ÎLE AUX CYGNES ISLAND

Map p414 (Isle of Swans; btwn Pont de Grenelle & Pont de Bir Hakeim, 15e; MJavel–André Citroën or Bir Hakeim) Paris' little-known third island, the artificially created Île aux Cygnes, was formed in 1827 to protect the river port and measures just 850m by 11m. On the western side of the Pont de Grenelle is a soaring one-quarter scale **Statue of Liberty replica** (Map p414), inaugurated in 1889. Walk east along the Allée des Cygnes – the tree-lined walkway that runs the length of the island – for knock-out Eiffel Tower views.

⊙ Place d'Italie & Chinatown

BIBLIOTHÈQUE NATIONALE DE FRANCE LIBRARY

Map p410 (📞01 53 79 59 59; www.bnf.fr; 11 quai François Mauriac, 13e; temporary exhibitions adult/child from €3/free; ⊗exhibitions 10am-7pm Tue-Sat, 1-7pm Sun, closed early-late Sep; 📶; MBibliothèque) With four glass towers shaped like half-open books, the National Library of France, opened in 1995, was one of President Mitterand's most ambitious and costliest *grands projets*. Some 12 million tomes are stored on 420km of shelves and the library can accommodate 2000 readers and 2000 researchers. Excellent temporary exhibitions (entrance E) revolve around 'the word' – from storytelling to bookbinding and French heroes. Exhibition admission includes free same-day access to the reference library.

No expense was spared to carry out the library's grand design, which many claimed defied logic. Books and historical documents are shelved in the sunny, 23-storey and 79m-high towers, while patrons sit in artificially lit basement halls built around a 'forest courtyard' of 140 50-year-old pines, trucked in from the countryside. The towers have since been fitted with a complex (and expensive) shutter system, but the basement is prone to flooding from the Seine.

GALERIE ITINERRANCE GALLERY

Map p410 (http://itinerrance.fr; 7bis rue René Goscinny, 13e; ⊗2-7pm Wed-Sat; MBibliothèque) Testament to the 13e's ongoing creative

---

TOP SIGHT
CIMETIÈRE DU MONTPARNASSE

Opened in 1824, Cimetière du Montparnasse, Paris' second-largest cemetery, sprawls over 19 hectares shaded by 1200 trees, including maples, ash, limes and conifers. Although it doesn't have the sheer scale of celebrities laid to rest as its bigger and better-known counterpart, there are still numerous famous graves.

Some of the illustrious 'residents' at Cimetière du Montparnasse include poet Charles Baudelaire, writer Guy de Maupassant, playwright Samuel Beckett, painter Chaim Soutine, photographer Man Ray, industrialist André Citroën, Captain Alfred Dreyfus of the infamous Dreyfus Affair, actress Jean Seberg, and philosophers, writers and life partners Jean-Paul Sartre and Simone de Beauvoir, who are buried together.

Like Père Lachaise, Cimetière du Montparnasse has its time-honoured tomb traditions. One of the most popular is fans leaving metro tickets atop the grave of crooner Serge Gainsbourg (in division 1, just off av Transversale), in reference to his 1958 song 'Le Poinçonneur des Lilas' (The Ticket Puncher of Lilas), depicting work-a-day monotony through the eyes of a metro ticket-puncher. Gainsbourg enacted the soul-destroying job on film when recording the song in the Porte des Lilas station.

DON'T MISS

➤ Charles Baudelaire's grave
➤ Samuel Beckett's grave
➤ Jean-Paul Sartre and Simone de Beauvoir's grave
➤ Serge Gainsbourg's grave

PRACTICALITIES

➤ Map p412, E3
➤ www.paris.fr
➤ 3 bd Edgar Quinet, 14e
➤ ⊗8am-6pm Mon-Fri, 8.30am-6pm Sat, 9am-6pm Sun
➤ MEdgar Quinet

LES MONTPARNOS

Peer long and hard (and long and hard again) around the unfortunate 1960s Gare Montparnasse complex and glimmers of the area's bohemian past occasionally emerge: after WWI, writers, poets and artists of the avant-garde abandoned Montmartre on the Right Bank and crossed the Seine, shifting the centre of Paris' artistic ferment to the area around bd du Montparnasse.

Known as les Montparnos, artists Chagall, Modigliani, Léger, Soutine, Miró, Matisse, Kandinsky and Picasso, composer Stravinsky, and writers Hemingway, Ezra Pound and Cocteau were among those who hung out here, talking endlessly in the cafes and restaurants for which the quarter became famous. It remained a creative hub until the mid-1930s.

Historic brasseries that recall les Montparnos' legacy include La Rotonde Montparnasse (p255); Le Select (p259); La Coupole (p257), with muralled columns painted by artists including Chagall; Hemingway's favourite, the hedged La Closerie des Lilas (p256); and Le Dôme (p257), where Gertrude Stein is said to have encouraged Matisse to open his artist academy (only for Matisse to later add his voice to the 1935 'Testimony Against Gertrude Stein' pamphlet, condemning Stein's interpretation of how cubism emerged in her 1933 *Autobiography of Alice B Toklas*).

renaissance, this very funky gallery in an unassuming backstreet showcases graffiti and street art, and can advise on self-guided and guided street-art tours of the neighbourhood that take in many landmark works by artists represented by the gallery. Exhibitions and events change regularly.

DOCKS EN SEINE
CULTURAL CENTRE

Map p410 (Cité de la Mode et du Design; www.citemodedesign.fr; 34 quai d'Austerlitz, 13e; ⏱10am-midnight; MGare d'Austerlitz) Framed by a lurid-lime wave-like glass facade, a transformed Seine-side warehouse now houses the French fashion institute, the Institut Français de la Mode (hence the docks' alternative name, Cité de la Mode et du Design), mounting fashion and design exhibitions and events throughout the year. Other draws include an entertainment-themed contemporary art museum Art Ludique-Le Musée (p251), along with ultra-hip bars, clubs and restaurants and huge riverside terraces.

The docks occupy a 20,000-sq-metre riverside warehouse built in 1907 (the first industrial complex in Paris to use reinforced concrete), where goods were delivered by barge.

For the best view of the water-facing facade, cross the Seine over Pont Charles de Gaulle.

ART LUDIQUE-LE MUSÉE
ART MUSEUM

Map p410 (www.artludique.com; Docks en Seine, 34 quai d'Austerlitz, 13e; adult/child €16.50/11; ⏱11am-7pm Mon, 11am-10pm Wed-Fri, 10am-10pm Sat & Sun; MGare d'Austerlitz) Comics, manga, video games and animated and live-action cinema are treated as seriously as any other art form at this contemporary art museum in the cutting-edge Docks en Seine complex. Chronologically arranged exhibits showing the evolution of the genre form the core of the permanent collection, but the real crowd-pleasers are the blockbuster temporary exhibitions such as a Pixar retrospective or Marvel superheros. Online bookings cost a euro extra but allow you to skip the queues. Hours can vary.

MANUFACTURE DES GOBELINS
FACTORY, GALLERY

Map p410 (☎01 44 08 53 49; www.mobiliernational.culture.gouv.fr; 42 av des Gobelins, 13e; gallery adult/child €8/6, gallery & tour €14/7; ⏱gallery 11am-6pm Tue-Sun, guided tours 2.30pm & 4pm Sat; MLes Gobelins) The Gobelins Factory has been weaving *haute lisse* (high relief) tapestries on specialised looms since the 18th century along with Beauvais-style *basse lisse* (low relief) tapestries and Savonnerie rugs. Superb examples are showcased in its gallery; one-hour guided factory visits take you through the *ateliers* (workshops) and exhibits of the thousands of carpets and tapestries woven here.

Turn up well ahead of time for same-day tour tickets.

PUITS ARTÉSIEN DE LA BUTTE AUX CAILLES
SPRING

Map p410 (place Paul Verlaine, 13e; ⏱24hr; MCorvisart) FREE You'll often see locals

LOCAL KNOWLEDGE

PETITE CEINTURE

Long before the tramway or even the metro, the 35km Petite Ceinture (Little Belt) steam railway encircled the city of Paris. Constructed during the reign of Napoléon III between 1852 and 1869 as a way to move troops and goods around the city's fortifications, it became a thriving passenger service until the metro arrived in 1900. Most passenger services ceased in 1934 and goods services in 1993, and the line became an overgrown wilderness. Until recently, access was forbidden (although that didn't stop maverick urban explorers scrambling along its tracks and tunnels). Of the line's original 29 stations, 17 survive (in various states of disrepair).

Plans for regenerating the Petite Ceinture railway corridor have seen the opening of three sections with walkways alongside the tracks. Other areas remain off limits.

In southern Paris, the **Petite Ceinture du 15e** (PC 15; Map p414; www.paris.fr; btwn rue Olivier de Serres & rue St-Charles, 15e; ⊙9am-8.30pm May-Aug, shorter hours rest of year; MBalard or Porte de Versailles) FREE stretches for 1.3km, with biodiverse habitats including forest, grassland and prairies supporting 220 species of flora and fauna. In addition to the end points, there are three lift/elevator-enabled access points along its route: 397ter rue de Vaugirard; opposite 82 rue Desnouettes; and place Robert Guillemard. Ultimately the goal is to open the entire section of track between parcs Georges Brassens and André-Citroën, around 3km in all.

On the eastern side of Parc Georges Brassens, a *promenade plantée* (planted walkway) travels atop a stretch of the Petite Ceinture's tracks by Porte de Vanves.

Sections of the track itself in eastern Paris, Petite Ceinture du 12e (PC 12, p182), near the Bois de Vincennes, and western Paris, Petite Ceinture du 16e (PC 16), near the Bois de Boulogne are also open to the public.

filling containers with the natural 28°C spring water that has bubbled up here from 600m below ground since 1893. It's free, safe to drink, and is said to have health-giving properties thanks to its rich iron fluorine content and low calcium levels (BYO bottle). The four-tap stainless-steel fountain was inaugurated in the year 2000; striking opaque panels describe the history of the *source* (spring).

BRASSERIE LA PARISIENNE   BREWERY

Map p410 (☑09 52 34 94 69; http://brasserie laparisienne.com; 10 rue Wurtz, 13e; tours €15; ⊙tours by reservation; MGlacière) After founding organic brewery Brasserie Artisanale du Luberon in Provence in 2011, Jean Barthélémy Chancel launched his Parisian craft brewery in 2014. Look out for its brews (a bio white and blonde, classic red, stout, white and blonde, as well as eight speciality and seasonal beers, such as an IPA, Belgian white ale, Scottish Export and coffee-infused stout) around town, or try them during a two-hour brewery tour (in French), which includes eight tastings. Book tour tickets at http://reservation.tourisme-valde marne.com/474-1761-visite-et-degustation-de-biere-a-la-brasserie-la-parisienne.html.

PARC MONTSOURIS   PARK

Map p410 (av Reille, 14e; ⊙8.30am-9.30pm May-Aug, shorter hours rest of year; MPorte d'Orléans or RER Cité-Universitaire) The name of this sprawling lakeside park – planted with horse-chestnut, yew, cedar, weeping beech and buttonwood trees – derives from *moque souris* (mice mockery) because the area was once overrun with the critters. Today it's a delightful picnic spot and has endearing playground areas, such as a concrete 'road system' where littlies can trundle matchbox cars (BYO cars), as well as a marionette (puppet) theatre and pony rides (Wednesday, Saturday and Sunday afternoons).

An abandoned section of the Petite Ceinture runs through the park.

The park neighbours the ground-breaking 1920s-built Cité Universitaire (student halls of residence), which you're free to wander.

PARC GEORGES BRASSENS   PARK

Map p414 (http://equipment.paris.fr; 2 place Jacques Marette, 15e; ⊙8am-sunset Mon-Fri, 9am-sunset Sat & Sun; MConvention, 🚇Georges Brassens) Covering 7.74 hectares, Parc Georges Brassens (named for the French singer-songwriter and poet, who lived nearby) has a large central pond bordered by lawns, and gardens featuring roses and medicinal and aromatic plants. The sloping hill is home to a wine-producing vineyard and an apiary; honey is sold on the first Saturday of each month at the entrance. On Wednesday, Saturday and Sunday kids can ride ponies (€3.50; 3pm to 6pm) and watch a marionette show (€4; 3.30pm and 4.30pm).

Also here is the Monfort theatre, with dance, circus and theatre performances, and the weekend book market, **Marché Georges Brassens** (Map p414; 104 rue Brancion, 15e; ⊙9am-6pm Sat & Sun; ⓂPorte de Vanves).

A honey and grape-harvest festival takes place on the first weekend in October.

EATING

Since the 1920s, bd du Montparnasse has been one of the city's premier avenues for enjoying Parisian pavement life, with legendary brasseries and cafes. The down-to-earth 15e cooks up fabulous bistro fare – key streets are rues de la Convention, de Vaugirard, St-Charles, du Commerce and south of bd de Grenelle. For Asian food, try Chinatown's avs de Choisy and d'Ivry and rue Baudricourt. The villagey Butte aux Cailles, 13e, south of Corvisart metro station, is chock-a-block with interesting addresses. Uberhip restaurants hide inside the Docks en Seine (p251).

✖ Montparnasse & 15e

L'ATELIER B
BURGERS €

Map p412 (www.latelierb.fr; 129 rue du Château, 14e; burgers €11-13; ⊙noon-2.30pm & 6pm-2am Tue-Sat; ⓂPernety) The best thing about this brilliant spot isn't the late closing time, friendly service or even the cocktails, wine and beers, but the burgers themselves. Choices include Mon Bougnat (black Angus, confit onion, ruccola and blue cheese), Mon Basse Cour (chicken, aubergine, red onion, pickles and homemade BBQ sauce) and Mon Bia (chickpea patty, coleslaw, spinach, mushrooms and brie).

Sides span fries to onion rings; save room for desserts, such as tiramisu, chocolate brownies and cheesecake.

PARIS RIVE GAUCHE

Paris' largest urban redevelopment since Haussmann's 19th-century reformation is gathering pace in the 13e *arrondissement* (city district). Centred on a once nondescript area south of the Latin Quarter spiralling out from big busy traffic hub place d'Italie, the renaissance of the area known as Paris Rive Gauche was heralded in the 1990s by the controversial Bibliothèque Nationale de France (p250) and the arrival of the high-speed Météor metro line. They were followed, among other additions, by the **MK2 entertainment complex** (Map p410; www.mk2.com; 128-162 av de France, 13e; ⓂBibliothèque), the Piscine Joséphine Baker swimming pool (p261) floating on the Seine, and the Passerelle Simone de Beauvoir (2006), providing a cycle and pedestrian link to the Right Bank. And work isn't slated to stop for several more years.

Pivotal to this 130-hectare redevelopment zone is the Paris 7 university campus hosting some 30,000 students. Other institutions to have moved in include the Institut Français de la Mode (the French fashion institute) in the stylised former warehouse Docks en Seine (p251).

As of spring 2016, the area is home to Paris' first floating hotel, Off Paris Seine (p292), an 80m-long catamaran-design structure with a 400 sq metre sun terrace, 15m-long swimming pool, bar, lounge, and 54 rooms and four suites.

The area's mainline train station, Gare d'Austerlitz, is getting a €600 million makeover from celebrated architect Jean Nouvel. Not only will the station itself be overhauled (including €200 million alone on the grand hall's glass roof, beneath which hot air balloons were manufactured during the 1870 siege of Paris), but shops, cafes and green spaces will fill the surrounding streets. The renovation is due to wrap up in 2021.

Track updates on the area at www.parisrivegauche.com.

LE FOURNIL DE LOURMEL   BOULANGERIE €

Map p414 (121 av Félix Faure, 15e; dishes €1.80-5.50; ⏰6.30am-8.30pm Mon-Sat; Ⓜ Lourmel) Situated a short stroll from the gates of Parc André Citroën, *boulangerie* Le Fournil de Lourmel is a handy pit stop for freshly baked picnic staples: luscious quiches (salmon, leek, tomato and onion, goat's cheese or classic ham-filled Lorraine), baguettes, and sweet treats including éclairs and *clafoutis* (cherry flan).

MARCHÉ EDGAR QUINET   MARKET €

Map p412 (bd Edgar Quinet, 14e; ⏰7am-2.30pm Wed, 7am-3pm Sat; Ⓜ Edgar Quinet, Montparnasse Bienvenüe) Opposite Tour Montparnasse, this open-air street market teems with neighbourhood shoppers. There's always a great range of cheeses, as well as stalls sizzling up snacks to eat on the run, from crêpes to spicy falafels.

POILÂNE   BOULANGERIE €

Map p414 (www.poilane.com; 49 bd de Grenelle, 15e; ⏰7.15am-8.15pm Tue-Sun; Ⓜ Dupleix) Pick up handcrafted sourdough bread from this branch of one of Paris' most famous bakeries (p234), as well as its delicious *punitions* (crispy butter biscuits).

★**LE CLOS Y**   MODERN FRENCH €€

Map p412 (📞01 45 49 07 35; www.leclosy.com; 27 av du Maine, 15e; 2-/3-course lunch menus €26/31, 4-/6-course dinner menus €45/65; ⏰noon-2pm & 7.30-10pm Tue-Sat; Ⓜ Montparnasse Bienvenüe) One of Paris' rapidly rising star chefs Yoshitaka Ikeda creates utterly original *menus* that change daily but might start with foie gras ice cream and move on to perch sashimi with beetroot, apple and powdered olive oil; green peas in pea jelly with mascarpone; smoked salmon and egg with raspberry foam; and Madeira-marinated beef with butternut squash and carrot purée.

The black-and-grey dining room with cherry-wood tables is streamlined and chic. Allergies and preferences can be catered for by prior request.

★**LE BEURRE NOISETTE**   NEOBISTRO €€

Map p414 (📞01 48 56 82 49; 68 rue Vasco de Gama, 15e; 2-/3-course lunch menus €23/32, mains €18; ⏰noon-2pm & 7-10.30pm Tue-Sat; Ⓜ Lourmel) *Beurre noisette* (brown butter sauce, named for its hazelnut colour) features in dishes such as scallops with cauliflower purée, and tender *bœuf fondante*

with artichokes, courgette and carrot at pedigreed chef Thierry Blanqui's neighbourhood neobistro. Other treats include homemade blood sausage with apple compote. Filled with locals, the chocolate-toned dining room is wonderfully convivial – be sure to book.

★**LE GRAND PAN**   NEOBISTRO €€

Map p414 (📞01 42 50 02 50; www.legrandpan.fr; 20 rue Rosenwald, 15e; mains €16-29; ⏰noon-2pm & 7-11pm Mon-Fri; Ⓜ Porte de Vanves) Red-leather banquettes, gorgeous mosaic-tiled floors and dark-timber tables set the stage for an atmospheric Parisian dining experience. The blackboard menu changes daily but stalwarts include foie gras ravioli with truffle shavings, *côte de veau* with cream sauce, and a chocolate cylinder filled with vanilla mousse and drizzled with salted caramel sauce. Its small-plates restaurant, **Le Petit Pan** (Map p414; 📞01 42 50 04 04; www.lepetitan.fr; 18 rue Rosenwald, 15e; 2-/3-course lunch menu €15/20, small plates €4-16; ⏰noon-2.30pm & 6-11.30pm Tue-Sat; Ⓜ Porte de Vanves), is directly opposite.

★**LE CASSE NOIX**   MODERN FRENCH €€

Map p414 (📞01 45 66 09 01; www.le-cassenoix.fr; 56 rue de la Fédération, 15e; 2-/3-course lunch menus €21/28, 3-course dinner menu €35; ⏰noon-2.30pm & 7-10.30pm Mon-Fri; Ⓜ Bir Hakeim) Proving that a location footsteps from the Eiffel Tower doesn't mean compromising on quality, quantity or authenticity, 'the nutcracker' is a neighbourhood gem with a cosy retro interior, affordable prices, and exceptional cuisine that changes by season and by the inspiration of owner-chef Pierre Olivier Lenormand, who has honed his skills in some of Paris' most fêted kitchens. Book ahead.

JEU DE QUILLES   BISTRO €€

Map p412 (📞01 53 90 76 22; 45 rue Boulard, 14e; 2-/3-course lunch menus €18/21, 4-course dinner menu €35, mains €23-37; ⏰8-10pm Tue, noon-2pm & 8-10pm Wed-Fri, noon-2pm & 7.30-10pm Sat; Ⓜ Mouton-Duvernet) When your next-door neighbour is the original premises of celebrated butcher Hugo Desnoyer, you have an inside track to serve exceptional meat-based dishes, and chef Benoît Reix does exactly that at this fabulous bistro. Creations such as artichoke-paste-encrusted pork or veal carpaccio pair with an extensive selection of natural wines. Reserve ahead: there are just 18 seats and locals love it.

JADIS
NEOBISTRO €€

Map p414 (☏01 45 57 73 20; www.bistrotjadis paris.com; 208 rue de la Croix Nivert, 15e; 3-course lunch menu €22, mains €16-34; ☺noon-2pm & 7-10pm Mon-Fri; Ⓜ Boucicaut) This crimson-fronted neobistro on the corner of an unassuming street is revered for traditional French dishes that pack a modern punch (pig trotter stew with calamari and chickpeas; beetroot-marinated pigeon with apple chutney) thanks to its risk-taking chef Guillaume Delage. The lunch *menu* is exceptional value and the chocolate soufflé – order it at the start of your meal – is divine.

LA ROTONDE MONTPARNASSE
BRASSERIE €€

(☏01 43 26 48 26; www.rotondemontparnasse. com; 105 bd du Montparnasse, 6e; 3-course menu €42, mains €15.50-42; ☺6am-2am, menus noon-3pm & 7-11pm; Ⓜ Vavin) Opened in 1911 and recently restored to its former glory, La Rotonde may be awash with the same Les Montparnos history as its famous brasserie neighbours like Le Select, but the real reason to come is for the superior food. Meat comes from Parisian butcher extraordinaire Hugo Desnoyer, salmon and chicken are organic, and brasserie classics are cooked to perfection.

AUX ENFANTS GÂTÉS
BISTRO €€

Map p412 (☏01 40 47 56 81; www.auxenfants-gates.fr; 4 rue Danville, 14e; 2-/3-course midweek lunch menu €28/36, mains €22; ☺noon-2pm & 7.30-10pm Tue-Sat; Ⓜ Denfert Rochereau) Just 20 seats at this neighbourhood bistro of bare boards, marine-blue walls and red banquettes means it's worth booking ahead to avoid missing out on its simple but delicious dishes, such as rabbit terrine with pickled vegetables, confit lamb shoulder with potato and broccoli, roast veal in red wine jus with fried polenta, and fondant cheesecake with homemade mango sorbet.

LA VÉRAISON
MODERN FRENCH €€

Map p414 (☏01 45 32 39 39; www.laveraison. com; 64 rue de la Croix Nivert, 15e; mains €18-26; ☺7.30-10pm Tue-Sat; Ⓜ Commerce) The elegant simplicity of owner-chef Ulla Bosse's welcoming neighbourhood bistro (bare boards, timber tables, pistachio-coloured walls) belies the outstanding cuisine she creates in her open kitchen. The starters

---

LOCAL KNOWLEDGE

RUE DAGUERRE

Paris' traditional village atmosphere thrives along rue Daguerre, 14e.

Tucked just southwest of the Denfert-Rochereau metro and RER stations, this narrow street – pedestrianised between av du Général-Leclerc and rue Boulard – is lined with florists, *fromageries* (cheese shops), *boulangeries* (bakeries), patisseries, greengrocers, delis (including Greek, Asian and Italian) and classic cafes where you can watch the local goings on.

Shops set up market stalls on the pavement; Sunday mornings are especially lively. It's a great option for lunch before or after visiting Les Catacombes, or packing a picnic to take to one of the area's parks and squares.

---

alone – truffled chestnut velouté, foie gras ravioli in cognac sauce, burrata cheese with orange, crispy 'Peking duck' morsels, Thai crab cakes with mango dip – are reason enough to return.

LA CERISAIE
REGIONAL CUISINE €€

Map p412 (☏01 43 20 98 98; www.restaurant-lacerisaie.com; 70 bd Edgar Quinet, 14e; mains €15-20; ☺noon-2pm & 7-10pm Mon-Fri; Ⓜ Edgar Quinet) Chef Cyril Lalanne shows how inventive southwestern French cuisine can be at this snug 22-seat restaurant behind a cherry-coloured facade. Starters such as snail cassoulet are followed by rich, often game-based mains (goose with spiced roast pear, for instance) and desserts like fig and shortbread crumble. The wine list is extensive and extremely well priced. Be sure to book.

LA GAULOISE
TRADITIONAL FRENCH €€

Map p414 (☏01 47 34 11 64; 59 av de la Motte-Picquet, 15e; 2-/3-course lunch menus €26/31, mains €19-31; ☺noon-2.30pm & 7-11pm; Ⓜ La Motte Picquet Grenelle) With a name like La Gauloise, you wouldn't expect this venerable, terrace-fronted restaurant to serve anything other than traditional fare, which it does, very well. From onion soup to pansautéed calf's liver, preserved foie gras with pear and mustard marmalade, and profiteroles or *îles flottantes* for dessert, it refines but doesn't reinvent the classics that make French cuisine iconic.

LOCAL KNOWLEDGE

'LITTLE BRITTANY'

Trains depart from Gare Montparnasse for the windswept region of Brittany, a couple of hours' west, but you don't have to leave the capital for authentic Breton crêpes. Due to the Breton population congregating in this area, the station's surrounding streets – especially rue du Montparnasse, 14e, and rue Odessa, 14e, one block west – are lined with dozens of crêperies.

Unlike the rolled-up crêpes sold on street corners, Breton crêpes are folded envelope-style at the edges, served flat on a plate and eaten using cutlery – and are best washed down with bowls of brut Breton cider. Savoury *galettes* use *blé noir* – (buckwheat flour; *sarrasin* in Breton), while both *galettes* and sweet crêpes made from white flour use salted Breton butter. Traditional toppings include *andouille* (Breton sausage), and *caramel au beurre salé* (salted caramel sauce; *salidou* in Breton).

Top picks:

Crêperie Josselin (Map p412; ☎01 43 20 93 50; 67 rue du Montparnasse, 14e; crêpes €7-10; ⊙11.30am-3pm & 5-11pm Tue-Fri, 11.30am-11pm Sat & Sun; 🖈; MEdgar Quinet) Filled with dark timber furniture, painted plates and screened by lace curtains, Josselin takes its name from the eastern Breton village crowned by a 14th-century castle. Locals crowd around the open kitchen waiting for a table. Savoury *galettes* include Roquefort with walnuts; enjoy it with a bowl of Breton cider and finish with a crêpe smothered in salted caramel.

Crêperie Plougastel (Map p412; ☎01 42 79 90 63; www.creperie-plougastel.com; 47 rue du Montparnasse, 14e; crêpes €3.10-10.90; ⊙noon-midnight; 🖈; MEdgar Quinet) Named for the Breton commune near Brest, Plougastel's decor might be spartan, but its *galettes* and crêpes are anything but, with generous toppings including St-Jacques scallops, or chicken breast, spinach and fried egg, and pears in syrup and Chantilly (cream whipped with sugar).

AU MOULIN VERT   TRADITIONAL FRENCH €€
Map p412 (☎01 45 39 31 31; www.aumoulinvert.com; 34bis rue des Plantes, 14e; 2-/3-course menus €19/35, seafood platters €44-56; ⊙noon-3pm & 7-11pm; MAlésia) The 19th-century 'green windmill' is a delightful, relaxed neighbourhood restaurant opening to a glass-paned winter garden and sunlit terrace. Luscious shellfish platters composed from the fresh seafood bar are complemented by chef Gérard Chagot's seasonal creations, like duck in cherries, cod in cider and snails in garlic, served by aproned waiters at white-clothed tables inside and on the terrace.

LE SÉVÉRO   BISTRO €€
Map p412 (☎01 45 40 40 91; www.lesevero.fr; 8 rue des Plantes, 14e; mains €17-36; ⊙noon-2pm & 7.30-10pm Mon-Fri; MMouton Duvernet) Steaks served with sensational *frites* (fries) are the mainstay of this upmarket bistro (it's run by ex-butcher William Bernet); other meat specialities include black pudding and pigs' trotters. Wash them down with any number of excellent wines, which are chalked on an entire wall. With just 30 seats, reconfirming advance reservations by noon is essential.

LA CABANE À HUÎTRES   SEAFOOD €€
Map p412 (☎01 45 49 47 27; 4 rue Antoine Bourdelle, 14e; dozen oysters €18, menu €22; ⊙noon-2.15pm & 7-10.15pm Wed-Sat; MMontparnasse Bienvenüe) Wonderfully rustic, this wooden-styled *cabane* (cabin) with just nine tables is the pride and joy of fifth-generation oyster farmer Françis Dubourg, who splits his time between the capital and his oyster farm in Arcachon on the Atlantic Coast. The fixed menu includes a dozen oysters, foie gras, *magret de canard fumé* (smoked duck breast) or smoked salmon.

LA CLOSERIE DES LILAS   BRASSERIE €€
Map p412 (☎01 40 51 34 50; www.closeriedeslilas.fr; 171 bd du Montparnasse, 6e; mains restaurant €28-55, brasserie €24-33; ⊙restaurant noon-2.30pm & 7-11.30pm, brasserie noon-12.30am, piano bar 11am-1.30am; MVavin or RER Port Royal) Brass plaques tell you exactly where Hemingway (who wrote much of *The Sun Also Rises* here) and luminaries like Picasso, Apollinaire, Man Ray, Jean-Paul Sartre and Samuel Beckett stood, sat or fell at the 'Lilac Enclosure' (opened 1847). It's split into a late-night piano bar, upmarket restaurant

and more lovable (and cheaper) brasserie with a hedged-in pavement terrace.

LA COUPOLE   BRASSERIE €€

Map p412 (℡01 43 20 14 20; www.lacoupole-paris. com; 102 bd du Montparnasse, 14e; lunch menus €31-59, mains €21-48; ⊙kitchen 8am-11pm Mon, 8am-midnight Tue-Fri, 8.30am-midnight Sat, 8.30am-11pm Sun; 🛜🚸; Ⓜ️Vavin) The reason for visiting this enormous, 450-seat brasserie, designed by the Solvet brothers and opened in 1927, is more history than gastronomy. Its famous mural-covered columns (painted by such artists as Brancusi and Chagall), dark wood panelling and soft lighting have hardly changed an iota since the days of Sartre, Soutine, Man Ray, Josephine Baker and other regulars.

You can also go dancing (p260) here.

LE DÔME   BRASSERIE €€€

Map p412 (℡01 43 35 25 81; 108 bd du Montparnasse, 14e; mains €44-66.50, seafood platters €75; ⊙noon-3pm & 7-11.30pm; Ⓜ️Vavin) A 1930s art deco extravaganza of the formal white-tablecloth and bow-tied waiter variety, monumental Le Dôme is one of the swishest places around for shellfish platters piled high with fresh oysters, king prawns, crab claws and much more, followed by traditional creamy homemade *millefeuille* for dessert, wheeled in on a trolley and cut in front of you.

LE CIEL DE PARIS   TRADITIONAL FRENCH €€€

Map p412 (℡01 40 64 77 64; www.cieldeparis. com; Level 56, Tour Montparnasse, 33 av du Maine, 14e; menus lunch/dinner from €30/45; ⊙7.30am-11pm; Ⓜ️Montparnasse Bienvenüe) Views don't get much better than 'the sky of Paris', the Tour Montparnasse's 56th-floor restaurant, accessed by private lift/elevator. Starters include snails and pigs' trotters; seafood is a speciality. The gastronomic Grand Écran menu (€136), available at dinner daily and Sunday lunch, includes a guaranteed window table and bottle of Champagne per person. The bar stays open until 1am.

🍴 Place d'Italie & Chinatown

LAURENT DUCHÊNE   BOULANGERIE, PATISSERIE €

Map p410 (www.laurent-duchene.com; 2 rue Wurtz, 13e; ⊙7.30am-8pm Mon-Sat; Ⓜ️Glacière) Prize-winning croissants made with *beurre*

Charentes-Poitou AOC butter are the speciality of this lauded *boulangerie* and patisserie, and its tantalising rainbow of macarons, tarts and intricately layered cakes taste even more luscious than they look.

THIENG HENG   VIETNAMESE, SANDWICHES €

Map p410 (50 av d'Ivry, 13e; sandwiches €2.40-3.80; ⊙8.30am-7pm; Ⓜ️Porte d'Ivry) You'll know you're in the vicinity of this takeaway joint when you see crowds of locals munching on giant *banh mi* (Vietnamese stuffed baguettes), which have earned Thieng Heng a cult following. Fillings include grilled marinated meats, such as pork or chicken, pickled veggies, fresh herbs and sweet, salty or spicy sauces. If you're famished, there's a super-size option.

PHO 14   VIETNAMESE €

Map p410 (129 av de Choisy, 13e; mains €7-10; ⊙9am-11pm; Ⓜ️Tolbiac) Factor in a wait at this small, simple restaurant (also known as Pho Banh Cuon 14) – it doesn't take bookings and is wildly popular with in-the-know locals for its authentic and astonishingly cheap *pho*. The steaming Vietnamese broth is richly flavoured with cinnamon and incorporates noodles and traditional beef or chicken.

LA CHINE MASSÉNA   CHINESE €

Map p410 (℡01 45 83 98 88; www.chinemassena. fr; 18 av de Choisy, 13e; menus lunch/dinner from €11/16, dim sum €4.80-7; ⊙noon-3pm & 7-11pm; Ⓜ️Porte de Choisy) Set back off the street adjoining a shopping mall, this enormous restaurant specialising in Cantonese and Chiu Chow cuisine is a real favourite in Chinatown, particularly with large groups (it has plenty of room to accommodate them). The live-tank seafood and traditional dim sum are especially good. Dancing accompanied by a live orchestra takes place on Friday and Saturday nights.

SIMONE   NEOBISTRO €€

Map p410 (℡01 43 37 82 70; www.simoneparis. com; 33 bd Arago, 13e; 2-/3-course lunch menus €21/24, mains €19-28; ⊙noon-2.30pm & 7.30-10.30pm Tue-Sat; Ⓜ️Les Gobelins) Bright pastel-coloured tables line the pavement outside this vibrant neighbourhood neobistro well off the tourist radar. Daily changing *menus* created in the open kitchen might incorporate langoustines with polenta, filet mignon with fig jus, or lamb with heirloom carrots cooked three ways. All-natural wines (also available to pick up from its wine shop next door) pair perfectly with each course.

TEMPERO — NEOBISTRO €€

Map p410 (☑09 54 17 48 88; http://tempero. fr; 5 rue Clisson, 13e; 2-/3-course lunch menus €15.50/21, mains €14-18; ☺noon-2.15pm Mon-Wed, noon-2.15pm & 7.30-10.30pm Thu & Fri; MChevaleret) Feisty fare at this stylish neobistro fuses the flavours of Asia and France in mains such as sea bass fillet with black rice shiitake risotto and carrot and lemon purée, and Gyoza marinated duck in miso bouillon, and out-there desserts like cardamom and pineapple soup or mango pannacotta with passionfruit compote. Its younger sibling, **Comptoir Tempero** (Map p410; ☑01 45 84 15 35; 124 bd Vincent Auriol, 13e; 2-/3-course lunch menus €15.50/21, mains €16-23; ☺noon-2.15pm Mon-Wed, noon-2.15 & 7.30-10pm Thu & Fri; MNationale), is close by.

AU PETIT MARGUERY — TRADITIONAL FRENCH €€

Map p410 (☑01 43 31 58 59; http://petitmarguery.com; 9 bd de Port Royal, 13e; menus lunch €24-29, dinner €32-37; ☺noon-2.15pm & 7.15-10.15pm; MLes Gobelins) This wonderfully traditional restaurant is a perfect choice for honest-to-goodness, heartily proportioned dishes like house-speciality roast partridge, pan-fried veal in chestnut sauce, lamb with parsley mash and red wine jus, and Grand Marnier soufflé. It's popular with locals; so popular that it's opened a casual dining space, **Le Comptoir Marguery** (Map p410; ☑01 42 17 43 43; http://comptoirmarguery. com; 9 bd de Port Royal, 13e; 2-/3-course menus €17.90/21.90; ☺noon-2.30pm & 6.30-10.30pm; MLes Gobelins), next door, so book ahead to avoid a lengthy wait.

L'OURCINE — NEOBISTRO €€

Map p410 (☑01 73 20 23 21; www.restaurantlourcine.fr; 92 rue Broca, 13e; menu €38; ☺noon-2.30pm & 7-11pm Tue-Sat; MLes Gobelins) With wine corks in the window, this intimate place may be casual (no dress code) and affordable but it takes its food seriously. The superb menu spans starters like spider crab ravioli with lemongrass to mains such as sautéed Breton squid with cuttlefish-ink risotto or pigeon roasted on the bone with seared foie gras, and desserts like traditional frangipane *galette*.

DRINKING & NIGHTLIFE

The comings and goings of the Gare Montparnasse train station and its historic brasseries keep things lively. Southwest of place d'Italie, rue de la Butte aux Cailles and the surrounding Butte aux Cailles molehill have a plethora of options popular with students and local residents; places here tend to die-hard regulars. Especially in summer, you can't beat the floating bars and clubs on the Seine.

Montparnasse & Southern Paris

★LE PETIT GORILLE — CAFE

Map p414 (46 rue de Cronstadt, 15e; ☺8.30am-2am Tue-Sun; ☏; MConvention) A statue of a gorilla with her baby on her back (the 'little gorilla' of the name) is the first clue to the kitschy-cool vibe at this fun new neighbourhood bar with a marine-blue facade and pavement seating in summer. Inside, the neoretro decor features downlights and a fire-engine-red feature wall. Great cocktails, beers and wines, plus bargain-priced food, too.

HEXAGON CAFÉ — COFFEE

Map p412 (121 rue du Château, 14e; ☺8am-6pm Mon-Fri, 10am-6pm Sat & Sun; ☏; MPernety) Parisian furniture maker David Guillon designed the industrial-inspired metal-framed bar stools and textured blonde-wood bar for this chilled spot, which uses award-winning Breton roaster Caffè Cataldi beans for its addictive espressos, drip-filters and cappuccinos, and also serves loose-leaf teas and pastries. Fast wi-fi, big picture windows and downlights make it a favourite with freelancers, students and creatives.

LA PLAGE PARISIENNE — BAR

Map p414 (www.laplageparisienne.fr; Port de Javel Haut, 15e; ☺noon-midnight Sun-Fri, 7pm-midnight Sat; MJavel–André Citroën) More upmarket than the floating bars in the 13e, La Plage Parisienne has a plush cruiseship-like interior, a snazzy menu of internationally inspired dishes, and an absolutely stunning, sun-soaked outdoor terrace with cream banquettes where you can sip a glass of wine or a cocktail (go for the house- or, rather, boat-speciality La Plage, with vodka, fresh strawberries and Champagne).

FÉLICIE
BAR

Map p412 (www.felicie.info; 174 av du Maine, 14e; ⏰7.15am-2am Mon-Fri, 8am-2am Sat & Sun; 🛜; ⓂLourmel) Chances are your first visit won't be your last at this unpretentious neighbourhood cafe with a big heated pavement terrace, fun-loving staff and a laid-back vibe. It's a quintessentially Parisian spot to hang out any time of day, but especially during Sunday brunch; lunches are built around bistro classics like steak tartare. Late at night is also good.

LE ROSEBUD
COCKTAIL BAR

Map p412 (11bis rue Delambre, 14e; ⏰7pm-2am; ⓂVavin) Like the sleigh of that name in *Citizen Kane*, Rosebud harks back to the past. In this case it's to Montparnasse's early-20th-century heyday (the decor has scarcely changed since Sartre drank here). Enjoy a Champagne cocktail amid the quiet elegance of polished wood and aged leather.

LE SELECT
CAFE

Map p412 (www.leselectmontparnasse.fr; 99 bd du Montparnasse, 6e; ⏰7am-3am; 🛜; ⓂVavin) Dating from 1923, this Montparnasse institution was the first of the area's grand cafes to stay open late into the night, and it still draws everyone from beer-swigging students to whisky-swilling politicians.

LE REDLIGHT
CLUB

Map p412 (www.leredlight.com; 34 rue du Départ, 14e; ⏰midnight to 6am Fri & Sat; ⓂMontparnasse Bienvenüe) Beneath Tour Montparnasse, this 1500-capacity, laser-lit venue – fittingly called *l'enfer* (hell) in a previous life and sharing space with Brazilian cabaret Brasil Tropical – is up there among Paris' busiest house, techno and electro clubs. Its podiums get packed out with a young, dance-mad crowd. Hours often vary depending on the *soirée*. Enter down the stairs across the street from Monoprix.

🍷 Place d'Italie & Chinatown

⭐LE BATOFAR
CLUB

Map p410 (www.batofar.org; opp 11 quai François Mauriac, 13e; ⏰bar noon-midnight, club 11.30pm-6am; ⓂQuai de la Gare, Bibliothèque)

This much-loved, red-metal tugboat has a rooftop bar that's terrific in summer, and a respected restaurant, while the club underneath provides memorable underwater acoustics between its metal walls and portholes. Le Batofar is known for its edgy, experimental music policy and live performances from 7pm, mostly electro-oriented but also incorporating hip-hop, new wave, rock, punk or jazz.

Happy hour is 5pm to 8pm. Food is served at the restaurant from noon to 2pm and 7pm to 11pm May to September (shorter hours from October to April).

LA DAME DE CANTON
CLUB

Map p410 (www.damedecanton.com; opp 11 quai François Mauriac, 13e; ⏰7pm-2am Tue-Thu, to dawn Fri & Sat; ⓂBibliothèque) This floating *boîte* (club) aboard a three-masted Chinese junk with a couple of world voyages under its belt bobs beneath the Bibliothèque Nationale de France. Concerts cover pop and indie to electro, hip-hop, reggae and rock; afterwards DJs keep the crowd hyped. There's also a popular bar and restaurant with wood-fired pizzas served on the terrace from May to September.

LE MERLE MOQUEUR
BAR

Map p410 (11 rue de la Butte aux Cailles, 13e; ⏰5pm-2am; ⓂCorvisart) The tiny, retro Mocking Magpie serves a huge selection of rum punches (more than 20 at last count) and unearths long-forgotten 1980s tracks from the musical vaults.

☆ ENTERTAINMENT

Many of the 13e's floating nightclubs have live music. Events regularly take place at Docks en Seine (p251).

CINÉMA LES FAUVETTES
CINEMA

Map p410 (www.cinemalesfauvettes.com; 58 av des Gobelins, 13e; tickets before/after noon €7/12; ⏰10.30am-12.30am; ⓂLes Gobelins) Classics from the silent era to contemporary films are the *raison d'être* of this five-screen cinema, which has a dedicated 3D screen and also hosts retrospectives, such as the entire James Bond catalogue or Best Picture Oscar winners. Movies are shown in French and original languages (including English) with subtitles; check the program online.

DISCOUNT DESIGNER OUTLETS

Save up to 70% off men's, women's and kids' fashions from previous seasons' collections, surpluses, prototypes and seconds by name-brand designers at the discounted outlet stores along rue d'Alésia, 14e, west of the Alésia metro station (particularly between av de Maine to rue Raymond-Losserand).

Shops pop up regularly and close just as often, so you can never be sure what you'll find, but look out for two shops stocking **Sonia Rykiel** (Map p412; www.soniarykiel.com; 110-112 rue d'Alésia, 14e; ⊙11am-7pm Tue-Sat; Ⓜ Alésia) designs. No 64 has lower-priced, more casual clothes, while No 110–112 has Sonia Rykiel's classic lines.

L'ENTREPÔT   CULTURAL CENTRE
Map p412 (✆01 45 40 07 50; www.lentrepot.fr; 7-9 rue Francis de Pressensé, 14e; Ⓜ Pernety) Everything from film screenings to jazz and world music concerts, poetry slams, photography, painting and sculpture exhibitions, art installations and much more take place at this dynamic cultural space. It's a fantastic place to eat, too, with a glassed-in conservatory and dozens of tables beneath the trees in its leafy back garden; Sunday brunch is especially popular.

DANCING LA COUPOLE   DANCING
Map p412 (✆01 43 20 14 20; www.lacoupole-paris.com; 102 bd du Montparnasse, 14e; Ⓜ Vavin) Swing, rumba, cha-cha, foxtrot, tango, roaring 1920s-style tea dances and more are held in the ballroom of the historic brasserie (p257) of the same name. Check its Facebook page or its website's *actualités* (current events) section for details, dates and times.

LE PETIT JOURNAL MONTPARNASSE   JAZZ, BLUES
Map p412 (✆01 43 21 56 70; http://petitjournal-montparnasse.com; 13 rue du Commandant René Mouchotte, 14e; from €15, incl 1 drink €25, with dinner €55; ⊙concerts from 9.30pm Mon-Sat; Ⓜ Gaîté) A fabulous range of jazz and blues concerts take place at this jazz and blues club near Gare Montparnasse. Its sister club Le Petit Journal St-Michel (p219) is situated in the Latin Quarter.

PETIT BAIN   LIVE MUSIC
Map p410 (7 Port de la Gare, 13e; Ⓜ Quai de la Gare) 'Floating cultural centre' Petit Bain has a packed program of DJs, club events and concerts – from soul, funk, punk, pop, rock and hip-hop to headbanging metal. Check the schedule on its Facebook page.

PÉNICHE L'IMPROVISTE   JAZZ, BLUES
Map p410 (✆06 50 32 63 54; http://clubmusique-improviste.wordpress.com; 36 quai d'Austerlitz, 13e; Ⓜ Gare d'Austerlitz) Many of the concerts aboard the barge containing this floating jazz club are free, including regular jam sessions.

SHOPPING

The concrete-block shopping mall opposite Gare Montparnasse includes a branch of department store Galeries Lafayette. Savvy fashion shoppers head to the southern 14e to shop for discount designer wear, while the 15e is filled with specialist addresses. In the 13e you'll find Asian grocery stores and supermarkets in Chinatown, and an enormous state-of-the-art shopping mall at place d'Italie.

★**ADAM MONTPARNASSE**   ART & CRAFTS
Map p412 (www.adamparis.com; 11 bd Edgar Quinet, 14e; ⊙9.30am-7pm Mon-Sat; Ⓜ Edgar Quinet) If Paris' art galleries have inspired you, pick up paintbrushes, charcoals, pastels, sketchpads, watercolours, oils, acrylics, canvases and more at this historic shop. Picasso, Brancusi and Giacometti were among Édouard Adam's clients. Another seminal client was Yves Klein, with whom Adam developed the ultramarine 'Klein blue' – the VLB25 'Klein Blue' varnish is sold exclusively here.

BIÉROCRATIE   DRINKS
Map p410 (www.bierocratie.com; 32 rue de l'Espérance, 13e; ⊙11am-8pm Tue & Thu-Sat, 4-8pm Wed; Ⓜ Corvisart) Craft beers from around the world (such as English Weird Beard, Canadian Dieu du Cieu, Danish Ianø, and Belgian Gulden Draak and Deus Brut des Flandres) but especially France (including Île-de-France-brewed La Baleine, Distrikt and Parisis) fill this bottle-lined specialist shop run by fun-loving young husband-and-wife team Jaclyn and Pierre. Regular events include beer and **Quatre-**

homme (Map p410; wwwquartrehomme.fr; 32 rue de l'Espérance, 13e; ⊘9am-1pm & 4-7.45pm Tue-Fri, 9am-7.45pm Sat, 9am-1pm Sun; Ⓜ Corvisart) cheese tastings.

COMPTOIR CORREZIEN   FOOD
Map p414 (8 rue des Volontaires, 15e; ⊘10.30am-1.30pm & 3-7.30pm Tue-Sat; Ⓜ Volontaires) Caviar, smoked salmon, foie gras, Corsican honey, wild duck and geese, fresh and dried mushrooms, Berthillon ice cream and truffles in season are among the mouthwatering products stocked at this head-spinning deli, which supplies some of the city's premier restaurants. If you're staying in a kitchen-equipped apartment, you can also pick up premade meals (soups, pastas) to dine *chez vous*.

LA CAVE DES PAPILLES   WINE
Map p412 (www.lacavedespapilles.com; 35 rue Daguerre, 14e; ⊘3.30-8.30pm Mon, 10am-1.30pm & 3.30-8.30pm Tue-Fri, 10am-8.30pm Sat, 10am-1.30pm Sun; Ⓜ Denfert Rochereau) All of the 1200-plus varieties of wine at this dazzling rue Daguerre (p255) wine shop are bio, organic or additive free. There's also a wonderfully chosen selection of rare whiskies, cognacs and brandies.

FROMAGERIE VACROUX ET FILS   CHEESE
Map p412 (5 rue Daguerre, 14e; ⊘8am-7.30pm Tue-Sat, to 1pm Sun; Ⓜ Denfert Rochereau) Almost 400 varieties of cheeses are stocked at this heady fromagerie on foodie street rue Daguerre (p255), along with other fresh dairy products (milk, cream), farm eggs, jams and Corsican charcuterie.

MARCHÉ AUX PUCES DE
LA PORTE DE VANVES   MARKET
(www.pucesdevanves.fr; av Georges Lafenestre & av Marc Sangnier, 14e; ⊘7am-2pm Sat & Sun; Ⓜ Porte de Vanves) The Porte de Vanves flea market is the smallest and one of the friendliest of the lot. Av Georges Lafenestre has lots of 'curios' that don't quite qualify as antiques. Av Marc Sangnier is lined with

stalls of new clothes, shoes, handbags and household items for sale.

TANG FRÈRES   SUPERMARKET
Map p410 (48 av d'Ivry, 13e; ⊘9am-8pm Tue-Sat, 8am-8pm Sun; Ⓜ Porte d'Ivry) Chinatown's beating heart centres on this enormous Asian supermarket, where you would be forgiven for thinking you'd been transported to another continent. Spices, sauces, freezers full of frozen dumplings, and kitchen utensils are imported from Asia along with beverages including Chinese beer. Ready-to-eat snacks are sold opposite the entrance.

 ## ACTIVITIES

PISCINE JOSÉPHINE BAKER   SWIMMING
Map p410 (🕿01 56 61 96 50; http://equipement. paris.fr/piscine-josephine-baker-2930; quai François Mauriac, 13e; adult/child pool €3.60/2, sauna €10/5; ⊘7-8.30am & 1-9pm Mon, Wed & Fri, 1-11pm Tue & Thu, 11am-8pm Sat, 10am-8pm Sun; Ⓜ Quai de la Gare) Floating on the Seine, this striking swimming pool is style indeed (named after the sensual 1920s American singer, what else could it be?). More of a spot to be seen than to thrash laps, the two 25m-by-10m pools lure Parisians like bees to a honey pot in summer when the roof slides back.

PISCINE DE LA BUTTE
AUX CAILLES   SWIMMING
Map p410 (🕿01 45 89 60 05; http://equipement. paris.fr/piscine-de-la-butte-aux-cailles.2927; 5 place Paul Verlaine, 13e; adult/child €3/1.70; ⊘hours vary; Ⓜ Place d'Italie) Built in 1924, this art deco swimming pool complex takes advantage of the lovely warm artesian well water nearby. Its spectacular vaulted indoor pool was recently restored to its former glory; come summer, its two outdoor pools buzz with swimmers frolicking in the sun. Hours fluctuate; check schedules online.

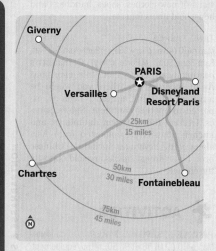

Giverny

PARIS

Versailles

Disneyland
Resort Paris

25km
15 miles

Chartres

50km
30 miles

Fontainebleau

75km
45 miles

Day Trips from Paris

Versailles (p263)

When it comes to over-the-top opulence, the colossal Château de Versailles is in a class of its own, even for France.

Disneyland Resort Paris (p269)

The 'party never stops' at Europe's Disneyland theme park, Disney Village's hotels, shops, restaurants and clubs, and Walt Disney Studios Park, bringing film, animation and TV production to life.

Fontainebleau (p270)

A lavish château and rambling forest grace the elegant town of Fontainebleau, and its international business school gives it a vibrant edge.

Chartres (p273)

Rising from fertile farmland, Chartres' Cathédrale Notre Dame, famed for its beautiful stained glass, dominates the charming medieval town.

Giverny (p276)

Art and/or garden lovers shouldn't miss Giverny's *maison et jardins de Claude Monet*, the former home and flower-filled gardens of the impressionist master.

TOP SIGHT
VERSAILLES

Louis XIV transformed his father's hunting lodge into the monumental Château de Versailles in the mid-17th century, and it remains France's most famous, grandest palace. Situated 22km southwest of Paris, the baroque château was the kingdom's political capital and the seat of the royal court from 1682 until the French Revolution in 1789.

Intending the château to house his court of 6000 people, Louis XIV hired four talented men to take on the gargantuan task: architect Louis Le Vau; Jules Hardouin-Mansart, who took over from Le Vau in the mid-1670s; painter and interior designer Charles Le Brun; and landscape designer André Le Nôtre, under whom entire hills were flattened, marshes drained and forests moved to create the seemingly endless gardens, ponds and fountains for which Versailles is so well known. It has been on Unesco's World Heritage list since 1979.

Sprawling over 900 hectares, the estate is divided into four main sections: the 580m-long palace; the gardens, canals and pools to the west of the palace; two smaller palaces, the Grand Trianon and the Petit Trianon, to the northwest; and the Hameau de la Reine (Queen's Hamlet) north of the Petit Trianon. Tickets include an English-language audioguide; free apps can be downloaded from the website.

Versailles is easy to reach from Paris. The most convenient option is to take RER C5 (€4.20, 40 minutes, frequent), which goes from Paris' Left Bank RER stations to Versailles-Château–Rive Gauche station.There are also other rail connections, buses and organised tours.

DON'T MISS

➡ Château de Versailles
➡ Gardens
➡ Marie-Antoinette's estate
➡ Trianon palaces

PRACTICALITIES

➡ ☎01 30 83 78 00
➡ www.chateau versailles.fr
➡ place d'Armes
➡ passport ticket incl estate-wide access adult/child €18/free, with musical events €25/free, palace €15/free
➡ ⊘9am-6.30pm Tue-Sun Apr-Oct, to 5.30pm Tue-Sun Nov-Mar
➡ Ⓜ RER Versailles-Château–Rive Gauche

Versailles

A DAY IN COURT

Visiting Versailles – even just the State Apartments – may seem overwhelming at first, but think of it as a house where people ate, drank, worked, slept and conspired and you'll be on the right path.

Some two decades into his long reign, Louis XIV began turning his father's hunting lodge into a palace large enough to house his entire court (to keep closer tabs on the 6000-strong army of courtiers). Sparing no expense, the Sun King employed the greatest artists and craftspeople of the day and by 1682 he'd created the most extravagant dormitory in history.

The royal schedule was as accurate and predictable as a Swiss watch. By following this itinerary of rooms you can recreate the king's day, starting with the **King's Bedchamber ❶** and the **Queen's Bedchamber ❷**, where the royal couple was roused at about the same time. The royal procession then leads through the **Hall of Mirrors ❸** to the **Royal Chapel ❹** for morning Mass and returns to the **Council Chamber ❺** for late-morning meetings with ministers. After lunch the king might ride or hunt or visit the **King's Library ❻**. Later he could join courtesans for an 'apartment evening' starting from the **Hercules Drawing Room ❼** or play billiards in the **Diana Drawing Room ❽** before supping at 10pm.

VERSAILLES BY NUMBERS

➡ **Rooms** 700 (11 hectares of roof)
➡ **Windows** 2153
➡ **Staircases** 67
➡ **Gardens and parks** 800 hectares
➡ **Trees** 200,000
➡ **Fountains** 50 (with 620 nozzles)
➡ **Paintings** 6300 (measuring 11km laid end to end)
➡ **Statues and sculptures** 2100
➡ **Objets d'art and furnishings** 5000
➡ **Visitors** 5.3 million per year

CHRISTOPHE LEHENAFF/GETTY IMAGES ©

Queen's Bedchamber
Chambre de la Reine
The queen's life was on constant public display and even the births of her children were watched by crowds of spectators in her own bedchamber. **DETOUR »** The Guardroom, with a dozen armed men at the ready.

LUNCH BREAK

Diner-style food at Sister's Café, crêpes at Le Phare St-Louis or picnic in the park.

Guardroom

South Wing

King's Library
Bibliothèque du Roi
The last resident, bibliophile Louis XVI, loved geography and his copy of *The Travels of James Cook* (in English, which he read fluently) is still on the shelf here.

DEA/G. DAGLI ORTI/GETTY IMAGES ©

SAVVY SIGHTSEEING

Avoid Versailles on Monday (closed), Tuesday (Paris' museums close, so visitors flock here) and Sunday, the busiest day. Also, book tickets online so you don't have to queue.

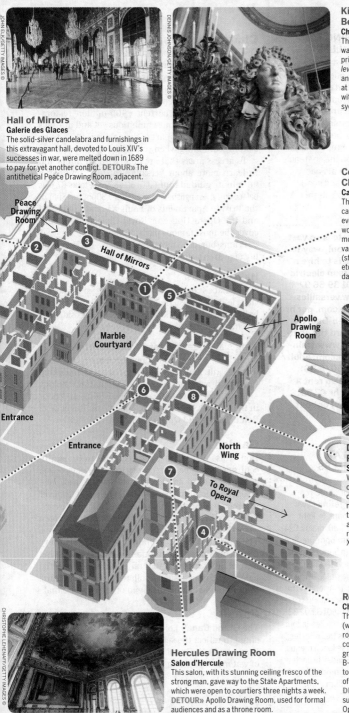

King's Bedchamber
Chambre du Roi
The king's daily life was anything but private and even his *lever* (rising) at 8am and *coucher* (retiring) at 11.30pm would be witnessed by up to 150 sycophantic courtiers.

Hall of Mirrors
Galerie des Glaces
The solid-silver candelabra and furnishings in this extravagant hall, devoted to Louis XIV's successes in war, were melted down in 1689 to pay for yet another conflict. **DETOUR»** The antithetical Peace Drawing Room, adjacent.

Council Chamber
Cabinet du Conseil
This chamber, with carved medallions evoking the king's work, is where the monarch met his various ministers (state, finance, religion etc) depending on the days of the week.

Diana Drawing Room
Salon de Diane
With walls and ceiling covered in frescos devoted to the mythical huntress, this room contained a large billiard table reserved for Louis XIV, a keen player.

Royal Chapel
Chapelle Royale
This two-storey chapel (with gallery for the royals and important courtiers, and the ground floor for the B-list) was dedicated to St Louis, patron of French monarchs. **DETOUR»** The sumptuous Royal Opera.

Hercules Drawing Room
Salon d'Hercule
This salon, with its stunning ceiling fresco of the strong man, gave way to the State Apartments, which were open to courtiers three nights a week. **DETOUR»** Apollo Drawing Room, used for formal audiences and as a throne room.

Peace Drawing Room

Hall of Mirrors

Marble Courtyard

Apollo Drawing Room

Entrance

Entrance

North Wing

To Royal Opera

PLANNING FOR VERSAILLES

By noon queues for tickets and entering the château spiral out of control: arrive early morning and avoid Tuesday, Saturday and Sunday. Prepurchase tickets on the château's website or at Fnac branches and head straight to Entrance A.

The estate is so vast that the only way to see it all is to hire a four-person electric car (01 39 66 97 66; www.versailles-tourisme.com; per hr €32; Feb-Dec) **or hop aboard the shuttle train (www.train-versailles.com; adult/child €7.50/5.80); you can also rent a bike (per hr €7.50; Feb-Nov) or boat (per hr €16).**

DINING AT VERSAILLES

Eateries include tea-room **Angelina** (www.angelina-paris.fr; light dishes €16-30, mains €24-36; 10am-6pm Tue-Sun Apr-Oct, to 5pm Tue-Sun Nov-Mar), with branches inside the palace and by the Petit Trianon. In the town of Versailles, try **La Cour** (01 39 02 33 09; www.versailles-lacour.fr; 7 rue des Deux Portes; 2-/3-course lunch menus €14/16, Sunday brunch €22; noon-6pm Tue-Sat, 11am-3pm Sun).

Château de Versailles

Few alterations have been made to the château since its construction, apart from most of the interior furnishings disappearing during the Revolution and many of the rooms being rebuilt by Louis-Philippe (r 1830–48), who opened part of the château to the public in 1837. The current €400-million restoration program is the most ambitious yet and until it's completed in 2020 a part of the palace is likely to be clad in scaffolding when you visit.

To access areas that are otherwise off limits and to learn more about Versailles' history, prebook a 90-minute **guided tour** (01 30 83 77 88; tours €7, plus palace entry; English-language tours 9.30pm Tue-Sun) of the Private Apartments of Louis XV and Louis XVI and the Opera House or Royal Chapel. Tours also cover the most famous parts of the palace.

Prams/buggies, metal-frame baby carriers and luggage aren't allowed inside the palace.

Hall of Mirrors

The palace's opulence peaks in its shimmering Galerie des Glaces (Hall of Mirrors). This 75m-long ballroom has 17 sparkling mirrors on one side and an equal number of windows on the other.

King's & Queen's State Apartments

Luxurious, ostentatious appointments – frescoes, marble, gilt and woodcarvings, with themes and symbols drawn from Greek and Roman mythology – adorn every moulding, cornice, ceiling and door in the palace's Grands Appartements du Roi et de la Reine (King's and Queen's State Apartments).

Gardens

Don't miss a stroll through the château's magnificent **gardens** (free except during musical events; gardens 8am-8.30pm Apr-Oct, to 6pm Nov-Mar, park 7am-8.30pm Apr-Oct, 8am-6pm Nov-Mar). The best view over the rectangular pools is from the Hall of Mirrors. Pathways include the Royal Walk's verdant 'green carpet', with smaller paths leading to leafy groves. The gardens' largest fountains are the 17th-century Bassin de Neptune (Neptune's Fountain), a dazzling mirage of 99 spouting fountains 300m north of the palace, and the Bassin d'Apollon (Apollo's Fountain), built in 1668 at the eastern end of the Grand Canal.

Canals

The **Grand Canal**, 1.6km long and 62m wide, is oriented to reflect the setting sun. It's traversed by the 1km-long **Petit Canal**, forming a cross-shaped body of water with a perimeter of more than 5.5km.

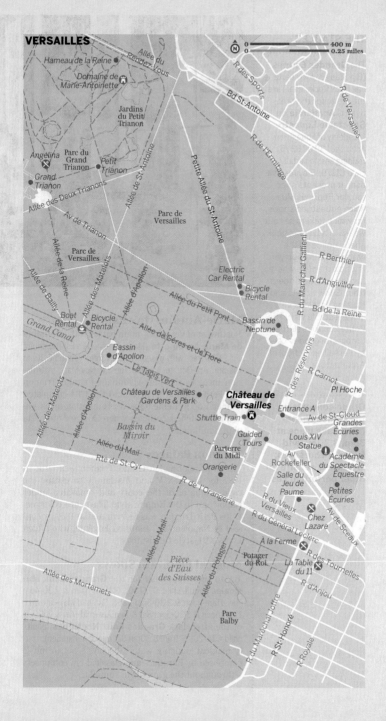

VERSAILLES

Hameau de la Reine

Domaine de Marie-Antoinette

Allée du Rendez-Vous

R des Sports

Bd St-Antoine

R de Versailles

Jardins du Petit Trianon

R de l'Ermitage

Angelina

Parc du Grand Trianon

Petit Trianon

Grand Trianon

Allée des Deux Trianons

Av de Trianon

Parc de Versailles

Allée de St-Antoine

Petite Allée du St-Antoine

Parc de Versailles

Allée de la Reine

Allée des Matelots

Allée d'Apollon

Electric Car Rental

Bicycle Rental

R du Maréchal Galliéni

R Berthier

R d'Angiviller

Bd de la Reine

Allée de Bailly

Boat Rental

Bicycle Rental

Grand Canal

Allée du Petit Pont

Bassin de Neptune

Allée de Cérès et de Flore

Bassin d'Apollon

Le Tapis Vert

R des Réservoirs

R Carnot

Pl Hoche

Allée des Matelots

Allée d'Apollon

Château de Versailles Gardens & Park

Château de Versailles

Shuttle Train

Entrance A

Av de St-Cloud

Grandes Écuries

Bassin du Miroir

Guided Tours

Louis XIV Statue

Académie du Spectacle Équestre

Allée du Mail

Rte de St-Cyr

Parterre du Midi

Orangerie

Av Rockefeller

Salle du Jeu de Paume

Petites Écuries

R de l'Orangerie

R du Vieux Versailles

R du Général Leclerc

Chez Lazare

Av de Sceaux

A la Ferme

Allée du Mail

Pièce d'Eau des Suisses

Allée du Potager

Potager du Roi

La Table du 11

R des Tournelles

R d'Anjou

Allée des Mortemets

Parc Balby

R du Maréchal Joffre

R St-Honoré

R Royale

0 ——— 400 m
0 ——— 0.25 miles

THE STABLES

The **Grandes Écuries** (Big Stables; www.barta bas.fr; av Rockefeller) are the stage for the prestigious **Académie du Spectacle Équestre** (Academy of Equestrian Arts; ☎01 39 02 62 75; training session adult/child €12/9; ⊘by reservation). It presents spectacular Reprises Musicales equestrian shows, for which tickets sell out weeks in advance; book ahead online. In the stables' main courtyard is a new manège where horses and their riders train. Show tickets and training sessions include a stable visit. The Petites Écuries (Little Stables) are today used by Versailles' School of Architecture.

Organ concerts in the palace chapel (free) take place at 3pm, 3.30pm and 5.30pm Thursdays; check the website for other performances.

Galerie des Glaces (p266)

Marie-Antoinette's Estate

Northwest of Versailles' main palace is the **Domaine de Marie-Antoinette** (Marie-Antoinette's Estate; adult/child €10/free, with passport ticket free; ⊘noon-6.30pm Tue-Sun Apr-Oct, to 5.30pm Tue-Sat Nov-Mar). Admission includes the pink-colonnaded Grand Trianon and Petit Trianon palaces, and the 1784-completed Hameau de la Reine (Queen's Hamlet), a mock village of thatched cottages where Marie-Antoinette played milkmaid.

Trianon Palaces

The pink-colonnaded Grand Trianon was built in 1687 for Louis XIV and his family to escape the rigid etiquette of the court and renovated under Napoléon I in the Empire style. The ochre-coloured, 1760s Petit Trianon was redecorated in 1867 by consort of Napoleon III, Empress Eugénie, who added Louis XVI–style furnishings

Musical Fountain Shows

Try to time your visit for the **Grandes Eaux Musicales** (adult/child €9/7.50; ⊘11am-noon & 2.30-4pm Tue, 11am-noon & 3.30-5pm Sat & Sun mid-May–late Jun, 11am-noon & 3.30-5pm Sat & Sun Apr–mid-May & Jul-Oct) or the after-dark **Grandes Eaux Nocturnes** (adult/child €24/20; ⊘from 8.30pm Sat mid-Jun–mid-Sep), truly magical 'dancing water' displays – set to music composed by Baroque- and classical-era composers – throughout the grounds in summer.

It took almost €4.6 billion to turn the beet fields 32km east of Paris into Europe's first Disney theme park. What started out as Euro-Disney in 1992 today comprises the traditional Disneyland Park theme park, the film-oriented Walt Disney Studios Park, and the hotel-, shop- and restaurant-filled Disney Village. And kids – and kids-at-heart – can't seem to get enough.

Basic one-day admission fees at Disneyland Resort Paris include unlimited access to attractions in either Disneyland Park or Walt Disney Studios Park. A multitude of multiday passes, special offers and packages are always available.

No picnic hampers/coolers are allowed but you can bring snacks, sandwiches, bottled water (refillable at water fountains) and the like. The resort also has 29 themed restaurants of varying quality and value; reservations are recommended and can be made online up to two months in advance.

Disneyland is easily reached by RER A4 (€7.50, 40 minutes to one hour, frequent), which runs from central Paris to Marne-la-Vallée/Chessy, Disneyland's RER station.

DON'T MISS

➜ Disneyland Park
➜ Walt Disney Studios Park

PRACTICALITIES

➜ 🗓hotel bookings 01 60 30 60 30, restaurant reservations 01 60 30 40 50
➜ www.disneylandparis.com
➜ 1 day single park adult/child €69/62, 1 day both parks €84/77, 2 days both parks €139/126
➜ ⊙hours vary

Disneyland Park

Disneyland Park (⊙10am-11pm May-Sep, to 7pm Oct-Apr, hours can vary) has five themed pays (lands): the 1900s-styled Main Street USA; Frontierland, home of the legendary Big Thunder Mountain ride; Adventureland, which evokes exotic lands in rides like the Pirates of the Caribbean and Indiana Jones and the Temple of Peril; Fantasyland, crowned by Sleeping Beauty's castle; and the high-tech Discoveryland, with massive-queue rides such as Space Mountain: Mission 2 and Buzz Lightyear Laser Blast. Star Wars Land is due to arrive in 2022.

Walt Disney Studios Park

The sound stage, production backlot and animation studios of **Walt Disney Studios Park** (⊙10am-9pm Jun-Sep, to 6pm Oct-May, hours can vary) provide an up-close insight into the production of films, TV programs and cartoons, with behind-the-scenes tours, larger-than-life characters and spine-tingling rides like the Twilight Zone Tower of Terror, as well as the outsized Ratatouille ride, based on the winsome 2007 film about a rat who dreams of becoming a top Parisian chef and offering a multisensory rat's perspective of Paris' rooftops and restaurant kitchens aboard a trackless 'ratmobile'.

Top Disney Tips

➜Crowds peak during European school holidays; visit www.schoolholidayseurope.eu to avoid them if possible.

➜Preplan your day on Disney's website or the excellent www.dlpguide.com, working out which rides, shows etc you really want to see.

➜Buy tickets in advance to avoid the ticket queue.

➜The free Disneyland Paris app provides real-time waiting time for attractions but note that free wi-fi is only available in limited areas within the park.

➜Once in, reserve your time slot on the busiest rides using FastPass, the park's ride-reservation system (limited to one reservation at a time).

➜Disney hotel guests are often entitled to two 'Magic hours' in Disneyland Park (usually from 8am May to October) before opening to the public, although not all rides run during these hours.

Fontainebleau

⊙10am-6pm Mon-Sat, 10am-1pm & 2-5pm Sun May-Oct, 10am-6pm Mon-Sat, 10am-1pm Sun Nov-Apr; 🛜)

Explore

Fresh air fills your lungs on arriving in the smart town of Fontainebleau. It's enveloped by the 200-sq-km Forêt de Fontainebleau, which is as big a playground today as it was in the 16th century, with superb walking and rock-climbing opportunities. The town grew up around its magnificent château, one of the most beautifully decorated and furnished in France. Although it's less crowded and pressured than Versailles, exploring it can still take the best part of a day. You'll also find a cosmopolitan drinking and dining scene, thanks to the town's lifeblood, the international graduate business school INSEAD.

The Best...

➡**Sight** Château de Fontainebleau (p272)
➡**Place to Eat** L'Axel (p270)
➡**Place to Drink** Le Grand Café (p271)

Top Tip

Importantly, train tickets to Fontainebleau/ Avon are sold at Paris' Gare de Lyon's SNCF Transilien counter/Billet Ile-de-France machines, not SNCF mainline counters/ machines. On returning to Paris, tickets include travel to any metro station.

Getting There & Around

➡**Train** Up to 40 daily SNCF Transilien (www.transilien.com) commuter trains link Paris' Gare de Lyon with Fontainebleau/Avon station (€8.85, 35 to 60 minutes).

➡**Bus** Local bus line A links the train station with Château de Fontainebleau (€2), 2km southwest, every 10 minutes; the stop is opposite the main entrance.

➡**Bike A la Petite Reine** (☑01 60 74 57 57; www.alapetitereine.com; 14 rue de la Paroisse; bike hire per hr/day €8/15; ⊙9am-7.30pm Tue-Sat, to 6pm Sun) rents bikes.

Need to Know

➡**Location** 69km southeast of Paris
➡**Tourist Office** (☑01 60 74 99 99; www. fontainebleau-tourisme.com; 4 rue Royale;

SIGHTS

Aside from its monumental château (p272), Fontainebleau's other big draw is the Forêt de Fontainebleau (p272).

🍴 EATING & DRINKING

There are lovely cafe terraces on place Napoléon Bonaparte and some appealing drinking options on rue de la Corne.

DARDONVILLE PATISSERIE, BOULANGERIE €
(www.dardonville-fontainebleau.com; 24 rue des Sablons; ⊙7am-1.30pm & 3.15-7.30pm Tue-Sat, 7am-1.30pm Sun) Melt-in-your-mouth macarons, in flavours like poppy seed and gingerbread, cost just €4.80 per dozen (per dozen!) at this beloved patisserie-*boulangerie* (bakery). Queues also form out the door for its amazing breads.

CRÊPERIE TY KOZ CRÊPERIE €
(☑01 64 22 00 55; www.creperiety-koz.com; 18 rue de la Cloche; crêpes & galettes €3-12.80; ⊙noon-2pm & 7-10pm Tue-Thu, noon-2pm & 7-10.30pm Fri & Sat, noon-2pm Sun) Tucked away in an attractive courtyard, this Breton hidey-hole cooks up authentic sweet crêpes and *simple* (single thickness) and *pourleth* (double thickness) *galettes* (savoury buckwheat crêpes). Wash them down with traditional Val de Rance cider.

★**L'AXEL** GASTRONOMY €€
(☑01 64 22 01 57; www.laxel-restaurant.com; 43 rue de France; 3-/5-/7-course menus €33/55/90; ⊙7.15-9.30pm Wed, 12.15-2pm & 7.15-9.30pm Thu-Sun) Chef Kunihisa Goto has caught the attention of foodies far and wide since opening here, and he's since gained a Michelin star for his astonishing creations incorporating unlikely but ultimately amazing flavour combinations: sea urchin and black-truffle soup; sesame-crusted sweetbreads with langoustines; sea bass with coco beans, Iberian ham and chilli purée; and strawberries with shortbread and green-tea chiffon cake sorbet.

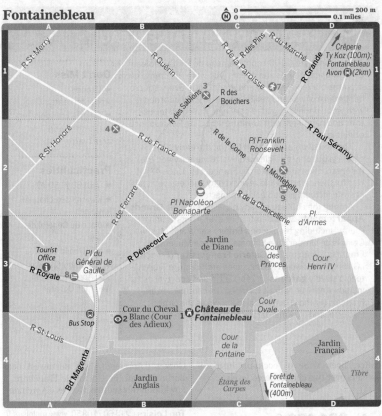

Fontainebleau

DAY TRIPS FROM PARIS FONTAINEBLEAU

LE BISTROT 9
BISTRO €€

(☏01 64 22 87 84; www.lebistrot9.fr; 9 rue Montebello; mains €16-29; ⊙noon-2.30pm & 7-10pm Mon-Thu, noon-2.30pm & 7-11pm Fri & Sat, noon-2.30pm Sun) Fronted by an awning-covered, timber-decked terrace (heated in winter), this locals' favourite has a cheerful red- and yellow-painted, bare-boards interior and delicious specialities including beef tartare, poached salmon in *beurre blanc* (white sauce), *sole meunière* (floured, fried sole served with butter sauce and lemon) and profiteroles for dessert, as well as oysters in season. Great value and lively vibe.

LE GRAND CAFÉ
CAFE

(http://legrandcafefontainebleau.fr; 33 place Napoléon Bonaparte; ⊙8am-midnight) In a dress-circle position on place Napoléon Bonaparte, this true-to-its-name cafe offers some of Fontainebleau's best people-watching from the huge terrace over a

TOP SIGHT
CHÂTEAU DE FONTAINEBLEAU

The resplendent, 1900-room Château de Fontainebleau once housed tenants and guests who were the crème de la crème of French royalty and aristocracy. Every square centimetre of wall and ceiling space is richly adorned with wood panelling, gilded carvings, frescoes, tapestries and paintings, with furniture including Renaissance originals.

The first château was built here in the early 12th century, but only a single medieval tower survived the reconstruction undertaken by François I (r 1515–47). It was further enlarged and reworked by successive heads of state including Napoléon Bonaparte.

Among the château's many highlights are the **Grands Appartements**, which embrace several outstanding rooms, including the Second Empire salon and Musée Chinois de l'Impératice Eugénie (Chinese Museum of Empress Eugénie). The **Galerie François 1er** (François I Gallery) is a jewel of Renaissance architecture. The château's stately **gardens** (⏲24hr) FREE and courtyards include André Le Nôtre's formal, 17th-century Jardin Français (French Garden), also known as the Grand Parterre, and informal Jardin Anglais (English Garden).

Don't Miss
→ Grands Appartements
→ Galerie François 1er
→ Gardens and courtyards

Practicalities
→ ✆01 60 71 50 70
→ www.musee-chateau-fontainebleau.fr
→ place du Général de Gaulle
→ adult/child €11/free
→ ⏲9.30am-6pm Wed-Mon Apr-Sep, to 5pm Wed-Mon Oct-Mar

---

coffee, beer, wine or cocktail. Inside it spreads over two chandeliered levels.

🏃 SPORTS & ACTIVITIES

Beginning just 500m south of the château and surrounding the town, the 200-sq-km **Forêt de Fontainebleau** (Fontainebleau Forest) is one of the prettiest woods in the region. The many trails – including parts of the GR1 and GR11 – are excellent for jogging, walking, cycling and horse riding; Fontainebleau's tourist office stocks maps and guides.

Rock-climbing enthusiasts have long come to the forest's sandstone ridges, rich in cliffs and overhangs, to hone their skills before setting off for the Alps. There are different grades marked by colours, starting with white ones, which are suitable for children, and going up to death-defying black boulders. The website Bleau.info (http://bleau.info) has stacks of information in English on climbing in Fontainebleau. Two gorges worth visiting are the

Gorges d'Apremont, 7km northwest near Barbizon, and the Gorges de Franchard, a few kilometres south of Gorges d'Apremont. If you want to give climbing a go, contact **Top Loisirs** (✆01 60 74 08 50; www.toploisirs.fr; 1 rue de Montchavant, Ecuelles; ⏲9am-6pm, hrs can vary) about equipment hire and instruction; pick-ups in Fontainebleau are possible by arrangement. The tourist office also sells comprehensive climbing guides.

🛏 SLEEPING

LA GUÉRINIÈRE
B&B €

(✆06 13 50 50 37; balestier.gerard@wanadoo.fr; 10 rue Montebello; d incl breakfast €70, f €100; @🛜🅿) This charming B&B provides some of the best-value accommodation in town. Owner Monsieur Balestier speaks English and has five en suite rooms, each named after a different flower and dressed in white linens and period furniture; some have wooden beams. Breakfast includes homemade jam and zesty marmalade. Two family rooms are available.

HÔTEL DE LONDRES HOTEL €€
(☎01 64 22 20 21; www.hoteldelondres.com; 1 place du Général de Gaulle; d €132-188; ✵ @ ⑤) Classy, cosy and beautifully kept, the 16-room 'Hotel London' is furnished in warm reds and royal blues. The priciest rooms (eg room 5) have balconies with dreamy château views. Breakfast is €16.

Chartres

Explore

Step off the train in Chartres and the two very different steeples – one Gothic, the other Romanesque – of its glorious 13th-century cathedral loom above. Follow them to check out the cathedral's dazzling blue stained-glass windows and its collection of relics, including the Sainte Voile (Holy Veil) said to have been worn by the Virgin Mary when she gave birth to Jesus, which have lured pilgrims since the Middle Ages.

After visiting the town's museums, don't miss a stroll around Chartres' carefully preserved old city. Adjacent to the cathedral, staircases and steep streets lined with half-timbered medieval houses lead downhill to the narrow western channel of the Eure River, romantically spanned by footbridges.

The Best...
➡**Sight** Cathédrale Notre Dame (p273)
➡**Place to Eat** Le Tripot (p274)
➡**Place to Drink** La Chocolaterie (p274)

Top Tip
Allow 1½ to two hours to walk the signposted *circuit touristique* (tourist circuit) taking in Chartres' key sights. Free town maps from the tourist office also mark the route.

Getting There & Away
➡**Train** Frequent SNCF trains link Paris' Gare Montparnasse (€16, 55 to 70 minutes) with Chartres, some of which stop at Versailles-Chantiers (€13.50, 45 to 60 minutes). The bus station is next to the train station.

TOP SIGHT
CATHÉDRALE NOTRE DAME

France's best-preserved medieval cathedral was built in Gothic style during the early 13th century to replace a Romanesque cathedral devastated by fire in 1194. Construction took just 30 years, resulting in a high degree of architectural unity.

Covering 2.6 sq km, the cathedral's 176 stained-glass windows are mostly 13th-century originals. Three over the west entrance, dating from 1150, are renowned for their brilliant 'Chartres blue' tones.

The 105m-high Clocher Vieux (Old Bell Tower) is the tallest Romanesque steeple still standing. The 112m-high Clocher Neuf (New Bell Tower; adult/child €7.50/free; ⊙9.30am-12.30pm & 2-6pm Mon-Sat, 2-6pm Sun May-Aug, 9.30am-12.30pm & 2-5pm Mon-Sat, 2-5pm Sun Sep-Apr) justifies the spiralling 350-step climb.

Look out for the Sainte Voile (Holy Veil), in Chartres since 876.

French-language tours of the 110m-long **crypt** (adult/child €3/2.40; ⊙up to 5 tours daily) – France's largest – run year-round. There are also seasonal **English-language guided tours** (☎02 37 28 15 58; millerchartres@aol.com; tours €10; ⊙noon & 2.45pm Mon-Sat Apr-Oct, noon Sat Nov-Mar) of the cathedral.

Don't Miss
➡ Stained glass
➡ Clocher Neuf
➡ Sainte Voile
➡ Crypt

Practicalities
➡ www.cathedrale-chartres.org
➡ place de la Cathédrale
➡ ⊙8.30am-7.30pm daily year-round, also to 10pm Tue, Fri & Sun Jun-Aug

Need to Know

➡**Location** 91km southwest of Paris

➡**Tourist Office** (📱02 37 18 26 26; www.chartres-tourisme.com; 8-10 rue de la Poissonnerie; ⏰10am-6pm Mon-Sat, to 5pm Sun)

 SIGHTS

Chartres' beautiful medieval old city is northeast and east of the cathedral. Highlights include the 12th-century Collégiale St-André (place St-André), a Romanesque church that's now an exhibition centre; rue de la Tannerie and its extension rue de la Foulerie, lined with flower gardens, mill-races and the restored remnants of riverside trades: wash houses, tanneries and the like; and rue des Écuyers, with many structures dating from around the 16th century.

 EATING

Food shops surround the **covered market** (place Billard; ⏰7am-1pm Wed & Sat), just off rue des Changes south of the cathedral. The cafes facing the cathedral are touristy but drinks here come with great views.

LA CHOCOLATERIE   PATISSERIE €
(www.lachocolaterie-chartres.com; 2 place du Cygne; dishes €3.80-5.50; ⏰8am-7.30pm Tue-Sat, 10am-7.30pm Sun & Mon) Soak up local life overlooking the open-air **flower market** (place du Cygne; ⏰8am-1pm Tue, Thu & Sat). This tearoom/patisserie's hot chocolate and macarons (flavoured with orange, apricot, peanut, pineapple and so on) are sublime, as are its sweet homemade crêpes and miniature madeleine cakes.

★LE TRIPOT   BISTRO €€
(📱02 37 36 60 11; http://letripot.wix.com; 11 place Jean Moulin; 2-/3-course lunch menus €15/18, 3-course dinner menus €29.50-45, mains €13.50-22; ⏰noon-1.45pm & 7.30-9.15pm Tue & Thu-Sat, noon-1.45pm Sun) Tucked off the tourist trail and easy to miss, even if you do chance down its narrow street, this atmospheric space with low beamed ceilings is a treat for authentic and adventurous French fare like saddle of rabbit stuffed with snails, and grilled turbot in truffled hollandaise sauce. Locals are onto it, so booking ahead is advised.

LES FEUILLANTINES   MODERN FRENCH €€
(📱02 37 30 22 21; 4 rue du Bourg; menus €23.50-33.50, mains €19-22; ⏰noon-1.30pm & 7-9.30pm Tue-Sat) Take a seat in the sleek interior or under a market umbrella in the rear courtyard to dine on superb dishes such as sea bream with potatoes and tomato emulsion, bacon-wrapped veal with lentils, roast duck with butternut squash and cider jus, before finishing with its house-speciality chocolate sphere served with orange sorbet and sweet Chantilly cream.

L'ESCALIER   BISTRO €€
(📱02 37 33 05 45; 1 rue du Bourg; 2-/3-course menus €18/22; ⏰noon-3pm & 7-10pm; 📞) On a steep corner near its namesake staircase in Chartres' hilly old city, this deceptively large, very local restaurant has a wonderful terrace for summertime dining and is worth the pre- or postmeal climb for its short but superb menu (succulent steaks and classic desserts like crème caramel). Look out for live jazz performances.

LE SAINT-HILAIRE   MODERN FRENCH €€
(📱02 37 30 97 57; www.restaurant-saint-hilaire.fr; 11 rue du Pont St-Hilaire; 3-course menus €29.50-49; ⏰noon-2pm & 7-9.30pm Tue-Sat) At this pistachio-painted, wood-beamed charmer, local products are ingeniously used in dishes such as scallops in hazelnut and foie gras sauce. Don't miss its lobster menu in season, or the aromatic cheese platters any time of year. A two-course lunch menu from Tuesday to Friday costs €19.

🛏 **SLEEPING**

HÔTEL DU BŒUF COURONNÉ   HOTEL €€
(📱02 37 18 06 06; www.leboeufcouronne.com; 15 place Châtelet; s €57-96, d €67-121; 📞) The red-curtained entrance lends a theatrical air to this two-star Logis guesthouse in the centre of everything. Its summertime terrace restaurant has cathedral-view dining and the XV bar mixes great cocktails.

TIMHOTEL CHARTRES CATHÉDRALE   HOTEL €€
(📱02 37 21 78 00; www.timhotel.com; 6-8 av Jehan de Beauce; d/f from €120/168; 🅿❄🛜🚻) A bullseye location footsteps from the ca-

Chartres

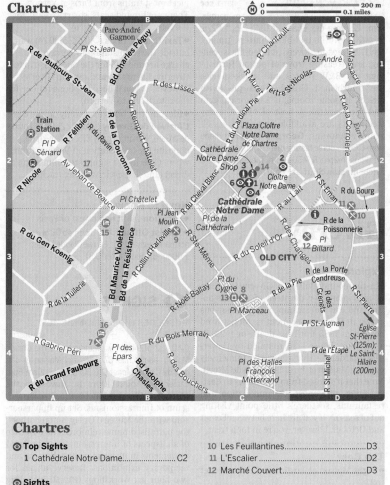

N 0 ————— 200 m
   0 ————— 0.1 miles

Chartres

◎ Top Sights
1 Cathédrale Notre Dame	C2

◎ Sights
2 Cathédrale Notre Dame Crypt	C2
3 Clocher Neuf	C2
4 Clocher Vieux	C2
5 Collégiale St-André	D1
6 Portail Royal	C2

⊗ Eating
7 Georges	A4
8 La Chocolaterie	C3
9 Le Tripot	B3

10 Les Feuillantines	D3
11 L'Escalier	D2
12 Marché Couvert	D3

🔒 Shopping
13 Flower Market	C3

🟢 Sports & Activities
14 Cathédrale Notre Dame Tours	C2

🛏 Sleeping
15 Hôtel du Bœuf Couronné	B3
16 Le Grand Monarque	B4
17 Timhotel Chartres Cathédrale	A2

thedral and train station, 48 unique rooms (some with cathedral views) and on-site parking make this hotel – part of a small French chain – a winning trifecta. Staff are welcoming, rooms are spacious and there's a small, private rear terrace. Breakfast costs €15. Rates are up to 50% cheaper on the hotel's website.

Several family rooms and baby cots are available.

LE GRAND MONARQUE   HOTEL **€€€**

(02 37 18 15 15; www.bw-grand-monarque. com; 22 place des Épars; d €145-215, f €275; ❄ ＠ ✆) With its teal-blue shutters gracing its 1779 facade, lovely stained-glass ceiling, and treasure trove of period furnishings, old B&W photos and knick-knacks, the refurbished Grand Monarque (with air-con in some rooms) is a historical gem and very central. A host of hydrotherapy treatments are available at its spa. Its elegant restaurant, **Georges** (4-course menu from €75, 8-course tasting menu €95, mains €38-41; ⊘noon-2pm & 7.30-10pm Tue-Sat), has a Michelin star. Staff are charming.

Giverny

Explore

The tiny country village of Giverny is a place of pilgrimage for devotees of impressionism, and can feel swamped by the tour-bus crowd in the summer months. Monet lived here from 1883 until his death in 1926, in a rambling house – surrounded by flower-filled gardens – that's now the immensely popular Maison et Jardins de Claude Monet. Note that it's closed from November to Easter, along with most accommodation and restaurants, so there's little point visiting out of season. If you are here between Easter and October, however, you're in for a treat.

The Best

➡**Sight** Maison et Jardins de Claude Monet (p276)

➡**Place to Paint** Musée des Impressionnismes Giverny (p277)

➡**Place to Eat** Le Jardin des Plumes (p277)

Top Tip

Be aware that the village has no public toilets, ATMs or bureaux de change.

Getting There & Away

➡**Train** From Paris' Gare St-Lazare there are up to 15 daily trains to Vernon (€14.70, 45 minutes to one hour), 7km to the west of Giverny.

➡**Bus** Shuttle buses (€8 return, 20 minutes, four daily Easter to October)

meet most trains from Paris at Vernon. There are limited seats, so arrive early for the return trip from Giverny.

➡**Taxi** Usually **Taxis** (02 32 51 10 24) wait outside the train station in Vernon and charge around €15 for the one-way trip to Giverny. There's no taxi rank in Giverny, however, so you'll need to phone for one for the return trip to Vernon.

➡**Bicycle** Rent bikes (cash only) at the **Café L'Arrivée de Giverny** (02 32 21 16 01; 1 place de la Gare, Vernon; per day €15; ⊘7am-11pm), opposite the train station in Vernon, from where Giverny is a signposted 5km along a direct (and flat) cycle/walking track.

Need to Know

➡**Location** 74km northwest of Paris

➡**Tourist Office** (02 32 64 45 01; www. normandie-giverny.fr; 80 rue Claude Monet; ⊘10am-5.45pm Easter-Oct)

SIGHTS

MUSÉE DES IMPRESSIONNISMES GIVERNY   ART MUSEUM

(02 32 51 94 65; www.mdig.fr; 99 rue Claude Monet; adult/child €7/4.50, incl Maison et Jardins de Claude Monet €16.50/8.50; ⊘10am-6pm Easter-Oct) About 100m northwest of the Maison de Claude Monet is the Giverny Museum of Impressionisms. Set up in partnership with the Musée d'Orsay, among others, the pluralised name reinforces its coverage of all aspects of impressionism and related movements in its permanent collection and temporary exhibitions. Reserve ahead for two-hour art workshops (€12.50 including materials) offering an introduction to watercolour, drawing, sketching or pastels. Lectures, readings, concerts and documentaries also take place regularly.

✗ EATING

Advance reservations are always a good idea from April to October due to the limited number of eateries.

★**LE JARDIN DES PLUMES**   MODERN FRENCH **€€€**

(02 32 54 26 35; www.jardindesplumes.fr; 1 rue du Milieu; 3-course/tasting menu €48/75,

TOP SIGHT
MAISON ET JARDINS DE CLAUDE MONET

The prized drawcard of tiny Giverny is the home and flower-filled garden of the seminal impressionist painter and his family from 1883 to 1926. Here Monet painted some of his most famous series, including *Décorations des Nymphéas* (Water Lilies).

Monet's hectare of land encompasses two distinct areas, cut by the Chemin du Roy but linked by a foot tunnel.

The artist's pastel-pink house and Water Lily studio stand on the periphery of the Clos Normand, with its symmetrically laid-out gardens bursting with flowers.

Monet bought the Jardin d'Eau (Water Garden) in 1895 and set about creating his trademark lily pond, as well as the famous Japanese bridge (since rebuilt). Draped with purple wisteria, the bridge blends into the asymmetrical foreground and background, creating the intimate atmosphere for which the 'painter of light' was renowned. The charmingly preserved house and beautiful bloom-filled gardens are the attractions here.

Combined tickets with Paris' **Musée Marmottan Monet** (p88) per adult/child cost €20.50/12, and combined adult tickets with Paris' Musée de l'Orangerie (p118) cost €18.50.

Don't Miss
➡ Clos Normand
➡ Jardin d'Eau

Practicalities
➡ ☏02 32 51 28 21
➡ http://fondation-monet.com
➡ 84 rue Claude Monet
➡ adult/child €9.50/5.50, incl Musée des Impressionnismes Giverny €16.50/8.50
➡ ⊙9.30am-6pm Easter-Oct

mains €32-48; ⊙12.15-1.45pm & 7.15-9pm Wed-Sun, hotel closed Mon & Tue Nov-Mar; 🛜🍴) This gorgeous sky-blue-trimmed property's airy white dining room sets the stage for chef Eric Guerin's exquisite, inventive and Michelin-starred cuisine, which justifies the trip from Paris alone.

It also has four rooms (€180 to €200) and four suites (€290 to €350) that combine vintage and contemporary furnishings. It's less than 10 minutes' walk to the Maison et Jardins de Claude Monet.

Little gourmands can get a three-course children's menu for €22.

🛌 SLEEPING

LA MUSARDIÈRE
HOTEL €€

(☏02 32 21 03 18; www.lamusardiere.fr; 123 rue Claude Monet; d €85-99, tr €125-149, f €149, 3-course menus €26-36; ⊙hotel Feb–mid-Dec, restaurant noon-10pm Apr-Oct; 🅿🛜🍴) This two-star 10-room hotel dating back to 1880 and evocatively called the 'Idler' is set amid a lovely garden less than 100m northeast

of the Maison et Jardins de Claude Monet. Breakfast costs €11. In season, savouring a crêpe in its restaurant is a pleasure. Family rooms sleep three or four people.

LA PLUIE DE ROSES
B&B €€

(☏02 32 51 10 67; www.givernylapluiederoses.fr; 14 rue Claude Monet; s/d/tr/f €120/135/193/251; 🅿🛜🍴) You'll be won over by this adorable private home cocooned in a dreamy, peaceful garden. Inside, the three rooms (two of which can accommodate families) are so comfy it's hard to wake up. Superb breakfast on a verandah awash with sunlight. Payment is by cash only.

LE CLOS FLEURI
B&B €€

(☏02 32 21 36 51; www.giverny-leclosfleuri.fr; 5 rue de la Dîme; s/d €93/98; ⊙Apr-Oct; 🅿🛜) Big rooms with king-size beds and exposed wood beams overlook the hedged gardens of this delightful B&B within strolling distance of the Maison et Jardins de Claude Monet. Each of its three rooms is named after a different flower; green-thumbed host Danielle speaks fluent English. Cash only.

Sleeping

Paris has a wealth of accommodation for all budgets, but it's often complet *(full) well in advance. Reservations are recommended year-round and essential during the warmer months (April to October) and all public and school holidays.*

Hotels

Hotels in Paris are inspected by government authorities and classified into six categories, from no star to five stars. The vast majority are two- and three-star hotels, which are generally well equipped. All hotels must display their rates, including TVA (*taxe sur la valeur ajoutée;* valued-added tax), though you'll often get *much* cheaper prices online, especially on the hotels' own websites, which invariably offer the best deals.

Parisian hotel rooms tend to be small by international standards. Families will probably need connecting rooms but if children are too young to stay in their own room, it's possible to make do with triples, quads or suites in some places.

Cheaper hotels may not have lifts/elevators and/or air-conditioning. Some don't accept credit cards.

Breakfast is rarely included in hotel rates; heading to a cafe often works out to be better value (and more atmospheric).

Hostels

Paris is awash with hostels, and standards are consistently improving. A wave of state-of-the-art hostels have recently opened their doors, such as the design-savvy 950-bed 'megahostel' by leading hostel chain Generator near Canal St-Martin, 10e, and, close by, two by the switched-on St Christopher's group.

Some of the more traditional (ie institutional) hostels have daytime lock-outs and curfews; some have a maximum three-night stay. Places that have upper age limits tend not to enforce them except at the busiest of times. Only the official *auberges de jeunesse* (youth hostels) require guests to present Hostelling International (HI) cards or their equivalent.

Not all hostels have self-catering kitchens but rates generally include basic breakfast.

B&Bs & Homestays

Bed-and-breakfast (B&B) accommodation (*chambres d'hôte* in French) is increasingly popular.

The city of Paris runs a scheme called **Paris Quality Hosts** (Hôtes Qualité Paris; www.hotesqualiteparis.fr), which fosters B&Bs, in part to ease the isolation of Parisians, some half of whom live alone. There's often a minimum stay of three or four nights.

Apartments

Families – and anyone wanting to self-cater – should consider renting a short-stay apartment. Paris has a number of excellent apartment hotels, such as the international chain Apart'hotels Citadines (www.citadines.com).

For an even more authentic Parisian experience, websites offer entire private apartments, some in unique locations such as houseboats. Rental agencies also list furnished residential apartments for stays of a few days to several months. Apartments often include facilities such as wi-fi and washing machines, and can be good value. Beware of direct-rental scams (above all, never send money via an untraceable money transfer).

Lonely Planet's Top Choices

Grand Amour Hôtel (p284) Hipster lifestyle hotel in the up-and-coming 10e.

Hôtel Providence (p284) Clandestine boutique hotel with bespoke in-room cocktail bars.

Edgar (p282) Twelve individually themed rooms, each by a different artist or designer.

L'Hôtel (p291) The stuff of romance, Parisian myths and urban legends.

Le Citizen Hotel (p285) Modern and tech-savvy, with a warm minimalist design.

Hôtel Henriette (p292) Unique rooms filled with vintage flea-market treasures.

Best by Budget

€

Cosmos Hôtel (p286) Cheap, brilliant value and footsteps from the nightlife of Le Marais' rue JPT.

Hôtel du Nord – Le Pari Vélo (p284) Bric-a-brac charm and bikes on loan.

Mama Shelter (p288) Philippe Starck–designed hipster haven with a cool in-house pizzeria.

Hôtel St-André des Arts (p290) Old-school charm in St-Germain's beating heart.

€€

Hôtel Exquis (p288) Surrealist design hotel east of Bastille.

Hôtel Amour (p285) Stylish choice for a romantic getaway.

Familia Hôtel (p289) Sepia murals and flower-bedecked balconies in the Latin Quarter.

Hôtel Jeanne d'Arc (p287) Gorgeous, like a family home in a quiet Marais backstreet.

€€€

Les Bains (p288) Nineteenth-century thermal baths turned nightclub, turned rockstar-hot lifestyle hotel.

Hôtel Molitor (p281) Stunningly restored art deco swimming pool with gallery-style poolside rooms.

Hôtel Crayon (p282) Line drawings, retro furnishings and coloured-glass shower doors.

Hôtel du Jeu de Paume (p289) Romantic haven on the serene Île St-Louis.

Best Historic Hotels

Hôtel Particulier Montmartre (p285) Designer suites in an elegant 19th-century mansion with walled garden in Montmartre.

Hôtel St-Merry (p282) Medieval charm in a former presbytery.

La Maison Favart (p283) Art nouveau elegance taking you back to the belle époque.

Hôtel d'Angleterre (p291) Exquisite former embassy hosting seminal guests.

Best Design Hotels

Joke Hôtel (p284) Playful childhood-themed hotel with a wheel of fortune behind the bed to spin.

Le Pigalle (p284) Channels the hipster spirit of Pigalle with vinyl and vintage turntables in some rooms.

Hôtel Joséphine (p284) Inspired by cabaret star Josephine Baker, with complimentary absinthe cocktails.

Grand Amour Hôtel (p284) All you need is love at this risqué hideaway.

Off Paris Seine (p292) Paris' first, fabulous floating hotel has docked.

NEED TO KNOW

Price Ranges
The following price ranges refer to a double room with en suite bathroom in high season (breakfast not included).

€	less than €130
€€	€130–250
€€€	over €250

Taxe de Séjour
The city of Paris levies a *taxe de séjour* (tourist tax) per person per night on all accommodation:
➡ Palaces (and similar): €4.40
➡ 5 stars: €3.30
➡ 4 stars €2.48
➡ 3 stars €1.65
➡ 2 stars: €0.99
➡ 1 star & B&Bs: €0.83
➡ Unrated/unclassified: €0.83
➡ 3- to 5-star campgrounds: € 0.61
➡ 1- and 2-star campgrounds and marinas: €0.22

Internet Access
Wi-fi (pronounced wee-fee in French) is virtually always free of charge at hotels and hostels. You may find that in some hotels, especially older ones, the higher the floor, the less reliable the wi-fi connection.

Smoking
Smoking is officially banned in all Paris hotels.

Where to Stay

NEIGHBOURHOOD	FOR	AGAINST
EIFFEL TOWER & WESTERN PARIS	Close to Paris' iconic tower and museums. Upmarket area with quiet residential streets.	Short on budget and midrange accommodation. Limited nightlife.
CHAMPS-ÉLYSÉES & GRANDS BOULEVARDS	Luxury hotels, famous boutiques and department stores, gastronomic restaurants, great nightlife.	Some areas extremely pricey. Nightlife hot spots can be noisy.
LOUVRE & LES HALLES	Epicentral location, excellent transport links, major museums, shopping galore.	Not many bargains. Noise can be an issue in some areas.
MONTMARTRE & NORTHERN PARIS	Village atmosphere and some lively multicultural areas. Many places have views across Paris.	Hilly streets, further out than some areas, some parts very touristy. The red-light district around Pigalle, although well lit and safe, won't appeal to all travellers.
LE MARAIS, MÉNILMONTANT & BELLEVILLE	Buzzing nightlife, hip shopping, fantastic eating options in all price ranges. Excellent museums. Lively gay and lesbian scene. Busier on Sundays than most areas. Very central.	Can be seriously noisy in areas where bars and clubs are concentrated.
BASTILLE & EASTERN PARIS	Few tourists, allowing you to see the 'real' Paris up close. Excellent markets, loads of nightlife options.	Some areas slightly out of the way.
THE ISLANDS	As geographically central as it gets. Accommodation centred on the peaceful, romantic Île St-Louis.	No metro station on the Île St-Louis. Limited self-catering shops, minimal nightlife.
LATIN QUARTER	Energetic student area, stacks of eating and drinking options, late-opening bookshops.	Popularity with students and visiting academics makes rooms hardest to find during conferences and seminars from March to June and in October.
ST-GERMAIN & LES INVALIDES	Stylish, central location, superb shopping, sophisticated dining, proximity to the Jardin du Luxembourg.	Budget accommodation is seriously short-changed.
MONTPARNASSE & SOUTHERN PARIS	Good value, few tourists, excellent links to both major airports.	Some areas out of the way and/ or not well served by metro.

⊨ Eiffel Tower & Western Paris

★HÔTEL FÉLICIEN BOUTIQUE HOTEL €€€

Map p366 (☑01 55 74 00 00; www.hotelfelicien
paris.com; 21 rue Félicien David, 16e; d €280-330,
ste from €470; ❋@🖥; MMirabeau) The price–
quality ratio at this chic boutique hotel, squirrelled away in a 1930s building, is outstanding. Exquisitely designed rooms feel more
five-star than four, with 'White' and 'Silver'
suites on the hotel's top 'Sky floor' more than
satisfying their promise of indulgent cocooning. Romantics, eat your heart out.

HÔTEL MOLITOR HISTORIC HOTEL €€€

Map p366 (☑01 56 07 08 67; www.mltr.fr; 2 av de
la porte Molitor, 16e; d from €490, ste €560-750;
❋@🖥🏊♿; MMichel Ange Molitor) Famed as
Paris' swishest swimming pool in the 1930s
(where the bikini made its first appearance,
no less) and a hot spot for graffiti art in the
1990s, the Molitor is one seriously legendary address. The art deco complex, built in
1929 and abandoned from 1989, has been
restored to stunning effect.

All 124 hotel rooms are arranged gallery-
style in a U shape overlooking the outdoor
pool (heated year-round). The rooftop cocktail bar, restaurant by Yannick Alléno, and
original changing cabins transformed into
contemporary artworks sign off the dramatic ensemble. A smaller indoor 'winter'
pool is also on the premises. Prices can
drop by half in low season.

⊨ Champs-Élysées & Grands Boulevards

HÔTEL FRANCE ALBION HOTEL €

Map p370 (☑01 45 26 00 81; www.albion-paris-
hotel.com; 11 rue Notre Dame de Lorette, 9e; s/d/q
from €107/127/227; ❋🖥; MSt-Georges) For the
quietest night's sleep, go for a room facing
the courtyard of this neat-as-a-pin budget
hotel. Its rooms all have private bathrooms
and, for Paris, are decently sized (doubles
from 14 sq metres), and staff are eager to
please. The location, near Opéra, is excellent.

HÔTEL MONTE CARLO HOTEL €

Map p370 (☑01 47 70 36 75; www.hotelmontecarlo.
fr; 44 rue du Faubourg Montmartre, 9e; s €88, d
€130-140, tr €176; 🖥; MLe Peletier) A unique
budget hotel, the Monte Carlo is a fabulous

deal, with 20 colourful, personalised rooms
and a great neighbourhood location. The
cheaper rooms don't have private bathroom
facilities, but overall it outclasses many of
the other choices in its price range. Prices
for a double drop below €100 out of season.

HOTEL ALISON HOTEL €€

Map p368 (☑01 42 65 54 00; www.hotelalison.
com; 21 rue de Surène, 8e; s €108, d €133-189, q
€264; ❋@🖥; MMadeleine) A pleasant surprise, this quiet hotel is a bargain just steps
from place de la Madeleine, the Champs-
Élysées and – in the event you've got an
early morning rendezvous with the *chef
d'état* (head of state) – the presidential palace. Rooms are bright and modern, though
they are on the petite side.

HÔTEL JOYCE DESIGN HOTEL €€

Map p370 (☑01 55 07 00 01; www.astotel.com;
29 rue la Bruyère, 9e; d €200-235; ❋@🖥; MSt-
Georges) 🌿 Located in a lovely residential
area between Montmartre and Opéra, this
place has all the modern design touches
(iPod docks, individually styled rooms, a
skylit breakfast room fitted out with old
Range Rover seats) and makes some ecofriendly claims – it relies on 50% renewable
energy and uses organic products.

HIDDEN HOTEL BOUTIQUE HOTEL €€€

Map p368 (☑01 40 55 03 57; www.hidden-hotel.
com; 28 rue de l'Arc de Triomphe, 17e; d €389-
454; ❋@🖥; MCharles de Gaulle–Étoile) 🌿 The
Hidden is one of the Champs-Élysées' best
secrets. It's serene, stylish, reasonably spacious, and it even sports green credentials:
the earth-coloured tones are the result of
natural pigments (no paint), and all rooms
feature handmade wooden furniture, stone
basins and linen curtains surrounding the
beds. The queen-size Emotion rooms are
among the most popular.

⊨ Louvre & Les Halles

HÔTEL TIQUETONNE HOTEL €

Map p376 (☑01 42 36 94 58; www.hoteltique
tonne.fr; 6 rue Tiquetonne, 2e; d €80, without
shower €65; 🖥; MÉtienne Marcel) What heart-
warmingly good value this 45-room chea-
pie is. This serious, well-tended address has
been in the hotel biz since the 1900s and is
much loved by a loyal clientele of all ages.
Rooms range across seven floors, are spick
and span, and sport an inoffensive mix of

vintage decor – roughly 1930s to 1980s, with brand-new bathrooms and parquet flooring in recently renovated rooms.

Ask for a room in the rooftops with a view of the Sacré-Cœur (701, 702 or 703) or Eiffel Tower (704 and 705)! Shared shower *jetons* (tokens) cost €5; ask at reception.

HÔTEL VIVIENNE
HOTEL €

Map p372 (☑01 42 33 13 26; www.hotel-vivienne. com; 40 rue Vivienne, 2e; d €100-150, tr & q €200; @🛜; MGrands Boulevards) This refurbished two-star hotel is amazingly good value for Paris. While the 45 rooms are not huge, they have all the mod cons; some even boast little balconies. Family rooms accommodate up to two children on a sofa bed.

★EDGAR
BOUTIQUE HOTEL €€

Map p376 (☑01 40 41 05 19; www.edgarparis. com; 31 rue d'Alexandrie, 2e; d €235-295; ✳🛜; MStrasbourg St-Denis) Twelve playful rooms, each decorated by a different team of artists or designers, await the lucky few who secure a reservation at this former convent/ seamstress workshop. Milagros conjures up all the magic of the Far West, while Dream echoes the rich imagination of childhood with surreal installations. Breakfast is served in the popular downstairs restaurant, and the hidden tree-shaded square is a fabulous location.

★HÔTEL CRAYON
BOUTIQUE HOTEL €€

Map p376 (☑01 42 36 54 19; www.hotelcrayon. com; 25 rue du Bouloi, 1er; s/d €203/229; ✳🛜; MLes Halles, Sentier) Line drawings by French artist Julie Gauthron bedeck walls and doors at this creative boutique hotel. The pencil *(le crayon)* is the theme, with 26 rooms sporting a different shade of each floor's chosen colour – we love the coloured-glass shower doors, and the books on the bedside table guests can swap and take home. Online deals often slash rates by up to 50%.

Beautiful pieces of 1950s and 1960s flea-market furniture add a dash of retro, and doodling on the walls is a unique perk for guests sleeping in the dazzling white-and-silver suite. Pick which fragrance you'd like your room perfumed with, help yourself to coffee or grab a drink from the fridge, and make yourself at home. *Quel bonheur!*

HÔTEL DU CONTINENT
DESIGN HOTEL €€

Map p372 (☑01 42 60 75 32; www.hotelcontinent. com; 30 rue du Mont-Thabor, 1er; s/d €187/277; ✳🛜; MConcorde) For a hotel designed by Christian Lacroix and located a block from the Jardin des Tuileries, this globetrotter's pick is a reasonable deal. Granted, rooms facing the street can be slightly noisy, but the colorful motifs and themed floors (each is dedicated to a particular continent or pole) will add a bit of *haute-couture* mystique to your stay.

HÔTEL ODYSSEY
BOUTIQUE HOTEL €€

Map p376 (☑01 42 36 04 02; http://hotelodyssey paris.com; 19 rue Hérold, 1er; r €229-288; ✳🛜; MSentier, Bourse) A futuristic refuge from the busy Paris streets, Hôtel Odyssey makes use of clever design to maximise small spaces. French designer Ora-Ito echoes the natural world with elegant curves and simple, ecofriendly materials, such as felt, oak and cork. Choose from one of three styles of room: Cocoon, Odyssey or the deluxe Galileo.

LE RELAIS DU LOUVRE
BOUTIQUE HOTEL €€

Map p376 (☑01 40 41 96 42; www.relaisdulouvre. com; 19 rue des Prêtres St-Germain l'Auxerrois, 1er; s €175, d €230-260, tr €260; ✳🛜; MPont Neuf) If you like style in a traditional sense, choose this lovely 21-room hotel just west of the Louvre and across the street from Église St-Germain l'Auxerrois with its melodious chime of bells. The nine rooms facing the street and church are petite, while room 2 has access to the garden.

HÔTEL ST-MERRY
HISTORIC HOTEL €€

Map p376 (☑01 42 78 14 15; www.saintmerry marais.com; 78 rue de la Verrerie, 4e; d €180-240, tr €286; ✳🛜; MChâtelet) The interior of this 12-room hostelry, with beamed ceilings, church pews and wrought-iron candelabra, is a neo-Goth's wet dream; you have to see the architectural elements of room 9 (flying buttress over the bed) and the furnishings of room 12 (choir-stall bed board) to believe them.

On the downside there is no lift connecting the postage-stamp lobby with the four upper floors, and not all rooms have air-con.

LE PRADEY
DESIGN HOTEL €€€

Map p372 (☑01 42 60 31 70; www.lepradey.com; 5 rue St-Roch, 1er; d €330-490; ✳@🛜; MTuileries) Enviably secreted behind the Louvre and Jardin des Tuileries on boutique-smart rue St-Honoré, this exclusive address is the last word in luxury hotel design. Guests linger over glossy art books in the understatedly chic mezzanine lounge – if they can drag themselves away from whichever individually themed suite they are staying in.

Exuberant Cabaret evokes the theatrical glamour of the Moulin Rouge with its frilly skirt bedspread, deep red walls and heart-shaped doorframe; while Opéra, elegantly dressed in pretty pinks and greys, treats guests to a magical night at the ballet.

LA MAISON FAVART
HISTORIC HOTEL €€€

Map p372 (☎01 42 97 59 83; www.lamaison favart.fr; 5 rue de Marivaux, 2e; d €370-500; ✳🐾🚭; MRichelieu Drouot) This peaceful art nouveau hotel facing the Opéra Comique feels like it never let go of the belle époque. It's an excellent choice if you're interested in shopping, and is within easy walking distance of the *grands magasins* (department stores) on bd Haussmann. Goya slept here in 1824. A small spa and pool are in the basement.

🛏 Montmartre & Northern Paris

⭐GENERATOR HOSTEL
HOSTEL €

Map p382 (☎01 70 98 84 00; www.generator hostels.com; 11 place du Colonel Fabien, 10e; dm €23-42, d €112-218; ✳ @ 🚭; MColonel Fabien) A short walk from the water, this buzzing hostel is a shout-out to design, street art and French *art de vivre* (art of living). From the stylish ground-floor cafe-restaurant and 9th-floor rooftop bar (spot Montmartre!) to the basement club and supercool bathrooms with 'I love you' tiling, this overwhelmingly contemporary hostel is sharp. Dorms have USB sockets, and the best doubles have fabulous terraces with views.

HÔTEL ELDORADO
HOTEL €

Map p385 (☎01 45 22 35 21; www.eldoradohotel. fr; 18 rue des Dames, 17e; s €70-120, d €80-140, tr €100-160; 🚭; MPlace de Clichy) Bohemian Eldorado is one of Paris' greatest finds: a welcoming, reasonably well-run hotel with 33 colourfully decorated and (often) ethnically themed rooms above the Bistro des Dames restaurant, with a private garden. Unfortunately rooms facing the back will probably be quite noisy as they look out onto the restaurant terrace – earplugs may be a good idea. Cheaper-category singles have washbasin only. Breakfast costs €9.

HÔTEL
DESIGN HOTEL €

Map p382 (☎01 42 08 20 09; www.hoteldistrict republique.com; 4 rue Lucien Sampaix, 10e; s/d/ tr €89/99/129; ✳🚭; MRépublique) Superb-value rates and a clean modern design make the District République – on a quiet backstreet behind place de la République, funnily enough – a top spot to stay in the trendsetting 10e. Its 33 rooms are comfortable and each has a much-appreciated courtesy tray with kettle, tea and coffee. Triples and superior doubles with fold-out sofa bed make it a good family choice.

ST CHRISTOPHER'S GARE DU NORD
HOSTEL €

Map p382 (☎01 70 08 52 22; www.st-christophers. co.uk/paris-hostels; 5 rue de Dunkerque, 10e; dm €15-50, d €96-240; @🚭; MGare du Nord) Steps from Gare du Nord, St Christopher's is a modern backpacker hostel with six floors of light-filled rooms (600 total). Dorms sleep four, six, eight or 10 but beds are pricey unless you reserve months in advance. Facilities include laundry, female-only floor and Belushi's bar and restaurant with live music and a buzzing happy hour (5pm to 10pm). No kitchen; breakfast included.

Bring a towel and padlock.

A ROOM IN PARIS
B&B €

Map p382 (☎06 33 10 25 78; www.aroomin paris.com; 130 rue La Fayette,10e; r €75-195; 🚭; MGare du Nord) Stay in a Parisian apartment at this cosy B&B near the Gare du Nord. Five rooms (three of which sleep up to four people) are available in a Haussmann-era building with herringbone parquet floors, period moulding and a fireplace. Three rooms share two bathrooms, the other two have private bathrooms. Thierry and Peet can also provide home-cooked dinners. Minimum stay two nights.

ST CHRISTOPHER'S CANAL
HOSTEL €

Map p384 (☎01 40 34 34 40; www.st-christo phers.co.uk/paris-hostels; 159 rue de Crimée, 19e; dm €15-50, d €96-240; @🚭; MRiquet, Jaurès) This is one of Paris' best, biggest (300 beds) and most up-to-date hostels, with modern design and four sizes of dorms (four to 12 beds, mixed and female floors). Doubles comes with or without en suite bathroom. Other perks include canalside cafe, bar, bike rental and organised day trips. Daily prices vary wildly; reserve in advance to secure reasonable prices. No kitchen.

HÔTEL DU NORD – LE PARI VÉLO   HOTEL €

Map p378 (☑01 42 01 66 00; www.hoteldunord-leparivelo.com; 47 rue Albert Thomas, 10e; s/d/q €73/86/125; ☎; MRépublique) This quaint address has 24 rooms decorated with flea-market antiques and 10 bikes for guests to borrow to ride around town. Beyond the bric-a-brac charm, Hôtel du Nord's other winning attribute is its prized location near place République. Ring and wait to enter. Breakfast costs €8.

★JOKE HÔTEL   DESIGN HOTEL €€

Map p378 (☑01 40 40 71 71; http://en.astotel.com/hotel/joke-hotel; rue Blanche, 9e; s/d €129/150; ❄@☎❢; MPlace de Clichy, Pigalle) No joke. This hotel is a serious contender for Paris' best-value, most fun address. Play 'scrabble' or spin the wheel of fortune above your bed each night, hunt for coins stuck in the floor, and generally frolic in the youthful ambience and striking design of this fabulous, childhood-themed hotel. Rates include breakfast and all-day complimentary drinks, cakes and fruit.

★LE PIGALLE   DESIGN HOTEL €€

Map p378 (☑01 48 78 37 14; http://lepigalle.paris/en; 9 rue Frochot, 9e; d €140-340; ❄@☎; MPigalle) This offbeat lifestyle hotel evokes the spirit of hipster Pigalle today. Edgy design reflects the neighbourhood's legendary nightlife, while carefully thought-out details like a postcard taped on the bathroom wall and a key ring jangling with Paris souvenirs add unique homely touches to the 40 stylish rooms. Each has an iPad loaded with music, and larger rooms have vintage turntables with an eclectic vinyl collection.

The ground-floor bar and restaurant is a happening space, with DJs spinning tropical music two nights a week and Sunday brunch packing out the place from 11am. Kudos for the good-value 'Pigalle 12' rooms – actually twins with bunk beds.

★HÔTEL PROVIDENCE   BOUTIQUE HOTEL €€

Map p382 (☑01 46 34 34 04; www.hotelprovidenceparis.com; 90 rue René Boulanger, 10e; d from €170; ❄☎; MStrasbourg-St-Denis, République) This luxurious hideaway, at home in a 19th-century townhouse in the increasingly trendy 10e, is exquisite. Its 18 individually decorated rooms come with rich House of Hackney velvet wallpaper and vintage flea-market finds; the smallest rooms are not nearly as 'Mini' (by Paris standards) as the name suggests. Utterly glorious

is the bespoke cocktail bar gracing each room, complete with suggested recipes and ingredients.

The downstairs bar, with fireplace and delightful summertime pavement terrace, doubles as reception and bistro.

GRAND AMOUR HÔTEL   DESIGN HOTEL €€

Map p382 (☑01 44 16 03 10; www.hotelamourparis.fr; 18 rue de la Fidelité, 10e; s/d from €145/230; ☎; MChâteau d'Eau) Younger sister to Pigalle's Hôtel Amour (p285), this hipster lifestyle hotel mixes vintage furniture from the flea market with phallic-symbol carpets and the striking B&W nude photography of graffiti artist André Saraiva. The result is an edgy hideaway for lovers in one of the city's most up-and-coming neighbourhoods. Breakfast is served in the hotel bistro, a trendy drinking and dining address in itself.

HÔTEL JOSÉPHINE   BOUTIQUE HOTEL €€

Map p378 (☑01 55 31 90 75; http://en.hotel-josephine.com; 67 rue Blanche, 9e; s/d/tr/q €133/145/182/260; ❄@☎; MPlace de Clichy, Pigalle) Life's a cabaret at this novel, four-star boutique address in Pigalle. Named after wildly popular 1920s cabaret star Josephine Baker, the hotel has 41 comfortable rooms dressed in a vivacious rainbow of rich colours and floral prints by French designer Julie Gauthron. B&W cabaret photos decorate walls, and downstairs in the enticing library-lounge, guests mingle over complimentary absinthe cocktails each evening at 6pm.

Rates fluctuate wildly so do check online for the best deal. Breakfast is €10.

9HÔTEL RÉPUBLIQUE   DESIGN HOTEL €€

Map p382 (☑01 40 18 11 00; www.le9hotel.com; 7-9 rue Pierre Chausson, 10e; s €89-399, d €109-439; ❄@☎; MJacques Bonsergent) This four-star lifestyle hotel is designed to feel very much like a posh home with open-plan living spaces, a library to browse and tea and cake at the ready for guests in the lounge. Its 48 rooms mix wooden parquet flooring with soft creamy linens and contemporary bathrooms with rainfall showers. Find it on a quiet side street, five minutes from Canal St-Martin.

The breakfast buffet costs €15.

HÔTEL PARADIS   BOUTIQUE HOTEL €€

Map p382 (☑01 45 23 08 22; www.hotelparadisparis.com; 41 rue des Petites Écuries, 10e;

s/d/tr €180/210/310; ✳ @ ☎; M Poissonnière)
An easy walk from Gare du Nord, this
chic three-star address resides on a quiet
street, with gourmet bistro Vivant (p145)
as neighbour and plenty more nearby. Soft
cream canapés and design books grace the
stylish ground-floor lounge, and stylishly
understated rooms mix warm colours and
elegant patterned wallpapers – only French
designer Dorothée Meilichzon could have
such impeccable taste. Breakfast costs €12
to €14.

For a romantic treat, check into the
6th-floor suite and peer across Parisian
rooftops all the way to Montmartre's Sacré-
Cœur. Doubles drop to as low as €88 in low
season.

HÔTEL AMOUR
BOUTIQUE HOTEL €€

Map p378 (☎01 48 78 31 80; www.hotelamour
paris.fr; 8 rue Navarin, 9e; d €170-230; ☎; M St-
Georges, Pigalle) Craving romance in Paris?
The inimitable black-clad Amour ('Love')
features original design and nude artwork
in each of the rooms, some more explicit
than others. The icing on the cake is the
hip ground-floor bistro with summer patio
garden, a tasty spot for breakfast, lunch or
dinner and everything in between. Rooms
don't have a TV, but who cares when you're
in love?

LOFT
APARTMENT €€

Map p378 (☎06 14 48 47 48; www.loft-paris.fr; 7
cité Véron,18e; 2-person apt €120-210, 4-person
apt 290; ☎; M Blanche) Book months in advance to secure one of the stylish apartments in this gem, which offers an intimacy
that simply cannot be replicated in a hotel.
Just around the corner from the Moulin
Rouge in an enchanting car-free alley typical of Montmartre, options range from a
two-person studio to a large loft for eight.
The owner, a culture journalist, is a great
resource.

HÔTEL BASSS
HOTEL €€

Map p378 (☎01 42 51 50 00; http://en.hotel-
basss.com; 57 rue des Abbeses, 18e; s €65-270,
d €75-280, tr €95-300; ✳ @ ☎; M Abbesses) An
original gold-stone doorway marks the entrance to this contemporary hotel inspired
by American graphic designer Saul Bass,
smart on main street rue Abbesses in the
heart of Montmartre. Soft greys and blues
dress its 36 modern rooms, complete with
funky chipboard desk and kettle-clad welcome tray. The complimentary coffee and

cakes in the lounge-lobby are a welcome
touch. Breakfast is €12.

LE CITIZEN HOTEL
BOUTIQUE HOTEL €€

Map p382 (☎01 83 62 55 50; www.lecitizenhotel.
com; 96 quai de Jemmapes, 10e; d from €149;
@ ☎ ♿; M Gare de l'Est, Jacques Bonsergent)
This alluring 12-room boutique hotel on the
banks of Canal St-Martin was the first to
bring iPads, filtered water and a warm minimalist design to this once-edgy part of town.
Every room has a courtesy tray with kettle,
tea and coffee, and the suite and apartments
are both great family choices. Rates, unusually for Paris, include breakfast.

HÔTEL DES ARTS
HOTEL €€

Map p378 (☎01 46 06 30 52; www.arts-hotel-
paris.com; 5 rue Tholozé, 18e; s €99-180, d €125-
275; ☎; M Abbesses, Blanche) Hôtel des Arts
is a friendly, attractive 50-room hotel with
handsome wooden shutters and flower boxes. It is well placed for both place Pigalle
and Montmartre, and its rooms are good
value – it is worth paying more for superior
rooms, which have nicer views. Just up the
street is the old-style windmill Moulin de la
Galette. Breakfast is €12.

★ HÔTEL PARTICULIER
MONTMARTRE
BOUTIQUE HOTEL €€€

Map p378 (☎01 53 41 81 40; http://hotel-
particulier-montmartre.com; 23 av Junot, 18e,
Pavillon D; d from €390; ✳ @ ☎; M Lamarck-
Caulaincourt) This secret mansion in Montmartre, hidden behind a high wall, only has
five rooms – or should we say, lavishly large
designer suites peppered with retro curiosi-
ties found in flea markets. Guests have free
access to the exclusive *pétanque* (similar
to the game of bowls) pitch next door, but
it's the hotel garden and fashionable cocktail bar that really stuns. Weekend brunch
(€38) is equally hot; reservations essential.

To find the hotel, tucked down an old
stone-paved alley, ring the buzzer outside
the unmarked black gated entrance at No 23.

★ GRAND HÔTEL
PIGALLE
BOUTIQUE HOTEL €€€

Map p378 (☎01 85 73 12 00; www.grandpigalle.
com; 29 rue Victor Massé, 9e; d from €275; ✳ @ ☎;
M Pigalle) 'Bed and beverage' is the thrust of
this elegant and outrageously hip hotel in
South Pigalle, or 'SoPi' to those in the know.
Love child of the Experimental group who
pioneered cocktails in Paris, this is a sophisticated lifestyle hotel with cocktail 'minibars'

in its 37 beautifully crafted rooms and a fabulous restaurant–wine bar with Italian chef Giovanni Passerini in the kitchen.

TERRASS HÔTEL
HOTEL €€€

Map p378 (📞01 46 06 72 85; www.terrass-hotel.com; 12 rue Joseph de Maistre,18e; d €400; ❋❄🗟; MBlanche) One of the best views of Paris can be enjoyed over cocktails in the rooftop bar of this stylish 85-room hotel, dating from 1911 and receiving a designer facelift in 2015. From the vast open-plan lobby with library-lounge, photo booth and playroom to the all-black corridors and running/cycling cabins, strikingly contemporary Terrass impresses. Breakfast on honey collected from beehives on the roof.

Online deals can drop rates by over 50%, making this a great choice.

🛏 Le Marais, Menilmontant & Belleville

⭐LES PIAULES
HOSTEL €

Map p390 (📞01 43 55 09 97; www.lespiaules.com; 59 bd de Belleville, 11e; dm €23-58, d €130-200; @❄🗟; MCouronnes) This thoroughly contemporary hostel is the Belleville hot spot to mingle with locals over Parisian craft beer, cosy up in front of the wood-burner with a good book, or lap up sun and stunning views from the 5th-floor rooftop terrace. Dorms are bright and cheery, with custom bunks and ample bedside plugs, but it's the sleek all-white rooftop doubles everyone really gushes over.

COSMOS HÔTEL
HOTEL €

Map p390 (📞01 43 57 25 88; www.cosmos-hotel-paris.com; 35 rue Jean-Pierre Timbaud, 11e; s €66, d €72-82, tr €93; 🗟; MRépublique) Cheap, brilliant value and just footsteps from the nightlife of rue JPT, Cosmos is a shiny star with retro style on the budget-hotel scene. It has been around for 30-odd years but, unlike most other hotels in the same price bracket, Cosmos has been treated to a thoroughly modern makeover this century. Breakfast costs €8.

MIJE FOURCY
HOSTEL €

Map p386 (📞01 42 74 23 45; www.mije.com; 6 rue de Fourcy, 4e; dm incl breakfast €33.50, s/d/tr €55/82/100.50; 🗟; MSt-Paul, Pont Marie) Sweep through the elegant front door of this *hôtel particulier* and congratulate yourself on scoring such magnificent digs. Fourcy

welcomes guests with clean rooms and a summer garden to breakfast/hang out in. It's one of three Marais hostels run by the Maison Internationale de la Jeunesse et des Étudiants, the others are **MIJE Le Fauconnier** (Map p386; 11 rue du Fauconnier, 4e; @❄🗟; MSt-Paul, Pont Marie) and **MIJE Maubuisson** (Map p386; 12 rue des Barres, 4e; @❄🗟; MHôtel de Ville, Pont Marie).

Rooms (closed noon to 3pm) have a shower but share toilets in the corridor. Curfew is 1am to 7am; no children under six years.

THE LOFT
HOSTEL €

Map p390 (📞01 42 02 42 02; http://theloft-paris.com; 70 rue Julien Lacroix, 20e; dm €20-35, d €60-85; @❄🗟; MBelleville) This bright, private hostel in Belleville has panache. Dorms sleeping four to eight are decorated with stylish patterned wallpaper, bold colours and contemporary furniture; those on the ground floor open onto an idyllic courtyard patio and one dorm upstairs has its own balcony to lounge on. Every room has its own bathroom, and a well-equipped kitchen, open until 2am, doubles as a bar.

HÔTEL DU HAUT MARAIS
B&B €

Map p386 (📞01 42 77 65 52; www.hotelhaut-marais.com; 7 rue des Vertus, 3e; d €100-129, tr €160-198, q €165-206; 🗟; MArts et Métiers) Otherwise called Chez Didier et Marc, this 15th-century townhouse is perfect for those seeking a stylish 'home away from home' experience. Didier, Marc and their pet dog live at this boutique address with eight rooms, each different in design and comfortably spread across five floors. Rates include breakfast (around a shared table in the cellar).

HÔTEL DE NICE
HOTEL €

Map p386 (📞01 42 78 55 29; www.hoteldenice.com; 42bis rue de Rivoli, 4e; s €80-100, d €100-250, tr €135-280; 🗟; MHôtel de Ville) This is a warm, family-run place with 23 comfy rooms full of Second Empire–style furniture, east Asian carpets and lamps with fringed shades. Some have balconies high above busy rue de Rivoli. Breakfast costs €8.

⭐HÔTEL GEORGETTE
DESIGN HOTEL €€

Map p386 (📞01 44 61 10 10; www.hotelgeorgette.com; 36 rue du Grenier St-Lazare, 3e; d from €190; ❋❄🗟; MRambuteau) Clearly seeking inspiration from the Centre Pompidou around the corner, this sweet little neighbourhood hotel is a steal. The lobby is bright and appealing, and rooms are a decorative ode to either Pop Art, Op Art, Dada or New Realism with lots of bold colours and funky touches like Andy Warhol–inspired Campbell's-soup-can lampshades.

★ HÔTEL JEANNE D'ARC
HOTEL €€

Map p386 (☎01 48 87 62 11; www.hoteljeannedarc. com; 3 rue de Jarente, 4e; s/d/q €120/195/420; ☎; MSt-Paul) About the only thing wrong with this gorgeous address is everyone knows about it; book well in advance. Games to play, a painted rocking chair for tots in the bijou lounge, knick-knacks everywhere and the most extraordinary mirror in the breakfast room create a real 'family home' air in this 35-room house.

The pièce de résistance: the 6th-floor attic room with sweeping Paris rooftop view.

HÔTEL JULES & JIM
DESIGN HOTEL €€

Map p386 (☎01 44 54 13 13; www.hoteljulesetjim. com; 11 Rue des Gravilliers, 3e; d from €240; ☀@☎; MRambuteau, Arts et Métiers) The subtle oyster-grey entrance to this hotel named after the cult 1962 Truffaut film hints at the sophisticated interior design. Contemporary rooms mix raw concrete with marble, wood, glass and other beautiful raw materials. Jim rooms open onto a fabulous interior courtyard with outdoor fireplace, while pricier Sous les Toits rooms peep across rooftops to hilltop Montmartre from their 8th-floor perch. Breakfast costs €19.

HÔTEL FABRIC
DESIGN HOTEL €€

Map p390 (☎01 43 57 27 00; www.hotelfabric. com; 31 rue de la Folie Méricourt, 11e; d from €240; ☀☎; MOberkampf) Four-star Hôtel Fabric is a stylish ode to its industrial heritage as a 19th-century textile factory. Steely pillars prop up the red-brick lounge area with *table d'hôte* (set menu at fixed price) dining table and vintage touches including a Singer sewing machine. Darkly carpeted corridors open onto 33 crisp, bright rooms with beautiful textiles and ubercool cupboards (upcycled packing crates!). Breakfast costs €18.

HÔTEL EMILE
DESIGN HOTEL €€

Map p386 (☎01 42 72 76 17; www.hotelemile. com; 2 rue Malher, 4e; d €135-218; ☀☎; MSt-Paul) Prepare to be dazzled – literally. Retro B&W, geometrically patterned carpets, curtains, wallpapers and drapes dress this chic hotel, wedged between boutiques and restaurants in the Marais. Pricier 'top floor' doubles are just that, complete with breath-taking outlooks over Parisian roofs and chimney pots. Breakfast, included in the price, is on bar stools in the lobby; open the cupboard to find the 'kitchen'.

HÔTEL CARON
HOTEL €€

Map p386 (☎01 40 29 02 94; www.hotelcaron. com; 3 rue Caron, 4e; d €245-255; ☀☎; MSt-Paul) Footsteps from delightful place du Marché Ste-Catherine, this is a solid mid-range hotel with convivial cosmopolitan neighbours (Scottish pub, Italian grocers and so on). Soft natural hues give its 18 double rooms instant appeal and the L'Occitane bathroom products are a sweet-smelling touch. Breakfast (€14) in the cream-stone, vaulted cellar is a highlight.

CASTEX HÔTEL
HOTEL €€

Map p386 (☎01 42 72 31 52; www.castexhotel.com; 5 rue Castex, 4e; s/d/tr €199/229/259; MBastille) Equidistant from the Bastille and the Marais, 30-room Castex retains a certain 17th-century charm with its vaulted stone cellar used as a breakfast room, terracotta floor tiles and toile de Jouy wallpaper. Try to get one of the independent doubles (Nos 1 and 2) or family-friendly two-room suite (No 3) off the lovely patio. Breakfast is €13.

HÔTEL DU VIEUX SAULE
HOTEL €€

Map p386 (☎01 42 72 01 14; www.hotelvieuxsaule. com; 6 rue de Picardie, 3e; s €115, d €155-255; ☎; MFilles du Calvaire) This flower-bedecked 27-room hostelry, just around the corner from the Marché aux Rouges Enfants, is something of a find because of its slightly off-the-beaten-track location. Breakfast (€12) is served in a 16th-century vaulted cellar. Book via its website to get the best rates.

HÔTEL DE LA PLACE DES VOSGES
HOTEL €€

Map p386 (☎01 42 72 60 46; www.hotelplace desvosges.com; 12 rue de Birague, 4e; s €95, d €150-220; ☎; MSt-Paul) This superbly situated 17-room hotel – stables to the nearby Bastille in the 16th century – is a hop and a skip from sublime place des Vosges. Ancient wood beams and exposed stone inject heaps of character into the hotel, which has 16 rooms and a loft suite (with a couple of pull-out beds for families) piled up on six floors. Breakfast is €8.

★ LES BAINS
DESIGN HOTEL €€€

(☎01 42 77 07 07; www.lesbains-paris.com; 7 rue du Bourg l'Abbé, 3e; d from €392; ☀@☎;

Ⓜ️Étienne Marcel, Rambuteau) Probably Paris' most fabulous lifestyle hotel, Les Bains opened in 1885 as thermal baths frequented by the literary likes of Marcel Proust. In 1978 the baths morphed into the Bains-Douches nightclub – an iconic address made famous by David Bowie, Mick Jagger and a host of other rock stars and celebs. Today's hotel remains rock-star hot.

Its 39 rooms are a showcase of vintage treasures, luxury fabrics and eclectic design touches. Concerts and DJs fill its club, Wednesday to Saturday evening (11pm to 5am), and hipsters enliven its restaurant for Sunday brunch (€48). Breakfast costs €25.

★HÔTEL DU
PETIT MOULIN   BOUTIQUE HOTEL €€€
Map p386 (☎01 42 74 10 10; www.hoteldupetit-moulin.com; 29-31 rue de Poitou, 3e; d €250-395; ☎; Ⓜ️Filles du Calvaire) This scrumptious 17-room hotel, a bakery at the time of Henri IV, was designed from head to toe by Christian Lacroix. Pick from medieval and rococo Marais (rooms sporting exposed beams and dressed in toile de Jouy wallpaper), or more modern surrounds with contemporary murals and heart-shaped mirrors just this side of kitsch.

🛏 Bastille & Eastern Paris

★MAMA SHELTER   DESIGN HOTEL €
(☎01 43 48 48 48; www.mamashelter.com; 109 rue de Bagnolet, 20e; s/d/tr from €89/99/139; ✳️@☎; 🚌76, Ⓜ️Alexandre Dumas, Gambetta) This former car park was coaxed into its current zany incarnation by uber-designer Philippe Starck. Its 170 cutting-edge rooms feature iMacs, catchy colour schemes, polished-concrete walls and free movies on demand. A rooftop terrace, pizzeria, and huge restaurant with live music and Sunday brunch only add to its street cred. Book as early as possible to get the best deal. Breakfast is €16.

The drawback? Mama Shelter is a hike from both central Paris and the nearest metro stop, but bus 76 from the centre via place de la Bastille drops you at the door.

★HÔTEL EXQUIS   DESIGN HOTEL €€
Map p394 (☎01 56 06 95 13; http://hotelexquisparis.com; 71 rue de Charonne, 11e; d/q from €178/404; ✳️☎; Ⓜ️Charonne) Surrealism is the theme of this excellent-value, three-star hotel near place de la Bastille and a cluster of top-choice dining addresses. A unique work of surrealist art decorates each room, where beautiful colour palettes, designer lighting and bathrooms with twinkling tile lights woo guests. Rates drop by as much as 50% in low season; check online for deals. Breakfast is €12.

HÔTEL DE LA PORTE DORÉE   HOTEL €€
(☎01 43 07 56 97; www.hoteldelaportedoree.com; 273 av Daumesnil, 12e; s/d/tr €132/136/170; ✳️@☎♿; Ⓜ️Porte Dorée) ♿ A few blocks inside the bd Périphérique ring road and footsteps from the Porte Dorée metro station, this country-manor-style hotel is as family friendly as you'll find, with crayons and paper at reception, toy boxes in the rooms and the beautiful Bois de Vincennes right next door. Some of the 43 hardwood-floored rooms have decorative period fireplaces.

STANDARD DESIGN HÔTEL   DESIGN HOTEL €€
Map p394 (☎01 48 05 30 97; www.standard-design-hotel-paris.com; 29 rue des Taillandiers, 11e; s/d/tr €111/134/180; ☎; Ⓜ️Bastille) Monochrome black-on-white or white-on-black stripes (think bar codes) rule at this sharp, contemporary hotel, broken up by splashes of colour. It's brilliantly located close to Bastille and Le Marais, with plenty of excellent dining and drinking choices on hand in the lively *quartier*. Its 37 rooms are well soundproofed but ask for a room back from the street if you need 100% tranquillity.

Online bookings almost always include breakfast.

★HÔTEL L'ANTOINE   DESIGN HOTEL €€€
Map p394 (☎01 55 28 30 11; www.hotelantoinebastilleparis.com; 12 rue de Charonne, 11e; s/d €280/380; ✳️@☎; Ⓜ️Bastille) Few hotels evoke the local 'hood quite like three-star, 38-room Antoine. A showcase for stunning contemporary decor by Christian Lacroix, its five floors reflect a different aspect of the Bastille – the 1950s, nightlife at the mythical Balajo (p191), romance, technology – where the French designer once lived. A luxury candle boutique fills part of the lobby and there's a basement sauna and fitness room.

If you love shocking pink, ask for an art-gallery-inspired room on the 2nd floor. Room rates can fluctuate by up to 50%; check the internet for deals. Breakfast costs €16.

🛏 The Islands

HÔTEL DES DEUX-ÎLES   HISTORIC HOTEL €€
Map p396 (✆01 43 26 13 35; www.deuxiles-paris-hotel.com; 59 rue Saint-Louis en l'Île, 4e; s/d from €210/240; ✸ 🖤; Ⓜ Pont Marie) A venerable 17th-century building shelters this intimate hotel with a vaulted stone guest lounge with a massive open fireplace and 17 spacious rooms with patterned wallpaper, screen-printed fabrics, original Portuguese *azulejos* (blue-and-white ceramic tiles) in some bathrooms, and ancient wooden beams. Breakfast (€14) is available in the lounge and, unusually for the same price, in the privacy of your room.

Top-floor rooms have enchanting views over the Parisian rooftops and chimney pots.

HÔTEL SAINT-LOUIS
EN L'ISLE   BOUTIQUE HOTEL €€
Map p396 (✆01 46 34 04 80; www.saintlouisen lisle.com; 75 rue St-Louis en l'Île, 4e; s €165-185, d €185-255; ✸ 🖤📶; Ⓜ Pont Marie) This elegant abode brandishes a pristine taupe facade and perfectly polished interior, while in-room home comforts such as kettles, complimentary tea and coffee and iPod docking stations next to the beds make it stand out. Room 52 on the 5th floor, with a balcony and timber beams, is dreamy, and the stone-cellar breakfast room is a 17th-century gem. Breakfast costs €13.

★ HÔTEL DU JEU
DE PAUME   BOUTIQUE HOTEL €€€
Map p396 (✆01 43 26 14 18; http://jeudepaume hotel.com; 54 rue St-Louis en l'Île, 4e; s €195-255, d €295-360; ✸ 🖤; Ⓜ Pont Marie) Romantically set in a courtyard off Île St-Louis' main street, this chic, contemporary four-star hotel occupies a 17th-century royal tennis court. Its 30 rooms are each inspired by a different modern artist. Panton chairs add a design edge to the historic beamed, exposed-stone-walled house, and its leafy patio garden is divine. Facilities include a wellness centre. Breakfast costs €18.

🛏 Latin Quarter

HÔTEL ESMERALDA   HOTEL €
Map p398 (✆01 43 54 19 20; www.hotel-esmer alda.fr; 4 rue St-Julien le Pauvre, 5e; s/d/tr from €85/125/150; 🖤; Ⓜ St-Michel) Tucked away in a quiet street with million-dollar views of Notre Dame (choose room 12!), this no-frills place is about as central to the Latin Quarter as it gets. At these prices, the 19 rooms are no great shakes (the cheapest singles have washbasin only) but they're popular – book well ahead.

★ FAMILIA HÔTEL   HOTEL €€
Map p398 (✆01 43 54 55 27; www.familiahotel. com; 11 rue des Écoles, 5e; s €110, d €134-152, tr €191, f €214; ✸ 🖤📶; Ⓜ Cardinal Lemoine) Sepia murals of Parisian landmarks, flower-bedecked windows and exposed rafters and stone walls make this friendly third-generation family-run hotel one of the most attractive 'almost budget' options on this side of the Seine. Eight rooms (on the 2nd, 5th and 6th floors; there's a lift/elevator) have little balconies offering glimpses of Notre Dame. Breakfast costs €7.

HÔTEL LA LANTERNE   BOUTIQUE HOTEL €€
Map p398 (✆01 53 19 88 39; www.hotel-la-lanterne.com; 12 rue de la Montagne Ste-Geneviève, 5e; d/ste from €170/390; ✸ @🖤✸; Ⓜ Maubert-Mutualité) A stunning swimming pool and hammam (Turkish steambath) in a vaulted stone cellar, a topiary-filled courtyard garden, contemporary guest rooms (some with small balconies) with black-and-white photos of Parisian architecture, and amenities, including Nespresso machines, and an honesty bar make this a jewel of a boutique hotel. Breakfast (€19) lets you choose from hot and cold buffets and includes Mariage Frères teas.

HÔTEL ATMOSPHÈRES   DESIGN HOTEL €€
Map p398 (✆01 43 26 56 02; www.hotelatmos pheres.com; 31 rue des Écoles, 5e; s/d/tr/ste from €126/144/174/229; ✸ @🖤; Ⓜ Maubert-Mutualité) Striking images by award-winning French photographer Thierry des Ouches are permanently exhibited at this haven, where cocooning rooms evoke different Parisian 'atmospheres', such as 'nature', 'monuments', the metro-inspired 'urban' and colourful *salon de thé* (tearoom)–style 'macaron'. There's a small gym and a sauna as well as an honesty bar. Breakfast costs €16.

HÔTEL DE NOTRE DAME   BOUTIQUE HOTEL €€
Map p398 (✆01 43 26 79 00; www.hotel-notre-dame-charmeparis.com; 19 rue Maître Albert, 5e; d from €240; ✸ @🖤; Ⓜ Maubert-Mutualité) Regular deals mean this charming bou-

SLEEPING THE ISLANDS

tique hotel invariably sits within midrange territory and offers excellent value for its location in a quiet street near Notre Dame. Some of its stylish rooms have rain showerheads, while others have deep tubs (with coloured fibre-optic lighting that you can change according to your mood). There's an on-site sauna and small gym.

HÔTEL LES DEGRÉS DE NOTRE DAME HOTEL €€

Map p398 (☑01 55 42 88 88; www.lesdegreshotel. com; 10 rue des Grands Degrés, 5e; d €140-200; ⍤; MMaubert-Mutualité) Wonderfully old-school, with a winding timber staircase (no lift/elevator) and charming staff, this 10-room hotel just a block from the Seine is good value. Breakfast (€10) comes with freshly squeezed orange juice. Rooms 47 and the spacious 501 have romantic views of Notre Dame. Rooms have not been renovated for some time, however.

HÔTEL MINERVE HOTEL €€

Map p398 (☑01 43 26 26 04; www.parishotel-minerve.com; 13 rue des Écoles, 5e; s/d/f from €161/197/394; ❋@⍤⍨; MCardinal Lemoine) Oriental carpets, antique books, frescoes of French monuments and wall tapestries make this family-run hotel a lovely place to stay. Room styles are a mix of traditional and modern (renovated earlier this decade); some have small balconies with views of Notre Dame, while the 1st-floor rooms all have parquet floors.

HÔTEL ST-JACQUES HOTEL €€

Map p398 (☑01 44 07 45 45; http://hotel-saint jacques.com; 35 rue des Écoles, 5e; s €188, d €206-290, tr €305; ❋@⍤; MMaubert-Mutualité) Framed reproductions of famous artworks line the walls of this belle époque–styled hotel, which retains original 19th-century details, such as trompe l'œil ceilings evoking cloud-filled skies, an iron staircase and balconies overlooking the Panthéon. Welcome touches include a cabaret-themed breakfast room (breakfast €14) and bowl of jelly beans in the lobby. Toulouse Lautrec (its bar) serves absinthe.

HÔTEL RÉSIDENCE HENRI IV HOTEL €€€

Map p398 (☑01 44 41 31 81; www.residence-henri4.com; 50 rue des Bernardins, 5e; d €299, ste €380-410; ❋⍤⍨; MMaubert-Mutualité) This exquisite late-19th-century cul-de-sac hotel has eight generously sized rooms (minimum 17 sq metres) and five two-room apartments (minimum 25 sq metres), done up with regal touches like draped fabrics and four-poster beds in some rooms. All are equipped with kitchenettes (induction cooktops, fridge, microwave and dishes), making them particularly handy for families and marketgoers.

FIVE HOTEL BOUTIQUE HOTEL €€€

Map p400 (☑01 43 31 74 21; http://thefivehotel. com; 3 rue Flatters, 5e; d/ste from €259/650; ❋@⍤; MLes Gobelins) Fibre-optic lighting enhances the small rooms at this contemporary romantic sanctum. Rooms become more spacious as you move up the price scale; its One By the Five suite has a phenomenal 'levitating' bed. In-room massages and beauty treatments can be arranged. Rates are often discounted by up to 50% online, making it a better deal than it first appears.

🛏 St-Germain & Les Invalides

HÔTEL ST-ANDRÉ DES ARTS HOTEL €

Map p402 (☑01 43 26 96 16; www.hotel-saint andredesarts.fr; 66 rue St-André des Arts, 6e; s/d/tr/q €95/115/156/181; ⍤; MOdéon) Located on a lively, restaurant-lined thoroughfare, this 31-room hotel is a veritable bargain in the centre of the action opposite the beautiful glass-roofed passage Cour du Commerce St André. The rooms are basic and there's no lift/elevator, but the public areas are very evocative of *vieux Paris* (old Paris), with beamed ceilings and ancient stone walls, and rates include breakfast.

LE BELLECHASSE DESIGN HOTEL €€

Map p406 (☑01 45 50 22 31; www.lebellechasse. com; 8 rue de Bellechasse, 7e; s/d €197/206; ❋⍤; MSolférino) Fashion (and, increasingly, interior) designer Christian Lacroix's entrancing room themes – including St-Germain, with brocades, zebra striping and faux-gold leafing; Tuileries, with trompe l'œil and palms; and Jeu de Paume, with giant playing-card motifs – give the impression you've stepped into a larger-than-life oil painting. Mod cons include docking stations and 200 TV channels. Rates include a glass of Champagne.

HÔTEL PERREYVE HOTEL €€

Map p402 (☑01 45 48 35 01; www.perreyve-hotel-paris-luxembourg.com; 63 rue Madame, 6e; s/d

€152/197; ❄️📶; Ⓜ️Rennes) A hop, skip and a jump from the Jardin du Luxembourg, this welcoming 1920s hotel is superb value given its coveted location. Cosy, carpeted rooms have enormous frescoes; on the ground floor, start the day in the pretty breakfast room with herringbone floors and fire-engine-red tables and chairs.

HÔTEL LE CLÉMENT
HOTEL €€

Map p402 (📞01 43 26 53 60; http://hotelclementparis.com; 6 rue Clément, 6e; d €115-159; ❄️📶; Ⓜ️St-Germain des Prés) Excellent value for the style and tranquillity it offers, the Clément has 28 stylish rooms (with beautiful printed wallpapers and fabrics), some of which overlook the Marché St-Germain (such as room 100). Rooms on the very top floor have sloping ceilings. The proprietors know what they're doing – this place has been in the same family for over a century.

HÔTEL DANEMARK
BOUTIQUE HOTEL €€

Map p402 (📞01 43 26 93 78; www.hoteldanemark.com; 21 rue Vavin, 6e; d €195-220; ❄️📶; Ⓜ️Vavin) In a peaceful location near the Jardin du Luxembourg, this stone-walled hotel has 15 scrumptious, eclectically furnished rooms. All are well soundproofed and at least 20 sq metres, which is bigger than many Parisians' apartments. Also unlike many residential apartments, all have bathtubs. Breakfast (€11) is served in the atmospheric vaulted cellar.

★L'HÔTEL
BOUTIQUE HOTEL €€€

Map p402 (📞01 44 41 99 00; www.l-hotel.com; 13 rue des Beaux Arts, 6e; d from €325; ❄️@📶🌀; Ⓜ️St-Germain des Prés) In a quiet quayside street, this award-winning hostelry is the stuff of romance, Parisian myths and urban legends. Rock- and film-star patrons fight to sleep in room 16, where Oscar Wilde died in 1900 and which is now decorated with a peacock motif, or in the art deco room 36 (where entertainer Mistinguett stayed once), with its huge mirrored bed.

A stunning, modern swimming pool occupies the ancient cellar. Guests and nonguests can soak up the atmosphere of the fantastic bar (often with live music by up-and-coming new talent) and Michelin-starred restaurant (called, what else, Le Restaurant) under a glass canopy.

LE SAINT
HOTEL €€€

Map p402 (📞01 42 61 01 51; http://lesainthotelparis.com; 3 rue du Pré aux Clercs, 7e; d from

€265; ❄️📶; Ⓜ️St-Germain des Prés) Live the St-Germain des Prés life at this 2016-opened hotel on a peaceful side street strolling distance from the area's churches, markets, literary cafes and the Seine. Some of its 54 rooms and suites have balconies or terraces; all have shimmering fabrics. An open fireplace blazes in the lounge; there's an in-house restaurant, Kult, and bar. Rates include organic breakfast.

LE SIX
BOUTIQUE HOTEL €€€

Map p402 (📞01 42 22 00 75; www.hotel-le-six.com; 14 rue Stanislas, 6e; d €310-460; ❄️📶🌀; Ⓜ️Notre Dame des Champs) From the funky red-leather reception bar to rotating art exhibitions, glass-topped courtyard salon and ultracool spa, this four-star hotel defines contemporary design. Beds are queen or king size and kids are warmly welcomed. But the biggest asset is the outstanding service on every level.

HÔTEL D'ANGLETERRE
HISTORIC HOTEL €€€

Map p402 (📞01 42 60 34 72; www.hotel-dangleterre.com; 44 rue Jacob, 6e; s €190, d €275-310; @📶; Ⓜ️St-Germain des Prés) If the walls could talk... This former garden of the British Embassy is where the Treaty of Paris ending the American Revolution was prepared in 1783. Hemingway lodged here in 1921, as did Charles Lindbergh in 1927 after completing the world's first solo nonstop flight from New York to Paris. Its 27 exquisite rooms are individually decorated. Rates include breakfast.

🛏 Montparnasse & Southern Paris

HÔTEL DE LA LOIRE
HOTEL €

Map p412 (📞01 45 40 66 88; www.hoteldelaloire-paris.com; 39bis rue du Moulin Vert, 14e; s €80, d €85-90, tr €105, apt €140; P📶🌀; Ⓜ️Alésia) Obviously at these prices don't expect luxury but do expect a warm welcome and clean, colourful en suite rooms (18 all-up) at this budget hotel of old. The lovely villagey location near Denfert-Rochereau makes it easy to reach both major airports and Gare du Nord, and there's a pretty table-set garden. The kitchen-equipped apartment sleeps four.

OOPS
HOSTEL €

Map p410 (📞01 47 07 47 00; www.oops-paris.com; 50 av des Gobelins, 13e; dm/d €43/115;

✳ 🛜; M Gobelins) A candyfloss-pink lift/ elevator scales the six colourful floors of Paris' first 'design hostel'. Good-size four- to six-bed dorms and doubles (from €27 and €70, respectively, outside high season) have en suites and are accessible all day. Some have Eiffel Tower views. Breakfast is included; there's also a self-catering kitchen, luggage room and lockers. No credit cards, no alcohol allowed.

HÔTEL CARLADEZ CAMBRONNE   HOTEL €

Map p414 (☑01 47 34 07 12; www.hotelcarladez. com; 3 place du Général Beuret, 15e; d €99-165, f €175-245; 🛜🛁; M Vaugirard) On a quintessentially Parisian cafe-clad square, this freshly renovated hotel has comfortable rooms with attractive wallpapers and fabrics. Higher-priced superior rooms come with bathtubs, more space and tend to be quieter. Communal coffee- and tea-making facilities let you make yourself at home. Very good value.

★ SUBLIM EIFFEL   DESIGN HOTEL €€

Map p412 (☑01 40 65 95 95; www.sublimeiffel. com; 94 bd Garibaldi, 15e; d from €146; ✳🛜; M Sèvres-Lecourbe) There's no forgetting what city you're in with the Eiffel Tower motifs in reception and rooms (along with Parisian street-map carpets and metro-tunnel-shaped bedheads) plus glittering tower views from upper-floor windows. Edgy design elements also include cobblestone staircase carpeting (there's also a lift/ elevator) and, fittingly in *la ville lumière* (the City of Light), technicoloured in-room fibre-optic lighting. The small wellness centre/hammam offers massages.

OFF PARIS SEINE   HOTEL €€

Map p410 (http://offparisseine.com; 20-22 Port d'Austerlitz, 13e; d/ste from €160/400; 🛜🛁; M Gare d'Austerlitz) If you like the idea of being gently rocked to sleep (not to mention staying right on the Seine), book into Paris' first floating hotel, an 80m-long catamaran-design structure by the Pont Charles de Gaulle with a panoramic 400-sq-metre sun terrace, 15m-long swimming pool, bar, lounge, and 54 stunningly appointed rooms and four even more stunning suites.

HÔTEL MAX   BOUTIQUE HOTEL €€

Map p412 (☑01 43 27 60 80; www.hotel-max.fr; 34 rue d'Alésia, 14e; d €175-240; ✳🛜; M Alésia)

Some of the 19 rooms at this delightful boutique hotel in the heart of the 14e have balconies and all have in-room Nespresso machines, stylised, contemporary decor, timber floors and Italian bathrooms. There's a small triangular garden at the entrance and another small rear garden adjacent to the breakfast room, where the morning buffet costs €12.

HÔTEL VIC EIFFEL   BOUTIQUE HOTEL €€

Map p412 (☑01 53 86 83 83; www.hotelvic eiffel.com; 92 bd Garibaldi, 15e; s/d €190/220; 🛜; M Sèvres-Lecourbe) A short walk from the Eiffel Tower, with the metro on the doorstep, this pristine hotel has chic orange and oyster-grey rooms (two of which are wheelchair accessible). Classic rooms are small but perfectly functional; Superior and Privilege rooms offer increased space. All have Nespresso coffee-making machines. Rates plummet outside high season. Breakfast, served in an atrium-style courtyard, costs €14.

Friendly staff go out of their way to help.

LA MAISON   BOUTIQUE HOTEL €€

Map p412 (☑01 45 42 11 39; http://lamaison-montparnasse.com; 53 rue de Gergovie, 14e; s €99-115, d €125-135, tr €145-165, f €175-210; ✳@🛜🛁; M Pernety) The House goes all out to recreate home, with homemade cakes and jams for breakfast in the open-plan kitchen-lounge or little courtyard garden. A candy-striped staircase leads to its 36 rooms (there's a box-sized lift/elevator too) with bold pinks, violets and soft neutral tones. Ask for an Eiffel Tower–view room. Prices peak from Monday to Thursday. Breakfast is €14.

★ HÔTEL HENRIETTE   DESIGN HOTEL €€€

Map p410 (☑01 47 07 26 90; www.hotelhenriette. com; 9 rue des Gobelins, 13e; s/d from €169/249; ✳🛜🛁; M Les Gobelins) Interior designer Vanessa Scoffier scoured Paris' flea markets for over a year sourcing unique pieces, such as Platner chairs and 1950s lighting, to give each of these 32 rooms a one-of-a-kind twist. The results are spellbinding, as is the light-bathed, glassed-in atrium, and adjoining plant-filled stone courtyard graced with wrought-iron furniture and a dazzling star made from multicoloured lightbulbs.

Understand Paris

Paris Today

The Latin motto *'fluctuat nec mergitur'* ('tossed but not sunk') was adopted by Paris around 1358. Officialised by Baron Haussmann in 1853, it still appears on the city's coat of arms. But it became emblematic of the city's spirit following the terrorist attacks of 2015. Paris' resilience came to the fore as defiant Parisians determined to uphold the city's cherished quality of life reclaimed cafe terraces and public spaces, and grand-scale plans for municipal infrastructure and greener living surge ahead.

Best on Film

Les 400 Coups (400 Blows; 1959) Moving portrayal of the magic and disillusionment of childhood.

La Haine (Hate; 1995) Mathieu Kassovitz's prescient take on social tensions in modern Paris.

Le Fabuleux Destin d'Amélie Poulain (Amélie; 2001) Endearing story of a winsome young Parisian.

La Môme (La Vie en Rose; 2007) Édith Piaf, from street urchin to international superstar.

Hugo (2011) A tribute to cinema and the legendary Georges Méliès.

Best in Print

Notre Dame de Paris (Victor Hugo; 1831) The classic tale of the hunchback of Notre Dame.

A Moveable Feast (Ernest Hemingway; 1964) Memoirs of the aspiring writer's life in Paris.

Life: A User's Manual (Georges Perec; 1978) Intricately structured novel about an apartment block's inhabitants between 1833 and 1975.

The Elegance of the Hedgehog (Muriel Barbery; 2008) French bestseller unveiling the world behind a Parisian facade.

Parisians: An Adventure History of Paris (Graham Robb; 2010) History tome and unexpected page turner.

Greater Paris

The Grand Paris (Greater Paris) redevelopment project got the green light in 2016 (although the governing authority won't be fully operational until 2020). The scheme connects the outer suburbs beyond the traffic-snarled bd Périphérique – the ring road that stands on the site of the former city walls – with the city proper. This is a significant break in the physical and conceptual barrier that the *périphérique* has imposed. But, due to the real estate boom that pushed many middle-class residents and large companies outside the ring road, the steadily growing suburban population (10.5 million, compared to 2.2 million inside the *périphérique*) has created a real need to redefine Paris, on both an administrative and infrastructural scale.

The crux of Grand Paris is a massive decentralised metro expansion, with 68 new stations and six suburban lines, with a target completion date of 2030. The principal goal is to connect the suburbs with one another, instead of relying on a central inner-city hub from which all lines radiate outwards (the current model). Progress is swift: tunnelling, which began in 2015, continues at a rate of some 12.5m per day.

Ultimately, the surrounding suburbs – Vincennes, Neuilly, Issy, St-Denis etc – will lose their autonomy and become part of a much larger Grand Paris governed by the Hôtel de Ville.

Smaller Paris

While Paris is spreading outwards, the city centre itself is – if voted in by parliament – shrinking, administratively at least. One of Mayor Anne Hidalgo's key reforms is to combine the 1er, 2e, 3e and 4e into one *arrondissement*. The move, which would come into operation in 2020, is intended to more evenly distribute services (such as childcare facilities) across the *arrondissements*.

Paris' *arrondissements* vary widely by size (the 2e is 1sq km, while the 16e is almost 8sq km) and population (the 1er has 17,000 residents, while the 15e has 240,000). While the plan would not do away with the *arrondissements* themselves (the postcodes and identities will stay the same), the four combined epicentral *arrondissements* would have a single mayor. Additionally, more city powers would be transferred to the *mairies* (town halls) of each *arrondissement*.

Greener Paris

Mayor Hidalgo's plans are inextricably tied to greening the city and reducing car traffic and pollution. Her predecessor, Bertrand Delanoë, introduced groundbreaking green transport initiatives during his tenure. These included the Vélib' bike share program, the Autolib' electric-car share program, and the creation of hundreds of kilometres of new bus and bike lanes. Delanoë's outgoing project was to close the riverside roads along the Left Bank and reinvent a new pedestrian-friendly public area, known as Les Berges de Seine. Hidalgo's agenda includes permanently pedestrianising 3.3km of Right Bank expressway between the Tuileries and Bastille, pedestrianising the Champs-Élysées on the first Sunday of each month, and an annual car-free day – along with reducing parking spaces by 55,000 per year, instigating a maximum speed limit of 30km per hour on the entire city, investing €150 million in cycling infrastructure and banning diesel cars by 2020.

Transport aside, other green initiatives include a goal of 100 hectares of green roofs, facades and vertical walls, a third of which will be devoted to urban agriculture. And the city is tackling food waste, too: restaurants are required to recycle food waste if they produce 10 metric tons per year, and the Union of Hospitality Trades and Industries now strongly recommends that doggy bags are provided by restaurants serving 150 to 200 covers per day.

Taller Paris

Architectural change doesn't come easy in Paris, given the need to balance the city's heritage with demands on space. But new projects continue to gather steam. The controversial Tour Triangle, a glittering glass triangular tower designed by Jacques Herzog and Pierre de Meuron, will be the first skyscraper in Paris since Tour Montparnasse in 1973 when it is completed at Porte de Versailles on the city's southwestern edge in 2018. Other high-rise projects include Duo, two Jean Nouvel–designed towers (180m and 122m) in the 13e, slated for completion in 2020. Countless other projects, both grand and small, highrise and low-rise, are in the works. Paris continues to not only survive but thrive.

if Paris were 100 people

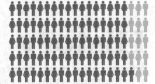

86 would be French
14 would be Foreign

living in Paris
(% of population by area)

Outer Arrondissements — 80
Central Paris — 20

population per sq km

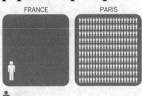

FRANCE   PARIS

 ≈ 100 people

History

With its cobbled streets, terraced cafes and iconic landmarks, Paris evokes a sense of timelessness, yet the city has changed and evolved dramatically over the centuries. Paris' history is a saga of battles, bloodshed, grand-scale excesses, revolution, reformation, resistance, renaissance and constant reinvention. This epic is not just consigned to museums and archives: reminders of the capital's and the country's history are evident all over the city.

Early Settlers: the Celts & Romans

The early history of Paris is murky, but the general consensus is that a Celtic tribe known as the Parisii established a fishing village in the area in the 3rd century BC. Years of conflict between the Gauls and Romans ended in 52 BC, when the latter took control of the territory after a decisive victory during Julius Caesar's eight-year Gallic Wars campaign. The Romans promptly established a new town – Lutetia (Lutèce in French) – with the main public buildings (forum, bathhouse, theatre and amphitheatre) all located on the Left Bank, near today's Panthéon. Remnants of both the bathhouse and amphitheatre are still visible.

Gallo-Roman Paris (Lutetia) features in several classic Asterix adventures, including *Asterix and the Golden Sickle*.

Though Lutetia was not the capital of its province, it was a prosperous town, with a population of around 8000. However, raids by the Franks and other Germanic tribes during the 3rd century AD left the settlement on the Left Bank scorched and pillaged, and its inhabitants fled to the Île de la Cité, subsequently fortified with stone walls. Christianity was introduced by St-Denis – decapitated on Montmartre in AD 250 for his efforts – and the first church was built on the western part of the island.

The Roman town held out until the late 5th century – mythically saved from Attila the Hun by the piety of Geneviève, who became the city's patron saint – only to fall when a second wave of Franks overran the area for good.

TIMELINE

3rd century BC	52 BC	AD 250
Celtic Gauls called Parisii arrive in the Paris area and set up wattle-and-daub huts on the Seine, possibly in the Nanterre area.	Roman legions under Titus Labienus crush a Celtic revolt on Mons Lutetius (site of today's Panthéon) and establish the town of Lutetia (Lutèce in French).	St-Denis, who brought Christianity to Lutetia, is executed on Montmartre. According to legend, he then carries his head 10km north, to the site of the future royal necropolis of St-Denis.

The Middle Ages: Paris as Capital

One of the key figures in early Parisian history was the Frankish king Clovis I (c 466–511). Clovis was the first ruler to unite what would later become France, to convert to Christianity and to declare Paris the capital. Under the Frankish kings the city once again began to expand, and important edifices such as the abbey of St-Germain des Prés and the abbey at St-Denis were erected.

However, the militaristic rulers of the succeeding Carolingian dynasty, beginning with Charles 'the Hammer' Martel (688–741), were almost permanently away fighting wars in the east, and Paris languished, controlled mostly by its counts. When Charles Martel's grandson, Charlemagne (768–814), moved his capital to Aix-la-Chapelle (today's Aachen in Germany), Paris' fate was sealed. Basically a group of separate villages with its centre on the Ile de la Cité, Paris was badly defended throughout the second half of the 9th century and was raided incessantly by Vikings, who eventually established control over northern and northwestern France.

The Paris counts, whose powers had grown as the Carolingians feuded among themselves, elected one of their own, Hugh Capet, as king at Senlis in 987. He made Paris the royal seat and lived in the renovated palace of the Roman governor on the Île de la Cité (site of the present Palais de Justice). Under the 800 years of Capetian rule that followed, Paris prospered as a centre of politics, commerce, trade, religion and culture.

The city's strategic riverside position ensured its importance throughout the Middle Ages. The first guilds were created in the 11th century, and in the mid-12th century the ship merchants' guild bought the principal river port, by today's Hôtel de Ville (City Hall), from the crown. Frenetic building marked the 12th and 13th centuries. The Basilique de St-Denis was commissioned in 1136 and less than three decades later work started on Notre Dame. During the reign of Philippe-Auguste (r 1180–1223), the city wall was expanded and fortified with 25 gates and hundreds of protective towers.

The swampy Marais was drained for agricultural use and settlement, prompting the eventual need for the food markets at Les Halles in 1183 and the Louvre as a riverside fortress in the 13th century. In a bid to resolve ghastly traffic congestion and stinking excrement (by 1200 the city had a population of 200,000), Philippe-Auguste paved four of Paris' main streets with metre-square sandstone blocks. Meanwhile, the Left Bank – particularly in the Latin Quarter – developed as a centre of European learning and erudition. Ill-fated lovers Pierre Abélard and

In the early Middle Ages, most of today's Paris was either a carpet of fields and vineyards or a boggy, waterlogged marsh.

HISTORY THE MIDDLE AGES: PARIS AS CAPITAL

In 1292 the medieval city of Paris counted 352 streets, 10 squares and 11 crossroads.

451	509	845–86	987
Attila the Hun unexpectedly turns away from Paris to march south; credit is given to the prayers of Geneviève, who later becomes the city's patron saint.	Clovis I becomes the first king of the Franks and the first Frankish ruler to convert to Christianity. He declares Paris the seat of his new kingdom.	Paris is repeatedly raided by Vikings for over four decades, including the siege of 885–86 by Siegfried the Saxon, which lasts 10 months but ends in victory for the French.	Five centuries of Merovingian and Carolingian rule ends with the crowning of Hugh Capet; a dynasty that will rule one of Europe's most powerful countries for the next eight centuries.

STAR-CROSSED LOVERS

He was a brilliant 39-year-old philosopher and logician with a reputation for controversial ideas. She was the beautiful niece of a canon at Notre Dame. And like Bogart and Bergman in *Casablanca* and Romeo and Juliet in Verona, they had to fall in love – in medieval Paris of all damned times and places.

In 1118 the wandering scholar Pierre Abélard (1079–1142) found his way to Paris, having clashed with yet another theologian in the provinces. There he was employed by Canon Fulbert of Notre Dame to tutor his niece Héloïse (1101–64). One thing led to another and a son, Astrolabe, was born. Abélard married his sweetheart in secret and when Fulbert found out he was outraged. He had Abélard castrated and sent Héloïse off to a convent where she eventually became abbess. Abélard took monastic vows at the abbey in St-Denis and continued his studies and controversial writings.

Yet, all the while, the star-crossed lovers corresponded: he sending tender advice on how to run the convent and she writing passionate, poetic letters to her lost lover. The two were reunited only in death: in 1817 their remains were disinterred and brought to Père Lachaise cemetery in the 20e, where they lie together beneath a neo-Gothic tombstone in division 7.

Héloïse penned the finest poetry of the age and treatises on philosophy, Thomas Aquinas taught at the new university, and the Sorbonne opened its scholarly doors.

Black Times: War & Death

Political tension and open insurrection were brought to Paris by the Hundred Years' War (1337–1453); the Black Death (1348–49), which killed over a third of Paris' population; and the development of free, independent cities elsewhere in Europe. In 1420 the dukes of Burgundy, allied with the English, occupied the capital and two years later John Plantagenet, duke of Bedford, was installed as regent of France for the English king, Henry VI, then an infant. Henry was crowned king of France at Notre Dame less than 10 years later, but Paris was almost continuously under siege from the French.

Around that time a 17-year-old peasant girl known to history as Jeanne d'Arc (Joan of Arc) persuaded the French pretender to the throne that she'd received a divine mission from God to expel the English from France and bring about his coronation as Charles VII. She rallied French troops and defeated the English north of Orléans, and Charles was crowned at Reims. But Joan of Arc failed to take Paris. In 1430 she was captured, convicted of witchcraft and heresy by a tribunal of French ecclesiastics and burned at the stake. Charles VII returned to

1066	1163	1358	1572
The so-called Norman Conquest of England ignites almost 300 years of conflict between the Normans in western and northern France and the Capetians in Paris.	Two centuries of non-stop building reaches its zenith with the start of Notre Dame Cathedral under Maurice de Sully, the bishop of Paris; construction takes over a century and a half.	The Hundred Years' War (1337–1453) between France and England and the devastation and poverty caused by the plague lead to the ill-fated peasants' revolt led by Étienne Marcel.	Some 3000 Huguenots who are in Paris to celebrate the wedding of the Protestant Henri of Navarre (the future Henri IV) are slaughtered on 23–24 August.

Paris in 1436, ending over 16 years of occupation, but the English were not entirely driven from French territory for another 17 years.

The Rise of the Royal Court

Under Louis XI (r 1461–83) the city's first printing press was installed at the Sorbonne and churches were built around the city in the Flamboyant Gothic style. But it was during the reign of François I in the early 16th century that Renaissance ideas of scientific and geographic scholarship and discovery really assumed a new importance, as did the value of secular matters over religious life. Writers such as Rabelais, Marot and Ronsard of La Pléiade were influential, as were artist and architect disciples of Michelangelo and Raphael who worked towards a new architectural style designed to reflect the splendour of the monarchy (which was fast moving towards absolutism) and of Paris as the capital of a powerful centralised state. At François I's chateau, superb artisans, many brought over from Italy, blended Italian and French styles to create what is known as the First School of Fontainebleau.

But all this grandeur and show of strength was not enough to stem the tide of Protestant Reformation sweeping Europe in the 1530s, strengthened in France by the ideas of John Calvin. Following the Edict of January 1562, which afforded the Protestants certain rights, the Wars of Religion, which lasted three dozen years, broke out between the Huguenots (French Protestants who received help from the English), the Catholic League (led by the House of Guise) and the Catholic monarchy. On 7 May 1588, on the 'Day of the Barricades', Henri III, who had granted many concessions to the Huguenots, was forced to flee from the Louvre when the Catholic League rose against him. He was assassinated the following year.

Henri IV, founder of the Bourbon dynasty, issued the controversial Edict of Nantes in 1598, guaranteeing the Huguenots many civil and political rights, notably freedom of conscience. Ultra-Catholic Paris refused to allow the new Protestant king to enter the city, and a siege of the capital continued for almost five years. Only when Henri IV embraced Catholicism at the cathedral in St-Denis – *'Paris vaut bien un messe'* (Paris is well worth a Mass), he is reputed to have said during Communion – did the capital submit to him. Henri's rule ended abruptly in 1610 when he was assassinated by a Catholic fanatic when his coach became stuck in traffic along rue de la Ferronnerie, south of Les Halles.

Arguably France's best-known king of this or any other century, Louis XIV (r 1643–1715) aka 'Le Roi Soleil' (the Sun King), ascended the throne at the tender age of five. He involved the kingdom in a series

The population of Paris at the start of François' reign in 1515 was 170,000 – still almost 20% less than it had been some three centuries before, when the Black Death had decimated the city population.

Paintings by Jules Hardouin-Mansart in the Royal Chapel at Versailles evoke the idea that the French king was chosen by God and is thus his lieutenant on earth – a divinity the 'Sun King' believed in devoutly.

HISTORY THE RISE OF THE ROYAL COURT

1589	1643	1756–63	14 July 1789
Henry IV, the first Bourbon king, ascends the throne after renouncing Protestantism.	'Sun King' Louis XIV ascends the throne aged five but only assumes absolute power in 1661.	The Seven Years' War sees France lose flourishing colonies in Canada, the West Indies and India.	The French Revolution begins when a mob arms itself with weapons taken from the Hôtel des Invalides and storms the prison at Bastille, freeing a total of just seven prisoners.

of costly, almost continuous wars with Holland, Austria and England, which gained France territory but nearly bankrupted the treasury. State taxation, imposed to refill the coffers, caused widespread poverty and vagrancy, especially in cities. In Versailles, Louis XIV built an extravagant palace and made his courtiers compete with each other for royal favour, thereby quashing the ambitious, feuding aristocracy and creating the first centralised French state. In 1685 he revoked the Edict of Nantes.

During Louis XIII's reign (1610–43) two uninhabited islets in the Seine – Île Notre Dame and Île aux Vaches – were joined to form the Île de St-Louis.

From Revolution to Republic

During the so-called Age of Enlightenment, the royal court moved back to Paris from Versailles and the city effectively became the centre of Europe. Yet as the 18th century progressed, new economic and social circumstances rendered the *ancien régime* dangerously out of step with the needs of the country.

By the late 1780s the indecisive Louis XVI and his dominating Vienna-born queen, Marie-Antoinette, had alienated virtually every segment of society. When they tried to neutralise the power of more reform-minded delegates at a meeting of the États-Généraux (States-General) in Versailles from May to June 1789, the masses – spurred by the oratory and inflammatory tracts circulating at places like the Café de Foy at Palais Royal – took to the streets of Paris. On 14 July a mob raided the armoury at the Hôtel des Invalides for rifles, seized 32,000 muskets and stormed the prison at Bastille. Enter the French Revolution.

At first the Revolution was in the hands of moderate republicans, the Girondins. France was declared a constitutional monarchy and reforms were introduced, including the adoption of the Déclaration des Droits de l'Homme and du Citoyen (Declaration of the Rights of Man and of the Citizen). But as the masses armed themselves against the external threat to the new government – posed by Austria, Prussia and the exiled French nobles – patriotism and nationalism mixed with extreme fervour and then popularised and radicalised the Revolution. It was not long before the Girondins lost out to the extremist Jacobins, who abolished the monarchy and declared the First Republic. The Assemblée Nationale was replaced by an elected Revolutionary Convention.

Louis XVI was convicted of 'conspiring against the liberty of the nation' in January 1793 and guillotined at place de la Révolution, today's place de la Concorde. Two months later the Jacobins set up the notorious Committee of Public Safety to deal with national defence and try 'traitors'. The subsequent Reign of Terror (September 1793 to July 1794) saw religious freedoms revoked, churches closed and desecrated, cathe-

In 1774 a 100ft section of the rue d'Enfer (today's av Denfert-Rochereau) disappeared into a sinkhole, revealing an inconceivably precarious network of mining tunnels upon which southern Paris had been built.

1793	1799	1815	1830
Louis XVI is tried and convicted as 'Louis Capet' (as all kings since Hugh Capet were declared to have ruled illegally) and executed; Marie-Antoinette's turn comes nine months later.	Napoléon Bonaparte overthrows the Directory and seizes control of the government in a coup d'état, opening the doors to 16 years of despotic rule, victory and then defeat.	British and Prussian forces under the Duke of Wellington defeat Napoléon at Waterloo; he is sent into exile for the second time, this time to a remote island in the South Atlantic.	During the July Revolution, revolutionaries seize Hôtel de Ville and overthrow Charles X (r 1824–30). Place de la Bastille's Colonne de Juillet honours those killed.

drals turned into 'Temples of Reason' and thousands incarcerated in dungeons in La Conciergerie before being beheaded.

After the Reign of Terror faded, a five-man delegation of moderate republicans set itself up to rule the republic as the Directory.

Napoléon & Empire

The post-Revolutionary government was far from stable and when Napoléon returned to Paris in 1799, he found a chaotic republic in which few citizens had any faith. In November, when it appeared that the Jacobins were again on the ascendancy in the legislature, Napoléon tricked the delegates into leaving Paris for St-Cloud to the southwest ('for their own protection'), overthrew the discredited Directory and assumed power.

At first, Napoléon took the post of First Consul. In a referendum three years later he was named 'Consul for Life' and his birthday became a national holiday. By December 1804, when he crowned himself 'Emperor of the French' in the presence of Pope Pius VII at Notre Dame, the scope and nature of Napoléon's ambitions were obvious to all. But to consolidate and legitimise his authority, Napoléon needed more victories on the battlefield. So began a seemingly endless series of wars and victories by which France would come to control most of Europe.

In 1812 Napoléon invaded Russia and captured Moscow, only for his army to be quickly wiped out by the brutal Russian winter. Two years later Allied armies entered Paris, exiled Napoléon to Elba and restored the House of Bourbon to the French throne at the Congress of Vienna (1814–15).

But in early 1815 Napoléon escaped the Mediterranean island, landed in southern France and gathered a large army as he marched towards Paris. On 1 June he reclaimed the throne at celebrations held at the Champs de Mars. But his reign came to an end just three weeks later when his forces were defeated at Waterloo in Belgium. Napoléon was exiled again, this time to St Helena in the South Atlantic, where he died in 1821. In 1840 his remains were moved to Paris' Église du Dôme.

The Second Republic was established and elections in 1848 brought in Napoléon's inept nephew, the German-reared (and -accented) Louis Napoléon Bonaparte, as president. In 1851 he staged a coup d'état and proclaimed himself Emperor Napoléon III of the Second Empire, which lasted until 1870.

France enjoyed significant economic growth at this time, and Paris was transformed by town planner Baron Haussmann (1809–91) into the modern city it is today. Huge swaths of the city were completely

HISTORY NAPOLÉON & EMPIRE

Haussmann revolutionised Paris' water-supply and sewage systems, and created some of the city's loveliest parks. The city's first department stores were built, as were Paris' delightful shop-strewn *passages couverts* (covered passages).

From 1784 to 1836 the duke of Chartres turned the now-dignified Palais Royal into one of Europe's foremost pleasure gardens – 'the capital of Paris' – home to theatres, casinos, shops, cafes and an estimated 2000 sex workers.

1848	1852–70	1871	1880s
After more than three decades of monarchy, King Louis-Philippe is ousted and the short-lived Second Republic is established with Napoléon's incompetent nephew at the helm.	Paris enjoys significant economic growth during the Second Empire of Napoléon III and much of the city is redesigned or rebuilt by Baron Haussmann as the Paris we know today.	Harsh terms inflicted on France by victor Prussia in the Franco-Prussian War leads to open revolt and anarchy during the Paris Commune.	The Third Republic ushers in the bloody-then-beautiful belle époque, a madly creative era that conceives bohemian Paris, with its decadent nightclubs and artistic cafes.

rebuilt (demolishing much of medieval Paris in the process), its chaotic narrow streets replaced with the handsome, arrow-straight and wide thoroughfares for which the city is now celebrated.

Essential Historical Encounters

Arènes de Lutèce (Latin Quarter)

Musée National du Moyen Âge (Latin Quarter)

Hôtel des Invalides (St-Germain & Les Invalides)

Les Catacombes (Montparnasse & Southern Paris)

The Belle Époque

Though it would usher in the glittering belle époque (beautiful age), there was nothing particularly attractive about the start of the Third Republic. Born as a provisional government of national defence in September 1870, it was quickly besieged by the Prussians, who laid siege to Paris and demanded National Assembly elections be held. Unfortunately, the first move made by the resultant monarchist-controlled assembly was to ratify the Treaty of Frankfurt, the harsh terms of which – a huge war indemnity and surrender of the provinces of Alsace and Lorraine – helped instigate a civil war between radical Parisians (known as Communards) and the national government. The Communards took control of the city, establishing the Paris Commune, but the French Army eventually regained the capital several months later. It was a chaotic period, with mass executions on both sides, exiles and rampant destruction (both the Palais des Tuileries and the Hôtel de Ville were burned down). The Wall of the Federalists in Cimetière du Père Lachaise is a deathly reminder of the bloodshed.

The belle époque launched art nouveau architecture, a whole field of artistic 'isms' from impressionism onwards, and advances in science and engineering, including the construction of the first metro line (1900). World Fairs were held in the capital in 1889 (showcasing the Eiffel Tower) and 1901 (in the purpose-built Petit Palais). The Paris of nightclubs and artistic cafes made its first appearance around this time, and Montmartre became a magnet for artists, writers, pimps and prostitutes.

In 1923 French women obtained the right to – wait for it – open their own mail. The right to vote didn't come until 1945, and a woman still needed her husband's permission to open a bank account or get a passport until 1964.

But all was not well in the republic. France was consumed with a desire for revenge after its defeat by Germany, and was looking for scapegoats. The so-called Dreyfus Affair began in 1894 when a Jewish army captain named Alfred Dreyfus was accused of betraying military secrets to Germany; he was then court-martialled and sentenced to life imprisonment on Devil's Island. Liberal politicians and writers succeeded in having the case reopened despite bitter opposition from the army command, right-wing politicians and many Catholic groups – and Dreyfus was vindicated in 1900. This resulted in more rigorous civilian control of the military and, in 1905, the legal separation of the church and the state. When he died in 1935 Dreyfus was laid to rest in the Cimetière de Montparnasse.

1889	1914	1918	1920s
The Eiffel Tower is completed in time for the opening of the Exposition Universelle (World Fair) but is vilified in the press and on the street as the 'metal asparagus' – or worse.	Germany and Austria-Hungary declare war on Russia and France. German troops reach the River Marne 15km east of Paris and the government moves to Bordeaux.	An armistice ending WWI signed 82km northeast of Paris returns Alsace and Lorraine; of the eight million French called to arms, 1.3 million die and another million are crippled.	Paris sparkles as centre of the avant-garde with its newfound liberalism, cutting-edge nightlife and painters pushing into new fields of art like cubism and surrealism.

WWII & Occupation

Two days after the German invasion of Poland on 1 September 1939, Britain and France declared war on Germany. For the first nine months Parisians joked about *le drôle de guerre* – what Britons called 'the phoney war' – in which nothing happened. But the battle for France began in earnest in May 1940 and by 14 June France had capitulated. Paris was occupied, and almost half the population fled the city by car, bicycle or on foot. The British expeditionary force sent to help the French barely managed to avoid capture by retreating to Dunkirk, described so vividly in Ian McEwan's *Atonement* (2001), and crossing the English Channel in small boats. The Maginot Line, a supposedly impregnable wall of fortifications along the Franco-German border, had proved useless – the German armoured divisions simply outflanked it by going through Belgium.

The Germans divided France into two: a zone under direct German rule (along the western coast and the north, including Paris); and a puppet state based in the spa town of Vichy and led by General Philippe Pétain, the ageing WWI hero of the Battle of Verdun. Pétain's collaborationist government and French police forces in German-occupied areas (including Paris) helped the Nazis round up 160,000 French Jews and others for deportation to concentration and extermination camps in Germany and Poland.

After the fall of Paris, General Charles de Gaulle, France's undersecretary of war, fled to London. He set up a French government-in-exile and established the Forces Françaises Libres (Free French Forces), a military force dedicated to fighting the Germans alongside the Allies.

The liberation of France started with the Allied landings in Normandy on D-day (Jour-J in French): 6 June 1944. On 15 August that same year, Allied forces also landed in southern France. After a brief insurrection by the Resistance and general strikes by the metro and police, Paris was liberated on 25 August by an Allied force spearheaded by Free French units – these units were sent in ahead of the Americans so that the French would have the honour of liberating the capital the following day. Hitler, who visited Paris in June 1940 and loved it, demanded that the city be burned towards the end of the war. It was an order that, thankfully, was not obeyed.

Postwar Instability

De Gaulle returned to Paris and established a provisional government. But in January 1946 he resigned as president, wrongly believing the move would provoke a popular outcry for his return. A few months later

Historians debate the overall military effectiveness of the Resistance. But it served as an enormous boost to French morale and continues to impact French literature and cinema.

The Extraordinary Adventures of Adèle Blanc-Sec features the swashbuckling adventures of Adèle in early-20th-century Paris. Originally a graphic novel series created by Tardi, it was released as a film in 2010.

1940	25 August 1944	1949	1958
After over 10 months of *le drôle de guerre* (phoney war), Germany launches the battle for France, and the four-year occupation of Paris under direct German rule begins.	Spearheaded by Free French units, Allied forces liberate Paris and the city escapes destruction, despite Hitler's orders that it be torched; the war in Europe will end nine months later.	Simone de Beauvoir publishes her groundbreaking and very influential study *Le Deuxième Sexe* (The Second Sex) just four years after French women win the right to vote.	De Gaulle returns to power after more than a dozen years in opposition, to form the Fifth Republic.

a new constitution was approved by referendum. De Gaulle formed his own party (Rassemblement du Peuple Français) and spent the next 13 years in opposition.

The Fourth Republic saw a series of unstable coalition cabinets following one after another with bewildering speed (on average, one every six months), and economic recovery, helped immeasurably by massive American aid. France's disastrous defeat in Vietnam in 1954 ended its colonial supremacy in Southeast Asia. France also tried to suppress an uprising by Arab nationalists in Algeria, where more than a million French settlers lived.

The Fourth Republic came to an end in 1958, when extreme right-wingers, furious at what they saw as defeatism as opposed to tough action in dealing with the uprising in Algeria, began conspiring in an effort to overthrow the government. De Gaulle was brought back to power to prevent a military coup and possible civil war. He drafted a new constitution that handed considerable powers to the president, at the expense of the National Assembly.

On 15 October 1959, then senator and future president François Mitterrand was involved in a staged assassination attempt on his own life, now known as the infamous Observatory Affair.

Charles de Gaulle & the Fifth Republic

The Fifth Republic was rocked in 1961 by an attempted coup staged in Algiers by a group of right-wing military officers. When it failed, the Organisation de l'Armée Secrète (OAS) – a group of French *colons* (colonists) and sympathisers opposed to Algerian independence – turned to terrorism, trying several times to assassinate de Gaulle and nearly succeeding in August 1962 in the town of Clamart just southwest of Paris.

In 1962, after more than 12,000 had died as a result of this 'civil war', de Gaulle negotiated an end to the war in Algeria. Some 750,000 *pieds noirs* (black feet), as Algerian-born French people are known in France, came to France and the capital. Meanwhile, almost all of the other French colonies and protectorates in Africa had demanded and achieved independence. Shrewdly, the French government began a program of economic and military aid to its former colonies to bolster France's waning importance internationally and to create a bloc of French-speaking nations – *la francophonie* – in the developing world.

The book and film *The Day of the Jackal* portray a fictional account of the attempts by the OAS (a renegade paramilitary group who fought against Algerian independence) to take de Gaulle's life.

Paris retained its position as a creative and intellectual centre, particularly in philosophy and film-making, and the 1960s saw large parts of the Marais beautifully restored.

A Pivotal Year: 1968

The year 1968 was a watershed. In March a large demonstration in Paris against the war in Vietnam gave impetus to the student movement, and protests by students of the University of Paris peppered the capital

1962	1968	1977	1978
War in Algeria is brought to an end after claiming the lives of more than 12,000 people; three-quarters of a million Algerian-born French citizens arrive in France.	Paris is rocked by student-led riots that bring the nation and the city to the brink of civil war; as a result de Gaulle is forced to resign the following year.	Jacques Chirac, the first Paris mayor to be elected with real power, assumes office.	The Centre Pompidou, the first of a string of *grands projets*, huge public edifices through which French leaders seek to immortalise themselves, opens to great controversy.

for most of spring. In May police broke up yet another demonstration, prompting angry students to occupy the Sorbonne and erect barricades in the Latin Quarter. Workers joined in very quickly, with six million people across France participating in a general strike that virtually paralysed the country. It was a period of creativity and new ideas with slogans like *'L'Imagination au Pouvoir'* (Put Imagination in Power) and *'Sous les Pavés, la Plage'* (Under the Cobblestones, the Beach) – a reference to Parisians' favoured material for building barricades and what they could expect to find beneath them – popping up everywhere.

But such an alliance between workers and students couldn't last long. While the former wanted to reap greater benefits from the consumer market, the latter supposedly wanted to destroy it. De Gaulle took advantage of this division and appealed to people's fear of anarchy. And just as Paris and the rest of France seemed on the verge of revolution, a mighty 100,000-strong crowd of Gaullists came out on the streets of Paris to show their support for the government, thus quashing any idea of revolution. Stability was restored.

Modern Society

Once stability was restored the government immediately decentralised the higher education system and implemented a series of reforms (including lowering the voting age to 18, and enacting an abortion law) throughout the 1970s to create the modern society France is today.

President Charles de Gaulle resigned in 1969 and was succeeded by the Gaullist leader Georges Pompidou and later Valéry Giscard d'Estaing. Socialist François Mitterrand became president in 1981 and immediately nationalised privately owned banks, large industrial groups and other parts of the economy. A more moderate economic policy in the mid-1980s ensured a second term in office for the then 69-year-old Mitterrand.

Jacques Chirac, mayor of Paris since 1977, took over the presidential baton in 1995 and received high marks in his first few months for his direct words and actions in EU matters and the war in Bosnia. But his decision to resume nuclear testing on the French Polynesian island of Mururoa and a nearby atoll was met with outrage in France and abroad, and when, in 1997, Chirac gambled with an early parliamentary election for June, the move backfired. Chirac remained president but his party, the Rassemblement Pour la République (RPR; Rally for the Republic), lost support, and a coalition of Socialists, Communists and Greens came to power – under whom France's infamous 35-hour working week was introduced.

Paris is run from the Hôtel de Ville (City Hall) by the *maire* (mayor) with help from 21 *adjoints* (deputy mayors), elected by 163 members of the Conseil de Paris (Council of Paris) and serving terms of six years.

HISTORY MODERN SOCIETY

1989	1998	2001	2002
President Mitterrand's *grand projet*, Opéra de Paris Bastille, opens to mark the bicentennial of the French Revolution; IM Pei's Grande Pyramide is unveiled at the Louvre.	France beats Brazil to win the World Cup at the spanking-new Stade de France (Stadium of France) in St-Denis north of central Paris.	Socialist Bertrand Delanoë becomes the first openly gay mayor of Paris (and of any European capital); he is wounded in a knife attack by a homophobic assailant the following year.	The French franc is thrown onto the scrap heap of history as the country adopts the euro as its official currency, along with 14 other EU member-states.

Chirac's second term, starting in 2002, was marred by some of the worst violence seen in Paris since WWII. In autumn 2005, following the death of two teenage boys of North African origin hiding in an electrical substation while on the run from the police, riots broke out in Paris' *cités,* the enormous housing estates encircling the capital where a dispossessed population lives. The violence quickly spread to other cities in France and the government called a state of emergency. Only 9000 burnt cars and buildings later was peace in Paris was restored.

The Presidential Pendulum

Presidential elections in 2007 ushered old-school Jacques Chirac out and the dynamic, ambitious and media-savvy Nicolas Sarkozy in. The former interior minister and chairperson of centre-right party Union pour un Mouvement Populaire (UMP) wooed voters with promises of reducing unemployment, job creation, lower income tax, a crackdown on crime and help for France's substantial immigrant population – something that had particular pulling power coming from the son of a Hungarian immigrant father and Greek Jewish-French mother. And the French, fed up with an economically stagnant, socially discontented France, wanted change. A new breed of French president was born.

Contrary to the rigorous economic reform platform on which he'd been elected and against the backdrop of the global recession, Sarkozy struggled to keep the French economy buoyant. Attempts to introduce reforms – eg the scaleback of the extremely generous French pension system – provoked widespread horror and a series of national strikes and protests. Sarkozy's popularity plummeted, paving the way for socialist Francois Hollande's victory in the 2012 presidential elections.

With France still struggling to restart the economy, Hollande pledged to end austerity measures and reduce unemployment. Many economic policies have thus far proved ineffectual though, and rising anger at Hollande's failure to deliver on campaign promises saw his popularity plunge even faster and further than Sarkozy's and resulted in a near-total wipeout for French socialists in the 2014 municipal elections. The 2014 election of Socialist Anne Hidalgo, Paris' first female mayor, meant the capital was one of the few cities to remain on the political left.

Turbulent Times

The year 2015 was a harrowing one for the French capital. On 7 January the offices of magazine *Charlie Hebdo* were attacked in response to satirical images it published of the prophet Muhammad. Eleven staff and one police officer were killed and a further 22 people injured. The at-

HISTORY THE PRESIDENTIAL PENDULUM

Bertrand Delanoë, a socialist backed by the Green Party, became the first openly gay mayor of Paris (and any European capital) in 2001. He was reelected for a second term in 2008.

Historical Reads

Seven Ages of Paris (Alistair Horne, 2002)

Suite Française (Irène Némirovsky, 2006)

The Paris Wife (Paula McLain, 2011)

2004	2005	2011	2012
France bans the wearing of crucifixes, the Islamic headscarf and other overtly religious symbols in state schools.	The French electorate overwhelmingly rejects the EU Constitution; the suburbs surrounding Paris are wracked by rioting youths.	The controversial French parliamentary ban on burkas in public comes into effect in April; Muslim women wearing the Islamic face-covering veil risk a fine.	France loses its top AAA credit rating. Economic policy becomes a campaign issue in the run-up to the 2012 presidential elections in late April.

tacks shocked the world and on 11 January over two million people, including 40 world leaders, held a rally of national unity in the streets of Paris. Millions more joined demonstrations across France. The hashtag #jesuischarlie (I am Charlie) became a slogan of support around the globe. The magazine printed 7.95 million copies of its following issue in six languages (compared with its usual 60,000 copies in French only).

But worse was to come. On the night of 13 November 2015 a series of coordinated terrorist attacks occurred in Paris and St-Denis – the deadliest on French soil since WWII. The attacks started at 9.20pm. Three explosions shook the Stade de France stadium during a football friendly match between Germany and France attended by 80,000 spectators including President Hollande. A series of neighbourhood restaurants and their outdoor terraces in the 10e and 11e *arrondissements* were attacked by suicide bombers and gunmen. At 9.40pm three gunmen fired into the audience of Le Bataclan, where American band Eagles of Death Metal were performing. Over the course of the evening's terror 130 people lost their lives (89 in Le Bataclan alone) and 368 were injured, 99 seriously. Many of the victims were young. Paris went into lockdown, the army was mobilised and a state of emergency declared. Several of the attackers were linked to atrocities that later took place in Brussels on 22 March 2016.

Parisians responded to the trauma by establishing memorials at the fatality sites and place de la République, which became the focal point for the city's outpouring of grief, and by taking to cafe terraces and other public spaces. The hashtag #jesuisenterrasse (I am on the terrace) represented Parisians' refusal to live in fear.

The city of Paris also refused to allow daily life to be disrupted. The long-planned United Nations Climate Change Conference (COP21) went ahead from 30 November to 12 December 2015. During the conference leaders from around the world reached an agreement to limit global warming to less than 2°C by the end of the century.

HISTORY TURBULENT TIMES

The French receive free education and health care, state-subsidised child care, travel concessions for families, ample leisure time and a 35-hour working week.

2012	2014	2015	2015
Socialist candidate François Hollande beats Nicolas Sarkozy to become France's new president but his popularity is short-lived.	Spanish-born Anne Hidalgo becomes the first female mayor of Paris after defeating Sarkozy protégé Nathalie Kosciusko-Morizet.	The year is bookended by deadly terrorist attacks, on staff at the offices of satirical magazine *Charlie Hebdo* on 7 January, and on civilians at multiple locations on 13 November.	Paris successfully hosts the United Nations Climate Change Conference (COP21), during which world leaders agree on measures to reduce global warming.

Fashion

Yves Saint Laurent once declared that fashion is a way of life, and most Parisians would agree. Dressing well is part of the Parisian DNA, the world's eyes are on the city during the bi-annual fashion weeks, and new labels spring up in the French capital every year. But what is less well known is that Parisian *haute couture* (literally 'high sewing') as it exists today was created by an Englishman.

**Fashion
Museums &
Exhibitions**

*Fondation Pierre
Bergé-Yves Saint
Laurent, 16e*

*Musée de la Mode
de la Ville de
Paris, 16e*

*Cité de la Mode et
du Design (Docks
en Seine), 13e*

Revolution & Drama

Nicknamed 'the Napoléon of costumers', 20-year-old Englishman Charles Frederick Worth (1825–95) arrived in Paris and revolutionised fashion by banishing the crinoline (stiffened petticoat), lifting hemlines to ankle length and presenting his creations on live models. The House of Worth stayed in the family for four generations until the 1950s.

In the 1990s highly creative, rebel-yell British designers such as Alexander McQueen (1969–2010) and John Galliano (b 1960) dominated Paris' fashion scene. One of the industry's biggest influencers, Gibraltar-born and London-raised Galliano moved to Paris in 1991 and became chief designer at Givenchy in 1995. A year later he moved to Dior, the legendary French fashion house responsible for re-establishing Paris as world fashion capital after WWII. Galliano's first women's collection for Dior was spectacular – models waltzed down a catwalk framed by 500 gold chairs and 4000 roses arranged to recreate the postwar glamour of Christian Dior's 1946 showroom on av Montaigne, 8e, in Paris' legendary Triangle d'Or (Golden Triangle).

The downfall of fashion's talented *enfant terrible* was dramatic. In 2011 Galliano was caught on camera casting public insults to punters at his local neighbourhood cafe-bar La Perle in Le Marais. He was dismissed by the House of Dior and later found guilty in court of anti-Semitic abuse.

Contemporary Fashion

Outlandish designs by young rising stars such as Serkan Cura (swiftly making a name for himself with work-of-art dresses crafted from feathers and Swarovski crystals) or world-famous couturiers like 'wild child' Jean Paul Gaultier (known for putting men in punky skirts and Madonna in her signature conical bra) might strut down the Paris catwalk during fashion week. But you encounter few Cura- or Gaultier-clad women rubbing shoulders in the metro: Parisian style is generally too conservative for that.

London-inspired streetwear jumps off the shelves in trendy shops around rue Étienne Marcel in the Louvre & Les Halles neighbourhood, and Le Marais. The Haut Marais, 3e, is known for its young designer boutiques. Names to watch and wear include Moon Young Hee, Valentine Gauthier, Yukiko and Sakina M'sa. Anne Elisabeth, a well-travelled Parisian designer with boutiques in the 1er, 3e and 6e, is a long-standing favourite. Parisian handbag designers include Nat & Nin, Clarisse (Pauline Pin), Kasia Dietz and Jamin Puech.

APC bag at Paris Fashion Week

BCBG & Intello

In upper-crust circles, the BCBG *(bon chic bon genre)* woman shops at department store Le Bon Marché or Chanel, and rarely ventures outside her preferred districts: the 7e, 8e and 16e.

The chic Left Bank *intello* (intellectual) shops for trendy but highly wearable fashion at upmarket high-street boutiques such as Agnès b (created in Paris in 1975 by Versailles designer Agnès Troublé – the 'b' gives a nod to her husband) and APC (Atelier de Production et de Création). Fast-growing brands like Kooples, Maje, Sandro, Comptoir des Cotonniers and Zadig & Voltaire are huge among BCBG.

Bobo & Hipster

Bastille, Le Marais and the 10e around Canal St-Martin are stomping grounds of the *bobo* (bourgeois bohemian) – modern bohemians with wealthy bourgeois parents whose style roots itself in nostalgia for that last voyage to India, Tibet or Senegal and that avowed commitment to free trade and beads. The wildest *bobos* wear Kate Mack and dress their kids in romantic rockesque designs by Liza Korn, at home in 10e.

Younger professional *bobos* frequent iconic concept store Colette or smaller concept stores with carefully curated collections like L'Éclaireur and the Broken Arm in Le Marais. Isabel Marant enjoys cult worship among Parisian *bobos* thanks to her chic but easy style that teams wearable-year-round floral dresses or denim mini skirts with loose knits and lush scarves. Another favourite is Vanessa Bruno, a Parisian brand again known for its wearable, if slightly edgy, fashion, such as crocheted bra tops, and cotton skirts with metallic thread to maintain shape. On the jewellery front, designs by Marion Vidal in the 9e are bold, funky and heavily architecture-influenced.

Paris coined the expression *lèche-vitrine* (literally 'window-licker') for window shopping. 'Tasting' without buying is an art like any other so don't be shy. The fancy couture houses on av Montaigne may seem daunting but, in most, no appointment is necessary and you can simply walk in.

THE SHOW OF SHOWS

The Paris fashion *haute-couture* shows fall in late January for the spring/summer collections and early July for autumn/winter ones. But most established couturiers presented a more affordable prêt-à-porter (ready-to-wear) line, and many have abandoned *haute couture* altogether. Prêt-à-porter shows are in late January and September. Shows are exclusive affairs, not open to the general public.

For alternative catwalk action, reserve a spot at the Friday-afternoon fashion show (March to June and September to December) at department store Galeries Lafayette, 9e.

Paris' Brooklyn-styled hipster is similar to a *bobo* but younger (typically aged 18 to 25 years) and often without the money. Parisian hipsters only drink juice that is freshly squeezed and flout big-name or known fashion labels for a 'purist', often vintage, look.

Ready to Wear

Céline, prided for its stylish and clever minimalism since 1945, is a luxury label so popular it's practically mainstream in its ready-to-wear, 'fashion for everyone' approach. Chloé is the other big ready-to-wear house, created in 1952 and the first *haute-couture* label to introduce (in 1956) a designer ready-to-wear collection. Paris' prêt-à-porter industry was born.

Nostalgia & Recycling

Hipster 'purism' gives an approving nod to secondhand and recycling, while the desire in less-uber-trendy circles to have an original Hermès scarf or Chanel black dress never tires.

Two films about fashion icon Yves Saint Laurent were released in 2014: the more innocous 'official' film, *Yves Saint Laurent,* directed by Jalil Lespert (using original costumes), and the edgier but much longer unauthorised film, *Saint Laurent,* directed by Bertrand Bonello.

Vintage

Parisian women play safe with classic designs and monotones, jazzed up by a scarf (often those by Hermès, founded by a saddle-maker in 1837) or other simple accessory, hence the fervent nostalgia for the practical designs and modern simplicity of interwar designer Coco Chanel (1883–1971), celebrated creator of the 1920s' 'little black dress'. Equal enthusiasm for pieces by Givenchy, Féraud and other designers from the 1950s heyday of Paris fashion contribute to the vintage clothing demand.

Twice a year Parisian auction house Hôtel Drouot hosts *haute-couture* auctions. Collector Didier Ludot has sold the city's finest couture creations of yesteryear in his exclusive boutique at Palais Royal since 1975. In St-Germain, Catherine B (p244) specialises in vintage fashion and accessories from fashion houses Chanel and Hermès only.

Postvintage

Postvintage fashion is about recycling. Art and fashion studio Andrea Crews, born between new millennium sex shops in Pigalle and now at home in Le Marais, was among the first to reinvent grandpa's discarded shirts and daughter's has-beens into new hip garments.

Trends of Tomorrow

Each year the city of Paris' Grand Prix Création de la Ville de Paris is awarded to the 'Best New Designer' (working in the trade for under three years) and 'Best Confirmed Designer' (at least three years in the fashion biz). The list of prize laureates is tantamount to a who's who of tomorrow's fashion scene.

Labels to watch include Each X Other, Vetements, Jacquemus, Etudes Studio, MiniMe Paris, Aleph Mendel and Amalgam.

Architecture

It took disease, clogged streets, an antiquated sewage system and Baron Georges-Eugène Haussmann to drag architectural Paris out of the Middle Ages and into the modern world – yet ever since Haussmann's radical transformation of the city in the 19th century, which saw entire sections razed and thousands of people displaced, Paris has never looked back. Its contemporary skyline shimmers with the whole gamut of architectural styles, from Roman arenas and Gothic cathedrals to postmodernist cubes and futuristic skyscrapers.

Gallo-Roman

Traces of Roman Paris can be seen in the residential foundations in the Crypte Archéologique in front of Notre Dame; in the Arènes de Lutèce; and in the *frigidarium* (cooling room) and other remains of Roman baths dating from around AD 200 at the Musée National du Moyen Âge.

Above: Panthéon (p209)

The latter museum also contains the *Pillier des Nautes* (Boatsmen's Pillar), one of the most valuable legacies of the Gallo-Roman period. It is a 2.5m-high monument dedicated to Jupiter and was erected by the boatmen's guild during the reign of Tiberius (AD 14–37) on the Île de la Cité. The boat has become the symbol of Paris, and the city's Latin motto is *'Fluctuat Nec Mergitur'* (Tossed by Waves but Does Not Sink).

Merovingian & Carolingian

Although quite a few churches were built in Paris during the Merovingian and Carolingian periods (6th to 10th centuries), very little of them remain.

When the Merovingian ruler Clovis I made Paris his seat in the early 6th century, he established an abbey on the south bank of the Seine. All that remains is the Tour Clovis, a heavily restored Romanesque tower within the grounds of the prestigious Lycée Henri IV just east of the Panthéon.

Archaeological excavations in the crypt of the 12th-century Basilique de St-Denis have uncovered extensive tombs from the Merovingian and Carolingian periods; the oldest dates from around AD 570.

Romanesque

A religious revival in the 11th century led to the construction of many *roman* (Romanesque) churches, typically with round arches, heavy walls, few (and small) windows and a lack of ornamentation that bordered on the austere.

No remaining building in Paris is entirely Romanesque but several have important representative elements. Église St-Germain des Prés, built in the 11th century on the site of the Merovingian ruler Childeric's 6th-century abbey, has been altered many times over the centuries, but the Romanesque bell tower above the west entrance has changed little since AD 1000. The choir, apse and truncated bell tower of Église St-Nicolas des Champs, now part of the Musée des Arts et Métiers, are Romanesque. Église St-Germain l'Auxerrois was built in a mixture of Gothic and Renaissance styles between the 13th and 16th centuries.

Gothic

The world's first Gothic building was Basilique de St-Denis, which combined various late-Romanesque elements to create a new kind of structural support in which each arch counteracted and complemented the next. The basilica served as a model for many 12th-century French cathedrals, including Notre Dame de Paris and Chartres cathedral.

In the 14th century, the Rayonnant – or Radiant – Gothic style, named after the radiating tracery of the rose windows, developed. Interiors became even lighter thanks to broader windows and more translucent stained glass. One of the most influential Rayonnant buildings was Sainte-Chapelle, whose stained glass forms a curtain of glazing on the 1st floor. The two transept facades of Cathédrale de Notre Dame de Paris and the vaulted Salle des Gens d'Armes (Cavalrymen's Hall) in the Conciergerie, the largest surviving medieval hall in Europe, are other fine examples of Rayonnant Gothic style.

By the 15th century, decorative extravagance led to Flamboyant Gothic, so named because the wavy stone carving made the towers appear to be blazing or flaming *(flamboyant)*. Beautifully lacy examples of Flamboyant architecture include the Clocher Neuf (New Bell Tower) at Chartres' cathedral, Église St-Séverin, and Tour St-Jacques, a 52m tower that is all that remains of an early-16th-century church. Inside

Must-See Buildings

....

Eiffel Tower (Eiffel Tower & Western Paris)

....

Louvre pyramid (Louvre & Les Halles)

....

Basilique du Sacré-Cœur (Montmartre & Northern Paris)

....

Centre Pompidou (Louvre & Les Halles)

....

Cité de l'Architecture et du Patrimoine (Eiffel Tower & Western Paris)

Grande Arche de la Défense (p87)

Église St-Eustache there's some outstanding Flamboyant Gothic arch work holding up the ceiling of the chancel. Several *hôtels particuliers* (private mansions) were also built in this style, including Hôtel de Cluny, now the Musée National du Moyen Âge.

Renaissance

The Renaissance set out to realise a 'rebirth' of classical Greek and Roman culture and first affected France at the end of the 15th century, when Charles VIII began a series of invasions of Italy, returning with some new ideas.

The Early Renaissance style, in which a variety of classical components and decorative motifs (columns, tunnel vaults, round arches, domes etc) were blended with the rich decoration of Flamboyant Gothic, is best exemplified in Paris by Église St-Eustache on the Right Bank and Église St-Étienne du Mont on the Left Bank.

Mannerism was introduced by Italian architects and artists brought to France around 1530 by François I. In 1546 Pierre Lescot designed the richly decorated southwestern corner of the Cour Carrée at the Musée du Louvre.

The Right Bank district of Le Marais remains the best area for Renaissance reminders in Paris proper.

Baroque

During the baroque period (tail end of the 16th to late 18th centuries), painting, sculpture and classical architecture were integrated to create structures and interiors of great subtlety, refinement and elegance. With the advent of the baroque, architecture became more pictorial,

The iconic apartment buildings that line the boulevards of central Paris, with their cream-coloured stone and curvy wrought-iron balconies, are the work of Baron Haussmann (1809–91), prefect of the Seine *département* between 1853 and 1870.

with painted church ceilings illustrating the Passion of Christ to the faithful, and palaces invoking the power and order of the state.

Salomon de Brosse, who designed the Palais du Luxembourg in the Jardin du Luxembourg in 1615, set the stage for two of France's most prominent early-baroque architects: François Mansart, designer of Église Notre Dame du Val-de-Grâce, and his young rival Louis Le Vau, architect of Château de Vaux-le-Vicomte, which served as a model for Louis XIV's palace at Versailles.

Other fine French-baroque examples include: Église St-Louis en l'Île, Chapelle de la Sorbonne, Palais Royal and Hôtel de Sully, with its inner courtyard decorated with allegorical figures.

A zany structure if ever there was one is auction house Hôtel Drouat. After a late-1970s surrealist facelift by architects Jean-Jacques Fernier and André Biro, the 19th-century Haussmann building was instantly hailed as a modern architectural gem.

Neoclassicism

Neoclassical architecture emerged about 1740 and had its roots in the renewed interest in classical forms – a search for order, reason and serenity through the adoption of forms and conventions of Graeco-Roman antiquity: columns, geometric forms and traditional ornamentation.

Among the earliest examples of this style are the Italianate facade of Église St-Sulpice, and the Petit Trianon at Versailles, designed by Jacques-Ange Gabriel for Louis XV in 1761. The domed building in Paris housing the Institut de France is a masterpiece of early French neoclassical architecture, but France's greatest neoclassical architect of the 18th century was Jacques-Germain Soufflot, creator of the Panthéon in the Latin Quarter.

Neoclassicism came into its own under Napoléon, who used it extensively for monumental architecture intended to embody the grandeur of imperial France and its capital: the Arc de Triomphe, the Arc de Triomphe du Carrousel, Église de Ste-Marie Madeleine, the Bourse de Commerce, and the Assemblée Nationale in the Palais Bourbon. Fittingly, the climax to this great 19th-century movement was Palais Garnier, the city's opera house designed by Charles Garnier.

Art Nouveau

Art nouveau, which emerged in Europe and the USA in the second half of the 19th century under various names (Jugendstil, Sezessionstil, Stile Liberty), caught on quickly in Paris, and its influence lasted until about 1910. It was characterised by sinuous curves and flowing, asymmetrical forms reminiscent of creeping vines, water lilies, the patterns on insect wings and the flowering boughs of trees. Influenced by the arrival of exotic objets d'art from Japan, art nouveau's French name came from a Paris gallery that featured works in the 'new art' style.

LA NOUVELLE SAMARITAINE

Founded in 1870 by Ernest Cognacq and Louise Jaÿ, La Samaritaine was, up until its closure in 2005, one of Paris' four big department stores. Bought by the LVMH group at the turn of the millennium and the subject of a bitter preservationist battle in the years that followed, it is finally preparing for its new lease on life – one in which the landmark will incorporate a luxury hotel (on the Seine side), a new department store (on the rue de Rivoli side), social housing, a crèche (nursery) and office space.

The project, awarded to the Pritzker Prize–winning Japanese firm Sanaa, will preserve an estimated 75% of the original art nouveau and art deco exterior, although the new rue de Rivoli facade, an immense etched-glass wall, offers a glimpse of La Nouvelle Samaritaine's modernist inclinations. Construction is expected to be completed in late 2018.

A lush and photogenic architectural style, art nouveau is expressed to perfection in Paris by Hector Guimard's graceful metro entrances and Le Marais synagogue, parts of the interiors in the Musée d'Orsay and the city's main department stores, Le Bon Marché and Galeries Lafayette.

Modern

France's best-known 20th-century architect, Charles-Édouard Jeanneret (aka Le Corbusier), was born in Switzerland but settled in Paris in 1917 at the age of 30. A radical modernist, he tried to adapt buildings to their functions in industrialised society without ignoring the human element. Most of Le Corbusier's work was done outside Paris, though he did design several private residences and the Pavillon Suisse, a dormitory for Swiss students at the Cité Internationale Universitaire in the 14e.

But until 1968, French architects were still being trained almost exclusively at the conformist École de Beaux-Arts, reflected in most of the early impersonal and forgettable 'lipstick tubes' and 'upended shoebox' structures erected in the skyscraper district of La Défense, the Unesco building (1958) in the 7e, and the 210m-tall Tour Montparnasse (1973).

Contemporary

For centuries France's leaders sought to immortalise themselves by erecting huge public edifices *('grands projets')* in Paris. Georges Pompidou commissioned the once reviled, now much-loved Centre Pompidou. His successor, Valéry Giscard d'Estaing, was instrumental in transforming the derelict Gare d'Orsay train station into the glorious Musée d'Orsay (1986). François Mitterrand surpassed all of the postwar presidents with monumental projects costing taxpayers €4.6 billion: Jean Nouvel's Institut du Monde Arabe (1987), built during this time, mixes modern Arab and Western elements and is arguably one of the city's most beautiful late-20th-century buildings. Jacques Chirac orchestrated the magnificent Musée du Quai Branly, a glass, wood and sod structure with 3-hectare experimental garden, also by Jean Nouvel.

Ground-Breaking Designs

Recent years have seen the construction of several modern Parisian landmarks: IM Pei's glass-pyramid entrance at the hitherto sacrosanct and untouchable Musée du Louvre, an architectural cause célèbre that paved the way for Mario Bellini and Rudy Ricciotti's magnificent 'flying carpet' roof atop the museum's Cour Visconti in 2012; the city's second opera house, tile-clad Opéra de Paris Bastille, designed by Uruguayan architect Carlos Ott in 1989; the monumental Grande Arche de la Défense by Danish architect Johan-Otto von Sprekelsen (1989); the delightful Conservatoire National Supérieur de Musique et de Danse (1990) and Cité de la Musique (1994), designed by Christian de Portzamparc in the whimsical Parc de la Villette; the four glass towers of the €2 billion Bibliothèque Nationale de France (Dominique Perrault, 1995); and neighbouring M2K Bibliothèque pleasure palace (Wilmotte & Namur, 2003) in a glass shoebox that glimmers at night.

The *grand projet* of the new millennium was Jean Nouvel's long-awaited Philharmonie de Paris, a state-of-the-art creation that took three years to build and cost €381 million. On a more human scale is the redeveloped warehouse district known as Masséna Nord, where narrow streets and open blocks link conversions such as the Grands Moulins (an old mill that is now the hub of the new Paris Diderot University), the former SNCF cold-storage warehouse of Les Frigos (now a colourful artists' community), and an old factory complete with smokestack (a new architecture school).

ARCHITECTURE MODERN

Interesting and frightening were Le Corbusier's plans for Paris that never left the drawing board. Plan Voisin (Neighbour Project; 1925) envisaged wide boulevards linking the Gare Montparnasse with the Seine and lined with skyscrapers. The project would have required bulldozing much of the Latin Quarter.

A signature architectural feature of Paris is the vertical garden, or *mur végétal* (vegetation wall). Seeming to defy gravity, these gardens clad walls in chic boutique interiors, outside museums, within spas and elsewhere. The Seine-facing garden at the Musée du Quai Branly, by Patrick Blanc, is Paris' most famous.

Literary Paris

Whether attending a reading at legendary bookshop Shakespeare & Company in the Latin Quarter, browsing bookshelves in a wine bar in Le Marais or poring over the latest *bande dessinée* (comic strip) in Fnac, Parisians have a deep appreciation for the written word, and literature remains essential to their sense of identity. Couple this with the mass of modern literature inspired by the 'City of Light' and Paris will never leave you short of a good read.

Medieval

Paris does not figure largely in early-medieval French literature, although the misadventures of Pierre Abélard and Héloïse took place in the capital, as did their mutual correspondence, which ended only with their deaths.

François Villon, the finest poet of the Middle Ages, received the equivalent of a Master of Arts degree from the Sorbonne before he turned 20. Involved in a series of brawls, robberies and illicit escapades, 'Master Villon' (as he became known) was sentenced to be hanged in 1462, supposedly for stabbing a lawyer. However, the sentence was commuted to banishment from Paris for 10 years, and he disappeared forever. Villon left behind a body of poems charged with a highly personal lyricism, among them *Ballade des Pendus* (Ballad of the Hanged Men), in which he writes his own epitaph, and *Ballade des Dames du Temps Jadis*, translated by the English poet and painter Dante Gabriel Rossetti as the 'Ballad of Dead Ladies'.

Literary Sights

....

Maison de Victor Hugo

....

Maison de Balzac

....

Musée de la Vie Romantique

....

Art Ludique-Le Musée

Renaissance

The great landmarks of French Renaissance literature are the works of François Rabelais, Pierre de Ronsard (and other poets of the Renaissance group of poets known as La Pléiade) and Michel de Montaigne. The exuberant narratives of erstwhile monk Rabelais blend coarse humour with erudition in a vast oeuvre that seems to include every kind of person, occupation and jargon to be found in the France of the early 16th century. Rabelais' publisher, Étienne Dolet, was convicted of heresy and blasphemy in 1546, hanged and burned on place Maubert, 5e.

Classical

During the 17th century, François de Malherbe, court poet under Henri IV, brought a new rigour to rhythm in literature. One of his better-known works is his sycophantic *Ode* (1600) to Marie de Médici. Transported by the perfection of Malherbe's verses, Jean de la Fontaine went on to write his charming *Fables* (1668) in the manner of Aesop – though he fell afoul of the Académie Française (French Academy) in the process. A mood of classical tragedy permeates *La Princesse de Clèves* (1678), by Marie de la Fayette, widely regarded as the precursor of the modern character novel.

Eighteenth Century

The literature of the 18th century is dominated by philosophers, among them Voltaire (François-Marie Arouet) and Jean-Jacques Rousseau. Voltaire's political writings, arguing that society is fundamentally opposed to nature, had a profound and lasting influence on the century, and he is buried in the Panthéon. Rousseau's sensitivity to landscape and its moods anticipated romanticism, and the insistence on his own singularity in *Les Confessions* (1782) made it the first modern autobiography. He, too, lies in the Panthéon.

French Romanticism

The 19th century produced poet and novelist Victor Hugo, who lived on place des Vosges before fleeing to the Channel Islands during the Second Empire. *Les Misérables* (1862) describes life among the poor of Paris in the early 19th century. *Notre Dame de Paris* (The Hunchback of Notre Dame; 1831), a medieval romance and tragedy revolving around the life of the celebrated cathedral, made Hugo the key figure of French romanticism.

Other influential 19th-century novelists include Stendhal (Marie-Henri Beyle), Honoré de Balzac, Amandine Aurore Lucile Dupin (aka George Sand) and, of course, Alexandre Dumas, who wrote the swashbuckling adventures *Le Comte de Monte Cristo* (The Count of Monte Cristo; 1844) and *Les Trois Mousquetaires* (The Three Musketeers; 1844).

In 1857 two landmarks of French literature were published: *Madame Bovary,* by Gustave Flaubert, and *Les Fleurs du Mal*, by Charles Baudelaire. Both writers were tried for the supposed immorality of their works. Flaubert won his case, and his novel was distributed without censorship. Baudelaire, who moonlighted as a translator in Paris, was obliged to cut half a dozen poems from his work and fined 300 francs.

The aim of Émile Zola, who came to Paris with his close friend, the artist Paul Cézanne, in 1858, was to transform novel-writing from an art to a science by the application of experimentation. His theory may now seem naive, but his work influenced most significant French writers of the late 19th century and is reflected in much 20th-century fiction as well. His novel *Nana* (1880) tells the decadent tale of a young woman who resorts to prostitution to survive the Paris of the Second Empire.

Symbolism & Surrealism

Paul Verlaine and Stéphane Mallarmé created the symbolist movement, which strove to express states of mind rather than simply detail daily reality. Arthur Rimbaud, in addition to crowding an extraordinary amount of exotic travel into his 37 years and having a tempestuous sexual relationship with Verlaine, produced two enduring pieces of work: *Une Saison en Enfer* (A Season in Hell; 1873) and *Illuminations* (1874). Verlaine died at 39 rue Descartes, 5e, in 1896.

Marcel Proust dominated the early 20th century with his seven-volume novel *À la Recherche du Temps Perdu* (Remembrance of Things Past; 1913–27), which explores the true meaning of past experience recovered from the unconscious by 'involuntary memory'. In 1907 Proust moved from the family home near av des Champs-Élysées to an apartment on bd Haussmann famous for its cork-lined bedroom. André Gide found his voice in the celebration of gay sensuality and, later, left-wing politics. *Les Faux-Monnayeurs* (The Counterfeiters; 1925) exposes the hypocrisy and self-deception to which people resort in order to fit in with others or deceive themselves.

L'Âge de Raison (The Age of Reason; 1945), the first volume of Jean-Paul Sartre's trilogy *Les Chemins de la Liberté* (The Roads to Freedom), is a superb Parisian novel. His subsequent volumes recall Paris immediately before and during WWII.

Histoire d'O (Story of O; 1954), Dominique Aury's erotic, sadomasochistic novel written under a pseudonym, has sold more copies outside France than any other contemporary French novel. Most believed it to be the work of a man; it was only 40 years after publication that the author revealed her identity.

FOREIGN LITERATURE: INTERWAR HEYDAY

Foreigners have found inspiration in Paris since Charles Dickens used the city along-side London as the backdrop to *A Tale of Two Cities* in 1859. The heyday of Paris as a literary setting, however, was the interwar period.

Ernest Hemingway's *The Sun Also Rises* (1926) and the posthumous *A Moveable Feast* (1964) portray bohemian life in Paris between the wars. So many vignettes in the latter – dissing Ford Madox Ford in a cafe, 'sizing up' F Scott Fitzgerald in a toilet in the Latin Quarter, and overhearing Gertrude Stein and her lover, Alice B Toklas, bitchin' at one another from the sitting room of their salon near the Jardin du Luxembourg – are classic and *très parisien*.

Gertrude Stein let her hair down by assuming her lover's identity in *The Autobiography of Alice B Toklas,* a fascinating account of the author's many years in Paris, her salon on rue de Fleurus, 6e, and her friendships with Matisse, Picasso, Braque, Hemingway and others.

Down and Out in Paris and London (1933) is George Orwell's account of the time he spent working as a *plongeur* (dishwasher) in Paris and living with tramps in the city in the 1930s. Henry Miller's *Tropic of Cancer* (1934) and *Quiet Days in Clichy* (1956) are steamy novels set partly in the French capital. Then there's Anaïs Nin's voluminous diaries and fiction; her published correspondence with Miller is particularly evocative of 1930s Paris.

André Breton wrote French surrealism's three manifestos, although the first use of the word 'surrealist' is attributed to the poet Guillaume Apollinaire, a fellow traveller of surrealism killed in action in WWI. Colette (Sidonie-Gabrielle Colette) enjoyed tweaking the nose of conventionally moral readers. Her best-known work is *Gigi* (1945) but far more interesting is *Paris de Ma Fenêtre* (Paris from My Window; 1944), dealing with the German occupation of Paris. Her view was from 9 rue de Beaujolais in the 1er, overlooking Jardin du Palais Royal.

Existentialism

After WWII, existentialism developed as a significant literary movement around Jean-Paul Sartre, Simone de Beauvoir and Albert Camus, who worked and conversed in the cafes of bd St-Germain in St-German des Prés. All three stressed the importance of the writer's political engagement. De Beauvoir, author of *Le Deuxième Sexe* (The Second Sex; 1949), had a profound influence on feminist thinking. Camus' novel *L'Étranger* (The Stranger; 1942) reveals that the absurd is the condition of modern man, who feels himself an outsider in his world.

Modern Literature

Literary Cafes

Café de Flore

Les Deux Magots

La Belle Hortense

In the late 1950s certain novelists began to look for new ways of organising narrative. The so-called *nouveau roman* (new novel) refers to the works of Nathalie Sarraute, Alain Robbe-Grillet, Boris Vian, Julien Gracq, Michel Butor and others. But these writers never formed a close-knit group, and their experiments took them in divergent directions.

In 1980 Marguerite Yourcenar, best known for her memorable historical novels including *Mémoires d'Hadrien* (Hadrian's Memoirs; 1951), became the first woman to be elected to the Académie Française. Marguerite Duras came to the notice of a larger public in 1984 when she won the Prix Goncourt for *L'Amant* (The Lover).

Philippe Sollers, an editor at *Tel Quel,* a highbrow, left-wing, Paris-based review, was very influential in the 1960s and early '70s. His 1960s novels were highly experimental, but with *Femmes* (Women; 1983) he returned to a conventional narrative style. Another *Tel Quel* editor, Julia Kristeva, became known for her theoretical writings on literature and psychoanalysis but subsequently turned her hand to fiction: *Les Samuraï* (The Samurai; 1990), a fictionalised account of the heady days of *Tel Quel*, is an interesting document on Paris intelligentsia life.

Roland Barthes and Michel Foucault are other notable 1960s and '70s authors and philosophers. In the 1990s French writing focused in a nihilistic way on what France had lost as a nation (identity, international prestige etc), and never more so than in the work of controversial writer Michel Houellebecq, who rose to national prominence in 1998 with his *Les Particules Élémentaires* (Atomised).

Contemporary Literature

Contemporary French writers include Jean Echenoz, Erik Orsenna, Christine Angot (dubbed *'la reine de l'autofiction'*, 'the queen of autobiography') and Paris-based comedian/dramatist Nelly Alard, who had her second novel *Moment d'un couple* (Moment of a Couple) published in 2013. Author Yasmina Khadra is actually a man – a former colonel in the Algerian army who adopted his wife's name as a nom de plume.

Delving into the mood and politics of the capital's notable ethnic population is Faïza Guène (b 1985), a French literary sensation who writes in an 'urban slang' style. Born and bred on a housing estate outside Paris, her debut novel, *Kiffe Kiffe Demain* (2004), sold in 27 countries and is published in English as *Just Like Tomorrow* (2006). Like the parents of most of her friends, Guène's father moved from a village in western Algeria to northern France in 1952, aged 17, to work in the mines. Only in the 1980s could he return to Algeria, where he met his wife. He returned to France with her – to Les Courtillières housing estate in Seine-St-Denis, where 6000-odd immigrants live like sardines in five-storey blocks stretching for 1.5km. Such is the setting for *Kiffe Kiffe Demain* and for Guène's second (semi-autobiographical) novel, *Du Rêve pour les Oufs* (2006), published in English as *Dreams from the Endz* (2008). Her third novel, *Les Gens du Balto* (2008), published in English as *Bar Balto* (2011), is a series of colloquial, first-person monologues by various characters who live on a street in a Parisian suburb. Her next work, *Un Homme, ça ne pleure pas* (2014), shifted to Nice, in southern France.

Ex–French border guard turned author Romain Puértolas (b 1975) had an instant best-selling hit with his surreal, partly Paris-set 2013 novel *L'Extraordinaire Voyage du Fakir Qui Était Resté Coincé Dans une Armoire Ikea* (The Extraordinary Journey of the Fakir Who Got Trapped in an Ikea Wardrobe), which won the Grand Prix Jules Verne in 2014. It was followed in 2015 by *La Petite Fille Qui Avait Avalé un Nuage Grand Comme la Tour Eiffel* (The Little Girl Who Swallowed a Cloud as Big as the Eiffel Tower) and the zany farce *Re-vive l'Empereur* (Re-live the Emperor), imagining the contemporary return of Napoléon Bonaparte.

In France the *bande dessinée* (comic strip) has a cult following – Paris even has a museum, Art Ludique-Le Musée, dedicated to the *neuvième art* ('ninth art'). The genre was originally for children, but comic strips for adults burst onto the scene in 1959 with René Goscinny and Albert Uderzo's now-iconic *Astérix* series.

One of France's top-selling writers is Parisian Marc Levy (b 1961). His first novel was filmed as 2005's *Just Like Heaven*, and his novels have been translated into 42 languages and sold more than 30 million copies worldwide. His latest, *Elle et Lui* (She and Him; 2015), is set in Paris.

Painting & Visual Arts

While art in Paris today means anything and everything – bold installations in the metro, monumental wall frescoes, mechanical sculpture, space invader tags and other gregarious street art – the city's rich art heritage has its roots firmly embedded in the traditional genres of painting and sculpture.

Baroque to Neoclassicism

Above: Gustave Courbet's *The Etretat Cliffs after the Storm*, housed in Musée d'Orsay (p224)

According to philosopher Voltaire, French painting proper began with baroque painter Nicolas Poussin (1594–1665), the greatest representative of 17th-century classicism, who frequently set scenes from ancient Rome, classical mythology and the Bible in ordered landscapes bathed in golden light.

In the field of sculpture, extravagant and monumental tombs had been commissioned by the nobility from the 14th century, and in Renaissance Paris Pierre Bontemps (c 1507–68) decorated the beautiful tomb of François I at Basilique de St-Denis, and Jean Goujon (c 1510–67) created the Fontaine des Innocents near the Forum des Halles. No sculpture better evokes baroque than the magnificent *Horses of Marly* of Guillaume Coustou (1677–1746), at the entrance to av des Champs-Élysées.

Modern still life pops up with Jean-Baptiste Chardin (1699–1779), who brought the humbler domesticity of the Dutch masters to French art. In 1785 neoclassical artist Jacques Louis David (1748–1825) wooed the public with his vast portraits with clear republican messages. A virtual dictator in matters of art, he advocated a precise, severe classicism.

Jean-Auguste-Dominique Ingres (1780–1867), David's most gifted pupil in Paris, continued the neoclassical tradition. His historical pictures (eg *Oedipus and the Sphinx*, the 1808 version of which is in the Louvre) are now regarded as inferior to his portraits.

Romanticism

One of the Louvre's most gripping paintings, *The Raft of the Medusa* by Théodore Géricault (1791–1824), hovers on the threshold of romanticism; if Géricault had not died early (aged 33), he probably would have become a leader of the movement, along with his friend Eugène Delacroix (1798–1863; find him in the Cimetière du Père Lachaise), best known for his masterpiece commemorating the July Revolution of 1830, *Liberty Leading the People*.

While romantics revamped the subject picture, the Barbizon School effected a parallel transformation of landscape painting. The school derived its name from a village near the Forêt de Fontainebleau where Jean-Baptiste Camille Corot (1796–1875) and Jean-François Millet (1814–75) painted in the open air. The son of a Norman peasant farmer, Millet took many of his subjects from peasant life; his *L'Angélus* (The Angelus; 1857) is one of the best-known French paintings from this period. View it in the Musée d'Orsay.

In sculpture, the work of Paris-born Auguste Rodin (1840–1917) overcame the conflict between neoclassicism and romanticism. One of Rodin's most gifted pupils was his lover Camille Claudel (1864–1943), whose work can be seen with Rodin's in the Musée Rodin.

Realism

The realists were all about social comment: Millet anticipated the realist program of Gustave Courbet (1819–77), a prominent member of the Paris Commune whose paintings depicted the drudgery and dignity of working-class lives. In 1850 he broke new ground with *A Burial at Ornans* (in the Musée d'Orsay), painted on a canvas of monumental size reserved until then exclusively for historical paintings.

Édouard Manet (1832–83) used realism to depict Parisian middle classes, yet he included in his pictures numerous references to the Old Masters. His *Déjeuner sur l'Herbe* and *Olympia* were both scandalous, largely because they broke with the traditional treatment of their subject matter. He was a pivotal figure in the transition from realism to impressionism.

One of the best sculptors of this period was François Rude (1784–1855), creator of the relief on the Arc de Triomphe and several pieces in the Musée d'Orsay. By the mid-19th century, memorial statues in public places had replaced sculpted tombs, making such statues all the rage.

Sculptor Jean-Baptiste Carpeaux (1827–75) began as a romantic, but his work in Paris – such as *The Dance* on the Palais Garnier and his fountain in the Jardin du Luxembourg – recalls the gaiety and flamboyance of the baroque era.

Painting Meccas
Musée du Louvre (Louvre & Les Halles)
Musée d'Orsay (St-Germain & Les Invalides)
Centre Pompidou (Louvre & Les Halles)
Musée Picasso (Le Marais, Ménilmontant & Belleville)

Sculpture Studios
Musée Rodin (St-Germain & Les Invalides)
Musée Atelier Zadkine (St-Germain & Les Invalides)
Atelier Brancusi (Louvre & Les Halles)
Musée Bourdelle (Montparnasse & Southern Paris)

Photographs
Maison Européenne de la Photographie (Le Marais, Ménilmontant & Belleville)
Fondation Henri Cartier-Bresson (Montparnasse & Southern Paris)
Jeu de Paume (Louvre & Les Halles)
Le Bal (Montmartre & Northern Paris)

PAINTING & VISUAL ARTS ROMANTICISM

Pommes et Biscuits by Paul Cézanne, on display at Musée de l'Orangerie (p118)

Impressionism

Paris' Musée d'Orsay is the crown jewel of impressionism. Initially a term of derision, 'impressionism' was taken from the title of an 1874 experimental painting, *Impression: Soleil Levant* (Impression: Sunrise) by Claude Monet (1840–1926). Monet was the leading figure of the school, and a visit to the Musée d'Orsay unveils a host of other members, among them Alfred Sisley (1839–99), Camille Pissarro (1830–1903), Pierre-Auguste Renoir (1841–1919) and Berthe Morisot (1841–95). The impressionists' main aim was to capture the effects of fleeting light, painting almost universally in the open air – and light came to dominate the content of their painting.

Edgar Degas (1834–1917), buried in Cimetière de Montmartre, was a fellow traveller of the impressionists, but he preferred painting cafe life (*Absinthe*) and in ballet studios (*The Dance Class*) than the great outdoors – several beautiful examples hang in the Musée d'Orsay.

Henri de Toulouse-Lautrec (1864–1901) was a great admirer of Degas but chose subjects one or two notches below: people in the bistros, brothels and music halls of Montmartre (eg *Au Moulin Rouge*). He is best known for his posters and lithographs, in which the distortion of the figures is both satirical and decorative.

Paul Cézanne (1839–1906) is celebrated for his still lifes and landscapes depicting southern France, though he spent many years in Paris after breaking with the impressionists. The name of Paul Gauguin (1848–1903) immediately conjures up studies of Tahitian and Breton women. Both Cézanne and Gauguin were postimpressionists, a catch-all term for the diverse styles that flowed from impressionism.

César Baldaccini (1921–98), known simply as César, used iron and scrap metal to create imaginary insects and animals, later graduating to pliable plastics. Among his best-known works are the Centaur statue in the 6e and the statuette handed to actors at the Césars (French cinema's equivalent of the Oscars).

Gustave Moreau's *Tyrtée Chantant Pendant le Combat*, at Musée National Gustave Moreau (p99)

Pointillism & Symbolism

Pointillism was a technique developed by Georges Seurat (1859–91), who applied paint in small dots or uniform brush strokes of unmixed colour to produce fine 'mosaics' of warm and cool tones. His tableaux *Une Baignade, Asnières* (Bathers at Asnières) is a perfect example.

Henri Rousseau (1844–1910) was a contemporary of the postimpressionists, but his 'naive' art was unaffected by them. His dreamlike pictures of the Paris suburbs and of jungle and desert scenes (eg *The Snake Charmer*) – in Musée d'Orsay – have influenced art right up to this century. The eerie treatment of mythological subjects by Gustave Moreau (1826–98) can be seen in the artist's studio, now within the Musée Gustave-Moreau in the 9e.

Twentieth-Century Art

Twentieth-century French painting is characterised by a bewildering diversity of styles, including fauvism, named after the slur of a critic who compared the exhibitors at the 1905 Salon d'Automne (Autumn Salon) in Paris with *fauves* (wild animals) because of their wild brushstrokes and radical use of intensely bright colours. Among these 'beastly' painters was Henri Matisse (1869–1954).

Cubism was launched in 1907 with *Les Demoiselles d'Avignon* by Spanish prodigy Pablo Picasso (1881–1973). Cubism, as developed by Picasso, Georges Braque (1882–1963) and Juan Gris (1887–1927), deconstructed the subject into a system of intersecting planes and presented various aspects simultaneously.

In the 1920s and '30s the École de Paris (School of Paris) was formed by a group of expressionists, mostly foreign born.

Keep abreast of current exhibitions, events and happenings with Paris' contemporary art and design magazine *Slash* (www.slash-paris.com), also on Twitter and Facebook.

No piece of French art better captures the rebellious, iconoclastic spirit of Dadism – a Swiss-born literary and artistic movement of revolt – than *Mona Lisa*, by Marcel Duchamp (1887–1968), complete with moustache and goatee. In 1922 German Dadaist Max Ernst (1891–1976) moved to Paris and worked on surrealism, a Dada offshoot that flourished between the wars. Drawing on the theories of Sigmund Freud, surrealism attempted to reunite the conscious and unconscious realms, to permeate everyday life with fantasies and dreams. The most influential of this style in Paris was Spanish-born artist Salvador Dalí (1904–89), who arrived in the French capital in 1929 and painted some of his most seminal works while residing here. To see his work, visit the Dalí Espace Montmartre.

One of the most influential pre-WWII sculptors to emerge in Paris was Romanian-born Constantin Brancusi (1876–1957); view his work at the Atelier Brancusi. Two other Paris-busy sculptors each have a museum devoted to their work: Ossip Zadkine (1890–1967) and Antoine Bourdelle (1861–1929).

WWII ended Paris' role as the world's artistic capital. Many artists left during the occupation, and though some returned after the war, the city never regained its old magnetism.

Contemporary Art

Artists in the 1990s turned to the minutiae of daily urban life to express social and political angst, using new mediums to let rip. Conceptual artist Daniel Buren (b 1938) reduced his painting to a signature series of vertical 8.7cm-wide stripes that he applies to every surface imaginable – white-marble columns in the courtyard of Paris' Palais Royal included. Partner-in-crime Michel Parmentier (1938–2000) insisted on monochrome painting – blue in 1966, grey in 1967 and red in 1968.

Paris-born conceptual artist Sophie Calle (b 1953) brazenly exposes her private life in public with eye-catching installations, such as 107 women reading and commenting on an email she received from her French lover, dumping her. The resultant work of art – compelling and addictive – was published in the artist's book *Take Care of Yourself*.

Street art is a current buzz word. In 2013 the world's largest collective street-art exhibition, La Tour Paris 13 (www.tourparis13.fr), opened in a derelict apartment block in the 13e *arrondissement*. Its 36 apartments on 13 floors were covered from head to toe with works by 100 international artists. The blockbuster exhibition ran for just one month, after which the tower was demolished in April 2014.

Another high-profile installation featured over 4000 portraits by French photographer JR, which covered the floor and walls of the Panthéon while it underwent renovation. Meanwhile, the famous Pont des Arts, once covered with lovers' padlocks, incorporated temporary panels in 2015 featuring the work of four different street artists.

Both Brazue and Picasso experimented with sculpture and, in the spirit of Dada, Marcel Duchamp exhibited 'found objects', one of which was a urinal, which he mounted, signed and dubbed *Fountain* in 1917.

A bill in 1936 provided for 'the creation of monumental decorations in public buildings' by allotting 1% of building costs to art. The concept mushroomed half a century later (with Daniel Buren) and now there's artwork everywhere: in the Jardin des Tuileries, La Défense, Parc de la Villette, the metro...

Film

Paris is one of the world's most cinematic cities. The French capital has produced a bevy of blockbuster film-makers and stars and is the filming location of countless box-office hits by both home-grown and foreign directors. Fabulous experiences for film buffs range from exploring behind the scenes at an art deco cinema to catching a classic retrospective in one of the Latin Quarter's many cinemas, or following in the footsteps of iconic screen heroine Amélie Poulain through the streets of Montmartre.

Movie-Makers & Stars

French cinema has not looked back since 2012 when *The Artist* (2011), a silent B&W romantic comedy set in 1920s Hollywood, won seven BAFTAs and five Oscars to become the most awarded film in French cinema history. Best Director went to Parisian Michel Hazanavicius (b 1967) and Best Original Score went to French composer-pianist Ludovic Bource (b 1970). Best Actor was awarded to charismatic Jean Dujardin (b 1972), who started with one-man shows in Paris' bars and cabarets, and made his name with roles as varied as surfer Brice waiting for his wave in *Brice de Nice* (2005), James Bond in *OSS 117: Le Caire, Nid d'Espions* (OSS 117: Cairo Nest of Spies; 2006), the sexiest cowboy around in *Lucky Luke* (2009) and a WWII French soldier in George Clooney's recent *The Monuments Men* (2014).

Another French blockbuster packed with Parisian talent is Anne Fontaine's *Coco Avant Chanel* (Coco Before Chanel; 2009). The movie tells the compelling life story of orphan-turned–fashion designer Coco Chanel, played by Audrey Tautou (b 1976), the waifish French actress who conquered stardom with her role as Montmartre cafe waitress Amélie in Jean-Pierre Jeunet's *Le Fabuleux Destin d'Amélie Poulain* (Amélie; 2001), an earlier Paris classic.

One of the most successful French-language films ever is *Intouchables* (Untouchable; 2011). Directed by Parisian Éric Toledano and Olivier Nakache, the comic drama is about a billionaire quadriplegic and his live-in Senegalese carer in Paris. Assuming the role of carer is charismatic Omar Sy (b 1978), raised in the Parisian suburbs by Senegalese Mauritian parents. The film scooped Best Foreign Film at both the Golden Globes and the BAFTA Awards in 2013.

France's leading lady is Parisian Marion Cotillard (b 1975), the first French woman since 1959 to win an

---

1920s
French film flourishes. Sound ushers in René Clair's (1898–1981) world of fantasy and satirical surrealism. Watch Abel Gance's antiwar blockbuster *J'Accuse!* (I Accuse!; 1919), filmed on actual WWI battlefields.

1930s
WWI inspires a new realism: portraits of ordinary lives dominate film. Watch *La Grande Illusion* (The Great Illusion; 1937), based on the trench-warfare experience of director Jean Renoir.

1940s
Surrealists eschew realism. Watch Jean Cocteau's *La Belle et la Bête* (Beauty and the Beast; 1946) and *Orphée* (Orpheus; 1950). WWII saps the film industry of both talent and money.

1950s
Nouvelle Vague (New Wave): small budgets, no stars and real-life subject matter produce uniquely personal films. Watch Jean-Luc Goddard's carefree, B&W celebration of Paris *À Bout de Souffle* (Breathless; 1959).

1980s
Big-name stars, slick production values and nostalgia: generous state subsidies see filmmakers switch to costume dramas and comedies in the face of growing competition from the USA.

2000s
Renaissance: *philanthrope* Amélie is the subject of Jean-Pierre Jeunet's *Le Fabuleux Destin d'Amélie Poulain* (2001), the first of a string of French-made films to succeed globally.

Oscar, for her role as Édith Piaf in Olivier Dahan's *La Môme* (La Vie en Rose; 2007). The versatile actress went on to play an amputee in art film *De Rouille et d'Os* (Rust and Bone; 2012) by Parisian director Jacques Audiard (b 1952). In *Deux Jours, Une Nuit* (Two Days, One Night; 2014), screened at the 2014 Cannes International Film Festival, Cotillard plays an employee in a solar-panel factory who learns she will lose her job if her co-workers don't each sacrifice €1000 bonuses offered to them.

Animated films have also enjoyed huge success; 2015's *Avril et de Monde Truqué* (April and the Extraordinary World) depicts a fictitious world in 1941 Paris under the rule of Napoléon V in the steam age. Marion Cotillard provides the voice of Avril, who, with her talking cat, searches for her missing scientist parents.

On Location

Cinematic Trips

Forum des Images

Cinémathèque Française

Le Grand Rex

Art Ludique-Le Musée

Paris is the perfect cinematic setting and a natural movie star: look no further than timeless French classics *Hôtel du Nord* (1938), set along the Canal St-Martin, and *Les Enfants du Paradis* (1946), set in 1840s Paris, both directed by Parisian filmmaker Marcel Carné (1906–96).

New Wave film director Jean-Luc Godard followed his B&W celebration of Paris in *À Bout de Souffle* (Breathless; 1959) with *Bande à Parte* (Band of Outsiders; 1964), an entertaining gangster film with marvellous scenes in the Louvre.

For decades 'Most Watched French Film' kudos went to *La Grand Vadrouille* (The Great Ramble; 1966), a French comedy in which five British airmen are shot down over German-occupied France in 1942. One is catapulted into Paris' Bois de Vincennes zoo, another into the orchestra pit of Paris' opera house, and so the comic tale unfurls.

In the 1990s Juliette Binoche (b 1964) catapulted to fame after diving into the shimmering, bright-turquoise water of Paris' art-deco swimming pool the Piscine de Pontoise in the 5e, in *Bleu* (Blue; 1993), the first in Krzysztof Kieślowski's *Trois Couleurs* (Three Colours) triology. A decade later Binoche wooed cinema-goers in equal measure with her role as a grieving mother in *Paris, je t'aime* (Paris, I Love You; 2006), a staggering work comprising 18 short films – each set in a different Parisian *arrondissement* (neighbourhood).

Honoured with the Palme d'Or at Cannes in 2008, Laurent Cantet's *Entre Les Murs* (The Class; 2008) portrays a year in the school life of pupils and teachers in a Parisian suburb. Based on the autobiographical novel of teacher François Begaudeau, the documentary-drama is a brilliant reflection of contemporary multi-ethnic society.

The city has always been popular with foreign film directors, whatever their genre: Bernardo Bertolucci's *Last Tango in Paris* (1972) stars Marlon Brando as a grief-stricken American. Roman Polanski's *Frantic* (1988) is a stylish thriller set in and around the city's seedier quarters that sees Harrison Ford enlist the help of a feisty Emmanuelle Seigner to help him track down his kidnapped wife. Doug Liman's fast-moving action flick *The Bourne Identity* (2002) features Matt Damon as an amnesiac government agent–turned-target in a gripping story that twists and turns against a fabulous backdrop of Paris. Woody Allen's *Everybody Says I love You* (1996) unfolded on the Left Bank's quai de la Tournelle, while *Midnight in Paris* (2011) evoked the city, along with Hemingway's 'Lost Generation', in the 1920s. Martin Scorsese's Oscar-winning children's film *Hugo* (2011) paid tribute to cinema and Parisian film pioneer Georges Méliès through the remarkable adventure of an orphan boy in the 1930s who tends the clocks at a Paris train station. The crazed antics of Gargamel et al in American movie *Smurfs 2* (2013) were shot on location in Paris at Cathédrale de Notre Dame.

Music

From organ recitals amid Gothic architectural splendour to a legendary jazz scene, stirring *chansons*, groundbreaking electronica, award-winning world music and some of the world's best rap, music is embedded deep in the Parisian soul. To understand the capital's musical heritage is to enrich your experience of a city where talented musicians have to audition even to perform in the metro.

Jazz & French Chansons

Jazz hit Paris in the 1920s with the banana-clad form of Josephine Baker, an African American cabaret dancer. In 1934 a chance meeting between Parisian jazz violinist Stéphane Grappelli (1908–97) and three-fingered Roma guitarist Django Reinhardt (1910–53) in a Montparnasse nightclub led to the formation of the Hot Club of France quintet. Claude Luter and his Dixieland band were hip in the 1950s.

The *chanson française*, a tradition dating from troubadours in the Middle Ages, was eclipsed by the music halls of the early 20th century but was revived in the 1930s by Édith Piaf (1915–63) and Charles Trenet (1913–2001), followed by 'France's Frank Sinatra', Charles Aznavour (b 1924). In the 1950s Left Bank cabarets nurtured singers like Léo Ferré (1916–63), Georges Brassens (1921–81), Claude Nougaro (1929–2004), Jacques Brel (1929–78), Barbara (1930–97) and the very sexy, very Parisian Serge Gainsbourg (1928–91). The genre was revived in the new millennium as *la nouvelle chanson française* by performers like Vincent Delerm (b 1976), Bénabar (b 1969), Jeanne Cherhal (b 1978), Camille (b 1978) and Zaz (Isabelle Geffroy; b 1980), who mixes jazz, soul, acoustic and traditional *chansons*.

Rock & Pop

French pop has come a long way since the yéyé (imitative rock) days of the 1960s as sung by Johnny Hallyday. The distinctive M is the son of singer Louis Chédid; Arthur H is the progeny of pop-rock musician Jacques Higelin; and Thomas Dutronc is the offspring of 1960s idols Jacques and Françoise Hardy. Serge Gainsbourg's daughter with Jane Birkin, songwriter-singer and actress Charlotte (b 1971), made her musical debut in 1984 with the single 'Lemon Incest' and – several albums later – released a cover version of the song 'Hey Joe' as soundtrack to the film *Nymphomaniac* (2013), in which she also starred.

Noir Désir was *the* sound of French rock until its lead vocalist, Bertrand Cantat (b 1964), was imprisoned in 2003 for the murder of his girlfriend. Following his early release from prison in 2007, Noir Désir limped along until 2010. The controversial singer, once dubbed the 'Jim Morrison of French rock', later formed the band Détroit with instrumentalist Pascal Humbert. Cantat's powerfully husky voice instantly won fans over: Détroit's first album *Horizons* (2013) sold 160,000 copies in just six months and the 2014 album *La Cigale* was equally well received.

Indie rock band Phoenix from Versailles – born in the late 1990s in a garage in the Paris suburbs – headlines festivals in the US and UK.

Top Five Albums

....

Histoire de Melody Nelson, Serge Gainsbourg

....

Moon Safari, AIR

....

Dante, Abd al Malik

....

Bankrupt, Phoenix

....

Paris by Night, Bob Sinclair

Lead singer Thomas Mars (b 1976), his schoolmate Chris Mazzalai (guitar), his brother Laurent Brancowitz (guitar and keyboards) and Deck d'Arcy (keyboards and brass) have five hugely successful albums under their belt and a much-coveted Grammy award.

Nosfell is one of France's most creative and intense musicians, who sings in his own invented language called 'le klokobetz'. His third album, *Massif Armour* (2014), opens and closes in 'le klokobetz' but otherwise woos listeners with powerful French love lyrics.

In 2011 Sylvie Hoarau and Aurélie Saada formed the indie folk duo Brigitte; their debut album *Et vous, tu m'aimes?* went platinum in France. Their 2014 album *A bouche que veux-tu* also achieved widespread success.

Electronica

Paris does dance music very well, computer-enhanced Chicago blues and Detroit techno often being mixed with 1960s lounge music and vintage tracks from the likes of Gainsbourg and Brassens to create a distinctly urban and highly portable sound.

Internationally successful bands such as Daft Punk and Justice head up the scene. Daft Punk (www.daftalive.com), originally from Versailles, adapts first-wave acid house and techno to its younger roots in pop and indie rock.

Electronica band Justice, aka talented duo Gaspard Michel Andre Augé and Xavier de Rosnay, burst onto the dance scene in 2007 with a debut album that used the band's signature crucifix as its title. Raved about for its rock and indie influences, Justice has released three albums since, most recently live album *Access All Arenas* (2013). Electronica duo from Versailles AIR (an acronym for 'Amour, Imagination, Rêve' meaning 'Love, Imagination, Dream') is another band to listen for.

David Guetta, Laurent Garnier, Martin Solveig and Bob Sinclair (aka Christophe Le Friant, originally nicknamed 'Chris the French Kiss') are top Parisian electronica producers and DJs who travel the international circuit. In the late 1990s David Guetta, with his wife, Cathy, directed Paris' legendary nightclub Les Bains Douches (now hotel, Les Bains) in Le Marais.

Breakbot (Thibaut Berland; b 1981) released his first album in 2012 and gained a rapid following for his remixes. His 2016-released album *Still Waters* includes the track Star Tripper, included in Disney's Star Wars-themed music album *Star Wars Headspace*.

Musical Pilgrimages

....

Serge Gainsbourg's grave, Cimetière du Montparnasse

Jim Morrison's grave, Cimetière du Père Lachaise

....

La Cigale, Montmartre

....

Les Bains, Le Marais

....

Musée de Édith Piaf, Belleville

World

Paris' world beat is strong: think Algerian raï (artists include Cheb Khaled, Natacha Atlas, Jamel, Cheb Mami), Senegalese *mbalax* (Youssou N'Dour), West Indian zouk (Kassav', Zouk Machine) and Cuban salsa. In the late 1980s bands Mano Negra and Les Négresses Vertes combined many of these elements with brilliant results, as did Manu Chao (b 1961; formerly frontman for Mano Negra), the Paris-born son of Spanish parents.

Magic System from Côte d'Ivoire popularised zouglou (a kind of West African rap and dance music) with its album *Premier Gaou*, and Congolese Koffi Olomide (b 1956) still packs the halls. Also try to catch blind singing couple Amadou and Mariam – Rokia Traoré – from Mali, and Franco-Algerian DJ-turned-singer Rachid Taha, whose music mixes Arab and Western musical styles with lyrics in English, Berber and French.

Paris-born Franco-Congolese rapper, slam poet and three-time Victoire de la Musique–award winner Abd al Malik has helped cement France's reputation in world music. His albums *Gibraltar* (2006), *Dante* (2008) and *Château Rouge* (2010) are classics; look out for his popular 2015 album, *Scarifications*.

Survival Guide

Transport

ARRIVING IN PARIS

Few roads *don't* lead to Paris, one of the most visited destinations on earth. Practically every major airline flies through one of its three airports, and most European train and bus routes cross it.

On public transport, children under four years travel free and those aged four to nine years (inclusive) pay half price; exceptions are noted.

Flights, tours and rail tickets can be booked online at www.lonelyplanet.com.

Air

Charles de Gaulle Airport

Most international airlines fly to **Aéroport de Charles de Gaulle** (CDG; ☑01 70 36 39 50; www.aeroportsdeparis.fr), 28km northeast of central Paris. In French the airport is commonly called 'Roissy' after the suburb in which it is located. A €1.7 billion project to create a high-speed train link between Charles de Gaulle and Gare de l'Est in central Paris is on the table, but no track will be laid until 2017. When complete in 2023, the CDG Express will cut the current 50-odd minute journey to 20 minutes. A fourth terminal is due to open in 2020.

TRAIN

CDG is served by the RER B line (€10, approximately 50 minutes, every 10 to 20 minutes), which connects with the Gare du Nord, Châtelet–Les Halles and St-Michel–Notre Dame stations in the city centre. Trains run from 5am to 11pm; there are fewer trains on weekends.

TAXI

A taxi to the city centre takes 40 minutes. From 2016, fares have been standardised to a flat rate: €50 to the Right Bank and €55 to the Left Bank. The fare increases by 15% between 5pm and 10am and on Sundays.

Only take taxis at a clearly marked rank. Never follow anyone who approaches you at the airport and claims to be a driver.

BUS

There are six main bus lines.

Le Bus Direct line 2 (€17, 1hr, every 30 minutes, 5.45am-11pm) Links the airport with the Arc de Triomphe via the Eiffel Tower and Trocadéro. Children under four travel free.

Le Bus Direct line 4 (€17, 50-80 minutes, every 30 minutes, 6am to 10.30pm from the airport, 5.30am to 10.30pm from Montparnasse) Links the airport with Gare Montparnasse (80 minutes) in southern Paris via Gare de Lyon (50 minutes) in eastern Paris. Under fours travel free.

CLIMATE CHANGE & TRAVEL

Every form of transport that relies on carbon-based fuel generates CO_2, the main cause of human-induced climate change. Modern travel is dependent on aeroplanes, which might use less fuel per kilometre per person than most cars but travel much greater distances. The altitude at which aircraft emit gases (including CO_2) and particles also contributes to their climate change impact. Many websites offer 'carbon calculators' that allow people to estimate the carbon emissions generated by their journey and, for those who wish to do so, to offset the impact of the greenhouse gases emitted with contributions to portfolios of climate-friendly initiatives throughout the world. Lonely Planet offsets the carbon footprint of all staff and author travel.

Noctilien bus 140 & 143 (€8 or 4 metro tickets, line 140 1¼hrs, line 143 2hrs, hourly, 12.30am-5.30am) Part of the RATP night service, Noctilien has two buses that go to CDG: bus 140 from Gare de l'Est, and 143 from Gare de l'Est and Gare du Nord.

RATP bus 350 (€6, 70 minutes, every 30 minutes, 5.30am-11pm) Links the airport with Gare de l'Est in northern Paris.

RATP bus 351 (€6, 70 minutes, every 30 minutes, 5.30am-11pm) Links the airport with place de la Nation in eastern Paris.

Roissybus (€11.50; 1 hour; from CDG every 15 minutes, 5.30am-10pm & every 30 minutes, 10pm &11pm; from Paris every 15 minutes, 5.15am-10pm & every 30mins, 10pm-12.30am) Links the airport with the Opéra.

Orly Airport

Aéroport d'Orly (ORY; ☏01 70 36 39 50; www.aeroports deparis.fr) is 19km south of central Paris but, despite being closer than CDG, it is not as frequently used by international airlines, and public transport options aren't quite as straightforward. That will change by 2024, when metro line 14 will be extended to the airport. A TGV station is due to arrive here in 2025.

Orly's south and west terminals are currently being unified into one large terminal suitable for bigger planes such as A380s; completion is due in 2018.

TRAIN
There is currently no direct train to/from Orly; you'll need to change halfway. Note that while it is possible to take a shuttle to the RER C line, this service is quite long and not recommended.

The **RER B** (€12.05, 35 minutes, every four to 12 minutes) line connects Orly with the St-Michel–Notre Dame, Châtelet–Les Halles and Gare du Nord stations in the city centre. In order to get from Orly to the RER station (Antony), you must first take the Orlyval automatic train. The service runs from 6am to 11pm (less frequently on weekends). You only need one ticket to take the two trains.

TAXI
A taxi to the city centre takes roughly 30 minutes. Standardised flat-rate fares since 2016 mean a taxi costs €30 to the Left Bank and €35 to the Right Bank. The fare increases by 15% between 5pm and 10am and on Sundays.

TRAM
The **Tramway T7** (€1.90, every six minutes, 40 minutes, 5.30am to 12.30am) links Orly with Villejuif-Louis Aragon metro station in southern Paris; buy tickets from the machine at the tram stop as no tickets are sold on board.

BUS
Two bus lines serve Orly:

Le Bus Direct line 1 (€12, one hour, every 20 minutes 5.50am to 11.30pm from Orly, 4.50am to 10.30pm from the Arc de Triomphe) Runs to/from the Arc de Triomphe (one hour) via Gare Montparnasse (40 minutes), La Motte-Picquet and Trocadéro. Under fours travel free.

Orlybus (€8, 30 minutes, every 15 minutes, 6am to 12.30pm from Orly, 5.35am to midnight from Paris) Runs to/from the metro station Denfert Rochereau in southern Paris, making several stops en route.

Beauvais Airport

Aéroport de Beauvais (BVA; ☏08 92 68 20 66; www.aero portbeauvais.com) is 75km north of Paris and is served by a few low-cost flights.

Before you snap up that bargain, consider if the post-arrival journey is worth it.

The Beauvais **shuttle** (€17, 1¼ hours) bus links the airport with metro station Porte de Maillot. See the airport website for details and tickets.

Train

Paris is the central point in the French rail network, Société Nationale des Chemins de Fer Français (SNCF), with six train stations that handle passenger traffic to different parts of France and Europe. Each is well connected to the Paris public transport system, the Régie Autonome des Transports Parisiens (RATP). To buy onward tickets from Paris, visit a station or go to Voyages SNCF (www.voyages-sncf.com). Most trains – and all Trains à Grande Vitesse (TGV) – require advance reservations. As with most tickets, the earlier you book, the better your chances of securing a discounted fare. Main-line stations in Paris have left-luggage offices and/or consignes (lockers) for a maximum of 72 hours.

Gare du Nord

Gare du Nord (rue de Dunkerque, 10e; Ⓜ Gare du Nord) is the terminus for northbound domestic trains as well as several international services. Located in northern Paris.

Eurostar (www.eurostar.com) The London–Paris line runs from St Pancras International to Gare du Nord. Voyages take 2¼ hours.

Thalys (www.thalys.com) Trains pull into Paris' Gare du Nord from Brussels, Amsterdam and Cologne.

Gare d'Austerlitz

Gare d'Austerlitz (bd de l'Hôpital, 13e; Ⓜ Gare

d'Austerlitz) is the terminus for a handful of trains from the south, including services from Orléans, Limoges and Toulouse. High-speed trains to/from Barcelona and Madrid also use Austerlitz. Current renovations will continue until 2021. Located in southeastern Paris.

Gare de l'Est

Gare de l'Est (bd de Strasbourg, 10e; MGare de l'Est) is the terminus for trains to/from Luxembourg, parts of Switzerland (Basel, Lucerne, Zürich), southern Germany (Frankfurt, Munich) and points further east; and for regular and TGV Est trains to areas of France east of Paris (Champagne, Alsace and Lorraine). Located in northern Paris.

Gare de Lyon

Gare de Lyon (bd Diderot, 12e; MGare de Lyon) is the terminus for trains from Provence, the Alps, the Riviera, Italy, Geneva and Zürich. Also has trains to/from Disneyland Paris Resort. Located in eastern Paris.

Gare Montparnasse

Gare Montparnasse (av du Maine & bd de Vaugirard, 15e; MMontparnasse Bienvenüe) is the terminus for trains from the southwest and west, including services from Brittany, the Loire, Bordeaux, Toulouse and Spain and Portugal. Some of these services will eventually move to Gare d'Austerlitz (by 2021, once refurbishment is complete). Located in southern Paris.

Gare St-Lazare

Gare St-Lazare (esplanade de la Gare St-Lazare, 8e; MSt-Lazare) is the terminus for trains from Normandy. Located in Clichy, northwestern Paris.

Bus

Eurolines (Map p398; www.eurolines.fr; 55 rue St-Jacques, 5e; ⊘ticket office 9.30am-6.30pm Mon-Fri, 10am-1pm & 2-5pm Sat; MCluny-La Sorbonne) connects all major European capitals to Paris' international bus terminal, **Gare Routiére Internationale de Paris-Galliéni** (☑08 92 89 90 91; 28 av du Général de Gaulle; MGalliéni). The terminal is in the eastern suburb of Bagnolet; it's about a 15-minute metro ride to the more central République station.

GETTING AROUND PARIS

Train

Paris' underground network is run by RATP and consists of two separate but linked systems: the metro and the Réseau Express Régional (RER) suburban train line. The metro has 14 numbered lines; the RER has five main lines (but you'll probably only need to use A, B and C). When buying tickets consider how many zones your journey will cover; there are five concentric transport zones rippling out from Paris (5 being the furthest); if you travel from Charles de Gaulle airport to Paris, for instance, you will have to buy a zone 1–5 ticket.

For information on the metro, RER and bus systems, visit www.ratp.fr. Metro maps of various sizes and degrees of detail are available for free at metro ticket windows; several can also be downloaded for free from the RATP website.

Metro

➡ Metro lines are identified by both their number (eg ligne 1; line 1) and their colour, listed on official metro signs and maps.

➡ Signs in metro and RER stations indicate the way to the correct platform for your line. The *direction* signs on each platform indicate the terminus. On lines that split into several branches (such as lines 7 and 13), the terminus of each train is indicated on the cars and on signs on each platform giving the number of minutes until the next and subsequent train.

➡ Signs marked *correspondance* (transfer) show how to reach connecting trains. At stations with many intersecting lines, like Châtelet and Montparnasse Bienvenüe, walking from one platform to the next can take a very long time.

➡ Different station exits are indicated by white-on-blue *sortie* (exit) signs. You can get your bearings by checking the *plan du quartier* (neighbourhood maps) posted at exits.

➡ Each line has its own schedule but trains usually start at around 5.30am, with the last train beginning its run between 12.35am and 1.15am (2.15am on Friday and Saturday).

RER

➡ The RER is faster than the metro but the stops are much further apart. Some attractions, particularly those on the Left Bank (eg the Musée d'Orsay, Eiffel Tower and Panthéon), can be reached far more conveniently by the RER than by the metro.

➡ If you're going out to the suburbs (eg Versailles, Disneyland), ask for help on the platform – finding the right train can be confusing. Also make sure your ticket is for the correct zone.

Tickets & Fares

➡ The same RATP tickets are valid on the metro, the RER (for travel within the city limits), buses, trams and the Montmartre funicular.

NAVIGO PASS

If you're staying in Paris for longer than a few days, the cheapest and easiest way to use public transport is to get a combined travel pass that allows unlimited travel on the metro, RER and buses for a week, a month or a year. Since September 2015, passes now cover all of the Île-de-France (that is, all zones).

Navigo (www.navigo.fr), like London's Oyster or Hong Kong's Octopus cards, is a system that provides you with a refillable weekly, monthly or yearly unlimited pass that you can recharge at machines in most metro stations. To pass through the station barrier, swipe the card across the electronic panel as you go through the turnstiles. Standard Navigo passes, available to anyone with an address in Île de France, are free but take up to three weeks to be issued; ask at the ticket counter for a form or order online via the Navigo website. Otherwise pay €5 for a Navigo Découverte (Navigo Discovery) card, which is issued on the spot but (unlike the standard Navigo pass) is not replaceable if lost or stolen. Both passes require a passport photo and can be recharged for periods of one week or more.

A weekly pass costs €22.15 and is valid Monday to Sunday. It can be purchased from the previous Friday until Thursday; from the next day weekly tickets are available for the following week only. Even if you're in Paris for three or four days, it may work out cheaper than buying *carnets* (books of tickets) and will certainly cost less than buying a daily Mobilis or Paris Visite pass. The monthly pass (€73) begins on the first day of each calendar month; you can buy one from the 20th of the preceding month. Both are sold in metro and RER stations from 6.30am to 10pm and at some bus terminals.

→ A ticket – white in colour and called *Le Ticket t+* – costs €1.90 (half price for children aged four to nine years) if bought individually and €14.50 for adults for a *carnet* (book) of 10.

→ Tickets are sold at all metro stations. Ticket windows accept most credit cards; however automated machines do not accept credit cards without embedded chips (and even then, not all foreign chip-embedded cards).

→ One ticket lets you travel between any two metro stations (no return journeys) for a period of 1½ hours, no matter how many transfers are required. You can also use it on the RER for travel within zone 1, which encompasses all of central Paris.

→ Transfers from the metro to bus or vice versa are not possible.

→ Always keep your ticket until you exit from your station; if you are stopped by a ticket inspector, you will have to pay a fine if you don't have a valid ticket.

TOURIST PASSES

The Mobilis and Paris Visite passes are valid on the metro, RER, SNCF's suburban lines, buses, night buses, trams and Montmartre funicular railway. No photo is needed, but write your full name and date of use on the ticket. Passes are sold at larger metro and RER stations, SNCF offices in Paris, and the airports.

Mobilis Allows unlimited travel for one day and costs €7.30 (two zones) to €17.30 (five zones). Buy it at any metro, RER or SNCF station in the Paris region. Depending on how many times you plan to hop on/off the metro in a day, a *carnet* might work out cheaper.

Paris Visite Allows unlimited travel as well as discounted entry to certain museums and other discounts and bonuses. The 'Paris+Suburbs+Airports' pass includes transport to/ from the airports and costs €24.50/37.25/52.20/63.90 for one/two/three/five days. The cheaper 'Paris Centre' pass, valid for zones 1 to 3, costs €11.65/18.95/25.85/37.25 for one/two/three/five days. Children aged four to 11 years pay half price.

Bicycle

Paris is increasingly bike-friendly, with more cycling lanes and efforts from the city of Paris to reduce the number of cars on the roads.

Vélib'

The **Vélib'** (☎01 30 79 79 30; http://en.velib.paris.fr; day/ week subscription €1.70/8, bike hire up to 30/60/90/120min free/€1/2/4) bike share scheme puts 23,600 bikes at the disposal of Parisians and visitors for getting around the city. There are some 1800 stations throughout Paris, each with anywhere from 20 to 70 bike stands. The bikes are accessible around the clock.

→ To get a bike, you first need to purchase a one- or seven-day subscription. There are two ways to do this: either at the terminals found at docking stations or online.

→ The terminals require a credit card with an embedded smart chip (which precludes many North American cards), and, even then, not all foreign chip-embedded cards will work. Alternatively, you can purchase a subscription online before you leave your hotel.

→ After you authorise a deposit (€150) to pay for the bike should it go missing, you'll receive an ID number and PIN code and you're ready to go.

→ Bikes are rented in 30-minute intervals. If you return a bike before a half-hour is up and then take a new one, you will not be charged.

→ If the station you want to return your bike to is full, log in to the terminal to get 15 minutes for free while you find another station.

→ Bikes are suitable for cyclists aged 14 and over, and are fitted with gears, an antitheft lock with key, reflective strips and front/rear lights. Bring your own helmet (they are not required by law).

→ P'tits Vélib' is a bike-sharing scheme for children aged two to 10 years, with bike stations at seven sites, including Bois de Bologne, Bois de Vincennes and Les Berges de Seine. Child helmets are always provided.

Rentals

Most rental places will require a deposit (usually €150). Take ID and your bank or credit card.

Au Point Vélo Hollandais (☑01 43 54 85 36; www. pointvelo.com; 83 bd St-Michel, 5e; per day €15; ⊙10.30am-7.30pm Mon-Sat; ⓂCluny-La Sorbonne or RER Luxembourg)

Freescoot (☑01 44 07 06 72; www.freescoot.com; 63 quai de la Tournelle, 5e; bike/tandem/electric bike per day from €20/35/40; ⊙9am-1pm & 2-7pm mid-Apr–mid-Sep,

closed Sun & Wed mid-Sep–mid-Apr; ⓂMaubert-Mutualité)

Gepetto et Vélos (☑01 43 54 19 95; www.gepetto-velos.com; 59 rue du Cardinal Lemoine, 5e; per day €16, child seat €5; ⊙9am-2pm & 3-7pm Tue-Sat year-round plus 10am-2pm & 3-7pm Sun mid-Apr–mid-Sep; ⓂCardinal Lemoine)

Paris à Vélo, C'est Sympa (☑01 48 87 60 01; www.parisvelosympa.com; 22 rue Alphonse Baudin, 11e; half-day/full day/24hrs from €12/15/20, electric bikes per half-day/full day/24hrs €20/30/40; ⊙9.30am-1pm & 2-6pm Mon-Fri, 9am-7pm Sat & Sun Apr-Oct, shorter hours winter; ⓂSt-Sébastien-Froissart)

Bus

Buses can be a scenic way to get around – and there are no stairs to climb, meaning they are more widely accessible – but they're slower and less intuitive to figure out than the metro.

Local Buses

Paris' bus system, operated by RATP, runs from 5.30am to 8.30pm Monday to Saturday; after that, certain evening-service lines continue until between midnight and 12.30am. Services are drastically reduced on Sunday and public holidays, when buses run from 7am to 8.30pm.

Night Buses

The RATP runs 47 night bus lines known as Noctilien (www.vianavigo.com), which depart hourly from 12.30am to 5.30am. The services pass through the main *gares* (train stations) and cross the major axes of the city before leading out to the suburbs. Look for navy-blue N or Noctilien signs at bus stops. There are two circular lines within Paris (the N01 and

N02) that link four main train stations – St-Lazare, Gare de l'Est, Gare de Lyon and Gare Montparnasse – as well as popular nightlife areas (Bastille, Champs-Elysées, Pigalle, St-Germain).

Noctilien services are included on your Mobilis or Paris Visite pass for the zones in which you are travelling. Otherwise you pay a certain number of standard €1.80 metro/bus tickets, depending on the length of your journey.

Tickets & Fares

→ Normal bus rides embracing one or two bus zones cost one metro ticket; longer rides require two or even three tickets.

→ Transfers to other buses – but not the metro – are allowed on the same ticket as long as the change takes place 1½ hours between the first and last validation. This does not apply to Noctilien services.

→ Whatever kind of single-journey ticket you have, you must validate it in the ticket machine near the driver. If you don't have a ticket, the driver can sell you one for €2 (correct change required).

→ If you have a Mobilis or Paris Visite pass, flash it at the driver when you board.

Boat

Batobus (www.batobus. com; adult/child 1-day pass €17/10, 2-day pass €19/10; ⊙10am-9.30pm Apr-Aug, to 7pm Sep-Mar) runs glassed-in trimarans that dock every 20 to 25 minutes at nine small piers along the Seine: Beaugrenelle, Eiffel Tower, Musée d'Orsay, St-Germain des Prés, Notre Dame, Jardin des Plantes/Cité de la Mode et du Design, Hôtel de Ville, Musée du Louvre and Champs-Élysées.

Buy tickets online, at ferry stops or at tourist offices.

You can also buy a two- or three-day Paris À La Carte Pass that includes L'Open Tour buses for €45 or €49.

Taxi

→ The *prise en charge* (flagfall) is €2.60. Within the city limits, it costs €1.04 per kilometre for travel between 10am and 5pm Monday to Saturday (*Tarif A*; white light on taxi roof and meter).

→ At night (5pm to 10am), on Sunday from 7am to midnight, and in the inner suburbs the rate is €1.27 per km (*Tarif B*; orange light).

→ Travel in the city limits and inner suburbs on Sunday night (midnight to 7am Monday) and in the outer suburbs is at *Tarif C*, €1.54 per kilometre (blue light).

→ The minimum taxi fare for a short trip is €6.86.

→ Flat fees have been introduced for taxis to/from the major airports, Charles de Gualle (p330) and Orly (p331).

→ There's a €3 surcharge for taking a fourth passenger, but drivers sometimes refuse for insurance reasons. The first piece of baggage is free; additional pieces over 5kg cost €1 extra.

→ Flagging down a taxi in Paris can be difficult; it's best to find an official taxi stand.

→ To order a taxi, call or reserve online with **Taxis G7** (☎01 41 27 66 99, 3607; www.taxisg7.com), **Taxis Bleus** (☎08 91 70 10 10, 3609; www.taxis-bleus.com) or **Alpha Taxis** (☎01 45 85 85 85; www.alphataxis.fr).

→ An alternative is the private driver system, Uber taxi (www.uber.com/cities/paris), whereby you order and pay via your smartphone. However, official taxis continue to protest about the service and there have been instances of Uber drivers and passengers being harassed.

Car & Motorcycle

Driving in Paris is defined by the triple hassle of navigation, heavy traffic and limited parking. Petrol stations are also difficult to locate and access. It doesn't make sense to use a car to get around, but if you're heading out of the city on an excursion, then your own set of wheels can certainly be useful. If you plan on hiring a car, it's best to do so online and in advance.

Autolib'

Paris' electric-car-share program, Autolib' (www.autolib.eu), is similar to bike-share scheme Vélib': pay €9 per half hour to rent a GPS-equipped car in 30-minute intervals, plus €1 per reservation. Its 3800 cars (most of which have more than a little wear and tear) can be picked up/dropped off at 1000 stations around the city and are designed only for short hops; the car battery is good for 250km. Carry your driving licence and photo ID.

Scooters

Cityscoot (www.cityscoot.eu; per minute/100 minutes €0.28/25; ☉7am-11pm) Since summer 2016, electric mopeds with a top speed of 45km per hour are available to rent as part of Paris' scooter-sharing scheme (similar to the Autolib' car-sharing program), with all bookings via smartphones.

Freescoot (☎01 44 07 06 72; www.freescoot.com; 63 quai de la Tournelle, 5e; 50/125cc scooters per 24hrs €55/65; ☉9am-1pm & 2-7pm mid-Apr–mid-Sep, closed Sun & Wed mid-Sep–mid-Apr; MMaubert-Mutualité) Rents 50/125cc scooters in various intervals. Prices include third-party insurance as well as helmets, locks, rain gear and gloves. You must be at least 23 years old

and leave a credit card deposit of €1000.

Left Bank Scooters (☎06 78 12 04 24; www.leftbankscooters.com; 50/125/300cc scooters per 24hrs €70/80/100) Rents Vespa XLV scooters including insurance, helmet and wet-weather gear. To rent a scooter, you must be at least 20 years old and have a car or motorcycle licence. Credit-card deposit is €1000. Scooter tours also available.

Parking

→ Parking meters in Paris do not accept coins; they require either a European-compatible chip-enabled credit card or a Paris Carte, available at any *tabac* (tobacconist) for €10 to €30. The machine will issue you a ticket for the allotted time, which should be placed on the dashboard behind the windscreen.

→ Municipal public car parks, of which there are more than 200 in Paris, charge between €2 and €6 an hour or €20 to €36 per 24 hours (cash and compatible credit cards accepted). Most are open 24 hours.

TOURS

As one of the world's most visited cities, Paris is well set up for visitors with a host of guided tours, from bike, boat, bus, scooter and walking tours (including some wonderful local-led options in off-the-beaten-track areas) to some more unusual themed options including photography tours, film location tours and treasure hunts.

Bicycle

Bike About Tours (Map p386; ☎06 18 80 84 92; www.bikeabouttours.com; 4 rue de Lobau, 4e, Vinci Parking; MHôtel de Ville) This expat-

SPECIALISED TOURS

Meeting the French (📞01 42 51 19 80; www.meetingthefrench.fr) Make-up workshops, backstage cabaret tours, fashion-designer showroom visits, French table decoration or art embroidery classes, market tours, baking with a Parisian baker: the repertoire of cultural and gourmet tours and behind-the-scene experiences offered by Meeting the French is truly outstanding. All courses and tours are in English.

THATLou (www.thatlou.com; per person excluding museum admission fees €20-25) Organises treasure hunts in English, French and more for two or more people in the Louvre, Musée d'Orsay (THATd'Or) and streets of the Latin Quarter (THATrue). Participants (playing alone or against another team) have to photograph themselves in front of 20 to 30 works of art ('treasure'). Hunts typically last 1½ to two hours. Kids packs (€15) also available.

Left Bank Scooters (📞06 78 12 04 24; www.leftbankscooters.com; 3hr tours per 1st/2nd passenger from €150/50) Runs a variety of scooter tours around Paris, both day and evening, as well as trips out to Versailles and sidecar tours. Car or motorcycle licence required.

Paris Photography Tours (📞06 17 08 54 45; www.parisphotographytours.com; 3hr day/ night tours for 1-4 people €150) Customised tours by professional photographers take into account your level of experience as well as what you most want to capture, such as nature, architecture or street life. Tours can incorporate lessons on how to improve your photographic skills.

Set in Paris (Map p398; 📞09 84 42 35 79; www.setinparis.com; 3 rue Maître Albert, 5e; 2hr tours €25; ⊙2hr tours 10am & 3pm; Ⓜ Maubert-Mutualité) From its cinema-style 'box-office' HQ in the Latin Quarter, Set in Paris' two-hour walking tours take you to locations throughout Paris where movies including *The Devil Wears Prada*, *The Bourne Identity*, *The Three Musketeers*, *The Hunchback of Notre Dame*, *Ratatouille*, *Before Sunset*, several James Bond instalments and many others were filmed. Advance reservations are recommended.

tour group offers daytime city tours (adult/child €32.50/30; 3½ hours), trips to Versailles (€85/65), e-bike tours to Champagne (€150/130) and private family tours.

Fat Tire Bike Tours (📞01 85 08 19 76; www.fattirebiketours.com; tours from €32) Day and night bike tours of the city, both in central Paris and further afield to Versailles and Monet's Garden in Giverny.

Paris à Vélo, C'est Sympa! (Map p386; 📞01 48 87 60 01; www.parisvelosympa.com; 22 rue Alphonse Baudin, 11e; Ⓜ St-Sébastien-Froissart) Three guided bike tours (adult/child €35/29; three hours): a Heart of Paris tour, Unusual Paris (taking in artist studios and mansions) and the Contrast tour, combining nature and modern architecture. Tours depart from its bike rental shop.

Boat

A boat cruise down the Seine is the most relaxing way to watch the city glide by – and is a wonderful way to acquaint or reacquaint yourself with the city's main monuments. An alternative to a regular tour is the hop-on, hop-off **Batobus** (www.batobus.com; adult/child 1-day pass €17/10, 2-day pass €19/10; ⊙10am-9.30pm Apr-Aug, to 7pm Sep-Mar).

Bateaux Parisiens (Map p366; www.bateauxparisiens.com; Port de la Bourdonnais, 7e; adult/child €14/6; Ⓜ Bir Hakeim or RER Pont de l'Alma) This vast operation runs 1½-hour river circuits with recorded commentary in 13 languages (every 30 minutes 10am to 10.30pm April to September, hourly 10am to 10pm October to March), and a host of themed lunch/dinner

cruises. It has two locations: one by the Eiffel Tower, the other south of Notre Dame.

Bateaux-Mouches (Map p368; 📞01 42 25 96 10; www.bateauxmouches.com; Port de la Conférence, 8e; adult/child €13.50/6; Ⓜ Alma Marceau) The largest river cruise company in Paris and a favourite with tour groups. Cruises (70 minutes) run regularly from 10.15am to 10.30pm April to September and 13 times a day between 11am and 9.20pm the rest of the year. Commentary is in French and English. It's located on the Right Bank, just east of the Pont de l'Alma.

Vedettes de Paris (Map p366; 📞01 44 18 19 50; www.vedettesdeparis.fr; Port de Suffren, 7e; adult/child €14/6; Ⓜ Bir Hakeim or RER Pont de l'Alma) It might be a small company, but its one-hour sightseeing cruises on smaller boats are second to none. It runs themed cruises too, including imaginative 'Mysteries of Paris' tours for kids (adult/child €14/8).

Vedettes du Pont Neuf
(Map p396; ☏01 46 33 98 38, classical-music cruises 01 42 77 65 65; www.vedettes-dupontneuf.com; square du Vert Galant, 1er; adult/child €14/7; Ⓜ Pont Neuf) One-hour cruises depart year-round from Vedettes' centrally located dock at the western tip of Île de la Cité; commentary is in French and English. Tickets are cheaper if you buy in advance online (adult/child morning cruises €9/5, afternoon cruises €11/5). Check the website for details of its wonderful 'Concerts en Seine' – classical music afloat after dusk (tickets €30 to €40).

Bus

Big Bus Paris (☏01 53 95 39 53; http://fra.bigbustours.com;

1-day pass adult/child €32/16) These hop-on, hop-off city bus tours make 11 stops around the city. Buses run from 9.40am to 9.30pm; commentary is in 11 languages. Download free apps for iPhone or Android.

L'Open Tour (☏01 42 66 56 56; www.paris.opentour.com; 1-day pass adult/child €32/16) Hop-on, hop-off bus tours aboard open-deck buses with four different circuits and 50 stops – good for a whirlwind city tour.

Walking

Ça Se Visite (☏01 43 57 59 50; www.ca-se-visite.fr; adult/child on foot €12/10, scooter €15/13) Meet local artists and craftspeople on resident-led 'urban discovery tours' of the northeast (Belleville, Ménilmontant, Canal St-Martin, Canal de l'Ourcq, Oberkampf, La Villette) – on foot or *trottinette* (scooter).

Eye Prefer Paris (☏06 31 12 86 20; www.eyepreferparis-

tours.com; 3-person 3hr tour €225) New Yorker–turned-Parisian Richard Nahem leads offbeat tours of the city. Full-day tours also available.

Localers (☏01 83 64 92 01; www.localers.com) Classic walking tours and behind-the-scenes urban discoveries with local Paris experts: *pétanque*, photo shoots, market tours, cooking classes, foie gras–tasting et al.

Parisien d'un jour – Paris Greeters (www.greeters.paris; by donation) See Paris through local eyes with these two- to three-hour city tours. Volunteers – knowledgeable Parisians passionate about their city in the main – lead groups (maximum six people) to their favourite spots. Minimum two weeks' notice needed.

Paris Walks (☏01 48 09 21 40; www.paris-walks.com; 2hr tours adult/child €15/8) Long established and well respected, Paris Walks offers two-hour thematic walking tours (art, fashion, chocolate, the French Revolution etc).

Directory A–Z

Discount Cards

Almost all museums and monuments in Paris have discounted tickets (*tarif réduit*) for students and seniors (generally over 60 years), provided they have valid ID. Children often get in for free; the cut-off age for 'child' is anywhere between six and 18 years.

EU citizens under 26 years get in for free at national monuments and museums.

Paris Museum Pass (en. parismuseumpass.com; 2/4/6 days €48/62/74) Gets you into 50-odd venues in and around Paris; a huge advantage is that pass holders usually enter larger sights at a different entrance meaning you bypass (or substantially reduce) ridiculously long ticket queues.

Paris Passlib' (www. parisinfo.com; 2/3/5 days €109/129/155) Sold at the Paris Convention & Visitors Bureau (p338) and on its website, this handy city pass covers unlimited public transport in zones 1 to 3, admission to some 50 museums in the Paris region (aka a Paris Museum Pass), a one-hour boat cruise along the Seine, and a one-day hop-on hop-off open-top bus sightseeing service around central Paris' key sights with **L'Open Tour** (☎01 42 66 56 56; www.paris.opentour.com;

1-day pass adult/child €32/16). There's an optional €15 supplement for a skip-the-line ticket to levels one and two of the Eiffel Tower, or €21.50 for all three Eiffel Tower platforms.

Electricity

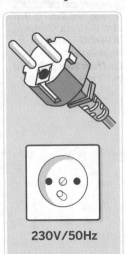

230V/50Hz

Emergency

Ambulance (SAMU)	☎15
Fire	☎18
Police	☎17
EU-wide emergency	☎112

Insurance

Comprehensive travel insurance to cover theft, loss and medical problems is highly recommended.

Worldwide travel insurance is available at www. lonelyplanet.com/travel-insurance. You can buy, extend and claim online anytime – even if you're already on the road.

Internet Access

➜ Wi-fi (pronounced 'wee-fee' in France) is available in most Paris hotels, usually at no extra cost, and in some museums.

➜ Free wi-fi is available in some 300 public places, including parks, libraries and municipal buildings, between 7am and 11pm daily. In parks look for a purple 'Zone Wi-Fi' sign near the entrance. To connect, select the 'PARIS_WI-FI_' network and connect; sessions are limited to two hours. For complete details and a map of hotspots see www. paris.fr/wifi.

➜ Expect to pay around €4 and €5 per hour for online access in internet cafes; **Milk** (www.milk-lub.com; 31 bd de Sébastopol, 1er; 15/60min €2.40/3.90; ⊙24hr; ⓂLes Halles) has several branches in central Paris.

➜ In our listings, the wi-fi symbol indicates that an establishment offers wi-fi access, while the internet symbol indicates there is an online computer available for guest use.

Legal Matters

If the police stop you for any reason, be polite and remain calm. They have wide powers of search and seizure and can, without any particular reason, decide to examine your passport, visa, *carte de séjour* (residence permit) and so on. (You are expected to have photo ID on you at *all* times.) Do *not* challenge them.

French police are strict about security. Do not leave baggage unattended; they are quite serious when they say that suspicious objects will be summarily blown up.

Medical Services
Hospitals

Paris has some 50 hospitals including the following:

American Hospital of Paris (☎01 46 41 25 25; www.american-hospital.org; 63 bd Victor Hugo, Neuilly-sur-Seine; MPont de Levallois) Private hospital; emergency 24-hour medical and dental care.

Hertford British Hospital (☎01 46 39 22 00; www.british-hospital.org; 3 rue Barbès, Levallois; MAnatole France) Less expensive, private, English-speaking option.

Hôpital Hôtel Dieu (☎01 42 34 82 34; www.aphp.fr; 1 place du Parvis Notre Dame, 4e; MCité) One of the city's main government-run public hospitals; after 8pm use the emergency entrance on rue de la Cité.

Pharmacies

Pharmacies (chemists) are marked by a large illuminated green cross outside. At least one in each neighbourhood is open for extended hours; find a complete night-owl listing on the Paris Convention & Visitors Bureau website (www.paris-info.com).

Pharmacie Bader (☎01 43 26 92 66; www.pharmaciebader.com; 10-12 bd St-Michel, 6e; ⊗8.30am-9pm; MSt-Michel)

Pharmacie de la Mairie (☎01 42 78 53 58; http://pharmacie-mairie-paris.com; 9 rue des Archives, 4e; ⊗9am-8pm; MHôtel de Ville)

Pharmacie Les Champs (☎01 45 62 02 41; Galerie des Champs-Élysées, 84 av des Champs-Élysées, 8e; ⊗24hrs; MGeorge V)

Money

France uses the euro (€), which is divided into 100 centimes. Denominations are €5, €10, €20, €50, €100, €200 and €500 notes, and €0.01, €0.02, €0.05, €0.10, €0.20, €0.50, €1 and €2 coins.

French vendors rarely accept bills larger than €50.

Check the latest exchange rates on websites such as www.xe.com.

ATMs

ATMs (*distributeur automatique de billets* in French) are widespread. Unless you have particularly high transaction fees, ATMs are usually the best and easiest way to deal with currency exchange; French banks don't generally charge fees to use their ATMs but check with your own bank before you travel to know if/how much they charge for international cash withdrawals.

Credit Cards

Visa/Carte Bleue is the most widely accepted credit card in Paris, followed by MasterCard (Eurocard). Amex cards are only accepted at more upmarket establishments.

Note that France uses a smartcard with an embedded microchip and PIN – few places accept swipe-and-signature. Some foreign chip-and-PIN-enabled cards require a signature – ask your bank before you leave. Chipless cards (and even some chip-embedded foreign cards) can't be used at automated machines (such as at a metro station or museum).

Tipping

Taxis Taxi drivers expect small tips of between 5% and 10% of the fare, though the usual procedure is to round up to the nearest €1 regardless of the fare.

Restaurants French law requires that restaurant, cafe and hotel bills include a service charge (usually 15%), and many people leave a few extra euros.

Bars & Cafes Not necessary at the bar. If drinks are brought to your table, tip as you would in a restaurant.

Hotels Bellhops usually expect €1 to €2 per bag; it's not necessary to tip the concierge, cleaners or front-desk staff.

Travellers Cheques

Travellers cheques are now very rarely used but can still be changed at many post offices.

Opening Hours

The following list shows *approximate* standard opening hours for businesses. Hours can vary by season. Many businesses close for the entire month of August for summer holidays.

Banks 9am to 1pm & 2 to 5pm Monday to Friday, some open on Saturday morning

Bars & Cafes 7am to 2am

Museums 10am to 6pm, closed Monday or Tuesday

Post Offices 8am to 7pm Monday to Friday, and until noon on Saturday

Restaurants noon to 2pm and 7.30 to 10.30pm

Shops (Clothing) 10am to 7pm Monday to Saturday, they occasionally close in the early afternoon for lunch and sometimes all day Monday

Shops (Food) 8am to 1pm and 4 to 7.30pm, closed Sunday afternoon and sometimes Monday

Post

➜ Most post offices *(bureaux de poste)* are open Monday to Saturday.

➜ *Tabacs* (tobacconists) usually sell postage stamps.

➜ The main **post office** (Map p376; www.laposte.fr; 52 rue du Louvre, 1er; ⊙24hr; MSentier, Les Halles), five blocks north of the eastern end of the Musée du Louvre, is open round the clock, but only for basic services such as sending letters. Other services, including currency exchange, are available only during regular opening hours. Be prepared for long queues.

➜ Each *arrondissement* has its own five-digit postcode, formed by prefixing the number of the *arrondissement* with '750' or '7500' (eg 75001 for the 1er *arrondissement*, 75019 for the 19e). The only exception is the 16e, which has two postcodes: 75016 and 75116. All mail to addresses in France *must* include the postcode.

Public Holidays

There is close to one public holiday a month in France and, in some years, up to four in May alone. Be aware, though, that unlike in the USA or UK, where public holidays usually fall on (or are shifted to) a Monday, in

France a *jour férié* (public holiday) is celebrated strictly on the day on which it falls. Thus if May Day falls on a Saturday or Sunday, no provision is made for an extra day off.

The following holidays are observed in Paris:

New Year's Day (Jour de l'An) 1 January

Easter Sunday & Monday (Pâques & Lundi de Pâques) Late March/April

May Day (Fête du Travail) 1 May

Victory in Europe Day (Victoire 1945) 8 May

Ascension Thursday (L'Ascension) May (celebrated on the 40th day after Easter)

Whit Monday (Lundi de Pentecôte) Mid-May to mid-June (seventh Monday after Easter)

Bastille Day/National Day (Fête Nationale) 14 July

Assumption Day (L'Assomption) 15 August

All Saints' Day (La Toussaint) 1 November

Armistice Day/Remembrance Day (Le Onze Novembre) 11 November

Christmas (Noël) 25 December

Safe Travel

In general, Paris is a safe city and random street assaults are rare. The city is generally well lit and there's no reason not to use the metro until it stops running, at some time between 12.30am and just past 1am (2.15am on weekends). Many women do travel on the metro alone, late at night, in most areas.

Pickpocketing is typically the biggest concern. *Always* be alert and take precautions: don't carry more money than you need, and keep your credit cards, passport and other documents in a concealed pouch, a hotel safe or a safe-deposit box.

Metro Safety

Metro stations best avoided late at night include Châtelet–Les Halles and its seemingly endless corridors, Château Rouge, Gare du Nord, Strasbourg St-Denis, Réaumur Sébastopol, Stalingrad and Montparnasse Bienvenüe.

Bornes d'alarme (alarm boxes) are located in the centre of each metro/RER platform and in some station corridors.

Pickpockets & Common Scams

Nonviolent crimes, such as pickpocketing and theft from handbags and packs, are a problem wherever there are crowds, especially of tourists. Places to be particularly careful include Montmartre (especially around Sacré Cœur); Pigalle; the areas around Forum des Halles and the Centre Pompidou; the Latin Quarter (especially the rectangle bounded by rue St-Jacques, bd St-Germain, bd St-Michel and quai St-Michel); beneath the Eiffel Tower; and on the metro during rush hour (particularly on line 4 and the western part of line 1).

Common 'distraction' scams employed by pickpockets include the following:

Gold Ring Scammers pretend to 'find' a gold ring (after subtly dropping it on the ground) and offer it to you as a diversionary tactic while they surreptitiously reach into your pockets or bags (variations include offering to sell you the ring for an outrageous price, or having the ring's 'owner' arrive and demand compensation).

Fake Petitions After approaching you to sign a 'petition', scammers will use the document to cover your belongings while they swipe them.

Dropped Items Often occurs on the metro. Someone will

drop something or spill a bag; your reaction might be to bend down and help them, while their accomplices rifle through your belongings.

Friendship Bracelets

Scammers approach you and tie a 'friendship bracelet' on your wrist, not only insisting that you pay for it, but taking the opportunity to fleece you of your valuables.

Taxes & Refunds

France's value-added tax (VAT) is known as TVA (*taxe sur la valeur ajoutée*) and is 20% on most goods with a few exceptions: for food products and books it's 5.5%, and for medicines it is 2.1%. Prices that include TVA are often marked TTC (*toutes taxes comprises;* literally 'all taxes included').

If you're not an EU resident, you can get a TVA refund provided that:

➡ you're aged over 15

➡ you'll be spending less than six months in France

➡ you purchase goods worth at least €175 at a single shop on the same day (not more than 10 of the same item)

➡ the goods fit into your luggage

➡ you are taking the goods out of France within three months of purchase

➡ the shop offers *vente en détaxe* (duty-free sales)

Present a passport at the time of purchase and ask for a *bordereau de vente à l'exportation* (export sales invoice) to be signed by the retailer and yourself. Most shops will refund less than the full amount (about 14%) to which you are entitled, in order to cover the time and expense involved in the refund procedure.

Some larger shops offer the refund on the spot (always ask). Alternatively, as you leave France or another

PRACTICALITIES

Classifieds Check FUSAC (France USA Contacts; www.fusac.fr) for classified ads about housing, babysitting, French lessons, part-time jobs and so forth.

Newspapers & Magazines Parisians read their news in centre-left *Le Monde* (www.lemonde.fr), right-leaning *Le Figaro* (www.lefigaro.fr) and left-leaning *Libération* (www.liberation.fr). *Metro* (readmetro.metrofrance.com) is the freebie to pick up outside metro stations, and *Le Parisien* (www.leparisien.fr) is the city-news read.

Smoking It's illegal to smoke in indoor public spaces, including restaurants and bars (hence the crowds of smokers in doorways and on pavement terraces outside).

Weights & Measures France uses the metric system.

EU country, have all three pages of the *bordereau* validated by the country's customs officials at the airport or at the border. Customs officials will take one sheet and hand you two. You must post one copy (the pink one) back to the shop and retain the other (green) sheet for your records in case there is any dispute. Once the shop where you made your purchase receives its stamped copy, it will send you a *virement* (fund transfer) in the form you have requested. Be prepared for a wait of up to three months.

If you're flying out of Orly or Charles de Gaulle, certain shops can arrange for you to receive your refund as you're leaving the country, though you must complete the steps outlined above. You must make such arrangements at the time of purchase.

For more information contact the **customs information centre** (☎08 11 20 44 44; www.douane.minefi.gouv.fr; ☷phone service 8.30am-6pm Mon-Fri).

Telephone

➡ There are no area codes in France – you always dial the 10-digit number.

➡ Telephone numbers in Paris always start with ☎01, unless the number is provided by an internet service provider (ISP), in which case it begins with ☎09.

➡ Mobile phones throughout France commence with either ☎06 or ☎07.

➡ France's country code is ☎33.

➡ To call abroad from Paris, dial France's international access code (00), the country code, the area code (usually without the initial '0', if there is one) and the local number. International Direct Dial (IDD) calls to almost anywhere in the world can be placed from public telephones. The international reduced rate applies from 7pm to 8am weekdays and all day at the weekend.

➡ Note that while numbers beginning with 08 00, 08 04, 08 05 and 08 09 are toll-free in France, other numbers beginning with 08 are not (costs per minute range from €0.09 to €0.75).

➡ Customer service numbers are generally more expensive than local rates.

➡ Most four-digit numbers starting with 10, 30 or 31 are free of charge.

➔ If you can read basic French, directory enquiries are best done via the *Yellow Pages* (www.pagesjaunes.fr; click on Pages Blanches for the *White Pages*), which will provide more information, including maps, for free. From a mobile phone, use the site mobile.pagesjaunes.fr.

Mobile Phones

Phone Compatibility You can use your mobile/cell phone (*portable*) in France provided it is GSM (the standard in Europe, which is becoming increasingly common elsewhere) and tri-band or quad-band. If your phone meets the requirements, you can check with your service provider about using it in France, but beware of roaming costs, especially for data.

Networks Rather than staying on your home network, it is usually more convenient to buy a local SIM card from a French provider, such as Orange (www.orange.fr), SFR (www.sfr.fr), Bouygues (www.bouyguestelecom.fr) or Free Mobile (mobile.free.fr), which will give you a local phone number. In order for this to work, you'll need to ensure your phone is 'unlocked', which means you can use another service provider.

Call Credit Count on paying between €1.90 and €5 for the initial SIM card (with a few minutes of calls included), then purchase a prepaid Mobicarte for phone credit. *Tabacs* (tobacconists), mobile phone outlets such as **La Boutique Orange** (16 place de la Madeleine, 8e; ⊗10am-7.30pm Mon-Sat; MMadeleine), supermarkets etc sell Mobicartes.

Time

➔ France uses the 24-hour clock in most cases, with the hours usually separated from the minutes by a lower-case 'h'. Thus, 15h30 is 3.30pm, 00h30 is 12.30am and so on.

➔ France is on Central European Time (like Berlin and Rome), which is one hour ahead of GMT.

➔ Daylight-saving time runs from the last Sunday in March to the last Sunday in October.

Toilets

➔ Public toilets in Paris are signposted *toilettes* or *WC*. The self-cleaning cylindrical toilets you see on Parisian pavements are open 24 hours, reasonably clean and free of charge, though, of course, they never seem to be around when you need them. Look for the words *libre* ('available'; green-coloured) or *occupé* ('occupied'; red-coloured).

➔ Cafe owners do not appreciate you using their facilities if you are not a paying customer (a coffee can be a good investment); however, if you have young children they may make an exception (ask first!). Other good bets are major department stores and big hotels.

➔ There are free public toilets in front of Notre Dame cathedral, near the Arc de Triomphe, east down the steps at Sacré-Cœur at the northwestern entrance to the Jardins des Tuileries.

Tourist Information

The main branch of the **Paris Convention & Visitors Bureau** (Office du Tourisme et des Congrès de Paris; Map p372; www.parisinfo.com; 27 rue des Pyramides, 1er; ⊗7am-7pm May-Oct, 10am-7pm Nov-Apr; MPyramides) is 500m northwest of the Louvre. It sells tickets for tours and several attractions, plus museum and transport passes. Also books accommodation.

The bureau maintains a handful of centres in Paris. In addition, find information desks at Charles de Gaulle Airport. For tourist information around Paris, see Paris Region (www.visitparisregion.com).

Anvers-Montmartre Welcome Desk (Map p378; http://en.parisinfo.com; opp 72 bd Rochechouart, 18e; ⊗10am-6pm; MAnvers) At the foot of Montmartre, next to Anvers metro station.

Gare de l'Est Welcome Desk (Map p382; place du 11 Novembre 1918, 10e; ⊗8am-7pm Mon-Sat; MGare de l'Est) Inside Gare de l'Est train station, facing platforms 1–2.

Gare de Lyon Welcome Desk (Map p394; 20 bd Diderot, 12e; ⊗8am-6pm Mon-Sat; MGare de Lyon) Inside Gare de Lyon train station, facing platforms L–M.

Gare du Nord Welcome Desk (Map p382; 18 rue de Dunkerque, 10e; ⊗8am-6pm; MGare du Nord) Inside Gare du Nord station, under the glass roof of the Île de France departure and arrival area (eastern end of station).

Syndicate d'Initiative de Montmartre (Map p378; ✆01 42 62 21 21; www.montmartre-guide.com; 21 place du Tertre, 18e; ⊗10am-6pm summer, 10am-4pm Mon-Thu, 10am-5pm Fri, 10am-1pm & 2-5pm Sat rest of year; MAbbesses) Locally run tourist office and shop on Montmartre's most picturesque square. It sells maps of Montmartre and organises guided tours.

Travellers with Disabilities

Paris is an ancient city and therefore not particularly well equipped for *visiteurs handicapés* (disabled visitors): kerb ramps are few and far between, older public facilities and budget hotels usually lack lifts, and the metro, dating back more than a century, is mostly inaccessible for those in a wheelchair (*fauteuil roulant*).

But efforts are being made. The tourist office continues its excellent 'Tourisme & Handicap' initiative, in which museums, cultural attractions, hotels and restaurants that provide access or special assistance or facilities for those with physical, mental, visual and/or hearing disabilities display a special logo at their entrances. For the ever-increasing list of places that qualify, visit the website of the Paris Convention & Visitors Bureau (www.parisinfo.com) and click on 'Practical Paris'.

Resources

➡ For information about which cultural venues in Paris are accessible to people with disabilities, surf Accès Culture (www.accesculture.org).

➡ *Access in Paris*, a 245-page guide to the French capital for people with disabilities, can be downloaded in PDF form at Access Project (www.accessinparis.org).

➡ **Mobile en Ville** (☑09 52 29 60 51; www.mobile-en-ville.asso.fr; 8 rue des Mariniers, 14e) works hard to make independent travel within the city easier for people in wheelchairs. Among other things it organises wheelchair *randonnées* (walks) in and around Paris; those in wheelchairs are pushed by 'walkers' on roller skates.

➡ Download Lonely Planet's free *Accessible Travel* guide from http://lptravel.to/AccessibleTravel.

Transport

The SNCF has made many of its train carriages more accessible to people with disabilities. A traveller in a wheelchair can travel in both the TGV (*train à grande vitesse;* high-speed train) and in the 1st-class carriage with a 2nd-class ticket on mainline trains provided they make a reservation by phone or at a train station at least a few hours before departure. Details are available in the SNCF booklet *Le Mémento du Voyageur Handicapé* (Handicapped Traveller Summary) available at all train stations. For advice on planning your journey from station to station, contact the SNCF service **Accès Plus** (☑08 90 64 06 50; www.accessibilite.sncf.com).

Line 14 of the metro was built to be wheelchair-accessible, although in reality it remains extremely challenging to navigate in a chair – unlike Paris buses, which are 100% accessible.

For information on the accessibility of all forms of public transport in the Paris region, get a copy of the *Guide Pratique à l'Usage des Personnes à Mobilité Réduite* (Practical Usage Guide for People with Reduced Mobility) from the Syndicate des Transports d'Île de France (www.stif.info). Its info service for travellers with disabilities, **Info Mobi** (☑09 70 81 83 85; www.infomobi.com), is especially useful.

Taxis G7 (☑01 41 27 66 99, 3607; www.taxisg7.com) has 120 cars especially adapted to carry wheelchairs, and drivers trained in helping passengers with disabilities.

Visas

There are no entry requirements for nationals of EU countries and a handful of other European countries (including Switzerland). Citizens of Australia, the USA, Canada and New Zealand do not need visas to visit France for up to 90 days.

Everyone else, including citizens of South Africa, needs a Schengen Visa, named after the Schengen Agreement that has abol-ished passport controls among 26 EU countries and which has also been ratified by the non-EU governments of Iceland, Norway and Switzerland. A visa for any of these countries should be valid throughout the Schengen area, but it pays to double-check with the embassy or consulate of each country you intend to visit. Note that the UK and Ireland are not Schengen countries.

Check www.france.diplomatie.fr for the latest visa regulations and the closest French embassy to your current residence.

Titre de Séjour

If you are issued a long-stay visa valid for six months or longer, you may need to apply for a *titre de séjour* (residence permit; also called a *carte de séjour*) after your arrival in France. If you are only staying for up to 12 months you may not need it, but you will need to register with the French Office of Immigration and Integration (www.ofii.fr). Check the website of the Préfecture de Police (www.prefecturedepolice.interieur.gouv.fr) or call ☑01 53 71 53 71 first for instructions.

Passport holders from one of 31 European countries who are seeking to take up residence in France don't need to acquire a *titre de séjour;* their passport or national ID card is sufficient. Check the Préfecture de Police website to see which countries are included.

Foreigners with non-European passports should check the website of the Préfecture de Police or call ☑01 53 71 53 71.

Visa Extensions

Tourist visas *cannot* be extended except in emergencies (such as medical problems). If you have an urgent problem, contact the Service Étranger (Foreigner Service) at the Préfecture de Police for guidance. If you entered France on the 90-day visa-waiver program (eg you are Australian, Canadian or American) and you have stayed for 90 days, you must leave the Schengen area for an additional 90 days before you can re-enter.

Work & Student Visas

If you would like to work, study or stay in France for longer than three months, apply to the French embassy or consulate nearest to you for the appropriate *long séjour* (long-stay) visa. Au pairs are granted student visas: they must be arranged *before* you leave home (unless you're an EU resident); the same goes for the year-long working holiday visa *(permis vacances travail)*.

Unless you hold an EU passport or are married to a French national, it's extremely difficult to get a visa that will allow you to work in France. For any sort of long-stay visa, begin the paperwork in your home country several months before you plan to leave. Applications usually cannot be made in a third country, nor can tourist visas be turned into student visas after you arrive in France. People with student visas can apply for permission to work part time; enquire at your place of study.

Women Travellers

➡ Women attract more unwanted attention than men, but female travellers need not walk around Paris in fear: people are rarely assaulted on the street. However, the French seem to have given relatively little thought to sexual harassment *(harcèlement sexuel)*, and many men still think that to stare suavely at a passing woman is to pay her a compliment.

➡ France's national rape crisis hotline, Viols Femmes Informations, is run by a group called **Collectif Féministe contre le Viol** (CFCV Feminist Collective Against Rape; ☑08 00 05 95 95; www.cfcv.asso.fr; ⊙10am-7pm Mon-Fri).

➡ In an emergency, call the police ☑17.

➡ **La Maison des Femmes de Paris** (Map p394; ☑01 43 43 41 13; https://mdfparis.wordpress.com; 163 rue de Charenton, 12e; ⊙11am-7pm Mon-Fri; Ⓜ Reuilly Diderot) is a meeting place for women of all ages and nationalities, with events, workshops and exhibitions scheduled throughout the week.

Language

The sounds used in spoken French can almost all be found in English. If you read our pronunciation guides as if they were English, you'll be understood just fine. There are a couple of sounds to take note of: nasal vowels (represented in our guides by o or u followed by an almost inaudible nasal consonant sound m, n or ng), the 'funny' u (ew in our guides) and the deep-in-the-throat r. Syllables in French words are, for the most part, equally stressed. As English speakers tend to stress the first syllable, try adding a light stress on the final syllable of French words to compensate.

BASICS

Hello.	Bonjour.	bon·zhoor
Goodbye.	Au revoir.	o·rer·vwa
Excuse me.	Excusez-moi.	ek·skew·zay·mwa
Sorry.	Pardon.	par·don
Yes./No.	Oui./Non.	wee/non
Please.	S'il vous plaît.	seel voo play
Thank you.	Merci.	mair·see
You're welcome.	De rien.	der ree·en

How are you?
Comment allez-vous?   ko·mon ta·lay·voo

Fine, and you?
Bien, merci. Et vous?   byun mair·see ay voo

What's your name?
Comment vous   ko·mon voo·
appelez-vous?   za·play voo

WANT MORE?

For in-depth language information and handy phrases, check out Lonely Planet's *French phrasebook*. You'll find it at **shop.lonelyplanet.com**, or you can buy Lonely Planet's iPhone phrasebooks at the Apple App Store.

My name is ...
Je m'appelle ...   zher ma·pel ...

Do you speak English?
Parlez-vous anglais?   par·lay·voo ong·glay

I don't understand.
Je ne comprends pas.   zher ner kom·pron pa

ACCOMMODATION

Do you have any rooms available?
Est-ce que vous avez   es·ker voo za·vay
des chambres libres?   day shom·brer lee·brer

How much is it per night/person?
Quel est le prix   kel ay ler pree
par nuit/personne?   par nwee/per·son

Is breakfast included?
Est-ce que le petit   es·ker ler per·tee
déjeuner est inclus?   day·zher·nay ayt en·klew

dorm	dortoir	dor·twar
guesthouse	pension	pon·syon
hotel	hôtel	o·tel
youth hostel	auberge de jeunesse	o·berzh der zher·nes

a ... room	une chambre ...	ewn shom·brer ...
single	à un lit	a un lee
double	avec un grand lit	a·vek un gron lee

with (a) ...	avec ...	a·vek ...
air-con	climatiseur	klee·ma·tee·zer
bathroom	une salle de bains	ewn sal der bun
window	fenêtre	fer·nay·trer

DIRECTIONS

Where's ...?   Où est ...?   oo ay ...

What's the address?   Quelle est l'adresse?   kel ay la·dres

Signs

Entrée	Entrance
Femmes	Women
Fermé	Closed
Hommes	Men
Interdit	Prohibited
Ouvert	Open
Renseignements	Information
Sortie	Exit
Toilettes/WC	Toilets

Can you write down the address, please?
Est-ce que vous pourriez es·ker voo poo·ryay
écrire l'adresse, ay·kreer la·dres
s'il vous plaît? seel voo play

Can you show me (on the map)?
Pouvez-vous m'indiquer poo·vay·voo mun·dee·kay
(sur la carte)? (sewr la kart)

at the corner	*au coin*	o kwun
at the traffic lights	*aux feux*	o fer
behind	*derrière*	dair·ryair
in front of	*devant*	der·von
far (from ...)	*loin (de ...)*	lwun (der ...)
left	*gauche*	gosh
near (to ...)	*près (de ...)*	pray (der ...)
next to ...	*à côté de ...*	a ko·tay der ...
opposite ...	*en face de ...*	on fas der ...
right	*droite*	drwat
straight ahead	*tout droit*	too drwa

EATING & DRINKING

What would you recommend?
Qu'est-ce que vous kes·ker voo
conseillez? kon·say·yay

What's in that dish?
Quels sont les kel son lay
ingrédients? zun·gray·dyon

I'm a vegetarian.
Je suis zher swee
végétarien/ vay·zhay·ta·ryun/
végétarienne. vay·zhay·ta·ryen (m/f)

I don't eat ...
Je ne mange pas ... zher ner monzh pa ...

Cheers!
Santé! son·tay

That was delicious.
C'était délicieux! say·tay day·lee·syer

Please bring the bill.
Apportez-moi a·por·tay·mwa
l'addition, la·dee·syon
s'il vous plaît. seel voo play

I'd like to reserve a table for ...	*Je voudrais réserver une table pour ...*	zher voo·dray ray·zair·vay ewn ta·bler poor ...
(eight) o'clock	*(vingt) heures*	(vungt) er
(two) people	*(deux) personnes*	(der) pair·son

Key Words

appetiser	*entrée*	on·tray
bottle	*bouteille*	boo·tay
breakfast	*petit déjeuner*	per·tee day·zher·nay
cold	*froid*	frwa
delicatessen	*traiteur*	tray·ter
dinner	*dîner*	dee·nay
fork	*fourchette*	foor·shet
glass	*verre*	vair
grocery store	*épicerie*	ay·pees·ree
hot	*chaud*	sho
knife	*couteau*	koo·to
lunch	*déjeuner*	day·zher·nay
market	*marché*	mar·shay
menu	*carte*	kart
plate	*assiette*	a·syet
spoon	*cuillère*	kwee·yair
wine list	*carte des vins*	kart day vun
with/without	*avec/sans*	a·vek/son

Meat & Fish

beef	*bœuf*	berf
chicken	*poulet*	poo·lay
crab	*crabe*	krab
lamb	*agneau*	a·nyo
oyster	*huître*	wee·trer
pork	*porc*	por
snail	*escargot*	es·kar·go
squid	*calmar*	kal·mar
turkey	*dinde*	dund
veal	*veau*	vo

Fruit & Vegetables

apple	*pomme*	pom
apricot	*abricot*	ab·ree·ko
asparagus	*asperge*	a·spairzh
beans	*haricots*	a·ree·ko
beetroot	*betterave*	be·trav

cabbage	chou	shoo
celery	céleri	sel·ree
cherry	cerise	ser·reez
corn	maïs	ma·ees
cucumber	concombre	kong·kom·brer
gherkin (pickle)	cornichon	kor·nee·shon
grape	raisin	ray·zun
leek	poireau	pwa·ro
lemon	citron	see·tron
lettuce	laitue	lay·tew
mushroom	champignon	shom·pee·nyon
peach	pêche	pesh
peas	petit pois	per·tee pwa
(red/green) pepper	poivron (rouge/vert)	pwa·vron (roozh/vair)
pineapple	ananas	a·na·nas
plum	prune	prewn
potato	pomme de terre	pom der tair
prune	pruneau	prew·no
pumpkin	citrouille	see·troo·yer
shallot	échalote	eh·sha·lot
spinach	épinards	eh·pee·nar
strawberry	fraise	frez
tomato	tomate	to·mat
turnip	navet	na·vay
vegetable	légume	lay·gewm

Other

bread	pain	pun
butter	beurre	ber
cheese	fromage	fro·mazh
egg	œuf	erf
honey	miel	myel
jam	confiture	kon·fee·tewr
oil	huile	weel
pepper	poivre	pwa·vrer
rice	riz	ree
salt	sel	sel
sugar	sucre	sew·krer
vinegar	vinaigre	vee·nay·grer

Drinks

beer	bière	bee·yair
coffee	café	ka·fay
(orange) juice	jus (d'orange)	zhew (do·ronzh)
milk	lait	lay

red wine	vin rouge	vun roozh
tea	thé	tay
(mineral) water	eau (minérale)	o (mee·nay·ral)
white wine	vin blanc	vun blong

EMERGENCIES

Help!
Au secours! · o skoor

Leave me alone!
Fichez-moi la paix! · fee·shay·mwa la pay

I'm lost.
Je suis perdu/perdue. · zhe swee·pair·dew (m/f)

Call a doctor.
Appelez un médecin. · a·play un mayd·sun

Call the police.
Appelez la police. · a·play la po·lees

I'm ill.
Je suis malade. · zher swee ma·lad

It hurts here.
J'ai une douleur ici. · zhay ewn doo·ler ee·see

I'm allergic (to ...).
Je suis allergique (à ...). · zher swee za·lair·zheek (a ...)

SHOPPING & SERVICES

I'd like to buy ...
Je voudrais acheter ... · zher voo·dray ash·tay ...

Can I look at it?
Est-ce que je peux le voir? · es·ker zher per ler vwar

I'm just looking.
Je regarde. · zher rer·gard

I don't like it.
Cela ne me plaît pas. · ser·la ner mer play pa

How much is it?
C'est combien? · say kom·byun

It's too expensive.
C'est trop cher. · say tro shair

There's a mistake in the bill.
Il y a une erreur dans la note. · eel ya ewn ay·rer don la not

bank	banque	bonk
internet cafe	cybercafé	see·bair·ka·fay
tourist office	office de tourisme	o·fees der too·rees·mer

Question Words		
What?	Quoi?	kwa
When?	Quand?	kon
Where?	Où?	oo
Who?	Qui?	kee
Why?	Pourquoi?	poor·kwa

TIME & DATES

What time is it?
Quelle heure est-il? kel er ay til

It's (eight) o'clock.
Il est (huit) heures. il ay (weet) er

Half past (10).
(Dix) heures et demie. (deez) er ay day·mee

morning	*matin*	ma·tun
afternoon	*après-midi*	a·pray·mee·dee
evening	*soir*	swar
yesterday	*hier*	yair
today	*aujourd'hui*	o·zhoor·dwee
tomorrow	*demain*	der·mun

Monday	*lundi*	lun·dee
Tuesday	*mardi*	mar·dee
Wednesday	*mercredi*	mair·krer·dee
Thursday	*jeudi*	zher·dee
Friday	*vendredi*	von·drer·dee
Saturday	*samedi*	sam·dee
Sunday	*dimanche*	dee·monsh

TRANSPORT

I want to go to ...
Je voudrais aller zher voo·dray a·lay
à ... a ...

Numbers

1	*un*	un
2	*deux*	der
3	*trois*	trwa
4	*quatre*	ka·trer
5	*cinq*	sungk
6	*six*	sees
7	*sept*	set
8	*huit*	weet
9	*neuf*	nerf
10	*dix*	dees
20	*vingt*	vung
30	*trente*	tront
40	*quarante*	ka·ront
50	*cinquante*	sung·kont
60	*soixante*	swa·sont
70	*soixante-dix*	swa·son·dees
80	*quatre-vingts*	ka·trer·vung
90	*quatre-vingt-dix*	ka·trer·vung·dees
100	*cent*	son
1000	*mille*	meel

Does it stop at ...?
Est-ce qu'il s'arrête à ...? es·kil sa·ret a ...

At what time does it leave/arrive?
À quelle heure est-ce a kel er es
qu'il part/arrive? kil par/a·reev

I want to get off here.
Je veux descendre zher ver day·son·drer
ici. ee·see

a ... ticket	*un billet ...*	un bee·yay ...
1st-class	*de première classe*	der prem·yair klas
2nd-class	*de deuxième classe*	der der·zyem klas
one-way	*simple*	sum·pler
return	*aller et retour*	a·lay ay rer·toor

aisle seat	*côté couloir*	ko·tay kool·war
boat	*bateau*	ba·to
bus	*bus*	bews
cancelled	*annulé*	a·new·lay
delayed	*en retard*	on rer·tar
first	*premier*	prer·myay
last	*dernier*	dair·nyay
plane	*avion*	a·vyon
platform	*quai*	kay
ticket office	*guichet*	gee·shay
timetable	*horaire*	o·rair
train	*train*	trun
window seat	*côté fenêtre*	ko·tay fe·ne·trer

I'd like to hire a ...	*Je voudrais louer ...*	zher voo·dray loo·way ...
car	*une voiture*	ewn vwa·tewr
bicycle	*un vélo*	un vay·lo
motorcycle	*une moto*	ewn mo·to

child seat	*siège-enfant*	syezh·on·fon
helmet	*casque*	kask
mechanic	*mécanicien*	may·ka·nee·syun
petrol/gas	*essence*	ay·sons
service station	*station-service*	sta·syon·ser·vees

Can I park here?
Est-ce que je peux es·ker zher per
stationner ici? sta·syo·nay ee·see

I have a flat tyre.
Mon pneu est à plat. mom pner ay ta pla

I've run out of petrol.
Je suis en panne zher swee zon pan
d'essence. day·sons

GLOSSARY

(m) indicates masculine gender, (f) feminine gender, (pl) plural and (adj) adjective

adjoint (m) – deputy mayor

ancien régime (m) – 'old order'; France under the monarchy before the Revolution

apéritif (m) – a drink taken before dinner

arrondissement (m) – one of 20 administrative divisions in Paris; abbreviated on street signs as 1er (1st arrondissement), 2e or 2ème (2nd) etc

auberge (de jeunesse) (f) – (youth) hostel

avenue (f) – avenue (abbreviated av)

banlieues (f pl) – suburbs

belle époque (f) – 'beautiful age'; era of elegance and gaiety characterising fashionable Parisian life roughly from 1870 to 1914

billet (m) – ticket

billeterie (f) – ticket office or window

biologique or **bio** (adj) – organic

boucherie (f) – butcher

boulangerie (f) – bakery

boules (f pl) – a game played with heavy metal balls on a sandy pitch; also called *pétanque*

brasserie (f) – 'brewery'; a restaurant that usually serves food all day long

brioche (f) – small roll or cake, sometimes made with nuts, currants or candied fruit

bureau de change (m) – currency exchange bureau

café du quartier (m) – neighbourhood café

carnet (m) – a book of (usually) 10 bus, tram, metro or other tickets sold at a reduced rate

carrefour (m) – crossroads, intersection

carte (f) – card; menu; map

carte de séjour (f) – residence permit

cave (f) – (wine) cellar

chambre (f) – room

chanson française (f) – 'French song'; traditional musical genre where lyrics are paramount

chansonnier (m) – cabaret singer

charcuterie (f) – a variety of meat products that are cured, smoked or processed, including sausages, hams, pâtés and rillettes; shop selling these products

cimetière (m) – cemetery

consigne (f) – left-luggage office

correspondance (f) – linking tunnel or walkway, eg in the metro; rail or bus connection

cour (f) – courtyard

couvert (m) – covered shopping arcade (also called *galerie*)

dégustation (f) – tasting, sampling

demi (m) – half; 330mL glass of beer

département (m) – administrative division of France

dessert (m) – dessert

eau (f) – water

église (f) – church

entrée (f) – entrance; first course or starter

épicerie (f) – small grocery store

espace (f) – space; outlet

exposition universelle (f) – world exhibition

fête (f) – festival; holiday

ficelle (f) – string; a thinner, crustier 200g version of the baguette not unlike a very thick breadstick

fin de siècle (adj) – 'end of the century'; characteristic of the last years of the 19th century and generally used to indicate decadence

forêt (f) – forest

formule (f) – similar to a *menu* but allows choice of whichever two of three courses you want (eg starter and main course or main course and dessert)

fromagerie (f) – cheese shop

galerie (f) – gallery; covered shopping arcade (also called *passage*)

galette (f) – a pancake or flat pastry, with a variety of (usually savoury) fillings

gare (f) – railway station

gare routière (f) – bus station

gendarmerie (f) – police station; police force

grand projet (m) – huge, public edifice erected by a government or politician generally in a bid to immortalise themselves

Grands Boulevards (m pl) – 'Great Boulevards'; the eight contiguous broad thoroughfares that stretch from place de la Madeleine eastwards to the place de la République

halles (f pl) – covered food market

hameau (m) – hamlet

hammam (m) – steam room, Turkish bath

haute couture (f) – literally 'high sewing'; the creations of leading designers

haute cuisine (f) – 'high cuisine'; classic French cooking style typified by elaborately prepared multicourse meals

hôtel de ville (m) – city or town hall

hôtel particulier (m) – private mansion

jardin (m) – garden

kir (m) – white wine sweetened with a blackcurrant (or other) liqueur

lycée (m) – secondary school

mairie (f) – city or town hall

marché (m) – market

marché aux puces (m) – flea market

menu (m) – fixed-price meal with two or more courses; see *formule*

musée (m) – museum

musette (f) – accordion music

nocturne (f) – late night opening at a museum, department store etc

orangerie (f) – conservatory for growing citrus fruit

pain (m) – bread

palais de justice (m) – law courts

parc (m) – park

parvis (m) – square in front of a church or public building passage

pastis (m) – an aniseed-flavoured aperitif mixed with water

pâté (m) – potted meat; a thickish paste, often of pork, cooked in a ceramic dish and served cold (similar to terrine)

pâtisserie (f) – cakes and pastries; shop selling these products

pelouse (f) – lawn

pétanque (f) – see boules

pied-noir (m) – 'black foot'; French colonial born in Algeria

place (f) – square or plaza

plan (m) – city map

plan du quartier (m) – map of nearby streets (hung on the wall near metro exits)

plat du jour (m) – daily special in a restaurant

poissonnerie (f) – fishmonger, fish shop

pont (m) – bridge

port (m) – harbour, port

port de plaisance (m) – boat harbour or marina

porte (f) – door; gate in a city wall

poste (f) – post office

préfecture (f) – prefecture; capital city of a département

produits biologique – organic food

quai (m) – quay

quartier (m) – quarter, district, neighbourhood

raï – a type of Algerian popular music

RATP – Régie Autonome des Transports Parisiens; Paris' public transport system

RER – Réseau Express Régional; Paris' suburban train network

résidence (f) – residence; hotel usually intended for longterm stays

rillettes (f pl) – shredded potted meat or fish

rive (f) – bank of a river

rond point (m) – roundabout

rue (f) – street or road

salle (f) – hall; room

salon de thé (m) – tearoom

SNCF – Société Nationale de Chemins de Fer; France's national railway organisation

soldes (m pl) – sale, the sales

sono mondiale (f) – world music

sortie (f) – exit

spectacle (m) – performance, play or theatrical show

square (m) – public garden

syndicat d'initiative (m) – tourist office

tabac (m) – tobacconist (which also sells bus tickets, phonecards etc)

tarif réduit (m) – reduced price (for students, seniors, children etc)

tartine (f) – a slice of bread with any topping or garnish

taxe de séjour (f) – municipal tourist tax

télécarte (f) – phonecard

TGV – train à grande vitesse; high-speed train

tour (f) – tower

tous les jours – every day (eg on timetables)

traiteur (m) – caterer, delicatessen

TVA – taxe sur la valeur ajoutée; value-added tax

Vélib' (m) – communal bicycle rental scheme in Paris

vélo (m) – bicycle

version française (m) – literally 'French version': a film dubbed in French

version originale – literally 'original version': a nondubbed film in its original language with French subtitles

Behind the Scenes

SEND US YOUR FEEDBACK

We love to hear from travellers – your comments keep us on our toes and help make our books better. Our well-travelled team reads every word on what you loved or loathed about this book. Although we cannot reply individually to your submissions, we always guarantee that your feedback goes straight to the appropriate authors, in time for the next edition. Each person who sends us information is thanked in the next edition – the most useful submissions are rewarded with a selection of digital PDF chapters.

Visit **lonelyplanet.com/contact** to submit your updates and suggestions or to ask for help. Our award-winning website also features inspirational travel stories, news and discussions.

Note: We may edit, reproduce and incorporate your comments in Lonely Planet products such as guidebooks, websites and digital products, so let us know if you don't want your comments reproduced or your name acknowledged. For a copy of our privacy policy visit lonelyplanet.com/privacy.

OUR READERS

Many thanks to the travellers who used the last edition and wrote to us with helpful hints, useful advice and interesting anecdotes: Alison Forrester, Claire Garon, Damien Richardot, Ellie Sanders, Georgia Richmond, Jill Drake, Laurence van Bilderbeek, Loren Buchanan, Pien Borghouts, Sain Alizada, Salim Abboud, Seraina Walser, Seth Blumenthal, Shoshana Baumgarten, Suzette Gresham

WRITER THANKS

Catherine Le Nevez

Un grand merci to my Paris co-writers Chris and Nicola. *Merci mille fois* to Julian, and all of the innumerable Parisians who offered insights and inspiration. In particular, *merci beaucoup* to Laurent for going above and beyond, and to Laurence for the same. Huge thanks also to Helen Elfer, Kate Morgan and everyone at LP. A heartfelt *merci encore* to my parents, brother, *belle-sœur* and *neveu* for sustaining my lifelong love of Paris.

Christopher Pitts

Special thanks to my two great co-writer for their advice and input and to all the crew at LP who have put much hard work into making this book what it is. *Bises* as well to the Pavillards and my dearest partners in crime: Perrine, Elliot and Celeste.

Nicola Williams

Un grand merci to the many in Paris who aided and abetted in tracking down the very best: font of all Parisian knowledge-extraordinaire Élodie Berta, Louvre treasure-hunt queen Daisy de Plume (THATLou), near-native Parisians Mary Winston Nicklin and Kasia Dietz. Kudos to my extra-special 'Paris with kids' research team Niko, Mischa & Kaya Luefkens.

ACKNOWLEDGEMENTS

Illustrations pp110-11, pp196-7 and pp264-5 by Javier Zarracina.

Cover photograph: IM Pei's Grande Pyramide at the Louvre, Francesco Carovillano/ 4Corners ©.

THIS BOOK

This 11th edition of Lonely Planet's *Paris* guidebook was curated by Catherine Le Nevez and researched and written by Catherine, Christopher Pitts and Nicola Williams, who also all wrote and researched the previous two editions. This guidebook was produced by the following:

Destination Editors Helen Elfer, Kate Morgan
Product Editors Kathryn Rowan, Anne Mason
Senior Cartographer Valentina Kremenchutskaya
Book Designer Mazzy Prinsep
Assisting Editors Janet Austin, Imogen Bannister, Nigel Chin, Andrea Dobbin, Ali Lemer, Kristin Odijk, Charlotte Orr, Maja Vatrić
Cover Researcher Naomi Parker
Thanks to Daniel Corbett, Ryan Evans, Andi Jones, Lauren Keith, Claire Naylor, Karyn Noble, Wayne Murphy, Anthony Phelan, Kirsten Rawlings, Tony Wheeler, Amanda Williamson

Index

See also separate subindexes for:

🍴 **EATING P356**

🍷 **DRINKING & NIGHTLIFE P358**

☆ **ENTERTAINMENT P359**

🛍 **SHOPPING P359**

🏃 **SPORTS & ACTIVITIES P360**

🛏 **SLEEPING P360**

🏃 SPORTS & ACTIVITIES

🛏 SLEEPING

Paris Maps

Sights
- Beach
- Bird Sanctuary
- Buddhist
- Castle/Palace
- Christian
- Confucian
- Hindu
- Islamic
- Jain
- Jewish
- Monument
- Museum/Gallery/Historic Building
- Ruin
- Shinto
- Sikh
- Taoist
- Winery/Vineyard
- Zoo/Wildlife Sanctuary
- Other Sight

Activities, Courses & Tours
- Bodysurfing
- Diving
- Canoeing/Kayaking
- Course/Tour
- Sento Hot Baths/Onsen
- Skiing
- Snorkelling
- Surfing
- Swimming/Pool
- Walking
- Windsurfing
- Other Activity

Sleeping
- Sleeping
- Camping

Eating
- Eating

Drinking & Nightlife
- Drinking & Nightlife
- Cafe

Entertainment
- Entertainment

Shopping
- Shopping

Information
- Bank
- Embassy/Consulate
- Hospital/Medical
- Internet
- Police
- Post Office
- Telephone
- Toilet
- Tourist Information
- Other Information

Geographic
- Beach
- Gate
- Hut/Shelter
- Lighthouse
- Lookout
- Mountain/Volcano
- Oasis
- Park
- Pass
- Picnic Area
- Waterfall

Population
- Capital (National)
- Capital (State/Province)
- City/Large Town
- Town/Village

Transport
- Airport
- Border crossing
- Bus
- Cable car/Funicular
- Cycling
- Ferry
- Metro station
- Monorail
- Parking
- Petrol station
- S-Bahn/Subway station
- Taxi
- T-bane/Tunnelbana station
- Train station/Railway
- Tram
- Tube station
- U-Bahn/Underground station
- Other Transport

Note: Not all symbols displayed above appear on the maps in this book

Routes
- Tollway
- Freeway
- Primary
- Secondary
- Tertiary
- Lane
- Unsealed road
- Road under construction
- Plaza/Mall
- Steps
- Tunnel
- Pedestrian overpass
- Walking Tour
- Walking Tour detour
- Path/Walking Trail

Boundaries
- International
- State/Province
- Disputed
- Regional/Suburb
- Marine Park
- Cliff
- Wall

Hydrography
- River, Creek
- Intermittent River
- Canal
- Water
- Dry/Salt/Intermittent Lake
- Reef

Areas
- Airport/Runway
- Beach/Desert
- Cemetery (Christian)
- Cemetery (Other)
- Glacier
- Mudflat
- Park/Forest
- Sight (Building)
- Sportsground
- Swamp/Mangrove

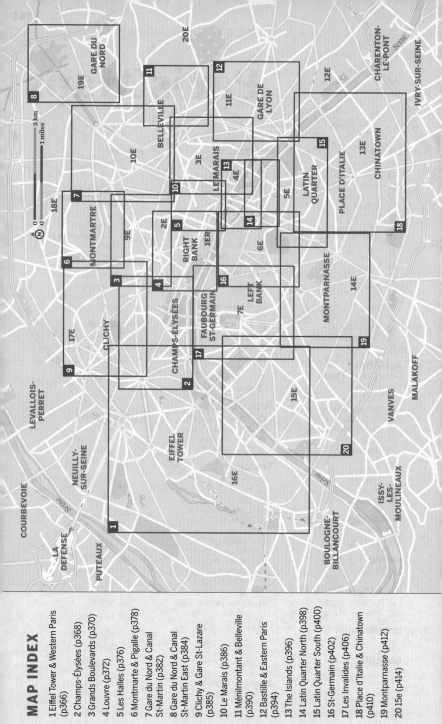

MAP INDEX

EIFFEL TOWER & WESTERN PARIS *Map on p366*

EIFFEL TOWER & WESTERN PARIS

EIFFEL TOWER & WESTERN PARIS

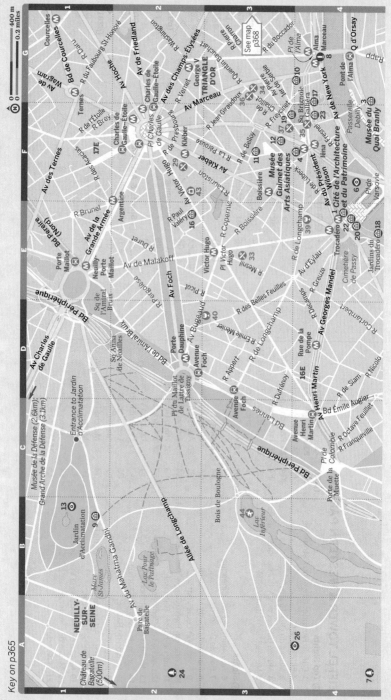

400 m
0.2 miles

See map p368

NEUILLY-
SUR-
SEINE

Château de
Bagatelle
(500m)

Musée de la Défense (2.6km)
Grand Arche de la Défense (3.1km)

Entrance to Jardin
d'Acclimatation

Jardin
d'Acclimatation

Parc de
Bagatelle

Av du Mahatma Gandhi

Mare St-James

Lac Pour
le Patinage

Bois de Boulogne

Allée de Longchamp

Lac
Inférieur

Porte de la
Muette

Bd Périphérique

Porte
Maillot

Av Charles
de Gaulle

Av de Ternes

Bd Pereire (Nord)

Av de la Grande Armée

Porte
Dauphine

Av Foch

Av de Malakoff

Sq de
l'Amiral
Bruix

Pl du Maillot
de Lattre de
Tassigny

Avenue
Foch

Bd Périphérique

Avenue
Henri
Martin

Bd Lannes

Av Georges Mandel

Av Henri Martin

R de la Pompe

Rue de
Longchamp

Av d'Eylau

R Greuze

R Dedar

Cimetière
de Passy

Jardins du
Trocadéro

R Octave Feuillet

R Tranqueville

Bd Émile Augier

R de Siam

R Nicolo

R Cortambert

R Scheffer

Pl du
Trocadéro

Av du Président Wilson

Av de New-York

Musée du
Quai Branly

Passerelle
Debilly

Pont de
l'Alma

Q d'Orsay

Rapp

Pl de
l'Alma

Pl de
Varsovie

Av Marceau

Av des Champs-Élysées

TRIANGLE
D'OR

Pl Charles
de Gaulle-Étoile

Charles de
Gaulle-Étoile

Av de Friedland

Bd de Courcelles

Courcelles

Ternes

Av de Wagram

R du Faubourg St-Honoré

R Balzac

Av Hoche

R de Courcelles

R de Presbourg

Av Kléber

Av Victor Hugo

Victor
Hugo

Pl Victor
Hugo

R Paul
Valéry

R Copernic

R Boissière

Boissière

Iéna

Cité de l'Architecture
et du Patrimoine

R de Longchamp

R de Belloy

R La Pérouse

Kléber

R Vernet

George V
R Quentin Bauchart

R Pierre
Charron

George V

R de Bassano

Av Marceau

R de Chaillot

R Jean Giraudoux

R Fresnel

R Freycinet

R Galilée

R Brunel

Argentine

R de l'Étoile

R Brey

R des Acacias

R Duret

R Pergolèse

R de la Faisanderie

R Picot

Av Bugeaud

R Appert

R Dufrénoy

Av de la Grande Armée

Neuilly
Porte
Maillot

R Lauriston

Sq Brignole-Galliera

Av du Président Kennedy

R de Longchamp

R des Belles Feuilles

Pte de la
Colombe

Porte de la
Muette

Sq Anna
de Noailles

Bd de l'Amiral Bruix

R Émile Menier

17E

16E

NEUILLY-
SUR-SEINE

24

13 ◎

9 🏛

26 ◎

7 🎭

44 🏊

40

33 ✕

16

43

29 ✕

36 ✕

34 ✕

37 🏛

12 🏛

11 🏛

Musée
Guimet des
Arts Asiatiques

10 🏛

17

23

35

4

1

22

20

18

6

3 🏛

8 🍴

39 🏛

EIFFEL TOWER & WESTERN PARIS

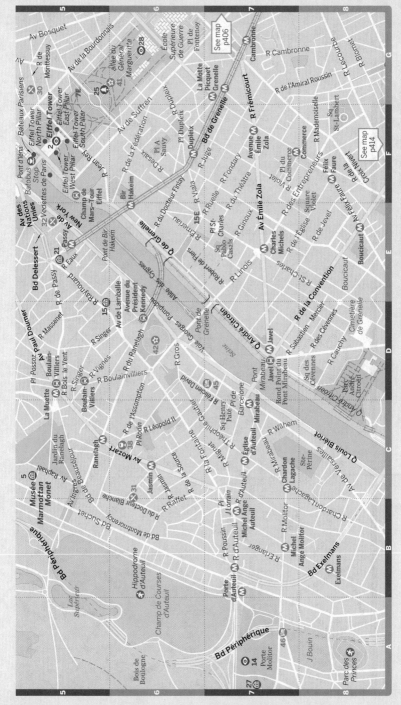

See map p406

See map p414

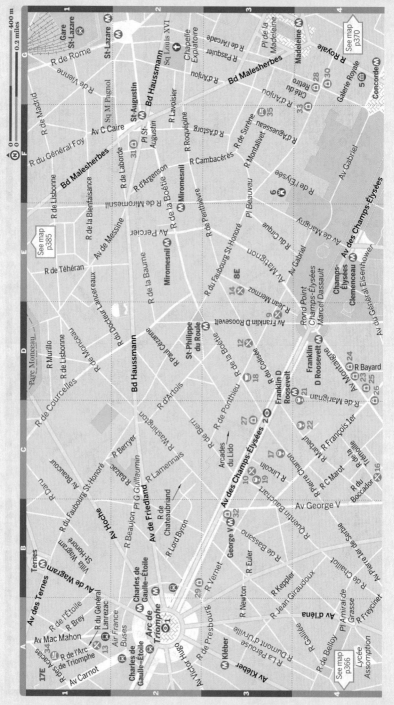

CHAMPS-ÉLYSÉES

See map p372

◎ **Top Sights** (p94)
1 Arc de Triomphe............A2

◎ **Sights** (p96)
2 Avenue des Champs-Élysées........C3
3 Grand Palais........E5
4 Jardin de la Nouvelle France........D5
5 Musée Maxim's........G4
6 Palais de l'Élysée........F3
7 Petit Palais........E5
8 Place de la Concorde........G5

✪ **Eating** (p99)
9 Framboise........D3
10 Ladurée........C3
11 Lasserre........D5

12 Le Boudoir........D3
13 Le Hide........A1
14 Makoto Aoki........E3
15 Mini Palais........E5
16 Philippe & Jean-Pierre........C4

◉ **Drinking & Nightlife** (p102)
17 Blaine........C3
18 La Baroche........D3
19 Queen........C3
20 ShowCase........E5
21 Wine by One........D4
22 Zig Zag Club........C4

◎ **Shopping** (p104)
23 Chanel........D4

24 Chloé........D4
25 Dior........D4
26 Givenchy........C3
27 Guerlain........G4
28 Hermès........B2
29 Lancel........G4
30 Lanvin........F2
31 Les Caves Augé........B3
32 Louis Vuitton........(see 29)
33 Saint Laurent........F4

🛏 **Sleeping** (p281)
34 Hidden Hotel........A1
35 Hotel Alison........F3

GRANDS BOULEVARDS

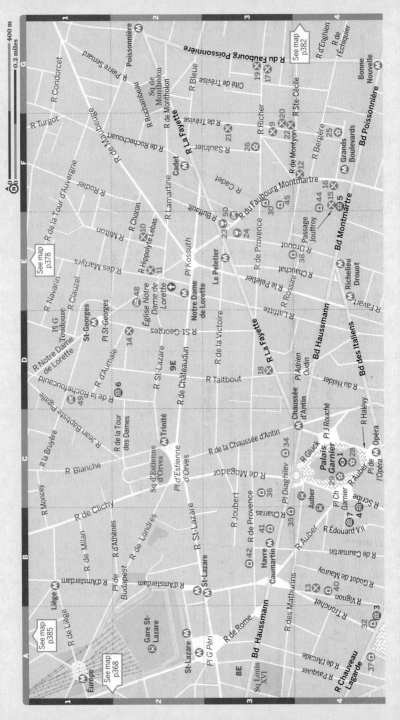

GRANDS BOULEVARDS

Key on p374

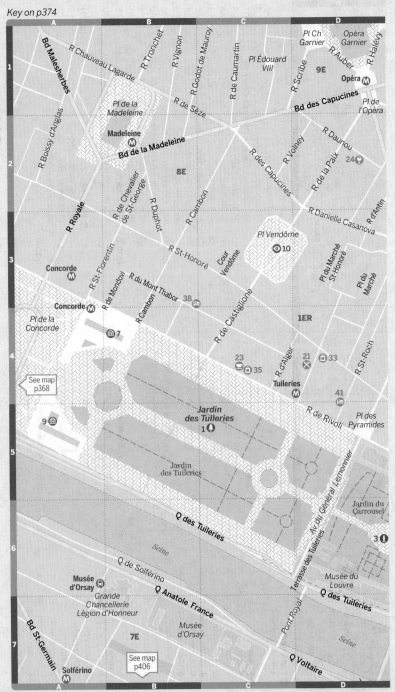

Bd Malesherbes

R Chauveau Lagarde

R Boissy d'Anglas

R Tronchet

R Vignon

R Godot de Mauroy

R de Caumartin

Pl Édouard VIII

Pl Ch Garnier

Opéra Garnier

R Auber

R Halévy

R Scribe

9E

Opéra Ⓜ

Pl de la Madeleine

R de Sèze

Bd des Capucines

Pl de l'Opéra

Madeleine Ⓜ

Bd de la Madeleine

R de Chevalier de St-George

8E

R des Capucines

R Volney

R Daunou

R de la Paix

24

R Royale

R Duphot

R Cambon

Pl Vendôme

R Danielle Casanova

R d'Antin

⊙10

R St-Honoré

Cour Vendôme

Pl du Marché St-Honoré

Pl du Marché

Concorde Ⓜ

R St-Florentin

R de Mondovi

R du Mont Thabor

R de Castiglione

1ER

R St-Roch

Concorde Ⓜ

R Cambon

38 🏛

Pl de la Concorde

🏛7

23 🖼 🏛35

R d'Alger

21 ⊗

🔒 33

See map p368

Tuileries Ⓜ

41 🏛

9 🏛

Jardin des Tuileries

1 🛈

R de Rivoli

Pl des Pyramides

Jardin des Tuileries

Av du Général Lemonnier

Jardin du Carrousel

Q des Tuileries

Seine

3 🛈

Q de Solférino

Terrasse des Tuileries

Musée d'Orsay 🖼

Q Anatole France

Musée du Louvre

Grande Chancellerie Légion d'Honneur

Q des Tuileries

Bd St-Germain

7E

Musée d'Orsay

Pont Royal

Seine

See map p406

Q Voltaire

Solférino Ⓜ

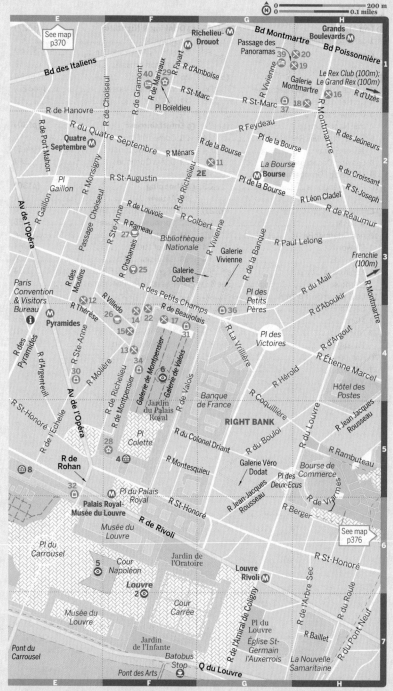

See map p370

Bd des Italiens

Richelieu-Drouot Ⓜ

Bd Montmartre

Grands Boulevards Ⓜ

Bd Poissonnière

Passage des Panoramas

Le Rex Club (100m);
Le Grand Rex (100m)

Galerie Montmartre

R d'Uzès

R de Gramont

R de Marivaux

R Favart

R d'Amboise

R St-Marc

Pl Boïeldieu

R St-Marc

R Vivienne

R Montmartre

R de Hanovre

R du Quatre Septembre

R de Choiseul

R Feydeau

R des Jeûneurs

Quatre Septembre Ⓜ

R de Port Mahon

R de Monsigny

R Ménars

R de la Bourse

Pl de la Bourse

R du Croissant

Pl Gaillon

R St-Augustin

R de Richelieu

11

2E

La Bourse

Bourse Ⓜ

R St-Joseph

Av de l'Opéra

Passage Choiseul

R Ste-Anne

R de Louvois

R Colbert

Pl de la Bourse

R Léon Cladel

R de Réaumur

R Rameau

27

Bibliothèque Nationale

R Vivienne

Galerie Vivienne

R Paul Lelong

Frenchie (100m)

R Chabanais

25

Galerie Colbert

R de la Banque

R du Mail

R Montmartre

Paris Convention & Visitors Bureau ⓘ

R des Moulins

R Villedo

R des Petits Champs

Pl des Petits Pères

36

R d'Aboukir

Pyramides Ⓜ

12

R Thérèse

26

14

22

R de Beaujolais

R La Vrillière

Pl des Victoires

R d'Argout

R Étienne Marcel

R des Pyramides

R d'Argenteuil

15

13

34

R Ste-Anne

R Molière

6

Galerie de Montpensier

Galerie de Valois

17

31

Banque de France

R Hérold

Hôtel des Postes

30

Av de l'Opéra

R de Richelieu

R de Montpensier

Jardin du Palais Royal

R de Valois

R Coquillière

R Jean Jacques Rousseau

R St-Honoré

R de l'Echelle

28

Pl Colette

RIGHT BANK

R du Louvre

R Rambuteau

8

4

Pl du Palais Royal

R du Colonel Driant

R du Bouloi

Bourse de Commerce

32

Galerie Véro Dodat

R de Viarmes

R de Rohan

Palais Royal-Musée du Louvre Ⓜ

R St-Honoré

R Montesquieu

Pl des Deux-Écus

R Berger

See map p376

Pl du Carrousel

Musée du Louvre

R de Rivoli

R Jean-Jacques Rousseau

R St-Honoré

Jardin de l'Oratoire

Louvre Rivoli Ⓜ

R de l'Arbre Sec

R du Roule

5

Cour Napoléon

Louvre 2

Jardin de l'Infante

Cour Carrée

Pl du Louvre

R du Pont Neuf

Musée du Louvre

Pont du Carrousel

Batobus Stop

Pont des Arts

Q du Louvre

Église St-Germain l'Auxerrois

La Nouvelle Samaritaine

R de l'Amiral de Coligny

R Baillet

LOUVRE *Map on p372*

LES HALLES

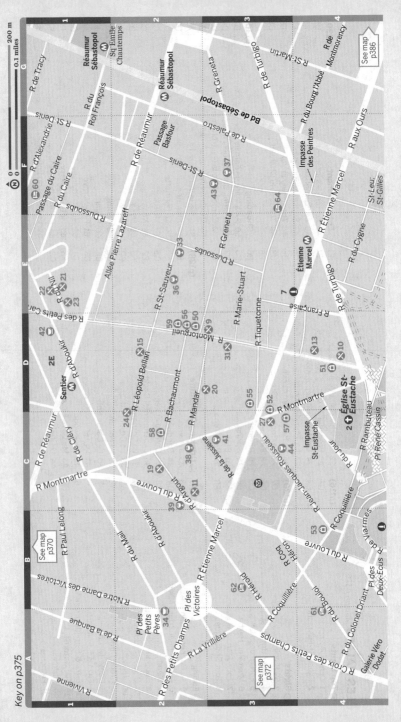

Key on p375

See map p370

See map p372

See map p386

0   200 m
0   0.1 miles

R Vivienne

R des Petits Champs

Pl des Petits Pères

Pl des Victoires

R La Vrillière

R de la Banque

R Notre Dame des Victoires

R du Mail

R Paul Lelong

R de Réaumur

R de Cléry

R Montmartre

R d'Aboukir

62

34

R Hérold

R Coq Héron

R Coquillière

R du Bouloi

19

53

R du Louvre

Galerie Véro Dodat

R Croix des Petits Champs

R du Colonel Driant

Pl des Deux-Écus

R de Viarmes

R Coquillière

R Renée Cassin

Pl René Cassin

R Rambuteau

R du Jour

Rambuteau

Église St-Eustache

2

Impasse St-Eustache

44

57

27

52

55

R Montmartre

51

R de Turbigo

10

13

7

Étienne Marcel

R Française

R Tiquetonne

R Marie-Stuart

R Montorgueil

9

50

56

59

31

15

R Léopold Bellan

R Bachaumont

R Mandar

20

38

41

R de la Jussienne

58

24

R d'Argout

39

61

11

R du Louvre

R Montmartre

R Étienne Marcel

2E

Sentier

R d'Aboukir

42

R des Petits Car

22

R Nil

21

23

Allée Pierre Lazareff

R St-Sauveur

36

R Greneta

R Dussoubs

33

R St-Denis

Passage du Caire

60

R du Caire

R Dussoubs

R d'Alexandrie

R St-Denis

R de Réaumur

R du Rol François

Sq Émile Chautemps

Réaumur Sébastopol

Réaumur Sébastopol

Bd de Sébastopol

Passage Basfour

R de Palestro

R Greneta

43

37

64

Impasse des Peintres

R Étienne Marcel

R du Bourg l'Abbé

R aux Ours

R de Montmorency

R St-Martin

R de Turbigo

St-Leu: St-Gilles

R du Cygne

R de Tracy

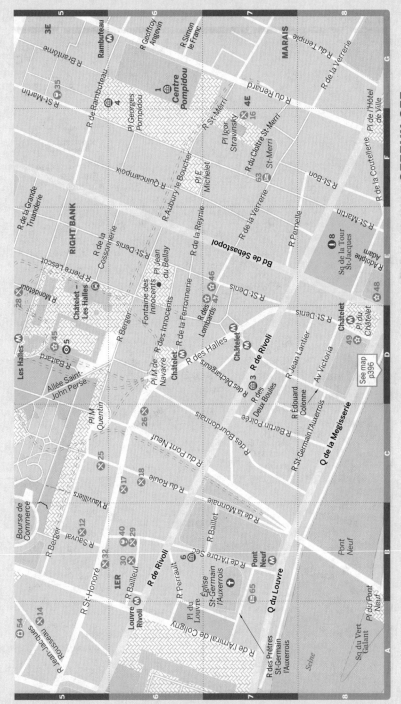

3E

Rambuteau Ⓜ

R Geoffroy Angevin

R Simon le Franc

MARAIS

R du Temple

R Brantôme

R St-Martin

Ⓜ 35

R de Rambuteau

Pl Georges Pompidou

Ⓣ 4

Centre Pompidou 1

R du Renard

R de la Verrerie

R St-Merri

Pl Igor Stravinsky

🍴 16

4E

R du Cloître St-Merri

St-Merri

Pl E Michelet

R Aubry le Boucher

🍴 63

R St-Bon

R de la Coutellerie

R de l'Hôtel de Ville

R de Quincampoix

R St-Martin

R de la Grande Truanderie

RIGHT BANK

R de la Cossonnerie

R St-Denis

R Pierre Lescot

R Mondétour

Châtelet – Les Halles Ⓜ

Fontaine des Innocents

Pl Jean du Bellay

R de la Reynie

R de la Verrerie

R Pernelle

R St-Martin

8 ⓘ

Sq de la Tour St-Jacques

R Adolphe Adam

28 ❌

☆ 45 5 ⓘ

Les Halles Ⓜ

R Baltard

Allée Saint-John Perse

R des Innocents

Pl M de Navarre

R de la Ferronnerie

R Berger

☆ 47

R des Lombards

46 ❌

R St-Denis

48 ❌

Pl du Châtelet

Châtelet

49 ☆

Ⓜ **Châtelet**

R St-Denis

R des Halles

R des Déchargeurs

R de Rivoli

3 🍴

R des Deux Boules

R Édouard Colonne

R Jean Lantier

Av Victoria

See map p396

Pl M Quentin

26 ❌

R des Bourdonnais

R Bertin Poirée

R St-Germain l'Auxerrois

Q de la Mégisserie

25 ❌

R du Pont Neuf

R du Roule

18 ❌

17 ❌

R Vauvilliers

R de la Monnaie

Bourse de Commerce

12 ❌

R Berger

R Sauval

40 ⓘ

29 ❌

32 ❌

30 🛍

1ER

R Bailleul

R de Rivoli

R St-Honoré

R Perrault

R de l'Arbre Sec

6 🛍

Pont Neuf Ⓜ

Pont Neuf

R Baillet

Pl du Louvre

Église St-Germain l'Auxerrois

🛏 65

Q du Louvre

54 ⓘ

14 ❌

R Jean-Jacques Rousseau

Louvre Rivoli Ⓜ

R de l'Amiral de Coligny

R des Prêtres St-Germain l'Auxerrois

Pl du Pont Neuf

Sq du Vert Galant

Seine

Key on p380

MONTMARTRE & PIGALLE

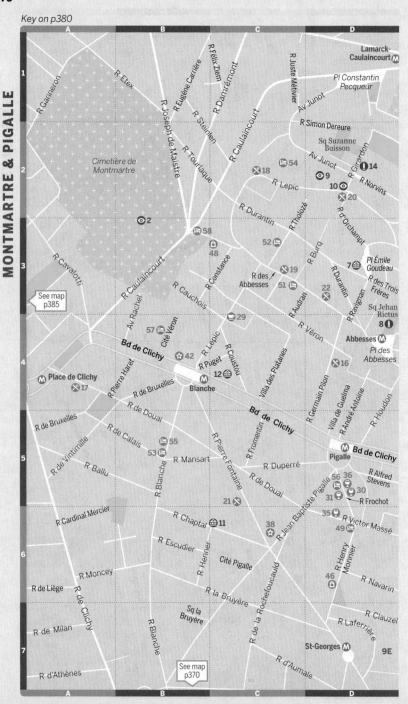

A B C D

1

R Ganneron
R Etex
R Eugène Carrière
R Félix Ziem
R Daunrémont
R Juste Métivier
Lamarck-
Caulaincourt M
Pl Constantin
Pecqueur

R Joseph de Maistre
R Steinlen
R Caulaincourt
Av Junot
R Simon Dereure
Sq Suzanne
Buisson
Av Junot
Girardon
14

2
Cimetière de
Montmartre
R Tourlaque
18
54
9
10
20
R Lepic
R Norvins

R Durantin
R Tholozé
R d'Orchampt

2
52
R Burq
7
Pl Émile
Goudeau

R Cavalotti
48
58
R Constance
19
R Durantin
R des Trois
Frères

See map
p385
R Caulaincourt
R Cauchois
R des
Abbesses
51
22
R Ranquan
Sq Jehan
Rictus
8

57
Cité Véron
29
R Véron
R Audran
Abbesses M

Bd de Clichy
42
R Lepic
R Coustou
R Puget
Villa des Platanes
16
Pl des
Abbesses

Place de Clichy M
17
R Pierre Haret
R de Bruxelles
12
Blanche
Bd de Clichy
R Germain Pilon
Villa de Guelma
R André Antoine
R Houdon

R de Bruxelles
R de Calais
R de Douai
R Fromentin
Pigalle
Bd de Clichy M

R de Victimille
R Ballu
R Blanche
55
53
R Mansart
R Pierre Fontaine
R Duperré
R de Douai
56 36
30
31
R Frochot
R Alfred
Stevens

R Cardinal Mercier
21
R Chaptal
11
38
R Jean Baptiste Pigalle
35
49
R Victor Massé

R Escudier
R Henner
Cité Pigalle
R Henry Monnier
R Navarin

R de Liège
R Moncey
R la Bruyère
R de la Rochefoucauld
46
R Clauzel

R de Clichy
R Blanche
Sq la
Bruyère
R Laferrière
9E

R de Milan
St-Georges M

R d'Athènes
See map
p370
R d'Aumale

A B C D

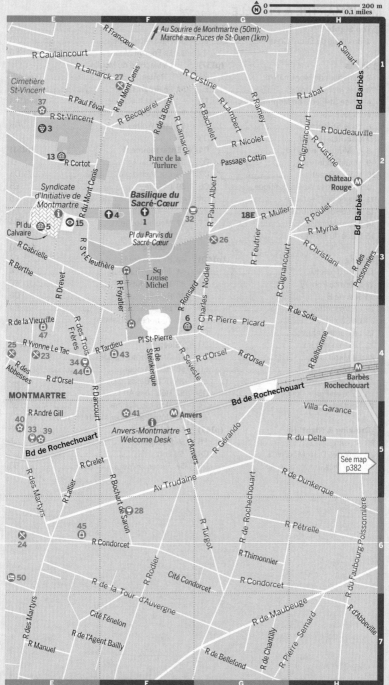

N 0   200 m
   0   0.1 miles

R Francœur

Au Sourire de Montmartre (50m);
Marché aux Puces de St-Ouen (1km)

R Caulaincourt

R Smart

R Lamarck 27

R du Mont Cenis

R Custine

R Labat

Bd Barbès

Cimetière
St-Vincent

R Paul Féval

R Lambert

R Ramey

R Clignancourt

R Doudeauville

R Custine

37

R St-Vincent

R Becquerel

R de la Bonne

R Bachelet

R Nicolet

Passage Cottin

Château
Rouge

3

13   R Cortot

Parc de la
Turlure

R Lamarck

R Poulet

Bd Barbès

Syndicate
d'Initiative de
Montmartre

R du Mont Cenis

**Basilique du
Sacré-Cœur**

R Paul Albert

18E   R Muller

R Myrha

R des Poissonniers

Pl du
Calvaire

5   15

4

1

32

26

R Christiani

R Gabrielle

R St-Eleuthère

Pl du Parvis du
Sacré-Cœur

R Feutrier

R Clignancourt

R Berthe

Sq
Louise
Michel

R Drevet

R Foyatier

R Ronsard

R Charles Nodier

R de Sofia

R de la Vieuville

47

R des Trois Frères

R Tardieu

6   R Pierre Picard

R Belhomme

25   23

34   43

Pl St-Pierre

R d'Orsel   R d'Orsel

M

44

R de Steinkerque

R Séveste

Barbès
Rochechouart

R des
Abbesses

R d'Orsel

R Dancourt

MONTMARTRE

Bd de Rochechouart

Villa Garance

40

R André Gill

41   M Anvers

33   39

Bd de Rochechouart

Anvers-Montmartre
Welcome Desk

R Gérando

R du Delta

R Crelet

R des Martyrs

Pl Lallier

R Bochart de Saron

Av Trudaine

R de Rochechouart

R de Dunkerque

See map
p382

24

28

R Turgot

R Pétrelle

45

R Condorcet

R Rodier

Cité Condorcet

R Thimonnier

R Condorcet

R du Faubourg Poissonnière

50

R de la Tour d'Auvergne

Cité Fénelon

R de Maubeuge

R d'Abbeville

R des Martyrs

R de l'Agent Bailly

R Manuel

R de Bellefond

R de Chantilly

R Pierre Semard

MONTMARTRE & PIGALLE *Map on p378*

GARE DU NORD & CANAL ST-MARTIN

GARE DU NORD & CANAL ST-MARTIN

Key on p381

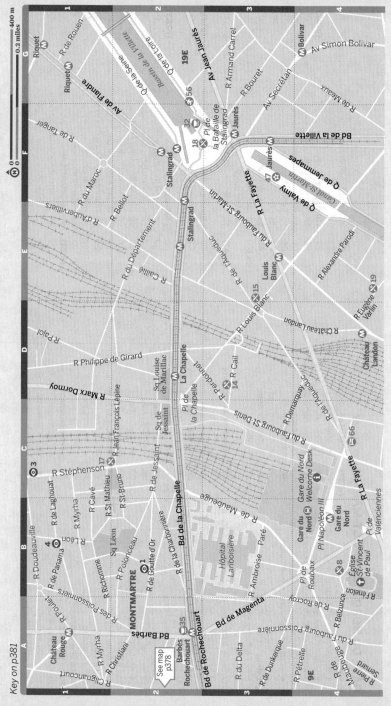

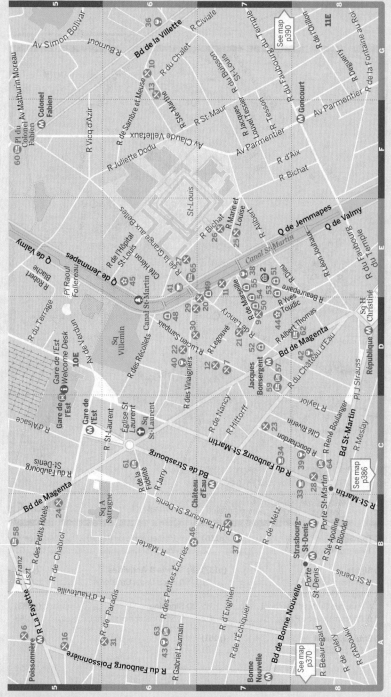

See map p390

11E

See map p886

See map p370

400 m
0.2 miles

PANTIN

Porte
de la
Villette

Corentin
Cariou

R Curial

R Alphonse Karr

Av Corentin Cariou

R de Cambrai

R de l'Ourcq

Av de Flandre

R de Nantes

Crimée

R de Joinville

R de Marne

Q de l'Oise

Canal de l'Ourcq

Q de Thionville

R de Crimée

Bassin de
la Villette

Q de la Loire

R Léon Giraud

R de l'Ourcq

R Tandou

Av Jean Jaurès

See map
p382

Laumière

R de Meaux

R Petit

Av de Laumière

R du Rhin

R Cavendish

R de Lorraine

R de Crimée

R Meynadier

R Armand Carrel

Pl A
Carrel

R Édouard Pailleron

R Manin

Belleville Brûlerie (550m);
Zoé Bouillon (600m)

R Botzaris

Canal St-Denis

R Rouvet

R de l'Argonne

Parc de
la Villette

Canal St-Denis

Galerie de l'Ourcq

Parc de
la Villette

Allée du Belvédère

Galerie de la Villette

R des Ardennes

19E

R du Hainaut

Ourcq

R Georges Auric

Pl F
Poulenc

R d'Hautpoul

R de Crimée

R Compans

Cimetière
de la
Villette

Allée Darius Milhaud

R Manin

R David d'Angers

R Miguel Hidalgo

R du Général
Brunet

Botzaris

Bd Macdonald

Bd Périphérique

Le Zénith

Allée du Zénith

Bd Sérurier

Porte de Pantin

Stade
Jules
Ladoumègue

R Edgar Varèse

R Eugène Jumin

Sente des Dorées

Bd Sérurier

Av de la Porte Chaumont

R Goubet

R de la Solidarité

Av Ambroise Rendu

Danube

R de Mouzaia

Bd Sérurier

Bd d'Algérie

Porte
du Pré
St-Gervais

Pré St-Gervais

Sq de la
Marseillaise

⊚ **Top Sights** (p136)
1 Parc de la Villette C1

⊙ **Sights** (p137)
2 Cité des Sciences C1
3 Musée de la Musique D3
4 Parc des Buttes-Chaumont B5
5 Philharmonie de Paris D2

⊙ **Entertainment** (p151)
6 Cabaret Sauvage C1

Philharmonie de Paris .... (see 3)
7 Rosa Bonheur B5

⊙ **Sports & Activities** (p141)
8 Paris Canal Croisières C2

⊙ **Sleeping** (p283)
9 St Christopher's Canal A3

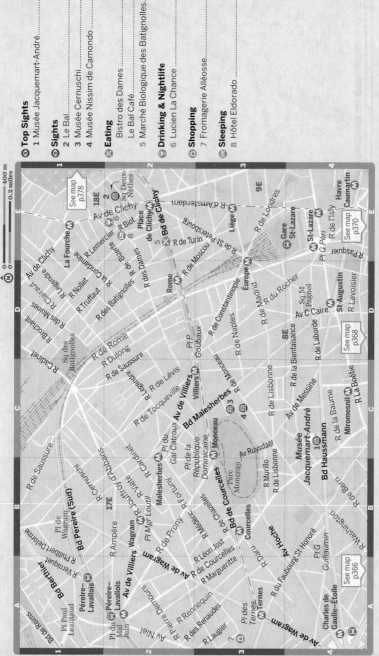

LE MARAIS

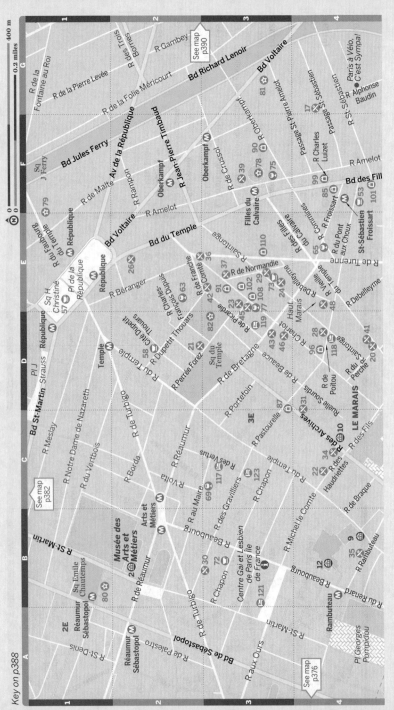

See map p390
See map p382
See map p376
See map p388

Key on p388

400 m
0.2 miles

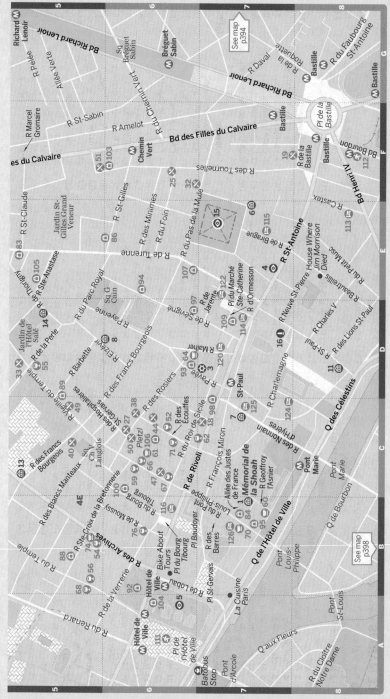

LE MARAIS

See map p394

See map p398

Richard Lenoir

Bd Richard Lenoir

R Pelée

Allée Verte

Sq Bréguet Sabin

Bréguet Sabin

R du Faubourg St-Antoine

R du Chemin Vert

R Daval

R de la Roquette

Bastille

Bastille

R Amelot

R St-Sabin

Bd des Filles du Calvaire

Chemin Vert

Pl de la Bastille

R Marcel Gromaire

R St-Claude

Jardin St-Gilles Grand Veneur

R St-Gilles

R des Minimes

R du Foin

R des Tournelles

51
103

25
32

15

6
115

R de la Bastille

Bd Bourdon

112

113

R Castex

Bd Henri IV

R du Petit Musc

Jim Morrison Died

R Neuve St-Pierre House Where

R de Birague

R St-Antoine

83

R de Turenne

R du Pas de la Mule

R de Thorigny

R Ste-Anastase

105

R du Parc Royal

Sq G Cain

R Payenne

R de Sévigné

94

107

122

Pl du Marché Ste-Catherine

R d'Ormesson

109

114

97

R de Jarente

Jardin de l'Hôtel Salé

R de la Perle

R Elzévir

R Barbette

R des Francs Bourgeois

14

8

33

R Vieille du Temple

55

89

49

R Mahler

R Pavée

64

93

3

120

16

R Charles V

R des Lions St-Paul

R St-Paul

11

R Charlemagne

4

St-Paul

125

124

Q des Célestins

13

R des Francs Bourgeois

40

R des Hospitaliers St-Gervais

27
38

R des Rosiers

Pletzl
106

R des Écouffes

52

62
18
98

7

Pont Marie

Pont Marie

Q de Bourbon

Ch Langlois

50

66
61

44

71

R du Roi de Sicile

R François Miron

4E

R des Blancs Manteaux

R Ste-Croix de la Bretonnerie

59

100

47
67

116

R du Bourg Tibourg

R du Temple

88

56

68

92

74
54

76

Bike About Tours

Pl du Bourg Tibourg

R des Barres

R St-Gervais

Pl St-Gervais

Mémorial de la Shoah

Allée des Justes de France

1

84

60

R Geoffroy l'Asnier

70
95

126

R du Pont Louis-Philippe

R Baudoyer

R des Nonnains d'Hyères

Pont Louis-Philippe

Q de l'Hôtel de Ville

Pont Marie

Hôtel de Ville

104

Pl de l'Hôtel de Ville

111

R du Renard

R de la Verrerie

Hôtel de Ville

5

R de Lobau

La Cuisine Paris

Q aux Fleurs

Batobus Stop

Pont d'Arcole

Pont St-Louis

Q du Cloître Notre Dame

LE MARAIS

MÉNILMONTANT & BELLEVILLE

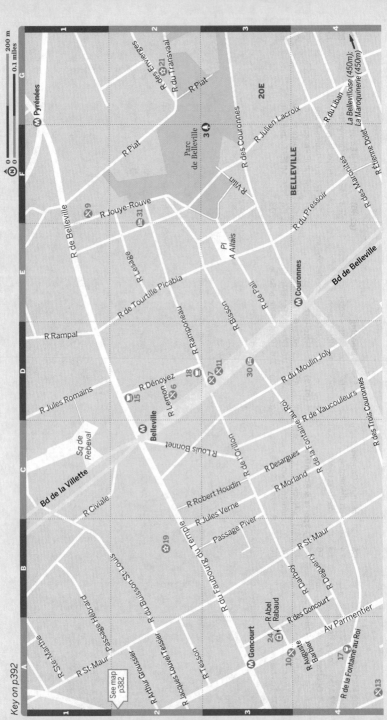

Key on p392

200 m
0.1 miles

See map p382

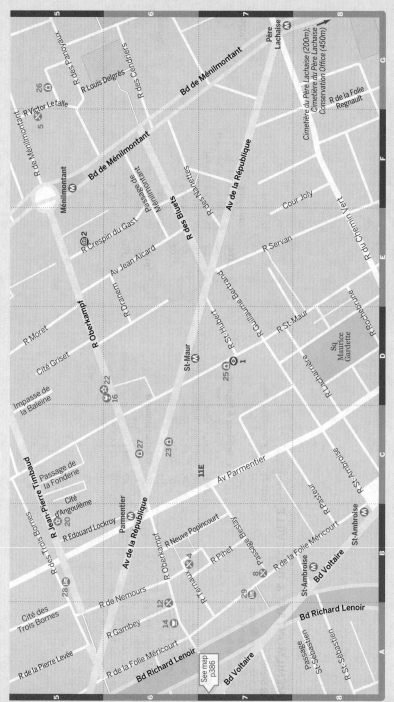

Cimetière du Père Lachaise (200m);
Cimetière du Père Lachaise
Conservation Office (450m)

R de la Folie
Regnault

Père
Lachaise

Bd de Ménilmontant

Av de la République

Bd de Ménilmontant

R des Panoyaux

R Louis Delgrès

R des Cendriers

R Victor Letalle

R de Ménilmontant

Ménilmontant

Bd de Ménilmontant

Passage de
Ménilmontant

R Crespin du Gast

Av Jean Aicard

R Dranem

R Moret

R Oberkampf

Cité Griset

Impasse de
la Baleine

R des Bluets

R des Nanettes

Cour Joly

R Servan

R du Chemin Vert

R Rochebrune

R St-Maur

G Guillaume Bertrand

R St-Hubert

St-Maur

Sq
Maurice
Gardette

R Lacharrière

R Lacharrière

Av Parmentier

11E

R Jean-Pierre Timbaud

Passage de
la Fonderie

Cité
d'Angoulême

R Edouard Lockroy

Parmentier

Av de la République

R des Trois Bornes

Cité des
Trois Bornes

R de la Pierre Levée

R de Nemours

R Gambey

R Oberkampf

R Ternaux

R Neuve Popincourt

R Plhet

Passage Beslay

R de la Folie Méricourt

R Pasteur

St-Ambroise

R St-Ambroise

Bd Voltaire

St-Ambroise

Bd Richard Lenoir

Bd Richard Lenoir

Passage
St-Sébastien

R St-Sébastien

Bd Voltaire

See map
p386

BASTILLE & EASTERN PARIS *Map on p394*

BASTILLE & EASTERN PARIS

BASTILLE & EASTERN PARIS

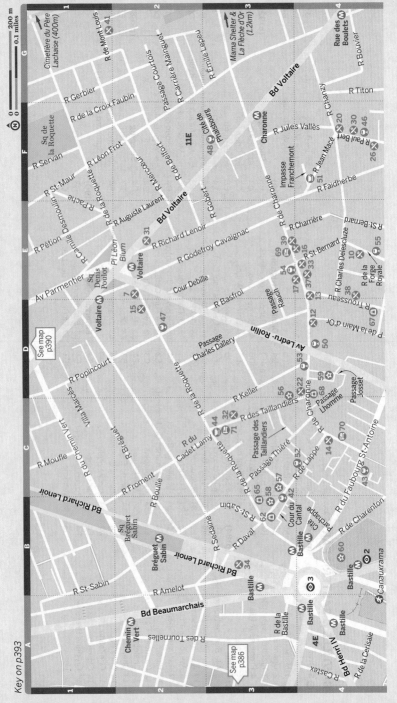

Key on p393

200 m
0.1 miles

See map p390

See map p386

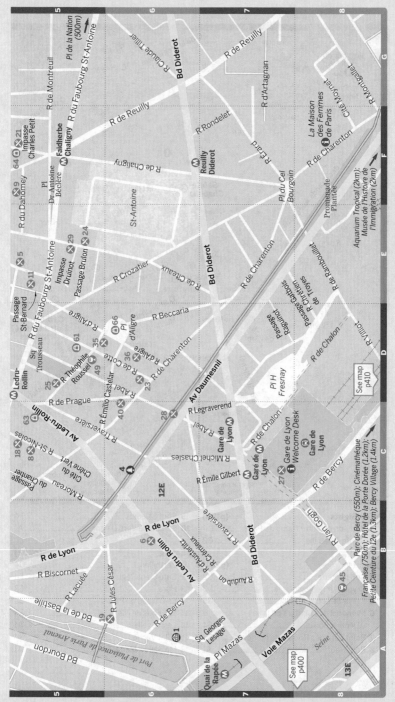

5
6
7
8

Pl de la Nation (500m)

R de Montreuil

R Claude Tillier

R du Faubourg St-Antoine

Bd Diderot

R de Reuilly

R d'Artagnan

R Montgallet

Cité Moynet

64 X 21
Impasse Charles Petit

Faidherbe Chaligny M

R du Faubourg St-Antoine

R de Reuilly

R Rondelet

La Maison des Femmes de Paris

9 X R du Dahomey

Pl Dr-Antoine Béclère

R de Chaligny

Reuilly Diderot M

R Féard

R de Charenton

St-Antoine

Pl du Cel Bourgoin

Promenade Plantée

Aquarium Tropical (2km); Musée de l'Histoire de l'Immigration (2km);

5 X
Impasse Druinot

29 X 24 X

Passage Brulon

Bd Diderot

R de Charenton

R de Charenton

11 X

Passage St-Bernard

R du Faubourg St-Antoine

R Crozatier

R de Créaux

R Beccaria

Passage Chéret de Troyes

Passage Résumé

Passage Chrétien d'Orléans

R de Vuillot

Ledru-Rollin M

66 Pl d'Aligre

R d'Aligre

61

35

36

49

R Théophile Roussel

R de Cotte

R d'Aligre

R Emilio Castelar

23

R de Charenton

R de Chalon

See map p410

25

R de Prague

40

R Traversière

Av Daumesnil

28 X

R Legraverend

Pl H Fresnay

Av Ledru-Rollin

R St-Nicolas

63

18 X

8 X

Cité du Chêne Vert

R Abel

Gare de Lyon M

R de Chalon

Gare de Lyon M

Gare de Lyon

Passage du Chantier

R Moreau

4

R Michel Chasles

R Abel

27 X

Gare de Lyon M

Welcome Desk

R de Bercy

12E

R Émile Gilbert

Parc de Bercy (550m); Cinémathèque Française (750m); Hôtel de la Porte Dorée (1.2km); Petite Ceinture du 12e (1.3km); Bercy Village (1.4km)

R de Lyon

Av Ledru Rollin

R d'Austerlitz

R Crémieux

R Traversière

9

Bd Diderot

R Audubon

R Van Gogh

45

R de Lyon

R Biscornet

R Lacuée

R Jules César

Bd de la Bastille

19

R de Bercy

1

Sq Georges Lesage

Pl Mazas

Seine

Voie Mazas

Bd Bourdon

Port de Plaisance de Paris Arsenal

Quai de la Rapée M

See map p400

13E

A
B
C
D
E
F
G

THE ISLANDS

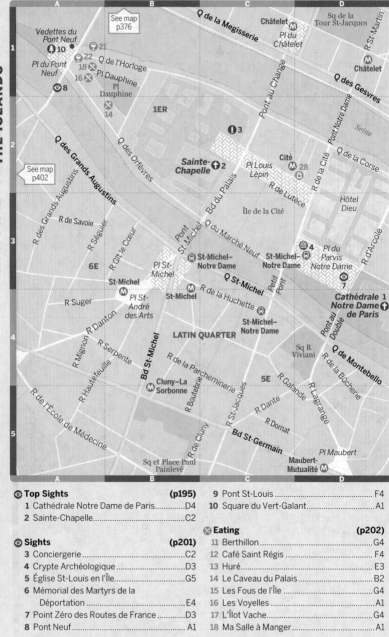

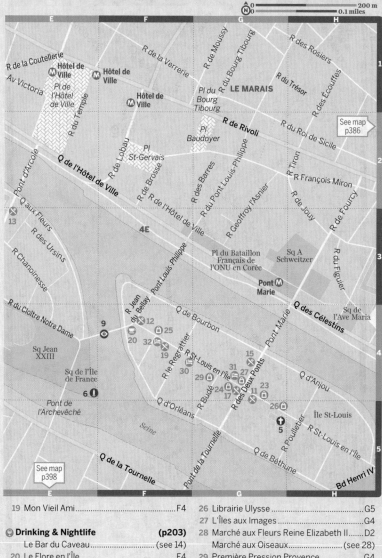

N
0   200 m
0   0.1 miles

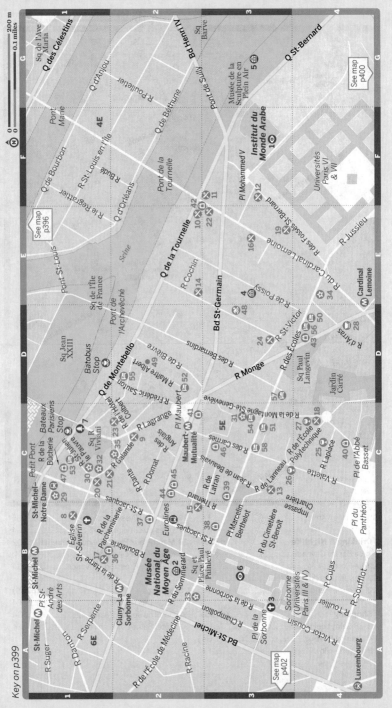

LATIN QUARTER NORTH

Key on p399

See map p396

See map p400

See map p402

LATIN QUARTER NORTH Map on p398

LATIN QUARTER SOUTH

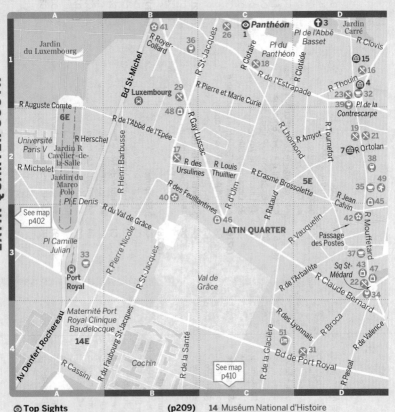

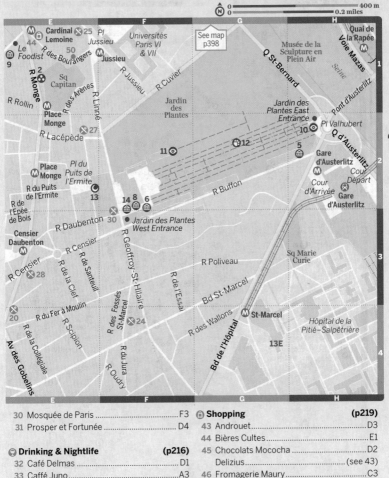

LATIN QUARTER SOUTH

ST-GERMAIN

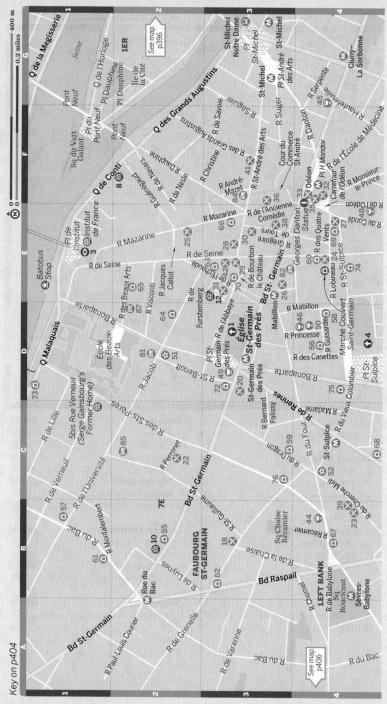

Key on p404

N
0   400 m
0   0.2 miles

Q de la Mégisserie

Seine

Pont Neuf

Sq du Vert Galant

Pl du Pont Neuf

Q du Conti

Institut de France

Pl de l'Institut

Q des Grands Augustins

Pl Dauphine
Q de l'Horloge
Q Dauphine
Île de la Cité

1ER

See map p396

St-Michel
Notre Dame

Pl St-Michel
St-Michel
St-Michel

Cluny–
La Sorbonne

R Serpente
45
R Hautefeuille

R de l'École de Médecine

R Monsieur-
le-Prince

Carrefour
de l'Odéon

Pl H Mondor
32
Odéon
33
35
Statue
Georges Danton
R de Condé
48
R de l'Odéon

R des Quatre Vents
60 69
24
R Lobineau
R St-Sulpice
74

R André-
Mazet
41
R St-André des Arts
R de l'Ancienne Comédie
36
38
R Grégoire
de Tours

R Mazarine
66
R de Seine
30
42
29
70
63
R de l'Échaudé
31
12
R de Furstemberg
R de l'Abbaye
Pl St-Germain
des Prés
Église
St-Germain
des Prés
St-Germain
des Prés
20
49
72
51

R de Nesle
R Dauphine
R de Nevers
R Guénégaud
R Christine
R de Savoie
R Séguier
R Suger
R St-André
Cour du
Commerce
St-André
R Danton

8

3

R Mazarine
25
R de Seine
65
R des Beaux Arts
87
R Visconti
64
R Jacques Callot
R de Seine

Batobus
Stop

Q Malaquais
73

Q Malaquais

École
des Beaux-
Arts
81
51

R Jacob
R St-Benoît
R des Sts-Pères

R de Lille
R de Verneuil
5bis Rue Verneuil
(Serge Gainsbourg's
Former Home)
R de l'Université
R du Bac
57
R Montalembert
85

R Perronet
22

R Bonaparte

R de Bourbon
le Château
R du Dragon
R du Four
59
76
52

Bd St-Germain
R St-Guillaume

7E

FAUBOURG
ST-GERMAIN

R de Luynes
62

R de la Chaise
18

10
55

Bd Raspail

Rue du
Bac

Bd St-Germain

R Paul-Louis Courier
R de Grenelle
R de Varenne

See map
p406

R du Bac

R du Bac

LEFT BANK

Sèvres–
Babylone
R de Babylone
Sq Boucicaut
R Chomel

Pl St-
Sulpice

Mabillon
26
R Mabillon
46
50
R Princesse
56
R Guisarde
58
Marché Couvert
Saint-Germain
R des Canettes
R Bernard
Palissy
75
R de Rennes
R Madame
R du Vieux Colombier
St-Sulpice
R du Cherche Midi
68
39
23
44
Sq Chaise
Récamier
R Récamier
67

Bd St-Germain

Mabillon
R de Seine
82
Bd St-Germain

4

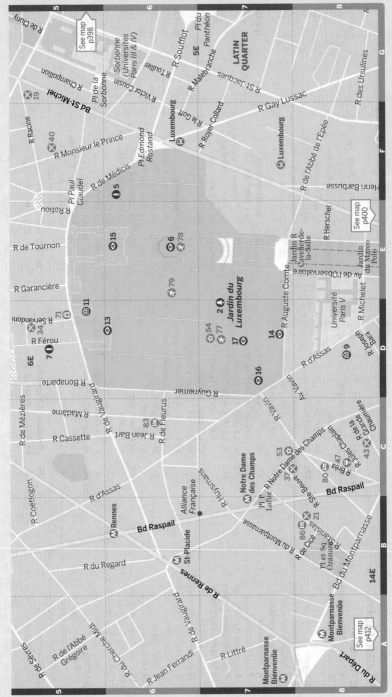

LES INVALIDES

Key on 408

See map p368

400 m
0.2 miles

Jardin des Tuileries

1ER

Q des Tuileries

Batobus Stop

Musée d'Orsay

Seine

Q Anatole France

Musée d'Orsay

R de la Légion d'Honneur

R de Solférino

R de Bellechasse

R de Lille

R de Verneuil

R de Poitiers

R de l'Université

Rue du Bac

R de Luynes

R de Grenelle

Assemblée Nationale

Bd St-Germain

Bd St-Germain

Solférino

Solférino

R de Bellechasse

R de St-Simon

FAUBOURG ST-GERMAIN

Pl du Prést E Harriot

R Aristide Briand

Assemblée Nationale

Pl du Palais Bourbon

R de l'Université

R St-Dominique

Basilique Ste-Clotilde

Sq S Rousseau

R de Martignac

R Casimir Périer

R Las Cases

R de Grenelle

R de Bourgogne

R de Constantine

R de Bellechasse

R de Varenne

R Barbet de Jouy

Cité Vaneau

Hôtel Matignon

R de Varenne

Musée Rodin

Pont de la Concorde

Q d'Orsay

Pont Alexandre III

Esplanade des Invalides

Le Bus Direct

Invalides

Invalides

Pl des Invalides

Sq Santiago du Chili

Sq d'Ajaccio

Varenne

Bd des Invalides

7E

Hôtel des Invalides

Jardin de l'Intendant

Pont des Invalides

Pl de Finlande

R Surcouf

Bd de la Tour Maubourg

R Fabert

Pl Santiago du Chili

La Tour Maubourg

R de la Comète

Sq de la Tour Maubourg

R Chevert

R Louis Codet

Av de Tourville

Av Robert Schuman

R de l'Université

R Jean-Nicot

Passage Jean Nicot

R Amélie

R de Grenelle

R Ernest Psichari

R Duvivier

R Cler

École Militaire

Av de la Motte-Picquet

R Malar

R Valadon

R du Champ de Mars

R Bosquet

R de la Passage de la Vierge

R Cognacq-Jay

R E Valentin

R St-Dominique

Passage Landrieu

Av Bosquet

R Sédillot

R de l'Exposition

R Augereau

Av de la Bourdonnais

Av Frédéric le Play

Allée Adrienne Lecouvreur

Av Anatole France

Pont de l'Alma

Av Rapp

Q d'Orsay

Pont de l'Alma

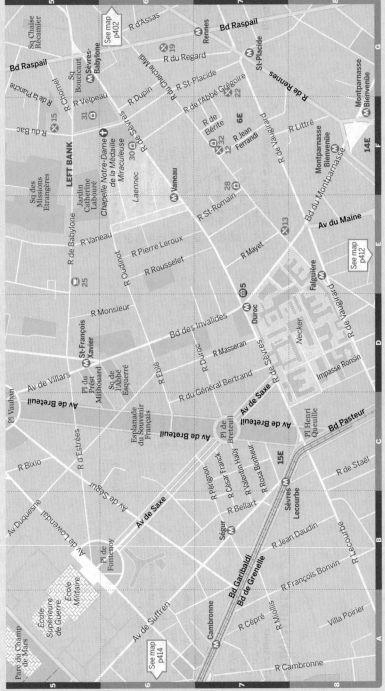

LES INVALIDES

See map p402

See map p412

See map p414

Pare du Champ de Mars

École Supérieure de Guerre

École Militaire

Pl de Fontenoy

Av de Suffren

Av de Lowendal

Av Duquesne

Av de Ségur

R Bixio

R d'Estrées

Pl Vauban

R Bellart

R Pérignon

R César Franck

R Valentin Haüy

R Rosa Bonheur

Ségur

Sèvres Lecourbe

Bd Garibaldi

Bd de Grenelle

Cambronne

R Cépré

R Miollis

R François Bonvin

R Jean Daudin

R de Staël

R Lecourbe

Villa Poirier

R Cambronne

15E

Pl Henri Queuille

Bd Pasteur

Impasse Ronsin

Necker

R de Vaugirard

Falguière

Av du Maine

13

R Littré

R de Rennes

Bd du Montparnasse

Montparnasse Bienvenue

Montparnasse Bienvenüe

14E

Montparnasse Bienvenüe

St-Placide

Bd Raspail

Rennes

R d'Assas

R du Regard

19

R St-Placide

R Cherche Midi

R du Cherche Midi

R Dupin

R de l'Abbé Grégoire

22

R de Bérite

R Jean Ferrandi

32

12

6E

R de Sèvres

R St-Romain

Vaneau

28

R Vaneau

R Oudinot

R Pierre Leroux

R Rousselet

R Mayet

Duroc

5

Bd des Invalides

R Monsieur

R Masseran

R Duroc

R Ebié

R du Général Bertrand

Av de Saxe

R de Sèvres

Necker

St-François Xavier

Pl du Prést Mithouard

Sq de l'Abbé Esquerré

Av de Villars

Av de Breteuil

Av de Breteuil

Av de Breteuil

Pl de Breteuil

Esplanade du Souvenir Français

Av de Saxe

Chapelle Notre-Dame de la Médaille Miraculeuse

Laennec

30

R de Sèvres

Jardin Catherine Labouré

Sq des Missions Étrangères

LEFT BANK

R de Babylone

25

R de Babylone

Sèvres-Babylone

Sq Boucicaut

R Chomel

R Velpeau

R de la Planche

Bd Raspail

Sq Chaise Récamier

15

R du Bac

31

LES INVALIDES

PLACE D'ITALIE & CHINATOWN *Map on p410*

Key on p409

PLACE D'ITALIE & CHINATOWN

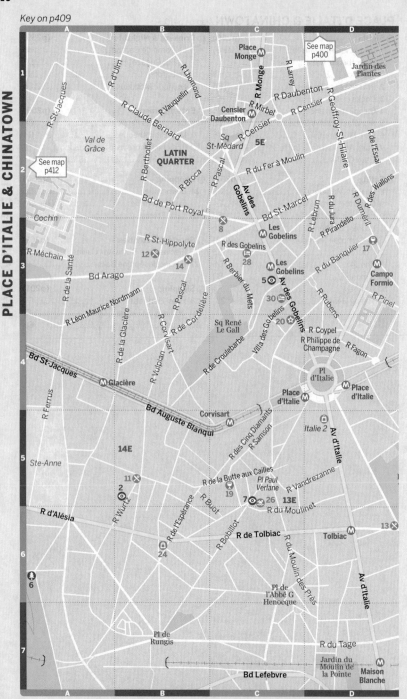

See map
p400

See map
p412

Place
Monge

R Monge

R Larrey

R Daubenton

Jardin des
Plantes

R St-Jacques

R d'Ulm

R Lhomond

R Vauquelin

R Claude Bernard

Censier
Daubenton

R Mirbel

R Censier

R Geoffroy-St-Hilaire

R de l'Essai

Val de
Grâce

R Berthollet

LATIN
QUARTER

Sq
St-Médard

R Censier

5E

R de Wallons

Cochin

R Broca

R Pascal

Av des
Gobelins

R du Fer à Moulin

R Lébrun

R du Jura

R Pirandello

R Duméril

Bd de Port Royal

Bd St-Marcel

Les
Gobelins

R Méchain

R St-Hippolyte

8

R des Gobelins

28

Les
Gobelins

R du Banquier

17

Campo
Formio

R de la Santé

12

14

Bd Arago

R Berbier du Mets

5

Av des Gobelins

30

R Rubens

R Pinel

R Léon Maurice Nordmann

R Pascal

R de Cordelière

Sq René
Le Gall

20

R Coypel
R Philippe de
Champagne

R Fagon

Bd St-Jacques

R de la Glacière

R Corvisart

R de Croulebarbe

Villa des Gobelins

Pl
d'Italie

R Ferrus

Glacière

Bd Auguste Blanqui

Corvisart

Place
d'Italie

Place
d'Italie

Ste-Anne

14E

R des Cinq Diamants

R Samson

Italie 2

Av d'Italie

11

2

R de la Butte aux Cailles

19

Pl Paul
Verlane

R Vandrezanne

R d'Alésia

R Wurtz

R de l'Espérance

R Buot

7

26

13E

R du Moulinet

13

24

R Bobillot

R de Tolbiac

R du Moulin des Prés

Tolbiac

6

Pl de
l'Abbé G
Henocque

Pl de
Rungis

R du Tage

Av d'Italie

Bd Lefebvre

Jardin du
Moulin de
la Pointe

Maison
Blanche

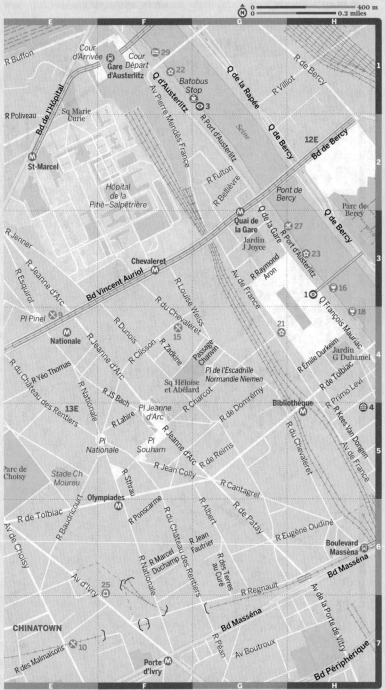

0   400 m
0   0.2 miles

E F G H

1

R Buffon

Cour
d'Arrivée
Cour
Départ
Gare
d'Austerlitz

29

22

Q d'Austerlitz

Batobus
Stop

3

R de Bercy

R Villiot

Q de la Rapée

Bd de l'Hôpital

R Poliveau

Sq Marie
Curie

Av Pierre-Mendès France

R Port d'Austerlitz

Seine

12E

Bd de Bercy

2

St-Marcel

Hôpital
de la
Pitié–Salpêtrière

R Fulton

R Bellièvre

Pont de
Bercy

Parc de
Bercy

Q de Bercy

R Jenner

R Jeanne d'Arc

R Esquirol

Chevaleret

Bd Vincent Auriol

R Louise Weiss

R du Chevaleret

Quai de
la Gare

Q de la Gare

Jardin
J Joyce

27

R Port d'Austerlitz

Av de France

R Raymond
Aron

23

Q de Bercy

3

Pl Pinel

9

Nationale

R Jeanne d'Arc

R Dunois

R Clisson

R Zadkine

15

R Château des Rentiers

R Yéo Thomas

R JS Bach

R Lahire

Pl Jeanne
d'Arc

Sq Héloïse
et Abélard

R Charcot

Passage
Chanvin

Pl de l'Escadrille
Normandie Niemen

R de Domrémy

1

16

Q François Mauriac

18

21

R Émile Durkeim

Jardin
G Duhamel

R de Tolbiac

R Primo Levi

4

13E

R Nationale

Pl
Nationale

Pl
Souham

R Jeanne d'Arc

R Sthrau

R de Reims

R Jean Colly

Bibliothèque

R du Chevaleret

R Kees Van Dongen

Av de France

4

5

Parc de
Choisy

Stade Ch
Moureu

Olympiades

R Baudricourt

R Ponscarme

R du Château des Rentiers

R Cantagrel

R de Patay

Av de Choisy

R de Tolbiac

R Marcel
Duchamp

R Jean
Fautrier

R des Terres
au Curé

R Albert

R Eugène Oudiné

Boulevard
Masséna

Bd Masséna

6

25

R Nationale

R Regnault

Bd Masséna

Av de la Porte de Vitry

CHINATOWN

10

R des Malmaisons

Porte
d'Ivry

R Péan

Av Boutroux

Bd Périphérique

7

E F G H

MONTPARNASSE

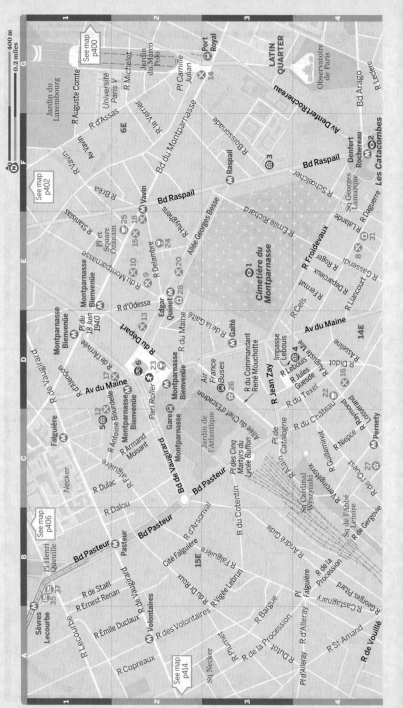

See map p400

See map p402

See map p406

See map p414

400 m
0.2 miles

Jardin du Luxembourg

R Auguste Comte

Pl Henri Queuille

Sèvres Lecourbe

Bd Pasteur

Pasteur

Bd Pasteur

R de Stael
R Ernest Renan

R Lecourbe

R Émile Duclaux

Volontaires

R de Vaugirard

R du Dr Roux

R Copreaux

Necker

R Falguière

R Dalou

R Dulac

Cité Falguière

15E

R d'Arsonval

R Falguière

R Vigée Lebrun

Sq Necker

R Pluma

R Dutot

R de la Procession

Pl d'Alleray

R d'Alleray

R de Vouillé

R St-Amand

R Castagnary

R Georges Pitard

Pl Falguière

R de la Procession

R Bargue

R du Cotentin

Bd de Vaugirard

Bd Pasteur

R André Gide

Pl des Cinq Martyrs du Lycée Buffon

Sq Cardinal Wyszynski

R Al...

Pl de Catalogne

R Vercingétorix

Sq de l'Abbé Lemire

R de Gergovie

R de l'Ouest

27

Pernety

Losserand

R Raymond

R du Château

R Niepce

22

Didot

R du Texel

R Jules Guesde

R Lebouis

R Auguste Mie

Impasse Lebouis

R Jean Zay

R du Commandant René Mouchotte

16

Gare Montparnasse

Pari Roller

Air France Buses

26

Jardin de l'Atlantique

Allée du Chef d'Escadron

Montparnasse Bienvenüe

Montparnasse Bienvenüe

Montparnasse Bienvenüe

23

6

8

17

Av du Maine

R Antoine Bourdelle

R Armand Moisant

R de l'Arrivée

Pl du 18 Juin 1940

R du Départ

R Vandamme

Montparnasse Bienvenüe

Falguière

5

12

R de Vanves

R d'Alençon

Montparnasse Bienvenüe

13

R d'Odessa

R du Montparnasse

Edgar Quinet

Gaîté

28

R de la Gaîté

R du Maine

9

10

20

24

15

18

25

R Delambre

Pl et Square Ozanam

R Stanislas

R Bréa

R Vavin

Vavin

Bd Raspail

Bd Raspail

Allée Georges Besse

R Huyghens

6E

R d'Assas

R le Verrier

Av Vavin

Université Paris V

Jardin du Marco Polo

Pl Camille Julian

14

Port Royal

LATIN QUARTER

Observatoire de Paris

Bd Arago

R Leclerc

Denfert Rochereau

Denfert Rochereau

Av Denfert Rochereau

Bd Raspail

3

R Boissonade

R Schœlcher

R Émile Richard

Cimetière du Montparnasse

1

Av du Maine

14E

R Cels

R Fermat

R Froidevaux

R Liancourt

R Daguerre

R Lalande

Sq Georges Lamarque

R Gassendi

R Roger

R Deparcieux

R Boulard

8

31

2

Les Catacombes

R Asseline

MONTPARNASSE

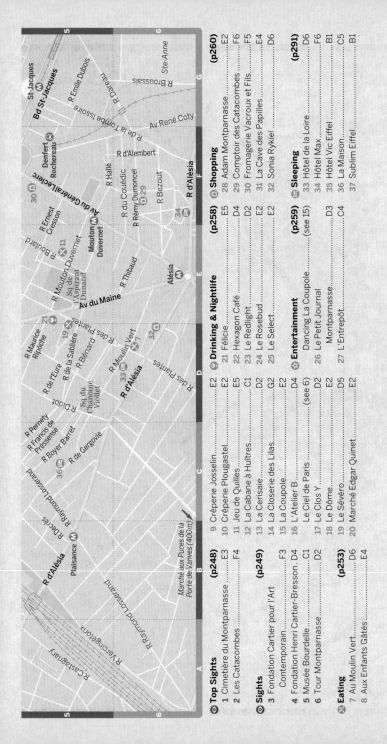

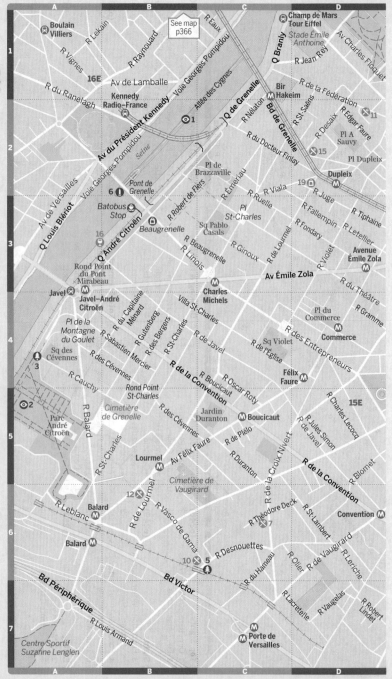

Our Story

A beat-up old car, a few dollars in the pocket and a sense of adventure. In 1972 that's all Tony and Maureen Wheeler needed for the trip of a lifetime – across Europe and Asia overland to Australia. It took several months, and at the end – broke but inspired – they sat at their kitchen table writing and stapling together their first travel guide, *Across Asia on the Cheap*. Within a week they'd sold 1500 copies. Lonely Planet was born.

Today, Lonely Planet has offices in Franklin, London, Melbourne, Oakland, Dublin, Beijing and Delhi, with more than 600 staff and writers. We share Tony's belief that 'a great guidebook should do three things: inform, educate and amuse'.

Our Writers

Catherine Le Nevez

Latin Quarter, Montparnasse & Southern Paris, St-Germain & Les Invalides, The Islands, Day Trips from Paris An award-winning, Paris-based travel writer, Catherine first lived in the French capital aged four and has been hitting the road at every opportunity, completing her Doctorate of Creative Arts in Writing, Masters in Professional Writing, and postgrad qualifications in Editing and Publishing along the way. Over the last dozen-plus years she's written scores of Lonely Planet guides, along with numerous print and online articles, covering Paris, France, Europe and far beyond. Wanderlust aside, Paris remains her favourite city on earth. Catherine also wrote the Plan, Understand and Survive sections of this guide.

Christopher Pitts

Eiffel Tower, Champs-Élysées & Grands Boulevards, Louvre & Les Halles Christopher Pitts first moved to Paris in 2001. He initially began writing about the city as a means to buy baguettes – and to impress a certain Parisian (it worked, they're now married with two kids). Over the past decade, he has written for various publications, in addition to working as a translator and editor. Visit him online at www.christopherpitts.net.

Nicola Williams

Le Marais, Ménilmontant & Belleville; Montmartre & Northern Paris; Bastille & Eastern Paris British writer and editorial consultant Nicola Williams has lived in France and written about it for more than a decade. From her hillside house on the southern shore of Lake Geneva, it's an easy hop to Paris where she has spent endless years revelling in its extraordinary art, urban architecture, boutique shopping and cuisine. Nicola has worked on numerous titles for Lonely Planet, including *France* and *Discover France*. Find Nicola on Twitter at @Tripalong.

Published by Lonely Planet Global Limited
CRN 554153
11th edition – Jan 2017
ISBN 978 1 78657 221 9
© Lonely Planet 2017 Photographs © as indicated 2017
10 9 8 7 6 5 4 3 2 1
Printed in China